Communications
in Computer and Information Science   211

Mark Zhou (Ed.)

Advances in Education and Management

International Symposium, ISAEBD 2011
Dalian, China, August 6-7, 2011
Proceedings, Part IV

 Springer

Volume Editor

Mark Zhou
Hong Kong Education Society
The Sherwood No.8 Fuk Hang Tsuen Road
Tuen Mun, Hong Kong, China
E-mail: zhoumarkhk@sina.com

ISSN 1865-0929   e-ISSN 1865-0937
ISBN 978-3-642-23061-5   e-ISBN 978-3-642-23062-2
DOI 10.1007/978-3-642-23062-2
Springer Heidelberg Dordrecht London New York

Library of Congress Control Number: 2011933608

CR Subject Classification (1998): H.4, I.2, H.3, C.2, D.2, J.1

Typesetting: Camera-ready by author, data conversion by Scientific Publishing Services, Chennai, India

Printed on acid-free paper

Springer is part of Springer Science+Business Media (www.springer.com)

Preface

It is our pleasure to welcome you to the proceedings of the 2011 International Symposium on Applied Economics, Business and Development (ISAEBD 2011) which was held in Dalian, China. ISAEBD 2011 was the first conference dedicated to issues related to applied economics, business and development. This conference aims to provide a high-level international forum for researchers to present and discuss the recent advances in related issues, covering various research areas including economics, management, education and its applications.

The conference is sponsored by the Hong Kong Education Society, International Material Science Society and Information Engineering Research Institute. Their support is very important for our conference.

The conference was both stimulating and informative with an interesting array of keynote and invited speakers from all over the world. Delegates had a wide range of sessions to choose from.

The program consisted of invited sessions, technical workshops and discussions with eminent speakers covering a wide range of topics in applied economics, business and development. This rich program provided all attendees with the opportunity to meet and interact with one another.

We would like to thank the organization staff, the members of the Program Committees and the reviewers for their hard work.

We hope the attendees of ISAEBD 2011 had an enjoyable scientific gathering in Dalian, China. We look forward to seeing all of you at the next ISAEBD event.

Qingyuan Zhou

ISAEBD 2011 Organization

Honorary Conference Chairs

Chin-Chen Chang   Feng Chia University, Taiwan
Chris Price   Aberystwyth University, UK

General Chairs

Qinyuan Zhou   Jiangsu Teachers University of Technology, China
Junwu Zhu   Yangzhou University, China

Program Chairs

Honghua Tan   Wuhan Institute of Technology , China
Qihai Zhou   Southwestern University of Finance and Economics, China

Publication Chair

Mark Zhou   Hong Kong Education Society, Hong Kong

Local Chair

He Ping   Liaoning Police Academy, China

International Program Committee

Ming-Jyi Jang   Far-East University, Taiwan
Tzuu-Hseng S. Li   National Cheng Kung University, Taiwan
Yanwen Wu   Huazhong Normal University, China
Teh-Lu Liao   National Cheng Kung University, Taiwan
Yi-Pin Kuo   Far-East University, Taiwan
Qingtang Liu   Huazhong Normal University, China
Wei-Chang Du   I-Shou University, Taiwan
Jiuming Yang   Huazhong Normal University, China
Hui Jiang   Wuhan Golden Bridge-Network Security Technocogy Co. Ltd., China
Zhonghua Wang   Huazhong Normal University, China
Jun-Juh Yan   Shu-Te University, Taiwan
Dong Huang   Huazhong University of Science and Technology, China
JunQi Wu   Huazhong Normal University, China

Table of Contents – Part IV

Sino-foreign Comparative Analysis of Environmental Compensation System

Yanli Li[1], Lijun Li[1], and Jinghui Hu[2]

[1] School of Economics and Management, Shijiazhuang Tiedao University,
17 Beierhuan east road, Shijiazhuang, China
qhdlyl@sohu.com, lilj@stdu.edu.cn
[2] Hebei Province urban Construction School, 283 Donggang road,
Shijiazhuang, China
llj56857@sohu.com

Abstract. This paper want to introduce the situations of environmental compensation in western countries, so that China can do it better. This paper compared and analysed the concept, theory, understanding and practice of environmental compensation in China and western countries. We consider that the western Payment for Environmental Services generally had more solid theoretical foundation and legal basis, and domestic research has made a series of achievements, compared with the international research on the mechanism of the environmental compensation, the studies in China should do much more.

Keywords: environmental compensation, ecological payment, comparative analysis, environmental capacity.

1 Introduction

Matter and energy flows and exchanges continually between natural system and human economic system, specifically speaking, all kinds of resources, energy and raw material flow to economic system from environmental system, and various industrial emissions, wastewater and waste residue flow to environmental system from economic system. The exchange about matter and energy is abnormal, and it causes rapid the prosperity of the economic life of the mankind while the deterioration in the face, structure and function of the natural environment, and ultimately endangers the survival of human beings. This paper compared the progress of environmental compensate (abb. EC) and recover natural system in China and western country.

2 Sino-foreign Cognitional Compare on the Notion of EC

Currently, the implications closed to EC are mainly PES and PEB. There are three special expressions about PES, that is Payment for Ecological/Environmental Services, Market for Ecological/Environmental Services, and Compensation for Ecological/Environmental Services. PEB can be translated into Payment for Ecological/Environmental Benefit. The meanings of these expressions are basically consistent. Their essence is that the users of

M. Zhou (Ed.): ISAEBD 2011, Part IV, CCIS 211, pp. 1–7, 2011.
© Springer-Verlag Berlin Heidelberg 2011

environmental production factors are lack of enthusiasm to provide a variety of environmental services (including flow regulation, biodiversity conservation and carbon storage, etc.) because of not obtaining compensation from them. Paying for the users can inspire the acts of protecting ecological environment and especially can provide the poor ones with extra incomes in order to improve their livelihoods. The ecology and the environment all used in the PES and the PEB are not very different.

At present, the concept of EC is less and directly used in domestic researches, instead of "ecological compensation", "eco-environmental compensation", "compensation for ecological benefit", "compensation for ecological value", "compensation for ecological services", "compensation for ecological resources" "compensation for the value of ecological resources " and so on. The common of these concepts is to concern "ecology", emphasizing to compensate for the ecological impact caused by the human activities. For narrative convenience, the paper refers to these statements by the general name of ecological compensation. In these studies, some focus on the compensation for the changes of the natural resourses because of being exploited and used, and the ecosystem imbalance and the reduction of the species, some focus on the collection of compensation fee and the compensation for ecological benefit or value in single or complex. Others use the concept of EC from the angle of environmental reparation, which aims at the subject' loss in life health and property caused by the environmental issues. There is a wide gap in cognition because of different scholars in these studies, and their specific content are also difficult to generalize, but they generally do not involve or seldom in the discussions on the environmental capacity.

Although the focuses of EC and ecological compensation are different, their meanings are very close to each other. The researches on ecological compensation started earlier gives more guidance and support to the studies of EC, therefore, their related contents are also included in the comparative analysis in this paper.

3   Sino-foreign Compare on the Research of EC

The foreign research on EC can be traced back to the thought of the internalization of external costs in externality, whose main representatives including Pigou, Coase and other economists. In 1970s, American economists Seneca and Tao Heeg thought that additional labor and capital needed to input for the restoration of the environmental quality; in the use of the environment high costs must be paid increasingly as compensation for ecological damage and wasted resources. If didn't account the environment, it could not accurately reflect the stock of reproduced capital and resources and also be difficult to obtain the data of "all the property of society", so in order to ensure the correct price, the price system must be the mechanism which can compensate for the future or even can consider the future of every generation in the future. In June, 1972, the first United Nations conference on human environment, published "Declaration on the Human Environment", and presented all nations should be responsible for the victims of environmental pollution and damage; and should raise funds to maintain and improve the environment. It marks that the consensus on ecological compensation is formed in international community. In 1992, "Declaration on Environment and Development" made in Rio de Janeiro also raised that it should make all the people participate in the solution of environmental problem by effectively using judicial and administrative procedures included redress and remedy.

In 1960s, the contents of EC are limited in the field of externality damage, including life health hazards and property damage. In 1977, Westman proposed the concept of "nature's services" and the problem of its value assessment. Subsequently, the most developed countries and international institutions (like the United Nations, World Bank and European Community, etc.) have done a lot of studies to it, and made a number of significant breakthroughs in the value system and evaluation method of environmental resource. Particularly the research of Pearce , Mc-Neely and Turne laid the basis of classification theory research on the natural capital and service value of the ecosystem. In 1997, Daily edited and published "Nature's services - the Community Depends on Natural Ecosystem", which makes the value assessment and compensation of the ecosystem services become a hot and cutting-edge of ecology and ecological economics. In the same year, the British scholar Hen Smets proposed to introduce a system of integrated criminal sanctions and new green super fund in the field of environmental protection, and to establish a comprehensive compensation system on accidental pollution damage; Peter Wetterstein put forward the issue of the division and comparison about the private-rights and the public-rights ,by comparing and analyzing the harm of the environmental assets owned to the private in the Law of Scandinavian and the cases of America. Goldstein and other scholars discussed in the policy constraints, the problems of whether the government should compensate the loss or not after reducing the environmental assets of the owner; Dunford and other scholars made research on complex issues such as who should be compensated, and how much should be compensated when the losses of public property are caused by environmental pollution, Thus, a new concept on EC formed, that is compensation for the replacement of ecological assets, and accordingly loss of ecological compensation evolves to the power of ecological compensation, and they impacted actively the practice of compensation for the value of ecological resources in greater area.

The research on ecological compensation in China begins in 1980s, and the early studies are in the stage of spontaneous exploratory, mainly from the perspective of natural science. Their main point is that extracting part of funds from the economic benefits to return ecosystems in the way of matter and energy, in order to maintain the dynamic equilibrium of the input and output of the matter and energy in the ecological systems. Some scholars proposed to give the value to the ecological benefits and compensate it, and advocated to extract a certain percentage of benefits from the relevant departments as a compensation fund, which made the ecological compensation with the main characteristics of economic significance. For example, to the forest, not only to calculate its value in the provision of timber and forest by-products, but also its ecological value in climate regulation, water conservation, soil and water conservation, air cleanup and environment beautify, and compensate for it. Other scholars called for piloting ecological compensation to the forest designated as eco-efficiency shelterbelt, and the benefit units (power plants, factories, transport, shipping, mining, etc.) at the downstream according to the amount of benefit undertake investment obligations to compensate for the construction requirements of the shelter, which has the idea of ecological compensation of the valley. However, the related research results have no bigger impact.

In 1992, in China "The Report on the Case of Attending at the United Nations Conference on Environment and Development and the Related Strategies" pointed out: "The government at all levels should better use economic means to achieve the purposes of protecting the environment. In accordance with the principle of using paid resources, they should gradually introduce compensation fees of the use of resources and carry out the research of the environmental taxes. They should also research and pilot the problem of bringing the natural resources and environment into the accounting system of the national economy for making the market prices accurately reflect the environmental costs caused by economic activities". In this context, the first climax on the research of ecological compensation occurred in our country, and many scholars appealed the necessity and urgency of the ecological compensation and carried out studies and discussions to a series of problems, such as the concept, meaning, purpose, significance of the ecological compensation and the collection basis and standards, the collection scope and targets, the collection methods and its impact to the price about the ecological (environmental) compensation fee. The focus of the studies is compensation for economic losses caused by the environmental damage, which is often the synonym of paying for compensation by the perpetrators to the eco-environment, and the field of the researches aimed at the ecological compensation of the mining and the public welfares, especially the later had an absolute percentage. The main characteristics in this stage are the meaning and scope of ecological compensation, the discussion of its theoretical basis and the practical discussion in limited areas such as the forest and the mining.

Many scholars researched the EC from the angle of ecology, environmental science, economics, management, law and other different disciplines. Mao Xianqiang, lv Zhongmei, Ma Yan, Zhao Jianlin, Ma Jinnan and other scholars put forward the related concept of EC, established the asset theory of ecological resources, proposed the compensation content of the rights of the assets, and deemed that establishing compensation mechanisms on the value of ecological resources in our country should deal well with the ten major relationships, including the relationship between the government and the market, the central and the local, the building of comprehensive platform and sector platform about ecological compensation, paying for ecology and compensating for damage, "new account" and "old account", ecological compensation and ecological poverty, "blood creation" and "blood transfusion", responsibility of upstream and downstream, the compensation standards and the compensation agreement, financial capital and social capital and so on. On this basis, they also raised to mainly establish ecological compensation mechanism from five aspects: the first is the system of transferring payment on finance which is helpful for protecting the environment, the second is the system of eco-friendly tax, the third is the mechanism of ecological compensation based on main functional areas, the fourth is the system of the internalization of environmental cost and the last one is to establish the mechanism of ecological compensation on the valley. In addition, there are some new trends in the theory and practice of ecological compensation, that is, advocating to establish the statistical methods of the green GDP to reflect the environmental costs of economic development in the economic statistics, and trying to promote the environmental protection in the way of the disclosure of the environmental information; concerning increasingly about the problem of the income distribution which relates to the realization of the value of ecological resources; paying attention to achieve the compensation of the value of ecological resources and environment management in the way of recycling waste and developing the circular economy.

4   Sino-foreign Compare on the Practice of EC

From the practical application of the theory of the compensation for environmental value internationally, the specific cases of PES mostly revolve the environmental services of the forest ecosystems, and mostly base on the market mechanism, specifically including direct public compensation, quota trading scheme, private direct compensation and eco-product certification plan. Direct public compensation is to provide directly compensation by the government for the owners of the rural land who supplied the services for environmental systems and other providers, such as in Switzerland, the government provides financial compensation for the protection of particular species, the maintain of the higher environmental standards, the development of organic agriculture and so on. Quota trading scheme indicates that the government or the regulatory body firstly set a quota to the eco-system degradation or the loss of destruction, and the perpetrator overrun can choose to fulfill the compensation obligation or finance the activities of environmental protection, such as the EU's emissions trading scheme. Private direct compensation is often called "voluntary compensation", and the business groups and (or) individual consumers participate in the work of such compensation out of charity, risk management and (or) the purpose of participating in market management.

From the application of the theory of compensation for environmental value, EC are mainly concentrated in the fields associated with agricultural activities, such as environmental protection, resource development in environmental protection, integrated management of the watershed, the protection of biological resources and natural landscape and compensation for pollution damage and so on. In agriculture, the U.S. government implemented the protective farmland plan and the protective conservation program. From 1985 to 2002, the U.S. Department of Agriculture paid about 1.5 billion U.S. dollars annually for the land rents and the costs of conversion in production mode, and the average amount of compensation is 116 U.S. dollars / ha per year; in the farmland, 60% to grass, 16% to woodland, 5% to wetland. In the EC of the basin, the Australia promoted the integrated management of the watershed in all provinces with the economic subsidies from federal government; in South Africa, the government input about 170 million U.S. dollars a year to hire the disadvantaged groups to carry out ecological protection in valley in order to improve water quality and increase water supply; New York invested 1.5 billion U.S. dollars and made the protection agreement about supplying high-quality water source for the city with the upstream areas of the river. In the EC of the development of mineral resources, Germany and the United States put forward that the government was responsible for governing the environmental damage before the legislation, and the developers was in charge of the part after the legislation. The EC abroad on natural protection such as biodiversity and others basically depended on the channels of the government and the foundations, and sometimes combined with agriculture, watershed and forests, Etc.. The typical compensation for pollution damage is Japan's "The Law on Compensation for Health Damage Caused by Pollution", which established a relatively comprehensive compensation system on external damage to the environment. "Comprehensive Environmental response, Compensation and Liability Act" (CERCLA) of the United States regulates, as long as the pollutants' harm occurred or possible, it will initiate investigations on the power, and implement effective measures to enforce the parties burden governance costs, including reparation/compensation fee. If it is difficult to investigate the responsible objects, or the governance and compensation costs beyond their capacity, which needs to use the grant of the Super Fund. According to statistics, after the establishment of Super-fund Program in 1980, to 1993, it cost about 20 billion U.S. dollars, most of which was invested to the 400 heavily polluted sites (regions).

The practice of EC in China can be summarized into three aspects: 1, it was implemented in the form of the national policy and promoted by the relevant ministries from the central government; 2, it showed the exploration of local autonomy in practice; 3, its participation in the international market transactions on EC started preliminary in recent years. In December, 2005, "the Determination of the State Council on Implementing the Scientific Concept of Development and Strengthening Environmental Protection" was issued, which required that the whole community should establish "ecological compensation mechanism," In the term of the focus of EC and practical work, it was recently concentrated in the field of the forest and nature reserve, watershed and mineral resources and so on.

In the EC of the forests and the nature reserve, the investors are mainly consisted by the central and local governments. In 1992 and 1993, the State Council issued twice the document and denoted clearly to establish the system of compensation for ecological benefit to the forest; in 1998, the Article VI in the amended "Forest Law" clearly marked "the fund of compensation for ecological benefit to the forest set by the state". In 2004, a central fund on EC was established by the Ministry of Finance and State Forestry Administration. In the EC of the valley, the cooperation on the protection of water resources between Beijing and Hebei Province, the compensation for the East River and other river's upstream in Guangdong Province, and the compensation for the basin of Xin'an River in Zhejiang Province. The main policy instruments applied are the financial transfer payment from the higher governments, or the horizontal intergovernmental transfers at the same level. At the same time, some places have also explored some market-based means of EC mechanism, such as water trading patterns. In the EC of the mineral resources, China's mineral resources tax and mineral resources compensation to some extent play the same role with the tax related to the EC. The security deposit system of mine's recovery and management established in 2000 also safeguarded the development of EC.

5 Conclusion

Overall, the west PES generally has more solid theoretical foundation and legal basis, and formed a more comprehensive system of EC, which includes a direct and one to one transaction, public compensation, quota trading market, charitable compensation and ecological cognition of the products and so on. The domestic research on EC made a series of achievements and promoted the process, mainly carried out the theoretical research and practice from the aspects of the formation mechanism of the ecological and environmental problems, determination of the value of natural assets, the assessment the value of ecosystem services, the construction of the mechanism of EC and so on. However, compared with the international research, the studies in China quite lag, most of which are the introductory studies, and there are many problems, for example, the breakthrough and systematic of the EC theory are deficiency; the overall framework of the compensation mechanism has not been established yet, the research on scientific evidence to determine the assessment of environmental valuation and compensation standards is insufficient; there are more studies on the visible physical EC but fewer on the compensation for environmental capacity; the virtue of public goods on the environment and the purchases compensation of the government are stressed, but little research on the application of market mechanisms and so on. From the development trend, the mechanism of EC in developed countries will make more use of the tool based on market mechanisms, which is just the experience referred by the related research and practice in China.

Acknowledgments. Funded by the humanities & social science research foundation for young people from Ministry of Education of the PRC, NO: 10YJC790138.

References

1. Guangmei, Y., Qinghua, M., Wenhua, L., Lin, Z.: The scientific issues in studies of ecological compensation in China. Ecology 27, 4289–4301 (2007)
2. Fengqi, H.: Research on ecology resources' value compensation mechanism. PhD thesis. Northwest University, 5–38 (2008)
3. Junping, Y.: The environmental problems and behavior measures of cross-ecentury and global, vol. 198. Science Press, Beijing (1999)
4. Roger, M.S., Yue, M., Macgillivray, J., Caumon, M., et al.: Natural resources and environmental economics, vol. 317. China Press, Beijing (2002)
5. Rungao, Y., Hongmei, L.: The research and practice on environmental cmpensation abroad. Environment and Sustainable Development 2, 39–41 (2006)
6. Westman, W.: How much are nature's services worth? Science 197, 960–964 (1977)
7. Linlin, C., Zhenqi, H., Lei, S.: The policy design on the eco-compensation mechanism of mineral resources in China. China Mining Magazine 4, 11–18 (2007)
8. Guoqing, T.: Approach on the Problems of Levying Ecological Environmental Compensation. Shanghai Environmental Science 14, 1–4 (1995)
9. Turner, K.: Economics and wet land management. Ambio 20, 59–61 (1991)
10. Daily, G.C.: Nature's Service:Societal dependence on natural ecosystems. Island Press, Washington, DC (1997)
11. Miller, R.L., Cross, F.B.: The legal and regulatory environment today:changing perspectives for business, pp. 551–577. West Publishing Company, St. Paul (1993)
12. Miller, R.L., Cross, F.B.: The legal and regulatory environment today: changing perspectives for business, pp. 551–577. West Publishing Company, St. Paul (1993)

On the Ways to Optimize Land Use Pattern by Basing on the Concept of Low Carbon Eco-city

Ya-li Luo[1] and Chang-xin Zhang[1,2]

[1] Huaiyin Institute of Technology, College of Civil Engineering and Architecture,
No. 89, Beijing Rord (North), 223001 Huai'an, Jiang Su Prov., China
[2] College of Public Administration, ZheJiang University, 310029 Hang zhou,
Zhe Jiang Prov., China
{Luoyl8502,zcx8502}@sohu.com

Abstract. Based on the comparative analysis of the related concepts such as sustainable development, ecological city, low carbon cities and low-carbon eco-city, the paper argues that low-carbon eco-city embodies the concept of the sustainable urban development and implements that of the low-carbon economy development mode and eco-development in the course of urban development. Grounded on the systematic analysis of the relationship between urban land use and carbon emissions, such as urban land cover, land use type, land use structure etc, the paper put forward some ways to optimize the using pattern of urban land, which include economization of land use, compactization of space, effective mix of land function, and viresecnce of land etc..

Keywords: low-carbon eco-city, urban land use pattern, steps.

1 Introduction

Global climate is experiencing a remarkable change, with the main characteristic of getting warm, which has never happened in the last thousand years. The pressure of commitment to reduce the greenhouse gas emission is increasing. Our country is in the accelerated phase of economic development and urbanization, urban size constantly breakthroughs planning bounds, encroaches upon the external farm land and ecological land etc; the energy consumption in the city has soared. In the meantime, source scarcity, environmental degradation etc has become barriers of a city's sustainable development, even has a direct bearing on human destiny in the future. Coping challenges of resources and environment, Qiu Bao-xing vice minister of China's Ministry of Housing and Urban-Rural Construction propose that we should develop low-carbon economy to change the traditional development mode, consumption patterns and way of life. China must establish green economy development model based on the lower energy consumption and lower pollution, lower emission and higher efficiency, higher efficiency, higher benefit. To take low-carbon ecological city development road, by adopting environmental friendly development mode and using new carbon neutral technology [1].

M. Zhou (Ed.): ISAEBD 2011, Part IV, CCIS 211, pp. 8–16, 2011.

2 The Connotation of Low Carbon Ecological City

Since the sustainable development idea becomes the common sense of the society, following the eco-city idea in 1970s to the circular economic development mode proposed in 1990s, finally to low-carbon city proposed in 21st century, Low- carbon ecological city as a kind of city development mode is increasingly paid attention by the public [2-5]. In order to better grasp the connotation of low-carbon ecological city, the paper briefly methodized and discriminated these ideas in the aspect of proposed background, main thoughts, embodiment in the city(Table 1).

Table 1. Comparisons between several related ideas about city development

Idea	Background and Time	Concept and Connotation	Embodiment in the city development
Sustainable development	60, 70 years 20th century, the emergence of public and energy crisis , people realize that separating environment from economy and society to seek development can only lead to devastating disaster. In 1987, the WECD published *our common future* and officially proposed the concept of sustainable development.	Concept: Development that meets the needs of the present without compromising the ability of future generations to meet their needs. Connotation: Coordinated development among economy, society and environment.	The guiding direction of human development; The basic principles of urban development;
Eco-city	In 1971 , the UNESCO proposed the concept of eco-city in *man and biosphere* plan and definitely proposed that we should study the city with the comprehensive ecological method from the angle of ecology.	Concept: the human settlements form with society harmony, economic efficiency and a virtuous circle of ecology, which is based on natural systems harmony , the harmony between human and nature. Connotation: To realize the harmony of human , society and nature; to pursuit the natural systems harmony, human and nature harmony is the groundwork; To realize interpersonal harmony is the basic purpose of 'Eco-city'.	The goals of urban development in the future; The development idea of economic and social development, the coordination of human development and mutual promotion;

Table 1. *(continued)*

Low-carbon city	To deal with global climate change and to reduce greenhouse gas emissions. The England first officially proposed the concept of 'low-carbon economy' in *the white paper of energy in 2003*. In 2007, Japan committed to the construction of low-carbon society; Afterwards, the academia, the international organizations and the governments begins to pay attention to 'low-carbon city' concept in the 2007.	Concept: Through the transformation of economic development mode , consumption idea and lifestyle, to ensure improvement of the life quality and to realize the urban construction mode and social development mode, which is beneficial to reduce carbon emissions. Connotation: Meet the development of urbanization and economy accelerating needs; Realize separating economy development from carbon emissions.	The approach to sustainable urban development; City with 'a low-carbon economy' as the development mode and 'low-carbon lifestyle' as the idea and behavioral characteristics, realizing urban economic development and reducing carbon emissions.
Low-carbon eco-city	Facing the constraints of resource and environment, China has been confronted with the realistic contradictions and future challenges during the urbanization.	Concept: Through the development mode of low-carbon economy , to promote economic development and reduce carbon emissions , realize the harmonious development among human, economy and nature. Connotation: Emphasize separating economic development from carbon emissions; The goals of development is realizing of harmonious development among people, society and nature.	The integration of guiding direction and specific measures of urban development; The integration of goals and approaches of urban development.

Through the analysis we can see , the low-carbon eco-city is a human, economy and nature harmonious city development idea which promotes economic development and reduces carbon emissions through development mode of low-carbon economy; it is also the embodiment of sustainable development idea in the city development and the implementation of development mode of low-carbon economy and ecological development idea in the city development. Low- carbon eco-city integrates many city development ideas together, such as sustainable development, ecological city, low-carbon city etc., which was proposed in the current city development; it permeate many social and economic development mode of urban circular economy, clean production, green development etc.; It also comprehensively embodies the basic thought of developing 'saving' and 'environmentally friendly' society and constructing the harmonious society under the guidance of the scientific development perspective at the present stage in our country. It not only is urban development concept inheritance, but also is a strong integration to ensure that the practical maneuverability.

3   Analysis on the Relationship between Urban Land Use Pattern and Carbon Emissions

3.1 Land Cover and Carbon Emissions

Land cover refers to a complex of surface elements covered by natural and artificial buildings. Land cover will produce radiation force to albedos rate and make a difference to local or global climate. An important feature of urbanization is through human actions to change arrangements and activities of land cover type, and corresponding measures to transform the natural state of land or artificial management to urban land use [6]. Constructions inevitably leads to a mass scale of reduction in natural soil resources in areas surrounding the cities and will inevitably occur surface airtight, and make the land exert its foundation to support function while completely lose it the original production and ecological 'carbon sink' function. Research has shown that it will increase 149.8 times of carbon emissions when converting one hectare of farmland into a construction land, however, it will increase the carbon emissions 929 times when converting one hectare forest land into a construction land.

3.2 The Type of Urban Land Use and Carbon Emissions

Urban land use not only reduce carbon sink function through surface covered airtight, but also make a difference to carbon emissions and climate change through the buildings on different types of land and corresponding human activities. Zhao Rong-qin(2009) researched into the influence carbon circulation when land use changes, by constructing mode between the carbon emissions with energy consumption to make a quantitative calculation on five years' energy consumption 'carbon footprint' of Jiang Su Province. He concluded the sequence of different types of land use 'foot print' from large to small is: residential and industrial land, transportation land, unused land and special land, agricultural land and water land. Also some researches have shown that without considering the carbon absorbing effect, the intensity of carbon emissions of general farmland is 0.37 t/ha, the forest land is 0.06t/ha, however, the construction land is 55.8 t/ha, among which the industrial land is up to 196 t/ha [7].

3.3 The Spatial Structure of Land Use and Carbon Emissions

The urban spatial structure is refers to internal mechanism in the space distribution and mutual interaction of city elements. Various activities in cities and the urban spatial structure have locking relationships. Once the physical environment is built, it will exert far-reaching influence on human social and economic activities, through affecting transportation distance, what affects carbon emissions (Fig. 1) [8]. The spatial relationships among the land of residential, working and rest, which decides transportation distance of urban residents, then to some extent decides the transportation mode. However, the different transportations mode has different carbon emissions, the carbon emissions of walking and cycling is almost zero, public transportation system ranks the second, and the carbon emissions of private cars and planes is the highest(Fig. 2). Therefore the urban land use structure based on reducing the transportation distance is beneficial to reducing carbon emissions.

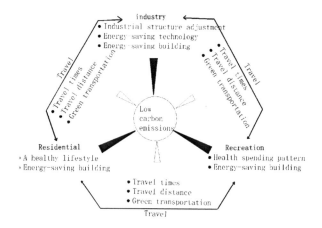

Fig. 1. Urban spatial structure and carbon emissions relations

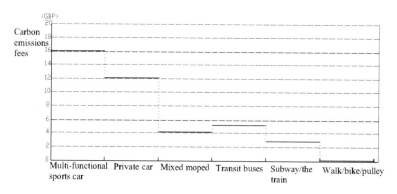

Fig. 2. 10 minutes commuter traffic 'carbon footprint' comparison (source: http://streetseducation .org/walkingschools)

4   The Approach to Optimize Urban Land Use Pattern Based on the Idea of Low-Carbon Ecological

4.1   Economize the Aggregate of Urban Land Use

Economize the urban land refers to careful calculation and strict budge on saving lands as far as possible, opposing to wasting lands, so as to reduce the aggregate demand of construction land sand slowing down the lose of land ecological functions, which is brought by non-agricultural transformation. First of all, we should make a scientific planning of different urban lands, reasonably forecast the land scale, reasonably determines the rate of building density, cubage and green land, strictly implements the national standards of construction and avoids planning wide street, big square and green belts etc. In addition, through the reform of villages in cities, land supply and the management in the section of construction to reserve lands and digest the free lands etc., all of these means are also the significant approach to save lands. Saving lands can reduce the consumption of land resource, thus effectively reduce the energy consumption and carbon emissions of each unit of land use.

4.2 Compact the Spatial of Urban Land Use

Based on the two most important theories : intensive form of urban helps reduce the erosion of ecological environment, thus reducing human's activities on the natural environment. Spatial compact cities can greatly reduce road traffic, especially relying on private cars, so as to mitigate the road traffic pressure and reduce the consumption of oil and other resources and reduce air pollution est. Meanwhile, scholars think that relatively improve the cities' compact degree of space density, functionality and physical form is beneficial to realize resources, service, infrastructure of sharing, reduce duplication of the construction which could occupy land and reduce the cost of energy and resources, so as to improve the sustainable development of the city, the compact city has been more and more recognized.

According to the urban structure scale, the compact space of urban land use reflects different space levels, respectively, four latitude : urban regional levels, urban space level, community space level and grouping space level and so on [8]. In urban regional levels, through reasonable distribution of urban space, organization of industrial structure and reasonable arrangement of infrastructures, guiding various elements of the city to the urban agglomeration, forming a regional spatial rank and levels of space pattern and different grades of lateral ties between cities reticular pattern; In urban space level, we should actively guide urban various functions and improve reasonable zoning layout of the infrastructures and avoid excessive outspread of city scale and the simplification of functions. In community space level, we should emphasize mixed use and the strategy of moderate high-density community development, break the traditional ways of functional zoning, different minimum functions as an urban community group and rely on public transport, reduce using cars and play an advantage of location in urban regions.

4.3 The Effective Mix of the Functions of Urban Land Use

Through the effective mix of the diversity and multiple function of urban land utilization can reduce long-distance traffic demand, and save transportation time, reducing cities' carbon emissions [9]. A healthy city's secret recipe by Jane. Jacobs is "the intricate and philosophical use of land can make between each other either economically or societies are constantly support mutually". Meanwhile hybrid land use can encourage taking public transportation, American scholars studied 59 office development project located large suburb in American and found that average increase 20% of the retail and commercial activities on the floor area, can cause carpool or public transportation increasing proportion of travel of 4.5%. The effective mix use of urban land function requires to break the traditional way of functional zone in urban planning, and to reasonably arrange work and living, have a rest sites in the community level , to make the traffic of each land at the range of walking and cycling, so as to reduce the usage of automobile, especially private cars and reach a effect of saving energy and reducing carbon emissions.(Fig. 3)

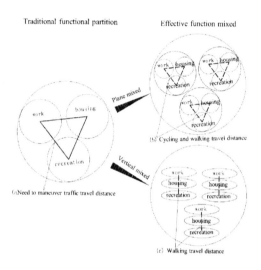

Fig. 3. Urban land functional zoning and function mixed

4.4   The Basal Greenization of Urban Land Use

Reduce ground hardening. While a lot of natural terrains were hardened to improve its support function in the urbanization process, however, they lost the original carbon function, directly led the land of carbon emissions soared[10]. Therefore, it is a necessary choice to reduce carbon emissions through reducing ground sclerosis. In construction, we should give full consideration to the land ecological value, minimize the use of hardened materials, in order to protect the ground ecological systems and ventilation permeable natural function. For the necessary sclerosis ground, we should probe to adopt new technology, new material to improve and make up,   take permeable material, maintain the ground to breathe smoothly to try and reduce its negative effects. For example, a sidewalk and bike lanes and walk street ground, we should adopt laying hydraulic permeability floor tile,   and use hydraulic permeability filler material between the brick and brick; Use grid ground shape parking lot , and fill with the soil humus into the bricky aperture, to help weeds grow and to maintain the carbon sink function of some of ground; Try to reduce large areas of hardening square, park, use more pebbles, and work with the natural material such as a natural landscape. These practices will help maintain the balance between rapid urbanization and ecological environment protection.

Increase stereo forestations. Stereo greening namely make full use of the site conditions, choose different climbing plants and other plants to plant and attach or stuck in various structures and other space structural virescence. Like many foreign countries, creating a 'ecological wall', the particular way is along the wall to scramble among planting trees, equidistance can climb a cane kind flowers and plants, wrought iron nets. This method saves labor and material, it is also a practical form, not only reaches the vertical virescence effect, but also plays a role through the green. And Chicago roof garden is worth using for reference, the Chicago design and build various roof garden, by designing a special multi-layer soil, and polystyrene materials, cone-shaped shell and waterproof membrane to ensure the roof withstand such soil, watering and plant the total weight of the leakage occurred. Roof garden can plant wild onions, safflower grass, sky blue aster and buffalo grass and other plants, so that it can save $ 40,000,000 in the cost of municipal government spent on the summer cooling.

Enhance the protection of urban open space and ecologically sensitive areas. By controlling the size of the accumulation of the secondary industry and limiting rural industry, centralizing towns and villages appropriately, the urban-rural handover area should undertake the task of agricultural production and protect natural environment. Agricultural Comprehensive Development Experimental Zone, the basic farmland protection areas should be strictly delineated the scope to prevent from being invaded, non-farmland protection areas delineated the scope of farmland to prevent the construction from encroaching; ecologically sensitive areas, such as national nature reserves, mountain forests, water sources, large reservoirs, coastal and tourist area of natural landscape, the local should prohibit industrial enterprises, large-scale real estate development projects entering, strictly control the development intensity.

5 Conclusions

Low-carbon eco-city is the embodiment of sustainable development idea during the city developing and is the implementation of development mode of low-carbon economy and ecological development idea in the city development. The urban land use pattern under the goal of low-carbon ecological refers to comprehensively consider the ecological value, economic value and social value of lands, to accomplish the goal of 'low emission, high efficiency, high benefit'. To give full play to land biological carbon absorbing effect, it is necessary to adopt advanced energy conservation and emission reduction technology to reduce carbon emissions on the various concrete process of land use; Meanwhile, through the mixed land use to improve the degree of land intensive use and social resources sharing; Through optimizing land use structure to deeply dig the value of land utilization and land economy, and finally realize the land use pattern of low-carbon economy, which is "low emission, high efficiency, high benefit".

References

1. Qiu, B.-x.: The tendency of China's urban development model Transformation – low-carbon eco-city. J. Urban Studies, 1–6 (2009)
2. Chen, Q.-y., Quan, Y.: The planning idea of constructing low carbon cities in China. Journal of Modern Urban Reasch, 17–19 (2009)
3. Ye, Z.-d.: The application of carbon emissions evaluating methods in the low carbon urban planning. Journal of modern urban studies, 20–26 (2009)
4. Quan, Z., Ye, X.-p., Chen, G.-w.: LOW-carbon urban planning: a new vision. J.urban planning review 41, 13–18 (2010)
5. Glaeser Edward, L., Kahn Matthew, E.: The Greenness of Cities: Carbon Dioxide Emissions and Urban Development.EB/OL, http://www.nber.org/papers
6. Liu, Y., Zhao, R.-q.: The advances and trends of land use and land cover change research. Journal of Hebei Normal University (Natural Science Edition), 310–315 (2004)
7. Zhao, H.-y., Guo, X.-m., Jun, C.: Low-Carbon Urban Planning from the Perspective of "CarbonFootprint". J. Planners, 9–15 (2010)
8. Pan, H.-x.: Urban spatial structure towards Low Carbon New Urban Transport and Land Use Model. Urban Studies, 40–45 (2010)
9. Fei, C., Zhu, D.-J.: Research on the Conternt Models and Strategies of Low Carbon Cities. Journal of urban planning, 71–79 (2009)
10. Xiao, Z.-a., Huan, P.: Low carbon economy path choice of land use patterns. J. Searchs, 85–86 (2010)

On the Sustainable Utilization of the World's Cultivated Land Resources in View of Food Security

Ya-li Luo[1] and Chang-xin Zhang[1,2]

[1] Huaiyin Institute of Technology, College of Civil Engineering and Architecture,
No. 89, Beijing Rord (North), 223001 Huai'an, Jiang Su Prov, China
[2] ZheJiang University, College of Public Administration,
310029 Hang zhou, Zhe Jiang Prov, China
{Luoyl8502,zcx8502}@sohu.com

Abstract. Based on the latest statistics, after giving a clear definition to food security, the paper argues that food security is threatened by the problems of poverty, rapid population growth, diet change and the increasing food demand which is caused by the bio-energy development. Meanwhile, the decrease of the average available arable land worldwide, the pessimistic growth potential of it, the reduction of it for food production, and its degradation, which all challenge the food security as well. In order to cope with this problem, the article focuses on promoting the ways of thinking of the sustainable use of cultivated land resources by the ways of maintaining the land ecological balance, optimizing land use structure, controlling the blind expansion of construction land and population growth, and by ways of changing the consumption patterns etc..

Keywords: Food security, The world, Cultivated land, Sustainable utilization.

1 Introduction

The food is not only important strategic mater which related the people's livelihood and national economic security, but also is the most basic life material to the masses. The outbreak of food crisis in 2008 caused hundreds of millions of people to endure hunger, more than 30 countries into a food shortage, even lead to social unrest in some countries. The World Bank's latest statistics show international prices for most crops sharp rise 15% from October 2010 to January 2011, and already approached all-time highs record set in 2008. The severe climate crisis, the explosion of the world's population, biological energy development, which lead to growing demand for food. Meanwhile the cultivated land supply is continuing to decrease. Those all challenge the food security [1].Focus on food security, the related research on the sustainable utilization of cultivated land resources are concerned by governments and scholars around the world.

2 Food Security and Food Crisis

Food security concept was defined by FAO in the 1974, and was amended in 1983 [2], and then was anew expressed in 1996. Now, the more complex definition is: "Food

M. Zhou (Ed.): ISAEBD 2011, Part IV, CCIS 211, pp. 17–24, 2011.
© Springer-Verlag Berlin Heidelberg 2011

security, at the individual, household, national, regional and global levels when all people, at all times, have physical and economic access to sufficient, safe and nutritious food to meet their dietary needs and food preferences for an active and healthy life" [3]. Compared to the previous concept, this notion added the demand for food quality. That is the food security is not only able to produce enough food to achieve a stable supply of food and asking people to eat more nutritious and healthier. The change of the concept of food security shows that the connotation and extension of food security is closely related to the international situation at different periods, and it is a dynamic international concept. Food crisis will happen once when the goal of world food security is seriously threatened. Generally, there are two aspects inducing food crisis, one is food prices and the other is food production and supply problems. In long term, the real food crisis is relative shortage of the food production and supply. As long as ensuring the stable development of grain production and adequate food supply, worldwide food crisis does not occur. On the contrary, the food crisis is inevitable [4].

3   Growing Demand for Food Threaten Food Security

3.1   World Poverty Population Demand for Food Have Not Yet Satisfied

In addition, the problem of the food and clothing for the world's poor is far from resolved, and the trend is very not optimistic. Adopted in 2000, the United Nations 'Millennium Declaration' established the United Nations Millennium Development Goals, the first of which was to "Eradicate extreme poverty and hunger". According to these goals, the level of world's poverty and hunger will be reduced by half in 2015. Unfortunately, the world's chronically hungry people have been increasing since 1995 (Fig.1). The world nutritional deficiencies rapidly increase due to the food crisis out breaking in 2007. By 2009, the world's undernourished populations have reached 1.02 billion, accounting for 15% of the total population, the most of which are in Asia-Pacific region, reaching 642 million, followed by sub-Saharan Africa, amounting to 265 million (Fig. 2). According to United Nations measurement standards, to reduce the world's undernourished population from the current 1020 million to 585 million requires about 7.8 million tons of food; and to eliminate under nutrition will need about 184 million

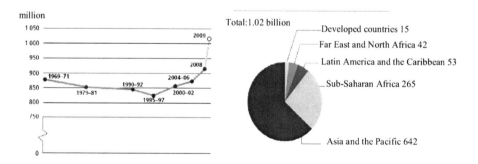

Fig.   1.   1969-2009   World   nutritional deficiencies toll (Source: FAO.2009b)

Fig. 2. 2009 according to region statistical nutritional deficiencies toll (Source: FAO.2009b)

tons of grain. To eliminate malnutrition and poverty is a long and difficult progress, which also form enormous pressure on the future world food demand and supply.

3.2 The Rapid Growth of Population and the Rigid Consumption for Food

The most basic function of food is to meet human food needs. The food supply must first meet demand for food consumption caused the world population growth, and the demand is rigid. According to UN statistics, the world's population increased by 1 billion people every 10 years in the past 30 years. World population was 6.115 billion people in 2000; the number is about 6.512 billion in 2006, 6.909 billion in 2010. According to the forecast, the world population will be 8.309 billion in 2030, the number will increase to 9.15 billion in 2050 (Fig. 3).

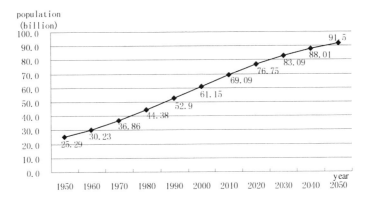

Fig. 3. The world population prospect(data source:World Population Prospects: The 2008 Revision, http://esa.un.org/unpp)

The world's population is on the rise, meanwhile the per capita consumption of grain is also increasing. The level of world food consumption per capita has grown from 2280 cal / d in the early 1960s up to now an average of 2800 cal/d. To meet the growing demand for food of human, world food production must be increased to more than 3,000 million tons by 2030. According to the MA (Millennium Ecosystem Assessment) prediction, the demand for food crops will grow 70% to 85% in the next 50 years [5]. To achieve such increase grain production is extremely difficult. But if it is not possible, the world's food supply should be a major problem.

3.3 Improvement of Dietary Structure Increases Demand for Food

With the improvement of people's consumption structure and change in eating habits since 1960s, the world has undergone major changes in dietary structure. The composition of diet has gradually been diversification, which includes the animal products (meat, eggs, milk), vegetable oil, fruits and vegetables etc. instead of the staple food such as grain, tubers and beans. By 2025, global meat demand will rapidly increase 138 million tons. According to statistics, to product 1kg beef production takes about 8kg grain feed, and producing 1kg chicken will take about 2kg grain feed. FAO predicted that the grain used to produce feed reach 756 million tons.

3.4 Biomass Energy Development Bring Huge Demand for Food

With non-renewable fossil energy resources depletion, more and more countries have put the development and utilization of biomass energy into national energy development strategy. For example, U.S. biomass energy policies and measures promote the rapid development of ethanol fuel industry. According to the World Agricultural Outlook 2007-2016 issued by OECD-FAO, the expansion of US ethanol production and corresponding use of maize have been upward trend since 1995 and for some time in the future (Fig. 4). Also, according to the "EU Strategy for Biofuels" plan, the proportion of biomass fuels is from 2% in 2005 to 5.75% in 2010, to 10% in 2020 in EU (Fig. 5). Therefore, the human should be alert to the relative food shortage and the relative arable land reduction and even the food crisis caused by the bio-energy development [6-7].

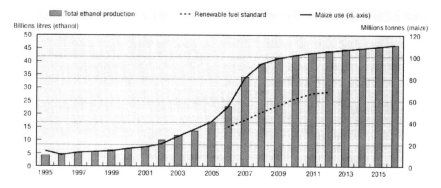

Fig. 4. Expansion of US ethanol production and corresponding use of maize (source: ERS)

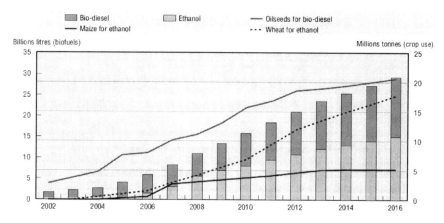

Fig. 5. Ethanol and bio-diesel use in the EU to increase – based on wheat, rapeseed and imports (Note: Ethanol and bio-diesel data before 2006 refer to production, from 2006 to 2016 to consumption. Source: EU Commission, OECD Secretariat)

4 Cultivated Land Resources Limited Supply Challenge Food Security

4.1 The per Capita Arable Land Decreased Rapidly

According to data published by FAO in 2009, the worldwide arable land area was about 1.411 billion hm^2 in 2007, accounting for 10.8% of global land area, the number was more 130 million hm^2 than 1.281 billion hm^2 in 1961, and is more 80 million hm^2 than 1.403 billion hm^2 in 1991. The total area of cultivated land was an upward trend, but the per capita arable land decreased rapidly because of the increase of world population. According to the United Nations statistics, the world population was about 3.085 billion in 1961, was 5.375 billion in 1991, and 6.671 billion in 2007. The per capita cultivated land area in the corresponding year was respectively about 0.415 ha, 0.261ha, 0.216ha. The cultivated land per capita decline rapidly.

4.2 The Pessimistic Growth Potential of Cultivated Area

From regional perspective, the cultivated land area of developed countries reduced at breakneck speed. From 1961 to 1991, it reduced 0.0467 million ha every year, and the number was 3.5 million ha from 1991 to 2007. In fact, the cultivated area expanded potential is little for the vast majority of developed countries, while the available land reserves in developing countries really is not much. The developing countries have about 2.8 billion hm^2 arable land area, of which 1.0 billion hm^2 arable land area has been cultivated. But the remaining 1.8 billion hm^2 no cultivate land can not be regarded as a land bank, because nearly 90% of them concentrated in South America and sub-Saharan Africa. Among of those no cultivate land, there are 45% of them are in the forest, 12% in natural resources conservation areas, 3% in the human settlements and areas prone to disease. So there is really not much for development.

4.3 The Supply of Land for Growing Food Show Tight Situation

There is almost no land can be reclaimed in South Asia, the Near East and North Africa, According to the International Food Policy Research Institute prediction, the land area that can be used to expand of grain cultivation could at most increase about 10%, and that is mainly in South America and Africa. By 2020, the world's grain acreage will grow by about 7%, of which the Sahara Desert Saharan Africa is expected to increase by 20 million hm^2, to increase 8 million hm^2 in Latin America, and other developing countries can only increase total 13 million hm^2. Overall, a substantial increase in cultivated area is unrealistic, the supply of land for growing food show tight situation.

4.4 The Quality of Cultivated Land Severely Degraded

According to a new research report by UNEP, in the past 45 years, because of agricultural activities, deforestation, over-grazing and so on, the degraded land area was near 1.2 billion hm^2, that accounted for about 11% of the earth surface area with vegetation. According to UNEP statistics, there are dry land 3.27 billion hm^2, among of them about 2.0 billion hm^2 have affected by desertification. There are more than 6 million hm^2 land became desert land and about 21 million hm^2 land loss economic value every year in the world. The desertification threat the more than 100 countries and 800 million populations.

5   To Promote Sustainable Utilization of World Cultivated Land Resources

5.1   Responding to Global Climate Change, to Maintain the Ecological Balance of Land

Ecological balance is the fundamental conditions that the biological depend on to maintain normal growth and development, procreation. Land ecosystem is the basis and the core of terrestrial ecosystems. Changes of land use lead to greenhouse gas source / sink change and surface albedo changes, which affect climate change [8]. Global climate change has significant impact on the global ecosystem and socio-economic system, and will continue to have far-reaching and significant impacts; many of them are negative or adverse [9,10]. Global climate change will make an unprecedented challenges facing humanity, and the agriculture depending on the natural is one of the industries that are hardest hit[11].

Therefore, all land development and utilization activities must maintain a balance of land ecosystems. The use of land resources must pay attention to the promotion and speed of the development of different land use types. Humans should focus on the world, to build regional collaboration restraint mechanism maintaining balance of land ecosystems, to specific responsibilities and obligations in all regions clear, and to regulate people's behavior of development and utilization of land.

5.2   Optimizing Land Use Structure, to Improve the Comprehensive Efficiency of Land Resources

Unreasonable land use structure will directly affect the combined effectiveness of the land. Development and utilization of land resources should based on the suitability evaluation of land resources. To optimize the allocation of land resources and to enhance the overall development performance, the land suitable for agricultural production is used as agricultural land, or as forest land, or as pastoral land etc..

5.3   Controlling Population Growth, to Ease Pressure on Man-Land Conflicts

With the rapid growth of world population and consumption, the conflict between population and resources, environment will become more complex; food security situation will be more and more serious. All countries of the world must focus on the carrying capacity of land resources, to coordinate Man-land relationship, to achieve the sustainable development of population.

Because of the obvious man-land conflicts and the rapid growth on food, energy consumption, and the developing countries should strictly control population growth, to reduce the rigid demand for food led by population growth. China has achieved historic success on controlling the population growth duo to the family planning policy for 30 years, which is worth learning to other countries. At the same time, facing to the cultivated land resources sharp drop and agricultural ecological environment worsening situation, it is very important to re-evaluate the lowest per-capita cultivated land and to build protection mechanism of cultivated land based on food safety at the global level.

5.4 Strictly Controlling Construction Land, to Contain Urban Sprawl Situation

The world is on the period of rapid urbanization. The conflicts among rapid urbanization reduce energy consumption and the protection of cultivated land will become increasingly serious. According to United Nations projections, world urbanization rate would be 68.7% and urban population would reach 6.286 billion in 2050. In terms of per capita 83 m^2 urban construction land, only urban construction land would be up to 25.8877 million hm^2, which does not include land occupied by transportation, water conservancy and other infrastructure.

Facing the urban sprawl, the traditional concept of urban development and governance model has become increasingly unsuited to new situation. It is the inevitable choice to improve the level of concentration of urban construction land and to strictly control the urban growth boundaries based on compact urban development concept. It is a new goal of urban development to achieve low-carbon urban construction, low-carbon energy development, low carbon economic development, low carbon social development and low carbon technology development through developing the green transportation, green building and green consumption.

5.5 Advocating Low Carbon Lifestyles, to Reduce the Excessive Consumption

A new low-carbon way of life is being vigorously promoted, which was proposed in the context of the serious challenge facing human survival and development to global warming. Low-carbon living emphasizes that to save fossil energy consumption and reduce carbon dioxide emissions in many ways. The essence of low-carbon life is advocating saving against over-consumption. Low-carbon lifestyle is bound to reduce energy consumption; ease the tremendous pressure on grain consumption. It will make a significant contribution to world food security.

References

1. Geng, X.-h.: International symposium of the food security and rural development in post-crisis era. Journal of Nanjing Agricultural University (Social Sciences Edition), 145–148 (2010)
2. Xuan, O., Jie, H.: Indicators analysis and countermeasure research of domestic and international food security. World Agriculture, 7–9 (2010)
3. Evolution of food security concept and its impact on China, http://www.cngrain.com
4. Yin, C.-j.: World Food Security: Global Food Crisis and Food Security in China. China Economic Publishing House, Beijing (2009)
5. Rosegrant, M.W., Cline, S.A., Valmonte-Santos, R.A.: Global water and Food Security: Megatrends and Emerging Issues (2010)

6. Li, L.-t., Xue, J.-l.: The changing tendency and forecasting of world food security. Journal of Shanghai University(Social sciences), 29–36 (2009)
7. Liu, G.-q., Yang, S.-q.: Analysis on the world food security and the coping strategy. Journal of Northwest A&F University(social science edition), 21–24 (2009)
8. Ding, Y.-h.: Human activities and global climate change and its impact on water resources. Observed facts of climate change, 20–27 (2008)
9. Dobson, A.P., Bradshaw, A.D., Baker, A.J.M.: Hopes for the future: Restoration ecology and conservation biology. Science 277, 515–521 (1997)
10. Hendrey, G., Lewin, K.F., Nagy, J.: Free air carbon dioxide enrichment: Development, progress, results.Vegetatio 104, 17–31 (1993)
11. Pang, J.-l., Huang, C.-c.: Study on palaeosol features in Xi'an area and climate change during the last 10,000 years. Plateau Meteorology, 79–83 (2003)

Option Pricing with Fuzzy Parameters via Monte Carlo Simulation

Michal Holčapek and Tomáš Tichý[*]

Institute for Research and Applications of Fuzzy Modeling
University of Ostrava, 30. dubna 22, 701 03 Ostrava, Czech Republic
michal.holcapek@osu.cz
Department of Finance, Faculty of Economics, Technical University Ostrava,
Sokolská 33, 701 21 Ostrava, Czech Republic
tomas.tichy@vsb.cz.

Abstract. Very nice applications of the stochastic simulation approach, both via MC and QMC, can be found in all areas that rely on modeling via stochastic processes, such as finance. However, since estimation of financial quantities is often very challenging, many scholars suggest to specify some parts of financial models by means of fuzzy sets theory. In this contribution the recent knowledge of fuzzy numbers and their approximation is utilized in order to suggest fuzzy-MC simulation approach to option price modeling in terms of fuzzy-random variables. In particular, we suggest to replace a crisp volatility parameter in the standard market model by a fuzzy random variable, which can be easily evaluated by Monte Carlo simulation. Application possibilities are shown on illustrative examples.

Keywords: fuzzy random variable, fuzzy stochastic process, option pricing.

1 Introduction

Options, a specific nonlinear type of a financial derivative, play an important role in the economy. In particular, the usage of options allows one to reach a higher level of efficiency in terms of risk-return trade-off. The option's holder can exercise his right, eg. buy or sell an underlying asset, when he finds it useful. Obviously, it is the case of positive cash flowing from the option exercising. Otherwise the option matures unexploited. By contrast, the seller of the option has to act according to the instructions of the holder. This asymmetry of buyer/seller rights implies the needs of advanced technique for option pricing and hedging.

The standard ways to option pricing, as well as replication and hedging, dates back to 70's to the seminal papers of Black and Scholes [3] and Merton [16], Cox et al. [6] or Boyle [4]. Although the aforementioned approaches slightly differ in details, eg. only the model of Cox et al. can be used directly to price American

---

[*] The support provided by VSB-TU Ostrava under the SGS project SP2011/7 is kindly announced.

M. Zhou (Ed.): ISAEBD 2011, Part IV, CCIS 211, pp. 25–33, 2011.
© Springer-Verlag Berlin Heidelberg 2011

options, the general frame is the same – the underlying process is derived from Gaussian distribution and all parameters are either deterministic or probabilistic, ie. particular probabilities are assigned to the set of real numbers. However, in the real world, it is often difficult to obtain reliable and stable estimates to input parameters. The reason can be that sufficiently long time series of data is lacking or the data are too heterogenous. Several research papers collected by Ribeiro et al. [18] suggested that the fuzzy sets theory proposed by Zadeh [23] can be useful for financial engineering problems of such kind.

One of the first attempts to utilize the fuzzy sets theory in option pricing dates back to Cherubini [5]. Later, for example, Zmeškal [24] applied a simplifying fuzzy-stochastic approach based on T-numbers to value a firm as a European call option (ie. a real option). By contrast, Yoshida [22] assumed European financial options so that only standard parameters (mainly riskless rate/drift and volatility) were specified as fuzzy. These papers were followed by many others, extending the analysis of Black-Scholes type models to eg. more general Lévy processes or even another direction of research dealing with discrete binomial-type models or utility functions. However, except recent, but brief contribution of Nowak and Romaniuk [17], there was no attempt to value an option with fuzzy parameters via Monte Carlo simulation approach.

In this paper, we try to fill this gap by suggesting a Monte Carlo methodology with fuzzy parameters to value a European option. More particularly, we assume (geometric) Brownian motion with fuzzy volatility as the option underling process. We proceed as follows. In the next section, we provide brief details about option pricing via plain Monte Carlo simulation within the risk neutral setting. Next, LU-fuzzy numbers are defined, including the basic operations with them. The definition of fuzzy random variables follows. Finally, the European option price is evaluated under fuzzy-stochastic process and compared to standard stochastic processes.

2 Standard Approach

Let us denote the underlying asset price at maturity time as S_T and the exercise price as K. Then we can denote the payoff function Ψ for European call ($p = 1$) and put ($p = -1$) options as $(p(S_T - K))^+$ with $(x)^+ \equiv \max(x, 0)$. For the option value at time $t < T$ it generally holds that:

$$f_t = e^{d_\tau} \mathbb{E}[\Psi_T^{vanilla\ call/put}] = e^{d_\tau} \mathbb{E}[(p(S_T - K))^+], \tag{1}$$

where a discount factor d_τ relates to the probability measure under which the expectation operator $\mathbb{E}$ is evaluated and $\tau = T - t$ denotes the remaining time to maturity. Commonly, $\mathbb{E}^\mathcal{P}$ denotes the real world expectation (under physical probability measure), while $\mathbb{E}^\mathcal{Q}$ is used within the risk-neutral world, ie. $e^{-r\tau}\mathbb{E}^\mathcal{Q}[S_T] = S_t$, where r is a riskless rate valid over time interval τ.

Since financial asset prices are often restricted to positive values only, geometric processes are commonly preferred. If, for example, $Z(t)$ denotes a stochastic process for log-returns of financial asset S, eg. a non-dividend paying stock, in order to model its price in time we have to evaluate the exponential function of $Z(t)$. It follows that under $\mathcal{Q}$ formula (1) can be rewritten into (assuming $p = 1$):

$$f_t = e^{-r\tau} \mathbb{E}^{\mathcal{Q}} \left[\left(S_t e^{r\tau + Z_\tau^{\mathcal{Q}}} - \mathcal{K} \right)^+ \right], \tag{2}$$

where $Z_\tau^{\mathcal{Q}}$ is a (potentially compensated) realization of a suitable stochastic process over τ such that it is ensured that $\mathbb{E}^{\mathcal{Q}}[S_t e^{Z_\tau^{\mathcal{Q}}}]$ is a martingale.

The optimal choice of $Z_\tau^{\mathcal{Q}}$ depends on the assumptions (observations) about the returns of the underlying asset. If the process is sufficiently tractable, (2) can be solved analytically leading to a closed form formula, see eg. risk-neutral derivation of Black-Scholes model in [20]. Alternatively, we can utilize the law of large numbers and evaluate the expectation in (2) via Monte Carlo simulation, ie. sufficiently large number N of independent scenarios is taken from the relevant probability distribution of $Z_\tau^{\mathcal{Q}}$ (see eg. [9]):

$$f_t = e^{-r\tau} \mathbb{E}^{\mathcal{Q}} \left[\left(S_t e^{r\tau + Z_\tau^{\mathcal{Q}}} - K \right)^+ \right] \approx \frac{e^{-r\tau}}{N} \sum_{i=1}^{N} \left(S_t e^{r\tau + Z_\tau^{\mathcal{Q}(i)}} - K \right)^+, \tag{3}$$

where superscript (i) refers to i-th scenario from a given probability space. Obviously, if the information available about the source of uncertainty are not sufficient to select a reliable candidate for its stochastic evolution, one can prefer to replace $Z_\tau^{\mathcal{Q}}$ by a fuzzy-stochastic variable.

3   LU-Fuzzy Number

Let $\mathbb{R}$ denotes the set of real numbers and $A : \mathbb{R} \to [0,1]$ be a mapping. We say that A is a *fuzzy number* if A is normal (ie. there exits an element x_0 such that $A(x_0) = 1$), convex (ie. $A(\lambda x + (1-\lambda)y) \geq \min(A(x), A(y))$ for any $x, y \in \mathbb{R}$ and $\lambda \in [0,1]$), upper semicontinuous and supp(A) is bounded, where supp$(A) = cl\{x \in \mathbb{R} \mid A(x) > 0\}$ and cl is the closure operator (see [12,7]). Note that the most popular models of fuzzy numbers are the triangular and trapezoidal shaped models investigated by Dubois and Prade in [8]. Their popularity follows from the simple calculus as addition or multiplication of fuzzy numbers which can be established for them. This is also a reason why we can find many recent papers on the approximation of fuzzy numbers by the aforementioned models (see eg. [1,2] and the references therein). In order to model fuzzy numbers we will use a more advanced model of fuzzy numbers based on the interpolation of given knots using rational splines that was proposed by Guerra and Stefanini in [11] and developed in [21]. This model generalizes triangular fuzzy numbers and provides a broad variety of shapes enabling more precise representation of fuzzy real data. Nevertheless, the calculus remains very simple.

Recall that a piecewise rational cubic Hermite parametric function $P \in C^1[\alpha_0, \alpha_n]$, with parameters v_i, w_i, $i = 0, \ldots, n - 1$, is defined for $\alpha \in [\alpha_i, \alpha_{i+1}]$, $i = 0, \ldots, n - 1$ by

$$P(\alpha) = P_i(\alpha, v_i, w_i) =$$

$$\frac{(1-\theta)^3 f_i + \theta(1-\theta)^2 (v_i f_i + h_i d_i) + \theta^2(1-\theta)(w_i f_{i+1} - h_i d_{i+1}) + \theta^3 f_{i+1}}{(1-\theta)^3 + v_i \theta(1-\theta)^2 + w_i \theta^2(1-\theta) + \theta^3},$$

where the notations f_i and d_i are, respectively, the real data values and the first derivative values (slopes) at the knots $\alpha_0 < \cdots < \alpha_n$, $h_i = \alpha_{i+1} - \alpha_i$, $\theta = (\alpha - \alpha_i)/h_i$ and $v_i, w_i \geq 0$. The parameters v_i and w_i are called the tension parameters.[1] In this work, we will use a global monotonicity setting (cf. [21]):

$$v_i = w_i = \begin{cases} \frac{d_{i+1} + d_i}{f_{i+1} - f_i}, & \text{if } f_{i+1} \neq f_i; \\ 0, & \text{otherwise.} \end{cases} \tag{4}$$

A main reason for this assumption is a natural calculus which can be introduced for fuzzy numbers based on this type of parametric functions. One can see that each such parametric function $P \in C^1[\alpha_0, \alpha_n]$ may be expressed in the matrix form consisting of parameters as follows:

$$\mathbf{P} = \begin{pmatrix} \mathbf{f} \\ \mathbf{d} \end{pmatrix} = \begin{pmatrix} f_{\alpha_0} & \cdots & f_{\alpha_n} \\ d_{\alpha_0} & \cdots & d_{\alpha_n} \end{pmatrix} \tag{5}$$

for a partition $\alpha_0 < \cdots < \alpha_n$ of the interval $[a_0, a_n]$.

In what follows, we will identify each parametric function $P \in C^1[\alpha_0, \alpha_n]$ satisfying the presumption on v_i and w_i given in (4) is satisfied, with a matrix $\mathbf{P}$ established above and simply write $P(\alpha) = \mathbf{P}(\alpha)$. Now we may define a special case of LU-fuzzy numbers introduced in [11]. Note that our definition is slightly different than the original one, but the idea remains the same. Recall that an α-cut of a fuzzy number A is a set $A_\alpha = \{x \in \mathbb{R} \mid A(x) \geq \alpha\}$.

Definition 1. *A fuzzy number A is an LU-fuzzy number, if there exist a partition $0 = a_0 < \cdots < \alpha_n = 1$ and $2 \times (n + 1)$ matrices $\mathbf{A}^-$ and $\mathbf{A}^+$ (in the form of (5)) such that*

1. *$A_\alpha = [\mathbf{A}^-(\alpha), \mathbf{A}^+(\alpha)]$ for any $\alpha \in [0, 1]$,*
2. *$f^-_{\alpha_{i+1}} \geq f^-_{\alpha_i}$ and $f^+_{\alpha_{i+1}} \leq f^+_{\alpha_i}$ for any $i = 0, \ldots, n - 1$, and $f^-_{\alpha_n} = f^+_{\alpha_n}$,*
3. *$d^-_{\alpha_i} \geq 0$ and $d^+_{\alpha_i} \leq 0$ for any $i = 0, \ldots, n$,*
4. *if $f^-_{\alpha_i} = f^-_{\alpha_{i+1}}$ (or $f^+_{\alpha_i} = f^+_{\alpha_{i+1}}$), then $d^-_{\alpha_i} = d^-_{\alpha_{i+1}}$ (or $d^+_{\alpha_i} = d^+_{\alpha_{i+1}}$).*

An LU-fuzzy number will be denoted by $\mathbf{A} = (\mathbf{A}^-, \mathbf{A}^+)$ and the set of all LU-fuzzy numbers defined over a partition $0 = a_0 < \cdots < \alpha_n = 1$ will be denoted by $\mathcal{F}_{LU}(\alpha_0, \ldots, \alpha_n)$.

---

[1] For details, we refer to [10,19].

Let $D \subseteq \mathbb{R}^m$ and $g : D \to \mathbb{R}$ be a real function which has all partial derivatives on the domain D, ie. $g'_{x_k}(a_1, \ldots, a_m) \in \mathbb{R}$ for any $(a_1, \ldots, a_m) \in D$ and $k = 1, \ldots, m$. A general procedura showing how to extend the function g to a function $\tilde{g} : \mathcal{D} \to \mathcal{F}_{LU}(\alpha_0, \ldots, \alpha_n)$, where $\mathcal{D} \subseteq \mathcal{F}_{LU}(\alpha_0, \ldots, \alpha_n)^m$ is a suitable domain, can be formulated within the two following steps:[2]

1. Put $\mathbf{m} = \{1, \ldots, m\}$, consider $\pi : \mathbf{m} \to \{-, +\}$ and define

$$
\mathbf{B}^{\pi(1), \ldots, \pi(m)} = \begin{pmatrix} f_{\alpha_0}^{\pi(1), \ldots, \pi(m)} & \cdots & f_{\alpha_n}^{\pi(1), \ldots, \pi(m)} \\ d_{\alpha_0}^{\pi(1), \ldots, \pi(m)} & \cdots & d_{\alpha_n}^{\pi(1), \ldots, \pi(m)} \end{pmatrix}, \tag{6}
$$

where (for any $k = 0, \ldots, n$)

$$
f_{\alpha_k}^{\pi(1), \ldots, \pi(m)} = g(f_{1\alpha_k}^{\pi(1)}, \ldots, f_{m\alpha_k}^{\pi(m)}),
$$
$$
d_{\alpha_k}^{\pi(1), \ldots, \pi(n)} = g'_{x_1}(f_{1\alpha_k}^{\pi(1)}, \ldots, f_{n\alpha_k}^{\pi(n)}) d_{1\alpha_k}^{\pi(1)} + \cdots + g'_{x_n}(f_{1\alpha_k}^{\pi(1)}, \ldots, f_{n\alpha_k}^{\pi(n)}) d_{n\alpha_k}^{\pi(n)}.
$$

2. Denote $\mathbf{B}_{\alpha_k} = (\mathbf{B}_{\alpha_k}^-, \mathbf{B}_{\alpha_k}^+)$ the pair of k-th columns of $\mathbf{B}^-$ and $\mathbf{B}^+$ and define

$$
\tilde{g}(\mathbf{A}_1, \ldots, \mathbf{A}_m) = \mathbf{B} = (\mathbf{B}^-, \mathbf{B}^+) \tag{7}
$$

such that, for any $k = 0, \ldots, n$, we have

$$
(\mathbf{B}_{\alpha_k}^-, \mathbf{B}_{\alpha_k}^+) = (\min_{\pi : \mathbf{m} \to \{-, +\}} \mathbf{B}_k^{\pi(1), \ldots, \pi(m)}, \max_{\pi : \mathbf{m} \to \{-, +\}} \mathbf{B}_k^{\pi(1), \ldots, \pi(m)}), \tag{8}
$$

where min (and analogously max) is defined by

$$
\min \left\{ \begin{pmatrix} a \\ b \end{pmatrix}, \begin{pmatrix} c \\ d \end{pmatrix} \right\} = \begin{pmatrix} a \\ b \end{pmatrix} \text{ if and only if } a \leq c \text{ or } (a = c \text{ and } b \leq d).
$$

Example 1. One can simply check that

1. $(\mathbf{A}^-, \mathbf{A}^+) + (\mathbf{B}^-, \mathbf{B}^+) = (\mathbf{A}^- + \mathbf{B}^-, \mathbf{A}^+ + \mathbf{B}^+)$,
2. $k(\mathbf{A}^-, \mathbf{A}^+) = (k\mathbf{A}^-, k\mathbf{A}^+)$ and $-k(\mathbf{A}^-, \mathbf{A}^+) = (-k\mathbf{A}^+, -k\mathbf{A}^-)$ for $k \geq 0$,
3. $\exp[(\mathbf{A}^-, \mathbf{A}^+)] = (\exp[\mathbf{A}^-], \exp[\mathbf{A}^+])$ with

$$
\exp[\mathbf{A}^-]_{\alpha_k} = \begin{pmatrix} \exp[f_{\alpha_k}^-] \\ \exp[f_{\alpha_k}^-] d_{\alpha_k}^- \end{pmatrix} \text{ and } \exp[\mathbf{A}^+]_{\alpha_k} = \begin{pmatrix} \exp[f_{\alpha_k}^+] \\ \exp[f_{\alpha_k}^+] d_{\alpha_k}^+ \end{pmatrix},
$$

where the usual addition of matrices and the usual scalar multiplication are applied.

---

[2] Let us stress that a careful choice of the domain $\mathcal{D}$ has to be given to unsure the correctness of the extended mapping $\tilde{g}$.

4   Fuzzy Random Variable

In order to define fuzzy random variables over LU-fuzzy numbers we follow the approach proposed by Kwakernaak [14,15] and later formalized in a clear way by Kruse and Meyer [13]. Since each LU-fuzzy number is uniquely determined by a pair of matrices $(\mathbf{A}^-, \mathbf{A}^+)$, we will define fuzzy random variable using random matrices as follows.

Definition 2. *Let* $(\Omega, \mathcal{A}, P)$ *be a probability spaces. A mapping* $X : \Omega \to \mathcal{F}_{LU}(\alpha_0, \ldots, \alpha_n)$ *is said to be a LU-fuzzy random variable (or FRV for short), if there exist mappings* $\mathbf{F}^-, \mathbf{F}^+, \mathbf{D}^-, \mathbf{D}^+ : \Omega \to \mathbb{R}^{n+1}$ *such that* $p_i \circ \mathbf{F}^-$, $p_i \circ \mathbf{F}^+$ *and* $p_i \circ \mathbf{D}^-$, $p_i \circ \mathbf{D}^+$, *where* p_i *denotes i-th projection, are real-valued random variables for any* $i = 1, \ldots, n+1$ *and*

$$X(\omega) = \left(\begin{pmatrix} \mathbf{F}^-(\omega) \\ \mathbf{D}^-(\omega) \end{pmatrix}, \begin{pmatrix} \mathbf{F}^+(\omega) \\ \mathbf{D}^+(\omega) \end{pmatrix} \right). \tag{9}$$

We say that two FRVs X and Y are *independent (identically distributed)*, if $p_i \circ \mathbf{F}_X^-$, $p_i \circ \mathbf{F}_X^+$, $p_i \circ \mathbf{D}_X^-$, $p_i \circ \mathbf{D}_X^+$ and $p_i \circ \mathbf{F}_Y^-$, $p_i \circ \mathbf{F}_Y^+$, $p_i \circ \mathbf{D}_Y^-$, $p_i \circ \mathbf{D}_Y^+$ are independent (identically distributed), respectively, for any $i = 1, \ldots, n+1$. On Fig. 1, we can see five pseudo-randomly generated LU-fuzzy numbers defined under the normal distribution (the kernels, ie. the points with the membership degree equal to 1, are determined from $N(0, 4)$, further values are determined in such way that the difference between $f_{\alpha_i}^\mp$ and $f_{\alpha_{i+1}}^\mp$ are random values from $N(0, 2)$, $d_{\alpha_i}^-$ and $-d_{\alpha_i}^+$ are determined from $U(0.01, 2)$ for $\alpha_i \neq 1$ and $d_1^- = -d_1^+ = 10000/x$, where x is a random value from $U(1, 1000)$).

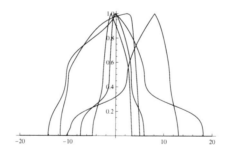

Fig. 1. Pseudo-random LU-fuzzy numbers

5   Option Pricing Illustration

As we have already argued, it can be very difficult to obtain reliable estimates for the parameters (eg. volatility or intensity of jumps) of the stochastic process $Z(t)$ in (2). It is the reason why many researchers suggest to define the underlying process in terms of fuzzy or fuzzy random variables. Assume the standard market model – a Brownian motion with drift μ and standard deviation σ:

$$Z(t) = \mu t + \sigma \sqrt{t}\varepsilon, \tag{10}$$

where $\varepsilon \sim N(0,1)$ (ie. it is of standard normal distribution). This is a standard market model for (log-)returns of financial asset prices, such as stocks, commodities or exchange rates, know as BS model [3]. Although the standard deviation σ need not be deterministic, but stochastic, it can be still difficult to obtain its reliable estimate. Hence, we can replace it by an LU-fuzzy number as bellow.

Standard market model with fuzzy parameter. Let σ_{LU} be an LU-fuzzy number defined around the crisp estimation of σ. Then we can model price returns by the following fuzzy-stochastic model:

$$Z(t) = \mu t + \sigma_{LU} \sqrt{t}\varepsilon. \tag{11}$$

In order to evaluate the risk-neutral expectation (3) via Monte Carlo simulation, we need to get (11) into the exponential and replace μ by r (a so called risk neutral setting). Moreover, it is important to choose a proper mean-correcting parameter ω_{LU} such that the complex process will be martingale, when discounted by the riskless rate. Obviously, since (11) is an LU-fuzzy random variable, parameter ω_{LU} has to be defined as LU-fuzzy number, too. Thus, we obtain:

$$S_T = S_t \exp[(r - \omega_{LU})\tau + \sigma_{LU} \sqrt{\tau}\varepsilon]. \tag{12}$$

Here, ω_{LU} denotes a mean correcting parameter that compensates $\sigma_{LU} \sqrt{\tau}$. Therefore, in order to evaluate the model, we have to apply several operations with fuzzy numbers to obtain S_T. Finally, assuming a call option the exercise prices is deduced from S_T and after that the positive part of the matrix is returned as an option payoff for a given scenario. Obviously, in line with (3) we have to evaluate a huge number of such scenarios to obtain a reliable estimate of option price as a mean of matrices – we recall that the payoff for each particular scenario must be a positive LU-fuzzy number or zero matrix.

Comparative results for call and put options are provided in Table 1. While crisp values are assumed for the initial price of the underlying asset ($S_0 = 100$), exercise price ($X = 100$), riskless rate ($r = 0$) and time to maturity ($T = 1$), volatility is defined as an LU-fuzzy number over normal distribution with mean value $\sigma_m = 0.25$ and two different standard deviations σ_s. The call and put option price according to BS model (and in line with (10)) is 9.9. Assuming $\alpha = 1$, we get very similar results for all options. Obviously, with increasing σ_s, resulting price estimates in terms of LU-fuzzy numbers are wider. However, we can observe, that the base of the fuzzy number is narrower when put options are considered (compare to call options). Moreover, the left slope of call option fuzzy-value is similar to the right slope of put option fuzzy-value and vice versa.

Table 1. Option pricing comparison

Call $\sigma_s = 0.1$	$\left(\begin{pmatrix} 0.5 & 2.7 & 8.8 \\ 128 & 149 & 8\ 719 \end{pmatrix}, \begin{pmatrix} 36.7 & 20.7 & 8.8 \\ -236 & -203 & -8\ 719 \end{pmatrix}\right)$
Call $\sigma_s = 0.01$	$\left(\begin{pmatrix} 8.0 & 9.0 & 10.0 \\ 169 & 171 & 11\ 947 \end{pmatrix}, \begin{pmatrix} 12.1 & 11.0 & 10.0 \\ -181 & -178 & -11\ 947 \end{pmatrix}\right)$
Put $\sigma_s = 0.1$	$\left(\begin{pmatrix} 1.1 & 3.8 & 8.8 \\ 235 & 202 & 8\ 723 \end{pmatrix}, \begin{pmatrix} 26.8 & 17.2 & 8.8 \\ -128 & -148 & -8\ 723 \end{pmatrix}\right)$
Put $\sigma_s = 0.01$	$\left(\begin{pmatrix} 8.6 & 9.3 & 10.0 \\ 182 & 178 & 11\ 929 \end{pmatrix}, \begin{pmatrix} 11.4 & 10.7 & 10.0 \\ -169 & -171 & -11\ 929 \end{pmatrix}\right)$

6   Conclusion

Many issues of financial modeling and decision making require some knowledge about the future states. However, sometimes it is very difficult to get reliable parametrization of stochastic models. In this contribution we suggested an alternative approach to option valuation problem via Monte Carlo simulation by volatility specified as an LU-fuzzy number.

References

1. Ban, A.I.: On the nearest parametric approximation of a fuzzy number – revisited. Fuzzy Sets Syst. 160(21), 3027–3047 (2009)
2. Ban, A.I.: Triangular and parametric approximations of fuzzy numbers – inadvertences and corrections. Fuzzy Sets Syst. 160(21), 3048–3058 (2009)
3. Black, F., Scholes, M.: The Pricing of Options and Corporate Liabilities. Journal of Political Economy 81, 637–659 (1973)
4. Boyle, P.: Options: a Monte Carlo approach. Journal of Financial Economics 4, 323–338 (1977)
5. Cherubini, U.: Fuzzy measures and asset prices: Accounting for information ambiguity. Applied Mathematical Finance 4, 135–149 (1997)
6. Cox, J.C., Ross, S.A., Rubinstein, M.: Option Pricing: A simplified approach. Journal of Financial Economics 7, 229–263 (1979)
7. Dubois, D., Prade, H.: Operations on fuzzy numbers. Int. J. Syst. Sci. 9, 613–626 (1978)
8. Dubois, D., Prade, H.: Fuzzy sets and systems. Theory and applications. In: Mathematics in Science and Engineering, vol. 144. Academic Press, New York (1980)
9. Glasserman, P.: Monte Carlo Methods in Financial Engineering. Springer, Heidelberg (2004)
10. Gregory, J.A.: Shape preserving spline interpolation. Comput. Aided Design 18, 53–57 (1986)
11. Guerra, M.L., Stefanini, L.: Approximate fuzzy arithmetic operations using monotonic interpolations. Fuzzy Sets Syst. 150(1), 5–33 (2005)
12. Klir, G.J., Yuan, B.: Fuzzy Sets and Fuzzy Logic: Theory and Applications. Prentice Hall, New Jersey (1995)
13. Kruse, R., Meyer, K.D.: Statistics with vague data. In: Theory and Decision Library. Series B: Mathematical and Statistical Methods, vol. 6, D. Reidel Publishing Company, Dordrecht (1987)

14. Kwakernaak, H.: Fuzzy random variables – I. Definitions and theorems. Inf. Sci. 15, 1–29 (1978)
15. Kwakernaak, H.: Fuzzy random variables – II. Algorithms and examples for the discrete case. Inf. Sci. 17, 253–278 (1979)
16. Merton, R.C.: Theory of rational option pricing. Bell Journal of Economics and Management Science 4, 141–183 (1973)
17. Nowak, P., Romaniuk, M.: Computing option price for Lévy process with fuzzy parameters. European Journal of Operational Research 201, 206–210 (2010)
18. Ribeiro, R.A., Zimmermann, H.-J., Yager, R.R., Kacprzyk, J.: Soft Computing in Financial Engineering. Physica-Verlag, Heidelberg (1999)
19. Sarfraz, M.: A rational cubic spline for the visualization of monotonic data. Comput. Graphics 24, 509–516 (2000)
20. Shreve, S.E.: Stochastic Calculus for Finance II: Continuous-Time Models. Springer, Heidelberg (2004)
21. Stefanini, L., Sorini, L., Guerra, M.L.: Parametric representation of fuzzy numbers and application to fuzzy calculus. Fuzzy Sets Syst. 157(18), 2423–2455 (2006)
22. Yoshida, Y.: The valuation of European options in uncertain environment. European Journal of Operational Research 145, 221–229 (2003)
23. Zadeh, L.A.: Fuzzy sets. Information and Control 8, 338–353 (1965)
24. Zmeškal, Z.: Application of the fuzzy stochastic methodology to appraising the firm value as a European calls option. European Journal of Operational Research 135(2), 303–310 (2001)

Legal Theoretical Analysis on the Market Economy Mode of China—Discussing from the Status of Market Economy in Anti-dumpling

XiaoChen Jin

Law School, Capital University of Economics and Business, Beijing, P.R. China

Abstract. Most of the discussion on Chinese market economy mode stayed in the representation, such as government-led and mixed economic model. However, the in-depth analysis of the reason for the formation of Chinese mode was rare. By means of cultural comparison and empirical analysis, this paper presents the reasons for Chinese mode. It analyzes and illustrates that it is the combined action of Chinese traditional culture, Marxism-Leninism, and Western free-market economic ideas that create the market economy mode with Chinese characteristics, namely the economic development mode with a variety of economy composition coexisting in the ownership aspect, strong government regulations at the macro level and sufficient competition from enterprise to locality at the microscopic level.

Keywords: The market economy mode, Legal theoretical analysis, Chinese traditional culture, Marxism-Leninism, Western market economic ideas.

1 Introduction

The author has been engaged in the study of international economic law yet is tangled with the status of China's market economy in the anti-dumping in international trade, China believes that it has already become a country with market economy, yet major western countries do not recognize that and they believe that, according to their standards, China is still not a country with complete market economy. This involves a problem: does market economy has only one mode? The mode of the western countries has arrived a perfect state and needs no improvements? Is it a "end of history" ? If a mode different from the western mode can more effectively promote the economy development of the whole world or certain countries, should we refuse it and follow the western principals? Of course, if the issue is raised to such a height, it is not only a technical issue affecting foreign trades, but also an issue to discuss how to construct a market economy system with Chinese characteristics.

Currently, there are totally three kinds of opinions about the market economy mode of China. The first opinion thinks that the market economy mode of China is still not perfect, it is only a transitional stage to the western market economic mode. The second opinion believes that the current market economy mode of China is only a making-up stage for the transition to the traditional socialism, when the conditions get mature in the future, it will eventually return to the "sophomore public" socialism[1];

M. Zhou (Ed.): ISAEBD 2011, Part IV, CCIS 211, pp. 34–40, 2011.

The third opinion thinks that although the market economy mode of China is still not perfect, its framework has been erected, it is not a transitional stage to any mode, it is an unique economy development mode in consistent with the actual situations of China. I support the last opinion and agree that it is necessary to discuss the ideological roots for the formation of such a mode, so that to carry out further study on its source, status and development.

From legal theoretical analysis, China's market economy mode has three sources, namely the impact of traditional Chinese culture, influence of socialist ideology and impact of western market economic thoughts. All the three sources will be analyzed below one by one.

2 Impact of Traditional Chinese Culture

In the past century, the traditional cultural of China experienced the processes of denial, improvement and reaffirmation. People attempts to improve the traditional culture to make it suitable to the market economy. Neo-Confucianism have done much useful work for this, yet most of such work is divorced from the reality of the mainland China, the experience summarized from the overseas Chinese, Taiwan, Hong Kong are unconvincing. However, the reform and opening practice of the mainland provides a stage to inherit, improve and develop our traditional culture.

First, to implement market economy, we must analyze the opinion of "developing agricultural and inhibiting commerce" in the traditional culture. I believe that philosophers in Qin Dynasty of China had profound understanding about the scarcity of resources. They believed that human resources, land resources and other resources are all limited, they can only satisfy the basic life demands of people, especially solving the problem of food and clothing. If encourage people to engage in productions or circulated activities associated with commodity economy, personnel engaged in agricultural production will be substantially reduced and people will not get enough food and clothing. Even input human resources in agricultural production, people's demands still can not be satisfied, because the resources available for consumption are quite limited.

The sages of course knew that business may enrich people, yet to inhibit the business development, the community designed a system to belittle the social status of businessmen and regarded business as a hangdog industry, erected obstacles for their offspring in political development, so that to balance their higher economic status. All these concepts inhibited the development of commodity economy in China, China experienced a long agricultural society. To satisfy the demands of agricultural production, other commodity production skill were all considered as tricks and wicked craft skills, this concept also seriously obstructed the scientific development in ancient China and promoted the spreading of the atmosphere of emphasizing distribution and ignoring creations. At that time, it was impossible for people to aware that adding science into the commodity production may produce dramatic wealth to satisfy people's demands. However, through constant cultural changes in recent years, people gradually recognized the importance of science and production and it was necessary to introduce it into Chinese culture. The way used by Neo-Confucianism to transform Chinese culture is to introduce science and democracy into Confucian culture.

The knowledge about science and economy development may increase material wealth is bound to change our opinions about wealth. We are no longer ashamed for speaking of benefits, we are proud of making wealth through legal channels. At the initial phase of reform and opening, the government proposed a slogan of "making some people gets rich first". Actually, Confucius had ever told us to obtain wealth through legal means in his "The Analects".

Secondly, traditional Chinese doctrine of mean guides us to correctly treat the relationship between the state, capital and individuals, we can neither adhere to the past "sophomore public" concept nor completely fall into the individualism of the western countries. The Confucianism and Taoism which have great influence on traditional Chinese culture are all associated with the "Book of Changes". The basic ideal of the "Book of Changes" is "Too much water drowned the miller", in other words, any thing will have opposite meaning after developing to a certain degree. The Confucianism adopted this concept and developed it to the doctrine of mean, while Daoism developed it to inaction. Before reform and opening, we departed from the doctrine of mean, extremely promoted the national and collective interests and completely ignored the personal interests, as a results, our national economy was at the brink of collapse. The so called reform and opening, in a certain manner, is to bring order out of chaos and return to the road of balancing the nation, capital and personal interests. Therefore, when various systems of market economy are established, at the micro level, we should grant the enterprises will full freedom, while on the macro level, we should implement macro regulations to overcome the defects of market economy.

I believe that there are still many problems with the market economy mode of the western countries, they ignore the balance between the national, capital and personal interests, this is just the root cause of the financial crisis. On the one hand, based on the instinct of the capitalist nations to protect capitals, they implement fundamentalist liberalism, turn a blind eye to the greed of capitals, lose effective supervision on the proliferation of various derivatives, all these create conditions for the occurrence of the financial crisis. On the other hand, considering the ballot papers, some populist trends need to be met. Subsequently, the load of the government and the community exceeds their capability, the subprime crisis as the fuse of the financial crisis is caused by the "bright" version of "Home Ownership" proposed by the U.S, it attracted many people who have no purchase ability participated in the housing purchase game. Compared with U.S, although the western European countries implement more effective regulations on capitals, yet the welfare system beyond the bearing ability of the government is the root cause for the currency crisis.

Of course, it was suspected ever that the development of China in recent years focused too much on economy, yet our government recognized this and proposed scientific development method. John ·Naisbitt summarized four basic points: the first prerequisite is development, the core is people-oriented, the basic requirement is overall coordinated and sustainable development, the basic method is making overall plans and take all factors into consideration.

Additionally, another important heritage of Chinese traditional cultural is people-oriented people's livelihood which has two ideological sources. The first source is the concept of "human" in the Confucian culture, it is the central idea of the Confucius and Mencius. The moral rules proposed by Confucius were originally for the rulers who were required to treat people kindly and show solicitude for the public. The second source is that the objective for loving people is to achieve national stability other than the kindness of the rulers.

The ancients also realized that the most important substance is to develop economy to satisfy the material demands of people. Only on such a basis, can the rulers require people to abide by the social regulations and keep the state stable. In additional, the ancients also recognized that nurturing the middle-class is beneficial for the social stability. Today, we emphasize economic development as the first task, overall improve people's material and cultural living standards, nurture and expand the middle class group, improve our social welfare system and give proper care for the vulnerable groups, these concepts of governance reflect that the ancient thoughts have profound influence on today's system construction.

Of course, the integrity and education concepts in the traditional culture all play an important role in guiding modern system construction, including the market economic system.

3 Influence of Socialist Ideology of Marx

The author believes that the reason for China to select socialism is there are many privities between the theory and practice of Marxist-Leninist and Chinese culture. In philosophy, the Dialectical Materialism of Marxist has similar opinions with the Atheism in Chinese Confucian culture and the simple Dialectics in the "Book of Changes". The criticism of Marx on the greedy nature of capital is easy to attract resonance of the Confucian culture which focus on justice other than profits. Marx pointed out the contradiction between the private ownership of capital and socialized production, the public representative naturally falls on the state, this is also in consistent with the concept of centralized power in China. Since the reform and opening, the Party and the government intentionally or unintentionally combine them, attempt to find a development way complying with Chinese characteristics and have achieved initial achievements.

In the guiding ideology, use the views related with main contradictions in the Marxist dialectics to rebuild the doctrines of mean, on the one hand, try to avoid the influence of any fundamentalism in the practice, yet agree to grasp the main contradictions in each development stage. At the initial stage of reform and opening, Deng Xiaoping realized that economic development is the current main tasks and pointed out that only development is of overriding importance. If we think it is not appropriate to accomplish something in theory in the initial stage of reform and opening, then for the period Jiang Zemin in power, it was a task that can not be evaded, thus came with the Three Represents, namely (1) The Communist Party must always represent the development requirements of China's advanced productive forces; (2) The Communist Party must always represent the forward direction of China's advanced culture; and (3) The Communist Party must always represent the Chinese people's fundamental interests. The transformation from a revolutionary party to a ruling party is initially completed. The New Deal of Hu-Wen is implemented after China has get certain economic development results and the government has the ability to transfer some resources to people's livelihood. Economic development solved the problem of efficiency, then the problem of solving fairness is naturally put on the agenda. The people-oriented scientific concept of development is the main program of New Deal of Hu-wen.

In economic system, we uphold the public ownership as the dominant body yet still maintain the pattern of co-existence of diverse economic elements, this represents that China is still a Socialist country, although we experienced constant changes in concepts about this problem. For private economy, it was only regarded as a supplement of the state-owned economy in the beginning, yet with the deepening of reform, its status has been increasingly improved and now it is enjoying an equal status with the state-own economy. However, major industries related with people's livelihood are still thriving in state-owned enterprises, this policy is not only affected by Marxism-Leninism, but also in consistent with Chinese tradition. For example, it was provided in ancient China that some industries associated with people's livelihood, such as salt and iron industries, must be controlled by the state, even in Taiwan, where the development of market economy is relatively complete, the public enterprises still control a large number o key industries, such as oil, electricity and aviation, etc. Many scholars agree that there are many adverse problems in China's state-owned enterprises, especially central enterprises, yet I believe that, as one of the characteristics of socialist market economy, the existence and role of the state-owned economy still can not be replaced by private economy, although it has many problems need to be eliminated through reform.

In China, protection to private property, in particular to capital, is still limited. Particularly, when the benefits pursuing behavior of the capital threatens the operation security of the national economy, the powerful intervention of the government will occur, according to the ruling ideal of the government and the public perception, necessary restrictions on private property or capital are acceptable.

4 Impact of Western Liberalism

In the initial stage of reform and opening, especially before and after entering WTO, the acceptance of China to western free economics is relatively comprehensive. For government officials, scholars and entrepreneurs, "connecting with the international" is a synonymous of political correctness. With the passing of time, the ideal of free economy has been accepted in different degrees, although a rejection phenomenon appeared with some ideas.

China has accepted private ownership system in a limited scope and articles about protecting private properties have been written into the Constitution, although some scholars not satisfied that the protection to production materials owned by privates are not listed in the Constitution. Private economy has been affirmed to be an important component of the socialist market economy. In the area of competition, the resource distribution and price formation are basically decided by the market, meanwhile, the major market economic rules are also developed by referring to the relevant laws of the western countries.

In distribution system, the previous system of defining rights according to grades is transferred to defining rights according to capitals. This enables the development of peoples no longer limited within the system, the market economy provides another stage for people to display their talents, there is enough space for selection in personal development.

Even for state-owned enterprises, they have enough momentum to participate in the market competitions because of the clearly defined assets rights and operation impendence. While the central government distributes rights among local governments and enterprises and an unique county competition pattern has been formed.

Describing the western influences, it is necessary to mention the intervention ideology of Tikai Burns. He believes that the state must invest directly to enable the investment amount to be equal to the savings under the full employment conditions, so that to solve the unemployment and crisis in the capitalism. After World War II, almost all western countries adopted the polices suggested by Keynesian in different degrees, yet the one who maximize it should be China. This is possibly because there are some similarities between the interventionist of Keynesian and the Marxism and stressing the role of the government in Chinese tradition. The government of China adopted and developed the theory of interfering economy by government, our government has strong intervention ability and has unique methods in micro economic regulation, the roles of anti-cycle control method, micro-invigorate and state-owned enterprises, especially the state-owned financial enterprises plays a good role in the health and orderly development of the national economy.

5   Conclusion

Under the combined effects of traditional Chinese culture, Marxism-Leninism and Western market economic ideas, we have established a market economy mode with Chinese characteristics, i.e. an economic development mode which allows the co-existence of multiple economic components under the powerful regulations of the government, enable the local governments and enterprises to fully take part in micro competitions. I believe that the framework of this mode has been erected, yet there is still space for constant improvements. We still need more efforts to accept the concept of Western free market economy, public economy, especially the operation of the state-owned enterprises, still needs to be constrained with proper laws and regulations, particularly the trend of entering the system of youths shall be inhibited, otherwise, it will create tremendous negative impact on maintaining social energy. However, I am not pessimistic, as long as the government and community have enough consensus on the existing problems, the Chinese system can be improved.

References

1. Su, W., Yang, F., Liu, S.W.: Chongqing Model. China Economic Publishing House, Beijing (2011)
2. Naisbitt, J., Naisbitt, D.: China's Megatrends—The 8 Pillars of a New Society. Jilin Publishing Group, China Industry & Commerce Associated Press, Beijing (2009)
3. Zhang, W.C.: The Economic System of China. China CITIC Press, Beijing (2009)

Risk Analysis on Cash Flow of Two Real Estate Projects Portfolio Development

Chuandong Geng, Hongliang Zhu, and Xinwu Zhang

Industrial and Commercial Bank of China Limited
Tsinghua University
{chuandong.geng,xinwu.zhang}@ICBC,
hongliang.zhu@TsinghuaUniversity

Abstract. A portfolio development cash flow model was constructed base on two real estate projects in this paper. According to the diverse equities resource, both of overlying type model and capital saving type model were built to qualitatively analyze the paying ability of two combination development type models. Furthermore, the characteristics of two projects portfolio development paying ability were summed up after calculating and analyzing the typical examples. At last, significant advices in risk management were given to commercial bank on loaning to real estate developments.

Keywords: Real estate, Cash flow, Risk of Credit.

1   Introduction

The real estate industry in China develops fast for the past few years. As a capital-intensive industry, the real estate industry's risk highly associated with the risk of overall economic. In recent years, Chinese governments continually publish the macro-control policies to reduce the risk of real estate industry. Related researches on risk management have caused scholar's attention. Tao etc used the PAC (principle components analysis) method to identify the financial risk of the real estate companies [1]. Li and Xu etc introduced VAR (value at risk) to carry out warning analysis [2]. Overall, the literatures studied on the cash flow in real estate development project are rare. Much of them mainly paid attention to the perspective of the real estate development and enterprises management, which are lack of quantitative analysis. Modeling methods were employed in this paper and took the macro-control policies and market conditions into consideration as the external affecting factors on the real estate development loans. Combining quantitative analysis and game theory, we researched the cash flow and solvency characteristics when two real estate project portfolio development.

2   Monthly Cash Flow Model on Portfolio Development

The real estate development usually used project as unit. When a project in the process of developing, the developer's cash flow constituted of various capital

M. Zhou (Ed.): ISAEBD 2011, Part IV, CCIS 211, pp. 41–48, 2011.

outflow used for project development and various capital inflow contained bank loan, sale revenue, and others. A real estate developer usually carries out several projects. The difference between the two projects developed together and two projects were developed respectively is the former can combine the capital of two projects together. There is the possibility that when one of the two projects occurring capital shortage or needed to pay the expenses of development and construction and repay the loan, the combined capital should payoff.

2.1   Monthly Cash Flow Function on Portfolio Development

Suppose that a property developer carry on two real-estate projects P_1 and P_2 at the same time. Project P_2 begins at one month after the project P_1 has been carried on. The investments of the two projects are I_1 and I_2, respectively. The construction cycle, project capital, bank loan, cost composition, project seals other variables of the two projects are the same. The cash flow of sub-projects of two projects is the function of time t, which is not a continuous function. Suppose the unit of time t is month and it is integer. t_{01} is the start month of project P_1 and t_{02} is the start month of Project P_2, where $t_{01} < t_{02}$. By the month i, the net cash flow of two project portfolio development is NCF_{ci}.

The net total cash of two projects:

$$NCF_{cn} = NCF_{n1} + NCF_{n2} - F_{cn} \tag{1}$$

where NCF_{n1} and NCF_{n2} mean the net cash flow by the month n of the projects P_1 and P_2 developed independently. F_{cn} is the payoff amount of combination cash when the project capital source shortage by the month n.

$$NCF_{cn} = \sum_{i=1}^{n} e_{i1} + l_{i1} + s_{i1} - c_{i1} - r_{i1} + e_{i2} + l_{i2} + s_{i2} - c_{i2} - r_{i2} - f_{ci} \tag{2}$$

where e_{i1} and e_{i1} indicate the amount of project capital fully funded in month i; s_{i1} and s_{i2} represent the amount of bank loan fully funded in month i; l_{i1} and l_{i2} mean the payment amount of booking and sale achieved in month i; c_{i1} and c_{i2} show the payment amount of construction period cost in month i; r_{i1} and r_{i2} are the repayment amount of bank loans in month i. f_{ci} is the payoff amount of combination cash when the project capital source shortage by the month i.

2.2   The Cash Flow Constraints of the Sub-project of Two Projects Portfolio Development

- Capital base e_{ij} Assume the total capital base amount of project $j (j = 1, 2)$ is E_j. From the month t_{0j} start to month t_{ej} put in place, the amount of cash base every month is e_{ij}. When $i > t_{0j} + t_{ej}, e_{ij} = 0$; at the same time

$$E_j = \sum_{i=t_{0j}}^{t_{0j}+t_{ej}-1} e_{ij}$$

– The cost of land and pre-project d_{ij} Assume the total cost amount of land and pre-project of the project j is D_j. From the month t_{0j} start to month t_{ej} pay, the amount of cost in every month is d_{ij}. When $i > t_{0j} + t_{ej}, e_{ij} = 0$; at the same time $D_j = \sum\limits_{i=t_{0j}}^{t_{0j}+t_{cj}-1} d_{ij}$

– The loan borrowed from bank l_{ij} Assume total amount of the loan borrowed from bank by project j is L_j. Begin at month $t_{0j} + t_{10j}$, put in place in t_{1j} months. The amount of bank loan every month is l_{ij} in month i. When $i > t_{0j} + t_{10j} + t_{1j}$ and $i < t_{0j} + t_{1j}, l_{ij} = 0$; at the same time $L_j = \sum\limits_{i=t_{0j}+t_{10j}}^{t_{0j}+t_{10j}+t_{1j}-1} l_{ij}$

– The cost of construct period c_{ij} Assume the total cost of construct period of the project j is C_j. It is divided into t_{cj} months and the payment is c_{ij} in per month from the month $t_{0j} + t_{c0j}$. When $i \geq t_{0j} + t_{c0j}$ and $i < t_{0j} + t_{c0j}$, $c_{ij} = 0$; at the same time $C_j = \sum\limits_{i=t_{0j}+t_{c0j}}^{t_{0j}+t_{c0j}+t_{cj}-1} c_{ij}$.

– The fund of sales revenue and advance sale s_{ij} Assume the total amount fund of the sales revenue and advance sale is S_j. The revenue realized in early days is S_{1j}, and the revenue realized in later period is S_{2j}. $S_j = S_{1j} + S_{2j}$, $S_{1j} = \sum\limits_{i=t_{0j}+t_{s0j}}^{t_{0j}+t_{s0j}+t_{sj}-1} s_{ij}$, $S_{2j} = \sum\limits_{i=t_{0j}+t_{s0j}+t_{s1j}}^{t_{0j}+t_{s0j}+t_{s1j}+t_{s2j}-1} s_{ij}$.

– The repay of bank loan r_{ij} The total amount of repay is L_j for project j equal to borrowed. Assume the payment begin at one month until all the loan pay back in the month $t_{0j} + t_{10j}t_{rj}$. The period divided into m_j months and the payment for each month is r_{ij}. When $i \geq t_{0j} + t_{10j}t_{rj}$ and $i < t_{0j} + t_{10j}t_{rj} - m_j$, $r_{ij} = 0$; at the same time $L_j = \sum\limits_{i=t_{0j}+t_{10j}+t_{rj}-m_j+1}^{t_{0j}+t_{10j}+t_{rj}} r_{ij}$.

– The balance relationship of capital The constitution of the project investment look from the perspective of cash outflow is $I_j = D_j + C_j$, from the perspective of cash inflow is $I_j = E_j + L_j + S_{Yj}$, where S_{Yj} indicate the booking income amount of another construct project.

2.3   The Index of Debt Paying Ability in Portfolio Development

– The net amount of minimum cash flow. The minimum cash flow of two projects portfolio development is $MinNCF_{cn}$ $n = 0, 1, 2, ...$
– The surplus. The surplus is the net amount cash flow when pay off a debt in two projects portfolio development.
  • **A** The surplus of first project.

$$M_{cl} = NCF_{crl} \tag{3}$$

where M_{cl} means the surplus pay off a debt; NCF_{crl} is the net amount of cash flow when first project pay off the debt.

$$M_{cl} = NCF_{r11} + NCF_{r12} + F_{crl} \tag{4}$$

where NCF_{r11} and NCF_{r12} are the net amount of cash flow of project 1 and project 2 respectively, when the first project pay off the debt. F_{cr1} is the amount of capital for developers use the method of combination development when the first project pay off the debt.

It is obvious in equation 5, the surplus of first project in combination development higher than developed individually when $NCF_{rl2} - F_{cr1} \geq 0$.

- **B** The surplus of second project.

$$M_{c2} = NCF_{cr2} \tag{5}$$

where M_{c2} indicate the surplus pay off a debt of the second project. NCF_{cr2} is the net cash flow amount of combination development when second project pay off the debt.

$$M_{c2} = NCF_{r21} + NCF_{r22} - F_{cr2} \tag{6}$$

where NCF_{r21} and NCF_{r22} are the net amount of cash flow of project 1 and project 2 respectively, when the second project pay off the debt. F_{cr2} is the amount of capital for developers use the method of combination development when the first project pay off the debt. Because the project period of project P_1 and P_2 are equal, $F_{cr2} = F_c$.

When $NCF_{r21} - F_{cr2} \geq 0$, the surplus of second project in combination development higher than develop individual.

- The safeguard multiples of debt service. Define the safeguard multiples of debt service of two projects in combination development condition are:

$$K_{c1} = \frac{M_{c1} + L_1}{L_1} \quad K_{c2} = \frac{M_{c2} + L_2}{L_2} \tag{7}$$

2.4   Two Special Mode of Portfolio Development

Based on the capital fund source of the second project, at first, we construct a simple overlying mode and give preliminary analysis. A capital saving mode which close to realistic situation is introduced to analyze the comprehensive ability debt paying in detail when two project portfolio development.

- **Mode 1:** simple overlying mode. The total capital fund of two projects is the equity funds of the developer. The capital fund of two projects E_1 and E_2 input to the portfolio development with the cash flow by the investment activity. The cash flow of two project portfolio development is the simple add with cash flow of two projects developed individually.

- **Mode 2:** capital saving mode. The developer put the capital fund of the first project into the portfolio development with the equity funds. The capital fund of the second project no longer put into. All the capital the second project need come from the comprehensive cash flow payment of the first project. The cash flow of two projects portfolio development consist of the cash flow simple overlying of the individual development two projects and the whole leakage of capital fund of the second project.

3   The Analysis on the Combination Cash Flow and the Debt Paying Ability of Simple Overlying Mode

3.1   The Qualitative Analysis on Cash Flow and the Debt Paying Ability

Under the general condition, the minimal cash flows of projects P_1 and P_2 are bigger than 0 when they developed individually. When two projects portfolio development using the overlying mode, the cash flow will higher than they developed individual. Furthermore, the debt paying ability will increase either.

3.2   The Computational Analysis and Typical Examples

- Typical simple constructed. Assume the capital fund, the cost of land and earlier fee, loan from the bank put in place and pays back at once. All the cost in construction period pay off uniformity and the revenue of advance sale and sale are obtained uniformity.

   Based on the statistical analysis, construct a typical example. Assume the total investment of the project is 100 million Yuan (RMB). The cost of land and earlier fee are 30 million, the cost of construction period is 70 million, the capital fund of the project is 35 million, loan from bank is 50 million, and the revenue of advance sale reinvestment 15 million. Assume advance sale and sale divided into two periods. The revenue of advance sale and sale is 102 million in the first period and the revenue of advance sale and sale is 18 million in the second period. The capital fund pays off the cost of land and earlier fee. The bank loan put in place in 3 months, length of maturity is 3 years. Pay the fee of construction period begins at the next month of bank loan punt in place. The period of construction is 2 years. The advance sale start one year later after constructing and divide into two periods. The first period lasts 2 years and the second period lasts 1 year.

- Sample computational analysis. Suppose the developer develop the two projects P_1 and P_2 with same size use the mode of simple overlying. t_{01} and t_{02} are the start time of projects P_1 and P_2.

   Assume project P_2 is posterior to project P_1 and the time lag of them is very short. We compute the net cash flow amount of the portfolio development in each month K_{c1} and K_{c2}, then compare them with K.

   The calculation results show that the mode using simple superposition combination of two projects development, the safeguard multiples of debt service of first project fluctuates greater. The safeguard multiples reach up to 3.4 at the peak. The second project in the different period of pay debt: rapid sales period, rapid advance sales period in construction period, not on advance sales in construction period, and early period of project. So the combination cash flow presents the larger fluctuation.

Comprehensive qualitative analysis and quantitative calculation results can be seen that if both of two projects have the debt paying ability, the paying ability in portfolio development used simple overlying mode lower than they developed individually at the under normal market and operating conditions.

3.3   Impact Analysis of Macroscopic Readjustment and Control

Combination pressure test analysis is employed for the macroscopic readjustment and control which reduce the ratio of capital fund and for both the sale price and speed descend which caused by the new possible macroeconomic control. Compute the safeguard multiplies of pay back debt of two projects based on the combination of different time interval.

- The ratio of the capital is 30%, sale price descent 3% and the sale speed descent 10%.

  Change both of the first and second projects. The debt paying ability of first project descent obviously. If the time interval between the two projects start in the 1-19 months or 26-36 months, the safeguard multiplies level of first project is higher than which is developed individually and unaffected by the policy.
- The ratio of the capital is 25%, sale price descent 10% and the sale speed descent 30%.

  Change both of the first and second projects. The debt paying ability of second project descent obviously. If the time interval between the two projects start less than 8 months,the safeguard multiplies of second project is less than 1.
- The ratio of the capital is 20%, sale price descent 15% and the sale speed descent 50%.

  Change both of the first and second projects. The debt paying ability of second project descent obviously. The safeguard multiplies of second project is less than 1.

Three kinds of pressure test demonstrate that the sale price and speed is affected more by the policy of macroscopic readjustment and control with the capital reduces, the risk of pay back debt on the commercial bank real estate loan is bigger. However, employed the simple overlying mode on combination development could improve the debt paying ability. Especially one of the projects is affected by regulate and control policy, that can reduce the risk of pay back debt. Commercial banks should pay close attention to the situation of combined development of developers in the loan risk management. This can prevent debt risk when the policy change for bank can take the repayment source of developer from other projects as a supplement of loan.

4   The Analysis of Combination Cash Flow and Debt Paying Ability on the Capital Saving Mode

4.1   The Qualitative Analysis of Combination Cash Flow and Debt Paying Ability on the Capital Saving Mode

- The debt paying ability of first project. Based on equation (5), $M_{c1} = M_1 + NCF_{r12} - F_{cr1}$, where $F_{cr1} \leq E_2$.

If in the pay off the debt date of first project, the net cash flow of second project developed individually larger than the capital of itself. $M_{c1} \geq M_1$, it indicates that the debt paying ability of first project in the combination development larger than it developed individually.

If the second project acquire the loan and haven't paid debt off. The possibility of $NCF_{r12} \geq E_2$ is bigger. Because of $M_1 = S_{R1} + E_1 - I + NCF_{r12} - E_2$, if the size of two projects are equal, $E_1 = E_2$. if $S_{R1} + E_1 - I \geq 0$, $M_{c1} \geq 0$.

If selling well, the sales revenue of first project can cover its total investment before the expiration of the first project loans. Even though NCF_{r12} very small, it will also have M_{c1} at this time. The first project has the solvency.

- The debt paying ability of second project. Based on equation (8), $M_{c2} = M_2 + NCF_{r21} - F_c$, where $F_c = E_2$. When $NCF_{r12} - E \geq 0$, $M_{c2} geq M_2$.
  If first project pay the debt before second project, the sales revenue of first project can cover its total investment before the expiration of the second project loans and it means $NCF_{r21} \geq E_1$. If the size of two projects are equal, $E_1 = E_2$, its means $M_{c2} \geq M_2$. Therefore, when two projects with same size developed combined and the first project selling well, the debt paying ability of second project can exceed it developed individually.

To sum up, when develop two projects with the mode of capital saving on portfolio development, if the size of two projects is same and selling well, the safeguard multiplies of pay debt of two projects increase than they develop themselves.

4.2 The Computational Analysis and Typical Examples on the Combination Capital Saving Development Mode

- Sample parameter selection. Suppose the developer develop the two projects P_1 and P_2 with same size use the mode of capital saving. The various cash flow values of two projects are equal to them which develop with the mode of simple overlying. At same time, the value of F_c and the second project's capital are equal. For any integer $i \geq 0$, the $F_{c(i+t_{02}-t_{01})} = e_{(i+t_{02}-t_{01})} = e_{i1}$.
- Sample computational analysis Assume project P_2 is posterior to project P_1 and the time lag of them is very short. We compute the net cash flow amount of the portfolio development in each month K_{c1} and K_{c2}, then compare them with K in different value of $t_{02} - t_{01}$.

The calculation results show that the mode using capital saving of two projects combination development, the safeguard multiples of debt service of two projects fluctuates higher than them develop themselves.

4.3 Impact Analysis of Macroscopic Readjustment and Control

Compute the safeguard multiplies of pay back debt of two projects twice based on the combination of different time interval.

- The ratio of the capital is 30%, sale price descent 3% and the sale speed descent 10%. Change both of the first and second projects. The debt paying ability of two projects is affected. The debt paying ability of second project descent obviously, but the safeguard multiplies is higher than 1.
- The ratio of the capital is 25%, sale price descent 10% and the sale speed descent 30%. Change both of the first and second projects. The safeguard multiplies of first project descent obviously. if and only if the time interval in 1 month and 33-36 months, the safeguard multiplies is larger than 1.
- The ratio of the capital is 20%, sale price descent 15% and the sale speed descent 50%. Change both of the first and second projects. The safeguard multiplies of two projects is less than 1 in any time intervals.

The pressure test of the capital saving mode demonstrate that the sale price and speed is affected more by the policy of macroscopic readjustment and control. The risk of pay back debt on the commercial bank real estate loan is higher than simple overlying mode for the debt paying ability descent quickly. At the same time, if the macroscopic readjustment and control effect part of the projects, the combination development can ensure the safeguard multiplies of two projects larger than 1. It demonstrate the portfolio development can resist the risk has a positive role.

5   Conclusions and Suggestions

According to the results of calculation and analysis based on the model, projects have the debt paying ability when they developed individually; they still have the paying ability when two projects portfolio development. The debt paying ability of two projects portfolio development use simple overlying type mode is higher than they respectively development. While the debt paying ability used capital saving mode in the appropriate combination modes can arrive even exceed they respectively development. In these situations, most of the developers chose the capital saving mode portfolio development in order to realize the maximization of capital gains. However, when the real estate industry suffer the harmful effects by the macro-control, the debt paying ability of capital saving mode descend faster compared to the overlying mode. Commercial bank should pay close attention to the risk characteristics of real estate industry; enhance the supervision of the funds for the real estate projects using in order to prevent the developer appropriated the loan to other purposes.

References

1. Tao, P., Chen, C., Sun, Y.: Research on Financial Risk Recognition and Dispose Measures for Real Estate Listed Company. Journal of Engineering Management 24(1), 107–112 (2010) (in Chinese)
2. Li, W., Xu, Y.: The application for risk value in real estate listed company financial crisis pre-warning model. Communication of Finance and Accounting 2009(02), 146–147 (2009) (in Chinese)

An Analysis on Spatial Differentiation and Spatial Expansion of County Economic Development in Hebei Province of China

HaiLong Ma[*]

Department of Economic, Tianjin Administrative Institute, Tianjin, China

Abstract. The article analyzes development of county economic in Hebei, in order to find spatial expansion direction of the region. By factor analysis and cluster analysis, it classifies 136 counties into four groups: developed, middle, lower-middle and less developed counties. Results show that county economic has no enough competition, significant differentiation between the southern and the northern, developed counties distributes along the principal axis, and less developed counties contiguous distribution, surrounding Beijing and Tianjin. Spatial expansion of county economic in Hebei should be along with three axes: the principal, the joint and ecological axis.

Keywords: country economy, spatial differentiation, spatial expansion, Hebei Province.

1 Introduction

County and county-level city is establishment unit for China to organize economic and social development. The development of country and county-level city plays extremely important role on promoting urban-rural integration. Now China is committed to promoting the development of rural areas. Therefore, a study on the difference between county economics of Hebei Province can help us make regional coordinated development strategy, and understand the rule of Chinese economic performance.

2 Research Areas, Methods and the Indicator System

This paper chooses 136 counties and county-level cities of Hebei Province as sample, and measures the level of economic development through statistical indicators which are chosen from 2010 Hebei Economic Yearbook, includes GDP per capita, per capita government revenue, per capita total investment in fixed assets, per capita total retail sales of consumer goods, per capita net income of rural residents, per capita wages of on-post staff and workers, per capita business value of post and telecommunications, civil motor vehicles per 100 persons.

---

[*] Doctor of science, vice professor of Tianjin Administrative Institute. His research fields are regional economy and governance.

M. Zhou (Ed.): ISAEBD 2011, Part IV, CCIS 211, pp. 49–52, 2011.
© Springer-Verlag Berlin Heidelberg 2011

In order to overcome multiple statistical indicators of information overlap between the variables and determine the index weight of human subjectivity, multiple statistical indicators are transformed into three mutually independent composite indicators by applying principal component analysis. Then takes the ratio of the variance contribution rate of the three principal components and cumulative variance contribution rate of all principal components as weight, which multiplied by the scores of the three principal components, the final comprehensive scores present the level of economic development of 136 counties and county-level cities.

3 Spatial Differentiation of County Economic Development of Hebei Province

3.1 The Calculation of County Economic Development Index

First, KMO test is used by SPSS 13.0 to determine whether selected indicators are appropriate to factor analysis. KMO test value is calculated by .851, with 28 degrees of freedom, significant level of .000, which is suitable for factor analysis.

Then the data of the 136 counties is analyzed by factor analysis, and extraction method is principal component analysis. Linear transformations of the original variables adopt correlation matrix and variance of the maximum orthogonal rotation. In the end, regression method is used to calculate the main principal component scores, and then with the weight of all the main components of the weighted summation of economic development level of county and city scores. The formula of Comprehensive score is $F= (42.564F1+21.296F2+17.763F3)/81.624$. The higher the score, indicating that the higher the level of the county's economic development, whereas lower.

From the results, there is 53 counties' economic development level is higher than average level (comprehensive score is more than 0), accounting for 38.97%, which is suggested that about 70 percent counties economic development are behind of average level. From the results, the difference of level of economic development between cities and counties is significant, and the most developed city is Qian'an City (2.451), the less developed counties is Kangbao County (-1.014).

3.2 The Types of Counties Economics

136 counties are divided into four types by K-means analysis: developed counties, middle developed counties, lower middle developed counties and less developed counties. Developed counties score above 0.8, a total of 19, accounting for 13.97 percent; middle developed counties score between 0.25 and 0.8, a total of 20 accounted for 14.71%; lower developed counties scores -0.55 ~ 0.25, a total of 61, accounting for 44.85%; less developed counties score below -0.55, a total of 36, accounting for 26.47 percent.

3.3 Spatial Differentiation of County Economics Development

Counties economics development of Hebei province has following characteristics:
First, weak competitiveness, significant differences between the North and the South
From spatial distribution, county economic development of Hebei province shows significant difference between the North and the South. Economic development in

northern counties is behind of the southern region. Most of the counties in north Hebei are less developed, and the rest are lower-middle developed.

Moreover, most of counties' economic strength is weak. Lower-middle developed counties area is 62109 KM^2, accounting for 33 percent; and has population 24 924 000, representing 36 percent of the province's population. The area of lower developed counties shares only 44 percent, and their GDP accounts for only 19 percent of the province.

Secondly, developed counties concentrated along the traffic axis

Developed counties mainly concentrated in three regions, and most of them are connected pieces. The first type of area is around Shijiazhuang City, capital of Hebei Province, and their social and economic development levels are the strongest city in Hebei Province. The development of Shijiazhuang City leads the development of the surrounding counties; the second type of area is surrounding Tangshan City. Tangshan City is in the axis of Beijing and Tianjin, and has obvious location advantages. Therefore, the rapid economic and social development of Tangshan City also pushes the development of surrounding cities and counties; the third type of region is between Beijing and Tianjin. Xianghe County, Sanhe City and Dachang County are enclave of Hebei Province and easy to accept the radiation of Beijing and Tianjin, relying on the strong development of Beijing and Tianjin, these counties also gain rapid development. Unique geographical location advantage of the region gain good development prospects.

Thirdly, less developed counties concentrate contiguously

Most of less developed counties are in northern Hebei, surrounding Beijing and Tianjin. These counties are mainly in the northern mountains and traditionally poor region.

4 Spatial Expansion of County Economic of Hebei Province

4.1 Shijiazhuang-Tangshan Axis

The highest level of economic development in Hebei Province is mainly distributed in Shijiazhuang - Tangshan main axis. The axis connects the three strongest economic strength counties: Baoding, Qinhuangdao, and Langfang. Besides, the main axis is across Beijing and Tianjin, and integration of the strategic axis of development of Beijing and Tianjin. These counties in the axis develop county economy, and fostered a number of competitive industries and specialized industry. The main axis of development can effectively promote the overall economic development in Hebei Province, lay a solid foundation of economic development in Hebei.

4.2 Handan-Xingtai-Hengshui-Cangzhou Joint Axis

This axis includes Handan, Xingtai, Hengshui and Cangzhou. Counties and cities are mainly lower-middle developed counties along the axis. The region is mainly plan, and has good natural conditions, developed transportation. Therefore, the region can be fostered a new economic growth belt.

4.3 Zhangjiakou-Chengde Ecological Axis

The western part of the axis belongs to Taihang Mountains, and the eastern belongs to Yanshan Mountains, the northern is Inner Mongolia Plateau dam. Natural and geographical environment is complex, and transport infrastructure is also underdeveloped. The region is always poor areas of Hebei Province historically. However, it is natural ecological barrier and water sources of Beijing and Tianjin, which has important strategic significance to the two cities. And the region has rich tourism resources to develop tourism.

5 Conclusions and Suggestions

According to economic development, counties can be divided four types: developed, middle developed lower-middle developed and less developed counties. Economic development of about 70 percent counties is below the average level of Hebei Province. County economic has no enough competition, and shows significant differentiation between the southern and the northern. From geographical distribution, developed counties are concentrated along the principal axis, and less developed counties contiguously distribute, surrounding Beijing and Tianjin.

Spatial expansion of county economic in Hebei should be along with three axes. The principal axis is Shijiazhuang-Tangshan axis, including Baoding, Qinhuangdao, and Langfang; the joint axis is across Handan, Xingtai, Hengshui and Cangzhou, named coastal development belt; the third axis is called ecological axis, is from Zhangjiakou to Chengde.

In addition, Hebei should actively participate in communication and cooperation of Beijing-Tianjin metropolitan area, strengthen economic ties between cities and counties.

Acknowledgments. The paper is supported by Nationally Social Science Foundation of China (Grant No.10CJL049).

References

1. Wu, M.L.: Statistic Apply and Practice of SPSS. China Railway Publishing House, Beijing (2001)
2. Peng, L., Qing, Q., Su, W.C.: Evaluation on spatial-temperal characteristics of comprehensive development level of counties in Chongqing. World Regional Studies 18, 61–67 (2009)
3. Qiu, F.D., Zhu, C.G.: Study on the Divergence and Temperal-Spatial Structure of Regional Economic Development in Jiangsu Province. Economic Geography 24, 468–476 (2004)
4. Wu, L.Y.: The Secondly Report on the Rural and Urban Spatial Development Planning Study for the Capital Region. Tsinghua University Press, Beijing (2006)
5. Wang, J., Jin, H., Ji, F.Y.: Comparative Study on the County Economic Competitiveness of Hebei. Journal of Hebei University of Technology 36, 51–59 (2007)
6. Guo, Y.T., Liao, H.P.: Progress in Research on Urban Spatial Expansion of China. Progress in Geography 28, 370–374 (2009)
7. Bo, X.N., Pang, B.Z.: Analysis of the Comprehensive Competition of County-Level Economy of Hebei Province by a Natural Area. Hebei Academic Journal 30, 194–197 (2010)

Quantitative Research on Brand Elements and Domestic Silk Brand Cognition Based on Silk Products

Rui Shi[1] and Guolian Liu [2]

[1] National Engineering Laboratory for Modern Silk,199 Ren Ai Road,
Suzhou 215123, P.R. China
[2] College of Textile and Clothing Engineering, Soochow University,
178 East GanJiang Road, Suzhou 215021, P.R. China
76067716@qq.com, liuguolian@suda.edu.cn

Abstract. This article designed a brand elements questionnaire combining the brand marketing theory from the point of consumers, analyzed the market research data with the structure equation model thought and analysis on SPSS13.0 software. Empirically researched the elements of silk brand and cognitive status on main silk products brand of domestic consumer.The results offered reference value for positioning China Silk brand, improving the Silk brand, and better implementing the strategic decision to brand marketing.

Keywords: silk products, brand elements, quantitative research, Structural equation model.

1 Introduction

Rich expressional form and the comprehensive connotation meaning of Brand is not from birth date, it is enriched with the development of the brand, which is a gradual process and a dynamic development, so brand is the embodiment of product or enterprise's core value. The domestic scholar Dou Jun-ling divided brand elements into intangible factors and tangible elements, thus formed the brand construction elements of the "trapezoid model", the tangible elements consistent with keller theory [1-3]. Maslow's hierarchy theory of needs showed that when consumer's basic physiological needs fulfilled, their consumption levels will increase, and then irrational consumption will produce[4].Therefore, silk brand is very important.

2 Research Content

The main content include two parts: points composing element of brand and cognitive of consumer on main domestic silk brand.

2.1 Analysis of the Components Factor

2.1.1 Analysis of Exploratory Factor

The analysis of preliminary exploratory by using software SPSS13.0 for factor [5]. Then get the clustering of each factor after exploratory factor analysis. Last get the rotating component matrix of 18 factors designed in questionnaire, parameters .

M. Zhou (Ed.): ISAEBD 2011, Part IV, CCIS 211, pp. 53–57, 2011.
© Springer-Verlag Berlin Heidelberg 2011

2.1.2 Confirmatory Factor Analysis

The factors clustering analysis and comprehensive comparison, see chart below (table 1). Also it's suitable for factor analysis after inspecting significantly (see table 2).

2.2 The Main Domestic Silk Brand Cognition of Consumers

Questionnaire, domestic main silk brand list for the following items. Using questionnaire about consumers of silk brand cognitive investigation data of domestic main silk, I found that consumer brand cognitive roughly status to see chart (figure 1) .

Table 1. Rotated Component Matrixa

	Component		
	1	2	3
Enterprise mechanism	.833		
Strategic positioning	.742		
loyalty	.729		
values	.619		
Brand logo		.732	
Advertising pr		.666	
source		.612	
popularity			.760
Consumer reflect degrees			.759

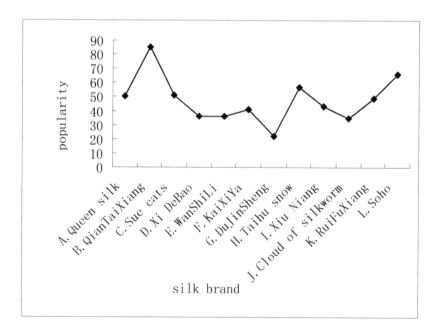

Fig. 1. Consumers' cognition of silk brand

Table 2. KMO and Bartlett's Test

Kaiser-Meyer-Olkin Measure of Sampling Adequacy.		.723
Bartlett's Test of Sphericity	Approx. Chi-Square	568.246
	df	36
	Sig.	.000

3   The Structural Equation Model of Brand Components

By using the thought of structural equation model [6], modeling and analyzing various elements. According to each factor elements of the clustering analysis and exploratory and confirmatory factor analysis results, now building structure equation model as follows.

3.1   Build SEM Models

According to the confirmatory factor analysis, it is concluded that the target factor the total covariance matrix, editor, import LISREL model, empirically software analysis, the analysis results are as follows(see table.3). According to the running result of LISREL program, we can get structure equation model and the factors statistical index, finally research model of indexes effect and the parameter.

3.2   Model Analysis

Table 3 shows each index result more ideal CFA, factor analysis and brand elements model can use. To analyze the model we need perfect it according to figure be fixed index.

Table 3. Statistical index

index	X^2	NFI	Df	IFI	GFI	CFI	RMSEA
Value	145.06	0.73	24	0.77	0.87	0.76	0.15

3.3   Modifying Model

From the Analysis of the model received (see figure 2).Component factor 1 of the four is VAR4 namely except for elements of main component factor 1 values is the outside, contribution to three factors (VAR1, 2, 3) contribution in general. Principal component factor 2 VAR7 contribution coefficients VAR6, is good, VAR5 and principal component factor 2 correlation weakly. VAR8, 9 correlative factors of Principal component factor 3 were good posture.

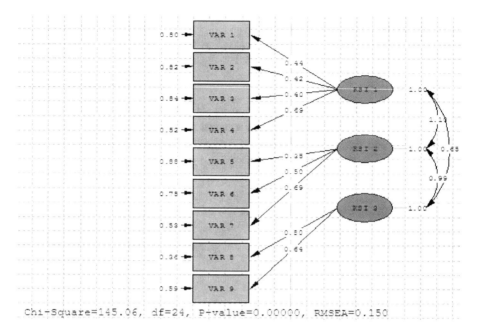

Fig. 2. The final structure model of brand components

4 Summary

Through this research and analysis, we can draw some conclusions as follow.

1. Chinese silk industry must implement brand development strategy, Advise businesses in silk products at the same time, will upgrade their silk brand and build good to win the positive market effect good solid foundation.
2. The study found that brand elements positive effect to brand itself, including the construction and development of culture construction of your brand identity is the source, brand values in the market, brand accumulated by the consumer reaction degree, these three key elements of silk brand of perfect is particularly important.

Acknowledgement. This research was funded by the First Phase of Jiangsu Universities' Distinctive Discipline Development Program for Textile Science and Engineering of Soochow University.

References

1. Leslie, D.E.: che(England), Tony. Brand to win. zhong xin press, Beijing (2002)
2. Yan, Z., Lu, T.: Industrial supplies brand elements and brand system integration. Economic and management research (8), 34–37 (2007)

3. Ying, W.: Brand elements of enterprise multiple combination and operation mechanism is discussed. The modern economy (4), 12–17 (2006)
4. Naiwen, Z.: Consumers of irrational behavior and marketing counter measure. Journal of enterprise vitality (4) (2010)
5. Jie, W.: Experimental design and SPSS application. chemical industry press, Beijing (2007)
6. Jietai, H., Zhonglin, W.: Structure equation model and its application, pp. 11–16. Education science press, Beijing (2005)

A Study on E-Commerce Outsourcing Research and WBS Internet Marketing

Sheng Cao and Erqin Mo

Management School, Donghu College, Wuhan University, Wuhan, 430212, China
{Sheng_cao,768239697}@qq.com

Abstract. With the electronic commerce outsourcing companies's appearance and development, the drawbacks in the electronic commerce and the internet marketing for SEMs also are becoming more remarkable, In view of this situation, the paper analyzes the respective advantages and disadvantages for both professional e-commerce outsourcing companies and enterprises doing e-commerce themselves, combined with the current development status of internet marketing, this paper made a summary, put forward WBS e-commerce marketing outsourced new mode. This mode through the comprehensive enterprise marketing type website, e-commerce integrated model and search engine marketing three as one to develop the internet promotion and online sales. Using the model neatly to carry out interner marketing activities can bring great benefits for enterprise.

Keywords: WBS, E-Commerce, Business, Website, outsourcing, Internet Marketing, SME.

Although with the continuous development and matures of e-commerce, there currently only has 24% of SMEs using the Internet to engage in internet marketing in China, and those who are able to do e-commerce internet marketing among s SMEs account for only 13% of the total, many companies do not develop their own e-commerce business.

With the continued refinement of operational structure of enterprises, more and more clear division of labor, business and how we can consolidate resources in order to enhance their competitiveness? "Obviously, due to the limit on the the capital, technology and human resources of our SMEs, the community needs to provide cost-effective universal e-commerce service, e-commerce outsourcing will become a mainstream of e-commerce development for SMEs." E-commerce Internet marketing outsourcing will become the first choice for SMEs to develop their e-commerce, it is a low-cost, high-yield information service model, is particularly suitable for some SMEs. Outsourcing can help companies solve problems of various kinds in e-commerce development. [2]

Enterprise hands over its product marketing and sales services to "e-commerce internet marketing professional outsourcing service providers", and take advantage of the internet operator skills learning from these new "e-commerce internet marketing outsourcing service providers."In order to expand business opportunities, increase sales of enterprise products, thus creating profits for the enterprise, Enterprise can use professional service provider resources advantages to Realize enterprise platform and

M. Zhou (Ed.): ISAEBD 2011, Part IV, CCIS 211, pp. 58–63, 2011.

national platform docking and integration, and break the bottleneck of e-commerce for SMEs. [3]However, with its wide spread development, e-commerce models become numerous, in actual practice of enterprise promotion, you may also meet many problems, gain little profits from it. With the development of e-commerce outsourcing, a new integrated e-commerce internet marketing model-WBS came into being, and it has been proved to be able to bring about a quick and great internet effectiveness in practice.

1 Analysis of E-Commerce Outsourcing Market

1.1 E-Commerce Situation of SMEs in China

With WEB2.0 era, by 2013 the scale of China's Internet users will reach 718 million, Internet users' penetration has surpassed half of the total population of the country, at 52.7%. As the internet is increasingly getting deep into the people's lives, internet users' consumer awareness is being enhanced, the internet showed a rapid growth trend in consumption, the consumption through internet for the first half of 2010 reached 473.4 billion total consumption, and to 1.1594 trillion throughout the year, online shopping expenditures in 2011 will exceed half of the total internet consumption (55.8%) and 2013 internet spending more than 2 trillion yuan. Online shopping will be the most important driving force for the internet consumption growth. [4]

1.2 E-Commerce Outsourcing Market Analysis

With the arrival of the era of individualistic consumption, consumers are increasingly affected trade. Electronic commerce future developments will eventually led by consumer, enterprise who wants to win in the industry must fully develop e-commerce, the setting up of enterprise brand. If an enterprise wants to rapidly develop its e-commerce business, it must choose a professional e-commerce internet marketing team. E-commerce outsourcing has broad prospects, and WBS e-commerce outsourcing is suitable for all kinds of SMEs.

2 E-Business New Model—WBS(Website-BMC-SEM)

WBS e-commerce integrated internet marketing new mode is a kind of such mode, it put the traditional internet marketing model and new internet marketing model combining, the construction of an independent enterprise Marketing websites, and using the BMC (Business-Marketing-Consumer) Integrated marketing model and SEM(search-engine-meting) to promote enterprise products and corporate brand, It can bring to the company faster more internet promotion and sales benefit on the internet.

2.1 Enterprise Marketing Website Optimization and Production (Website)

Website's structure, layout, website code are the key factors which will directly influence enterprise web browsing's speed and the effectiveness of SEM, and marketing Web is a dynamic system after the construction of static and then a static website, is very conducive to the search engines to crawl, marketing type of Website can realize background based website management, management systems will be fully integrated into the most advanced search engine optimization ideas, Let SEO (search engine optimization) technology for enterprise use. In internet marketing oriented enterprise website construction should be comprehensively uses standards, make full use of CSS + DIV exclusively website advantage, for in the future the orders increase lay a better foundation. [4]

2.1.1 BMC(Business-Marketing-Consumer) Integrated Mode

B=Business, refer to enterprises, M=Marketing, here refers to the marketing. C=Consumer, refers to consumers, internet retail agents, terminal, It is a multidimensional, unlimited conversion join-point website and the consumer, will, the enterprise and terminal, the enterprise and the channel agents, according to the different demands organically combined to form interests, creating win-win interaction of a kind of marketing operation model.

The new model BMC is committed to product promotion and corporate brand building, recruit online retailers through the new modell-B2C, Execute "Internet affiliate marketing" [5] to bring more common remark hits and potential customers, using the model-- B2C2C to develop the internet marketing activities, using the model— C2B to carry out the product design and quantitative production activities, and using the model-- B2B to carry out the activities of large sales.

2.1.2 SEM (Search Engine Marketing)

SEM is a new kind of Internet marketing form SEM should be comprehensive and effective use of search engines for online marketing and promotions.SEM pursuit of the highest cost, with minimal investment, maximize the traffic from search engines and generate business value. [6]

SEM search engine can maintain the brand, reduce the negative information to the brand as little as possible, can prevent competitors on the internet malicious framed, Also can undertake again positive business information promotion, then achieve brand promotion goals.

3 Enterprise Developments or Outsourcing Analysis

3.1 Enterprise Independent Develop E-Commerce Analysis

"Aeryn nets (http://www.iresearch.cn/) study found: according to the state administration of industry and commerce data, by 2009, with the e-commerce application ability of small and medium-sized enterprises, number has reached 3995.6 , Increase in the number of 3.8 compared with 2008[7] " It said China began to develop e-business of SMEs, although more, but can actually do more successful less.

3.2 E-Commerce Outsourcing Successful Case Study

January 2010 Wuhan Maoren Dress Co., Ltd limited by shares, bought Alipay mall ready to widen product online sales business, with no professional management, the Internet mall did not see any benefit after more than half a year.

Using e-commerce marketing model flexibly -- WBS can obtain good marketing benefits. we began to construct and operate online distribution mall for wuhan Maoren Dress Co., Ltd （www.umaoren.com） through using WBS internet marketing new model at the end of July 2010. We optimized the keywords and the website for the mall, formulated the search engine marketing planning, we made keywords and website optimization for the mall, formulated the search engine marketing planning, taken recruitment online retailers and affiliate marketing strategy, [8] Let the web pages of Wuhan cat people corporation online distribution mall be collected 76 page by baidu, Important keywords SOSO (A famous search engine in China) ranked the first page in article 1, Mall, PV traffic at present more than 4000, At present the daily sales of over 30,000 yuan, Every day the highest sales breakthrough 40,000 yuan, the monthly sales close to 270,000 RMB. The number of online retail agent reached more than 3000.We have a lot of distributors, which in an underwear shop in the taobao mall occupy 90%.

4   Detail Analysis of WBS

By companies are different. Using the BMC e-commerce integrated model for promotion enterprise product sales, easy to transport and has a bigger profit space products, production enterprises should build distribution mall, Through the form of "affiliate marketing" and recruitment internet product sales agent of to expand enterprise brand, and enhance product sales, for sales, difficult to transport or small luxury category products, the producer or agent is suitable for constructing product retailers, through the "internet affiliate marketing", "viral marketing", "internet" word-of-mouth marketing "marketing way to promote enterprise internet product sales and brand.

As for the agent retailers' recruitment, the agent's quality and quantity of will significantly affect sales of the enterprise internet. The Distribution mall of Wuhan cat people joint stock limited company Began to build In the end of July 2010, In early August, began to upload products, make the product packets, recruitment online agents.

Through two months nearly three months agent recruiting work, make its internet products retail agent number reached 3456, there are nearly 200 agents have not to open my own online, there are nearly 600 agents have not or not fully upload the product coming from wuhan Maoren Dress Co.,Ltd, and nearly 1000 agents have not done window recommended and product promotion for wuhan Maoren Dress Co.,Ltd. Most online agents are amateurs or Part-time staff and they did not have enough experience on online marketing and distribution of the goods, and they not own a stable supply of goods. After planning we regularly held internet training seminars, inviting agents free to participate in, and provide special training course In order to make it more loyal to our product's sales agent while enhancing the agent internet sales skill and experience. Now the total number of agents increased by about 20 times than the activities carried out before. After the first training, agents increased many working passion, Mall monthly sales reached nearly 7 million yuan In September 2010, agent reach more than

1,000 people. October internets reach more than 2,000 agents, sales exceeded 25 million yuan. November more than 3,000 agents, too much orders every day, leading to accumulation of goods in logistics transportation, can not be timely delivered to end consumers. Caused each link negligent, its monthly sales for 24.5 million, nearly half the number of agents increased, but sales are down compared to the previous month. So in the management of agents we improved our requirements, for a month, no sales agents will cancel the agent qualification, and increase the number of managers, having done this, Malls operation again smooth rise.

The number of distribution agents mall is not sure, the number of recruiting agents to some extent also related to specific products. General distribution of the number of control agents Mall around 2000 is the most appropriate.

5 Conclusion

WBS integrated e-commerce internet marketing model, is a very new model. Professional e-commerce internet marketing outsourcing company in the operation model WBS status according to the specific business model to take the appropriate internet of sales and marketing, for enterprises in a short time a large number of online orders and traffic, enhance brand online Visibility, to seize more market share in the internet, reduce cost of sales promotion.

With the continuous development of e-commerce, business survival and development are no longer isolated; the majority of SMEs have to rely on e-commerce outsourcing model into the information age among the economic ecosystem. WBS integrated e-commerce internet marketing model, is a very new model. Professional e-commerce internet marketing outsourcing company in the operation model WBS status according to the specific business model to take the appropriate internet of sales and marketing, for enterprises in a short time a large number of online orders and traffic, enhance brand online Visibility, to seize more market share in the internet, reduce cost of sales promotion.

References

1. Alibaba (China) internet technology Co., LTD. The Chinese small and medium-sized enterprise electronic commerce development report (2010), http://news.mbalib.com/story/24669 (March 17, 2010)
2. Bao, W., Li, Z.: Based on outsourcing of small and medium-sized enterprises, e-commerce development trend. The northern economic (4), 46–47 (2008)
3. HuaGong, C.: The enterprise electronic commerce model selection. Modelrn marketing marketing macmillan 12(2) (2009)
4. Feng, Y.: The internet marketing basis and practical, 3rd edn., pp. 136–137. Tsinghua university press, Beijing (2007)
5. Feng, Y.: The internet marketing basis and practical, 3rd edn., pp. 74–75. Tsinghua university press, Beijing (2007)

6. Feng, Y.: The internet marketing basis and practical, 3rd edn., pp. 156–225. Tsinghua university press, Beijing (2007)
7. Aeryn advisory group. 2009-2010 Chinese small and medium-sized enterprise B2B e-commerce industry development report (2010),
   `http://wenku.baidu.com/view/fdaacbef5ef7ba0d4a733b3c.`
   `htmlsss2010-9-6`
8. Feng, Y.: The internet marketing basis and practical, 3rd edn., vol. 70. Tsinghua university press, Beijing (2007)

An Analysis on Influencing Factors of Express Company's Customer Loyalty

Hongyu Lu, Jingbo Shao, and Keke Chen

School of Management, Harbin Institute of Technology,
150001, Harbin, P.R.China

Abstract. Due to the great development potential of express delivery industry, the competition between the express companies is increasingly fierce. Hence, adjusting marketing strategies to enhance customer loyalty is a key measure to maintain long-term dynamic of express companies. This paper chose the express industry as the research object, and, in combination with the analysis on the characteristics of the express service, summarized the crucial influencing factors on customer loyalty of companies in this industry, analyzed the mechanism of impact of various factors on the express customer loyalty and conceptualized the impacts of different factors on customer loyalty in a structural model, in order to better illustrate the relationships between them.

Keywords: customer loyalty, express company, influencing factors.

1 Introduction

As a major theme of modern marketing strategy, customer loyalty means considerable potential profits to companies. Loyal customers protect the company against the fierce competition in industry and serve as a solid foundation for the long-term survival of companies. In traditional marketing theories, customer loyalty is generally defined as the repetitiveness and continuity of repurchase behavior. Besides direct repeat purchasing behavior, customer loyalty is also reflected in the attitude, intention and commitment towards the service provider.

Prior to the study on customer loyalty, understanding the express customers' characteristics is necessary. In general, the express customers are characterized by large number, dispersed customer base, and "bilaterality". The bilaterality of express customers refers to the existence of two clients in a specific delivery transaction: the shipper and the consignee. It is difficult to satisfy both of them in an intertemporal and cross-domain context. And the exchange of information between the shipper and the consignee makes it possible that the assessment of either party on the express service quality would be influenced by the subjective views of the other side. Therefore, customer satisfaction plays a significant role in the building process of express company's customer loyalty. Besides, customers that express company faces include enterprises and individuals across industries and across countries. In different geographical areas, the levels of economic development and cultural environment are different. Thus, customers' demand for express services, requirements of service

M. Zhou (Ed.): ISAEBD 2011, Part IV, CCIS 211, pp. 64–70, 2011.

quality and the affordability of delivery costs are surely different. Similarly, in different industries, the product mix is necessarily different. So the demand for express delivery services will also vary by customer. In addition, the customers' ownership will directly impact on the cost of market expansion, complexity of cooperation and customer retention and so on. In a word, the significance of market segmentation and customer characteristics identification cannot be ignored in the research of customer loyalty in express delivery industry.

Currently, researches on influencing factors of customer loyalty are focused in retailing, banking, telecommunication and third-party logistics industry. Though the express delivery industry has many similar features with the third-party logistics industry, they are not completely same. Generally, the goods transported by express delivery industry are lighter, smaller, and the speed requirement for transport is higher. In addition, there are differences in the clientele structure between the two industries. Thus, the degree of impacts on customer loyalty of different influencing factors could be various.

In combination with the analysis on the characteristics of the express service, this paper conceptualize the impacts of different factors on customer loyalty in a structural model, in order to better illustrate the relationships between them. The influencing factors which have been studied most include customer satisfaction, customer trust, service quality and customer value. Meanwhile, switching cost and corporate reputation are supposed to be the main factors driving customer loyalty in many cases. Besides, many express companies began to use reward program so as to improve customer loyalty. Thus, in this paper, loyalty program is treated as an influencing factor on customer loyalty as well. In the following part of this paper, we will analyze these factors in sequences.

2 Theoretical Framework

2.1 Customer Satisfaction

Rust and Oliver (1994) defined customer satisfaction as customers' perception of the degree of positive emotion brought by using the product or service [1]. Oliver (1999) concerned about the customers' cumulative experience and pointed that cumulative satisfaction is a key factor that influence customer loyalty [2]. Customer satisfaction is a psychological state. Customers could be pleased or disappointed when they compare the perception of the effect of product or service with their desired outcomes. Also, customer satisfaction is a psychological reaction, a judgment on the level that the product or service meets one's need. The level of express service customers' satisfaction depends primarily on the following parts: whether the customer is pleased when they use the express delivery service of a certain express company; the overall satisfaction on the quality of previous express delivery services and the discrepancy perceived between expectation and perception of outcomes in a specific transaction. Obviously, customers satisfied are more probable to re-use the express service provided by the original company; on the contrary, customers dissatisfied may possibly turn to another express company. McDougall and Levesque (2000) pointed out that the level of customer satisfaction directly determines the increase or decrease of future purchase intention [3]. Therefore, in the conceptual model in this paper, we assume that customer satisfaction has a positive influence on the express company's customer loyalty.

2.2 Service Quality

In theory, customers' perception of service quality is measured as the discrepancy between what customers expected and what customers actually received. Parasuraman, Zeithaml and Berry (1988) indicated five determinants of service quality: tangibles, reliability, responsiveness, assurance and empathy [4]. As to measurement of courier service quality, we focused mainly on the courier's attitude, the efficiency of courier service, their ability to respond to emergencies, the company's facilities equipment and the convenience provided to customers (time flexibility, network coverage, personalized service, etc). Heskett, James and Loveman (1994) believe that service quality has indirect impact through customer satisfaction on customer loyalty [5]. Parasuraman, Zeithaml and Berry (1996) found that there is a positive correlation between service quality and customers' willingness to pay a higher price and to remain loyal when price increases [6]. In addition, the relationship between service quality and purchasing frequency was proved to be positive by Boulding, Kalra, Staelin et al. (1993)[7]. Hence, in this paper, we assume that service quality has not only direct impact, but also indirect impact through customer satisfaction on express company's customer loyalty.

2.3 Customer Value

Customer value is defined by Zeithaml(1988) as the overall evaluation of the product or service based on customers' perception of tradeoff of "get" versus "give-up"[8]. According to Grewal, Monroe and Krishnan (1998), buyers' willingness to buy is "positively linked to their perception of acquisition and transaction value [9]". In order to investigate customers' perceived value of courier service, we should find out their "perceived benefits" including the fundamental benefits that customers received by using courier service, for example, saving time or money and the benefits derived in choosing fitting personalized service. Simultaneously, we should take in account the perceived costs including monetary cost like freight paid and implicit cost, for example, the risks that customers have to face. Several researchers believe that customer perceived value is a key driving factor of customer retention and customer loyalty (Cronin et al, 2000; Parasuraman, 1997; Woodruff, 1997) [10][11][12]. In a way, customer perceived value derived in courier transportation is both functional and hedonic, so we supposed that it has both direct and indirect impact (via customer satisfaction) on customer loyalty.

2.4 Trust

Morgan and Hunt (1994) defined trust "as existing when one party has confidence in an exchange partner's reliability and integrity" [13]. To obtain customer trust, express companies should stand in the customers' position to provide customers with reliable express delivery services and to meet customers' need for the sake of customers' benefits. Johnson and Grayson (2005) posited that consumer trust is based on service provider expertise, product performance, corporate reputation, satisfaction, and similarity in influencing customer's perception [14]. In fact, when a customer said that he trust in an express company, it means that he had confidence on the company's expertise and he had much belief that the goods could be sent to destination in time and in security. Besides, when a customer trusts an express company, he would engage in self-disclosure with couriers and set up a more intimate relationship with the company. Harris and Goode (2004) demonstrated that trust has direct and indirect effects on customer loyalty [15]. It is also a core driver of customer loyalty. In express delivery industry, if the courier company's performance can't win the trust of customers, it will be difficult to establish long-term relationship with them. In other words, when customers have full confidence in an express company, customer loyalty will be enhanced.

2.5 Switching Cost

When a customer ends the relationship with a company and turn to another competitor, switching cost engenders spontaneously, for instance, new service supplier information search costs and loss of interest cost due to relationship breakdown with the original. In the express delivery industry, the possible sources of switching cost are as follows: lost-performance cost (i.e., the loss of preferential treatment provided by the original company), uncertainty cost (i.e., the risks that customers have to face in dealing with a new service provider), pre-switching search cost, post-switching cognitive costs, etc. Among them, uncertainty cost and pre-switching search cost are most common in daily express transaction. Yini and Xujun (2010) considered switching cost as a adjusting factor of customer turnover behavior [16]. Beerli, Martin and Quintana (2004) proved that switching costs, as well as customer satisfaction, can be regarded as customer loyalty antecedents[17]. The two factors determine jointly customers' repurchasing behavior. When customer satisfaction towards a service provider is relatively low, switching cost plays an important role to ensure customers' behavioral loyalty. In other words, switching cost affect directly behavioral loyalty. Thus, we assume that switching cost has direct influence on customer loyalty of express company.

2.6 Corporate Reputation

Corporate reputation reflects the company's position in the market. Good corporate reputation can effectively convey the signals to customers that the company provides guarantee and commitment on the quality of product or service, which reduce pre-consumption risk perception and transaction cost. Corporate reputation is an influencing factor to customer loyalty of express company. In general, the express company provides "door-to-door" service. So when customers need to use express delivery service, they will contact the most familiar or the most heard express company without considering the other companies. Therefore, the more loyal customers recommend this company to others, the greater the number of potential customers. Their recommendation will contribute to wide spread of express company's reputation. Morgan and Hunt (1994) pointed out that both customers' choice of brand and repurchasing behavior are related to corporate reputation [13]. Nguyen and Leblanc (2001) found in their empirical study in service industry that there is a positive correlation between corporate reputation and customer loyalty [18]. After analysis, we assume that it has influence on both customer loyalty and trust of express company.

2.7 Loyalty Program

Currently, many express companies implement customer relationship management strategy and offer loyalty program to customers for purpose of reward and encourage their loyal behavior. For example, SF Express provided points redemption program to their customers in 2009 and 2010. Theoretically, loyalty programs can create different barriers to prevent the loss of customers. These obstacles manifest as both monetary and psychological switching costs to express service customers. For them, whether to participate in loyalty program depends on their perception of potential benefits in this program. For instance, if participating a program give the customer 10% discount in the future transaction with a certain express company, the customer will prefer to consume in this company rather than another which provides no reimburse. Therefore, it is practical to use customer perceived benefits of a loyalty program as an index to measure the effectiveness of this program in driving customer loyalty. We hypothesize that loyalty program impacts on customer loyalty through customer value and switching cost.

3 Conceptual Model

In order to illustrate more clearly the relationship between the influencing factors, we design a conceptual model as shown in Fig. 1.

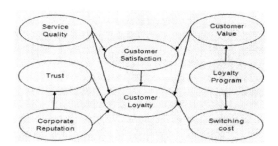

Fig. 1. Conceptual model of express company's customer loyalty

There are three main differences between the conceptual model in this paper and the models previously used in the researches concerning influencing factors on customer loyalty:

In the first place, in the previous theoretical and empirical studies on customer loyalty, few researchers will take all these factors in a model to comprehensively analyze their impacts on customer loyalty in a certain industry. However, the purpose of building this model is not just to illustrate the theoretical impact path of different influencing factors, but also to provide a basis for the future empirical study on express company's customer loyalty. We could distinguish the factors which contribute most to build customer loyalty and which are relatively less important. In this way, we could provide a reference to the manager of express company which implies a strategic direction in developing a marketing plan.

In the second place, by observing the conceptual model we could find that customer satisfaction is located in a core position in the relationship among these influencing factors. That is because in most existing academic papers, customer satisfaction is always deemed as the most important one. The other influencing factors like service quality and customer value are supposed to exercise influence over customer loyalty indirectly through customer satisfaction, due to its positive effect customer purchasing behavior and future purchasing intention.

In the third place, regarding loyalty program as an influencing factor of express company's customer loyalty is an innovation point in this paper. In general, loyalty program functions as a marketing tool to increase customer retention rate in the literature. However, the express company's marketing tool is relatively few. Nowadays, more and more express companies like SF Express and FedEx begin to use points redemption program and other concession terms to attract client and reinforce customer retention and then improve customer loyalty. Therefore, in the analysis on influencing factors on express company's customer loyalty, we treated loyalty program as a separate factor so as to investigate its effectiveness on building customer loyalty.

4 Conclusion

With the increasingly fierce market competition, customer retention and customer loyalty become the key theme in express company's marketing strategies. Through the theoretical analysis and conceptual model building above, we have drawn a conclusion in a way comprehensive about the influencing factors (customer satisfaction, service quality, customer value, trust, switching cost, corporate reputation and loyalty program) of express company's customer loyalty and the way that they impact on customer loyalty. However, the conceptual model and the analysis of relationship between influencing factors and customer loyalty are solely on the basis of theories and we haven't tested these hypotheses via empirical analysis yet. In the follow-up studies, we will collect data related to this model by sampling and test the hypotheses in the context of express delivery industry through the use of quantitative methods, for the purpose of providing a reliable basis for the establishment of conceptual model.

Acknowledgments. The authors thank to National Natural Science Foundation of China for financial support (71031003, 70802018).

References

1. Rust, R.T., Oliver, R.L.: Service Quality: New Directions in Theory and Practice, pp. 1–19. Sage, London (1994)
2. Oliver, R.L.: Whence Consumer Loyalty? The Journal of Marketing 63, 33–44 (1999)
3. McDougall, G.H.G., Levesque, T.: Customer Satisfaction with Services: Putting Perceived Value into the Equation. Journal of Services Marketing 14(5), 392–410 (2000)
4. Parasuraman, A., Zeithaml, V.A., Berry, L.: SERVQUAL: A Multiple-item Scale for Measuring Consumer Perceptions of Service Quality. Journal of Retailing 64(1), 12–37 (1988)
5. Heskett, L.J., James, T.O., Loveman, G.W., et al.: Putting the Service-Profit Chain to Work. Harvard Business Review 2, 164–174 (1994)
6. Parasuraman, A., Zeithaml, V.A., Berry, L.L.: The Behavior Consequences of Service Quality. Journal of Marketing 60(2), 25–50 (1996)
7. Boulding, W., Kalra, A., Staelin, R., et al.: A Dynamic Process Model of Service Quality: From Expectation to Behavioral Intentions. Journal of Marketing Research 30(1), 7–27 (1993)
8. Zeithaml, V.A.: Consumer Perceptions of Price, Quality, and Value: A Means-End Model and Synthesis of Evidence. The Journal of Marketing 52(3), 2–22 (1988)
9. Grewal, D., Monroe, K.B., Krishnan, R.: The Effects of Price-Comparison Advertising on Buyers, Perceptions of Acquisition Value, Transaction Value, and Behavioral Intentions. The Journal of Marketing 62(2), 46–59 (1998)
10. Cronin, J.J., Brady, K.M., Hult, G.M.T.: Assessing the Effects of Quality, Value, and Customer Satisfaction on Consumer Behavioral Intentions in Service Environments. Journal of Retailing 76(2), 193–218 (2000)
11. Parasuraman, A.: Reflections on Gaining Competitive Advantage through Customer Value. Journal of the Academy of Marketing Science 25(2), 154–161 (1997)
12. Woodruff, B.R.: Customer Value: The Next Source for Competitive Advantage. Journal of the Academy of Marketing Science 25(2), 139–153 (1997)
13. Morgan, R.M., Hunt, S.D.: The Commitment-trust Theory of Relationship Marketing. Journal of Marketing 58(3), 20–38 (1994)
14. Johnson, D., Grayson, K.: Cognitive and Affective Trust in Service Relationships. Journal of Business Research 58(4), 500–507 (2005)
15. Harris, L.C., Goode, M.M.H.: The Four Levels of Loyalty and the Pivotal Role of Trust: a Study of Online Service Dynamics. Journal of Retailing 80(2), 139–158 (2004)
16. Yini, C., Xujun, H.: Empirical Research on Integrated Model of Customer Switching Behavior in Service Industry. Scientific Decision Making 12, 61–68 (2010)
17. Beerli, A., Martin, J.D., Quintana, A.: A Model of Customer Loyalty in Retail Banking Market. European Journal of Marketing 38(1/2), 253–275 (2004)
18. Nguyen, N., Leblanc, G.: Corporate Image and Corporate Reputation in Customers' Retention Decisions in Services. Journal of Retailing and Consumer Services 8(4), 227–236 (2001)

The Research of the Impact from China-ASEAN Financial Cooperation on the Development of Bilateral Trade

Xuanqi Ou

701 10# building, 5th courtyard, BeiFengWo Road, HaiDian district Beijing, China
Ouxuanqi621@sohu.com

Abstract. In this article we first introduce the development of financial cooperation between China and ASEAN. Then we apply the method of panel data analysis by utilizing STATA to find out which financial factors we select significantly influence the trade volume between China and ASEAN and the conclusions are FDI as well as international reserve. After the empirical analysis we further explain the economic meanings of the model and discuss the policies that may promote the bilateral trade volume in the future by controlling those significant financial factors effectively.

Keywords: ChiangMai Initiative, International Reserve, FDI.

1 Introduction

During the two decades since 1990, with the financial cooperation between China and ASEAN deepened, the bilateral trade volume increases rapidly except the year 1998 and 2009 when the global financial crisis affected international trade severely. However, even in 2009 when the world's economy suffered a lot from the subprime crisis, bilateral trade volume ,though decreased to 213 billion $ as compared with 2008, still accounted for 9.7% on the total external trade volume of China while ASEAN kept the fourth trade partner, the fourth export market as well as the third import market of China.

1.1 CMI

In May 2000, ASEAN and China, Japan as well as Korea formally signed ChiangMai Initiative in the annual meeting of ADB, and reached broad agreement on consolidating CMI in the following finance ministers' meeting. CMI has become a foundation stone in the financial cooperation between China and ASEAN. From the aspect of building up currency swap net to stabilize regional finance market, CMI advocates enlarging the scale of currency swap among ASEAN and calls on the member countries to establish bilateral currency swap agreement in order to provide the relieving foreign exchange fund for each other in case of emergency. CMI puts forward the idea of regional financial cooperation in form of currency cooperation. Later on, governments among eastern Asian continues try relevant affairs based on CMI so as to

M. Zhou (Ed.): ISAEBD 2011, Part IV, CCIS 211, pp. 71–77, 2011.
© Springer-Verlag Berlin Heidelberg 2011

make foundational arrangement for further financial cooperation. CMI includes two important contents: First, perfect ASA (ASEAN Swap Arrangement) and make it cover all the member countries of ASEAN. The total money of ASA was added from 0.2billion $to 1billion $(in 2005 this number increased to 2 billion$). Second, build up BSA (Network of Bilateral Swaps and Repurchase Agreements) among "10+3" countries and promise to provide appropriate amount of money to member countries when it is necessary to help them solve the problem of short term international payments imbalance as well as capital flowability. So far, all of the member countries have participated the ASEAN multilateral swap arrangement and China has set up swap agreements with some of the ASEAN members respectively. By the end of November 2008, the total scale of CMI has reached 85.5 billion $(including the 2 billion $ of ASA) and China has signed several bilateral swap agreements with Thailand, Malaysia, Philippines, Indonesia respectively, totaled 9.5billion$.

1.2 E.A. Forex Reserve Pool

In March 2010, Chiang Mai multilateral agreement took effect formally. According to this agreement, the establishment of a multilateral foreign exchange (Forex) reserve not only helps to integrate East Asian financial resources and improve the regional common response to financial risks, but is also important in maintaining the steady growth of regional economy and spurring the multilateral process of East Asian cooperation. The 10 member countries of ASEAN plus China, Japan and the Republic of Korea (ROK) altogether collected 120 billion$ to establish Forex reserve, with 38.4 billion$ from China, the same contribution as Japan, which accounts for 32%, 19.2 billion $ from ROK, accounting for 16% and 24 billion $ from ASEAN, accounting for 20%. Along with the institution of 120 billion dollars regional Forex reserve, the East Asian financial cooperation was escalated from a bilateral to multilateral leap.

2 The Empirical Analysis

In this section we utilize the method of panel data analysis by STATA to establish econometric model with the relevant financial indexes in order to find out the indexes that impact bilateral trade volume significantly, then we theoretically explain the transmission mechanism of the indexes. The data are selected mainly from the ASEAN statistical Year Book 2008 and IMF's publication International Financial Statistics as well as the World Bank's publication World Development Indicators 2009. On the basis of proofreading we processed the data collection into panel data with the time span from 2000 to 2008. The 11 countries here include China and 10 ASEAN member countries.

2.1 The Introduction of Indicator System

i. In_gdppc

GDP per capita is gross domestic product divided by midyear population. GDP is the sum of gross value added by all resident producers in the economy plus any product taxes and minus any subsidies not included in the value of the products. It is calculated without making deductions for depreciation of fabricated assets or for depletion and degradation of natural resources. Data are in current U.S. dollars. In this article we take logarithm of GDP per capita, noting for In_gdppc.

ii. Deposit rate

Deposit interest rate is the rate paid by commercial or similar banks for demand, time, or savings deposits.

iii. Lending rate

Lending rate is the rate at which financial institutes lend money. It constitutes the base from which banks then lend money to the final customer.

iv. M2 growth rate

M2 growth rate is the average annual growth rate in money and quasi money. Money and quasi money comprise the sum of currency outside banks, demand deposits other than those of the central government, and the time, savings, and foreign currency deposits of resident sectors other than the central government. The change in the money supply is measured as the difference in end-of-year totals relative to the level of M2 in the preceding year.

v. Exchange rate

Exchange rate is the price of native currency in relation to another's (US$ here). It is the number of units of one currency that buys one unit of another currency. In this article the exchange rate is the average number of a year. The determination of exchange rates is a complex process that has economic impact on imports and exports.

vi. FDI（Foreign direct investment）

Foreign direct investment is the net inflow of investment to acquire a lasting management interest in an enterprise operating in an economy other than that of the investors. It is the sum of equity capital, reinvestment of earnings, other long-term capital, and short-term capital as shown in the balance of payments.

vii. International reserve

Theoretically, international reserve comprise holdings of monetary gold, special drawing rights, reserves of IMF members held by the IMF, and holdings of foreign exchange under the control of monetary authorities. However, in order to analogize E.A.Forex reserve, we exclude monetary gold so the international reserve here could be generally regarded as foreign exchange reserve.

viii. Trade volume

Trade volume is the total volume of the import and export of a country in a year.

2.2 Panel Data Analysis

In this article we choose the trade volume to be the explained variable while the explanatory variables are in_gdp, deposit rate, lending rate, m2 growth rate, FDI, exchange rate as well as international reserve. Now we utilize STATA to set up random effect regression model and fixed effect regression model.

	(1) trade volume	(2) trade volume
ln_gdppc	0. 298	0. 423
	(7002. 9)	(9931. 1)
deposit rate	−0. 285	−0. 419
	(1472. 3)	(1738. 4)
lending rate	−0. 311	0. 337
	(1718. 5)	(2806. 8)
m2growthrate	0. 438	0. 473
	(234. 9)	(250. 8)
fdi	0. 088***	0. 085**
	(3. 392)	(3. 573)
exchange rate	2. 835*	−4. 629**
	(2. 540)	(5. 292)
international reserve	0. 089***	0. 078***
	(0. 0145)	(0. 0161)
_cons	−0. 204	−0. 301
	(63087. 6)	(85289. 7)
N	77	77

Standard errors in parentheses * p < 0.10, ** p < 0.05, *** p < 0.01

Rank (1) lists the coefficients of the random effect regression model while rank (2) lists the coefficients of the fixed effect regression model. We can conclude primarily from the list that FDI and international reserve have strong correlation with trade volume whereas the correlation between trade volume and deposit rate is comparatively week. However, which model is more suitable as to the panel data of this article? We can conduct hausman inspection:

	(b) Fixed	(B) Random	(b-B) Difference	sqrt(diag(V_b- V_B)) S.E.
ln_gdppc	0. 423	0. 298	0. 125	69.72
deposit rate	−0. 419	−0. 285	−0. 134	9.078
lending rate	0. 337	−0. 311	0. 648	22.01
m2growthrate	0. 473	0. 438	0. 035	0.843
fdi	0. 085	0. 088	−0. 003	1.067
exchange rate	−4. 629	2. 835	−7. 464	4.612
international reserve	0. 078	0. 089	−0. 011	0.006

Chi2(5)   =   (b-B)'[(V_b-V_B)^(-1)](b-B)

                =   5.90

Prob>chi2   =   0.3158

From the result of hausman inspection, we can see that null hypothesis cannot be rejected. Because the null hypothesis of hausman inspection is that the fixed effect does not exist, the random effect regression model here is more suitable to this article.

2.3 Appreciation of Research Results

i. GDP percapita represents the level of economic development and level of income per capita in a country. Since the coefficient is positive, the research shows a positive correlation between a country's export capabilities as well as purchasing power trade and volume.

ii. The coefficient of interest rate is negative. Because raising interest rates suppresses the growth of credit and private investment. Financing cost rising forces the export-oriented corporations give up lower profit rate projects and reduce amount of using credit. Meanwhile, the prices of export products will increase, which cause exporting losing price competitiveness. Therefore export volume declines in corporations and vice versa. In sum, the transitive relation is center bank sets the interest rate policy, and then adjusts loan scale, so that commercial banks give response to the policies, loan rationing and loan direction adjust, export corporations give response to the policies and adjust productive investment so foreign trade scale changes accordingly.

iii. The coefficient of the money supply is positive. Because the increasing money supply may lead to the rising of domestic price, thus the foreign goods become relatively cheap and a short term beneficial to import .On the other hand, the increasing money supply gives an impetus to the growth of credit and investments in general, thus promotes the output level of the domestic enterprise which is beneficial to export, and finally promotes the growth of the volume of foreign trade in the long run.

iv. The major influences of FDI on international Trade are as follows: changes in foreign exchange rates due to large capital flows would impact the price and amount of goods; foreign corporations may lead local companies to produce intermediate goods, which are imported from overseas, so an increasing of the goods causes a raise of the volume of export. Foreign corporations use products made by local companies, which need import intermediate goods, so that the volume of import increases. Rapidly developing FDI, which is relative equilibrium in import and export, influences the promotion of trade balance, when the RMB increases in value and vice versa.

v. Exchange rate affects both the prices of export products in foreign market and the prices of foreign products in domestic market, and further affects volume of sales of both domestic goods in foreign market and foreign goods in domestic market. For developing countries, some degree of domestic currency depreciation at a managed exchange rate, limits importing goods to some extent and promote exporting goods. If a country performs direct foreign exchange quotation, its exchange rate increase lead domestic currency to depreciate, therefore the relative price of import goods goes up and the same quantity of foreign currency buy more domestic goods. Foreign customers give response to the price movement. Their requirement of exporting goods increases. So the rising exports may further promote trade volume.

vi. Each country creates foreign-exchange reserves in order to cover temporary increases in payments over receipts in international trade. There are four main functions in foreign exchange reserves:

a. Adjust international balance of payments, guarantee outgoing payment;
b. Intervene in the foreign exchange, stabilize domestic exchange rate;
c. Maintenance international credit, enhancing the overall national strength and capability of against risk.

Foreign exchange reserves are an important manner which is used to regulate macroeconomic and made ends meets by government. When domestic macroeconomic imbalances and aggregate supply is greater than aggregate demand, the government may import by using foreign exchange, therefore regulates the relation between aggregate demand and aggregate supply, promote balance of macro-economic The presence of foreign-exchange reserves determines the so-called international liquidity of a country, that is, its ability to make payments on foreign accounts regularly. So the foreign-exchange reserves have a strong influence on international trade.

3 The Future of China-ASEAN Financial Cooperation

3.1 Enlarge the Scale of E.A. Forex Reserve Pool

The establishment of multilateral Forex reserve is conducive to maintaining regional economic stability and growth and spurring the transformation of economic structure in East Asia. The region has long since relied mainly on external markets to achieve economic growth, but this growth pattern cannot guarantee the stable economic development because of greater risks it faces. Forex reserve not only helps to integrate East Asian financial resources and improve the regional common response to financial risks, but is also significant for maintaining the steady growth of regional economy and spurring the multilateral process of East Asian cooperation. The advancement of multilateral financial cooperation in East Asia offers a very good inspiration or much enlightment for people around the region to think of. Firstly, the institution of regional Forex reserve is brought about by an endeavor of each East Asian nation to alienate part of the national interest and assume more responsibilities. Secondly, the materialization of multilateral financial cooperation in East Asia fully proves that the East Asian nations can transcend their disparities to pursue or seek their common good. However, the scale of the Forex reserve is much less than the reserve level of these East Asian countries. So the problem is whether the reserve at current level can provide enough financial protection for the countries when the economic crisis breaks out. How to enlarge the scale of the reserve as well as optimizing the ratio of contributions are the urgent topics that need to be discussed right now.

3.2 Better the Investment Environment and Maintain the Momentum of Increasing the Bilateral Direct Investment

Since the establishment of China ASEAN Free Trade Area (CAFTA), the bilateral trade has increased rapidly. In 2010, the trade volume between China and ASEAN totaled 292.78 billion$ and hit the historical record. By now China has become the largest trade partner of ASEAN. However, unmatched with the robust growth of bilateral trade, China-ASEAN bilateral investment still remains at a low level. According to ASEAN Statistics, direct investment from China only takes up a share of 1.5% among all the FDI inflows that ASEAN has ever received between 2000 and 2008.

Theoretically, FDI provides not only the financial resource for the fixed assets investments but also the necessary technology as well as management skills for native corporations, which enable it to become an important factor in economic growth. Meanwhile, FDI promotes the host countries to utilize various kinds of nets, such as marketing nets, production nets and information nets of foreign companies. So the host countries may obtain high productivity and tremendous market. In fact, in order to gain more profits from FDI, many ASEAN members have drawn up more liberalized policies to attract FDI.

However, there are now still many problems and risks that are restraining Chinese enterprises' direct investment in ASEAN. To overcome these unfavorable factors, Chinese government should accelerate the bilateral negotiations on investment with ASEAN countries on one side, and widen financing channels for free flow and optimized allocation of capital on the other hand; while the industry associations should strengthen researches and study over the ASEAN markets so as to provide concrete investment advices for enterprises. Only in this way, can they enlarge direct investment in ASEAN and thus promote bilateral trade finally.

References

1. Aizenman, J., Lee, Y., Rhee, Y.: International Reserves Management and Capital Mobility in a Volatile World: Policy Consideration sand a Case Study of Korea. Journal of the Japanese and InternationalEconomies 21(1) (2007)
2. Zhi, L.: Participating the Construction of China-ASEAN Free Trade Area and Promoting the Development of Yunnan Economy. Chinese Book Company, Beijing (2004)
3. Root, F.R.: International Trade and Investment, pp. 448–471. South-western Publishing Co. (1984)
4. United Nations Conference on Trade and Development (UNCTAD). World Investment Report (2001-2004)
5. Weidong, H.: Study on China-ASEAN Free Trade Area. Southwestern University of Finance and Economics, Chengdu (2005)
6. Association of Southeast Asian Nations, http://www.aseansec.org
7. Asia Develop Bank (ADB), Monetary And Financial Integration In East Asia. Economic Science Press (2005)

Research on Small and Medium-Sized Enterprises (SMEs) Financing Based on the Game Theory

Hui-hui Sun[1,2] and Yu Zhang[3]

[1] School of Accounting, Chongqing Technology and Business University
400067 Chongqing, China
[2] School of Economics and Business Administration, Chongqing University
400044 Chongqing, China
[3] School of Arts and Communication, Southwest Jiaotong University,
610031 Chengdu, China
zjy_cq2@163.com

Abstract. The information asymmetric leads to the risk of bank credit increased and exacerbate the financing difficulties of Small and Medium-sized Enterprises (SMEs). Reputation is a strategic intangible asset and is an effective mechanism for information transmission. We can use the conduction effects of the reputation to reduce the information asymmetry caused by the credit risk. Therefore, under the assumption of rational expectations, the model of Barro and Vickers is deformed simply in this paper, and the game model of the SMEs financing behaviors, which take reputation into account, is established. Through the analysis of the reputation impacts on the SMEs, some good suggestions have been proposed in this paper.

Keywords: Small and Medium-sized Enterprises (SMEs), reputation, financing, asymmetric information, game.

1 Introduction

In the finance market, finance companies have more information on financing, such as the quality of corporate finance, investment risk and so on, but the banks and other lending institutions do not have. After lending funds, the lending corporations did not receive any immediate benefits. They only received the commitments to repay interest in the future. And the behavior of the borrowers to repay the loan will directly determine the bank's future earnings. To reduce credit risk caused by information asymmetry, the banks are more likely to shrink the money supply. This practice exacerbated the difficulty of SME financing. How to solve the uneven between supply and demand in the credit because of information asymmetry is the key to solve the problem of credit for SMEs.

The reputation research provides a new idea for us to solve the SMEs` financing problems. Under the assumption of rational expectations, the model of Barro and Vickers is deformed simply in this paper. The game model of SMEs banks finance the behavior is established. Through the analysis of the reputation impacts on the SMEs, some good suggestions have been proposed in this paper.

M. Zhou (Ed.): ISAEBD 2011, Part IV, CCIS 211, pp. 78–84, 2011.

2   The MODEL of the Reputation Effect

2.1   The Hypothesis

Firstly, the two sides of the game - the financing side (SMEs) and lenders (banks) constitute the two players in the game.

Secondly, Bank believes that as the financing side, the SMEs have two types: honest type and treacherous type. The honest type of financing parties will never repudiation and adhere to repay the loans; but the treacherous type of financing parties maybe not repay the loans to seek temporary repudiation interests under certain conditions. But the treacherous type of financing party may build a reputation to repay the loans forever by pretending to be an honest type of financing parties.

Thirdly, the banks do not know the type of financing companies, but can be inferred by observing the rate of Repudiation type of financing enterprises.

The last, once the SMEs Repudiation situation occurred, the bank will think the company is fraudulent enterprise, and the SMEs will not obtain loans in the subsequent stages.

2.2   The Game Model

In order to analyze the impact of the SEMs` reputation on the level of bank loans, we deform the model of Barro and Vickers simply. Assuming the single-stage cost function of the financing side (the SEMs) is following:

$$u = w^2 - 2b(w - w^e) \qquad (1)$$

w is the actual Repudiation rate of the SMEs, w^e is expected Repudiation rate of financing, b is the type of financing SMEs: $b = 0$ represents it is an honest enterprise; $b = 1$ represents it is a treacherous enterprise. Assume that the prior probability that the banks consider financing SMEs is an honest enterprise side ($b = 0$) is P, and assume that the prior probability that the banks consider financing SMEs is a treacherous enterprise side ($b = 1$) is $(1 - P)$.

2.2.1   The Single-Stage Game
When we derivative (2), we can get the best Repudiation rate of the single-stage:

$$du/dw = 2w - 2b = 0 \qquad (2)$$

So $w = b = 1$, and $u = 1^2 - 2 \times 1 \times (1 - 1) = 1$

2.2.2   Multi-stage Repeated Game

Let us assume that the game will repeat T times. y_t is the probability that the treacherous enterprise select to be zero probability of Repudiation. x_t is the probability that the bank think the treacherous enterprise will select to be never Repudiation; when equilibrium, $x_t = y_t$.

So, if in the t phase the bank does not observe the financing side SME to be Repudiation, according to Bayes rule, in the t +1 period the posterior probability that the public think the financing SEMs to be an honest enterprise is:

$$\tilde{P}_{t+1}(b=0|w_t=0) = \frac{prob(b=0, w_t=0)}{prob(w_t=0)}$$

$$= \frac{prob(w_t=0|b=0)prob(b=0)}{prob(w_t=0|b=0)prob(b=0) + prob(w_t=0|b=1)prob(b=1)} \quad (3)$$

$$= \frac{1 \times \tilde{P}_t}{1 \times \tilde{P}_t + x_t(1-\tilde{P}_t)}$$

Because   of $1 \times \tilde{P}_t + (1-\tilde{P}_t) \in [x_t, 1]$,   so $1 \times \tilde{P}_t + (1-\tilde{P}_t) \leq 1$,   i.e.

$\tilde{P}_{t+1}(b=0|_t=0) \geq \tilde{P}_t$, That is, if the financiers did not repudiate in the t phase, then in the period t +1 the probability that the banks think the SEM to be honest type will increase. However, if the financiers repudiated in the t phase, then:

$$\tilde{P}_{t+1}(b=0|w_t=1)$$

$$= \frac{prob(w_t=1|b=0)prob(b=0)}{prob(w_t=1|b=0)prob(b=0) + prob(w_t=1|b=1)prob(b=1)} \quad (4)$$

$$= 0$$

In other words, once the bank observed that the financing side SME to repudiate, the bank will think the SME to be a treacherous enterprise. Now, let us solve multi-stage game equilibrium with the backward induction method.

2.3   Game Model Solution

2.3.1   Solution in the Final Stage (the T Stage)

In the final stage, because game has entered the final stage, whether to maintain the reputation of not deadbeat has been not necessary, therefore, the optimal choice of treacherous enterprise must be $w_t = b = 1$. The expected Repudiation rate of the bank thinks the SME to be is $w_t^e = 1 - \tilde{P}$ .The repudiation cost of SMEs in T stage is:

$u_t = 1^2 - 2[1 - (1 - \tilde{P}_t)] = 1 - 2\tilde{P}_t$.

Because $\partial w_t / \partial P_t = -2 < 0$, so, u_t is the decreasing function of P_t. That is the better the reputation, the lower the cost of financing side of corporate finance. This is the reason that the treacherous enterprise try to establish the reputation of an honesty enterprise.

2.3.2 Solution of the Penultimate Stage (the T-1 Stage)

Assuming treacherous enterprise before the T-1 stage is not deadbeat, so $\tilde{P}_{t-1} > 0$, the expected repudiation rate is: $w_{t-1}^e = 1 \times (1 - \tilde{P}_{t-1})(1 - x_{t-1})$.

1 is the optimal Repudiation rate of treacherous enterprise, $(1 - \tilde{P}_{t-1})$ is the probability that the enterprise to be a treacherous enterprise. $(1 - x_{t-1})$ is the probability that the bank think treacherous enterprises choose to repudiate.

δ is the discount factor of the enterprise. First to consider the pure strategy game, that treacherous enterprises choose to repudiation or not, that is the case $y_t = 0$, or $=1$ (because the game in the mixed strategy equilibrium, only two pure strategies when the expected utility equal, people would be involved in Select mixed strategy. so we know the optimal conditions for pure strategy also know that a mixed strategy condition).

If the fraudulent enterprise in selected T-1 stage Repudiation ($y_{t-1} = 0$, so $w_{t-1} = 1$) , then: $\tilde{P}_t = 0$ (observed in the T-1 stage to the corporate deadbeat, the banks know that the financing party can not be honest enterprises SMEs). Given the bank is expected to be treacherous business deadbeat enterprise w_{t-1}^e total cost of financing:

$$u_{t-1}(1) + \delta u_t(1) = \left[1 - 2(1 - w_{t-1}^e) \right] + \delta = -1 + 2w_{t-1}^e + \delta \tag{5}$$

If the fraudulent enterprise in stage T-1 choose not to deadbeat, that is $y_{t-1} = 1$, so $w_{t-1} = 0$, then the treacherous type of financing the total cost of the financing of enterprises:

$$u_{t-1}(0) + \delta u_t(1) = 2w_{t-1}^e + \delta(1 - 2\tilde{P}_t) \tag{6}$$

Therefore, if and only if the following conditions are true, the election $w_{t-1} = 0$ (not deadbeat) is lower than the cost of financing election $w_{t-1} = 1$ (Repudiation) financing costs:

$$2w_{t-1}^e + \delta(1 - 2\tilde{P}_t) \le -1 + 2w_{t-1}^e + \delta \leftrightarrow \tilde{P}_t \ge 1/2\delta \tag{7}$$

Because in equilibrium, the expected deadbeat rate x_{t-1} that the banks thinks corporate to be is equal to the choice of enterprise y_{t-1} , therefore, if

$y_{t-1} = 1$ constitutes a treacherous enterprise's equilibrium strategy, then $x_{t-1} = y_{t-1} = 1$, $P_t = P_{t+1}$. The above conditions mean that: $\tilde{P}_{t-1} \geq 1/2\delta$. That is, if in the T-1 stage the probability that the bank think the enterprise is an honest enterprise, the repudiation cost will be less than the refund cost. Then the enterprise must choose to refund, and the enterprise will pretend to be an honest type Enterprises. That is, better corporate reputation, higher the better the reputation of companies (namely banks that the business is the greater the probability of honest enterprise), then the enthusiasm of enterprises to maintain the reputation of the higher (more enterprises want to pretend to be honest enterprise), the more obvious the role of reputation.

If $\tilde{P}_{t-1} = 1/2\delta$, then the above analysis shows that the T-1 stage treacherous enterprise does not pretend to be honest to pretend, or the cost is the same, the enterprise will be randomly selected probability $y_{t-1} = 1$ or 0 any optimal mixed strategy is that any $y_{t-1} \in [0,1]$ are the most Excellent. But because of balance requirements $x_{t-1} = y_{t-1}$, will be substituted $\tilde{P}_{t-1} = 1/2\delta$ into the formula before the Bayes rule, we have:

$$\tilde{P}_t = \tilde{P}(b = 0 | w_{t-1} = 0) = (\tilde{P}_{t-1} \times 1)/(\tilde{P}_{t-1} \times 1 + (1 - \tilde{P}_{t-1})x_{t-1})$$
$$y_{t-1} = x_{t-1} = (2\delta - 1)\tilde{P}_{t-1}/(1 - \tilde{P}_{t-1})$$

(8)

Because x_{t-1} is the increasing function with $\tilde{P}_{t-1}$, so the more that the bank financing of SMEs is the honest enterprise side, treacherous enterprises choose not to, the higher the probability of Repudiation (assuming $2\delta - 1, i.e. \delta > 1/2$). Especially, when $\tilde{P}_{t-1} \rightarrow 1/2\delta$, $y_{t-1} \rightarrow 1$. This is because the fraudulent enterprise in the repayment phase of T-1 decision faced with immediate and long-term interests of the trade-off. Financing of a given bank does not know the type of enterprise (that is, the expected rate of Repudiation $w_{t-1}^e < 1$), if the fraudulent enterprise at this stage to use the reputation (i.e. selection $w_{t-1} = 1$), the enterprise at this stage of the financing costs for the T-1 is $u_{t-1}(1) = -1 + 2w_{t-1}^e < 1$. However, after the destruction of reputation, corporate financing costs for the next phase of T = 1 is $u_t(1) = 1 > 1 - 2\tilde{P}_t$. Therefore, enterprises face the treacherous at this stage whether the use of their reputation or the reputation of the next phase of the problem using their own. Especially when $\tilde{P}_{t-1}$ is large enough, sufficiently close to 1, the treacherous enterprise selection is the next stage of the optimal use of their reputation, not at this stage to use their reputation.

2.3.3 The Optimal Solution before T-1 Stage

If assume that when $t \leq T-1$, which the SME financing side of zero, repudiation is the best choice. Using mathematical induction can prove the following:

If the government does not repudiation of choice (i.e. zero-repudiation rate) is the optimal solution, we can draw the conclusion that repudiation of Choice is not the best when all $t < T-1$ (the proving process is Omitted).

2.4 Summary

- **The first case.** if $P_0 \geq 1/2\delta$, the honest corporate will select $w_0 = w_1 = \cdots = w_{t-1} = w_t = 0$, the honest corporate will never select to repudiate; The treacherous corporate will select $w_0 = w_1 = \cdots = w_{t-1} = 0$, $w_t = 1$. That is before T stage, the treacherous corporate will never select to repudiate, but at final stage the treacherous corporate will repudiate. The expected repudiation rate that the bank thinks the financing is $w_0^e = w_1^e = \cdots = w_{t-1}^e = 0, w_t^e = 1 - \tilde{P}_t = 1 - P_0$. In the equilibrium path, the posterior probability is $\tilde{P}_t = \tilde{P}_{t-1} = \cdots = P_0$; In the non-equilibrium path, if $w_1 = 1$, $P_{t+1} = 0$. The total financing cost of the honest type business (discounted value): $\sum_{t=0}^{T} \delta^t u_t = 0$; The total financing cost of the treacherous type business (discounted value): $\sum_{t=0}^{T} \delta^t u_t = 0 + 0 + \cdots + \delta^t(1 - 2P_0) = \delta^t(1 - 2P_0)$

- **The second case.** If $P_0 < 1/2\delta$, The game equilibrium is separating equilibrium the honest type business will select $w_0 = w_1 = \cdots = w_{t-1} = w_t = 0$; the treacherous type business will select $w_0 = w_1 = \cdots = w_{t-1}$. The expected repudiation rate that the bank thinks the financing to be is $w_0^e = 1 - P_0, w_1^e = \cdots = w_{t-1}^e = w_t^e = \begin{cases} 1, w_0 = 1 \\ 0, w_0 = 0 \end{cases}$; The posterior probability is $\tilde{P}_t = \tilde{P}_{t-1} = \cdots = P_1 = \begin{cases} 0, w_0 = 1 \\ 1, w_0 = 0 \end{cases}$. The total financing cost of the honest type business (discounted value) : $\sum_{t=0}^{T} \delta^t u_t = 0$; The total financing cost of the treacherous type business (discounted value): $\sum_{t=0}^{T} \delta^t u_t = (1 - 2P_0) + \delta + \delta^2 + \cdots + \delta^t = -2P_0 + (1 - \delta^{t'})(1 - \delta)$.

3 The Model Implications and Policy Recommendations

3.1 Accelerate the Collection of Reputation Information

Reputation mechanism ensures the effective function of the reputation of the first collection of information to solve the problem. One can learn from foreign companies profit widespread credit bureaus, credit rating agencies, by their credit history according to the SMEs, operations and financial condition and other factors, the credit situation of SMEs to collect, organize, form the basis of reputation information, and then paid to provide this information to the lending bank or other financial institutions. On the other hand, the banks themselves can also review and oversight activities to obtain information. Banks and financial institutions themselves experts in the production of information, in part, the production advantages of information banks and other financial institutions can be the basis for the emergence and existence. For SMEs to open bank accounts in the settlement activities, the bank may also be made to obtain the financial situation of SMEs and trade useful information, compared to other agencies more information superiority.

3.2 Expand the Reputation of the Transmission Channels of Information

With a reputation based on the information, how to ensure effective transfer of reputation information, the role of reputation mechanism is an indispensable factor. We can take advantage of profitable enterprises in addition to credit bureaus, credit rating agencies to pass information to the reputation of foreign sales information, you can expand the reputation of the government level through the delivery channel to improve the reputation of transfer efficiency, specifically from the two levels of information to establish the reputation of the corresponding integrated Query library: The first level is the establishment of a large national financial institutions for the repository, to store all corporate customers, financial institutions and credit information. When faced with a private financial institution loans to business applications, can be paid by way of access to information in the database of credit information companies in the past; second level is the establishment of regional information base to address local financial institutions and local non-state Problem of asymmetric information between enterprises.

References

1. Barro, R.: Reputation in a Model of Monetary Policy with Incomplete Information. Journal of Monetary Economics 17, 3–20 (1986)
2. Kane, E.J.: Impact of Regulation on Economic Behavior. Journal of Monetary Credit and Banking (9), 355–367 (1981)
3. Yu, J.-j.: Commentary on Theory of Modern Western reputation. Current Financial (11), 18–22 (2003)
4. Zhang, W.-y.: The Game Theory and Information Economics. Sdxjoint Publishing, Shanghai (1996)

Impacts of Political Connections on Earnings Quality of Chinese Private Listed Companies

Yu Song[1,2], Lina Wang[3], and Zi Yan[1]

[1] School of Economics and Management, Nanjing University of Science and Technology, Nanjing, 210094, China
songyu6186@sina.com
[2] School of Business Nanjing University, Nanjing, 210093, China
wanglina2002@vip.sina.com
[3] School of Accounting, Hebei University of Business and Economics, Shijiazhuang, 050061, China
5295134@qq.com

Abstract. This paper examined empirically the impacts of political connections on earnings quality, taking the private listed companies with or without political connections in 2006-2008 as the sample. We define the political connections are that the chairman of the board or CEO is one of government officials or members of People's Congress or Chinese People's Political Consultative Conference. We use accruals quality and earnings response coefficients to proxy the earnings quality. The results show that the accruals quality of the private listed companies with political connections is better than those without political connections. The inhibition of political connections on the earnings management is mainly reflected in the inhibition of "downward" earnings management, and its role in the "upward" earnings management is not that significant. From the view of market, political connections can improve the reaction extent of earnings in returns and increase earnings response coefficients.

Keywords: political connections, private listed companies, accruals quality, earnings response coefficients.

1 Introduction

In recent years, earnings management has been one of the focuses of accounting scholars. There are a series of research results in this area. For example, some empirical evidences on the motives of earnings management shows that corporations often conduct earnings management for the following reasons: public offering of securities, to increase the manager's compensation and job security, to avoid the violating lending contracts, or to reduce regulatory costs or to increase regulatory benefits (Healy and Wahlen, 1999). In china, earnings management occurs especially in the area of equity financing (Xiaoyue Chen et al., 2000). However some scholars found that securities regulators in china began to focus on the earnings quality of corporations, and to a certain extent, can identify earnings fraud of the listed companies, and gradually improve its supervisory capacity (Chen and Yuan, 2004).

M. Zhou (Ed.): ISAEBD 2011, Part IV, CCIS 211, pp. 85–92, 2011.
© Springer-Verlag Berlin Heidelberg 2011

So, when the earnings management of listed companies have to consider the adverse consequences if being disclosed, they will probably achieve their aims by other means, rather than by the direct earnings management activities. Some scholars began to study the economic consequences, especially the impact on the earnings quality caused by the politics, which provides new ideas for the studies in this area.

The studies on political connections have generally recognized that the company's political connections really have an impact on all levels of the companies, and this effect is widespread. For example, the political connections have an impact on a country's financial market development and corporate financing strategy (Dinc, 2005; Leuz and Oberholzer-Gee, 2006), on corporate governance and firm performance (Johnson and Mitton, 2003; Fan, Wong and Zhang, 2007) and so on. In view of the usefulness of accounting information in decision-making, many scholars discussed the relationship between political connection and earnings quality from the perspective of political cost (Jones, 1991; Key, 1997; Han and Wang, 1997; Monem, 2003). However, such studies are very different from the studies on political connections which are generally concerned currently study.

In addition, in transition stage of economic system of china, the role of government gradually retreated behind the scenes. However, there are still residual imprints left by the planned economy in China's market economy. Especially for private enterprises, they encountered a lot of obstacles that affect their business during the stage of economic restructuring. For example, Johnson et al. (2000) indicates that private enterprises are often unable to obtain a large number of bank loans or lower interest because most of the loans are provided to state-owned enterprise, or subject to stringent regulations restricting by the government. In addition to the imperfections of the market mechanism, the legal system is too weak to protect the property rights of private enterprises and the implementation of the contract. In such circumstances, the close relationship with the government may be able to help companies overcome some of the failure of market mechanisms and avoid ideological discrimination. But at present, academic researches related to this area have just started in recent years in china, and have not formed a systematic research framework. So, the research space is still wide.

This article defined the corporations whose chairmen of the board or CEOs are now served in the government sectors, or act as NPC(National People's Congress) or CPPCC (National People's Political Consultative Conference)members as having political connection. Based on the A-share private listed companies in 2006-2008, this article examined the impact of executives' political connection on the earnings quality through regression analysis from two perspectives: the accrual quality and earnings response coefficients. The results show that: the accrual quality in private enterprises with political connection is better than private enterprises without political connection, and the role of political connection is mainly reflected in inhibiting the "downward" earnings management. In the "upward" earnings management, the role is smaller. From the view of market, political connections can improve the reaction extent of earnings in returns and increase earnings response coefficients.

Other parts of this paper are structured as follows: The second part includes relevant theoretical analysis and literature review and on this basis, theoretical hypotheses will be putted forward to be tested. The third part introduces the research methods and data description. The fourth part is the empirical results and interpretation. The fifth part summarizes the full text.

2 Theoretical Analysis and Literature Review

Some papers about the impact of political connections on earnings quality are mostly from the view of political cost, and rarely from the view of the political background of senior managements. In this case, the corporations with political connections are often consciously or unconsciously treated as a mechanism to transfer wealth. The existence of political costs will encourage listed companies to conduct earnings management in order to maximize their own interests. For example, Jones (1991) found that corporations would carry out "downward" earnings management to reduce their profits during the investigation by government in order to receive the subsidies of government for imports. Key (1997) found that the cable companies would reduce their profits to avoid political risk when the United States Congress began to investigate the cable industry. Based on the Persian Gulf crisis in 1990, Han and Wang (1998) investigated the differences of sensitivity to political environment among the natural oil industry and oil refining industry. There are more political interferences in the oil refining industry, which makes the industry reduce quarterly earnings by accrual basis, and break the convention of releasing good news earlier. Johnson et al. (2000) found that bureaucratic corruption in a country was significantly related to the hidden production and sales of domestic corporations, which can avoid the exploitation of the bureaucracy. Monem (2003) studied the case of Australian government imposing income tax on gold mining industry, and found that the corporations would reduce their profits to avoid tax increases during the period when government develop and review policies.

Since 2006, central government in China has stressed the need to promote the healthy development of non-state ownership economy, and introduced some measures to encourage non-state capital to enter the field of related industries. There are many disadvantages of perfect mechanisms because of a short time economic reform even though a lot of policies supporting for private business development have been published. Private enterprises are discriminated in the political or social status, or cannot receive the actual economic benefits, or become the victim of a local government seeking to enhance their own performance. In such a market environment, political connections as a special social resource may be able to help private enterprises solve some practical problems through informal channels to safeguard the development of private enterprises.

First, the political connections could become the "umbrella" for the enterprises. At this stage, local government still holds a large number of economic resources and administrative resources which are necessary to the development of non-state enterprise enterprises. The allocation of these resources is often opaque, and lack of judicial oversight. To get these resources, non-state business will need to work through various channels to establish good relations with local governments. The state credit instead of business credit guarantees the quality of enterprises because of the lack of credit in our society. On the other hand, enterprises can reduce the interference of local governments by virtue of the personal connections and social resources because the senior managements with political background can carry out more effective communication with government officials, which may enhance earnings quality.

Second, political connections may be able to become self-bound sign. With the development of society, it becomes one of the hot issues of social concern for government officials to be in business. Because these officials may seek personal gains by using public resources and public authority which they hold in the past, it becomes the focus of social concern. The concern is higher in the enterprises with political connections than in those without political connections. On the other hand, private entrepreneurs began to be interested in political arena, and became NPC deputies or CPPCC members. The Likelihood of entrepreneur's political participation will decline when the market environment improves. The kind of political connections, as a "signal" and "signs ", improve the degree of social concern, and enhance the social supervision. As a listed company, the external supervision become self-constraint in order to maintain a good public image to get its own stable development in the stock market. In view of this, private enterprises with political connections may need necessary control of earnings quality in order to maintain their good public images.

So the political connection is a bridge of mutual benefit between private enterprises and local government. According to the above analysis, we propose the following hypothesis:

Hypothesis 1: Other conditions limited, earnings quality of the private listed companies with political connections is higher than those without political connections.

3   Data Source and Model Design

3.1   Selection of Samples

This paper selects the A-share private listed companies in 2006-2008 as the sample in China. The financial data in this paper are from CCER (China Center for Economic Research) and WIND information database of the Shanghai Wind Information Technology Co., Ltd.. Data to whether the private listed companies have political connections are hand-collected. The method of collection is to search the personal resumes of executives disclosed by websites including "finance.sina.com.cn", "money.163.com" and "business.sohu.com". The information in these three websites is complementary. There are some principles when selecting the samples: (1) Excludes the ST sample of listed companies; (2) Excluding financial listed companies in the sample; (3) Removing the missing data sample of listed companies; (4) removing samples which were listed current year.

3.2   Model Tested

We investigated the impact of political connection on accruals quality through model (1), and examined the impact of political connection on the earnings response coefficient through model (2). The specific definition of the variables is shown in

Table 1. We expected the coefficient α_1 in model (1) should be significantly negative, and the coefficient β_2 in model (2) should be significantly positive.

$$|DA| = \alpha_0 + \alpha_1 PolC + \alpha_2 First + \alpha_3 First^2 + \alpha_4 Size + \alpha_5 Lev$$
$$+ \alpha_6 Cycle + \alpha_7 Year_{07} + \alpha_8 Year_{08} + \varepsilon \tag{1}$$

$$Re_{turn} = \beta_0 + \beta_1 \frac{EPS}{Pr_{ice}} + \beta_2 \frac{EPS}{Pr_{ice}} \times PolC + \beta_3 Beta + \beta_4 Size$$
$$+ \beta_5 Lev + \beta_6 Year_{07} + \beta_7 Year_{08} + \varepsilon \tag{2}$$

Table 1. Selection and Definition of Variables

Variables	Definition of variables	Method of calculation
$|DA|$	absolute value of manipulative accruals	Taking the absolute value based on cross-section modified Jones model
PolC	political connections	If the company has political connections, the value is 1, otherwise 0
First	percent of shares hold by the largest shareholder	The number of shares hold by the largest shareholder/total number of shares
First^2	square of percent of shares hold by the largest shareholder	The square of variable First
Size	size of the company	Natural logarithm of average total assets of the company
Lev	financial leverage	Average asset-liability ratio=average total liabilities/ average total assets
Cycle	operating cycle	Accounts receivable turnover days plus inventory turnover days and then take the natural logarithm
Year	annual control variables	When the sample belongs to the 2007/2008 , Yeary07/Year08 takes value of 1 respectively, and 0 otherwise
Return	annual return ratio	Cumulative rate of return on stocks from May this year to April the following year
EPS	earnings per share	Net profit/total shares
Price	closing price	Adjusted closing price of individual stocks at the end of April (taking into account dividends)
Beta	systematic risk coefficient β	β value of last 24 months

This paper takes on the senior managements' background in government as the standards determining if the corporations have political connections. Specific criteria are as follows: If the chairman of the board or the CEO in a company is now or had been employed by government, this company has political connection. In addition, if the chairman of the board or the CEO in a company is now or had been one of the NPC or the CPPCC members, this company also has political connection. It is because the NPC and the CPPCC while not a government department, but play a pivotal role in national politics.

4   Empirical Results and Analysis

4.1   Results of Multiple Linear Regression

Table 2 shows the regression results about the level of earnings management by using annually cross-section data and panel data respectively. PolC, the explanatory variable, is negatively correlated with the level of earnings management during 2006-2008 in the three regression equations. Regression results indicate that the level of earnings management in the private enterprise with political connections is lower than in those without political connections.

Table 2. Regression Results based on the Model of Accruals Quality

Variables	Expect Sign	2006	2007	2008	2006-2008
intercept		0.160**	0.069	0.125**	0.079**
		(2.507)	(1.051)	(2.050)	(2.259)
PolC	-	-0.011	-0.019**	-0.016**	-0.015***
		(-1.410)	(-2.203)	(-2.012)	(-3.203)
First	+	0.053*	0.027	-0.205*	0.041**
		(1.733)	(0.840)	(-1.797)	(2.374)
$First^2$	+	0.001*	0.000	0.327**	0.000**
		(1.725)	(0.841)	(2.226)	(2.374)
Size	-	-0.016***	-0.007	-0.009*	-0.010***
		(-3.014)	(-1.381)	(-1.926)	(-3.377)
Lev	+	0.049**	0.052**	0.030	0.042***
		(2.086)	(2.108)	(1.226)	(2.968)
Cycle	+	0.012***	0.016***	0.018***	0.015***
		(2.872)	(3.728)	(4.782)	(6.717)
Year					control
F value		4.520***	4.776***	6.767***	12.841***
Adjusted R^2		0.054	0.053	0.069	0.071

Note: ***,**,* represent the statistical significance at the level of respectively 1%, 5%, 10%.

Table 3 shows the regression results about earnings response coefficients by using annually cross-section data and panel data respectively. Results show that the coefficients of earnings per share multiplied by PolC are significantly positive. That is, earnings information content in the private enterprise with political connections is higher than in those without political connections.

Table 3. Regression Results based on earnings response coefficients

Variables	Expect sign	2006	2007	2008	2006-2008
intercept		-0.186	-0.542	0.233*	-0.123
		(-0.336)	(-0.700)	(1.757)	(-0.387)
EPS/Price	+	0.918*	4.646**	0.718	1.150**
		(1.659)	(2.059)	(1.614)	(2.195)
(EPS/Price)*PolC	+	1.342*	5.786*	1.103*	1.762**
		(1.735)	(1.793)	(1.808)	(2.394)
Beta	-	1.397***	1.513***	-0.414***	1.130***
		(11.365)	(7.572)	(-8.143)	(12.931)
Size	-	0.007	0.017	-0.029***	0.015
		(0.128)	(0.255)	(-2.669)	(0.509)
Lev	-	0.211	0.622*	-0.005	0.226
		(0.922)	(1.874)	(-0.094)	(1.623)
Year					control
F value		33.235***	15.783***	19.651***	308.509***
Adjusted R^2		0.302	0.167	0.204	0.660

Note: ***,**,* represent the statistical significance at the level of respectively 1%, 5%, 10%.

4.2 Robustness Check

To verify the robustness of the model, we also conducted the following additional tests. We divided the samples into two sub-samples according to the value of DA. When the value of DA is positive we defined it as DA+ group, otherwise as DA- group. DA+ group that has 638 samples stands for "upward" earnings management, and DA- group that has 599 samples stands for "downward" earnings management. Empirical results indicate that the inhibition of political connections on the earnings management is mainly reflected in the inhibition of "downward" earnings management, and its role in the "upward" earnings management is not that significant. Because the main reasons of managing earnings upward are to prevent Special Treatment (ST), or to meet mandatory requirements of SEO. The private listed companies with political connections also have to meet these mandatory requirements, so the role of political connections is smaller in DA+ group. On the contrary, the private listed companies are to reap their own benefits to manipulate the earnings, and the role of political connections is better in DA- group.

5 Conclusion

For a private enterprise, political connections are implicit resources which can protect it as an informal mechanism in the imperfect market system. Meanwhile, they are also some kind of unofficial signs, and make people to link a private enterprise to government indirectly. Therefore, political connections may play "resources" and "signs" of these two roles at same time. The "resources" role of political connections reduces the motives of private enterprises to hidden earnings information purposely, while the "signs" role of political connections can promote private enterprise to disclose higher quality earnings information. We used discretion accruals and earnings response coefficient to measure earnings quality, and tested above hypothesis. Further tests showed that the role of the political connections to restrain earnings management is mainly played in the "downward" earnings management.

Acknowledgments. This paper is supported by the Humanities and Social Science Young Researchers Fund of the Ministry of Education of PRC (NO. 10YJCZH131), Social Science Fund of Hebei Province (NO. HB09BYJ028), Jiangsu Education Planned Projects of Philosophy and Social Science (NO. 09SJD790031) and NUST Research Funding (NO. 2010ZYTS038).

References

1. Chen, K.C.W., Yuan, H.: Earnings Management and Capital Resource Allocation: Evidence from China's Accounting-Based Regulation of Rights Issues. The Accounting Review 79(3), 645–665 (2004)
2. Dinc, I.S.: Politicians and Banks, Political Influences on Government-owned Banks in Emerging Markets. Journal of Financial Economics 77, 453–479 (2005)
3. Fan, J.P.H., Wong, T.J.: Politically Connected CEOs, Corporate Governance, and Post-IPO Performance of China's Newly Partially Privatized Firms. Journal of Financial Economic 84, 330–357 (2007)
4. Han, J.C., Wang, S.: Political costs and earnings management of oil companies during the 1990 Persian Gulf Crisis. The Accounting Review 73(1), 103–118 (1998)
5. Healy, P.M., Wahlen, J.M.: A Review of the Earnings Management Literature and its Implications for Standards Setting. Accounting Horizons 13, 365–383 (1999)
6. Johnson, S., Kaufmann, D., McMillan, J., Woodruff, C.: Why do Firms Hide? Bribes and Unofficial Activity after Communism. Journal of Public Economics 76, 495–520 (2000)
7. Johnson, S., Mitton, T.: Cronyism and Capital Controls: Evidence from Malaysia. Journal of Financial Economics 67, 351–382 (2003)
8. Jones, J.J.: Earnings Management during Import Relief Investigations. Journal of Accounting Research 29(2), 193–228 (1991)
9. Key, Galligan, K.: Political Cost Incentives for Earnings Management in the Cable Television Industry. Journal of Accounting and Economics 23(3), 309–337 (1997)
10. Leuz, C., Oberholzer-Gee, F.: Political Relationships, Global Financing, and Corporate Transparency: Evidence from Indonesia. Journal of Financial Economics 81, 411–439 (2006)
11. Monem, R.M.: Earnings Management in Response to the Introduction of the Australian Gold Tax. Contemporary Accounting Research 20(4), 747–774 (2003)
12. Xiaoyue, C., Xing, X., Xiaoyan, G.: Rights of Rights Issues and Profit Manipulation. Economic Research Journal 1, 30–36 (2000) (in Chinese)

The Empirical Analysis of Economic Sustainable Development in Henan Province[*]

Ming-can Dang

Department of Economic and Trade,
Henan Institute of Engineering, P.R.China, 451191
13007530146@163.com

Abstract. Economic sustainable development is an inherent requirement of the regional economic development. The purpose of this article is to correctly understand the capacity of sustainable economic development in Henan Province, then for promoting better sustainable development in the future. Instead of using subjective evaluation index system, this paper used the method of Social & Ecological Accounting Matrix, the framework based on social accounting matrix, additional resources accounts, environmental accounts and other elements. Through comparative analyses of some relevant economic data of Henan Province from 2001 to 2009, including growth rate of GDP, high energy consumption and high pollution industry, energy production and energy consumption, the results shows the capacity of economic sustainable development in Henan Province gradually increases capacity in recent years, but still is in the weakness of the range.

Keywords: Social & Ecological Accounting Matrix, Economic sustainable development, Sustainability analysis.

1 Introduction

Since 2003, Henan Province has achieved sustained and rapid economic development. GDP growth rate is at more than 10% annually, exceeding the national average over the same period. GDP steady fifth in the country and exceeded 2 trillion Yuan more in 2010. However, with careful study of economic growth in Henan Province in recent years, it is not difficult to find that there are still some problems in the economic operation. Such as unit GDP energy consumption is still above the national average, the percentage of the industrial structure is below the national average. Under the impact of financial crisis in the United States, the economic impact in Henan Province is expressed as "more later, more slowly and more deeper ". Major economic indicators fell sharply in the end of 2008 and early 2009.The province's GDP growth rate fell sharply by 7.8% in the fourth quarter of 2008, lower than the national average at 3.3

---

[*] This paper is supported by Bid Project for Government Decision of Henan Province in 2009, China(B395) and by Henan Planning Program of Philosophy and Social Sciences, China (2010FJJ031).

percentage points. The province's GDP growth rate further fell to 6.6% in the first quarter of 2009, compared with 2008 down 5.5 percentage points. It is the key time for the country to readjust the economic structure, transform the mode of economic development in the next five years. It is also the key time for Henan Province to achieve the "two high and one low" development goals, and maintain the critical five-year leap-forward development. Therefore, what is the current momentum of economic development in Henan Province? What is the sustainability of economic development in Henan Province? This article is based on these issues, and use Social & Ecological Accounting Matrix (SEAM) to estimate the sustainability of economic development in Henan Province, in order to understand the situation and promote better sustainable development in the future.

2   Overview of the Theory of Economic Sustainable Development

Economic sustainable development is widely accepted proposed and produced with the concept of sustainable development. Sustainable development includes ecological sustainability, economic sustainability and social sustainability. Economic sustainable development is the core of the whole system. Economic sustainable development provides material conditions for ecological and social sustainable development. Only to do economic sustainability could form the sustainable development of the whole system. In theory, economic sustainable development is only one aspect of sustainable development; they are a part and whole. However, when the economic sustainable development is into an independent research issues at the right time, economic sustainable development of the research is not equivalent to the content of the economic sustainable development of sustainable development. Although there are many scholars say about the specific definition of economic sustainable development in the time, they all include two basic points: First, in the contemporary process of economic development must maintain the quality and quantity of natural resources, or that the contemporary Economic development should not be with the cost of resources waste and environmental pollution; the second is to meet the contemporary needs of economic development must take into account the needs of future generations of economic development, so that present and future generations have the same resource base, development opportunities and benefits of output . In recent years, our government initiated intensive economic growth mode, scientific development concept and building a harmonious society are in line with the concept of economic sustainable development.

There are many aspects on research and application of economic sustainable development at home and abroad, a crucial issue of which is how to evaluate the level of economic sustainable development of regional. Currently most scholars with different needs and goals, and the application of different focus areas, have built a lot of kinds of index system to assess the extent of the sustainable development of regional economy, but there is no scientific and feasible evaluation system widely accepted by everyone. Therefore, this article will use some ways of the Social & Ecological

Accounting Matrix (SEAM) to assess the extent of economic sustainable development in Henan Province.

Social & Ecological Accounting Matrix is the theoretical framework of including resources accounts, environmental accounts and other elements, which is based on input-output analysis, social accounting matrix, etc. In general, the criteria of economic sustainability theory is: when economic growth associated with the improvement of ecological environment, economic development has strong sustainability; when the environment has been consumed, but the rate of economic growth exceeds the consumption rate of ecological, economic development has weak sustainability; when economic growth can not compensate for the damage to ecosystems and even lead to economic recession, economic development has non-sustainability.

3   The Evaluation of Economic Sustained Development in Henan Province

For the use of SEAM to evaluate the level of economic sustained development in Henan Province, we use GDP growth rate as economic growth. With a direct loss of ecological assets assessment not to be expressed, considering the availability of data, we are using high energy consumption and high pollution industry growth rate, and the rate of energy production and consumption to measure the change rate of ecological consumption.

3.1   Comparative Analyses among GDP Growth Rate, High Energy Consumption Growth Rate and High Pollution Industry Growth Rate

High energy consumption and high pollution industry occupies a large proportion in the industrial structure in Henan Province. Here we use cement, crude steel and pig iron to represent high energy consumption and high pollution industry.

Table 1. The table of GDP growth rate, cement steel growth rate, Cement growth rate and Pig iron growth rate[1] (units:%)

date	GDP growth rate	Crude steel growth rate	Cement growth rate	Pig iron growth rate
2001	9.00	31.16	12.83	6.14
2002	9.50	26.60	6.67	11.92
2003	13.70	26.71	5.40	8.99
2004	10.70	14.44	14.27	20.06
2005	14.20	25.84	15.08	22.99
2006	14.40	41.92	19.37	50.13
2007	14.60	30.09	26.07	31.81
2008	12.10	-3.39	9.41	-10.88
2009	10.50	6.45	14.51	13.32

[1] The data are from Henan Statistical Yearbook 2010.

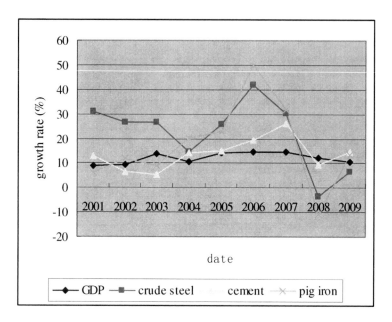

Fig. 1. The figure of GDP growth rate, cement steel growth rate, Cement growth rate and Pig iron growth rate

From the above chart it is not difficult to see that GDP growth remained at high running smoothly since Henan Province entered the new century, and the crude steel, pig iron is relatively sharp fluctuations in growth rates, especially during the financial crisis, the growth rate of the cement is relatively stable. To comparisons between growth rates, except in 2008, the three high energy consumption and high pollution industry growth rate is essentially higher than the growth rate of GDP, and it reached a local peak value in 2006. In general, when the growth rate of eco-consuming industries is severely higher than the GDP growth rate, it often appears excessive low-end products, environmental pollution and resource waste situation, and is not conducive to economic sustained development.

3.2 Comparative Analyses between GDP Growth Rate and Rate of Energy Production and Consumption

Consideration of data availability, we use the energy supply elasticity, demand elasticity and power supply elasticity, demand elasticity for energy production and consumption rates when compared. Among them, we use the sum of coal production, oil production, gas production, water and power production as the energy production.

Table 2. The table of the energy supply, demand elasticity and power supply, demand elasticity[2]

date	energy supply elasticity	Energy demand elasticity	power supply elasticity	power demand elasticity
2001	1.09	0.63	1.42	1.41
2002	1.57	0.87	1.52	1.55
2003	2.60	1.59	1.19	1.28
2004	1.58	1.71	1.77	1.63
2005	0.78	0.84	0.80	0.53
2006	0.23	0.76	0.88	0.73
2007	-0.18	0.68	1.36	1.47
2008	0.50	0.44	0.18	0.99
2009	0.90	0.38	0.56	0.53

The GDP elasticity shows that when each GDP increase at 1 percentage point, energy output and the percentage change in consumption. When elasticity is greater than 0, the change in the energy production or consumption is in the same direction with the change in GDP. That is, when GDP increases, the energy production or consumption also increased. When elasticity is less than 0, the change in the energy production or consumption is in the reverse direction with the change in GDP. That is, as GDP increases, the energy production or consumption reduced.

From the above data it is not difficult to find until 2004, the energy output and the demand elasticity, the electricity supply and the demand elasticity in Henan Province are greater than 1, but basically the supply elasticity of energy greater than the demand elasticity (supply elasticity and demand elasticity of power varying between), which indicates that the growth rate of province's energy supply and consumption of electricity is greater than the growth rate of GDP, and energy supply more than demand. Therefore, the province's GDP is extensive growth, and energy use efficiency is low. After 2004, the province's energy, power output and demand elasticity is less than 1 (except for electricity in 2007), the demand elasticity of energy is greater than supply elasticity , but after 2008 less than the supply elasticity. Elasticity of electricity supply and electricity demand has still no relationship between the rules. As the growth rate of the province's energy supply and consumption of electricity is less than the growth rate of GDP, we can conclude that the quality of our province's economic growth is increasing.

According to the above analysis, taking into account the trajectory changes in the rate of energy consumption and changes in production rate of high energy consumption and high pollution industry, we believe that the economic sustainable development in Henan Province is gradually increased, and the capacity of economic sustainable development is still in the range of a relatively weak capacity.

4   Conclusions

According to our analysis results with the use of SEAM, we can conclude although the sustainable economic development in Henan Province in recent years gradually

---

[2] The data are from Henan Statistical Yearbook 2010.

increased capacity, the ability of economic sustainable development is still in the range of weak capacity at present. Therefore, we should change the economic development mode as soon as possible, eliminate the constraints of economic sustainable development in Henan province as soon as possible, continue to enhance the capacity of economic sustainable development, so that the economic development in Henan province is to be a new level.

References

1. Yang, J.: The Theory of The Economic Sustainable Development. China Environmental Press, Beijing (2002)
2. Na, S-c.: Economic Sustainable Development Assessment and Strategic Studies. D. Hebei University of Technology (2008)
3. Hou, X-s.: Henan Regional Economy and Sustainable Development. D. Zhengzhou University (2007)
4. He, J.: Henan Sustainable Development and with Five Other Central Comparative Province. Henan Social Sciences 5, 137–139 (2006)
5. Henan Academy of Social Sciences: The Counter Measures and Thinking of Promoting Economic growth Mode Transformation in Henan. Learning Forum 2, 57–60 (2007)
6. Henan Bureau of Statistics: Henan Statistical Yearbook 2010. China Statistics Press, Beijing (2010)

Current Situation, Problems and Reflections on Sustainable Development and Utilization of Land Resources in China

Chang-xin Zhang[1,2], Wei-dong Liu[1], and Ya-li Luo[2]

[1] ZheJiang University, College of Public Administration,
310029 Hang zhou, China
[2] Huai-yin Institute of Technology, College of Civil Engineering and Architecture,
223001 Huai-an city China
Zcx8502@sohu.com

Abstract. China feeds the 21% of the world's population, while China's land resources account for 6.4% of the worlds. The contradiction between man and land is the basic national conditions that China has to face. Comparing with other countries, China is one of the countries with the sharpest man-land-contradiction. Although having made remarkable achievements for years, China has outstanding problems on the development and utilization of land resources, such as rapid decrease in arable land, the low levels of construction land intensive use, lack of ecological land, grim situation of land degradation, lack of arable land reserve resources etc., which seriously impact the sustainable use of land resources. To solve these problems, this paper proposes some countermeasures, such as perfecting a more scientific mechanism supporting the land resources, building a mechanism for evaluation and restriction on the intensive use of urban construction land, a coordination mechanism on maintaining the ecological balance of land and improving the evaluation mechanism of land-use efficiency.

Keywords: China, land resources, development and utilization, current situation.

1 Introduction

The contradiction between man and land is the most prominent social problem. Over the past 30 years of the implementation of reform and opening-up policy, China has fed the 21% of the world's population with only 6.4% of the world's land resources and achieved rapid economic and social development .It has made remarkable achievements. But with China's increasing population and the rapid advance of industrialization and urbanization, the contradiction between man and land will become increasingly serious, and even threaten China's food security. It is expected that knowing the development and utilization of land resources of the Current Situation

M. Zhou (Ed.): ISAEBD 2011, Part IV, CCIS 211, pp. 99–107, 2011.

and development trend in China, analysis of the problems to the future sustainable development and utilization of land resources in China will benefit the theoretical research and practical exploration of it.

2 International Comparison of the Current Contradiction between Man and Land of China

At present, China ranks third in the world land area, fourth in the world arable land, second in the world grassland, eighth in the forest, but the per capita land area, arable land, forest land and grassland, are respectively, only 35%, 43%, 25% and 38% of the world average level. . Compared with the U.S which equivalent land area with china., per capita land area, cultivated area, forest area and grass area are only 24%,16%, 15% and 26%of the United States. And it is further less than that of Russia. Compared with India which has large population, the per capita amount of land, forest and grassland in China is more, but arable land is only 64% of that in India. In Japan, population living density is particularly high and the per capita land area, arable land and grassland in China are more than it, but the forest is only about 77% of that in Japan (Table 1). This shows that China suffers from the world's sharpest man-land-contradiction, so the scientific and rational use of land resources in China is extremely important.

Table 1. China's land resources in comparison with the world and some other countries (2001-2005)

	type	World	China	U.S	Russia	India
	Population (10 thousand)	651227.6	131225.3	30274.1	14317	113061.8
land resources	area（10 thousand hm^2）	1338700	95970	93640	170750	32880
	per capita (hm^2)	2.06	0.73	3.09	11.93	0.29
cultivated land	area (10 thousand hm^2)	139765.6	12177.6	17601.8	12437.4	16055.5
	percentage of China's total land area (%)	10.44	12.69	18.80	7.28	48.83
	per capita (hm^2)	0.21	0.09	0.58	0.87	0.14
forest	area (10 thousand hm^2)	395202.5	19729	30308.9	80879	6770.1
	percentage of China's total land area (%)	30.3	21.2	33.1	47.9	22.8
	per capita (hm^2)	0.599	0.149	1.001	5.647	0.059
grassland	area (10hm^2)	344207.8	26214.4	23400	9092.4	1104
	percentage of China's total land area (%)	25.71	27.32	24.99	5.32	3.36
	per capita (hm^2)	0.53	0.20	0.77	0.64	0.01

Data source: UN, FAO, China Land and Resources Bulletin.

3 The Current Pattern and Achievements of China's Land Resources Development and Utilization

According to the 2008 Bulletin of China Land and Resources, the basic pattern of China's land resources development and utilization is: 1826 million mu of cultivated land, 177 million mu of orchard, 3597 million mu of forest land, 3927 million mu of grassland, the other 383 million mu of agricultural land, 404 million mu of residential and independent industrial land, 37 million mu of transport, 55 million mu of water conservancy facilities, and 4049 million mu the remaining unused land.

China has accomplished remarkable achievements in the Development and utilization of land resources. China has not only fed the 21% of the world's population with only 6.4% of the world's land resources, but also achieved sustained and rapid economic growth in three decades. Per capita GDP has exceeded 4,000 U.S. dollars and various social undertakings have also made considerable progress. According to the China Bureau of Statistics China's cereal output in 2007 was 456 324 000t (including rice 186 034 000t, wheat 109 298 000t, corn 152 300 000t), meat production was 68 657 000t, sugarcane was 712 280 000t and milk was 36 334 000t. Since 2000, China's total production of grain, meat, cotton, peanut, rapeseed, fruit and other agricultural production has been highest in the world.

4 Analysis of the Main Problems on China's Land Resources Development and Utilization

4.1 Rapid Development of Industrialization, Urbanization and Shape Reduction of Arable Land

Since the implementation of the reform and opening-up policy more than 30 years ago, industrialization and urbanization have developed rapidly. The process of industrial development shows that it took 25 years for China entering the middle stage of industrialization, going into the initial stage of industrialization in 1978, and in 2003 to mid industrialization. In 2005, China's industrialization level composite index reached 50. That is, in the Tenth Five-Year Period, China's industrialization was in the high growth phase, average annual growth rate of the level of industrialization composite index close to 5.Developing under this rate, by 2015 ~ 2018, After 10 to 13 years of development, Composite Index level of industrialization in China will reach 100 which shows that China will generally realize industrialization [1]. The process of urbanization shows that the level of urbanization in China in 1950 was 11.80% ,and in 1978 it rose slowly to 19.36%.For nearly three decades, it had increased by only less than 8 percent, but Since the implementation of the reform and opening-up policy ,the process of urbanization had speeded up. In 2009, the urbanization level was close to 46%,It is expected that it will reach 54.97 percent in 2020, 73.23% in 2050, close to the level of urbanization in developed countries.

China's rapid development of industrialization and urbanization needs a large number of non-agricultural construction lands. From 1997 to 2005, China's new industrial and mining land construction sites in the proportion accounted for 40% or even up to 60% in some areas, an excessive growth of industrial land. In 2009, the construction land approved by the government was 576,000 hectares, an increase of 44.6%[2]. About 60% of China's non-agricultural construction land increased from cultivated land, of which more than 70% located in the high grain-producing areas such as northeast, north, coastal areas and so on. This has a serious threat to China's food safety[3]. From 2001 to 2008, the cultivated land in China fell from 19.14 million mu to 18.26 million mu must almost equal to China's 18 million mu of arable land red line (Figure1). In the future, processes of industrialization and urbanization will put bigger and bigger pressure on cultivated land protection in China.

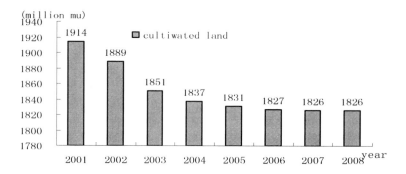

Fig. 1. 2001-2008 changes in cultivated area in China(Data source: 2008 China Land and Resources Bulletin)

4.2 The Expansion of Construction Land to the Scale-Based, Low Levels of Intensive Land Use

China's urban construction land use rate is not high. From 1990 to 2004, China's urban construction land expanded from 13,000 square kilometers to nearly 34,000 square kilometers. The scale elasticity of urban land (urban land use growth / urban population growth rate) increased from 2.13 to 2.28 in 1986-1991.This has been much higher than 1.12, the reasonable level. Compared to the construction land per capita, the largest cities are 115.6 m2, large cities are 99.1 m^2, big cities are 120.5 m^2 , medium-sized cities are 129.1 m^2, a small city is 164.1 m^2, the average level is 124.9 m2, far higher than the per capita 82.4 m^2 in developed countries and 83.3 m^2 in developing countries[4]. In particular, the level of using urban construction land in small and medium cities is significantly lower.

China's rural land for construction waste is a prominent problem. In the rural areas, particularly in the South, residential areas mostly distributes in hash-style, small scale, ranking points, and in close proximity. Intensive land is inhabited by the low level. In 2004, National Village construction land is 2.48 million mu. If it is calculated according to the agricultural population by the year, the per capita village land is 218 square meters. It is higher than the highest national scale (150 sq m / person) 45.3%. However, in New York, the per capita area including the suburbs is only 112.5 square meters. According to the survey in 1999, Chinese urban use land is hm2, and rural residential land is 16.5 million hm^2. Rural residential land is 5.5 times than that of urban construction land; if based on the per capita, rural land is 2.5 times than that of urban construction land. From 1997 to 2005, 9633 million population declined in rural China, and rural residential land has increased by nearly 117,500 hm^2 (170 acres). Thus, there are some problems in managing construction land in rural China.

China's "threshold "of industrial land is too low. People are affected by the development concept "no work, not rich". These all lead to the large proportion of industrial land, excessive growth, low efficient land use and productivity. In foreign countries, the city's industrial land is generally not more than 15% of urban area. While the proportion of industrial land in Chinese cities is on average more than 20% of industrial land and for the project volume was only 0.3-0.6.

4.3 Lack of the Total Amount of Ecological Land and Strict Protection

4.3.1 The Forest Area Has Gone Up, But the Overall Quality Is Not High
According to China's Seventh National Forest Resource Inventory Report, total forest area is 195 452 200 hm2. Forest cover is 20.36%. From the forest inventory data which has launched seven times by China, we can see steady rises of overall forest area and the forest coverage rate from 12.7% to 20.36% .At present, an increase is of 7.66 percentage points. It is a good development trend (Table 2).

Table 2. Outlook of the 7th Forest resource investigation

previous investigation	investigation time	area of woods (ten thousand hm2)	standing forest reserve volumn (100 million m3)	Forest reserve volumn (100 million m3)	rate of forest coverage (%)
First inventory	1973~1976	12186.00	95.32	86.56	12.70
Second inventory	1977~1981	11527.74	102.61	90.28	12.00
Third inventory	1984~1988	12465.28	105.72	91.41	12.98
Forth inventory	1989~1993	13370.35	117.85	101.37	13.92
Fifith inventory	1994~1998	15894.09	124.88	112.67	16.55
Sixth inventory	1999~2003	17490.92	136.18	124.56	18.21
Seventh inventory	2004~2008	19545.22	149.13	137.21	20.36

Data sources: China's Report on Previous Forestry Investigation.

However, protection and development of forest resources still face some prominent problems: First is shortage of total forest resource, china's forest coverage just covers 2/3 of the global average, ranking 139th in the world, personal forest coverage is 0.145 hm2 , which is far from 1/4 of the global coverage per capita; personal forest reserve volume is 10.15 m3 , and only account for 1/7 of global average .Second is low quality ,the ecological function index of arbor forests is 0.54 and those of good quality merely occupy 11.31%, thus we haven't reserve the state of fragile ecology. Third, afforestation will be more difficult. China's appropriate forests of good quality now available only take up 13%, while those of bad quality make up 52%; 60% of national forests was laid in Mongolia and northwest district, there greatly affected by natural environment.

4.3.2 Shrinkage of Grassland and Sustainability of Degradation

With the influence of multiple factors as latitudinal zonality, longitudinal zonality and zonality on the Qinghai-Tibet Plateau. China's natural grasslands were typed into three zones: grassland in northern temperate region, grassland on the Qinghai-Tibet Plateau, and secondary grassland in the south and east. But, near half natural grasslands are not suitable for grazing or exploitation, as most grassland were situated in arid and semiarid regions in the north with poor hydrothermal condition and shortage of water. According to the data of survey of land-using change in 1996, the pasture area was 266.06 million hm^2. .Comparing with that number, pasture area of 2005, has decreased by 3.921 million hm^2 .Though total area of grassland is quite large, per capita is just 3 mu, far away from 8 mu which is the global average.

Degradation of natural grassland in China is quite prominent. The causes leading to such degradation are overgrazing, deforestation, grassland salinization and others. In 2008, in china's important natural grassland, livestock overloading rate still reached 32%. Because of the overuse of grassland and the popular phenomena of degradation, from 1996~2005, grassland of Mongolia has decreased by 2405.3 thousand hm^2.

4.3.3 Limited Wetland Resources Need Frothed Protection

Wetland is called "natural storage of water" and "kidneys of the earth" for its powerful eco-service function and multiple benefits. According to china's first survey of wetland resource in1995~2001, available national wetland is 5.94.17mill hm^2 within the survey, among it 36.2005million hm^2 is the area of natural wetland(costal wetland area is5.9417million hm^2 , lake wetland area is 8.3515million hm^2, swamp wetland area is 13.7003million hm^2), which only takes up 3.77% of the national territory.

China's natural wetlands are shrinking. Among all the wetlands sources, the shrinkage of rivers, reed lands and tidal flats is a very serious problem. In the process of the shrinkage of wetlands, the most important reason is the transformation from wetlands to cultivated land, which has the proportion more than 50 percent. And the later is the use by uncultivated construction with its proportion 25.7 percent.

4.4 The Degradation of Land Is Complex and Varied

4.4.1 The Losing of Soil and Water Erodes a Large Amount of Lands

In China, there is serious soil erosion in almost all of the major drainage basin. In early 2002,survey results by remote sensing of soil erosion unveiled by China's ministry of water resources show that: the area of soil erosion is $3.56 \times 106 km^2$, which is 37.1 % percent of the total land areas of the country, the water-eroded area is $1.65 \times 106 km^2$ and the area of wind erosion is $1.91 \times 106 km^2$ .Every year Soil loss makes the loss of land 5 billion tons which eliminating the world, and take away lots of nitrogen, phosphate and potassium nutrition elements, which led to the land acidification phenomenon is so serious. In china, the "rocky desertification" is highlight due to the continuous erosion of soil resources which has deteriorated not only agricultural production conditions but ecological environment, and made the masses loss of the basic living condition, thus some places have to consider "ecological migrants", linen mountainous area of Guizhou province is a typical example. Rocky desertification is now the most serious problem of economic development and the recovery and reconstruction of ecology in China's western region, and human interference and sabotage are the main reason and direct foreign power [5].

4.4.2 Expansion of Land Desertification Has Not Been Curbed Effectively

In 2002, the area which influenced by desertification is about $3.33 \times 106 km^2$ which is one third of the total land areas of the country, and it is still expanding at rate of $2300 km^2$ per year. The rapidly expanding of land desertification causes not only land quality degradation and reduction of the available land resources; but also makes a serious threat of urban construction, and brings a series of economic and social problems. Since 1990, the production of farmland influenced by desertification has universally fallen 70% to 80%, the loss of nutrition in all kinds of desertification lands is 1.339 billion tons, the area of the degenerative grassland is 1.05 million km^2, and the degenerative cultivated land is 77 thousand km^2.

4.4.3 Land Pollution Diversification, Seriously Affecting the Quality of Land

China's land pollution problem is mainly manifested in the four aspects: The first is industrial "the three wastes" discharge of water pollution and quotation from a contaminated water and sewage pollution of farmland irrigation caused for land pollution. The second is the use of fertilizer, pesticides for agriculture in a large amount leading to land pollution. The usage of chemical fertilizer in unit of the crop acreage is more than triple of the world average usage, the usage of pesticides in unit of the crop acreage is over twice of the United States, and the application rates of these chemical fertilizer and pesticides increase unlimitedly every year. The third is acid rain pollution. In the 1980s, China's acid rain area is about $1.7 *106 km^2$. In 1990s, the number has expanded to $2.7*106 km^2$, and the domain has expanded from some part of southwest to the whole southwest, central China, south China and north China, and become the most seriously polluted region by acid rain that only to Europe and North America in the world. The fourth is salinization disasters. China's land of agriculture, forestry and livestock polluted by is 36.3 million hm2, and the farmland is 9.21 million hm^2, the woodlands is 1.42million hm^2, and the grassland is 23.2 million hm^2.

4.5 There Is No Adequate Resource for Farmland, and It Is difficult to Exploit

According to the possible supply of reserve land resources, they can be divided into three major categories: reserve land resources, land resources to be reclaimed and reserve land resources to be finished. According to the survey on change of land utilization conducted by former State Land Administration in 1996 ,the current reserve land resources for development, about 9.3 million hectares of grassland, marsh, saline land in unexplored land ,the reed land and beaches in water land, mainly locating in the northwest, the arid Tibetan Plateau area, semi-arid region and the North East and other hilly areas, as well as in the steep mountains of thin soil, the drought West in short of water or low humidity waterlogged depressions, so it is very difficult to exploit land resources.

5 Some Ideas on Sustainable Development and Utilization of Land Resources in China

5.1 Establishments of a More Sound and Scientific Support Mechanism for Land Resources

Protection of arable land is China's basic national policy. By the year 2033 China's population is expected to achieve zero population growth, reaching 1.5 billion [6]. The conflicts between the Chinese people and food will become more and more acute. However, the farmland protection is a "systematic project". Although the implementation of China's macro-control policy on maintaining balance of total arable land is of great strategic significance, it is irreversible that the differences in comparative advantage between cultivated land for construction and farmland as well as the rapid development of economy and society leading to decline in farmland, the balance in the amount of cultivated land is often difficult to achieve [7]. To solve the rooted clauses of land protection, we should establish a structural and long-term response mechanism that economic and social development is in harmony with the protection of farmland, build a fair and equal relationship of responsibilities, rights and interests between government, community and individual in the aspect of arable land protection, connect governments' will and farmers passion to protect farmland from top to bottom so as to improve the effectiveness of land protection.

5.2 Construction of the a Constraint, Utilized and Evaluated Mechanism for Urban and Rural Construction Land

Because of the lack of a strict and constraint mechanism for land construction, a considerable number of towns vigorously construct development zones, industrial parks, education areas, ecological parks, residential areas, and even unrealistically rebuild roads, squares. Priority should be given to build a Intensive and restraint mechanism on the construction of urban and rural land, combing it with the economic, social and ecological benefits .In urban areas, we should strictly control the scale and scope of industrial land, promote the industry to focus on the park, take the road of gathering production; meanwhile, we should control the land for housing construction, encourage the development, purchase of small family houses through policy. We also should promote a free and competitive market construction in urban and rural construction land, and it will help to improve the level of non-agricultural construction land use, if the Chinese urban and rural construction land market transmits from monopoly to competition [8-9].

5.3 Construction of a Regional Mechanism to Maintain Ecological Balance for Land Protection

Ecological balance is the basic condition for human existence and development. Land ecosystem is the basis and the core of terrestrial ecosystems. In face of the diversity and the severity of land degradation in China, we must strengthen the protection of the natural environment, and put maintaining a balance of land ecosystems at the first place. China enjoys a vast land, complex natural environment and distinctive land resources; we must pay attention to the ratio and the speed of the different land utilization type in the development of land, implementing differentiated land use policy. More importantly, we must strengthen the links and coordination between regions to establish a legal, regional mechanism to maintain the ecological balance and coordination of land, achieving complementarities, benefits sharing, and coordinated development between regions.

5.4 Improvement of Mechanism for Land Use Efficiency Evaluation

Land is of versatility, the same is true with the land-use efficiency. For a long time, because of people's unawareness of land use efficiency, and their special attention to economic benefits rather than ecological and social benefits, arable land, grassland, forest land and other agricultural land and ecosystems now face serious threats. Therefore, we must improve the mechanism for land use efficiency evaluation, set up different types of income compensation systems for land use and realize the fairness of development and utilization of various lands so as to radically prevent people from destructing the agricultural land.

References

1. Industrialization, information technology, urbanization, marketization and internationalization of China,
   http://www.sznews.com/zhuanti/content/2007-11/28/
   content_1680807.htm
2. The Ministry of Land and Resources. China Land and Resources Bulletin (2009)
3. Zhang, K.-f., Li, X.-w., Zhang, D.-x.: Spatial-Temporal Dynamic Change of Land Resource Degradation in China. Environment Science 27(6), 1244–1250 (2006)
4. China's urban construction land, http://www.chinagate.com.cn
5. Wang, D.-l., Zhu, S.-q., Huang, B.-l.: Discussion on the Conception and Connotation of Rocky Desertification. Journal of Nanjing Forestry University(Natural Sciences Edition) 28(6), 87–90 (2004)
6. Development Trend of China's population,
   http://www.chinapop.gov.cn/dfgz/200801/t2008-0122_46198.html
7. Long, C.Y., Qiang, F.z., Dai, E.-b.: Regional minimum cultivated land per capita area and cultivated land resources regulation. Geographical Journal 57(2), 127–134 (2002)
8. Kai, M., Tao, L.L., Yuhong, Y.: China's urban and rural land-use evolution law of market research. China's population, Resources and Environment 19(3), 75–81 (2009)
9. Qian, Z.-h., Kai, M.: China's urban and rural land-use market: monopoly, separation and integration. Management world (6), 38–44 (2007)

A View of Democratic Management in Colleges and Universities from the Perspective of Communication

Chengbo Hu and Xiaoou Liu

Shenyang Aerospace University
110136, Shenyang, China
huchengbo79@yahoo.com.cn

Abstract. People need to communicate with each other, so do organizations. University, or college, serves as an important social organization in the society. Communication, being an essential part of management, plays an important role in university management. Traditional management in colleges and universities conducts organizations and communications in forms of meeting, written media, telephone and others, which fail to form a good information feedback mechanism. By taking full advantage of the network, it is able to overcome negative effects in interpersonal communication and form a favorable upward communication mechanism, so as to establish a democratic and scientific management of colleges and universities.

Keywords: communication, colleges and universities, democratic, management.

1 Introduction

People need to communicate with each other, so do organizations. As a unit of the society, it is bound to contact and communicate with other people or organizations. The importance of communication is obvious. Some people even reckon that the primary cause of conflicts in countries, societies and races is communication. That is to say, the biggest failure of human lies in the fact that they cannot get help or understanding from others. Throughout all kinds of functions and specific activities of management, there are abundant communicative activities. Communication is primary means, method and tool which guarantee the implementation of management. Management and communication have so many close internal relations that there are lots of similarities and common things between them. Thus, communication, as an importance aspect of management, is included into management theory.

2 The Concept of Communication

Communication refers to the exchange of ideas or information, from which people get mutual understanding and trust as well as establishing good interpersonal relationship. Meanwhile, communication also serves as the foundation that guarantees coordination in common activities of people. Essential factors of communication include content,

M. Zhou (Ed.): ISAEBD 2011, Part IV, CCIS 211, pp. 108–113, 2011.
© Springer-Verlag Berlin Heidelberg 2011

method and motion. In terms of its influence, content takes the smallest proportion which is 7%; motion takes the biggest which is 55%; method lies in between that it takes 38%. Existence and development of all kinds of organizations are based on communications among members. Communication is needed to guarantee the coordination of motions as long as common activities are conducted by more than two people. Management aims at making communication regular and ordered so as to ensure that the operation of management system lies in the sound development that all departments coordinate and interact with each other.

As for communication, different people give different definitions from various perspectives. goldhaber, an American researcher of communication, defines communication from the pespective of organization in this way: "Organizational communication is the network formed from a variety of dependent relationships and the process of dealing with environmental uncertainty and exchanging information". However, from the perspective of human being, he reckons that "Communication refers to the process of exchanging ideas and information among people. In short, it refers to conveying information from one person to another". These definitions reflect the content and the essence of communication from different sides.

During the process of organizational management, communication is one of the important aspects. It is the premise and the foundation of a right decision, the tool for uniting ideas and actions, and the key to establish favorable interpersonal relationship among members, especially relationship between leaders and those who are led. In the meantime, communication also serves as the bridge that builds up relationship between organization and external environment. A famous remark of Konosuke Matsushita goes like this: Communication existed in, is existing in and will always exist in business management. The real job of a manager is to communicate. Management in colleges and universities should never be separated from communication at any time.

Functions of communication in management of colleges and universities contain information transfer, emotional exchange and control. University, being an important social organization, cannot do without communication in effective internal management. There are various kinds of communication methods in internal management of colleges and universities, which intersect with each other and become an indispensable aspect. Analyzing features of organizational communication in colleges and universities is to the benefit of giving full play to their organizing function.

3 Types and Obstacles of Communication Is Colleges and Universities

There are different classifications of communication in university management from different perspectives. As for communication of internal management in colleges and universities, it can be divided into three types according to flowing direction: downward communication, upward communication and horizontal communication. The downward communication refers to the one from top to bottom that superior informs subordinate of goals, tasks, principles and policies relating to work in colleges and universities; the upward communication refers to the one from bottom to top that lower level department reports to superior about situations, problems, suggestions and support request; the horizontal communication, namely lateral communication, refers to communications among departments of equal level. All these communications are generally called formal communication, which represents organization and should be discreet. The other kind is informal communication, which is realized by personal contact rather than organizational system.

In actural management, obstacles of communication are ubiquitous and always perplex managers, declining their efficiency of management. Obstacles of information communication prevent the transmission of message or misrepresent message. These obstacles might come from information senders or environmental factors. However, the continuity and the availability of the entire information communication chain would be destroyed, no matter where obstacles come from. According to actural situations of internal management in colleges and universities, it is not difficult to find that traditional communications of internal organizations in colleges and universities are realized mainly by written media (documents, reports, etc.), meeting, telephone, school newspaper and others. Yet there are many obstacles and insufficiencies in internal management of university where communications are realized by these media.

The downward communication is easy while the upward one is difficult; transmission of message to lower level is easy while feedback is difficult. In internal management of colleges and universities, there are three aspects of authority governing system: party committee, school administration, academic evaluation mechanism (academic authority). Normally, if the leadership is of high level and the democratic consciousness is strong, the internal management of the school is scientific and standard. Discourse powers of the three aspects are not in contradiction with each other. However, it is prone to dislocation of management function once the leadership is poor in quality, low in level and unscientific in management. The three would be in a tangle and it is likely to make the mistake of bureaucracy. As a result, everything will be decided by one man's say or unprofessionals become in charge of professionals. Thus, a sound information feedback system cannot be established, which is likely to cause deformation and degeneration of work information. Especially for some schools with numerous administrative levels and complicated departments, mistakes are more likely to made because of transmission of verbal message from one level to another, let alone the improvement of work efficiency (such as meeting, telephone and etc.).

The situation of low speed, time waste and low work efficiency of information dissemination would also cause formalism and officialism. Obstacles of communicating way are mainly embodied in low efficiency or ineffectiveness of communication caused by improper choice of communicating way. In addition, there are might be obstacles of communication like overload of language and information or interference of environmental "noise". By investigating its deep reason, it can be found that position difference caused by organization structure is the objective obstacle of communication. Particularly in strictly hierarchical organizations, only downward communication can be realized and upward communication is quite difficult.

Besides, communication of informal channel inside schools are also likely to bring negative effects to management. Take interpersonal communication for instance. It is likely to bring about information loss and distortion, and is also likely to be affected by interpersonal relationship. Because it is impossible to be supervised, many reports of situation are spreading embroidered stories and malicious gossip and becoming the transmission of slanderous talk. When leaders get information that are mixed with subjective opinions of all levels of spreaders, misunderstanding and bias, and even hostility among staff, departments and leaders will be easily aroused. Thus, it will affect the unity and form sectarianism and cliquish. In many schools, principal and secretary are in bad terms over a long period of time, the reason of which is interpersonal communication.

4 Management and Communication of Colleges and Universities

During the process of communication, there are such six steps for information transmission as conceptualization, information organizing (refining or processing), information sending, information receiving, thinking and response organizing (feedback). In this cyclic process, each part is essential. Listener would feel unintelligible and cannot get the point without information organizing, namely the process of refining and processing. And thus feedback cannot be given correctly. This sort of problem is the most common thing in our daily life that we call it information accumulation. If listener is not given enough time or opportunities for thinking, the effect of information transmission would also decrease largely. During the process of communication, the operating speed of brain is much faster than the speed of talking and information can not make the brain think, so listener would always be "absent-minded" or "thinking alone" and, definitely, the effect of communication is poor. This kind of situation is also common, which is usually called "self-communication". These two kinds of cases are quite common in our work and there is a variation to a certain extent. Therefore, solutions are needed to make some improvements. It can be seen that the major problem of communication among internal organizations of colleges and universities is how to enhance the communication efficiency and how to form a sound environment for upward communication.

Management of colleges and universities is a very complicated systematic engineering. Workers of university management are faced with a complicated "information environment". As for the so-called information environment, Goto Kazuhiko, a Japanese scholar, holds that information environment is the symbol part of social environment that controls behaviors of social members directly or indirectly. It is different from natural environment. In other words, what managerial staff in colleges and universities are faced with is a knowledge environment, a scientific and cultural environment and a talent environment composed by various kinds of professional research personnel. It is a complicated work to make judgement and conclusion in this complex environment. The more relax the information environment is, the more opinions faculty and staff in the school will get. And more abundant content will make it easier to judge what is right and what is wrong, as well as making it more likely to get close to the truth. As the saying goes, bth sides must present their opinions. The truth will become more convincing with more debates. This principle can be also illustrated by the theory of communicative action of Hamas, who holds that discourse consensus should meet the following conditions: on the premise of giving up consciously the use of rights and violence, each subject with language and behavior capacity should follow the three principles of authenticity, correctness and sincerity and participate in discussion and argument freely and equally so as to get close to the truth. One of the biggest advantage of doing this is that manager is able to make rules through discourse consensus. These rules are easy to be accepted by people. Therefore, a relax and democratic speech environment helps to form a sound community in a school.

5 The Establishment of Communication Mechanism and Its Functions

The degree if informatization increases with the development of human society. Communicative action is of vital importance in managerial behavior. In such a situation, communication is bound to draw more and more attentions of managers and management scientists.

Build up a sound communication mechanism so as to make faculty and staff express theirown opinions and suggestions actively and freely. This requires two conditions: one is to keep everyone away from oppression and pressure brought by certain bureaucratists who are relying on organization system; the other is to provide them with a window throught which they can get a quick understanding of school policies and managerial work as well as a platform where they can make quick expression and feedback of information. Thus, the flow of interpersonal communication of informal channel inside organization will be guided correctly. At present, the most effective way of solving the two problems is to take advantage of net communication in school management. Facts have shown that it has obvious superiority to use net communication in information transmission organization of colleges and universities.

By taking advantage of the network, information can be transmitted quickly and management efficiency can be improved largely. School uses website to search for information, uses electronic bulletin board to issue, check, discuss and exchange information and uses e-mail and file transfer protocol to interchange documents. What's more, quantitative analysis can be carried out on information, so that a lot of time and manpower will be saved and the management efficiency will be improved.

The directness of information transmission is able to streamline managerial administration. Traditional managerial administration in colleges and universities is divided into many levels and numerous departments, forming a complicated and redundant "hierarchy", namely bureaucracy, with a bunch of division heads and section chiefs. This kind of administration is structures pyramidally with fewer staff of upper management and more staff of lower level. By taking advantage of net communication, a large number of middle and lower managerial staff can be reduced and the middle level of management that processes and transmits information will also vanish. Hence, a new reticulate and flat management structure will be formed.

Interaction of information transmission helps to promote the democratization and scientification of decision-making. School sets up bulletin board system on its own website, enabling students and staff of the whole school to make discussion freely and independently about school policies and important clerical work, as well as absorbing wisdom of everyone for management work of the school. Thus, it will bring administrative transparency, democratic decision-making and scientific management.

Multimedia of information transmission make the information environment more plentiful and lively. The information form of net communication can be character, picture, voice or graphic. The vivid and abundant information environment will enhance the influence of information transmission.

References

1. Jianlin, Z.: Management Tutorial, vol. 7. Shanghai Finance University Press (2001) (in Chinese)
2. Chengbo, H., Xiaoou, L.: Scanning the University Democracy Administration with communication. Journal of Shenyang Institute of Aeronautical Engineering (6) (2004) (in Chinese)
3. Yu, C., Xiaodong, Y.: Information and Social, vol. (5). China Renmin University Press (2009) (in Chinese)
4. Guofeng, Z.: Interview with Hamas. Foreign Literature Review (1) (1999, 2000) (in Chinese)
5. Tianxiang, X.: Higher Education Management. Guangxi Normal University Press (2001) (in Chinese)

College Student Management in Credit System

Chengbo Hu and Yue Wang

Shenyang Aerospace University
110136, Shenyang, China
huchengbo79@yahoo.com.cn

Abstract. Credit system reform is the direction of our college and university education and brings a huge challenge to student management. Colleges and universities should gradually explore a suitable credit system reform based on national and their own conditions. Under the new student management characteristics and requirements of credit system, counselors, other school department personals and related regulations need to change correspondingly, which will fully reflect student-centered school educational management and teaching guidelines.

Keywords: credit system, education, student management, tutorial system.

1 Introduction

The credit system was produced as a teaching management system in the late 19th century American, and introduced to china's colleges and universities in the early 20th century, and in 1952 it was repealed because of "Learn from Soviet Union Movement". In 1978, credit system was restarted in part of universities and extended to self-examination, college courses broadcast on television and adult education. It is flexibly adapt to needs of socialist market economy for talents, and widely accepted by various forms of higher education, but some universities are suffering from not getting the essence of credit system and blindly implementing it or even not know how to start with.

It is widely known that credit system is a fundamental reform to traditional scholastic year system, so it is a huge transformation project. The features of credit system is uniformity, and centralized management, as a standard teaching management system, credit is the unit for calculating quantity of study, there is a minimum necessary credit for graduation and obtaining a degree. So credit system is a flexible teaching management system and teaching plans adapted to individual differences.

2 Restraint Factors of Credit System Development

The key for current college and university education reform is credit system reform, it fully implement the principle of teaching by the student's ability, which actively promotes educational reform. But under current educational circumstances there are

M. Zhou (Ed.): ISAEBD 2011, Part IV, CCIS 211, pp. 114–119, 2011.
© Springer-Verlag Berlin Heidelberg 2011

many factors and obstacles restricting the development of credit system which cannot be ignored. For example: course system imperfection, low proportion of elective courses, short supply of courses, teachers' incompetency, as well as inside and outside school environment all restrain study time and leaning content selection.

Lack of educational hardware resources is another restraint factor of credit system. The implementation gives students freedom to select courses, and each class time is no longer uniformed. Students require extending computer rooms, laboratories, libraries, other academic support department, restaurants, bathrooms and other logistics service sectors, which are especially important for quantity and specifications of classroom and more modern teaching methods, if these problems are not properly solved, they would seriously affect the smooth implementation of credit system. Some students with low self-study consciousness and self-management capacity may not effectively arrange time, which may lead to a poor academic performance. These factors put up with more stringent requirements for school education and teaching management, which bring us a great challenge in student management.

In addition, there is a lack of guidance from education administrative departments. Because flexible educational system is a very important aspect of credit system and general public has inertia thinking for traditional system, because there are no corresponding released administrative files to regulate flexible educational system, it leads to social misunderstanding from employers and gives adverse effects on student employment and social evaluation. So the implementation of credit system is not just about colleges and universities but develop with policies from all sectors of society.

Although there are some constraints to implement credit system in colleges and universities, which brings a huge challenge to our student management, but we should recognize that the credit system is the direction of higher education reform, colleges and universities should gradually explore a suitable credit system based on national and university conditions to improve student management and gear our higher education development to the international conventions.

3   Student Management Changes with Credit System

Credit system is a flexible teaching plan and management system adapted to individual differences, it uses objective management method to test and mange teaching results, and pass the exam can obtain credit, complete prescribed credit can graduate. The objective management of credit system can not only focus on targets but also create a relaxed learning process, which requires students with high self-awareness and capacities. Next we will get some perspectives on what changes credit system has brought to our student management.

3.1   Changes of Student Relations

In scholastic year system, student relation is within class that students in same grade with same major composed into a group (each class with about 30 students), they go to class together, attend class activities. They are familiar with each other and have a strong sense of team spirit with cohesion. Student relations have changed in credit system, sense of class is gradually weakening because student choose different courses, there are students from different class and professionals to attend the same class, those with same grade and major may be appointed to 4, 5 or more classrooms. The original concept of class does not exist actually and is replaced by "dormitory", "association" and "community", which result in low sense of collective consciousness and sense of group honor, but personal awareness and more conscious of small groups arise.

3.2 Changes of Living Style

Students can independently choose curriculum based on their own ability/interests and arrange study in credit system, which is more autonomous than scholastic year system. But for students in the lower grades and not enough self-conciseness, they are tend to passively study and cannot arrange time properly and efficiently, so they may get lost with independent study and poor academic performance if there is no proper guidance. Instructors should help them to make reasonable course selection, so tutorial system is a very important part to achieve objective management quality control in credit system that counselors can give instructions to students on how to scientifically and reasonably arrange time to study, entertainment and rest. Many students have psychological disorders because of life style changes and pressures from family, economy, study and interpersonal relations, and those disorders become more subtle in credit system and cannot be easily detected by counselor, which may cause some events that should not have happened.

3.3 Changes of Student Management Style

Student management in credit system become more difficult and suddenly increases. The gap among students gets bigger in continuous learning, study locations are dispersed and class time is significantly different, all these lead to a series of problems: class leaders cannot find a single time to assemble the whole class to hold a class meeting or other activities, problems to conduct quality education and the education about Communist Party of China and the Communist Youth League.

3.4 Changes from Form-Teacher to Tutorial System

Colleges and universities appoint instructors based on a student quota in credit system which is called tutorial system. It is commonly seen in graduate education, but in recent years, it is introduced into undergraduate education. To conduct tutorial system in undergraduate education can eliminate some drawbacks. For example, teachers have little time to communicate with students in spare time, they even do not know student name, let along exchange ideas, explore the academic subject or inspire student. The objective of tutorial system is to explore a new way to foster students with independent thinking, establish innovation awareness and improve practical abilities, which enable students to change from "passive learning" to "active learning". However, colleges and universities are systematically strict with teaching and research evaluation, tutors work become more and more formality, it is very common for teachers to meet with student once or twice a semester, some student even do not know instructors and their work, all these are against the original intention of tutorial system.

4 Student Management Mode in Credit System

The fundamental issue for colleges and universities to implement credit system is not about calculating credit or designing teaching management procedure but reexamining education theories/concept and university management system. Even though credit system brings some difficulties for student management but its advantages are very obvious, and this is why it is widely promoted. Counselors, personals in other administrative departments and related systems need to change correspondingly under the new student management characteristics and requirements of credit system, we should fully take use of credit system advantages to make up its deficiencies and maximize credit system performance.

4.1 Work Mode

With the popularity of network, online working is a necessary and must for counselors. Now many universities have established network within campus, some even into dormitory. Online office is no longer a new stuff, while counselors work online is still a blank, so it will become the future trend, the key to solve this problem is renewal concept and fund. Network communication can overcome barriers of time and space, and also greatly improve work efficiency.

Counselors should adjust their work schedule because of work mode changes. Counselors work time should not rigidly adhere to normal school time, because in credit system, students may attend class or rest anytime, counselors work hours maybe in lunch, dinner or even weekend. So they need to flexibly adjust work time: (1) time to deal with routine affairs; (2) a settled period each day to handle miscellaneous and online psychological counseling; (3) how to contact counselors with urgent matters.

4.2 Work Centrality

Respecting the personality of higher education and emphasizing the personality development of students are important features of credit system and the fundamental reason why credit is everlasting. Credit is a learning system which emphasis on personality development and focus on training and improvement of students' self-management ability. From the nature of work, counselors are thought and act as instructors and reliable friends of students. So instructors should be fully connected to students and understand their state of mind.

In order to develop high-quality elites with modern consciousness, skills, spirit and innovation abilities, we should emphasize the quality and innovative education in education management. Set elective courses without professional restraints, such as liberal arts and science cross curriculum and arts curriculum. This will help to change the situation of "only know one of them" and train compound talents.

Integrate featured extra-curricular activities into quality education, universities enhance quality education, strengthen humanity education and professional knowledge at the same time, and strive to cultivate students into compound talents with "knowledge, ability and quality". In short, counselors do not have to be "hands on everything", and they even do not have enough time to do it, but rather implement student management work on a higher level and focus on improving "Three -Self" ability.

4.3 Ideology

Credit system is a wide-range and systematic project, student management cannot be conducted by counselors along, but corporations from all other administrative departments. For example, instructors are strict with attendance and study style, which can effectively avoid skipping. Other faculties should change their ideas and establish service awareness, get rid of the bureaucracy of "crudeness, obduracy and non-flexibility" to create a better soft environment for students. All university affairs should be student-oriented; counselors establish the awareness of "service, education, and management", change old preaching method and treat students as friends. For those with great psychological pressure, poor academic performance and economically disadvantaged students, counseling content should vary with individual situations and solve specific problems. In a word, everything must be about student interests, express student wishes and establish a sense for service for students and help them grow healthily.

4.4 Monitorial System

The so-called monitorial system is to select a certain number of outstanding graduates or senior undergraduates by referral process to be responsible for student management, ideological and political works which are mainly education and guidance-based, and they are also students, so it is called monitorial system. Now many universities use counselor system, and conduct work by class, major or grade, which focuses on common culture. Some universities adopt tutorial system with emphasis on respecting differences, teaching by the student's ability and guiding academic progress. But with gradual deepening of education system reform and university continuous increase enrollment, both modes are more and more difficult to implement, in particular the implementation of tutorial system, that qualified teacher are hard to guarantee.

With new features of this problem, advantages of replacing monitoring system to tutorial system are obvious: (1) selected senior students are with high ideological and professional qualities, there is no gap of grade or identity, they are psychologically the same and more easily to communicate with each other; (2) guidance students are seniors with the same status, and there is no identity and dignity of teachers, they can easily be accepted, students tend to say many stuff that they are unwilling to talk to teachers or parents;(3) guidance students learn the same or similar major as the class they are in charge of, they are not only familiar with credit system features, requirements and related curriculum but also self-development objective, study basis and learning abilities, so they will be more convincing than teacher based on their own experiences.

5 Conclusion

In summary, combined with university actual situations, the mode of "tutorial system+ monitoring system" can better promote college student management. It is more advance and effective than single implementation of tutorial system or counselor system. The promotion of this now mode will fully represent student-oriented educational management and teaching guidelines as well as college respect for student personality and independence, and it also maximize student autonomy and their personality development. We believe that student management will get a breakthrough with all efforts by governance at all levels and various social circles, which writes a new chapter in student management great-leap-forward development.

References

1. Maoyuan, P.: Higher Education. Fujian Education Press (1984) (in Chinese)
2. Lingling, Z.: Credit is difficult to resolve the issue of adult learning. Market News (March 30, 2003) (in Chinese)
3. Zou, X.-P., Jian, L., Hong, L., Hong, L.: Problems and Countermeasures of Credit Management. China Higher Education Research (7) (2001) (in Chinese)
4. Guanghua, Z.: To implement the credit system as a breakthrough point to promote the teaching management reform. China Higher Education Research 5 (2003) (in Chinese)
5. Jun, L., Xiaoping, S.: Thoughts and Countermeasures of Credit System. China Higher Education Research (2) (2004) (in Chinese)
6. Ting, L.: Practice and Reflection Tutorial System. Business (1) (2008) (in Chinese)

Concept Definition and Improving Measures of Industrial Clusters

Chengbo Hu[1] and Li Zhou[2]

[1] Shenyang Aerospace University
110136, Shenyang, China
huchengbo79@yahoo.com.cn
[2] University of South China
421001, Hengyang, China
174068598@qq.com

Abstract. The industrial clusters are a group of enterprises and related organizations in a particular area, which are geographically close and have relevance with each other. Their formation and development depend not only on market mechanisms but also on government regulation. This paper described the historical origin and the theoretical basis of industrial clusters, made a scientific definition of the concept of industrial clusters, proposed measures to promote industrial clusters and then obtained the conclusions that developing industrial clusters of large scale is the inevitable choice of enhancing industrial competitiveness.

Keywords: industrial clusters, regional economy, measures.

1 Introduction

Industrial cluster is the phenomenon of industrial areas, occurring under the conditions of the global division of labor and information technology revolution after the mid-80s in the 20th century and linked to such theories of new regional doctrine as the theory of industrial areas, the theory of regional innovation system and others. As technology advances and economic globalization develops, enterprises' competitive environment has undergone profound changes, prompting workers in the circles of theory and practice to reflect on traditional theory and its policy implications. Industrial cluster becomes the attention hotspot of academic, political and business circles as an important field of "new regionalism ".

In the early 21st century, the phrase of "industrial clusters" has waked into the economic life of people. Whether in the government sector of the economy, or in the enterprises' decision-making departments and industry associations, a growing number of people are concerned about it. The concept of "industrial clusters" is not only seen in the monographs and research papers of geography, economy, management, sociology and other subjects, but also frequently in the various types of media reports, even being popular among government research reports and official documents. However, due to the complexity of industrial clusters and the variety of

M. Zhou (Ed.): ISAEBD 2011, Part IV, CCIS 211, pp. 120–125, 2011.

options of research perspective on industrial clusters, different places and different people often have different understanding of industrial clusters, and then the concept of industrial clusters is also apparently of diversity.

Currently, strong interest all around the world is attached to the development of industrial clusters. Although the upsurge of academic research on industrial clusters is a matter discussed in the last decade, the number excursion and the apparent success of international industrial clusters is one of the most important economic phenomena observed in the past 30 years. Both in developed and developing countries, there are a large number of industrial clusters and the number is still increasing, especially in developing countries, industrial clusters are constantly emerging, which led to the constant changing of the "mosaic" pattern of world economic map.

2   Concept Definition of Industrial Clusters

Concept of "industrial clusters" comes from the summary of the successful experience of regional economy in developed Western countries and has rich connotations. Although the first recognition of the phenomenon of cluster comes from 100 years ago, the famous British economist, Marshall (Marshall, 1891) who proposed the concept of industrial district. Marshall in his classic "Principles of Economics" calls the specialized specific industrial cluster districts "industrial zones". Influenced by the theory of Marshall Industrial District, the later scholars call the social areas with high degree of aggregation of some small and medium enterprises, both competition and cooperation among enterprises and widespread formal and informal contact with each other, representative of "the third Italy" as the "new industrial zone." However, it was Professor Porter of Harvard Business School that first clearly proposed the concept and strictly defined the concept of industrial clusters. Porter proposed it in "Competitive Advantage of Nations" published in 1990. Porter believes that industrial clusters are a collection of companies and institutions inter-linked in a particular field and geographically focused. Industrial clusters extend to sales channels and customers top-down and laterally extend to the manufacturers of ancillary products, as well as the industry companies related to technical skills or inputs. Clusters often include downstream industrial companies, manufacturers of complementary products, suppliers of specialized infrastructure and other agencies to provide training, education, information, research and technical support. Porter defines the concept of industrial clusters mainly from the perspective of management and industry chain. He believes that clusters have become a new way of thinking for promoting economic development and also a means of causing changes. As a result, different analysts have to choose their own different elements to suit different types of clusters, with different ways of empirical observation of the phenomenon of industrial clusters, which has generated considerable discussion and deeper thinking in the international academic community.

Development of industrial clusters involved many aspects, such as the impact on foreign-funded enterprises, linkages with local suppliers, enterprises' international connections, and even the linkages between local industry clusters and foreign industrial clusters and so on. Therefore, how to implement industrial cluster strategy, fostering business cooperation network to ensure the sustainable development of industrial clusters, how to upgrade the industrial clusters, how to improve the competitiveness of industrial clusters, how to make industrial clusters "home plate" to participate in international competition as China's enterprises, how to play the role of government, which are all issues placed in front of the development of China's industrial clusters. In view of the development of industrial clusters in China are facing various problems, the strategy of making the industrial clusters economic resources union and the enterprise group shared brand has become urgent and inevitable need. Industrial cluster are a collection of companies and relevant institutions geographically close to and related in a particular field. Clusters include a series of linked industries and other major competitors, with a large number of relevant enterprises and institutions focus on a specific geographical area according to certain economic ties, forming a similar biological organism community. Industrial clusters cannot only become the lead of regional economic development but also can improve a country's international industrial competitiveness.

In summary, industry cluster is the system of complex industrial organization of space, which is a flexible specialization among regional enterprises, a close formed network of cooperation and rooted in local social and cultural environment of constant innovation, with a large number of similar or related business and their stakeholders (companies, universities, research institutions, financial institutions, intermediaries, industry organizations and governments, etc.) interacting with each other and then gathered in order to obtain certain economic and social interests in a particular location.

3   Improving Measures of Industrial Clusters

The industry clusters mostly form spontaneously in the role of market mechanism. But in the respects of guiding the rational and orderly development of industrial clusters, creating a good external environment conducive to innovation and preventing degradation and even recession of industrial clusters and so on, the role of government policy is very important. The formation and development of industrial clusters depend not only on market mechanisms, but also depend on the government's regulation. Because knowledge spillovers and its externalities exist, the private benefits of innovative firms is less than its social benefits, when there is no government intervention, economic growth is usually only a sub-optimal growth, only through government regulation and the elimination of distorted allocation of resources caused by market mechanisms, the social effect optimization can be achieved. So how to upgrade the industry clusters?

3.1   Make Scientific Plan of the Development of Industry Cluster

Industry cluster is a complex organic system, the production of industrial clusters have certain conditions, when the industry gathered at a region and has been closely linked to industrial competitiveness, forced proposal of this industry will greatly increase the probability of failure if a region does not have conditions of an industry cluster. Industrial cluster is the organic integration of industry and region, it is stuck in the national and even global mobility of factors of production then located in the local through the local-specific, non-mobile factors of production, thus forming the effective allocation of resources. The industries suitable for the developments are different in different regions. And the factors of production owned by different regions are not the same. Many areas are keen to set up large enterprises and groups, but the benefits are not ideal. Industrial clusters provided a new perspective for our new understanding of SMEs, regional development, industry associations and so on, but also poured cold water to "heat of big business ". In fact, for firm size, the great size has great difficulties, but also has great advantages; the small has benefits, but also has shortcomings. Therefore, the Government should formulate a distinctive development plan of industry cluster based on the specific local situation, and create some local non-mobile factors of production as much as possible, to greatly develop industrial clusters in the way of top-down while stimulating spontaneous emerging of industrial clusters. The industrial projects planned to be launched should be considered whether they are of the industry competitiveness in the region and so competition in the market competition has evolved from the strategic competition of business development to the development of industry cluster. Regional characteristics of industrial cluster are industrial competitiveness with high degree of association. Within a region, the important means of developing economic for local government lie in how to promote the formation and development of industrial clusters, and make scientific plans of the development of industry cluster according to local characteristics and advantages of industrial development.

3.2 Increase the Innovation Degree of the System of Government

The development of industrial clusters is the result reacted by environmental factors, demand conditions, production factors and related and supporting industries together. But this does not mean the Government in the development of industrial clusters is nothing, left to its origin, development and destruction. On the contrary, the Government has played a very important role in the process of the emergence and development of industrial clusters. The role is mainly reflected in: First, the industry clusters require the Government to be indirectly involved in the development of clusters. Under the laws of the market, the Government should not be directly involved in the formation of industrial clusters. However, during the development period of industrial clusters, in the fierce market competition, if there is no effective government nutrition, the development of the clusters will be very difficult, they may even die. Second, the industry clusters require the Government to improve the atmosphere of industrial clusters. Misconduct within the cluster, the improvement of social service system, industrial upgrading and the opportunistic behavior of enterprises and the external cluster market environment construction are inseparable from the involvement of the Government. Innovation of the system is the key to the implementation of strategies of industry clusters. The question placed in front of the Government is how to help entrepreneurs to professional development, reduce transaction costs, facilitate inter-firm division of labor and improve the competitiveness of enterprises through the innovation of system, and how to develop industrial clusters through regional marketing, etc. Innovation of system of the Government is to form a system for policy control, indirect intervention and service, to offer a "fair, just and open" development platform for forming the industrial clusters, thus addressing issues such as risk financing, intermediary services, cooperation of production, academic and research, information support, industrial space layout and other issues. Local government provides a favorable internal and external environment for industrial clusters, technological progress and enterprises' innovation primarily through innovation of system, including the policy innovation and service innovation and optimization and innovation of environment.

3.3 Start the Industrial Cluster Policy Alternative to Industrial Policy

After China's entering WTO, not only high-tech industries but also clothing, toys and many other industries have experienced a more intense international competition, the cluster strategy reveals to us that the development of enterprises' clusters of these industries and improving the capacity of innovation has particular significance. To fully understand the importance of industrial clusters and seriously study and summarize the success of the development of industrial clusters in Zhejiang and Guangdong provinces, in addition to the necessary strategic industries, we should also reduce the preference for certain industrial sectors and develop special industries with innovative features and competitive advantages. Within the scope of the region, to replace the industrial policy to the industrial cluster policy, the real key is to take promoting the cluster, improving the market competitiveness and sustainable development as the goal, to encourage and limit the policy to be targeted at the enterprise within the industrial cluster, rather than the implementation of policy across the board within the whole region. We support the establishment of Productivity Center, Innovation Center, Technology Development Center, Information Service Center, Network Center, Financing Guarantee Institutions, Industry Associations, Chambers of Commerce and other organizations of intermediary services in the specialized town or in the specialized industrial zones, as well as promoting successful experiences much closely associated with universities and research institutions.

3.4 Strengthen the Regional Innovation System Construction

Regional innovation system is a composite system of the main body of innovation, organizations and institutions in an economic zone directly related to and having intrinsic relationship with the production, diffusion and application of the technological innovation. Prerequisite for its success is based on local innovation network, namely based on the long-term cooperation between enterprises and between enterprises and research institutions. Whether it is national or regional innovation system, the goal is to promote technological innovation through the effective accumulation, heritage and growth of knowledge, resulting in a substantial increase in productivity. The method is to constitute an effective network and interactive innovation through the main body of innovation system. The effective operation of the regional innovation system can accelerate the formation of industrial clusters and spatial agglomeration, resulting in agglomeration economy. Therefore, as a system of creation, diffusion and application of knowledge, in essence, industrial cluster is a regional innovation system and an important model for regional innovation system.

3.5 Foster the Regional Culture of Industrial Clusters

The industrial cluster has embeddedness, whose formation and development is based on the institutional culture in the region. Important criterion to judge industry cluster is the high degree of internal relations between a regional internal economic and social relations, namely the webs adjacent within the enterprises in a region, resulting in trust and willingness to cooperate. However, there is a long time institutional cultural shortcomings as fragmentation, imperfection of the market mechanism, lack of social capital, low trust, high transaction costs and imperfect system of various laws of related industrial enterprises, and then in some China's regions and enterprises only focus on using internal resources, improving the adaptability and flexibility within the enterprise, rather than on looking for external resources for enterprise, thus leading to difficulties to make and implement industrial cluster policy and to effectively develop industrial clusters. Therefore, for those regional industry clusters which have not formed the local advantages, it is important to foster the region's entrepreneurs and institutional cultural atmosphere conducive to innovation; for the industry clusters region which has formed local advantages, it also needs to attach importance to institutional cultural innovation, thus playing the competitive advantage of industrial clusters.

4 Conclusion

After the association degree of industry clusters with industrial competitiveness significantly increased, for a region, how to promote the local industry clusters has become the basic problem of the industry and overall economic development. Therefore, to greatly develop the industry clusters and enhance the competitiveness of China's industry competitiveness with the advantages of industry clusters has become an inevitable choice. Although industry clusters mostly form spontaneously in the role of market mechanism, in the respects of guiding the rational and orderly development of industrial clusters, creating a good external environment conducive to innovation and preventing industrial clusters degrading even moving to recession and so on, the role of government policy is very important.

References

1. Chengbo, H., Lin, C.: Industrial clusters Higher Vocational Education Dual Study. Jilin University Press (2009) (in chinese)
2. Ruoxiang, J.: Concept of industrial cluster and its role in regional development. China Economic Times (November 1,2005) (in chinese)
3. Minglong, Z.: Industrial Clusters and Regional Development. China Economic Publishing House (2008) (in Chinese)
4. From to, http://www.gmw.cn/content/2008-09/04/content_826425.htm

Project Knowledge Management Research Based on the Lifecycle

Genyi Niu

School of Information Management, Wuhan University,
430072 Wuhan, China
niugenyi@163.com

Abstract. The temporality and uniqueness of project-based organizations are major obstacle for organizational learning, and leading to massive loss of organizational knowledge. In order to solve this problem, strengthening the project knowledge management is very important. This paper described the meaning and function of project knowledge management, introduced lifecycle and knowledge management into project management, and forwarded project knowledge management integrated model based project lifecycle. The model includes project layer knowledge management model and organization layer knowledge management model. The aim of project layer knowledge management is to realize knowledge accumulation. The purpose of organization layer knowledge management is to realize knowledge sharing of organizations so as to improve organizational project management ability and learning ability through team learning and organizational learning.

Keywords: Knowledge Management, Project Management, Lifecycle, Project Knowledge Management.

1 Introduction

Knowledge management and project management are two branches developing rapidly of contemporary management science .The new concept project knowledge management raised for the close relationship between project management and knowledge management. Project knowledge management, especially in complex projects, is one of the main success factors in project management. Lack of project knowledge management is one of the main reasons for project failure. Knowledge about project management, explicit as well as tacit, plays a decisive role in understanding this discipline [1]. American scholar Srikanth conducted the research to project knowledge management early, he said: Knowledge have important inheritance role in project activities, and advised performing project management with knowledge strategy to control project "island" phenomenon. Chinese scholar ZhongTuo Wang thinks project knowledge is valuable experience for the organization's future. Through effective knowledge management means for project management knowledge identification, preparation and transmission, can avoid organization repeating previous error or doing of repetition in a follow-up projects. It emphasizes the importance of project knowledge management [2].

M. Zhou (Ed.): ISAEBD 2011, Part IV, CCIS 211, pp. 126–133, 2011.
© Springer-Verlag Berlin Heidelberg 2011

2   Knowledge Management and Project Knowledge Management

2.1   The Concept of Knowledge Management and Project Management and the Relationship between Them

There are a variety of categories of definition of Knowledge Management (KM) in the literature since people have realized its significance. About the concepts of knowledge management, a relatively new definition thinks: Knowledge management is a method of controlling processes of knowledge creation, its codification, ordering, storing, retrieval, processing, transfer, and application (2008)[1].According to the PMBOK (Project Management Body of Knowledge) , project management（PM）is the application of knowledge, skills, tools, and techniques to project activities to meet project requirements[3].Under the knowledge-based economy background, there is a close connection between knowledge management and project management. Project management may be seen as knowledge management process. KM should also be added to the PM theory and become an essential part, especially to a project-based organization.

2.2   The Meaning and Function of Project Knowledge Management

Conceptually, knowledge is the most important resource needed for project management. Project management is itself a knowledge management process, project management competence stems from the unique knowledge that enterprises have, and the ability to use knowledge. The literature [4] suggested that project knowledge management (PKM) is knowledge management in project situations and thus the link between the principles of knowledge management and project management.

The capability of obtaining, creating, transmitting and using knowledge would be the crucial factors to promote the success of project, which requires organization to take project knowledge management. Project knowledge management through the knowledge acquisition and accumulation, knowledge sharing and innovation and applied to project activities to realize the maximization of the value of project.

The main characteristics of project knowledge management: Project knowledge management is a process oriented management; According to the project life cycle organization and management knowledge; Project different participation body and management levels have different project knowledge needs [2].

The role of project knowledge management : Apart from cutting costs, several other objectives of PKM can be summarized in five aims: increasing work efficiency and reducing risk; A continuous learning process; Continuous improvement; the identification and fostering of innovation[4].

The core of project knowledge management: Converting the knowledge coming from project into organization knowledge, and serve project more efficiently; obtaining external knowledge needed to complete project activities, and integrating these knowledge in the process of project implementation.

3 Project Lifecycle and Knowledge Construction

3.1 The Concept of Project Lifecycle

The lifecycle concept is originally used to describe a period of one generation of organism in biological system. The term of lifecycle is the description of all activities that a subject is involved in a period from its birth to its end. Since the 1950s, based on biological evolution, the lifecycle theory is now seen as a kind of powerful theoretical research tool by many domestic and foreign scholars, and is widely used in many fields, formed the enterprise lifecycle theory, product lifecycle theory, etc. Similarly, project management also has a dynamic lifecycle process. The lifecycle concept has been applied into project management area. According to Schwalbe, a project lifecycle is a collection of project phases such as concept, development, implementation, and close-out [5].There are many project lifecycle models with various phase names and numbers of phases, the most common lifecycle is the one with four distinct phases: conceptual, planning, execution and termination. In this paper, the project lifecycle can be divided into four stages: Project decision-making, project planning, project implementation and project evaluation.

3.2 Project Lifecycle Knowledge Construction

Project management knowledge is the process, in which knowledge flow concept has carried through to each stage of whole project lifecycle, and knowledge can be managed more efficiently. Proper knowledge is a basic prerequisite for effective project management. All projects have one thing in common—knowledge. The Japanese project management standard recognizes knowledge and experience as the main sources of project value. The different stages of project have different knowledge management goals and contents. Chinese scholars Zhong Tuo Wang thinks knowledge needed and used in every stage of the project lifecycle are with different characteristics [2]. The literature [4] suggested that the relevant types of knowledge in projects differ along the stages of the project lifecycle. Experience from subsequent projects, information about the buying team, and knowledge about technology and markets are examples of knowledge types that are of particular importance for the early phases of the project. Knowledge about existing (technical) solutions, experience from scheduling, and the application of tools might be more interesting at the stage of implementation.

The Project Management Body of Knowledge has defined the fundamental basis of project management knowledge within the nine knowledge areas. The nine knowledge areas are: scope management; time management; cost management; quality management; human resource management; communications management; risk management; procurement management; integration management [6].

4 Project Knowledge Management Model Based on the Lifecycle

4.1 The Integrated Model of Project Knowledge Management

Project knowledge management based on the lifecycle can be divided into project layer knowledge management and organization layer knowledge management. The former is carried knowledge management activity around project activities process, its major purpose is to realize the accumulation of knowledge, and the latter is long-term organization promote cross-project knowledge sharing and reuse through knowledge management [7]. Project management as a process oriented management mode, management process itself contain knowledge management factors. Project management process is the movement process of knowledge, knowledge flow throughout project life period always. Combined with lifecycle and knowledge construction and project knowledge management process, we can build project knowledge management integrated model (see Figure 1).

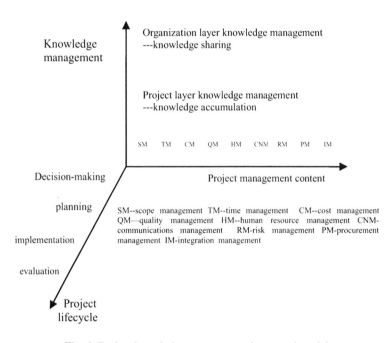

Fig. 1. Project knowledge management integrated model

The integrated model of project knowledge management merge project lifecycle, knowledge management process and project management content into a three-dimensional model. Project lifecycle consist of project decision-making, project planning, project implementation and project evaluation four stages. Project knowledge management includes two phases. The first stage is project layer knowledge management and the second stage is organization layer knowledge management. Project management content involve scope management, time management, cost management, quality management, risk management, human resources management, communication management, procurement management and integrated management 9 fields, each field has the corresponding knowledge content.

4.2 Project Layer Knowledge Management---To Realize the Accumulation of Knowledge

Project management can be divided into four phases: project decision-making, project planning, project implementation and project evaluation. Generally speaking, the process of knowledge management involves knowledge acquisition, knowledge transfer, knowledge sharing and knowledge innovation. Project layer knowledge management consists of knowledge acquisition, knowledge integration, knowledge sharing, knowledge innovation and the accumulation of knowledge. Knowledge as one of the important factors of production is the connection between project management and knowledge management. Project knowledge management obtains knowledge from all phases of project management operation. After the knowledge transfer, knowledge sharing and knowledge innovation reapply to projects and constantly storage and update knowledge base so as to promote further project management. Project layer knowledge management model (see Figure 2).

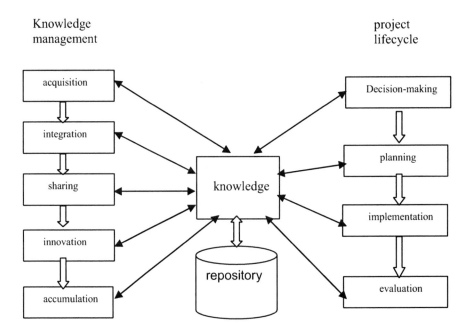

Fig. 2. Project layer knowledge management model

Project layer knowledge management model is a model by knowledge bridge links project knowledge activities and project lifecycle. On the one hand, getting the knowledge necessary to all phases of the project lifecycle through various channels, and accumulating knowledge produced by each stage in project lifecycle to rich and update project repository for follow-on projects sharing and reuse. On the other hand, through project knowledge management, integrating, sharing and innovating all kinds of knowledge produced in project knowledge management activities then used in project knowledge management.

4.3 Organization Layer Knowledge Management---To Realize the Sharing of Knowledge

Projects are unique and temporary undertakings with changing work force. Moreover, projects are often short-term oriented and integrating internal and external experts and knowledge. Project participants have to adapt quickly to new conditions and contents of work. The temporality and uniqueness is a major obstacle for organizational learning. This is particularly true for projects which therefore lack an organizational memory, routines and other mechanisms of organizational learning. From these conditions, the importance of a process of securing project knowledge for the overall organization seems obvious.

From the project organization perspective, the temporary nature of project organization forms knowledge islands. Organization layer project knowledge management is through knowledge sharing to solve this problem. Through knowledge management to timely translate knowledge existing in individual and project team into organization knowledge, and through constructing project repository for subsequent project service.

Knowledge in organization layer knowledge management can be divided into two categories: personal knowledge and organizational knowledge. Knowledge sharing in organization is to realize the transformation between knowledge content and the transfer of knowledge between different individuals, project teams and organizations utilizing the means such as   knowledge network, team learning etc. In essence, this is the knowledge type conversion and knowledge transfer and innovation process between different main bodies [8]. The literature [9] suggested that knowledge transfer and sharing of organization are divided into four forms:

- Knowledge sharing between individuals: realizing knowledge sharing through the communication between individuals.
- Knowledge sharing between individuals and project teams: This sharing are mainly manifested in two aspects. On the one hand, Personal knowledge increased to project knowledge. On the other hand, individual within project obtains project knowledge and internalizes our own tacit knowledge.
- knowledge sharing between project teams: Knowledge dissemination and sharing process from a project organization and its team members to another project organization.
- knowledge sharing between the project teams and enterprise organizations: This is a two-way diffusion mechanism of knowledge. On the one hand, systematic recording and organizing project knowledge and integrating into enterprise knowledge; On the other hand, the enterprise knowledge diffusing downward so as to reuse for the subsequent project and reduce project risk in the project implementation. Organization layer knowledge management model (see Figure 3).

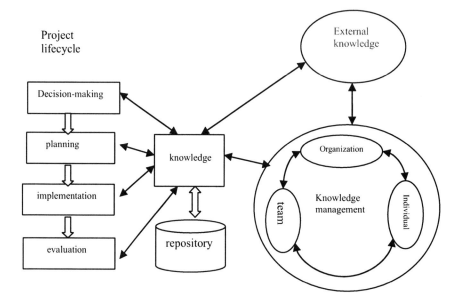

Fig. 3. Organization layer knowledge management model

Project layer knowledge management model combines knowledge management process with project process in microscopic level. Organization layer knowledge management model introduces knowledge management to the macroscopic level of project organization. The project organization, with many participants constitute a temporary network organization outside the organization, thus obtain external knowledge. Within the organization, a layered organization formed, in which individual, project teams and organizations as the main body of knowledge diffusion and sharing. Organization layer knowledge management model integrate project life cycle with project organization so as to facilitate organizational learning, knowledge transfer and sharing between projects, and using the integrated team knowledge to update repository.

5   Conclusion

The temporality and uniqueness of project-based organizations are major obstacle for organizational learning, and leading to massive loss of organizational knowledge. In order to solve this problem, this paper put forward project knowledge management integrated model based project lifecycle. Project layer knowledge management model merged knowledge acquisition, knowledge integration, knowledge sharing, knowledge creation and the knowledge accumulation process into the project management process, the aim is to realize knowledge accumulation; Organization layers knowledge management model blend knowledge management objectives into single project target system, the purpose is to realize knowledge sharing of organizations and improve organizational project management ability through team and organizational learning. In theory, this article frees learning disabilities of project-based organization, and provides the theory basis and System Structure for organization in implementing knowledge management.

References

1. Gasik, S.: A Model of Project Knowledge Management. Project Management Journal Online in Wiley Online Library (March 2011)
2. He, J.: Review of Project Knowledge Management Research. Library and Information Service 14, 45–49 (2010)
3. Project Management Institute, Edition): A Guide to the Project Management Body of Knowledge (PMBOK® Guide.) 3 edn., USA (2004)
4. Hanisch, B., Lindner, F., Mueller, A., Wald, A., Mueller, A., Wald, A.: Knowledge management in project environments. Journal of knowledge management 4, 148–160 (2009)
5. Schwalbe, K.: Information Technology Project Management. Thomson Course Technology, Boston (2004)
6. Frank, H.: Cervone: Standard methodology in digital library project management. OCLC Systems & Services 1, 30–34 (2007)
7. He, J.: Project Process—based knowledge management model construction research on library science. J. 10, 98–99 (2010)
8. Xiong, D.: Study of Organization Knowledge Sharing Models and Technologies. Library and Information Service 20, 114–117 (2010)
9. Li, Z., Zhao, J.: Knowledge Management in Projects Based on OCPT Model. Journal of Intelligence 11, 141–145 (2010)

Specification of Housing Bubbles Based on Markov Switching Mechanism: A Case of Beijing

Lei Feng and Wei Li

School of Public Administration, Renmin University of China, Beijing, P.R.C.

Abstract. Applying Markov switching mechanism to housing price model and ADF test, this paper determines the phases of housing bubble in Beijing from 1998 to 2010. The conclusions are as follows. After 2005, Beijing's housing market entered the stage of bubble accumulation. There are serious bubbles in 2007, 2009 and 2010. Disposable income and price expectation have significantly positive influences on housing price. Deposit and mortgage rates are of stationary features in the MS-ADF test, and the fluctuation of housing price is mainly caused by changes of income. The non-stationary supply of land strengthens the expectation of increase of housing price, and credit growth and long-term low interest rates contribute to the expansion of housing bubbles.

Keywords: rational bubble, Markov switching mechanism, housing price.

1 Introduction

Since 1998, China's real estate investment has maintained double-digit growth rate. In 2010, the central government made multiple policies with respects to land, finance and buyer qualification to regulate real estate market. Beijing, Shanghai etc. also issued "restriction order". However, housing prices of Beijing and Shanghai were still rising sharply throughout the year with the growth rate of 42% and 44% respectively. What are deep reasons of the fast growing housing prices? Was it due to fundamental factors such as urbanization and income growth, or caused by excessive speculation?

Scholars have used a variety of methods to specify housing bubbles from different angles which can be divided into three categories: direct test, indirect test and index method. Direct test has good theoretical basis and the existence of bubbles can be determined by comparing fundamental price and actual price. However, it is difficult to obtain the rent and discount rate. Indirect test analyzes the statistical features of indicators, of which the defect is the inability of measuring the size of price bubbles. By analyzing indicators of real estate industry, Index method finds out the existence of bubble. It is straightforward and relatively simple, but the choices of indicators mainly base on subjective experience.

This paper uses housing price model of Garino and Sarno (2004) and specifies housing bubbles in Beijing from 1998 to 2010. The remainder of the paper is as follows. In Section 2, we apply Markov switching mechanism to housing price model and ADF test, and also the estimate method and procedure are presented. In Section 3, both traditional method and varying parameter method are used to find out the

M. Zhou (Ed.): ISAEBD 2011, Part IV, CCIS 211, pp. 134–140, 2011.
© Springer-Verlag Berlin Heidelberg 2011

intrinsic link between the indicators. Using monthly data from February 1998 to November 2010 of Beijing, we conduct the MS-ADF test to find out the phases with existence of housing bubbles. Section 4 concludes.

2 Markov Switching Mechanism

2.1 Estimate Method

Evans (1991) shows that conintegraion test and unit-root test are unable to detect an important class of rational bubbles by simulation which normally concludes that prices will not be more explosive than dividends, even though the bubbles are substantial in magnitude and volatility. Suppose the typical historical behavior could be described as a first-order regression. At some point, there was a significant change in the average level of the series. Hence, it needs a model encompassing both periods:

$y_t = c_{s_t} + \phi y_{t-1} + \varepsilon_t$, where the regime change of the process is controlled by the

random variable s_t . Assuming that s_t can't be observed directly and can only be

inferred by the observed behavior of y_t , the parameters of model and state transition

probability. The simplest specification is that s_t is the realization of a two-state

Markov chain. The potential value of s_t can be $[0,1]$. The probability of a change in

regime depends on the past only through the value of the most recent regime. The

transition probability matrix is as follows: $\begin{bmatrix} p_{00} & 1-p_{11} \\ 1-p_{00} & p_{11} \end{bmatrix}$.

There can be state changes in other parameters such as ϕ and σ^2 during specific model configuration.

Let the regime that a given process is in any date t be indexed by an unobserved

random variable s_t , where there are two possible regimes. When the process is in

regime 0, the observed variable y_t is presumed to have been drawn from a

$N(\mu_0, \sigma_0^2)$ distribution. Hence, the density of y_t conditional on the random variable

s_t taking on the value j is:

$$f(y_t \mid s_t = j; \theta) = \frac{1}{\sqrt{2\pi}\sigma_j} e^{-\frac{(y_t-\mu_j)^2}{2\sigma_j^2}} \tag{1}$$

s_t is presumed to have been generated by some probability distribution, and the

unconditional probability of s_t is:

$$P\{s_t = j; \theta\} = \pi_j \tag{2}$$

where $\theta \equiv (\mu_0, \mu_1, \sigma_0^2, \sigma_1^2, \pi_1, \pi_2)'$.

The joint distribution probability of y_t and s_t is:

$$p(y_t, s_t = j; \theta) = f(y_t \mid s_t = j; \theta)P\{s_t = j; \theta\} \tag{3}$$

The unconditional probability of y_t can be found by summing (3), and the function can be given as follows:

$$f(y_t; \theta) = \frac{\pi_0}{\sqrt{2\pi}\sigma_0}e^{-\frac{(y_t-\mu_0)^2}{2\sigma_0^2}} + \frac{\pi_1}{\sqrt{2\pi}\sigma_1}e^{-\frac{(y_t-\mu_1)^2}{2\sigma_1^2}} \tag{4}$$

If the regime variable s_t is distributed i.i.d across different time, the log likelihood for the observed data can be calculated as follows:

$$L(\theta) = \sum_{t=1}^{T} \log f(y_t; \theta) \tag{5}$$

The maximum likelihood estimate of parameter θ in (5) is obtained by maximizing (5) subject to the constraints that $\pi_1 + \pi_2 = 1$ and $\pi_j \geq 0$.

2.2 Estimate Procedure

The optimal probabilistic inference of regime variable is calculated by Hamilton filter, which is a generalization of the Expectation Maximization algorithm. It can be summarized as follows:

Step 1: Calculate the joint density $p(S_t \mid I_{t-1})$ of the current and m past states conditional on past information $I_t = \{y_{t-1}, y_{t-2}, \ldots y_0\}$.

Step 2: Calculate the joint conditional distribution of y_t and s_t :

$$p(y_t, S_t \mid I_{t-1}) = p(y_t \mid S_t, I_{t-1})p(S_t \mid I_{t-1}).$$

Step 3: Calculate the marginal density of y_t :

$$p(y_t, S_t \mid I_{t-1}) = p(y_t \mid S_t, I_{t-1})p(S_t \mid I_{t-1}).$$

Step 4: Calculate the joint density function of the state conditional on current and past information:

$$p(S_t \mid I_t) = \frac{p(y_t, S_t \mid I_{t-1})}{p(y_t \mid I_{t-1})}.$$

Step 5: Compute the output of the filter: $p(S_t^- \mid I_t) = \sum_{s_{t-m}=0}^{1} p(S_t \mid I_t)$.

Using the results from step 5 we iterate the procedure. Here the parameters are required during the iteration process by maximization likelihood estimate.

3 Empirical Analysis of Housing Bubbles in Beijing

3.1 Variables and Data

The data set comprises monthly time series for the Beijing seasonally adjusted average new residential sales price, personal disposable income per capita, one-year deposit interest rate and mortgage rate over the sample period from 1998:2 through 2010:11. The nominal income per capita variable was converted into real value by using CPI (2008:1=100). The saving and mortgage interest rate was reduced by inflation rate. The time series of interest in the empirical analysis are the natural logarithm of the average new house price p , the natural logarithm of the real personal disposable income per capita inc , the real one-year saving interest rate is which we use as a proxy for the risk-free rate, and the real mortgage rate im .

We apply traditional model and varying parameter model to study the intrinsic link among housing price, income and interest rate, and use MS-ADF test to determine the existence of rational bubble.

3.2 Results of Fixed Parameter Estimate

Based on housing price theory in the former part, we establish the econometric model. Taking into account the possible autocorrelation and heteroskedasticity, two lagged terms of housing price are added into our model. The model is converted to:

$$\lg p = c_{s_t} + a_{s_t} * \lg inc + b_{s_t} * is + f_{s_t} * im + d1_{s_t} * \lg p(-1) + d2_{s_t} * \lg p(-2) + \varepsilon_{s_t} \quad (6)$$

For the regression effect, the residual shows stationary feature and no autocorrelation. The estimation results are in Table 1.

Table 1. Fixed Parameter Estimate

Panel A: The Estimated Values of Model Parameter

Parameter	c_{s_t}	a_{s_t}	b_{s_t}	f_{s_t}	$d1_{s_t}$	$d2_{s_t}$
Value	-0.3604***	0.0438***	-0.0511***	0.0492***	0.6836***	0.3010***

***, **, * represents significant at the 1%, 5%, 10% level respectively

Panel B: Effect of Model Estimation

R-squared	SD	F	P-Value(F)	DW
0.9699	0.0618	588.7713	0.0000	2.0968

In Figure 1, we graph the residuals from the regression of $\lg p$ onto $\lg inc$, is , im , $\lg p(-1)$ and $\lg p(-2)$. The probability of bubble existing is large during the phase where the residual sequence fluctuates a lot.

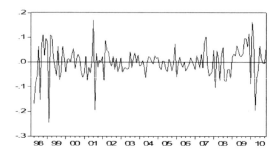

Fig. 1. The Residual Sequence of Fixed Parameter Model

3.3 Results of Varying Parameter Model Estimate

Then we apply Markov switching mechanism to model estimation. In order to make comparison with traditional method, we still add the two lagged terms. By doing this, we can find out the impact of expectation on housing price and alleviate the possible autocorrelation. The model estimation is achieved by using maximum likelihood estimation with Matlab. Table 2 is for the MS estimated model parameters with intercept and without intercept.

Table 2. The Comparison of Varying Parameter Model

Parameter	Value-Intercept	Value-No intercept	Parameter	Value-Intercept	Value-No intercept
c_1	8.6966 (0.00)	-	f_1	0.0101 (0.00)	-0.0113 (0.00)
c_2	8.6964 (0.00)	-	f_2	-0.5931 (0.00)	0.0088 (0.00)
a_1	0.0663 (0.00)	0.0254 (0.00)	$d1_1$	0.5933 (0.00)	0.7826 (0.00)
a_2	-0.0158 (0.00)	-0.0620 (0.00)	$d1_2$	0.3731 (0.00)	-0.0720 (0.00)
b_1	-0.0056 (0.00)	0.0161 (0.00)	$d2_1$	0.3814 (0.00)	0.2023 (0.00)
b_2	0.5721 (0.00)	-0.0125 (0.00)	$d2_2$	-0.0626 (0.00)	-0.0626 (0.00)

Value in () is the P-Value of the estimated parameters.

Whether there is intercept or not, the model over the sample period shows no changes in regime. The model with intercept is in regime 2, whereas the one with no intercept is in regime 1. However, the estimated values of parameter with intercept are not consistent with our theoretical expectation. Hence, we choose the no-intercept model. Again we graph the residual time series in Figure 2.

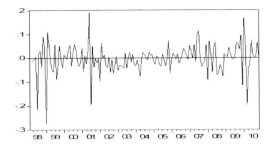

Fig. 2. The Residual Sequence of Varying Parameter Model

Comparing the two residual time series figures, we find out that the volatility of varying parameter model residual is slightly higher than that of the fixed one. But the trend of residual fluctuation is consistent, and draws the same conclusion: Due to institutional factors, residuals fluctuate significantly from the second half of 1998 through 1999, but there are no bubbles. In 2007, 2009 and the first half of 2010, both figures show excessive fluctuations, and the period has feature of bubbles obviously.

3.4 MS-ADF Test

MS-ADF test is based on a generalization of the Dickey-Fuller procedure, which makes use of the class of the Markov regime switching models and is proposed by Hall, Psaradakis, and Sola (1999).

MS-ADF test allows for the possibility that the dynamic behavior of Δy_t may be different for different parts of the sample. Assuming the parameters of ADF regression are time varying and change with an unobserved indicator $s_t \in \{0,1\}$, the regression form is as follows:

$$\Delta y_t = \mu_0(1-s_t) + \mu_1 s_t + \left[\phi_0(1-s_t) + \phi_1 s_t\right] y_{t-1} + \sum_{j=1}^{k}\left[\varphi_{oj}(1-s_t) + \varphi_{1j} s_t\right]\Delta y_{t-j} + \sigma_e e_t \quad (7)$$

With this change in the regression form, we can describe the process better when there is periodically collapsing bubble, where the two regimes correspond to the expanding and collapsing phase of the bubble. In Markov switching ADF test, the null hypothesis is $\phi_0 = 0$ or $\phi_1 = 0$, $\phi_0 = 0$ and $\phi_1 = 0$, which means there is unit root in y_t and no explosive rational bubble. And the existence of bubbles is consistent with $\phi_0 > 0$ or $\phi_1 > 0$, $\phi_0 > 0$ and $\phi_1 > 0$ indicating that one or both of the regime governing the underlying process is characterized by the presence of an explosive component. If the state transition possibility chart of housing price is the same with that of other fundamental variables, there is no rational bubble and the fluctuation of housing prices is caused by other fundamental variables. On the contrary, we can conclude there are explosive rational bubbles.

According to the statistical features of four indicators, we select different form of MS-ADF test for each indicator. All the four tests are with no trend term and no intercept. The k value of the ADF regression is chosen by AIC values of data series' autoregressive process. The estimated values of saving and mortgage rates in both regimes are not positive, and could not reject the null hypothesis. Therefore, the abnormal price fluctuation has nothing to do with interest rates. The estimated values of parameters of price and income data are significantly positive, and both of them show explosive features. Hence we compare the state transition possibility chart of price and income to find out the explosive fluctuations in price series is due to income changes or periodically collapsing rational bubbles.

The main conclusions of MS-ADF test are as follows. The residential market entered a bubble accumulation stage after the second half of 2005; the size of price bubbles in 2007, the second half of 2009 and 2010 was large; but the bubble percentage of housing price in 2008 was declining.

4 Conclusions

Applying Markov switching mechanism to housing price model and ADF test, we determine the phases of housing bubble in Beijing from 1998 to 2010. The conclusions are as follows. (1) After the second half of 2005, Beijing's housing market entered the stage of bubble accumulation. There are serious bubbles in 2007, the second half of 2009 and 2010. (2) Disposable income and price expectation have significantly positive influences on housing price. (3) Deposit and mortgage rates are of stationary features in the MS-ADF test, and the fluctuation of housing price is mainly caused by changes of income. (4) The non-stationary supply of land strengthens the expectation of increasing of housing price, and credit growth and long-term low interest rates contribute the expansion of housing bubbles.

References

1. Muellbauer, J., Murphy, A.: Booms and Busts in the UK Housing Market. The Economical Journal 107(455), 1701–1727 (1997)
2. Smith, M.H., Smith, G.: Bubble, Bubble, Where's the Housing Bubble. Brookings Papers Economic Activity, 1–50 (2006)
3. Chan, H.L., Lee, S.K.: Detecting Rational Bubbles in the Residential Housing Markets in Hong Kong. Economic Modeling 18, 61–73 (2001)
4. Abraham, J.M.: Patric H.Hendershott. Bubbles in Metropolitan Housing Markets. Journal of Housing Research 2(7), 191–207 (1996)
5. Lee, J.S.: An Ordo-liberal Perspective on land problems in Korea. Urban Studies 34, 1084–1971 (1997)
6. Black, A., Fraser, P., Hoesli, M.: House Prices, Fundamentals and bubbles. Journal of Business Finance & Accounting 33(9&10), 1535–1555 (2006)
7. Xiao, Q., Wang, T.G.: Signal Extraction with Kalman Filter: A study of the Hong Kong property price bubbles. Nanyang Technological University EGC Working Paper Series (2006)
8. Jiang, C.h.: The Empirical Analysis of Speculative Bubbles in China Real Estate Market. Management World 12, 71–84 (2005)
9. Yang, Z.C.: China Real Estate Bubbles Empirical Research Based on SSpace Model. Finance Teaching and Research 2, 41–68 (2010)

The Antecedents and Consequences of Job Satisfaction in China

Ren-Tao Miao[1], Xi-Lin Hou[1], and Daeup Kim[2]

[1] School of Business Administration, University of Science and Technology Liaoning,
Qianshan Zhong Road. 185, 114051 Anshan, China
[2] Department of Business Administration, Gyeongsang National University,
Gajwa-dong. 900, 660701 Jinju, South Korea
{Ren-Tao Miao,mrtmiao}@hotmail.com

Abstract. This study extends social exchange theory to develop a model in Chinese context that positions job satisfaction as a mediator of the relationships between four antecedents and four volitional workplace behaviors. All four classes of antecedents (perceived organizational support (POS), procedural, distributive and interactional justice) except for procedural justice contributed uniquely to the prediction of satisfaction. Job satisfaction is also shown to mediate most antecedent-consequence relationships; although two important exceptions are evident, Such as POS－turnover relationship and procedural justice－consequences relationships. Furthermore, only four direct links from POS to citizenship behaviors directed at individuals, distributive justice to turnover intention, interactional justice to citizenship behaviors directed at organizations and turnover, suggest that job satisfaction does not fully mediate the relationships between POS, distributive justice, interactional justice and volitional workplace behaviors.

Keywords: Job satisfaction, POS, organizational justice, work outcomes, China.

1 Introduction

Decades of research on job satisfaction have resulted in a sound understanding of how both organizational support factors (e.g., POS) and organizational fairness factors (e.g., procedural, distributive, and interactional justice) affect employees' level of job satisfaction and how job satisfaction, in turn, influences a variety of important workplace behaviors. For the most part, job satisfaction is thus positioned either as a determinant of workplace behavior (e.g., an independent variable) or as a desirable outcome in its own right (i.e., a dependent variable). While we recognize the intrinsic value of these two perspectives, we argue in this paper that an additional important role of job satisfaction lies in its role as mediator of the relationships between justices and organizational outcomes. This mediating role is not only a logical extension of the manner in which job satisfaction is positioned within the nomological network, but is also consistent with various theoretical frameworks that focus on the manner in which an individual's actions toward an attitude object (e.g., organization, coworkers,

M. Zhou (Ed.): ISAEBD 2011, Part IV, CCIS 211, pp. 141–147, 2011.
© Springer-Verlag Berlin Heidelberg 2011

supervisors) are informed by the manner in which the attitude object is perceived to have acted toward the individual.

2 Literature Review and Hypothesis

2.1 Job Satisfaction as Mediator

Our position that job satisfaction functions as a mediator within the nomological network has seldom been explicitly articulated in the organizational literature. It has however been implicitly presented in both important theoretical reviews and empirically oriented work. It is also consistent with Social-Exchange Theory, the Norm of Reciprocity, and perceptions of the fairness.

These theories, when applied to the employee-employer relationship, predict that employees respond to perceived favorable working conditions by behaving in ways that benefit the organization and/or other employees (i.e., organizational citizenship behavior, in-role behaviors, and organizational commitment). Equally, employees retaliate against dissatisfying conditions by engaging in harmful behavior (i.e., counterproductive work behavior). In addition, employees may even retaliate against extremely dissatisfying conditions by deciding to quit or by engaging in behavior commensurate with preparations to quit (i.e., turnover intention).

2.2 Antecedents of Job Satisfaction

Hulin and Judge (2003) define job satisfaction as being '…multidimensional psychological responses to one's job. These responses have cognitive (evaluative), affective (emotional), and behavioral components. Job satisfactions refer to internal cognitive and affective states…'. We argue here that these cognitive and affective states can be traced to multiple influences, ranging from factor that is highly proximal to support to employee (i.e., POS) to factors that are the perceptions of fairness (i.e., organizational justice).

Past findings have strongly associated POS with job satisfaction. For instance, POS appears to play an important role in the development and helps to explain the relationship with job satisfaction levels. A strong positive relationship between POS and overall job satisfaction is documented by Eisenberger et al., (1997). And in a meta-analysis, Riggle et al. (2009) examined the significant effect of POS on job satisfaction. Hence, we hypothesize that:

H_1: There is a significant direct and positive effect of POS on job satisfaction.

Davy et al. (1991) found that the higher perceived fairness of layoffs, the higher employees' job satisfaction. Recent initial research gives credence to this proposition finding that organizational justice influences employee's attitudes in sport organizations [1]. Colquitt et al.'s (2001) meta-analysis confirmed that organizational justice is a consistent and strong predictor of job satisfaction. In addition, available literature supports the links between job satisfaction and fair treatment received from the supervisor and coworkers. We hypothesize that:

H₂: There are significant direct and positive effects of organizational justice (a) distributive justice, (b) procedural justice (c) interactional justice on job satisfaction.

2.3   Consequences of Job Satisfaction

Several researchers have concluded that employees who are more satisfied with their jobs are more likely to display OCB [2] [3] and to be satisfied with their lives overall. Employees who are more committed are less likely to plan to leave their jobs or to actually leave. They are less likely to experience stress and are more likely to perform well (Mathieu & Zajac, 1990).

Organ (1988) and Organ and Konovsky (1989) have argued for and provided empirical evidence supporting a relationship between satisfaction and OCB, as did Williams and Anderson (1991) and others (Moorman et al., 1998; Skarlicki & Latham, 1997) have provided preliminary evidence for the differential effects of the extrinsic and intrinsic components of job satisfaction on OCBOs (i.e., generalized compliance) and OCBIs (i.e., altruism), respectively. Therefore, we hypothesize that:

H₃: Job satisfaction has a significant direct and positive effect on OCBs (a) OCBI, (b) OCBO.

Meta-analyses of the relationship between job satisfaction and job performance have reported a wide range of results (i.e., r =.14 to .31) with the recent meta-analysis reporting a relatively strong relationship (r =.30) between job satisfaction and job performance. The most recent study [4] reported a stronger correlation between the two variables of .29 which is consistent with a more recent meta-analysis performed by Judge, Thoresen, Bono, and Patton (2001). Thus, we hypothesize that:

H₄: Job satisfaction has a significant direct and positive effect on job performance.

Yavas and Bodur (1999) and Yousef (2001) found strong association between satisfaction and organizational commitment. Then, a study done by Yousef (2002) on job satisfaction as mediator of the relationship between role stressors and organizational commitment, found that job satisfaction directly and positively influenced affective and normative commitment and negatively influences continuous commitment. Thus, we hypothesize that:

H₅: Job satisfaction has a significant direct and positive effect on organizational commitment.

Using meta-analytic procedures, Hellman (1997) found that the job satisfaction-turnover intent relationship was "significantly different from zero and consistently negative". There is also a substantial body of literature that has reported that job satisfaction is negatively related to turnover intention. Khatri and Fern (2001) and Sarminah (2006) concluded a modest negative correlation between job satisfaction and turnover intentions. Brough and Frame (2004) suggested job satisfaction is a strong predictor of turnover intentions, and Korunka, Hoonakker and Carayon (2005) found a significant negative association between two variables. Therefore, we hypothesize that:

H₆: Job satisfaction has a significant direct and negative effect on turnover intentions.

3 Methodology

3.1 Procedures and Sample

Initially, employees were systematically selected from various SMEs in Qindao of China and then distributed 339 samples to these employees and collected, among which 294 units (86.7 %) were returned. Among of them, 176 units were drawn from paper survey and 118 units were drawn from on-line survey, and 33 units contained multiple missing items and were thus excluded, only 261 valid units were obtained.

3.2 Measures

Job satisfaction. Nine-item scale taken from Spector (1994) measured satisfaction.

Justice. Procedural justice. The Niehoff and Moorman (1993) six-item formal procedures assessment and one question from Moorman (1991) measured procedural justice. *Distributive justice.* Six questions from the six-item distributive justice index by Price and Mueller (2002) and one question from Spector (2002) measured distributive justice. *Interactional justice.* Also taken from the Niehoff and Moorman (1993) scale were seven of nine questions assessing interactional justice.

OCBs. OCBI. The six-item helping consideration directed-at-peers scale from Podsakoff et al. (1990) and Williams and Shiaw (1999) measured employee intentions to enact OCBI. *OCBO.* The seven-item civic virtue scale from Williams and Shiaw (1999) measured employee intentions to enact OCBO.

Job performance. The seven items from Brockner, Tyler, and Cooper-Schneider (1992) and May, Korczynski, and Frenkel (2002) were selected to measure job performance.

Organizational commitment. Measurement of this variable consisted of eight items from the Mowday et al.'s (1979) Organizational Commitment Questionnaire (OCQ).

Turnover intention. Measurement of this variable consisted of six-item by Mobley et al., (1979).

3.3 Analysis

Measurement Model. We performed confirmatory factory analysis to assess the factor structure of the scales employed in this study. Every construct in the measurement model was measured using three indicator variables. The overall goodness-of-fit indices indicated that the fits of the model was acceptable from an empirical aspect.

Structural Model. Following the first step of measurement model testing, the second step of analyzing the structural model was performed. Table 1 listed the test results for the structural models across direct, indirect, and total effects, indicating that the direct path from job satisfaction to procedure justice was not significant. In addition, the fit indices of the model all suggest a good fit with the data.

Table 1. Coefficients of Direct, Indirect, and Total Effects

Variables		JS	OCBI	OCBO	TI	OC	JP
Interactional Justice	DE	.228***					
	IE		.070***	.048**	−.049***	.083***	.049**
	TE	.228***	.070***	.048**	−.049***	.083***	.049**
Distributive Justice	DE	.186**					
	IE		.057**	.040**	−.040**	.068**	.040**
	TE	.186**	.057**	.040**	−.040**	.068**	.040**
Procedural Justice	DE	.083					
	IE		.025	.018	−.018	.030	.018
	TE	.083	.025	.018	−.018	.030	.018
POS	DE	.330***					
	IE		.101***	.070**	−.071***	.121***	.071**
	TE	.330***	.101***	.070**	−.071***	.121***	.071**
Job Satisfaction	DE		.307***	.213**	−.216***	.367***	.215**
	IE						
	TE		.307***	.213**	−.216***	.367***	.215**

Note. $*p < .10$, $**p < .05$, $***p < .01$; β values are standardized regression coefficients with two-tailed significance (PC). DE: direct effects; IE: indirect effects; TE: total effects.

4 Results

The path estimates for the general model illustrate that job satisfaction was related to all two proposed classes (four factors) of antecedents. The paths of POS to job satisfaction was .330 ($p<.01$), indicating that higher levels of perceived organizational support, was associated to with higher levels of job satisfaction. Similarly, the paths of .186 ($p<.05$) between distributive justice and job satisfaction, and .228 ($p<.01$) between interactional justice and job satisfaction indicate that distributive justice has moderate relationships with job satisfaction, and interactional justice has strong relationship with job satisfaction. Interestingly, the path from procedural justice to job satisfaction was non-significant ($\gamma =.083$, *ns.*).

Strong standardized path coefficients were found for the links between job satisfaction and OCBI ($\beta=.307$, $p<.01$), job satisfaction and OCBO ($\beta=.213$, $p<.05$), job satisfaction and job performance ($\beta=.215$, $p<.05$), job satisfaction and organizational commitment ($\beta=.367$, $p<.01$). These findings suggest that high levels of job satisfaction are associated with a slightly greater tendency to engage in OCBs, obtain job performance, and show organizational commitment. A strong link of -.216 ($p<.01$) was found between job satisfaction and turnover intentions, indicating that low levels of job satisfaction are associated with a greater intention to quit.

The results indicate that interactional justice has a significant indirect impact on turnover intention ($\gamma = -.049$, $p < .01$), OCBI ($\gamma = .070$, $p < .01$), organizational commitment ($\gamma = .083$, $p < .01$), OCBO ($\gamma = .048$, $p < .05$), and job performance ($\gamma = .049$, $p < .05$). Distributive justice, also have significant indirect impacts on turnover intentions ($\gamma = -.040$, $p < .05$), OCBI ($\gamma = .057$, $p < .05$), organizational commitment ($\gamma = .068$, $p < .05$), OCBO ($\gamma = .040$, $p < .05$), and job performance ($\gamma = .040$, $p < .05$), respectively. And POS also has significant indirect impacts on turnover intentions ($\gamma = -.071$, $p < .01$), OCBI ($\gamma = .101$, $p < .01$), organizational commitment ($\gamma = .121$, $p < .01$), OCBO ($\gamma = .070$, $p < .05$), and job performance ($\gamma = .071$, $p < .05$), respectively. While same to the non-significant direct effect between procedural justice and job satisfaction, there are non-significant indirect effects between procedural justice and turnover intentions ($\gamma = -.018$, $ns.$), OCBI ($\gamma = .025$, $ns.$), organizational commitment ($\gamma = .030$, $ns.$), OCBO ($\gamma = .018$, $ns.$), and job performance ($\gamma = .018$, $ns.$).

And finally, Table 2 presents the change in Chi-square for all mediation tests as well as the strength of the direct antecedent-consequence path except for procedural justice-consequences links when a direct path is included in the model. A joint consideration of the change in Chi-square statistics and the strength of the direct path suggest that job satisfaction acts as a nearly full mediator of several antecedent-consequence relationships. Results also suggest that job satisfaction only acts as a partial mediator of many of the relationships.

Table 2. $\Delta\chi^2$ Tests of all possible Antecedent-Consequences Relationships

Antecedents	Consequences	$\Delta\chi^2$	Direct path	S. E.	C. R.
Perceived Organizational Support	OCBI	1.225	.080	.070	1.137
	OCBO	7.982	.184***	.065	2.811
	JP	5.786	.181**	.074	2.454
	OC	22.894	.276***	.062	4.443
Distributive justice	OCBI	3.406	.131*	.070	1.864
	OCBO	10.868	.211***	.066	3.191
	JP	22.395	.344***	.074	4.658
	OC	4.544	.128**	.060	2.147
	TI	.304	−.055	.100	-.552
Interactional justice	OCBI	4.070	.169**	.084	2.022
	OCBO	.333	.045	.075	.591
	JP	4.560	.188**	.088	2.146
	OC	8.050	.201***	.072	2.795
	TI	.771	−.105	.119	−.882

Note. *$p < .10$, **$p < .05$, ***$p < .01$; $\Delta d.f. = 390-389 = 1$; Direct path refers to the standardized path coefficient of the direct path between the antecedent and consequence.

5 Discussion

The present study examined job satisfaction as a mediator in the relationships between POS, organizational justice and employee's workplace outcomes. The results make several theoretical and practical implications to our understanding of the job satisfaction within the organization.

First, although prior to this study, there was little clear evidence in the literature job satisfaction as mediator of two (POS and turnover intentions, POS and performance) of the antecedent-consequence relationship, we have shown that the influence of employees' perceptions of organizational support on volitional workplace attitudes and behaviors are largely mediated through job satisfaction. That is an important confirmation of employees' job satisfaction's implicit position within the organization.

In addition, our findings represent an extension of social exchange frameworks in that we have shown that employees' behaviors and attitudes are not only influenced by perceptions of organizational support but also by factors that reflect employees' perceptions of fairness (i.e., distributive and interactional justice). Understanding that there is a relationship between fairness and the satisfaction of employees is a significant step in providing better strategies for instituting fairness throughout the organization. By addressing the perceptions of employees regarding distributive justice, interactional justice and supervision satisfaction, administrators should first re-examine their corporate culture and create conducive organizational norms, because a corporate culture and norms encouraging employees to enhance the well-being and perceptions of work (e.g., organizational support and fairness), then improve employees' work-related satisfaction, and employees further will likely lead to a willingness to show more citizenship behaviors, hard at work, commitment to organization and stay in organization, and ultimately, the organization will likely acquire a series of better work outcomes and achievements.

Second, attempts to improve the job attitudes of employees based on any one of the three approaches (POS, distributive and interactional justice) to job satisfaction are likely to exhibit only limited effectiveness given that job satisfaction is determined by internal factors as well as multiple levels of external variables. It is evident from our results that the conceptual antecedents of job satisfaction do not act in a fully compensatory manner but rather explain unique variance in job satisfaction.

Third, the study was shown us that interactional ties is more likely to be adequate in accounting for job satisfaction in the context of the Chinese social structure. Because the Chinese social structure can be traced back to the five fundamental relationships (*wulun*) emphasized in Confucianism. Yang (1993) suggested about *wulun*: neither government nor political institutions are part of these five fundamental relationships, thus the concepts of organization and related notions of commitment are relatively rare in traditional Chinese society. Instead, traditional Chinese individuals related to people; they related to the emperor, but not to the organization or government, as subjects. The Chinese are expected to relate to an organization through the particular relationships that exist between individuals and their superiors.

References

1. Smucker, M.K., Whisenant, W.A., Pedersen, P.M.: An investigation of job satisfaction and female sports journalists. Sex Roles 49, 401–407 (2003)
2. Miao, R.T., Kim, H.G.: Gender as a moderator of the relationship between organizational citizenship behavior and team effectiveness in China. Asian Social Science 5, 98–108 (2009)
3. Miao, R.T.: Perceived organizational support, job satisfaction, task performance and organizational citizenship behavior in China. Journal of Behavioral and Applied Management 12, 105–127 (2011)
4. Muse, L.A., Stamper, C.L.: Perceived organizational support: evidence for a mediated association with work performance. Journal of Managerial Issues XIX, 517–535 (2007)

Study on the Countermeasures of China-EU Textile Trade Frictions

Min Yao

Shandong Vocational College of Science & Technology, Weifang, Shandong, China
ymbang1999@163.com

Abstract. The textile trade frictions between China and the EU are getting frequent and intense, which makes serious influence on the development of China's textile industry. Textile trade frictions between China and the EU will exist for a long time. This thesis gives some suggestions for China to deal with the frictions. To break through the restrictions, government, trade associations and enterprises in China should cooperate, under the WTO framework to promote multilateral and bilateral trade negotiations, strengthen information communication, implement international standards and improve the core competitive abilities of textile products.

Keywords: Textile trade, Friction, China-EU.

1 Introduction

Since 2004, the European Union has become China's largest trading partner instead of the United States and Japan. However, with trade growth, trade friction has not really stopped, especially the textile trade: Using import quotas to restrict Chinese textile to Europe in MFA and ATC, asking high price in negotiations of China's accession to WTO; anti-dumping on Chinese chemical fibers and shoes; imposing green barriers and restrictions on Chinese textiles during the so-called post-quota era and so on.

Analyzing EU, international economic trends, WTO rules and China-EU textile trade, we find that China-EU textile trade frictions are mainly due to: first, trade protectionism still exists in the EU, which is even severe during economic downturn. The European Union take measures to restrict the import of Chinese textiles and apparel in pursuit of economic and political benefits; Second, globalization of trade friction makes it inevitable in textile trade between China and EU; Third, some terms about exceptions in WTO are a bit fuzzy. They are used as excuses to import restrictions by the EU, which lead to more frictions. Especially the three articles in " PROTOCOL ON THE ACCESSION OF THE PEOPLE'S REPUBLIC OF CHINA" and "REPORT OF THE WORKING PARTY ON THE ACCESSION OF CHINA TABLE OF CONTENTS" which put China's textile exports to a passive position; Finally, China's shortcoming in textile products and export markets also increases the chance of EU-China trade frictions. In this paper we discuss the strategies of China to deal with the frictions under the framework of WTO.

M. Zhou (Ed.): ISAEBD 2011, Part IV, CCIS 211, pp. 148–153, 2011.
© Springer-Verlag Berlin Heidelberg 2011

2 Strategies of Chinese Government

2.1 To Promote Multilateral and Bilateral Negotiations

Since trade protectionism is the source of trade frictions and effective multilateral trade rules can restrain trade protectionism, it is the fundamental way to resolve trade frictions for China. Chinese government should actively participates in multilateral and bilateral trade negotiations to achieve worldwide trade liberalization step by step, and provide a stable favorable international environment for textile and other industries in China.

As a member of WTO, China has many rights in WTO multilateral negotiations, such as amending old rules and developing new rules, as well as adapting the existing rules passively. In this process, China communicates more with developed countries, and coordinate and cooperate with other developing countries. While safeguarding the interests of developing countries, we benefit more from the multilateral trading system, and make it more fair and equitable to promote the development of our national economy. In fact, China acted as an active participant in the Doha Round. In the course of negotiations on many issues, China put forward many proposals on behalf of the interests of developing countries and new members.

China made some tactical concessions in the negotiations of accession to WTO. On the whole, these concessions are worthy and necessary, but they are constraints on Chinese textile trade from the view of dealing with trade frictions, which is one of the main tasks for China in WTO negotiations in the future. That is to perfect the relevant laws and rules of China's accession to WTO. Some WTO members abuse anti-dumping, special safeguard measures and other trade restrictions in the flawed rules on Chinese textile and apparel products. China should learn to bargain in multilateral trade negotiations to avoid the frictions.

There is a good experience in bilateral negotiations between China and the EU. At the beginning of 2005, as ATC terminated, Chinese textiles export increased sharply and the EU imposed more restrictions. China-EU textile trade frictions exploded. After 10 hours of negotiations, China and EU reached an agreement and achieved a win-win situation on June 10. There were three major achievements for China. First, China got a favorable textile export base and a reasonable growth rate. Second, China got a package of arrangements with a low cost. Third, China urged the EU to use "Paragraph 242"of the report of the working party on the accession of China as little as possible, which opened a gap among all the members of WTO. The success of the negotiations offered a stable development environment for China's textile export to the EU, and it is conducive to the healthy development of China's textile industry. It also showed China's large country style in foreign negotiations.

2.2 To Make Full Use of the WTO Dispute Settlement Mechanism

The WTO dispute settlement system is a effective way for its members to solve trade frictions and safeguard their own rights. During the 16 years of WTO, both developed and developing countries have repeatedly proposed complaints to the dispute settlement mechanism, or complained by other WTO members. Most disputes got satisfactory results. From the practice of WTO disputes settlement, developing countries involved have been protected both as the complaint and as the respondent in trade disputes. China succeeded in some cases, such as the case of US Steel Safeguard Measures in 2002, but comparing with other developing countries, including Brazil, India and Mexico, China doesn't make full use of the Dispute Settlement Mechanism as a WTO member. In the face of the increasingly frequent international trade frictions, we must change ideas, fully understand WTO rules, use the WTO dispute settlement mechanism to solve trade frictions, and safeguard our legitimate interests. If the other members break or abuse WTO rules, damage our interest, we should dare to resort to the dispute settlement mechanism for our interests. On the other hand, we should also dare to deal with the deputes against us, and carry out effective defences.

3 The Roles of Industry Associations and Chambers of Commerce

Governments, enterprises and Industry associations, chambers of commerce and other non-governmental organizations are known as the "Three Pillars of Modern Society." A developed system of Industry associations is part of a mutual market economy system, an important part. With the deepening of reform, the government will gradually weaken its intervention or guidance to companies. And the roles of trade associations or chambers of commerce will be enhanced. In China, many textile enterprises are medium or small-sized. Many of them lack of experience in overseas markets and they know little of international practice, formulation and legislative procedure of international product standards. Industry associations are between the government and enterprises, and they are relatively independent and impartial. They have advantage on the relevant legal procedures and information acquisition. So it becomes a top priority to strengthen the construction of industry associations and chambers of commerce and make it a representative of the interests of enterprises.

3.1 To Make Full Use of the Its Role of Bridge

Trade association is one of the social organizations between governments, enterprises and individuals. The role as a link is its primary function. Under conditions of a market economy, the social division is getting more and more detailed, social and economic relations are getting increasingly complex, diverse. Therefore, it is more and more important for the market participants to communicate, coordinate and supervise. The role of industry associations is more prominent.

Based on investigations and researches, industry associations can put forward some suggestions on economic and social development policies and legislation. They participate in the research and establishment of relevant laws, the macroeconomic regulation and industrial policies. They can also reflect demands of industries and enterprises to the government and safeguard their legal rights.

3.2 To Strengthen Industry Self-regulation

Industry associations provide convenience for the enterprises to be early warned and to break all kinds of restrictions and technical barriers, to deal with anti-dumping and expand exports. EU anti-dumping is one of the main frictions between China and EU in textile trade. Enterprises can avoid facing EU anti-dumping, if Industry associations establish effective anti-dumping early warning mechanism. Through the early warning mechanisms, they can grasp the number, prices and distribution of export products, learn about the prices of similar products in the importing country and the situation of EU anti-dumping. When we get all these information, we can avoid or reduce the EU's anti-dumping on China. Industry associations should prevent the enterprises from cutting prices for market share, if necessary, they can make a minimum price to guard against malicious acts of unfair competition. The establishment of such a warning system can maintain a normal new order of international trade and reduce trade frictions.

3.3 To Fulfill the Tenet of Serving Enterprises Practically

Industry associations can carry out industry statistics to get hold of industry development trends at home and abroad, collect and release information of this industry, provide consulting service on statutes, policies, technology, management, marketing and so on for enterprises. They can also take investigations about anti-dumping anti-subsidy and safeguard measures, bring lawsuit or respond to lawsuit, so they provide effectively help to enterprises in trade frictions.

3.4 To Help Enterprises Exploit the Target Market

Industry association can grasp the new trends of industrial international standard and advanced company standard in EU in time, and adjust company standard according to the tendency of demand of international market, which plays a very important role for China's enterprises to exploit market in EU and change the passive position in the international trade war occured while contending for markets.

4 The Choices of Enterprises

4.1 To Pay More Attentions to International Standards of Textiles and Garments

Since the international standards of textiles and garments are numerous and complicated, it is a fundamental approach for enterprises to evade trade barriers to apply for international certification and certification by the target countries. Enterprises must strengthen the collection and research on technical regulations, standards, inspection and certification system of other countries and international organizations, then absorb the contents related to the exporting commodities and add to their own product standards. If the products are organized strictly based on the standards, they surely have the ability to break the technical barriers. Enterprises should increase investment of manual labor, material resources and financial resources in the progress of standard collecting, analyzing, researching, standards setting, equipment updating, and manufacturing, and get the international market permit as soon as possible.

4.2 To Adjust Composition of Export Commodity

It is one of the main causes of trade frictions between China and EU That China has continued textile trade surplus over EU. While such surplus is mainly accumulation of export quantity, China do not have much margin actually. This is because that textiles and garments exported from China are labor-intensive products.

When the percentage of production factors is different in the manufacturing process of textiles, this industry manifests different characteristics of different elements. Today, the pattern of international division of labor is: that developed countries have advanced textile production equipments, master advanced productive forces. So textile industry manifests capital and technology intensive performance characteristics there, and EU is one of the typical representatives. While many developing countries, including China, mainly undertake the textile production and processing sector, and their textile industries manifest labor-intensive performance characteristics.

Profit of textiles and garments industry chain shows a "V" character pattern, the Smiling Curve.

Added value

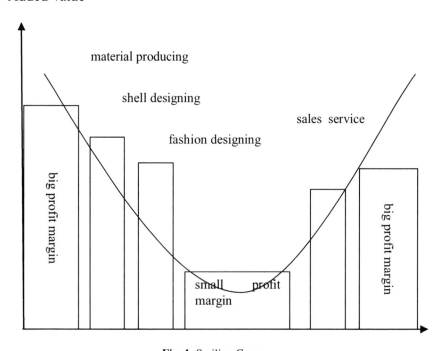

Fig. 1. Smiling Curve

The added value of products is high in upstream of the product designing and in downstream of brand operating and sales promoting, while in the middle, processing part is low-tech and has small profit margin because it is labor-intensive. Furthermore, with the popularization of textile technology and the standardization development of textile machinery, more and more developing countries will participate in this area, and the aggravation of competition would further compress the profit space of this intermediate sector. And at present, Chinese textile and garment industry is most lacking of the improvement technology of raw material and the development ability of new materials. In high-end clothing, domestic shell fabrics still cannot replace imported shell fabric, which seriously affected the development of China's garment industry, besides, China's garment industry is also relatively backward in brand operating and international network marketing. After Special Safeguard Measures on Chinese Textile expire, EU will take more anti-dumping measures. If Chinese enterprises don't pay enough attention to the situation that they export labour- intensive textiles and garments at low prices in large quantity, China will inevitably become the anti-dumping worst-hit area.

Consequently, in the process of changing from textile country to textile leading power, China must face and follow the development trend. We should not only keep the production and export of traditional staple textiles but also accelerate increasing the products' technological content and added value.

5 Conclusion

As the largest textile and garment market in the world, the Europe Union is the largest trading partner of China, and China is the largest supplier of textile to the EU. On the whole, in the process of global textile trade liberalization, textile trade is increasing between China and the EU. However, in recent years the EU frequently use quota, anti-dumping, green barriers and other measures to interdict Chinese textiles. EU's trade protection measures and restrictions have an adverse effect on Chinese textile imports and exports. Therefore, studying how to deal with these trade frictions has an important practical significance for textile and garment enterprises in China. To break through the restrictions, government, trade associations and enterprises in China should cooperate, under the WTO framework to promote multilateral and bilateral trade negotiations, strengthen information communication, implement international standards and improve the core competitive abilities of textile products.

References

1. Leamer, E., Levinsohn, J.: International Trade Theory: the Evidence, NBER Working Paper No.4940 (1994)
2. Guell, R.C.: Issues in Economics Today. Wuhan University Press, Wuhan (2007)
3. Gao, C.: Modern Textile Economy and Textile Trade. China Textile Press (2008)
4. Information on, http://www.wto.org
5. Yao, M.: Strategy of Chinese Textile and Garment for New International Trade Berries. Journal of Market Forum (04) (2006)
6. Information on, http://www.ctei.gov.cn/

The Dimensions of Romanian Consumers' Interest in Adopting High-Tech Products

Lavinia Dovleac, Marius Balasescu, Simona Balasescu, and Carmen Anton

Transilvania University of Brasov, str. Colinei, nr.1, Building A, Brasov, Romania
dovleaclavinia@yahoo.co.uk, marbalasescu@yahoo.com,
simona_balasescu@yahoo.com, anton_carmen@yahoo.com,

Abstract. This paper is based on a quantitative marketing research conducted in Romania in 2010 about the attitude of consumers from Brasov city regarding the acquisition of high technology products for personal consumption. High-tech products industry is in a continuous process of development and the pace of developing new products in this area is very rapid. But it raises the issue of the extent to which these products are accepted by the market. This paper aims to explore using a multivariate method, the main factors that define the current behavior of consumers across the high-tech products.

Keywords: high-tech products, consumer behavior, marketing research, factor analysis.

1 Introduction

High technology products have complex features that determine the consumers to look with suspicion when they are launched on the market. Buying a high-tech products involve different risks: financial risk, risk related to the satisfaction offered, the risk related to the understanding of functioning, etc. Such a product has to convince consumers of the benefits it provides, so they can adopt it and use it constantly. The main purpose of this paper is to present some of the results of a marketing research on the acquisition of high-tech products by Romanian consumers. These results will be processed in a factor analysis, based on theoretical and methodological considerations from works of marketing specialists.

In the first part of the paper it will be defined the concept of high technology product and will be briefly presented the main features of this type of product.

2 Characteristics of High-Tech Products

The concept of "high technology" refers to an industry that produce technology or technology-intensive industry. One of the definitions (given in 1982 in the United States Congress) characterizes high-tech industry as "the industry involved in creating, developing and introducing new products and/or innovative manufacturing processes through the systematic application of scientific and technical knowledge."

M. Zhou (Ed.): ISAEBD 2011, Part IV, CCIS 211, pp. 154–160, 2011.
© Springer-Verlag Berlin Heidelberg 2011

The "high-tech product" is defined rather by the perception that consumers have about it, perception which is guided by several concepts [1]: The product is not yet well understood or easily accepted as a solution to a particular problem; there is no certainty about how this product will solve a problem; the resources required to develop this product is provided by highly qualified specialists; the company producing these products has a technological orientation.

Similarly, the high-tech product is an innovation in the field, referring to a new product that aims to provide value both for the producer and consumer and to solve a series of problems.

High tech industry includes industries like: information technology, hardware components (physical), software, telecommunications and Internet infrastructure and consumer electronic products such as audio or video products, entertainment products or games, etc. [2]

The defining characteristics of high-tech products are: a shortened product life cycle, high risk in respect of changes in user behavior, indispensability of infrastructure, lack of clearly defined industry standards, uncertainty regarding the functionality of the product. [3]

3 Theoretical Considerations on Principal Components Analysis

Multivariate statistical methods allow the researcher to consider the effects of more than one variable at the same time. [4]

The goal of interdependence methods of analysis is to give meaning to a set of variables. N. Malhotra defines factor analysis as a general name denoting a class of procedures primarily used for data reduction and summarization. Relationships among sets of many interrelated variables are examined and represented in terms of a few underlying factors. These factors are new, more abstract variables created by combining the basic structure of a domain and a substantive interpretation to the underlying dimensions.

There are two approaches to locating underlying dimensions of a data set: factor analysis and principal components analysis. These techniques differ in the communalities estimates that are used. Principal Components Analysis is concerned with establishing which linear components exist within the data and how a particular variable might contribute to that component. [5] This method is recommended when the primary concern is to determine the minimum number of factors that will account for maximum variance in the data for use in the subsequent multivariate analysis. The factors are called "principal components".

There are several ways to determine the number of factors to extract: Prori Determination; Determination Based on Eigenvalues; Determination based on Scree Plot; Determination Based on the Percentage of Variance; Determination Based on Split-Half Reliability; Determination Based on Significance Tests. [6]

The steps involved in conducting factor analysis are: formulate the problem, construct the correlation matrix, determine the method of factor analysis, determine the number of factors, rotate the factors, interpret the factors.

Statistics associated with factor analysis:

Bartlett's test of sphericity is a test statistic used to examine the hypothesis that the variables are uncorrelated in the population. *Correlation Matrix* shows the simple correlations, r, between all possible pairs of variables included in the analysis. *Communality* is the amount of variance a variable shares with all the other variables being considered. This is also the proportion of variance explained by the common factors. *Eigenvalue* represent the total variance explained by each factor. *Factor loadings* are simple correlations between the variables and the factors. *Factor matrix* contains the factor loadings of all the variables on all the factors extracted. *Factor scores* are composite scores estimated for each respondent on the derived factors. *Kaiser-Meyer-Olkin (KMO) measure of sampling adequacy* – is an index used to examine the appropriateness of factor analysis; high values (between 0.5 and 1.0) indicate factor analysis is appropriate.

4   Methodological Considerations on the Conducted Marketing Research

The theme of the quantitative marketing research is "Attitudes, opinions and behaviors of people in Brasov on the purchase of high technology products for household consumption"

The research has been conducted on a sample survey which aimed to know the buying behavior of people in Brasov regarding the high-tech products. The investigation was based on a questionnaire consisting of 49 questions. The process of data collection was carried out between September 1st to October 15th, 2010. The population considered in this research consists of all persons aged 15 years residing in the city of Brasov. The sampling method is a combination of group sampling and systematic sampling. The main objectives related to research theme are: Identifying the types of high technology products held in Brasov households, determining the reasons for purchasing high-tech products and determining if economic crisis will influence the purchase decision of high-tech products in the future.

The data processing involved both an univariate analysis and a bivariate analysis to capture the respondents' points of view about many issues related to high technology products. But we considered that analysis should be deepened in order to clarify what is actually the general attitude of consumers towards the products of high technology. For this we used a multivariable analysis method: principal components analysis.

5   Principal Components Analysis. Application

The variables considered for this analysis are: the importance of owning high-tech products in the household; the opinion about the fact that high-tech products are hard to use; the necessity of a demonstration about using the high-tech product; the degree of satisfaction regarding the information received from the specialized staff from the sale point; the measure of contribution of high-tech products to a better living; the permanent interest for high-tech products; the reasons of considering the owners of high-tech products as having a superior status; the opinion about the danger represented by high-tech products.

The value of KMO Measure of Sampling Adequacy is 0,72 , a bigger value than 0,5, which indicates that the factor analysis in appropriate.

Bartlett's measure tests the null hypothesis that the original correlation matrix is an identity matrix. A significant test tells us that R-matrix is not an identity matrix. From our case results that Bartlett's test is highly significant (Sig. =.000), so there are some relationships between the variables we could include in the analysis. This means that the factor analysis is once again appropriate.

Factor extraction
Table 1 includes the communalities before and after extraction. Principal Components Analysis works on the initial assumption that all variance is common, so, before extractions communalities are all 1. After extraction (in the second column) we can state that 74,9% of the variance associated to the question "the importance of owning high-tech products in the household" is common variance.

Table 1. The values for communalities before and after the extraction process

Communalities

	Initial	Extraction
the importance of owning high-tech products in the household;	1,000	,749
the opinion about hte fact that high-tech products are hard to use	1,000	,574
the necessity of a demonstration about using the high-tech product;	1,000	,721
the degree of satisfaction regarding the information received from the specialised staff from the sale point;	1,000	,478
the measure of contribution of high-tech products to a better living;	1,000	,742
the permanent interest for high-tech products;	1,000	,679
the reasons of considering the owners of high-tech products as having a superior status;	1,000	,489
the opinion about the danger represented by high-tech products	1,000	,496

Extraction Method: Principal Component Analysis.

The following table show the eigenvalues associated with each linear component (factor) before extraction, after extraction and after rotation.

The eigenvalues associated with each factor represent the variance explained by that particular linear component. So, factor 1 explains 41,28% of total variance and the second factor explains 20,31% of total variance). The two factors explain together 61,60% of variance. The information contained by the last factors is very small by comparison with the first two factors. [7]

After the rotation of factors, the variances explained by the first and the second factors doesn't change substantially. [8] The Component Matrix contains the coefficients used to express the standardized variables in terms of the factors.

Table 2. The eigenvalues for each variable and the percent of variance explained by each factor

Total Variance Explained

Comp onent	Initial Eigenvalues			Extraction Sums of Squared Loadings			Rotation Sums of Squared Loadings		
	Total	% of Variance	Cumulative %	Total	% of Variance	Cumulative %	Total	% of Variance	Cumulative %
1	3,303	41,287	41,287	3,303	41,287	41,287	3,284	41,045	41,045
2	1,625	20,314	61,601	1,625	20,314	61,601	1,645	20,556	61,601
3	,877	10,968	72,569						
4	,741	9,258	81,827						
5	,538	6,721	88,548						
6	,411	5,132	93,680						
7	,335	4,183	97,864						
8	,171	2,136	100,000						

Extraction Method: Principal Component Analysis.

There are three variables loading on the first factor and two variables loading on the second factor. So, for the first factor we have: the importance of owning high-tech products in the household; the measure of contribution of high-tech products to a better living; the degree of satisfaction regarding the information received from the specialized staff from the sale point. For the second factor we have: the reasons of considering the owners of high-tech products as having a superior status; the necessity of a demonstration about using the high-tech product.

The results changes if we rotate the factors using Quartimax: there are 3 variables loading on the first factor and 3 variables loading on the second factor.

Interpretation of factors
We identified the variables that have large loadings on the same factor. We named the factors as follows:

Factor 1 "Positive and open attitude regarding the adoption of high-tech products in daily consumption" explains 41,28% of total varance. The variables loading on this factor are: the importance of owning high-tech products in the hosehold; the measure of contribution of high-tech products to a better living; the permanent interest for high-tech products.

Factor 2 "Suspicious and reserved attitude regarding the adoption of high-tech products in daily consumption" explains 20,31% of total variance. The variables loading on this factor are: the necessity of a demonstration about using the high-tech product; the reasons of considering the owners of high-tech products as having a superior status; the opinion about the danger represented by high-tech products.

Together, the two factors explain 61,60% of total variance. These two factors are those common and latent elements which stay at the basis of variables intercorrelation. [9]

Next figure is a graphic representation of the two factors in the rotated space. It shows the same results: the variables at the end of the axis are those that have high loadings on only that factor.

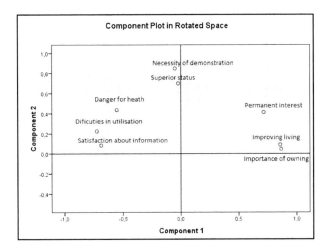

Fig. 1. The disposal of variables in the rotated space

5 Conclusions

The purpose of high-tech manufacturers is to create new products which could be more easily adopted by consumers. The adoption process involves a recognition of the benefits they offer. In general, high-tech products have an elegant and sophisticated design, they are made of materials that pollute as little as possible, they have relatively high price at launch. Consumers are increasingly interested in these products which could help them doing better and rapidly domestic tasks, or help them solve work's problems, or they are simply a way of entertainment. But consumer preferences for high-tech products are influenced by characteristics such as age, education level, current occupation, income level, etc. Consumer views across issues that concern high-tech products can be explained by performing univariate and bivariate analysis.

But a holistic attitude can be analyzed using Principal Components Analysis. The two main factors (principal components) identified for the model developed in this paper have been named: Factor 1 - *Positive and open attitude regarding the adoption of high-tech products in the daily consumption* and Factor 2 - *Suspicious and reserved attitude regarding the adoption of high-tech products in daily consumption*. Open and positive attitude is given by the big importance that consumers attach to owning high-tech products in the household and by the perception of high technology products as elements that contribute substantially to improving the living. Reserved attitude of consumers is given by the necessity of a demonstration of how high-tech products work and by the fact that people who own high-tech products have a superior status in the community.

These views represent an impediment to the adoption of high technology products by consumers. Manufacturers and retailers have to defeat the consumer fear over high-tech products, they must pay more attention about the launching new products, so customers don't feel confused and disoriented. Dealers must give consumers the opportunity to test new products, they have to assist them and give them advice. Also, producers must properly position the high-tech products in the market. Only luxury high tech products must be seen by consumers as superior products that address only to a segment of consumers with high incomes, with a certain social status or a certain level of education. Otherwise, every consumer must believe he is entitled to want, to buy and use high technology products which meet his needs.

Acknowledgments. For the first author, this paper is supported by the Sectoral Operational Programme Human Resources Development (SOP HRD), financed from the European Social Fund and by the Romanian Government under the contract number POSDRU/6/1.5/S/6.

References

1. Hyde, R.: Key Issues in High-Tech Marketing,
   `http://www.3rdperspective.com/documents/`
   `KeyIssuesHighTechMarketing.doc`
2. Mohr, J., Sengupta, S., Slater, S.: Marketing of High Technology Products and Innovations, 3rd edn. Prentice Hall, Englewood Cliffs (2010)
3. Sahadev, S., Jayachandran, S.: Managing the distribution channels for high-technology products. European Journal of Marketing 38(1/2), 121–149 (2004)
4. Zikmund, W.K.: Exploring Marketing Research, 5th edn. The Dryden Press (1994)
5. Field, A.: Discovering Statistics Using SPSS, 2nd edn. SAGE Publications, Thousand Oaks (2005)
6. Malhotra, N.K.: Marketing Research. An Apllied Orientation, 4th edn. Prentice Hall, Englewood Cliffs (2004)
7. Petcu, N.: Statistica. Teorie si aplicatii in SPSS. Infomarket. Brasov (2003)
8. Constantin, C.: Sisteme Informatice de Marketing. Aplicatii in SPSS. Infomarket, Brasov (2006)
9. Lefter, C.: Cercetarea de marketing. Teorie si aplicatii. Infomarket, Brasov (2004)

The Research of Facility Management Based on Organization Strategy Perspective

Xing Gao and Ji-ming Cao

School of Economics and Management, Tongji University,
Shanghai, China
gx2005@sina.com

Abstract. Owing to diversification of Facility Management roles and responsi-bilities, Facility Management industry is facing a serious identity crisis. Based on organization strategy perspective, a conception frame model was conceived from strategic facility planning, space management & service outsourcing, and management audit. The purpose of the paper is to help people recognize the es-sence and core value of facility management. At the same time, the paper is helpful to research facility management theory knowledge.

Keywords: Facility Management, strategic facility planning, space manage-ment, service outsourcing, management audit.

1 Introduction

Facility Management (FM) is a profession that encompasses multiple disciplines to ensure functionality of the built environment by integrating people, place, process and technology [1]. Simultaneously, FM is also a process by which an organization inte-grates its people, work process and physical assets to serve its strategic objectives [2].

In the past several decades, FM has been a professional integrated approach to assist a lot of business organizations, educational institutions and government departments in managing property facilities effectively and providing a high degree of support services. However, with rapid development of this profession, FM is suffering from an acute identity crisis. Nutt [3] pointed out that FM operates in "an ever widening and ill-defined sphere of activity". For example, Chotipanich [4] provided a diversified scope of FM services, which is composed of nine groups and 61 services. The diversification of FM services has severely impeded the recognition of the essence and core value in FM. Nutt [5] contended that the lack of a unique knowledge base is the cause of the identity crisis. Based on organization strategy perspective, a conception frame model was conceived to help people recognize the essence and core value of FM. At the same time, the paper is helpful to research facility management theory knowledge.

2 Literature Review

So far, the definition of FM has not reached a consensus. A lot of scholars and indus-try associations proposed respective definitions to illustrate FM's goals and scopes, as shown Table 1[6] and Table 2.

M. Zhou (Ed.): ISAEBD 2011, Part IV, CCIS 211, pp. 161–167, 2011.

Table 1. FM definition from scholar

scholar	the definition of FM
Becker	FM is responsible for coordinating all efforts related to planning, designing and managing buildings and their systems, equipment and furniture to enhance the organization's ability to compete successfully in a rapidly changing world.
Nourse	FM unit is seldom aware of the overall corporate strategic planning, and does not have a bottom-line emphasis.
NHS Estates	The practice of coordinating the physical workplace with the people and work of an organization; integrates the principles of business administration, architecture, and the behavioral and engineering science.
Alexander	The scope of the discipline covers all aspects of property, space, environmental control, health and safety, and support services.
Then	The practice of FM is concerned with the delivery of the enabling workplace environment—the optimum functional space that supports the business processes and human management.
Hinks and MeNay	…common interpretations of the FM remit: maintenance management; space management and accommodation standards; project management for new-build and alterations; the general premises management of the building stock; and the administration of associated support services.
Varcoe	…a focus on the management and delivery of the business "outputs" of both these entities [the real estate and construction industry]; namely the productive use of building assets as workplaces.
Nutt	The primary function of FM is resource management, at strategic and operational levels of support. Generic types of resource management central to the FM function are the management of financial resources, physical resources, human resources, and the management of resource of information and knowledge.
Linda Tay and Joseph T. L. Ooi	FM is the integrated management of the workplace to enhance the performance of the organization.

Table 2. FM definition from industry association

Industry association	the definition of FM
International Facility Management Association	Facility management is a profession that encompasses multiple disciplines to ensure functionality of the built environment by integrating people, place, process and technology [1].
British institute of Facility Management	Facilities management is the integration of processes within an organization to maintain and develop the agreed services which support and improve the effectiveness of its primary activities [7].
German facility management association	FM is a management discipline which fulfils people's basic requirements at work, supports companies' primary processes and increases return on capital by economic use of facilities and services within the framework of planned, managed and controlled facility processes [8].

Table 2. *(continued)*

Facility Management Association of Australia	Facilities can be generally defined as buildings, properties and major infrastructure, also referred to within the Facility Management industry as the "built environment". The primary function of FM is to manage and maintain the efficient operation of this "built environment"[9].
Japan Facility Management Promotion Association	FM is a comprehensive management approach for the optimization of the ownership, utilization, operation, and maintenance of the business real properties (land, buildings, structures, equipment, etc.) and maintain them in optimal conditions (minimum costs & maximum effects), so that they could contribute to the overall management of the business [10].

From Table 1 and Table 2, FM has many various definitions. In fact, there are considerable differences in responsibilities among different facility managers, so that many facility managers are confused with their responsibilities in organizations. However, in other traditional disciplines in construction and real estate industry, such as architecture, project management and town planning, the confusion was rarely.

Nutt [11] raised the concern on the knowledge deficiency of FM: "FM continues to be reliant on borrowed management concepts on one hand, and on the results of building performance research on the other." Grimshaw[12], on the other hand, argued that FM is to manage the changes that are taking place in the relationship between organizations, their employees and their facilities. Nutt [5] reconciled Grimshaw's strategic approach and re-engineered FM as a "resource management at strategic and operational levels of support."Nutt reiterated the lack of "a distinctive knowledge-base in FM to underpin best practice, to advance the field, and to bridge the gap between its promise and performance."Price [13] also attributed the fad-decay of FM to the over-diversification of the meaning of FM. McLennan [14] posited that "the lack of conceptual management framework is the reason why FM remains misunderstood in the general business sector."Chotipanich [15] reviewed comprehensively on models which link FM to the core business of the organization at the strategic level.

More evidences have indicated that FM must have its own distinctive knowledge-base and a unique identity in contrast with that of building professionals, if it is going to sustain and evolve [16].

3   Facility Management Based on Organization Strategy Perspective

The fundamental purpose of FM is support organization strategy and core business to enhance organization's economic benefits and core competence. Therefore, FM should be guided according to organization strategy and FM strategy is part of organization overall strategy. Figure 1 shows the position of FM strategy in organization strategy frame.

Under the guidance of organization strategy, FM will possess functions of integrating organization resources. Without the guidance of organization strategy, facilities managers will have great difficulty in recognizing the essence and core value in FM from the diversification of FM services. Based on organization strategy perspective, a conception frame model was conceived from strategic facility planning, space management & service outsourcing, and management audit. The three aspects composed a strategic circulation process. Figure 2 shows the FM strategic circulation model.

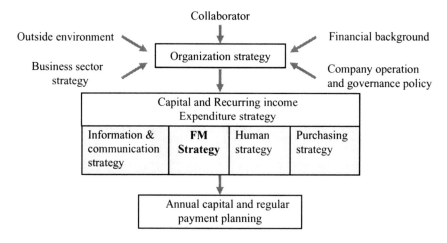

Fig. 1. The position of FM in organization strategy

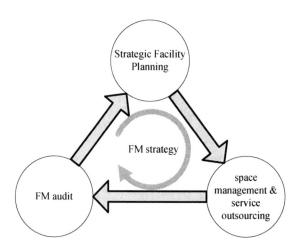

Fig. 2. FM strategic circulation model

3.1 FM Strategy Establishment---Strategic Facility Planning

International Facility Management Association (IFMA) defines the strategic facility plan: "A strategic facility plan (SFP) is defined as a two-to-five year facilities plan encompassing an entire portfolio of owned and/or leased space that sets strategic facility goals based on the organization's strategic (business) objectives. The strategic facilities goals, in turn, determine short-term tactical plans, including prioritization of, and funding for, annual facility related projects."[17]

The SFP identifies the type, quantity and location of spaces required to fully support the organization's business initiatives and should be framed within the organization's vision. The SFP includes three primary components: (1)an understanding of the organization's culture and core values and an analysis of how existing and new facilities must manifest that culture and core values within the physical space or support their change; (2)an in-depth analysis of existing facilities—including location, capability, utilization and condition; (3)an achievable and affordable (approved) plan that translates the goals of the business plan into an appropriate facility response.

Once the organization's business plan has been established, and a clear understanding of assets and capabilities has been gathered, it is possible to identify which strategic business goals require a facility response.

3.2 Strategy Execution—Space Management and Service Outsourcing

(1) Space management is the main content of facility strategy execution.

From the aspect of facilities strategy demands, the essence of FM is to provide a well-operating space environment. The facilities demand of core business is to require a well-operating space environment, rather than a sort of facilities or some facilities. Therefore, facilities managers shouldn't only concern physical space, more aspects should be considered, such as hardware, software, human resources, business process, etc. Facilities managers must comprehensively consider various factors to achieve the strategy goal of FM.

Based on strategy perspective, the connotation and extension of space management have been greatly expanded. Space management is not limited to allocation and use of physical space and facilities managers must recognize space management from Life Cycle Costing (LCC) of FM, including demand analysis, planning, design, budget, building/lease, operation & maintenance, reforming, valuation and disposition. This change of understanding is helpful to form common FM knowledge system and avoid the difference of understanding among different organizations and different facilities.

(2) Service Outsourcing is an important means of facility strategy execution.

Outsourcing is a sort of management model, by which organizations can integrate and utilize outer excellent professional resources to acquire the goals of reducing costs, improving efficiency, making full use of core competitiveness and enhancing rapid response ability to the environment.

Service Outsourcing is an important means of facility strategy execution. The outsourcing of FM is that facilities managers transfer some non-core support services to outer organization and utilize outer excellent professional resources to get acquire the goals of reducing costs, improving facilities service quality, enhancing rapid response ability to organization strategy and providing sufficient support for organization strategy development.

With the rapid development of FM, the scope of FM outsourcing is increasingly expanded. Figure 3 shows the change of FM outsourcing scope.

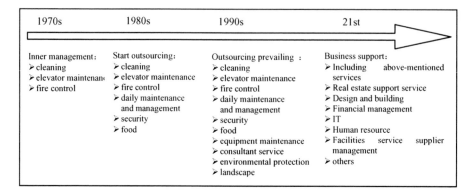

Fig. 3. The change of FM Outsourcing scope

3.3 Strategy Assessment—FM Audit

A facility management audit follows an orderly, objective process to compare an organization's FM resources – staffing, services, physical facilities, and financial performance– to internal expectations and external benchmarks. Facility audit can help organization identify the condition of property operating, find the deficiency of FM and establish future facility management plan. So facility management audit has vital strategic significance.

The objects of FM audit mainly include construction facilities, energy, environment, business process, etc. According to the audit content, facility management audit may be divided into two categories: professional audit and comprehensive audit.

(1) Professional system audit

Professional system audit mainly investigates a sort of facilities system, which includes air-conditioning/ electrical system audit, space audit, energy audit, etc. The common means include interview, questionnaire, photo/Video Recorder, Physical measurement, etc. Professional system audit may last several months and the time it takes will depend on the quantity of auditor and the client's organization size.

(2) Comprehensive audit

Comprehensive audit is more overall audit model, which poses some distinctive features including the longest time, the most thorough investigation, and the Maximum expense. Comprehensive audit will overall investigate hardware facilities, financial management, project management, management process, quality assurance system, etc. It will last several months or one year, even longer. The conclusion and suggestion from comprehensive audit have a long term strategic value. The goal of comprehensive audit is not only to improve some available problems, but also to assess organization facilities service performance level and provide decision support for future facilities management planning.

4 Conclusion

FM is an emerging profession and its development is very rapid. The theoretical research is far behind practice demand, which caused the difference of recognition and misunderstanding. In the paper, a conception frame model was conceived from strategy perspective. It is helpful to recognize the essence of facilities management and to enriching facilities management theory knowledge.

Acknowledgments. The authors are grateful to the editor and anonymous reviewers for the comprehensive reviews and constructive comments.

References

1. IFMA, What is FM?, http://www.ifma.org/what_is_fm/index.cfm
2. HKIFM, What is FM?, http://www.hkifm.org.hk/public_html/about.html/underline
3. Nutt, B.: Linking FM practice and research. Facilities 17(1/2), 11–17 (1999)
4. Chotipanich, S.: Positioning facility management. Facilities 22(13/14), 364–372 (2004)
5. Nutt, B.: Four competing futures for facility management. Facilities 18(3/4), 124–132 (2000)
6. Tay, L., Ooi, J.T.: Facilities management:a jack of all trades. Facilities 19(10), 357–362 (2001)
7. British institute of Facility Management, Facility Management introduction, http://www.bifm.org.uk/bifm/about/facilities
8. German facility management association, Definition facility management, http://www.gefma.de/definition.html
9. Facility Management Association of Australia, What is Facility management?, http://www.fma.com.au/cms/index.php
10. Japan Facility Management Promotion Association, What is FM?, http://www.jfma.or.jp/en/
11. Nutt, B.: Moving targets. Facilities Management World (11), 25–28 (1998)
12. Grimshaw, B.: Facilities management: the wider implications of managing change. Facilities 17(1/2), 24–30 (1999)
13. Price, I.: Can FM evolve? If not, what future? Journal of Facilities Management 1(1), 56–69 (2002)
14. McLennan, P.: Service operations management as a conceptual framework for facility management. Facilities 22(13/14), 344–348 (2004)
15. Chotipanich, S.: Positioning facility management. Facilities 22(13/14), 364–372 (2004)
16. Yiu, C.Y.: A conceptual link among facilities management, strategic management and project management. Facilities 26(13/14), 501–511 (2008)
17. IFMA, Strategic Facility Planning: A White Paper on Strategic Facility Planning (2009)

On the Longevity Risk in the Annuity Market: Some Mathematical Models

Iulian Mircea[1] and Mihaela Covrig[2]

The Bucharest Academy of Economic Studies,
[1] Department of Mathematics, [2] Department of Statistics and Econometrics,
Piata Romana, 6, 010374 Bucharest, Romania
{iulian.mircea,mihaela.covrig}@csie.ase.ro

Abstract. The insurance industry is facing some specific challenges related to longevity risk. More and more capital has to be constituted to face this long-term risk, and new regulations in Europe, together with the recent financial crisis only amplify this phenomenon. Hence, it has become more important for insurance companies and pension funds to find a suitable and efficient way to cross-hedge or to transfer part of the longevity risk to reinsurers or to financial markets. In this study, we analyze some models of mortality rates and pricing the longevity risk. We make some remarks regarding forecasting mortality rates using the Lee-Carter model and our own developed model. Also, we deal with the securitization of longevity risk through the longevity bonds (the straight bonds), the interest being split between the annuity provider and the investors depending on the realized mortality at each future time, by a Special Purpose Company (SPC).

Keywords: stochastic mortality model, Lee-Carter model, longevity risk, longevity bonds (straight bonds).

1 Introduction

One of the largest sources of risk faced by life insurance companies and pension funds is the longevity risk: the risk that members of some reference population might live longer on average than anticipated, affecting their pricing and reserving calculations. The risk of outliving one's savings or other financial resources to cover expenses during retirement could also be understood as some sort of individual longevity risk. However, the term aggregate longevity risk has been used rather to refer to the additional uncertainty about changes in the underlying patterns, and this particular risk can be considered a major concern for insurers.

Nevertheless, this risk should be carefully considered also when dealing with insurance covers, especially within the area of health insurance. In particular, the longevity risk affects sickness benefits for the elderly (for example, post-retirement sickness benefits) and long-term care (LTC) annuities. A moving scenario, in which both future mortality and future senescent disability are random, constitutes the appropriate context for pricing and reserving for LTC products. Reinsurance policies and capital allocation can provide appropriate tools to face this risk.

M. Zhou (Ed.): ISAEBD 2011, Part IV, CCIS 211, pp. 168–175, 2011.

These unanticipated improvements in life expectancy have proved to be of greatest significance at higher ages, and have caused life offices (and pension plan sponsors in the case where the plan provides the pension) to incur losses on their life annuity business. As a result, life offices are paying out for much longer than was anticipated, and their profit margins are being eroded in the process. The insurance industry is therefore bearing the costs of unexpectedly greater longevity. Exposure to longevity risk is therefore a serious issue, and yet, traditionally, life companies and pensions funds have had few means of managing it: until recently, longevity risks were never securitized and there were no longevity derivatives that these institutions could use to hedge their longevity risk exposures. However, this state of affairs is changing, and markets for longevity derivatives are starting to develop. Most prominent amongst these are longevity bonds (LBs). The idea of using the capital markets to securitize and trade specific insurance risks is relatively new, and picked up momentum in the 1990's with a number of securitizations of non-life insurance risks. In December 2003, Swiss Re issued the first bond to link payments to mortality risk: specifically short-term, catastrophic mortality risk. Also an important issue in actuarial theory is to study the ruin probability of an insurance company when the management has the possibility of investing in the financial market. In [1], this problem is treated assuming that part of the surplus is invested in the risky asset.

Increased life expectancy indicates the possible risk of underestimating insurance premiums on the basis of period mortality tables for life annuity policies. Actuaries must therefore use for pricing and reserving life insurance policies cohort mortality tables to compute pure premiums for annuity products. There are thus required stochastic mortality models or mortality projections. Understanding the dynamics of future mortality is very important for an actuary in the activity of pricing and reserving. Recent years have seen considerable developments in the modelling and forecasting of mortality rates. Pioneering work [7] has been supplemented by a variety of alternatives that might be considered improvements on the single-factor Lee-Carter model according to a variety of criteria, [11], [2]. In [9], it has been developed a parametric model which incorporates both the effect of age on mortality and of underlying time trends on mortality rates so that the model captures the evolution of the mortality curve over time.

The main impact of longevity risk on the net pension liabilities of employer-provided private pension plans is through their annuity payments. The capital and investment proceeds are generally tax-deferred. There are many categories of annuities. Longevity risk would have its larger effect on annuities that are fixed, deferred and for the lifetime of the annuitant once retirement age is reached. Unfortunately, the impact of longevity risk is compounded as few pension plans account for future changes in mortality and life expectancy. Moreover, the task of assessing the best way to account for improvements in mortality and life expectancy is complicated by the lack of a common methodology to account for longevity risk.

From this point, the paper contains two main sections and the conclusions. Section 2 presents some important models for the estimation of the force of mortality with a numerical application for Romanian population. In Section 3, we develop a model for computing the premium and the price paid by the insurers and investors for the securitization of longevity risk through the bonds.

2 Stochastic Mortality Models

Mortality analysis has a long tradition in actuarial science. Conventional actuarial practice uses parametric graduation techniques to smooth out wild fluctuations when estimating probabilities of death for a given population. Graduation allows us to obtain a clear picture of the mortality curve, in other words the probability of death as a function of age.

The prediction of mortality is a subject of great interest as a result of the persistent tendency of decrease of the mortality rates during the last century, respectively the effects upon the expenses of the social insurance systems. An approach in forecasting mortality rates was proposed by Lee and Carter, in [7], and used initially for projections of the age-specific mortality rates in the United States. Specific to the Lee-Carter method is the extrapolation in perspective of the behavior recorded in the past. The method consists in decomposing the age-specific mortality in two components, a time-varying index of mortality k_t and a set of age-specific constant β_x.

We will use the following notations: $T_x(t)$ is the remaining lifetime of an x-aged individual in calendar year t; $L_{x,t}$ is the number of individuals aged x alive on January 1 of year t; $D_{x,t}$ is the number of deaths at age x during year t; $ETR_{x,t}$ is the exposure-to-risk at age x during year t; $q_x(t)$ is the probability that an x-aged individual dies in calendar year t; $p_x(t)=1-q_x(t)$ is the corresponding survival probability; $m_{x,t}$ the central death rates for age x in year t, it is estimated by the ratio between $D_{x,t}$ and the total number of person-years lived in the interval $[x,x+1)$ during calendar year t; $\mu_x(t)$ is the mortality force at age x during calendar year t. We assume that $\mu_{x+\xi}(t+\tau)=\mu_x(t)$ for $0\leq\xi,\tau<1$ and integer x and t.

We have $p_x(t)=\exp(-\mu_x(t))$, $m_{x,t}=\mu_x(t)$ and $ETR_{x,t}=-L_{x,t}\cdot q_x(t)/\ln p_x(t)$.

Gompertz proposed a simple model of mortality with age:

$$\mu(x) = A \cdot e^{\alpha \cdot x} \ . \tag{1}$$

where $\mu(x)dx$ is the probability that an individual who has reached the age x dies until age $x+dx$. The function μ is the force of mortality, also known as the hazard rate function.

Makeham completed this model adding a constant to model age-independent mortality. This appears to fit reasonably well with human between sexual maturity and some advanced age. As direct calculation of mortality rates at advanced ages is problematic due to sampling error inherent in small surviving cohort sizes, other models are substituted for the highest ages.

The classical model Makeham states that

$$\mu_x(t) = a_t + b_t \cdot c_t^x \ , \tag{2}$$

and the Lee-Carter model gives

$$\ln \hat{\mu}_x(t) = \ln \mu_x(t) + \varepsilon_x(t) \ , \tag{3}$$

where $\mu_x(t)=\exp(\alpha_x+\beta_x\cdot k_t)$ and the error terms $\varepsilon_x(t)\sim N(0,\sigma^2)$; parameters must fulfill the conditions that the sum of k_t is equal to 0 and the sum of β_x is equal to 1; α_x is the mean of $\mu_x(t)$, age specific parameter that indicates the average level of mortality; k_t is a time specific parameter, i.e. an index of the level of mortality; β_x is an age specific parameter that indicates the responsiveness of each age to the time parameter k_t. Some ages decline in mortality quicker then others.

The mortality $\mu_x(t)$ is estimated by $\hat{\mu}_x(t) = \dfrac{D_{x,t}}{ETR_{x,t}}$, where $ETR_{x,t} = -\dfrac{l_x(t) \cdot \hat{q}_x(t)}{\ln(1 - \hat{q}_x(t))}$

for $x = x_{min}, \ldots, x_{max}$ and $t = t_{min}, \ldots, t_{max}$. Thus, $\hat{\mu}_x(t) = \alpha_x + \beta_x \cdot k_t + \varepsilon_x(t)$.

Differentiating with respect to α_x, we obtain

$$\sum_{t=t_{min}}^{t=t_{max}} \ln \hat{\mu}_x(t) = (t_{max} - t_{min} + 1) \cdot \alpha_x \, , \tag{4}$$

so α_x will be estimated by

$$\hat{\alpha}_x = \frac{1}{t_{max} - t_{min} + 1} \sum_{t=t_{min}}^{t=t_{max}} \ln \hat{\mu}_x(t) \, . \tag{5}$$

Let Z be a matrix $(x_{max}-x_{min}+1) \times (t_{max}-t_{min}+1)$ with the elements $z_{xt} = \ln \hat{\mu}_x(t) - \hat{\alpha}_x$. Let u_1 (respective v_1) a normed eigenvector of $Z^t \cdot Z$ (respective $Z \cdot Z^t$) corresponding to the maximal eigenvalue λ_1. We estimate β and k with the decomposition $Z = U \cdot D \cdot V^t \, Z$, where D is a diagonal matrix. Thus,

$$\hat{\beta}_x = \frac{U(x,1)}{\sum_x U(x,1)} \text{ and } \hat{k}_t = V(t,1) \cdot \left(\sum_x U(x,1) \right) \cdot D(1,1) \, . \tag{6}$$

In the second step, using the estimates found previously, we search an estimate of k_t so that for t we have:

$$\sum_x D_{x,t} = \sum_x ETR_{x,t} \cdot \exp\left(\hat{\alpha}_x + \hat{\beta}_x \cdot \hat{k}_t \right), \tag{7}$$

The Lee-Carter model is generalized in [11] to include a cohort effect as follows:

$$\ln \mu_x(t) = \alpha_x + \beta_x^{(1)} \cdot k_t + \beta_x^{(2)} \cdot \gamma_{t-x} \, , \tag{8}$$

An autoregressive-integrated-moving average model (ARIMA) is fitted for the time series k_t. Lee and Carter used a random walk $k_t = k_{t-1} + d + e_t$, where d is annual average transformation and the errors are uncorrelated. Our purpose is to obtain predictions $\hat{k}_{T+h}, h = 1,2,\ldots$ for the estimated mortality to time horizon h.

In the numerical applications that we considered, we used as the reference population the Romanian population. Figure 1 shows the graph of the cumulated death risk, for ages between 10 and 40 years old, corresponding to the four basic populations: urban men (Q1x), rural men (Q3x), urban women (Q2x), rural women (Q4x).

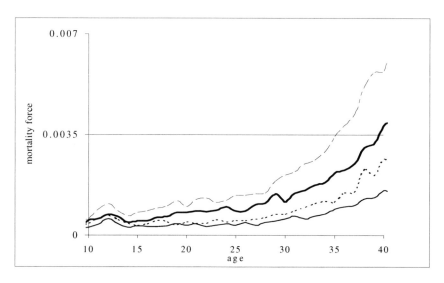

Fig. 1. The graph of mortality risks on residence and on gender (10-40 years old): rural men (*the highest line*), urban men (*the second highest*), rural women (*the third line*), and urban women (*the lowest line*)

3 Securitization of Longevity Risk through the Bonds

The first bond with cash flows linked to the realization of a composite mortality index, M_t, was the Swiss Re bond [3] issued in December 2003. This bond had a maturity of three years, a principal of $400m, and offered investors a floating coupon of LIBOR+135 basis points. In return for this coupon rate, the principal repayment is dependent on the realized value of a weighted index of mortality rates, M_t. The principal is repayable in full only if the mortality index does not exceed 1.3 times the 2002 base level during any year of the bond's life, and is otherwise dependent on the realized values of the mortality index, that is, the bond is a principal-at-risk bond. The bond was issued through a special purpose vehicle (SPV) called Vita Capital: this was convenient from Swiss Re's point of view because it kept the cash flows off-balance sheet, but also helped to reduce the credit risk faced by investors.

The main characteristics of this bond can be summarized as follows: the bond was designed to be a hedge to the issuer; the issuer gains if M_t is extremely high (the buyer gains if M_t is not extremely high); the bond is a short-term bond designed to protect the issuer against an extreme increase in mortality, such as that associated with an influenza pandemic; the bond is a standard coupon-plus-principal bond in which the coupons float with LIBOR and only the principal is at risk from a mortality deterioration that might occur during the period until the bond matures, and it is the spread over LIBOR that compensates the holder for allowing the principal to be at risk.

The precise payment schedules are given by the following functions:

$$f_t(\cdot) = \begin{cases} LIBOR + spread, & t = 1,...,T-1 \\ LIBOR + spread + \max\left(0.1\% - \sum_j L_j\right), & t = T \end{cases} \quad , \tag{9}$$

where L_j is the loss function.

Now, we develop a mathematical model to compute the premium and the price paid by the insurers and investors. Let S be the compensation paid to the insurer for each survivor annuitant over the estimated number, B_t the number of compensations (benefits) granted, N_s the threshold for the number of living annuitants, l_{x_0} the number of annuitants aged x_0 at the initial moment, l_{x_0+t} the number of annuitants alive at the time moment t, and $\hat{l}_{x_0+t}$ the estimated number of annuitants alive at moment t. The insurer is at risk of systematic biases between l_{x_0+t} and $\hat{l}_{x_0+t}$, taking into account the fact that premiums are calculated based on the estimated number (usually the mean). These are the losses of the insurer at time t. These damages may be limited by the so-called securities or straight bonds, i.e. bonds with no other incentives for the investor than the annual interest coupon along with the promise to repay the nominal value at the ransom date. They are called longevity bonds because they have the interest rate inversely proportional to the excess number of survivors. We denote this interest by D_t, and we have:

$$D_t = \frac{S(N_s - B_t)}{N} = \begin{cases} 0, & \text{if } l_{x_0} - \hat{l}_{x_0} > N_s \\ D_t^{(1)}, & \text{if } 0 < l_{x_0} - \hat{l}_{x_0} \le N_s \\ \frac{S \cdot N_s}{N}, & \text{if } l_{x_0} - \hat{l}_{x_0} \le 0 \end{cases} \tag{10}$$

where $D_t^{(1)} = \frac{S}{N}\left(N_s - \left(l_{x_0} - \hat{l}_{x_0}\right)\right)$.

The scheme to limit the losses of the insurer and the investment in bonds is made through a special purpose company (SPC), i.e. a government company specially created to issue and sell bonds. In exchange for a premium P from the insurer, SPC ensure its support with the amount $S \cdot B_t$, where:

$$B_t = \begin{cases} N_s, & \text{if } l_{x_0} - \hat{l}_{x_0} > N_s \\ l_{x_0} - \hat{l}_{x_0}, & \text{if } 0 < l_{x_0} - \hat{l}_{x_0} \le N_s \\ 0, & \text{if } l_{x_0} - \hat{l}_{x_0} \le 0 \end{cases} \tag{11}$$

We denote by: N the number of bonds sold, P the premium paid by the insurer, W the total value of the loan bond, V the price paid by the investors (the nominal value).

The profitability of the operation requires $P+V \ge W$, and we will consider a nonprofit operation, if $P+V=W$. Let SF be the principal (the amount of the loan at maturity) and $d(0,t)$ the discount factor at moment 0 of the amount at time t (for example, $d(0,t)=1/(1+i)^t$, where i is the interest rate). The total amount paid by the clearing house at moment t is $S \cdot B_t + N \cdot D_t = S \cdot N_s = C_t = C$, we will consider this cash-flow constant (the value divided between the insurer and investor). We have:

$$W = SF \cdot d(0,t) + \sum_{t=1}^{T} C_t \cdot d(0,t) ,$$ (12)

If $l_{x_0+t} > \hat{l}_{x_0+t}$, then the insurer has the loss $Loss(t) = S \cdot \left(l_{x_0+t} - \hat{l}_{x_0+t} \right)$.

If the insurer pays for the bond issue, then its loss is reduced by the received compensation $Loss^{LB}(t) = Loss(t) - S \cdot B_t$ (in our hypotheses it cancels).

The premium P and the price V are computed according to:

$$P = S \cdot \sum_{t=1}^{T} E[B_t] \cdot d(0,t) ,$$ (13)

$$V = SF \cdot d(0,t) + \sum_{t=1}^{T} N \cdot E[D_t] \cdot d(0,t) ,$$ (14)

where the expected values are taken for the estimated risk.

4 Conclusions

The European insurance industry will soon have to comply to some new solvency regulations, namely Solvency II, that will be effective by late 2012 and certainly enhance the development of alternative risk transfer solutions for insurance risk in general and for longevity risk in particular. Those regulations and standards lay the emphasis on the way risks endorsed by an insurance company should be handled in order to face adverse economic and demographic situations. Thus, the pricing methodologies for insurance related transactions, and in particular longevity linked securities will be impacted as more and more alternative solutions appear in the market. Today, the longevity market is an immature and incomplete market, with an evident lack of liquidity. Standard replication strategies are impossible, making the classical financial methodology not applicable. In this case, indifference pricing, involving utility maximization, seems to be a more appropriate point of view to adopt. Besides, due to the long maturities of the underlying risk, the modeling of long term interest rate becomes also unavoidable and adds to the complexity of the problem. Mortality forecasts are needed as inputs for economic, fiscal, environmental, and social policy planning. They are needed also by insurance companies for pricing of and reserving for annuities and pension products as accurately as possible.

References

1. Azcue, P., Muler, N.: Optimal investment strategy to minimize the ruin probability of an insurance company under borrowing constraints. Insurance: Mathematics and Economics 44, 26–34 (2009)

2. Blake, D., Cairns, A., Dowd, K., MacMin, R.: Longevity Bonds: Financial Engineering, Valuation and Hedging. British Actuarial Journal 12, 153–228 (2006)
3. Blake, D., Cairns, A.J., Dowd, K.: Living With Mortality: Longevity Bonds and Other Mortality-Linked Securities. Institute of Actuaries, London (2006)
4. Cox, S., Lin, Y., Wang, S.: Pricing longevity bonds. In: The 1st International Conference on Longevity Risk and Capital Market Solutions, pp. 20–21. Cass Business School, London (2005)
5. Denuit, M., Devolder, P., Goderniaux, A.C.: Securitization of Longevity Risk: Pricing Survivor Bonds With Wang Transform in The Lee-Carter Framework. The Journal of Risk and Insurance 74, 87–113 (2007)
6. Fledelius, P., Guillen, M., Nielsen, J.P., Vogelius, M.: Two-dimensional Hazard Estimation for Longevity Analysis. Scandinavian Actuarial Journal 2, 133–156 (2004)
7. Lee, R.D., Carter, L.R.: Modeling and forecasting the time series of U.S. mortality. Journal of the American Statistical Association 38, 659–671 (1992)
8. Levantesi, S., Menzietti, M., Torri, T.: Longevity bond pricing models: an application to the Italian annuity market and pension schemes (2008),
   http://www.italian-actuaries.org/
9. Loeys, J., Panigirtzoglou, N., Ribeiro, R.M.: Longevity: a market in the making. JPMorgan Research Paper (2007), http://www.jpmorgan.com/lifemetrics
10. Mircea, I., Todose, D., Şerban, R.: Hedging against longevity risk: applications to Romanian annuity market and pension schemes. In: 5th International Conference on Applied Statistics, Bucharest (2010)
11. Renshaw, A.E., Haberman, S.: A cohort-based extension to the Lee-Carter model for mortality reduction factors. Insurance: Mathematics and Economics 38, 556–570 (2006)
12. Wang, S.S.: A universal framework for pricing financial and insurance risks. ASTIN Bulletin 32, 213–234 (2002)

Evolutionary Path of Innovation Fund for Agricultural Science and Technology in China: Based on International Comparative Study

Min Li[1] and Tao Shi[2]

[1] The Center of Financial Developmet and Financial Security in Hubei province,
430205, Wuhan, China
[2] Zhongnan University of Economy and Law, Economy School, 40074, Wuhan, China
limin9888888@163.com, 106326570@qq.com

Abstract. The innovation of Agricultural Science and Technology is the key factor in agricultural development, and agricultural technological innovation needs financial support. The current reality difficulties of lacking funds in agricultural technology transformation in China, urgently need to establish a suitable agricultural technology innovation fund, which perfect fit with the reality. This paper compared the Agricultural Science and Technology Innovation Agency and relevant national Fund and other development trends from the international perspective, and put forward evolutionary path of Agricultural Science and Technology Innovation Fund (ASTIF) in China. We think they must deepen three paths for Agricultural Science and Technology Innovation Fund in raising, supporting and regulation aspect in China.

Keywords: Agricultural Science and Technology, Innovation Fund, Evolutionary Path.

1 Introduction

Agricultural development had made significantly development in developing countries. The technology-driven paradigm, which represented by the "green revolution" mode (Ruttan, 1977) and "Training - Study" mode (Traing-and-Visit) (Benor et al, 1977), based on the linear transfer of top-down way, gone into the mainstream In 1960s and 1970s. That gradually development in the 1980s, but the small-scale farmers and community were largely excluded from the corresponding development (Chambers et al, 1989). At the same time, economic globalization, population growth and climate change, exacerbated the imbalance between the resources and the small-scale farmers (Mclntyre et al, 2009). In order to suit these changes, the corresponding alternative methods of agricultural development emerged, which aim to improve agricultural sustainable development by small farmers` cooperation. They are also some related research include diverse participation of farmers, technology or innovation development (PTD / PID), action research and collaborative design, etc. (Faure et al 2010). Although these methods have their own particularity, but a common

M. Zhou (Ed.): ISAEBD 2011, Part IV, CCIS 211, pp. 176–182, 2011.
© Springer-Verlag Berlin Heidelberg 2011

understanding of their innovation is that they are followed non-linear, unpredictable process, which need the worker of the source of knowledge and technology design have no significant differences, and require the knowledge and technology from the benefit (Roling, 2008). The Innovation System (World Bank, 2006) emerged recently undertake the views about the complexity and diversity of innovation process and methods. Many government agency and non-governmental organizations (NGOs) and the Agriculture Development (ARD) program are actively involved into the action of introduce the multi-stock approach to agricultural innovational development recently, although this has yet to become mainstream.

Agriculture is still the basic industry in developing countries, agricultural science and technology innovation is the key factor in agricultural development (Bezemer & Headey, 2008). In the past two decade, the development of science and technology innovation fund had experienced two stages: The first stage, the total amount of tech-nological innovation fund to optimize the investment; The second stage, optimize the limited resources allocated to the appropriate mechanism for action (Huffman and Evenson, 1993 ; Pardeyet al., 2006). And the innovation fund mechanism attracted great concern in the academic community (Huffman and Just, 2000). The General public funds for two purposes: First, improve social welfare; Second, maximize the fund size and income. Huffman and Just (2000) explain that existed the alternative mechanisms of agricultural public funds, the contract signed with the main course in the funds, which also include two significant features in Technology Innovation Fund: asymmetric information and high risk (Materia, 2008). But the tax system can be solved the problem in the development of agricultural science and technology innova-tion fund above (Laurens Klerkx, Cees Leeuwis, 2008).

To the existing literature in China recently, few scholars researched the fund sys-tem of agricultural technology innovation. But there are many problems existed in Agricultural Science and Technology Innovation Fund in China, and mostly problem is there have no perfect mechanism suit to Chinese reality (see the official report in China). This paper compared the Agricultural Science and Technology Innovation Agency and relevant Fund and other development trends from the international per-spective, and put forward evolutionary path of Agricultural Science and Technology Innovation Fund in China. We think they must go deepen three paths for Agricultural Science and Technology Innovation Fund in raising, supporting and regulation aspect in China. In following chapter, we compare the agricultural technology innovation system intermediary role from the international perspective in second chapter; We Compare the Agricultural Science and Technology Innovation Fund from the interna-tional perspective in third chapter; Make a Fund path in China in the fourth chapter; and the conclusions in the fifth part.

2   The International Comparison of the Agricultural Technology Innovation System (ATIS) Intermediary Role

Excepted the main factor in the ATIS, the intermediary organizations also plays an important role in ATIS.

2.1 The Formal Intermediary Organization

Governmental organization and Association. Such as a government organization——
SIBTA (Sistema Boliviano de Tecnología Agropecuaria) organizations in Bolivia,
which aim to raise funds for the local agricultural information sharing projects, and
the scientific and technological innovation projects (Hartwich, Monge Pérez, Ampu-
ero Ramos and Soto, 2007). There also similar funds organization in Mexico (Vera-
Cruz, Dutrénit, Ekboir, Martínez, and Torres-Vargas, 2008).

National Laboratory research and extension programs. There are agricultural extension projects and National Agricultural Advisory Services (NAADS) in Uganda
(Hall and Yoganand, 2004). The NAADS aims to providing fund for employing
farmers and training the private sector to be the innovational broker, and providing
technical and marketing support. The National Agricultural Innovation Project in Indian Council of Agricultural Research focused on the establishment of agricultural
development alliance.

Research institutions and branches. Hocdé, Triomphe, Faure and Dulcire (2008) studied the research institutions as agents of innovation. Van Mele (2008) explained that
the innovation broker will be a new role in the CGIAR. Spielman et al. (2007) research about the "AGRONATURA", which act as an science and technology pool of
Tropical Agriculture Research Center. Devaux et al (2009) research the role of
"AGRONATURA" in the potato industry chain of Andina project.

2.2 The Informal Intermediary Organization

National non-governmental organizations. Goldberger (2008) describes how the
agricultural non-governmental organizations in Kenya facilitate the transition from
primitive agriculture to exported organic horticulture agriculture. Cabero and Van
Immerzeel (2007) states the "Pachamama Raym" act as an netwoke broker in the in-
digenous knowledge transmission program of Bolivia.

International non-governmental organizations. Such as international non-
governmental organizations - International Development Enterprises engaged in the
packaging, low-cost irrigation and innovative pump management activities in India
and Bangladesh, respectively (Clark, Hall, Sulaiman & Naik, 2003; Hall, Clark &
Naik, 2007). In addition, the international non-governmental organizations also including "PROLINNOVA" organization (Waters-Bayer, Van Veldhuizen, Wong-
tschowski & Wettasinha, 2008) and Latin America Cooperation (Ramirez & Pino,
2008).

International donor agencies. Development agencies such as Denmark and the Dan-
ish International Development Agency in Ghana and Van Leeuwen make a broker
between companies (Kuada and Sørensen, 2005). These also play an important role in
agricultural development in Latin American countries.

Industry organizations. Heemskerk and Wennink (2004) studied the role of farmer
organizations in promoting the farmer join it, as well as communicate with other organizations, and connecting it to the formal agricultural research and extend it. The
Cut flower business in Colombia, the "Ceniflores" Innovation Centre established by

the producers' association, which act as an independent broker between enterprises and research institution, provide requirements and information platform (Lee & González, 2006). Other similar research about agricultural market, innovation system and its development include Wennink and Schrader (2007) and Abramovay, Magalhães & Schröder (2008).

The brokers based on information and communication technology (ICT). Although compared to strategy (innovation) the ICT has a higher operational level (market and production information), a series of ICT-based brokerage has already played on the role of middlemen (Rao, 2007), such as information box in India, which farmers can get the information of cattle's health (Ramkumar, Garforth, Rao, and Heffernan, 2007).

No matter which broker above, they aim to promote the development of agricultural science and technology innovation.

3   The International Comparison of the Agricultural Science and Technology Innovation Fund

3.1   Trends in Developing Countries

The Agricultural Technology Fund in *Indian* has three changing in the sources and the using: First, the state has increased the funds, the proportion of the total fund has exceeded 50%; Second, increase the supporting of agricultural development in arid areas; Third, India Introduced competition mechanisms in the allocation of funds to improve the efficiency of the fund. At the same time, strengthen the intellectual property protection in agriculture.

The fund of *Brazilian* Agricultural Research Corporation mostly comes from the federal government and partly from the state-owned institutions. Although these fund allocated by competitive mechanism between the federal and state apportionment. Another source of funds, including the increased internal resources recently, but that still maintains only a limited proportion.

Argentina's agricultural research relies heavily on government funding, and the government substantially increased the input of agricultural research and development between 2002 and 2006. The Inter-American Development Bank (IDB) in Argentina plays an important role in financing of agricultural science and technology in recent years. And the private sector also participated in the national financial and research institutions of higher education financing program.

3.2   Trends in Developed Countries

Australia spends about 1.3 billion dollars annually to research and development into agricultural science and technology with a growth rate of 2.2%, and the Science and Innovation Budget is 85.8 billion Australian dollars in 2009-2010, increase of 25%. The Agriculture R & D factor mainly include: the Universities, the Commonwealth Scientific and Industrial Research Organisation (CSIRO), government organizations, the Cooperative Research Centre (CRCs) and the private sector. And the main sources of funds are the government and the private sector. The government stated they will increase the proportion of innovation which enterprises participate to 25%, and improve the innovation performance of SMEs through the commercial financing, while strengthening the cooperation with the private sector to increase the supply of venture capital.

The agricultural science and technology innovation development in *Europe* mainly use the" government and private investment and management together" model. And the source of the model largely comes from government financial support and private sector assistance. The government gives special funding supports, tax reduced and other incentive items for agricultural innovational development, and rational using the human, material and financial resources of technology research and development to improve the "Enterprise Europe Network" role and to accelerate the transformation of agricultural science and technology.

4   Evolutionary Path of Innovation Fund for Agricultural Science and Technology in China

4.1   The Evolutionary Path of the ASTIF's Raising

The conversion of agricultural science and technology is a systematic project, in the marketing economy, the need the cooperation between the government and the market. After compared the Innovation Fund for Agricultural Science and Technology in worldwide, we find that foreign ASTIF is basically a government-led, market assisted funding model, because of agriculture itself is a high risk industry, the research and development of agricultural science and technology must meet some risk, that need for government-led. The level of agricultural development is still low recently in China, the risk of agricultural R & D risk is greater, and the agricultural project itself is a welfare program. Therefore we must follow the traditional recruitment path, which funding mainly from government. However, at the high level of agricultural development in China, we must change the path of development, induce the dependent level which agricultural R&D and transformation rely on government, and change to model, which is market supplying and demanding mechanism under the range of government, improving the efficiency of fund raising, change the funds raising source model from single source into multi-channel diversified source. Of course, this requires the development of agricultural science and technology has a certain stability path.

4.2   The Evolutionary Path of the ASTIF's Supporting

Agriculture is the foundation of a national economy, because the conversion of agricultural science and technology can solve livelihood problems. So the agricultural R&D and transforming projects itself certainly with a welfare nature, that requires the projects, which Agricultural Science and Technology supported, must have welfare nature. In the agricultural science and technology projects , which involving people's livelihood, we must adhere to the principle of maximizing social welfare, and to the projects, which have commercial nature, such as processing of agricultural products and so on, we must use the fund to support early science and technology innovation to maximize the commercial value. That's because: Firstly, maximizing the business value can inspire business R & D power and the enthusiasm of farmers planting; Secondly, can effectively increase the accumulation of capital in agriculture, increasing agricultural science and technology R & D capabilities. We can expect that path of the ASTIF is: at the initial period, pre-support income-generating agricultural high technology to stimulate further research and development; at certain development level, we must under the social welfare is maximized principal, to support the agricultural Science and Technology Innovation projects in initial time.

4.3 The Evolutionary Path of the ASTIF's Regulation

The set up of ASTIF must strengthen its regulation. The main purposes of regulation are: Firstly, to increase efficiency in the use of funds and distribution efficiency; Secondly, to prevent asymmetric information case; Thirdly, to prevent the funds departure from the policy direction. The problems in the use of the ASTIF at home and abroad mainly are funding is not in place, funds were misappropriated and used in the wrong direction. The traditional regulatory model is: the government and fund management departments to strengthen the regulatory approval for the agricultural technology innovation projects; In the project implementation process, strengthen the financial and auditing of financial regulation. This regulatory approach reduces the efficiency of capital using, and not well to prevent the occurrence of negative externalities. So, combined with foreign regulatory approach of agricultural science and technology innovation fund, the regulatory path of ASTIF in China should be: Firstly, to establish and improve the laws, making the operation of the Fund according to the law; Secondly, under the supervision of the government and fund department, should promote the using of agricultural orientation; Thirdly, innovative forms of regulation, to make full use of modern financial management methods, and directly pay to the Fund Planning Committee; Fourth, to strengthen the incentives mechanism which for the agricultural technology project-related staff to promote agricultural science and technology innovation.

5   Conclusion

In this paper, we compared the intermediary role of ATIS, and the ASTIF from the international perspective. We make a conclusion that we should improve the fund raising role multiply, make the fund suit to society mark, and enhance the regulation for the fund. Confronting the reality, we also following that aspect to solve the problem, which exist in China. But through the development of China, there will appear many other problems in ATIS, which need future working, this is not the emphasis in this paper.acknowledgement.

Acknowledgments. This paper gain from the two emphasis research program in Huber province, China,such as"the Reform of Rural Finance-the Research of Communities Loan Model"(series:2009DE053) and t"the Research of Agricultural Technology Innovation Fund "(like above.)(series:D20091902).

References

1. Ruttan, V.W.: The Green Revolution: seven generalizations. International Development Review 19, 16–23 (1977)
2. WORLD BANK, Enhancing agricultural innovation: how to go beyond the strengthening of research systems. World Bank, Washington, DC (2006)
3. Klerkx, L., Leeuwis, C.: Institutionalizing end-user demand steering in agricultural R&D: Farmer levy funding of R&D in The Netherlands. Research Policy 37, 460–472 (2008)
4. Vera-Cruz, A.O., Dutrénit, G., Ekboir, J., Martínez, G., Torres-Vargas, A.: Virtues and limits of competitive funds to finance research and innovation: the case of Mexican agriculture. Science and Public Policy 35(7), 501–513 (2008)
5. Devaux, A., Horton, D., Velasco, C., Thiele, G., Lopez, G., Bernet, T., et al.: Collective action for market chain innovation in the Andes. Food Policy 34(1), 31–38 (2009)
6. Goldberger, J.: Non-governmental organizations, strategic bridge building, and the "scientization" of organic agriculture in Kenya. Agriculture and Human Values 25(2), 271–289 (2008)

New Delicacy Management Theory

Xueying Zhang[*]

Henan University of Urban Construction, Business-management Department,
Ping Dingshan 467001
Tel.: 13837566037
Zhangxueying2004@tom.com

Abstract. This paper briefly expounds the market information disclosure of all kinds of basic theory of characteristics, advantages and disadvantages, this article summarizes the present stock market information disclosure system can satisfy investors to disclose information true, timely, overall demand, appropriate aggrandizement mandatory disclosure system theory, establish can satisfy the demand of the market, investors information disclosure of legal system.

Keywords: Investors demand information disclosure of information disclosure system, disclosure system theory.

The important content of enterprise transformation is about the transformation of the way enterprises operate and manage, and the conversion of extensive management to delicacy management. This article holds that the delicacy management plays an vital role in the transformation of management and enterprises and the rapid economic transition.

1 Connotation of Delicacy Management and Significance of Implementation of It

1.1 Significance of Delicacy Management

Delicacy is contrary to extension. The meaning of extension in 'extensive economy' can be connected to the agricultural phenomenon of extensive cultivation. In contrast,

---

[*] Born in 1965, Female, Degree: Graduate, Depute professor titles. The main research: Management ,Economics, Accounting, Etc, Main product: Hosted completing task One, Coal enterprise Learning Organization to Create and continuous operation of research in August 2006 through HeNan science and technology hall appraisal, the domestic leading by August 2007 science and technology progress, PingDingShan city, the first prize Two, coal enterprise circular economy and conservation issues research in August 2008 through HeNan science and technology hall appraisal, leading in the domestic in August 2009 by science and technology progress, PingDingShan city, the first prize Three, coal enterprise energy conservation and emission reduction and intensification of research in 2011 February through HeNan science and technology hall appraisal, leading in the domestic. Paper: International academic papers 6 articles, core periodical 12 articles, etc.

M. Zhou (Ed.): ISAEBD 2011, Part IV, CCIS 211, pp. 183–187, 2011.
© Springer-Verlag Berlin Heidelberg 2011

the meaning of delicacy in 'intensive economy' is related to the intensive cultivation or accurate agriculture. Now it is expanded to the way of operation and management, in which modern way of management and advanced technique are adopted, work-collaborations are in detail, capital and resources are efficiently used, emissions and wastes are reduced, and environment protection is better. Obviously, delicacy management is of the same origin with intensive one in the origin, expression and connotation, while it is on the opposite side with extensive one. Therefore, in the development of the conversion of extensive economy to intensive economy, delicacy management plays an important role since it highlights the feature and connotation of the intensive economy and has strong pertinence, which can facilitate the rapid economic transition. And now is the optimal and urgent moment to promote delicacy management.

1.2 Delicacy Management Is Conform to the Raw of Development in the Natural Society

All things are originated and developed from tiny. Giant tree grows from saplings, big river converges from drops. Substances consist of molecular and atom. The power of micro droplet founded surprises the world. Nanotechnology shows the wonderful function of tiny composition, which is the spirituality of the substance. The animation and energy of the living things exists in the cells, whose animation and energy determine organism's rise and fall. The enterprises are one kind of organism. It is the raw of development that all things are originated and developed from tiny. This is one point. And the second point is that the mystery of those things exists in their tiny. Thus, we should never ignore the slight aspects of the things when understanding them. The falling of one leaf heralds the autumn. A small sign can indicate a great trend. No details, no success. A bolt and a node sometimes destroy huge space vehicle and large scale equipment. Those are the lessons we must learn. The evolution of human is on the way with the continuing subdivision of subjective world, which is the main solution of recognizing the world. The third point is that the slight aspects of things contain energy, information, animation and energy. In order to make things developed, we must focus on the tiny to find the potential energy, information, animation and energy. Delicacy management is put forward under this raw of subject world.

1.3 Connotation Df Delicacy Management

Delicacy management has a long history as well as intensive economy and it is conform to the law of development of subject world, as well as the raw of recognition, in which people get to know something from shallow level to the deep one. Words with the meaning of delicacy vary. In addition to 'delicate', 'precise', 'meticulous', there are also 'fine', 'exquisite', 'sophisticated', which are related to delicacy management. Especially those reflect one's spirit, as attentive, critiqued, .intensive, are very important for they decide the effectiveness of delicacy management. The process of delicacy management is just the process of rejecting the dross and assimilating the essence. Apparently, the essence of delicacy management is accurate. In order to assimilate the essence, we must subdivide the management target, like we human chew those foods to make it absorbed. It is a prerequisite that we must first subdivide things, and then make it possible to start delicacy management. Subdivision is the essential route to get to know something, and delicacy is the indispensable part. And this is how to make delicacy management successful, which means we must dig out the potential power and information from the slight aspect of the management target to mobilize the animation and energy. Then by adjusting, optimizing, regulating and coordinating, we can organize those and take advantage of it effectively. That's the essence or connotation of delicacy management.

2   The Route of Promoting Delicacy Management in Enterprises

To develop and mobilize enterprises' energy and animation, feasible route are in emergency need. In order to find it out, we have to start with the connotation of the delicacy management and the original connection with the intensive economy. Those enterprises who had already implement delicacy management received average effect. Possible reasons lie in the thought and habit we formed in the extensive economy cannot reflect the connotation of delicacy management. In the day of rapid economic transition, we should change the way we think, or it is impossible to find the feasible route or hard to implement even with the feasible route.

2.1   Subdivision of the Management Target

To reach the goal of management, we should set up the marks according to the goal and classify the whole producing system or vital subsystem in comply with the requirement of delicacy management. For instance, if we set energy-saving as the goal, except that we update the energy-consuming equipment according to the national regulation, we should also divide the energy-consuming subsystem marked by the energy consumed. In comply with the production link and process activity, we divide those large scale equipment system into start, speed up, working speed, speed down, stop and other workers' operation, motion and even elements. Those different operations, motion consume energy in different volumes. Materials show that car driving in our country consume 10%~15% more oil than that in the foreign countries, which is related to the maintenance and the driving-technique. So do the large scale equipment. As a scientific classification, delicacy management is applicable to every level of enterprises and every position, if only the mark is appropriately selected. The main point is still that to dig out the potential power, information, animation and energy from the tiny and to focus on the interaction, cooperation and the developing working ability of workers' innovation and craftsmanship.

2.2   Field Study about the above Targets: Observe Those Targets Qualitatively and Quantitatively and Record the Data

Which includes resource, time, workforce occupied, positive or negative significance to the management targets, appropriate and inappropriate part and the necessary instructions. Since there are different ways to reach the same goal, there exist different detail targets with in one management goal. Some targets focus on promoting the advanced operating methods, trick and knack. Some target on the repeated procedures, activities and record data to analyze in order to redesign the activities and improve the techniques. Some focus on the vital position to record data all day long for analysis and adjust the regulation if necessary. Those different targets share the same principles and methods, but differ in implementation. However, all of them have to be repeated for times in case of contingency in order to guarantee the data's reliability. The observation can be recorded through camera, manual work or combined, which is chosen by the required accuracy, convenience and cost. However method chosen, it should be carefully organized, including the communication between the observed to reach close cooperation, normal ground organization and the selective preparation of observer and measurement.

2.3 Analysis, Regular Design and Experiment Amendment and Setting

Gather statistics and start data processing to reject the dross and assimilate the essence. Then reorganize and optimize the essence in order to form new activity structure, new processes to regulate procedure, or new type of organizations. And finally amend and form new project to implement.

Those discussed above are the fundamental structure to deepen delicacy management. Study further by combining with manufacturing technique, ergonomic, work psychology, work environment, management theory, economic probability statistics, value engineering and other kind of science. That further study to the realistic production, producers and the workers, together with that application of science is the essential condition to guarantee it's scientific and reliability. The feasibility and effectiveness are with no doubt, but are in need of enormous efforts and the down-to-earth attitude when implemented. Well beginning is half success. Whenever started, we can harvest more than we seed, just as the proverb says, Effort halved, result doubled. However, delicacy management needs endless effort to maintain the good results.

3 Firmly Implement Delicacy Management and Bring Its Functions into Play

Every overarching management method has various kinds of functions, so does delicacy management. Thus enterprises have to implement it firmly to bring its functions into play.

3.1 Take Advantage of Delicacy Management to Facilitate the Transformation of Enterprises' Operating and Managing Method: Extensive Economy Basically Mlays on Resource and Investments

It gain the economic increases at the cost of cheap workforce and its striving feature is material-centered. Therefore, the direction of transition is to improve the efficiency of resource utilization, protect environment and minimize material-consuming in order to contribute to the economy. From material-centered to human-resource-centered, we should facilitate the development of human resource, and promote innovation. Further implementation directs to the start and development of enterprises' energy, information and animation, which is weakening the material-centered thought and strengthening the human-resource-centered thought. Meanwhile, the implementation of delicacy management, make the scientific outlook on development more than just paper work, which are deeply relying on the management functions of delicacy management.

3.2 Delicacy Management Is the Cradle of the Vocational Schools and Skilled Craftsman

The further implementation of delicacy management is aiming at the public acknowledged productive activity and various positions' techniques. Thus, it can improve all kinds of workers with their professional level, and make more and more tricks obvious. Actually, delicacy management and education of skilled workers share the same principle and method, except that the latter is classified into education. We should lay emphasis on the role of delicacy management plays on the education of skilled workers to improve the entire level of competence.

3.3 Delicacy Management Plays as the Culture

The further implementations of delicacy management will forester the habit of preciseness, honesty, critiqued and efficiency. And those habits would form fashion, avocation and spirit, which are called the enterprise culture. This kind of culture is established on delicacy management and will be easier to form and much realistic. Thus, we must lay emphasis on the role of delicacy management plays on the forester of enterprise culture.

References

1. National Economy and Social Development, the recommendations of Twelfth Five-Year Plan, Guangming Daily (October 28, 2010)
2. Xueying, Z.: Project: Study of Intensive management of coal enterprises energy saving mechanisms. Identification of Science and Technology Department of Henan Province (February 15, 2011)
3. Taylor, F.W.: Principles of Scientific Management, p. 239,257,232. Social and Scientific Management Publishing House of China (1984)
4. Qinglian, C., et al.: Industrial production management, vol. 1, pp. 1–24. Wuhan University Press, Wuhan (1991)
5. Tinggao, L.: Modern team management, vol. 3, ch. 4. Electronic Industry Press, Bingjing (1991)
6. Pu, S.: Management Philosophy, vol. (1), ch. 1, pp. 61–78. Mechanical Press (2006)
7. Fayol, H.: Taylor: Principles of Scientific Management, pp. 239, 257, 232. China Social Sciences Publishing House (1984)
8. Koontz, H.: Management, pp. 15–16. China Social Sciences Publishing House (1984)
9. Pascal, R., Assos, A.: Art of Japanese Enterprises' management. Translation Publishing House of Science and Technology of China (1985)
10. Drucker, P.: Effective managers, pp. 85–100. China Social Sciences Publishing House (1982)
11. Where is 'human resource' in the economic transition-—Scholars from Beijing, Ningxia, Shanghai at 'Zhongshan Forum', Guangming Daily, vol (10) (June 29, 2010)
12. Wenzhao, Y.: Management Philosophy, vol. (2), pp. 18–24. Gansu People's Publishing House (May 1989)

Service Decision with Consideration of Price in Competitive Market

Youlong Luo, Guihua Nie, and Tang Yuanyi

Management school, Wuhan university of technology,
430070, Wuhan, China
luoyoulong@gmail.com

Abstract. When a new service composition is introduced, the new service product will lead competition to service market available. Both service integrator who introduce the new service and its competitor have to face the competive challenge. Therefore, we establish a model with two object in which one is to maximize benefit growth by introduction of new service composition, the other is to minimize reduction to profit available of the service integrator itself. The model focus on goods attribute of service composition which is scarcely involved in recent research on service composition. Finally, we present a algorithm to solve the model and an example is given, the result indicates that the model and algorithm can get approximate solution effectively.

Keywords: Composition, competitive, equilibrium, cluster.

1   Introduction

With continuous development of business and enhanced information exchange between different users, single web service cannot meet development of most users. Only by combination of multiple services, can it reduce development costs and achieve value-added service and play potential ability of each service .At present, how to assemble web services effectively has become a focus of industry and academy.

Web service composition is a new technology which is to choose relatively simple, usable web services or non-web services and build them up to a service composition. It can speed development, bring cost savings, adapt to dynamic changes of network and meet the needs of users quickly. As we known, prices of service composition alternatives even within a well-defined category vary widely. Intuitively, the variation in prices are caused in part by the quality of service or attributes of the product, customers' sensitivity to price, and the intensity of competition. However, the literature of service choice pays great attention to the direct impact of the quality of service or intensity of competition, but does not formally link these factors to the optimal price of a service composition and reach any consensus around them regarding their—inhibitory or attraction—effect [1].

In a monopolistic market, the optimal price is expressed as the marginal cost of the product plus a mark up that depends upon customer price sensitivity. In the case of perfect competition, price approaches the marginal cost. However, no such expression

M. Zhou (Ed.): ISAEBD 2011, Part IV, CCIS 211, pp. 188–194, 2011.

for optimal price exists for typical situations where there is an intermediate level of competition among qualities within a category.

In the model, we fully consider factor in competitive market. The model compose of two competitions ,one is competion between service composition provided by competitors and the service composition newly introduced by integrator, the other is competition between service composition newly introduced by integrator and exist service composition of his own. Therefore, the model compose of two object, one is to optimize market profit of newly introduced service composition, the second is to minimize erosion to exist profit caused by newly introduced service composition. [2].

The rest of the paper is organized as follows: Section 2 provides decision model with two object involved in competitive factors. Section 3 describes the computational method. Section 4 describes the simulation-based result for deciding at the service composition and concluding remarks are given in Section 5.

2   Model Description and Notation

2.1   Utility of Service Composition

We assume that there are M potential customers in the market. Each customer selects one of n+1 options: buy one unit from one of n qualities, or buy nothing at all. We model the utility of service composition j for a customer h as follows:

$$u_{ij} = \alpha(V_{ij} - P_j) \tag{1}$$

α is price sensitivity ; V_{ij} is perpective value of service composition quality j given by user i; P_j is the price of service composition quality j. The customer chooses the option that maximizes his utility u_{ij} in Eq.(1).

2.2   Utility of Gathered Quality of Service Compositions

Assume exist service composition quality set of the integrator himself is S, exist service composition quality set which is attributed to the competitor is C, candidate service composition quality set which do not appear in current maret is T. We can draw a conclusion that the newly-introduced service set is E($E = C \bigcup T$), it is that we can introduce a service composition whose function and quality is similar to a service composition attributed to competitor(C) or never appear in current market(T).

If the newly-introduced service compositions are similar to n type of existed services, there are not only competition but also scale effect brought by cluster of similar service compositions .For gathered and popular service compositions will attract users more, the enhanced attraction in market and optimal integration of related resource brought by gathered service compositions will lower users' search cost and expand uses cluster. Therefore the ultility of gathered service will get a growth $\gamma(\gamma \geq 0)$.

Therefore, ultility function of newly-introduced service composition is

$$u_{ij} = \alpha(\gamma W_j - P_j) \qquad (i = 1...M, j \in C) \tag{2}$$

$$u_{ij} = \alpha(Q_j - P_j) \qquad (i = 1...M, j \in T) \tag{3}$$

To users i, total ultility of service composition j in current market ($j \in S \cup C$) is

$$u_i = \sum_{j \in S \cup C} u_{ij} \tag{4}$$

According to gravity model, The probability that user i choose service composition j in current market is,

$$\frac{u_{ij}}{u_i} \tag{5}$$

which is also regarded as share of quality j

$$S_j = \sum_{i=1}^{m} \frac{u_{ij}}{u_i} \tag{6}$$

To users i, total ultility of Service composition j after new service composition have been introduced is

$$u'_i = u_i + \sum_{x \in C \cup T} u_{ix} \tag{7}$$

Similar to (6), the share of service composition j after new service composition have been introduced is

$$S'_j = \sum_{i=1}^{m} \frac{u_{ij}}{u'_i} \tag{8}$$

We assume that the marginal cost of a unit of service compostion j is a constant, C_j. As the demand for service composition quality j is M*Sj units, the contribution generated by service composition quality j is given by

$$\Pi_j = M * S_j * (P_j - C_j) \tag{9}$$

For simplicity and without loss of generality, we assume that fixed costs are zero; that is contribution equals profit. Hence the optimal (i.e. profit maximizing) prices are given by Nash equilibrium: for j=1...n. It can be shown (e.g. see Anderson et al., 1992; Besanko et al., 1998)[3],[4] [5]that at Nash equilibrium.

$$P_j - C_j = \frac{1}{\alpha(1 - S_j)} \tag{10}$$

The term (10) is the optimal mark-up on marginal cost for quality j. Note that the larger the market share of a quality, the higher is its optimal margin. Also, lower the price sensitivity of the market (i.e., the larger the $1/\alpha$, the higher is the margin. Finally, when market share of a quality is very small, the optimal margin approaches $1/\alpha$.

2.3 Objective Function

$$\max Z_1 = \sum_{x \in C} \sum_{i=1}^{n} \omega_i g(u_i) S_x'(P_x - C_x) + \sum_{x \in T} \sum_{i=1}^{n} \omega_i g(u_i) S_x'(P_x - C_x) + \sum_{l \in S} \sum_{i=1}^{n} \omega_i g(u_i) S_l'(P_l - C_l)$$

(11)

$$\min \quad Z_2 = (\sum_{l \in S} \sum_{i=1}^{n} \omega_i g(u_i) S_l - \sum_{l \in S} \sum_{i=1}^{n} \omega_i g(u_i) S_l') * (P_l - C_l) \qquad (12)$$

S.T.

$$\sum_{x \in C \cup T} y_x = M \qquad (13)$$

$$y_x = \{0, 1\} \qquad (14)$$

Once new service compositions are introduced, profit of integrator compose of three parts. Therefore, the formula (11) is divided into three parts. The first part is profit of one type of newly introduced service composition quality in which demand growth are involved. It is that newly introduced service product are similar to some service compositon of competitior. The cluster service compositon have more chance be choosed because they attract more users. The second parts is profit of another type of newly introduced service product. we do not consider growth because it is not similar to exist service compositon of competitor .The third part is profit of exist service of service integrator itself. Formula (11) ensure the max market profit of integrator his own.

The formula (12) is divided into two parts. The first is share of exist service produce before new service is introduced. The second part is erosion of exist share caused by newly introduced service composition product. To sum up, the formular (12) is to minimize negative effect of current market share brought by newly introduced service product.

Constraints (13) show the sum of newly introduced service product is M

Following is the notation used in the model:

ω_i: the number of customers i ; $g(u_i)$;demand function of type of customer i

$$g(u_i) = \sum_{x \in C \cup T} \sum_{i=1}^{n} \omega_i (1 - \exp(-\lambda u_i)) \qquad (15)$$

3   Solution Methodology

We transform the multi-objective function to a single objective function as below:

$$\min z = w * z1 - (1 - w) * z2 \tag{16}$$

The overall procedure of the proposed solution method is described as follow:

Step 1: initialize chromosomes, we use traditional bit bunch to code chromosomes,arrange decision variables in sequence.

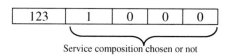

Fig. 1. Chromosome

To ensure the feasibility of chromosomes,we setup following constrants for the initializtion .It is that sum of bits between 2th with (c+r+1)th m,which denote that only m new service composition may be chosen from composition scheme from competitor and candidate .Among chromosome ,there are c +r bits denote type of composition may be chosen. It is that the the number of competitors' composition is c and the number of candidate composition is r.

Step 2: Calculate objective function value according to initial chrommosomes.

Step 3: Calculate every chromosome's fitness extent. Confirm next generation by circumvolving roulette wheel pop -size time,according to the fitness extent. Finally, we obtain a new chromosome.

Step 4: Divide the group of father generations into pairs, define Pc as the probability of intercross operation, and update chromosomes by intercross operation. If these two children chromosomes belong to the constrants of the model, we could use them to substitute their parents. If not, we have to give up these two children chromosomes, and repeat intercross operation until the children chromosomes meets the constraints. Finally, new chromosomes come into being;

Step 5: Renew chromosomes through variation operation. As the above step, firstly, define a parameter Pm as the probability of variation, and repeat the following process from i=1 to N: produce a stochastic number q from [0,1], if q<Pm , choose chromosome as one father generation and operate one-point variation in the selected father generation, then a new child chromosome will be produced.

Step 6: Repeat step 2 to step 5 in terms of the given circulation times, and at last we gain a group of new chromosomes.

4 Sample

The article assume there exist three service composition of the integrator itself S1,S2,S3, three service composition of competitor C1,C2,C3 and two candidate service composition scheme T1,T2, the price and cost are showed in table1 and table2 below. Obviously, the new service composition should be chosen from candidate scheme and service product of competitor.

Table 1. Price of Service Composition

	T1	T2	S1	S2	S3	C1	C2	C3
price	1000	800	750	900	450	550	670	790

Table 2. Cost of Service Composition

	T1	T2	S1	S2	S3	C1	C2	C3
cost	400	340	590	560	200	450	510	450

Table 3. Attract of Service

Exist composition of intergrator itself				Exist composition of competitor			
product	S1	S2	S3	product	C1	C2	C3
attract	120	150	250	attract	105	185	234

We program genetic algorithm in matlab, set the number of chromosome 30, iterations150,weight w is 1,0.8 and 0.6 ,the result compose of composition chosen and the objective value is in table 4 as below:

Table 4. Caculating Result

w	α (price sensitive)	Z	Z1	Z2
1	0.1	104.0995	104.0995	70. 7664
1	0.15	130.4866	130.4866	80.7542
1	0.18	140.5643	140. 5643	86.7908
0.8	0.1	100.4435	77.2498	33.3266
0.8	0.15	108.7468	86.4732	37.5575
0.8	0.18	128.9463	96.4757	53.6547
0	0.1	-44.6754	56.4678	44.6754
0	0.15	-67.5574	76.6658	67.5574
0	0.18	-75.4464	86.5574	75.4464

From these computational results in table 4, we know when discount decrease caused by composition cluster, then not only benefit but also loss will increase gradually. The integrator will choose composition similar to c2 if the object is maxmization benefit ,and the loss is most. In a contrary, the integrator will choose composition similar to r1 if the object is minimization loss, and the benefit is largest. Therefore ,integrator should choose the composition in compound way.

5 Conclusion

In this paper, we build a two object model with conderation cluster of service composition and competition of composition product quality. In one hand,we try to maximze share after the new service compositon is introduced .In the other hand ,we are to minimize the negative effect of current market and consider the rearrange of current market ,but also the scale effect caused by composition cluster which is the innovation of the article.

In this paper we utilize a standard logit model. However, this model may be extended to include nested logit models. Further, we consider a market that consists of single-quality marketers, attempting to maximize single-period profits. In most empirical studies that employ logit, this is a standard assumption. In certain instances this assumption may not be appropriate, where firms set prices strategically over time and for multi-product profit maximization. We leave these issues for future research.

Acknowledgments. This paper is supported by the self-determined and innovative research funds of WUT(2010-Ib-035), National Natural Science Foundation of China (NSF)under grants(71072077).

References

1. Liu, D.: A distributed data-flow model for composing software services. PhD Thesis, Department of Electrical Engineering, Stanford University (2003)
2. Liu, D., Sample, N., Peng, J., Law, K.H., Wiederhold, G.: Active mediation technology for service composition. In: Proceedings of workshop on component-based business information systems engineering (CBBISE 2003), Geneva,Switzerland (2003)
3. Anderson, S., de Palma, A., Jacques-Francois, T.: Discrete Choice Theory of Product Differentiation. The MIT Press, Cambridge (1992)
4. Youlong, L., Guihua, N.: Cost Optimatize Algorithm for Hub-and-Spoke Logistic Network. In: International Conference on Management and Service Science (MASS), pp. 1–4 (August 2010)
5. Chunlin, L., Layuan, L.: Utility based QoS Optimisation Strategy For Multi-Criteria Scheduling on the Grid. Journal of Parallel and Distributed Computing 67(2), 142–153 (2007)

Restructuring of Production Allocation Choice and Industrial Division of Multinational Firms in East Asia

Daming Xu and Qing Yuan

School of Architecture, Harbin Institute of Technology, Harbin,
Heilongjiang, 150001, China
xudm1202@gmail.com

Abstract. Through the analysis on new characteristics of regional trade in the development of regional economic integration of East Asia and the role of multinational firms in trade growth of East Asia, this paper studies the restructuring features of multinational firms in production allocation choice and industrial organizational model. From the aspects of FDI, outsourcing, fragmentation and other international production organization forms of multinational firms, it conducts classification analysis on industrial chain organizational patterns of multinational firms and their features. Finally, it proposes the forecast to future researches about the impacts of industrial allocation relocation of multinational firms and industrial chain organizational pattern restructuring on the environment, employment, leading industry formation of East Asia countries, as well as on the social responsibilities of multinational firms.

Keywords: Restructuring, production allocation, industrial division, multinational firms, East Asia.

1 Introduction

In recent years, free trade area of East Asia becomes more and more mature, attracting a large number of multinational firms to transfer their production and manufacturing industry to East Asia. Through the investment and trade in East Asia, multinational firms promote the development of manufacturing industrial cluster in East Asia, and meanwhile, they improve the intra-regional trade ratio in East Asia. In 2003, intra-regional trade ratios of three free trade areas in the world--East Asia, EU15, NAFTA--were respectively 54.2%, 60.3%, and 44.9% [1]. East Asia has officially become one of the three free trade areas in the world, paralleling with EU and NAFTA. However, the study on intra-regional trade characteristic of East Asia shows that in intra-regional trade of East Asia of 2005, the intermediate goods trade ratio accounted for 60.5% [1] in total trade volume, and in intra-regional trade products of EU and NAFTA, intermediate goods only took up 49.8% and 48.2% [1] respectively. Intermediate products, components and parts trade have become the main part of intra-regional trade in East Asia.

M. Zhou (Ed.): ISAEBD 2011, Part IV, CCIS 211, pp. 195–201, 2011.

The distribution of industrial organization activities of multinational firms in East Asia has promoted the formation of characteristics of intra-regional trade with the main body of intermediate trade in East Asia. In recent years, with the evolvement of ASEAN+3 East Asia free trade area, the countries in the domain have formulated the preferential policies to attract foreign investment, appealing multinational firms to transfer their manufacturing industry to East Asia. Besides, they have advocated the multinational firms to take full advantage of differentiated capital, technologies, resources, labors and other labor advantages to allocate different production process to various regions. Multinational firms have ongoing restructuring in investment domains and forms in East Asia. The industrial division and cooperation production system in East Asia have undergone restructuring and reorganization, led by investment choice of multinational firms. Restructuring of industrial organization in multinational firms mainly shows in the continual growth of industrial chain, closer industrial division and cooperation in and out of East Asia, more and more involvement of countries and regions in industrial division system in world economy with the main body of multinational firms. Besides, the investment model and production pattern also convert from single FDI to FDI, outsourcing, fragmentation production and other forms. The accumulative effect and scale economies effect brought by manufacturing industrial cluster in East Asia attract more multinational firms to transfer production and manufacture process to East Asia. This further promotes the industrial division and cooperation restructuring in East Asia.

This paper firstly analyzes the impact of multinational firms in the economic and trade development in East Asia, then, it studies the various industrial division characteristics of FDI, outsourcing, fragmentation production of multinational firms in East Asia, elaborating the restructuring characteristics of production organization system of multinational firms in East Asia.

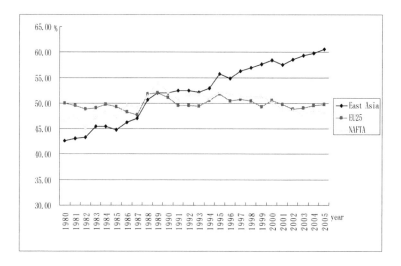

Fig. 1. The rate of intermediate goods trade in East Asia, EU and NAFTA

2 Leading Role of Multinational Firms in Economic Development of East Asia

In recent years, through modular design of components and parts production, fragmented management of production process and other various industrial organization restructuring, multinational firms have clustered the production and manufacturing to East Asia, gradually forming industrial division network system of East Asia. This has promoted the industrial division formation of East Asia in world economy. For example, East Asia has large production share in the fields of transportation machinery industry, electronic industry, computer industry and clothing industry in the world.

With the expansion of industrial activities of multinational firms in East Asia, the intra-regional trade of East Asia also grows rapidly. In the trade composition of many countries, the trade ratio among multinational firms is on increase, becoming the main body of East Asian trade. For instance, China, as the world manufacturing base and world workshop, has increases in trade volume year by year. However, through the analysis on export volume proportion of multinational firms in China (figure-2), it can be found that the proportions of multinational firms export are on increase in China's export year by year. In 2006, the export volume of multinational firms has reached 58.2% in the total volume in China. The analysis on trade data of China shows that through global information logistic system, multinational firms tightly combine the production capital, labor production technologies, labors in different regions and other production capitals in East Asia. Through industrial production network in East Asia, multinational firms finish the production process and make the products enter the international markets by globalized logistics system.

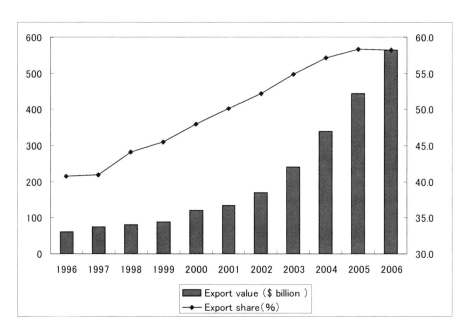

Fig. 2. Export share and value of multinational firms in china

3 The Production Organization Model Characteristics of Multinational Firms in East Asia

With the evolvement of more and more complex production organization structure of multinational firms, the investment locations and production division patterns of multinational firms in East Asia are also undergoing reform. Information technology development, lower transportation cost and establishment of FTA in East Asia all promote the continuous adjustment of optimal pattern of production organization network system and production organization model of multinational firms worldwide. With the deepening of specialized division of products and increase of industrialized production chain, production process can be divided into several modular components and production stages. According to modular production model that can carry out independent production, the production organization structure of multinational firms worldwide becomes more and more complicated. In East Asia, multinational firms conduct industrial organization restructuring of complex industrial chain in the world by FDI, outsourcing, fragmentation, and other forms.

3.1 FDI

In the recent 20 years, foreign direct investment of multinational firms grows rapidly. The early foreign direct investment (FDI) causes of multinational firms are approaching consumption market, pursuing low cost labor factors in investment regions, avoiding limitations of trade policies, etc. In these years, in FDI, multinational firms also take on diversified trends. According to the industrial division relations, they can be divided into horizontal direct investment and vertical direct investment. Horizontal direct investment refers to the multi-investment and multi-production in different regions with same production process and service. This is mostly seen in countries and regions that have similar labor advantage resources, or have relatively high trade barrier, difficulty in transportation and other industries. Vertical direct investment means that multinational firms organize the optimal intermediate goods production organization model by industrial chain and parts trade and other forms. This is mostly used in countries with huge disparity in labor advantage resources, or these countries have low transportation cost or low trade barrier.

3.2 Outsourcing

From 1990s, enterprise production and service outsourcing have grown greatly worldwide. When economist Mankiw was the economic adviser in U.S., he pointed out "outsourcing is a new trend of trade, which is beneficial to USA." Potter's research shows that outsourcing of a part of high cost, low efficiency, and non-core operation in value chain of multinational firms can improve the core competition of enterprises and promote the internationalized process of outsourcing operation of multinational firms. Meanwhile, it facilitates more specialized small and medium sized enterprises in the world to participate in the industrial activities in world economy. Dell, Adidas and other multinational firms have intensified outsourcing activities. Market research, R&D, design, parts production, assembling, logistics and after-sale service in enterprise activities all have characteristics of outsourcing enterprises participation and enterprises organization activities.

What factors promote the outsourcing of enterprises? The survey shows that though the purposes of outsourcing of multinational firms are different, they are mainly reduction of production cost, improvement of organization efficiency, strengthening of market competiveness, etc. Through the outsourcing worldwide, multinational firms can focus on the core competiveness of enterprises, improving industrial organizational efficiency, and reducing production cost. Therefore, they can gain more market share in the world.

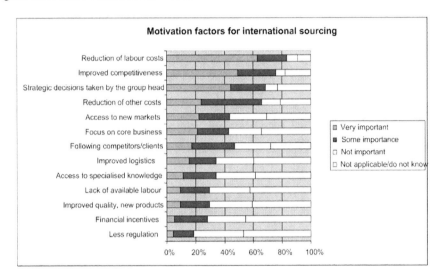

Fig. 3. The motivations of outsourcing

3.3   Fragmentation

With the possibility of modular production, components and parts of products, as well as production process can gradually establish unified and standardized production standard, enabling the fragmentation of production processes and parts in different regions. In particular, the low-cost communication technology and large scale transportation technology development, as well as the growing number of WTO member states give the possibilities of distribution of many intermediate products, final assembling operations and other production operation process to other parts of the world by multinational firms by the influencing factors in production processes, such as labor intensive degree, capital intensive degree, raw material intensive degree and wage level and other production factors. The optimal production organization network in the world is established by searching for the best parts supplier and production process collaborators in the world. Through fragmentation, the capital, technology, labor, natural resources and other advantageous factors in developed and developing countries can achieve fine integration, promoting the rapid development of world trade and attracting more developing countries to take part in the world economic activities.

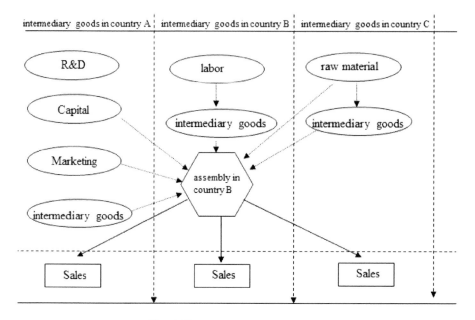

intermediary goods in country A | intermediary goods in country B | intermediary goods in country C

Fig. 4. The structure of fragmentation

4   Conclusion

With the investment and operation of multinational firms in the East Asia, the multinational corporation is restructuring the industrial organization in East Asia through FDI, outsourcing, fragmentation and other various optimal production organization models. Multinational firms promote the economic and trade growth in East Asian countries, as well as the formation of industrial cluster in East Asia. Nevertheless, investment and production in East Asia cause the environment pollution; industrial transfer leads to industrial workers unemployment and unbalanced trade between developed countries and developing countries. The social responsibility issues brought by the investment of multinational firms in East Asia deserve our future study. Faced with the huge impact of multinational firms and a series of deriving issues brought by social and economic development in East Asian countries, we should analyze the development characteristic of multinational firms and their impacts on East Asian regional economy by empirical researches and theoretical perspective.

Acknowledgements. This research have supported by NSFC (National Natural Science Foundation of China No. 41001096) and NSFHPC (Natural Science Foundation of Heilongjiang Province of China No. E200945).

References

1. world investment report (2008), http://www.unctad.org/
2. Hasan, S.F., Xu, D., Matsushima, K., Kobayashi, K.: Global Infrastructure and Optimum Production Allocation by Multi-national Firms. In: Khairuddin, A.R. (ed.) Research in the Malaysian Construction Industry and Built Environment, pp. 502–521 (2008)

3. van Gessel-Dabekaussen, G., Vancauteren, M.: Employment effects of International Sourcing in the Netherlands: a first look at the data, Statistics Netherlands, Division of B usiness Statistics (2008)
4. Kiyota, K., Urata, S.: The Role of Multinational Firms in International Trade:The Case of Japan, RIETI Discussion Paper Series 05-E-012 (2005)
5. Ryuhei, W.: International economics. Iwanami Shoten Publishers (2009)
6. Ministry of Economy, Trade and Industry, Japan: White Paper on International Economy and Trade (2006)

China's Energy Intensity of Industrial Sectors Based on Gray Clustering Analysis

Xindong Hao

College of Economy & Management, Wuhan University, Wuhan, 430072, China

Abstract. Energy is one of the critical and strategic issues for China's long-term development. In this paper, I divided all China's industrial sectors into two kinds by the perspective of energy intensity. Then I analyzed the relationship of energy intensity and industrial added value by means of gray clustering method. Based upon these analyses as well as the Chinese government's policy orientation, it is important to pay attention on the development of "win-win" industrial sectors which both increasing industrial output and reducing energy intensity.

Keywords: Energy Intensity, Industrial Sector, Gray Clustering, China.

1 Introduction

China is facing severe challenges from energy supply gap and environment pollution due to heavy dependence on energy. The study of China's economic development and related energy issues is vital not only for China itself but also for the rest of the world. Although China has made many progresses in industrial restructuring in recent years, the secondary industry in China remains proportionally high in GDP at present, and in 2009 the proportion of GDP of primary, secondary and tertiary industry was 10.3%, 46.3% and 43.4%. Promoting by investment in fixed assets, the scale of industrial production, in particular high energy consumption products, is rapidly enlarging. The industrial energy consumption in China now accounts for about 70% of the total energy consumption. The rapid development of steel, nonferrous metal, building materials, chemical and other high energy consumption industrial sectors is the main reason for the rapid rise in the total energy consumption in China recently.

Since the industrial sector plays a dominant role in total energy consumption, many studies have focus on this problem. A brief literature review as follows. Sinton and Levine (1994) examined China's industrial energy intensity issue for the period of 1980-1990 and found that the main reason for the decline of industrial energy intensity was the improvement in energy efficiency. Garbaccio et al (1999) employed the input-output approach to constructing an index on energy intensity and pointed to technological changes being responsible for the decline in energy intensity. Fisher et al (2004) studied China's energy intensity based on sample data collected on a large number of industrial enterprises and found that production structure changes were extremely important for the decline in energy intensity. Ma and Stern (2008) analyzed the data set on energy intensity between 1980 and 2003 level in China and pointed out

M. Zhou (Ed.): ISAEBD 2011, Part IV, CCIS 211, pp. 202–207, 2011.

that technological progress was one of the major factors for knock-down industrial sector energy intensity. Zha et al (2009) analyzed the energy consumption of 36 China industrial sub-sectors from 1993 to 2003 and argued that industrial structure played a important role in China's energy intensity. Similar results were also found by Li and Zhou (2006) for the period of 1980-2003, Qi and Chen (2006) for the period of 1993-2003.

In this paper, I goes through the main studies of previous literature, and then I explore the relationship between industrial energy intensity and industrial added value basing on gray correlation analysis, so as to determine which industrial sectors should be the priority development ones by the perspective of energy intensity. Finally I draw conclusions. Nowadays we have become a very energy greedy generation and our demands for economic development are also very high. Therefore, my goal in this paper is to identify the key industrial sectors of "win-win" which both increasing industrial output and reducing energy intensity.

2   A Clustering Analysis on China's Industrial Energy Intensity

2.1   China's Industrial Sectors

China's industrial sector has traditionally been disaggregated into 39 sub-sectors, which is roughly equivalent to the 2-digit standard industry classification (SIC) level. Because of the data availability, I drop three sub-sectors of "arms and ammunition manufacturing", "waste of resources and waste materials recycling industry" and "other mining industry". Such practice should not have significant impacts on final results due to minimal gross output shares of these sub-sectors in the whole industry.

According to the requirement of clustering analysis, the name and code of remaining 36 industrial sectors can be as follows: coal mining and extraction industry(H1), oil and gas mining industry(H2), ferrous metals mining and extraction industry(H3), nonferrous metals mining and extraction industry(H4), nonmetal mining and extraction industry(H5), agricultural byproduct processing industry(H6), food manufacturing industry(H7), beverage manufacturing industry(H8), tobacco manufacturing industry(H9), textiles industry(H10), garments, shoes, caps manufacturing industry(H11), leather, furs, feathers manufacturing industry(H12), wood, bamboo, timber processing industry(H13), furniture manufacturing industry(H14), papermaking and paper products industry(H15), printing and copying industry(H16), cultural, educational, sporting articles manufacturing industry(H17), oil processing, coking and nuclear fuel processing industry(H18), chemical raw materials and chemical products manufacturing industry(H19), pharmaceuticals manufacturing industry(H20), chemical fiber manufacturing industry(H21), rubber products industry(H22), plastic products industry(H23), nonmetal mineral products industry(H24), ferrous metals smelting and rolling processing industry(H25), nonferrous metals smelting and rolling processing industry(H26), metal products industry(H27), universal equipment manufacturing industry(H28), special equipment manufacturing industry(H29), transportation equipment manufacturing industry(H30), electrical machinery and equipment manufacturing industry(H31), communication equipment, computer and other electronic equipment manufacturing industry(H32), instrumentation and culture, office equipment manufacturing industry

(H33), electric power, hot power producing and supplying industry(H34), gas producing and supplying industry(H35), water processing and supplying industry(H36).

2.2 Data and Treatment

Basing on data availability and purpose of analysis, I have selected 1998-2009 as my
study period and the sub-sector data on industrial final energy consumption, industrial
GDP and industrial added value from 1998 to 2009 are collected accordingly. The
data is collected from China Statistical Yearbooks (CSY, 1999-2010), China Energy
Statistical Yearbooks (CESY, 1999-2010) and China Industrial Economic Statistical
Yearbook (CIESY, 1999-2010).

In order to ensure the effectiveness of empirical analysis, I divide the 36 industrial
sectors by stratification cluster method into high energy intensity industries and low
ones. The high energy intensity industry includes H1, H3, H5, H15, H18 H19, H21,
H24, H25, H26, H34, H35 and H36; and the low energy intensity industry includes
H2, H4, H6, H7, H8, H9, H10, H11 H13, H14 H12, and H16, H17, H20, H22, H23,
H27, H28, H29, H30, H31, H32 and H33.

2.3 Result and Analysis

The Fig. 1 and Fig. 2 give us the energy intensity of high energy intensity industries
and low energy intensity industries in 1998 and 2009. The third curve is average energy intensity in 1998-2009. The gas production and supply industry (the highest
industry) was 4.6 times more than water production and supply industry energy intensity (the lowest industry) in the high energy intensity industries in 1998. The figures
in the low energy intensity industries are as follows: rubber products industry (the
highest industry) was 8.8 times more than tobacco manufacturing industry (the lowest
industry). In the high energy intensity industries in 2009, ferrous metals smelting and

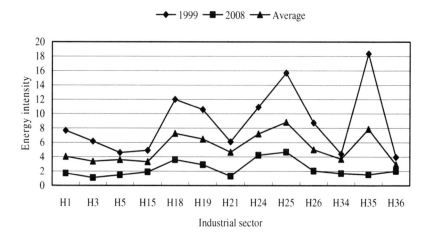

Fig. 1. High energy intensity industries

rolling processing industry(the highest industry) was 4.3 times more than ferrous metals mining and extraction industry(the lowest industry). In the low energy intensity industries in 1998, textiles industry (the highest industry) was 16.1 times more than beverage manufacturing industry (the lowest industry). The high energy intensity industry average energy intensity was 5.2538, and the low one average energy intensity was 0.9478 in 2009. The former was about 5.5 times more than the latter.

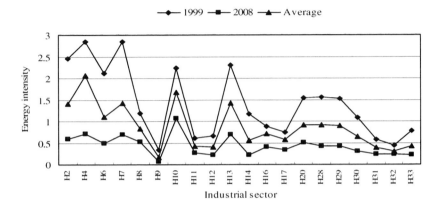

Fig. 2. Low energy intensity industries

3   Industrial Energy Intensity Based on Gray Correlation Analysis

In the paper, the gray system theory analysis is adopted to evaluate the relationship between energy intensity of China's industrial sectors and their industrial added values by calculating gray correlation coefficient and establishing gray associated sequence. Firstly, I sort the energy intensity of 36 industrial sectors in ascending. Then, I give a gray correlation analysis by taking this energy intensity ranking list as reference series and taking the industrial added value in the same time as compare one. The results in Table 1.

We can see from the Table 1 that there are some differences in the two series of energy intensity and grey correlation degree. The top rank industrial sectors in the series are tobacco industry, oil and gas mining industry, pharmaceutical products industry, food manufacturing industry which being "win-win" industry both in energy intensity and industrial added value. This kind of industrial sectors should be given priority to development. Referring to the other sectors, we should pay attention to those low energy intensity ones. Some sectors rank bottom in grey correlation degree but they rank top in energy intensity, such as transportation equipment manufacturing industry, electrical machinery and equipment manufacturing industry, nonferrous metals mining and extraction industry. Although such sectors can not play a important role in create industrial added value, but they consume less energy and have low energy intensity and play a important role in the development of low-carbon economy in China.

Table 1. The Gray Correlation Degree of Energy Intensity and Industrial Add Value

Sectors	Energy intensity	Sort	correlation degree	Sort	Sectors	Energy intensity	Sort	correlation degree	Sort
H9	0.061	1	0.893	6	H3	0.858	19	0.896	3
H2	0.127	2	0.910	2	H17	0.923	20	0.850	18
H30	0.283	3	0.830	29	H19	0.982	21	0.849	19
H1	0.379	4	0.727	34	H6	1.063	22	0.878	9
H33	0.445	5	0.841	25	H5	1.258	23	0.894	5
H31	0.454	6	0.840	27	H23	1.370	24	0.842	24
H20	0.623	7	0.895	4	H26	1.386	25	0.833	28
H28	0.664	8	0.845	22	H13	1.403	26	0.827	30
H29	0.667	9	0.843	23	H36	1.529	27	0.823	31
H11	0.678	10	0.854	16	H22	1.658	28	0.864	12
H8	0.681	11	0.917	1	H21	1.780	29	0.820	32
H12	0.687	12	0.856	13	H10	1.946	30	0.889	8
H7	0.724	13	0.876	10	H34	2.106	31	0.841	26
H32	0.769	14	0.850	17	H15	2.448	32	0.855	15
H4	0.771	15	0.713	35	H35	3.308	33	0.685	36
H14	0.776	16	0.856	14	H18	4.306	34	0.846	20
H16	0.776	17	0.890	7	H24	5.797	35	0.845	21
H27	0.847	18	0.867	11	H25	6.013	36	0.813	33

4 Conclusion

This study examines China's industrial energy consumption during 1998-2009 using the gray clustering analysis method and it give us a new way of thinking(win-win)for breaking through China's energy bottlenecks. I found that on the one hand, the high energy demand in industrial sectors is mainly attributed to expansion of production scale, especially in energy-intensive industries. On the other hand, energy saving mainly comes from efficiency improvement, with energy-intensive sectors making the largest contribution.

Since China's reform and opening, with the rapid development of the heavy manufacturing and high energy consumption industry, energy consumption also increases significantly. However, in the energy consumption process, out-dated technology lead to high energy consumption of the unit GDP and the environmental pollution, which have directly influenced the sustainable development of China's energy, economy and society. So we should put more technology into the energy consumption to realize the changes towards tech-intensive China's energy consumption.

References

1. Sinton, J.E., Levine, M.D.: Changing Energy Intensity in Chinese Industry; the Relative Importance of Structural Shift and Intensity Change. Energy Policy 22, 239–255 (1994)
2. Garbaccio, R., Ho, M., Jorgenson, D.: Why has the Energy-Output Ratio Fallen in China. The Energy Journal 20, 63–91 (1999)
3. Fisher, K., Jefferson, G., Liu, H., Tao, Q.: What is Driving China's Decline in Energy Intensity. Resource and Energy Economics 26, 77–97 (2004)
4. Ma, C.B., Stern, D.I.: China's Changing Energy Intensity Trend: a Decomposition Analysis. Energy Economics 30, 1037–1053 (2008)
5. Zha, D.L., Zhou, D.Q., Ding, N.: The Contribution Degree of Sub-sectors to Structure Effect and Intensity Effects on Industry Energy Intensity in China from 1993 to 2003. Renewable & Sustainable Energy Reviews 13(4), 895–902 (2009)
6. Li, L.S., Zhou, Y.: Can Energy Efficiency be Improved by Technological Changes. Management World 10, 82–89 (2006)
7. Qi, Z.X., Chen, W.Y.: Structure Adjustment or Technical Progress. Shanghai Economic Study 6, 8–16 (2006)

Path Analysis on China Farmland Tenure System Reform

Shu-qing Zhou

Academic Management Department
Chongqing Three Gorges College,
wanzhou, chongqing, China
zhshing6588@163.com

Abstract. As far as land tenure system in China is concerned, some serious problems exist objectively, for instance, the absent subject, Incomplete property right and decentralized management. We should adhere to collective ownership of farmland in the purpose of providing protection for social stability and security as well as economic development. The reform of land tenure system probably is implemented through the joint-stock form, which may by grouped by villages and villagers.

Keywords: Land tenure system, collective ownership, joint-stock form.

1 Adaptablity of Land Tenure in China

China's land tenure system has experienced three times of changes significantly. The system initiated with implementation of rural land reform, followed by rural collectivization campaign as well as the household contract responsibility system. The performance of household system has stimulated the farmers' enthusiasm of production greatly, and then released productivity tremendously. During the period from 1978 to 1984, the growth rate contributed to agricultural output by the household system varied from 35.6% to 75%, thus in 1980s, the rural social output value increased as fast as nearly 5 times, which showed the incentive effects of system changes on agricultural development.[1] Since then, the growth of agricultural production and farmers' incomes slowed down gradually. During the period from 1995 to 2003, the ratio of agricultural income to the farmers' total earnings declined continuously, meanwhile the proportion of per capita disposable income of urban residents to that of farmers' expanded from 1.86:1 in 1985 to 3.23:1 in 2003.[2] The dissipation of agricultural land system potential evolved into more and more serious "three rural issues" in the mid of 1990s. It seems that the household contract system is not adaptable to the development of society in the following several areas.

(1) Absent subject in land tenure, prevailing short-term investments and predatory operation

According to the existing law, the title of agricultural land "belongs to the rural collective'', otherwise, the current legislation and practice haven't stipulated clearly who is the representative of the ownership. Though the land is owned nominally collectively, in fact, nobody is entitled to deal with the property right, which goes against

M. Zhou (Ed.): ISAEBD 2011, Part IV, CCIS 211, pp. 208–211, 2011.

the principle of exclusivity of property rights seriously, and the absence of ownership exists objectively as a result.

Considering the vague land ownership, farmers is not willing to invest in the land, furthermore, the rural collective economic organizations are not in a position to protect the land property right for the contracted household effectively, consequently the farmers is lack of confidence in long-term management of land. It's inevitable that the short-term investments and predatory running would be prevailed in the land operation.

(2) Incomplete property rights result to the damage of land expropriation to farmers' interests

Owing to the incomplete agricultural collective property rights, the relevant laws and regulations have stated that any organization or individual neither can trade and transfer land property, nor lease and mortgage land, hence the rural collective land ownership is in a completely somewhat "virtual property", which can not be measured with price. Simultaneously, the law also states that the State can requisition land owned collectively. In accordance with this provision, the final disposal rights of rural collective land are actually owned by the Government. In the process of expropriation, it's not others but merely the government has the right to decide the land price consistent with their own standards, the transferred land price to the industrial, commercial, real estates from the government is rather higher in contrast to the low requisitioned price remarkably. In fact, the farmers' profiting rights of collective have been deprived of. According to the statistics, the government took from 2 trillion Yuan from the farmers through land requisition since economic reform and opening in our state.[3]

(3) Decentralized operations prevents from taking full advantage of scale economy effects

Since the introduction of the household contract system in rural areas, the land has been assigned to the family unit respectively, what's more, agricultural land has been fragmented to pieces dispersedly on account of averaging the different endowment of the distributed land.

In the economically developed areas, the form of single family land management constrains the investment of capital and technology on land; the dispersed management exactly is a hinder in the proceeding of the development of market-oriented rural economy. The prominent result from the above shows that it's increasingly difficult for farmers to increase income, and the growth of the rural economy is close to the limits of traditional system contiguously.

2 Adherence to the Ownership of Collective — The Rational Choice for the Rural Land Tenure System

Personally, I argue that collective ownership is the rational choice for the rural land tenure system in line with China's national conditions. In view of Chinese history and reality, agricultural land has been granted social responsibilities of reducing the employment pressure, providing life-support and food provisions as well as industrial capital; it bears the functions of stabilizing the society, protecting social security and fastening economic development etc...Why we must uphold the collective ownership of farmland is determined by the social responsibility and social functions the land bears in our country.

Reasonable land system acts as the mechanism of social stability. China is an agricultural country with large population in essence, and two-thirds of the total populations are farming persons, therefore, how to maintain social stability in rural areas to guarantee the farmers food to eat and land to plough available, becomes a priority for the selected factors of the land system. The prevailing land system characterized with collective ownership and households operation is distinguished for the huge benefits from maintaining social stability. It is not only solved the food problem for the large population basically in China, but also created more job opportunities for the rural labors. To a great extent, it is probably regarded as a reservoir to hold hidden unemployed in wide rural areas.

It's the current dual urban-rural social structure that has determined the farmers have to be feed on land fundamentally in that a comprehensive social security system in rural areas hasn't been established yet, and the prominent protection function of the land as a social "stabilizer", has highlighted the vital contribution to the development of the whole urban areas. It's necessary for us to persist in the collective ownership of land instead of implementation of land privatization results from very serious social problems which may derived from a large amount of concentrated of land as well as landless farming workers.

The function of agriculture is of particular importance in terms of the contribution to the economic development in the course of social development in China. At the early years of PRC, the fast development of rural economy has not only provided a favorable external environment for the guideline of priority to the industrial development, but also accumulated initial capital preparing for the agricultural industrialization. It's undoubted that the development of rural economy plays a crucial role in the process of China's industrialization irreplaceably. As production potential of the family contract system almost approached to the limit, we must reform the current land system under the policy of collective ownership to change the long-term stagnated rural incomes and agricultural development, to achieve economic development due.

3 China's Rural Land Tenure Reform

Current agricultural land tenure system reform in China focuses on how to solve the difficulty of collective land ownership of the "virtual proprietorship" issue. Personally I reckon that the establishment of collective economic organizations grouped by villages for the farming workers themselves is not only the realistic and feasible choice to realize the farmers' land rights, but also a definitely natural choice to stimulate the agricultural development by returning the land back to farmers.

The establishment of collective economic organizations grouped by villages is operable generally in that the number of families varies from 40 to 60, while the villagers from 200 to 400. The organization within such a range can easily separate the engagement from administrative authorities and agencies, to realize the real separation of rural collective economy from administration functions, thus is capable of suppressing the improper public force from collective right on the economy. As to its scale, is exactly in line with China's national condition basically.

The form of joint-stock is available to set up the collective economic organizations based on their common property, ie, commonly running farmland, participated by the farming workers with the group. As one independent legal person, the group members enjoy the ownership of land within its scope and fulfill their rights and obligations externally. With regard to the issues of common interests involving in the whole group, for instance, using, leasing, contracting, sharing and transfer the land etc…, should be voted by all members according to the fair and democratic principle.

It can't be denied that such a group will promote the development of land tapping and development and construction of water conservancy; and such a pattern will guarantee the income of rent used as group members' benefits and bonus. By this means, the land ownership is returned to the farmers in deed in that such a group within the villagers represents the farmers' rights directly,

The collective economic groups based on villages and villagers facilitate settling the conflicts between the large-scale agricultural community production and small-scale land operation. Literally, the collective group can be operated together as one person in view of common interests, particularly in the developed rural areas where are suitable for agricultural modernization, industrialization with a large scale production.

As to the remote and backward mountain areas, where are difficult to realize modernization and industrialization, the household contracting operation is feasible and realistic. As a commonly owned organization, it's a good way to the collect land rent by collective economic group for the public agricultural facilities and benefits for members.

References

[1] Wen, T.: Three rural issues: reflection upon the end of century. Reading (12) (1999)
[2] Lu, X., Shun, B.: Research on the new contradiction from rural property right in the rural economic development. Mayor's reference (2) (2007)
[3] Wang, Y.: The new beginning of land policy. Decision-making consultation (10) (2004)

A Study of Design Team Management Based on Communication and Cooperation

Yu Hao[1], Pengfei Chen[2], and Min Luo[3]

[1] School of Art, Taiyuan University of Science and Technology, Taiyuan, China
haoyu1024@gmail.com
[2] School of Machinery and Electronic Engineering, Taiyuan University of Science
and Technology, Taiyuan, China
rainbow20081230@126.com
[3] School of Design and Art, Beijing Institute of Technology, Beijing, China
ourminmin@gmail.com

Abstract. This paper aims at discussing problems and practice methods that design managers met when managing design team, which are beneficial to the establishment of an efficient design team. Focusing on the poor communication among team members caused by inherent characteristics of this industry and the concept of humanistic management, it analyzed designer's characteristics, the composition and features of an efficient team. Based on this analysis, it summarized the key points of communication and coordination mechanism in management, talent management that meet the requirements of designers and the pyramid-like management structure of design team.

Keywords: Design team, design management, communication, humanistic management.

1 Introduction

With the acceleration of the process of knowledge economy and global economic integration, design has penetrated into all aspects of enterprise, of which the design department generates the core competitiveness. Team construction has also become one of the most popular organizational development strategies at present. From the perspective of enterprise development, spirit and strength of team serve as one of the internal motivations of enterprise sustainable development. Therefore, it is of vital importance to create an efficient design team for an enterprise. With the effective management of design team, the general effect of an organization can be improved so as to achieve such effects as innovative, efficient, integrated and adventurous.

The construction of an efficient design team requires each excellent designer not only to communicate and cooperate with others, but also to conduct deployment and coordination. This paper is going to explore how managers can effectively manage their design team so that each member can give full play to their vitality and creativity, and the advantages of the team can be maximized [1].

M. Zhou (Ed.): ISAEBD 2011, Part IV, CCIS 211, pp. 212–218, 2011.
© Springer-Verlag Berlin Heidelberg 2011

2   Cooperation of Design Team

Designers, who are major components of design team, are full of creativity and imagination. They continuously put forward new ideas. They are enlighteners and innovators of team. Because modern consumer demand has converted from simple material needs to affection needs and products are focusing more on satisfying people's needs, design activity is becoming more and more complex that cannot be accomplished by a single designer or a certain type of designer. It requires various types of designers, along with professionals of other fields, to cooperate wholeheartedly [1]. For example, many excellent products design genes come from full cooperation between designers and marketers, who actively present market needs and feedbacks so as to provide important information for innovative design and development of products [2].

Communication is extremely important in this process. For teams, communication is the flocculant that coordinates all individuals and all factors for making the team a whole. Communication is the lubricant that facilitates the normal operation by solving internal team contradictions. Communication is also the basic approach for managers to inspire designers and perform management functions. Designers are knowledge workers, which is a special group. They are always obsessed with individual creativity because of features of their "original" work, neglecting the coherence of the whole work [3]. For this reason, managers must possess managerial qualities and skills that are suitable for this type of group. However, corresponding strategies should also be adopted in specific management process so that effective results can be achieved.

Meanwhile, designers have to integrate their own personality into the team so as to avoid being difficult to accept suggestions of others because of being obsessed with personal innovative ideas. They should not only keep their inherent independent creativity, but also cooperate with other designers and staffs of different perspectives, being mutually respected and understood as well as developing together.

3   Construction of Efficient Design Team

Efficient team usually has the following characteristics:

Shared vision and clear understanding of team goal: This is an inspirational strength deep in the heart of every team member. It is supported by all members, bringing the feeling of all in one, and also it is implemented intangibly in all activities of the team. Thus, the whole organization will be able to make astonishing achievements.

Definite roles and responsibilities of members: Each member should have a profound and clear understanding of their own role and responsibility as well as of others. Members should be willing to take responsibility, finish individual task and approve others. Pay attention to knowledge and skills of each other and combine them effectively in the work.

Obvious effect of goal orientation: There is not only an overall goal for a team, but also quantified and verifiable objectives that should be decomposed. Responsibilities are specifically assigned to each member so as to play the role of the goal as guidance and encouragement.

High degree of cooperation and mutual assistance: A team usually needs open, straight-out and timely communications. Members should be willing to exchange information, ideas and feelings, be willing to ask for help, and also be willing to help others sincerely. Thus, the team will be full of creativity and able to make right and timely decision when solving problems.

High level of creativity: It is because of above-mentioned advantages that an efficient design team usually shows a high level of creativity. On this account, the team will improve its ability of developing new products and services and expanding new market. What's more, it will also present outstanding performance to establish a good reputation [4].

It can be concluded from the above five factors combined with design team features that an efficient design team possesses high level of cohesiveness and creativity. Cohesiveness plays an important role in team development. Creativity is reflected on the basis of cohesiveness. Cohesiveness is based on effective cooperation of team members and favorable communications with other departments and leaders. As the bond between communication and management, design manager emerges at the right time. Design management involves internal and external work throughout all levels. They are not only coordinators but also monitors of team. Design manager should pay special attention to communication and coordination as well as humanistic management methods based on characteristics of designers. In this way, it is beneficial to the enhancement of team cohesiveness and the development of team creativity, providing safeguard for the construction of an efficient team.

Fig. 1. The equation of high efficient design team

4   The Role of Design Manager in Efficient Team Construction

4.1   Establishment of Communication and Coordination Mechanism between Manager and Designer

The primary purpose of design management is to coordinate design resources, give full play to ideas and talents of designers and create the most excellent design. Coordination of design resources can be only implemented effectively through communication [5]. As for a team, both information exchange and emotional contact between design manager and designer cannot be separated from communication activities. Good communication between design manager and designer serves as an important foundation for further management and efficient team construction.

Difficulties of design communication will be more or less reflected in some design organizations. In order to overcome these problems and make some improvements, design managers should attach great importance to the following points.

Firstly, to create the common language for communication. Due to the lack of common language for communication, problems of design that lie between manager and designer or between design group and non-design group cannot be effectively communicated at a deeper level. As a result, it is hard to reach a consensus on design standards, location, especially requirements of social and cultural level. To solve this problem, designers are required to be equipped with managerial knowledge and managers to be equipped with design knowledge, so that personnel involved in design and design management understand or be familiar with knowledge relating to design and management. They can only work together to build a platform for exchange and communication on this foundation.

Secondly, to create an environment conducive to communication. Both situations and effects of communication in design organizations have close relationship with managers. Design managers should not only be clear about the importance of design, but also work together with other design participants at an equal level. They should learn to accept opinions of others and never view themselves as leaders. Designers should foster an organizational climate which is full of vitality, freedom and interaction in organization. They are required to be familiar with characteristics of designers and fully respect them, which means being flexible in formulating management standards in design organization and being as much as suitable for designer's thinking characteristics and personality of pursuing innovation. Managers should pay attention to skills of communication during the process. For example, encourage each participant to take part in the role of communication. Mistakes are allowed and different opinions should be accepted. Managers should listen patiently when other people express their suggestions. They should not deny opinions of others rashly nor make premature conclusion.

In terms of communication channels, modern communication technology can be used. With the extensive application of digital technology, computer, multimedia and the Internet Network technology are gradually becoming forms of media commonly used in design communication. By taking advantage of modern communication technology, it is able to change communication occasions, geographical positions and environment. It shortens the communication time and makes it possible to carry out design exchange, transmission, management and other activities of long distance or between two places. Making use of modern communication technology is an important measure to improve communication efficiency.

The most important thing is to establish the system of regular communication. It is an effective method to establish the system of regular communication in design organization for preventing the lack of communication. For example, during the process of implementing design, it is obliged to stipulate specific agenda of design conference, discussion and communication according to each design stage. Then, make sure that design communication will be carried out timely and regularly by specific agenda or time schedule.

4.2 Humanistic Management of Designer

Humanistic management is a new type of management model that has become popular all over the world since 1980s, of which the rise and the prosperity show the trend of combination of management studies and ethics [6]. The core values of humanistic management is putting people first, namely respecting people, caring people, inspiring people's enthusiasm and meeting reasonable needs of people. Cooperation and coordination, which are based on credit, trust and reputation, can generate cohesion and driving force that continuously activate the positivity, initiative and creativity of staff. With a common goal and shared values, it motivates employees to reach a consensus on way of act so as to form an organic whole of coordination, harmony, mutual trust and high efficiency, as well as generate huge productivity and strong competitiveness [7].

In design industry, competition of enterprises is actually competition of talents. How to attract and retain talent is not only a vital task for designer but also the prerequisite for stable development of team. In order to retain talent, enterprises are required to build up a sound personnel training mechanism and provide designers with space for growth. So, a long-term cooperative partnership between designers and enterprise, who share weal and woe, can be established.

Respect and understand the work of designer

First of all, originality of designer should be properly respected if product design has no effect on the whole situation. And provide designers with certain design space without too much interference and falsification. Second, offer designers opportunities of making mistakes, which refer to mistakes of trivial matters in ordinary times and those relative ones of profession. Trivial matters are mainly things relating to designers from design planning to sample molding. Due to the increasingly complex design work, designers have much more trivial matters. Especially for designers who have no design assistant, it is very likely to have a mistake. Professionally relative mistakes refer to the unsatisfactory market of design style. With regard to the above mentioned mistakes affected by subjective and objective factors, managers, together with designers, should calm down in order to solve problems and find out their roots. Give designers appropriate opportunities to get back on track instead of blindly denying and hitting. Because designers are always sentimental, too much hits and setbacks would cause a tense atmosphere. Bad mood of designer affect directly work efficiency.

Attach importance to personal development needs of designer

Firstly, offer designers certain opportunities of training. With the accelerating pace of the times, designers should not only learn by themselves but also be provided with various kinds of training opportunities. Apart from training on professional skills, aesthetic appreciation, thinking and other aspects of consciousness should also be trained. For example, provide designers with opportunities of participating all kinds of fashion pageants; invite some experts and professors to communicate and explore with designers; encourage and support designers to take part in different design competitions. Properly arrange some opportunities of investigating abroad if conditions allow, so as to improve their comprehensive ability. From a certain perspective, it depends on the ability that what achievement a designer will get.

Secondly, create opportunities properly for promoting the occupational status of designer and enlarging individual development space. The unyielding pursuit of knowledge, individual and career development of a designer exceeds the pursuit of realizing the organization goal to a certain extent. Hence, in the premise of paying attention to personal development needs, managers are required to provide designers with learning opportunities for receiving education and constantly improving skills.

On the other hand, enterprises have to fully understand individual needs and vocational development will of designers, and then offer them with suitable path of improvement, create individual development space for them and give them more rights and responsibilities. Only when designers clearly see their prospects in the organization, can they have greater impetus to contribute themselves wholeheartedly. Therefore, it is obliged to provide designers with sufficient space for achieving success according to related post resources [8].

Fig. 2. Pyramid-like management structure of design team

5 Conclusion

In order to effectively manage a design team, managers would build a pyramid-like structure for the team management to improve team's cohesion and creation. In that structure, creating good communication environment, respect and understanding for designers and giving enough development space to meet their individual needs will be highlighted. Specifically, effective communication, which is the foundation of the structure, would make significant contribution to improve mutual understanding and respect. Then team members will get a good chance to be satisfied. Team's efficiency is a mirror of every team member's performance. Therefore, if every member in the team tries to do their best, the force of team will be largely strengthened.

Through establishing the communication and coordination mechanism of design team and humanistic management methods concerning designer needs, design manager is able to strengthen the cohesiveness of the team so as to increase the creativity of the team. This also requires design managers to grope and explore continuously in practice. In order to construct an efficient design team, except for the above two points, it still needs to further enhance the team cohesiveness and belongingness of members, find out other problems of the team, adopt solutions timely according to practical situation and take special measures to develop creativity of the team under the guide of enterprise brand strategy and the core competitiveness. Thus, it is possible to realize the "sustainable development" of the team construction.

Acknowledgements. We would like to thank Professor Baozhen Tian at the School of Art for her intensive guidance during our work. Our thanks also go out to Professor Hengying Li at the School of Business for her critical comments and suggestions on the theme and structure of the paper.

References

1. Tang, W.: Designers and Managers in Design Management. China Collective Economy 2 (2009)
2. Lee, L., Yue, Z.: New Idea for Construction of Business Design Team. Market Modernization 533, Mid-month (2008)
3. Wang, Y.: A study on managerial strategy of knowledge worker—an example of management of designer. Journal of Guangdong Education Institute 26(2) (April 2006)
4. Wang, X.: A brief study on approaches of constructing efficient team. China Collective Economy (30) (2009)
5. Yang, J., Du, H.: Establishment of effective communication mode based on design management. Packing Engineering 28(2) (2007)
6. Shen, J.: The combination of management and ethics: A new trend of modern business management. Scientific Management Research 9(4) (2001)
7. Cheng, J.: Core Value of HR Management. Policy-making Reference 15(1) (February 2002)
8. Wang, Z.: The change of the role of designer. Art of Design (2) (2009)

Review of Consumer Stickiness Research from Influence Factor Perspective*,**

Xiaohua Ou, Qun Wang, and Jun Xue

School of economic and management
Xi'an University of Posts & Telecommunications/Northwest University
Xi'an, China
Xo2005ok@163.com

Abstract. This paper reviews influence factors of the stickiness from the web-site, consumers and demographic factor perspective. In view of the website, this paper stress on the website should be concerned about web credibility, web monitoring and web service quality in order to increase consumers stickiness to the website; In view of consumers' perspective, customer's satisfaction, trust and customer commitment are main influence factors in this paper; It's especially concerned that the demographic statistics variables affect the stickiness of has been analyzed such as gender, age and educational level. At last, the future research directions are put forward.

Keywords: Customer stickiness, customer factor, website factor, demographic factor.

1 Introduction

Some scholars had studied influencing factors of the stickiness from the website and consumers perspective. In view of the website scholars stressed the website of the property or characteristic of helping to attract visitors in order to extend the access time and increase the access times, the more representative research is that the website should be concerned about the content and form of information, the speed of renew, and buildup interaction in order to increase the time consumers staying in the website (valczuch 2001); In view of consumers' perspective, there are a little study literature on stickiness, and influence factors focus on satisfaction, trust, commitment, and customer preference. Moreover some literatures research on online customers' repeat purchasing, the others explore potential customers' purchasing intentions. It is thus obvious that the conflict of stickiness intention to understand. Some scholars pointed out that consumers' attitude and satisfaction may affect the network stickiness, even purchase intention (Judy chuan-chuan Lin, 2007) other scholars research that three aspects of the general

---

 * Be funded by Chinese National Social Science Foundation Project, 10BGL099.
** Be funded by the Foundation Project for Young and Middle-aged Teachers of Xi'an Univer-sity of Posts & Telecommunications, ZL2002-32.

M. Zhou (Ed.): ISAEBD 2011, Part IV, CCIS 211, pp. 219–224, 2011.
© Springer-Verlag Berlin Heidelberg 2011

satisfaction of the product itself, sales processes and after-sale service and interactivity influence on network stickiness (khalifa, 2002). In addition, some scholars confirmed the network recreational and consumers' satisfaction on the with sticky forming a direct impact by empirical studies (kurniawan, 2000, 2001). Although the demographic impact is not the point, DahuiLi (2006) think that demographic role can't be ignored. It's concerned that the role demographic statistics variables affect network stickiness of has been proved (Li et al, 2006).

2   Consumer's Factor

2.1   Consumer's Satisfaction

Consumer's satisfaction is often used to measure consumers 'evaluation to what they contact. And it often leads to positive behavior. So it is also an important factor in studying online consumer's behavior. Mohamed and Vanessa measured overall satisfaction's effects on consumer's stickiness. Some factors composed the antecedents of overall satisfaction from online process: product satisfaction, sale process satisfaction and after sale service satisfaction. Their empirical analysis indicated that overall satisfaction and habit altogether explained 33% variance. Similarly, Sri Hastuti Kurniawan also studied customer satisfaction's effect on consumer's stickiness. And he found that customer satisfaction's role was weak. Website appealing, community atmosphere, convenience offered by online shop, website entertainment and satisfaction altogether explained 27%variance in consumer's stickiness. The effect of entertainment was stronger than satisfaction. Compared to assuring customer satisfaction to stick to a special website, making customers enjoy the pleasure about website and purchase process is more important.

2.2   Consumer's Trust

Trust is defined as 'the willingness of a party to be vulnerable to the actions of another party based on the expectation that the other will perform a particular action important to the trustor, irrespective of the agility to monitor or control that other party' (Mayer et al.1995). It is 'the psychological status of involved parties who are willing to pursue further interactions to achieve a planned goal' (Turban et al. 2002, p.131). Prior studies have shown that trust is one critical success factor for e-commerce (e.g. Lee and Turban 2001, McKnight et al.2002, Lin and Wu 2001).It not only increases the user's intention to revisit (Suh and Han 2003) and make a purchase on the website (Gefen 2000, Pavlou 2003), but it is also one of the significant determinants for customer's loyalty towards the business (Berry and Parasuraman 1991). Zott et al. (2000) further suggested that to create stickiness, online companies should focus on establishing trust, among other determinants. Therefore, the more a web user trusts a particular website, the stickier this user will be towards this website (Judy Chuan-Chuan LIN, 2007).

2.3   Consumer's Commitment

Commitment and trust are core element in relationship marketing. They are indicators to research relationship quality between website and its users from relationship perspective. Judy proved that consumer trust in the website was the antecedent of website stickiness .And Li, Browne and Wether be adopted relationship view to examine the role of commitment and trust and put forward that consumers stick to a website through a process developing relationship with it. So stickiness reflects the continuing relationship between websites and consumers. But the effect of commitment was higher than trust. This implied the important of commitment. Applying commitment and trust to online context can test whether there are relationships between a website and its consumers. It may offer beneficial help to customer relationship management practice. Research on trust is more than commitment in the e-commerce context. The main reasons lie in the nature of the Internet environment. Only consumers perceived risk is in their control, can they trust in the e-tailors and make transaction. Trust is a necessary element to study online consumer's behavior. But the study on commitment limits to the sustained development of relationship. The relationship perspective seldom is used in the online context. This shows that it is important to research online relationship.

3   Website Factor

3.1   Web Credibility

Web credibility is defined as perceived expertise and trustworthiness of a web site. In Information Sciences literature, two qualities of a web site are thought to contribute to web credibility of that site: cognitive qualities and technical qualities. Cognitive qualities are those related to the messages delivered, sources of delivered messages, or receivers of the messages .Technical qualities are those related to web design features. Among cognitive qualities, source factors have been studied across different fields. It is generally accepted that trust in the source, be it retailers of an ecommerce site or the organization that built the content web sites, affects user perception and behavior. In ecommerce sites, common trust-building measures include convincing the buyers that cheating is not beneficial to the seller, designing sites that meet buyers' expectations in similar situations, and offering structural assurances such as guarantees and self-regulatory polices. In online auction context, trust-building mechanisms include feedback, escrow services, credit card guarantees, and intermediaries. For content web sites, trust-building measures are employed to build trust in the organization that built the web site. The premise of trust-building is that trust improves web credibility, which in turn improves web stickiness (Zhiping Walter, 2007).

3.2   Web Monitoring

Pavlou (2002), in his organizational exchange relationship study, proposes an institution-based trust model. He refers to monitoring as a series of activities which ensure that all website affairs adhere to generally agreed to rules and regulations. Simply, monitoring is the management of a website; monitoring makes detailed checks of participants' activities in the website, takes action against unacceptable behavior, and rewards good behavior to stop speculation and cheating, thus facilitating smooth operation of the site. Zucker (1986) believes that monitoring is a basic form of institutional structure that promotes responsible behavior in both parties. Das and Teng (1998) strongly emphasize that trust is not the only factor that encourages individuals to cooperate; appropriate monitoring can also encourage cooperation. Mayer et al. (1995) point out that individuals also cooperate with each other in circumstances that have control mechanisms but lack other alternatives, although without trust. Therefore healthy monitoring can prevent speculation and let members know that the cost of speculation is greater than the potential profits; this facilitates trust building. This research takes the monitoring portion of the institution-based trust model (Pavlou 2002) as one of its two institutional trust factors.

3.3 Website Service Quality

Parasuraman et al. (1985; 1988a) measured service quality (SERVQUAL) in the following five phases: tangibility, reliability, responsiveness, assurance and empathy (Parasuraman et al., 1988a,b). In electronic commerce, service quality measures have been applied to assess the quality of search engines and factors associated with website success. Yang et al. (2008) used four dimensions of SERVQUAL to measure the users' cognition of SERVQUAL online. Keeney (1999) developed a means-ends objectives network for internet commerce. Relevant to service dimensions of the website, Devaraj et al. (2002) reported results of a study that measured consumer satisfaction with the e-commerce channel through constructs prescribed. This study found empirical support for the assurance dimension of SERVQUAL as a determinant in e-commerce channel satisfaction. Lai et al. (2007) suggested that when customers perceive better website service quality, such as special treatment benefits, they will have more e-satisfaction; when customers feel e-satisfaction with the website, they will feel more e-loyalty; and when the website is responsive, it will directly influence the customers' e-loyalty. Furthermore, Oliveira (2007) employed structural equation modelling to examine the link between website service quality and customer loyalty. His research found a strong and significant link between the two constructs.

4 Demographic Factor

Most researches on stickiness didn't put much emphasis on demographic characteristics' influence and it is often as a control variable. Li, Browne and Wether be revealed its complex effects on stickiness intention.

4.1 Gender

Several studies have examined gender issues in network anxiety and attitudes, and their results can perhaps be extended to the context of the Internet. Qureshi and Hoppel (1995) found that there are some gender differences in how students feel about computers. Similarly, Harrison and Rainer (1992) found some relationship between gender and level of computer skills, with males more likely to have better computer skills. Elder et al.(1987)found that females are more likely to experience technostress (physical and emotional burnout caused by inability to adapt to new technology)in using PCs compared to males. Some studies have found that females reported greater computer anxiety than males (Igbaria and Chakrabarti, 1990; Gilroy and Desai, 1986) while others found no gender differences (Parasuraman and Igbaria, 1990; Howard and Smith, 1986). In the context of the Internet, studies have generally shown that users are predominantly males and that men took to the Internet faster than women (Straits Times, 1996). Based on these findings, coupled with past research on computer predispositions which have generally shown that males are more interested in learning about computers than females (Qureshi and Hoppel,1995;Wilder et al., 1985), we can, by extension to the Internet, postulate that males are more interested in the Internet than females. Consequently, we may expect that males are more likely to use the Internet for various activities compared to females.

4.2 Age

In a study on the use of computers in government finance organizations, Elder et al. (1987) found that older workers are more likely to experience techno stress compared to younger workers. Similarly, Harrison and Rainer (1992) examined individual differences on skill in end-user computing and found that age is negatively correlated with skill level. Zeffane and Cheek's (1993) study of computer usage in an Australian telecommunications organization found that age is negatively correlated with computer usage. In the context of the Internet, studies have shown that users tend to be young adults (Straits Times, 1996).

4.3 Educational Level

There is a limited amount of research that examines the relationship between educational level and computer usage. In most cases, educational level is not among the main constructs and is usually measured as part of demographic characteristics or as a control variable in data analysis(e.g. Igbaria et al.,1995).Furthermore, researchers commonly relate educational level to usage indirectly via computer anxiety. Igbaria(1993)found that educational level has a significant negative effect on computer anxiety and a significant positive effect on perceived usefulness. Computer anxiety was found to have a strong negative effect on perceived usefulness and behavioral intentions while perceived usefulness was found to have positive effects on attitudes, behavioral intentions and user acceptance. Taken together, these results imply that higher educational level is likely to have a positive relationship with usage. Furthermore, higher educational level may result in greater knowledge about computers, thereby facilitating Internet usage. This notion is supported by Brancheau and Wetherbe(1990) who found that early adopters of spreadsheet software are likely to be more highly educated than late adopters.

5 Conclusion

This paper reviews influence factors of the stickiness from the website, consumers and demographic factor perspective. In view of the website, this paper stress on the website should be concerned about web credibility, web monitoring and web service quality in order to increase consumers stickiness to the website; In view of consumers' perspective, customer's satisfaction, trust and customer commitment are main influence factors in this paper; It's especially concerned that the demographic statistics variables affect the stickiness of has been analyzed such as gender, age and educational level. The influence factors researched are not systematic. Some literatures directly set out factors and are short of any theory support. Satisfaction is not the strong antecedent factor; there are also other important factors to be studied such as switching obstacles, former behavior or experience etc. Especially in Chinese online context, there are few literatures discussing switching cost's effects. So in the future, these factors can be studied in detail. Furthermore, developing good theory perhaps is more important in the future.

References

1. Lin, J.C.-C.: Online Stickiness: Its Antecedents and Effect on Purchasing Intention. Behavior &Information Technology 26(6), 507, 509–516 (2007)
2. Wathen, C.N., Burkell, J.: Believe it or not: factors influencing credibility on the web. Journal of the American Society for Information Science and Technology 53(2), 134–144 (2002)
3. Gefen, D., Straub, D.W.: Managing user trust in B2C e-services. e-Service, 7–24 (2003)
4. Pavlou, P.A., Gefen, D.: Building effective online marketplaces with institution-based trust. Information Systems esearch 15(1), 37–59 (2004)
5. Gefen, D., Straub, D.W.: Consumer trust in B2C e-commerce and the importance of social presence: Experiments in e-products and e-services. Omega 32, 407–424 (2004)
6. Brown, J., Morgan, J.: Reputation in online auctions: The market for trust. California Management Review 49(1), 61–81 (2006)
7. Yang, Z., Cai, S., Zhou, Z., Zhou, N.: Development and validation of an instrument to measure user perceived service quality of information presenting Web portals. Information&Management 42(4), 575–589 (2005)
8. Lin, G.T.R., Sun, C.-C.: Factors influencing satisfaction and loyalty in online shopping: an integrated model. Online information review 33(3), 458–475 (2009)
9. Teo, T.S.H.: Demographic and motivation variables associated with internet usage activities. Internet Research: Electronic Networking Applications and Policy 11(2), 125–137 (2001)
10. Wang, H.: Review of Online Stickiness Research from Consumer Perspective. In: International Conference on Networking and Digital Society, pp. 116–119 (2010)
11. Khalifa, M., Liu, V.: Determinants of Satisfaction at Different Adoption Stages of Internet-based Services. Journal of the Association for Information Systems 4(5), 206–232 (2003)
12. Bansal Harvir, S., McDougall, Gordon, H.G., Dikolli Shane, S., Sedatole Karen, L.: Relating E-satisfaction to Behavioral Outcomes: an Empirical Study. Journal of Services Marketing 18(4), 290–302 (2004)
13. Kurniawan, S.H.: Merged Structural Equation Model of Online Retailer's Customer Preference and Stickiness. Communications of the ACM 39, 341–346 (2000)
14. Fogg, B.J.: Persuasive Technologies: Using Computers to Change What We Think and Do. Morgan Kaufmann Publishers, San Francisco (2003)

Spatial Distribution of Branches, Internet Impact and the Performance of Investment Banks

Jianhuan Huang[1] and Zhujia Yin[2]

[1] School of Economics and Trade, Hunan University, 410079, Changsha, China
myhotpot@163.com
[2] School of Economics and Management, Changsha University of Technology & Science,
410004, Changsha, China
yinzhujia@126.com

Abstract. This paper examines the relationship between the performance of investment banks and their branches with regional factors and spatial distribution of branches in the internet era. A theoretical hypothesis is put forward and the empirical test verifies it that regional factors do matter to the performance and internet plays positive role and the influence of different regional factors varies. We also find that the bigger size of branch network is associated with lower performance.

Keywords: Spatial Distribution, Regional Factors, Internet Impact, Performance, Investment Bank, Branch.

1   Introduction

According to the traditional location theory, the right place selected to set up branches is essential to financial firms. Yet in recent decades, many questions and challenge were raised about the role of bricks-and-mortar branches by the advent of internet and other innovations. It seems that spatial factors or distance may affect little on the performance of firms than before since the boundary between cities become obscure in such an internet era.

However, the number of bank branches has grown steadily over time on the contrary way in many countries. Since 2008 the number of internet users in China has risen to the largest one in the world, and it expanded to 420 million in the middle of 2010, comparing to only 26.5 million in the middle of 2001. Great impact has been brought by rapid growing of internet, so does to bank industry, especially on the online trading. Yet from 2002 to 2009, the number of investment banks (IBs) in China decreased 30%, from 143 to 100, while the branches of them increased 14% from 2,880 to 3,296. Such trend also took place in the U.S (FDIC, 2004). Evidence shows that the banks were adopting a branch network growth strategy (Hirtle, 2007).

This paper focuses on how regional factors and spatial distribution of branches influence the outputs and efficiency of banks and their branches. We put forward a theoretical hypothesis that the performance of investment banks is influenced by regional factors or spatial distribution of branches, together with the important influence

M. Zhou (Ed.): ISAEBD 2011, Part IV, CCIS 211, pp. 225–232, 2011.
© Springer-Verlag Berlin Heidelberg 2011

from internet. Then we identify a series of comprehensive indicators based on model analysis, which integrate spatial information of all branches belonging to a certain investment bank and the information of regional factors, and the competition situation in cities, and use them as explanatory variables at bank or branch level to find out the relationship between the performance of investment banks and their branches. The rest of paper is organized as follows. Section 2 provides a brief review of related literature. Section 3 describes the methodology and data. The empirical result from cross-sectional models is summarized and analyzed in section 4. And the last section is conclusions.

2   A Brief Review of the Academic Literature

The concern about the interaction between the performance of banks and internet was aroused when internet was used as a new widespread channel to delivery financial services, as well as the relationship between distance or location and internet. Does Internet channel, 'clicks-and-mortar', plays a complement role to or serve as a substitute for the physical branches? There is a relative dearth of empirical studies about the impact of the internet on banks' financial performance with quantitative analysis (Ignacio et al, 2007), so little was known about the impact of internet channel on bank performance (DeYoung et al, 2007).

Yet the interests on this issue gradually catch scholars' attention in recent years. Many papers draw the conclusion that internet factor plays a positive role to the bank's performance from different aspects (Ignacio et al, 2007; DeYoung et al, 2007; Ram et al, 2008; Ken et al, 2009). At the same time, it is documented that the death-of-distance prophecy failed in internet banking by Guido (2009) based on the Italian household level data in 2002. So it is more convincing that internet plays a complementary role instead of a substitutive one (Claudia, 2005; Ignacio et al, 2007; DeYoung et al, 2007).

Internet is just one of important factors influencing banking. On the other side, the research on the performance of bank and their branches, location and other determinants is relatively abundant, involving extensive problems and results. There are two main related strands of these literatures: one concerns how branch location affects performance and the other focuses on the determinants of branches location.

In the first strand, some literatures focus on the relationships among branch location and factors such as industrial structure, market characteristics, and demographic factors (Ali & Greenbaum, 1977; Doyle et al., 1981; Boufounou, 1995). Other topics include the association between consolidation and changes in levels of bank branching (Avery et al.,1999), and the branching strategy in an oligopolistic setting and the branch network's influence on the market(Moshe & Bent,2001),and cost efficiency impact of bank branch characteristics and location (Giokas, 2008). An interesting and meaningful subject has appeared in recent years, focusing on the relationship between the performance and the bank branches network location. Examining the impact of branch banking by assessing the cost efficiency of individual bank branches held within a branch network, some early articles found increasing returns to scale for individual bank branches (Zardhoohi & Kolari, 1994; Berger et al., 1997; Athanassopoulos, 1998). Yet large branch networks may be inefficient from the perspective of minimizing costs, although they may be effective at generating revenue (Berger et al., 1997). Hirtle (2007) examined the impact of network size on bank branch performance, finding that banks with mid-sized branch networks may be at a competitive disadvantage in branching activities, and there is no systematic relationship between branch network size and overall institutional profitability.

As to the other strand, some studies show much interest in optimal location for a financial institution with models (Mahajan et al. ,1985; Paraskevi,1995), and spatial decision support method like GIS was introduced to the field(Willer ,1990). Yet many other studies focus on location of branch network and its determinants. GIS-based spatial interaction mode was widely used to enhance the management of branch network in many countries such as Netherlands (Hopmans, 1986), America (Min, 1989), and New Zealand (Morrison & O'Brien, 2001), Japan (Lee & Fukui, 2003) and Okeahalam (2009). However, income fact does not show similar importance according to the result of ordered probit model applied by Cohen et al (2010). They find that the size of branch networks of depository institutions and investment strategies are highly correlated with market structure and product differentiation.

Although the literature on spatial analysis in banking is extensive (Okeahalam, 2009), there is few comprehensive research on the determinants of performance including the spatial distribution of branches, internet and regional factors together. That is what we are trying to do in this paper. By testing the relationship, we also want to unravel the location selection question in a macro way, i.e. in which city instead of a position in a city.

3 Theory Hypothesis and Empirical Model

3.1 Theory Hypothesis

The relationship between internet and local branches mainly depends on whether branches are necessary for demander and suppler to keep interaction such as product choosing, trade negotiating and execution, and services support, which varies among industries and regions, and products. The role of internet will be substitute to branches when local branch is unnecessary. Otherwise Internet channel may be complement to traditional one. Based on characteristic of securities industry in china, we suggest a theoretical hypothesis that the performance of investment banks may be influenced significantly by regional factors or spatial distribution of branches, as well as impacted by internet factor. Our reasons and logic are listed below.

First of all, the customer structure is the key factor to the performance of securities branches, for it is the source of income for branches. And there exists a chain, "regional factors - local customer characteristics - performance of local branches - performance of investment banks", since the characteristic of local customer is mainly influenced by regional socio-economic factors. The location and spatial distribution of branches are important to the performance of banks when this chain works well. Then the point is whether the customer structure of branches is greatly changed by internet, which depends on the choice of securities investors in the new era. Secondly, most investors may be still inclined to choose local branches at the city where they live, instead of branches in other cities because of four factors. (1) Institutional arrangement. Investors must be on the spot when opening a securities account or handle some new business at a branch, although they are allowed to open one stock account at any branch in any city. They have to pay more cost and time relatively when they open an account other than the city where they live. (2) Consideration of capital security. Investors are more likely to choose a safe place to open their security accounts since the security investment involves a lot of money. A branch nearby at sight every day or at least in the same city will be a better choice, especially for public investors. (3) Convenience and custom of investors. Chinese investors, many of them are retired, have got use to stay together in a branch every day, exchanging information and transacting. Obviously a branch nearby is more convenient and economy for them to "work". Since investors still want to keep close interaction with branches, the local branches are still preferred by investors.

In such situation, "local branch & clicks" may be a better choice for investors for it helps to reduce their cost, and monitor their capital, as well as enjoy the convenience. Then most customers of branches are local ones and online trading is also popular. So the chain works as before, and both regional factors and internet may be important to the performance of branches and banks.

3.2 Empirical Model

We construct two cross-section models to test the above hypothesis. One model is the IBs performance model:

$$Y_b = Y(W_1, W_1, SM) = \varphi_0 + \varphi_1 W_1 + \varphi_2 W_2 + \varphi_3 SM + \varepsilon \tag{1}$$

Here Y_b is the dependent variable reflecting the performance of branches or banks, which is represented by Income from brokerage per branch (*PBIFB*). W_1 is a comprehensive indicator integrating spatial information of all branches belong to the IB z and the competition in cities, for which represents the centralization or competition in cities weighted by the number of branches of IB in each city. W_2 is more comprehensive and integrates spatial information of all branches belong to the IB z and regional factors, together with the competition in cities, for which represents the average regional factors in cities weighted by the number of branches of IB in each city. *SM* includes total assets (*ASSET*) and assets liability ratio (*ALR*), and branch network size of IBS'. To reduce heteroskedasiticity and gain robust results, their log forms are used.

Another model is the performance model of IBs branches:

$$TV = \phi_0 + \phi_1 INTERNET + \phi_2 RF + \phi_3 SM + \varepsilon \tag{2}$$

TV is Transaction Value per Branch, *INTERNET* is the number of Internet Users and *RF* represents some factors reflecting the feature of city and region.

4   Empirical Results

Table 1 is the summary of significant parameters of model (1) from 2006 to 2008. Because of the high correlation of *INTERNET* and *RS*, we estimate them in two different equations in every year. The results shows: firstly, internet shows positive role in all models. Secondly, most of regional factors enter models with significance. *GGDP* and *IC* appear significantly in about half models, and the number of significant times increases a little from 2006 to 2008. And *SN* enters with positive sign significantly in all models, which means regional competition structure is important to the output of banks. At last, dummy variablesare significantly positive, which indicates the *PBIFB* of middle and small IBs is higher.

Table 1. Regression Estimates of Investment Company Equation

Variables	Variable Meaning	2008M1	2008M2	2007M1	2007M2	2006M1	2006M2
INTERNET	Weighted Number of Internet Users		0.135		0.289**		0.136
RS	Weighted Resident Savings	0.282*		0.393*		0.073	
GGDP	Weighted Growth of GDP	1.06**	1.09**	0.406	0.522	0.477	0.562
IC	Weighted Investment Propensity	0.345**	0.244	0.352**	0.213*	0.175	0.168
SN	Weighted Share of Branch numbers	0.11***	0.109***	0.086**	0.063	0.047	0.029
ASSET	Total Assets	0.609***	0.621***	0.582***	0.58***	0.546***	0.54***
AGE	Years Founded	0.014	0.023	0.111**	0.126**	0.128***	0.13***
ALR	Assets Liability Ratio	0.828***	0.825***	0.573*	0.642**	0.333*	0.311*
nb2	Dummy variable for number of	0.683***	0.702***	0.73***	0.74***	0.495***	0.48***
nb3	branches (nb), nb2=1 if 20<nb	1.01***	1.00***	1.05***	1.03***	0.79***	0.77***
nb4	≤45, nb3=1 if 10<nb≤20, nb4=1 if 3≤nb≤10, Else is 0.	1.43***	1.51***	1.29***	1.31***	1.19***	1.16***
Constant		-10.1***	-7.60***	-9.0***	-6.7***	-4.26*	-4.78**
R-squared		0.776	0.772	0.780	0.784	0.701	0.705
F		29.80	28.32	31.09	30.26	14.09	14.19
P		0	0	0	0	0	0

Note: ①*** $p<0.01$, ** $p<0.05$, * $p<0.1$; ② among the independent variables, *SNB* represents W_1 and *GGDP*, *RS*, *IC* and *INTERNET* represent W_2; ③ all variables are log forms except *ALR*.

Table 2 is the results of model (2). From it we can find internet factor is strongly positive in all models, which indicates it plays important role on *TV* (transaction value) of branches. *RS*, *GGDP* and *IC* also have significantly positive influence on *TV*. Further more, the stiffer is the *COMPETETION*, the lower is the *TV*. The results demonstrate our findings of table 1. For dummy variables, most coefficients of *nb2* and *nb4* are significantly negative while those of *nb3* are not, which means compare to the IBs of the biggest internet size, the *TV* of IBs of smaller size is lower. The difference between model (1) and model (2) implies that although average *TV* of big IBs is high, their *PBIFB* is not necessarily higher than that of small IBs because of the high extent competence and low commission rate of big cities, which proves the importance of location and competence factor to IBs. Finally, the new independent factor *POP_CLUSTER* is negatively but not significantly correlative to *TV*, which indicates the cluster of population makes little influence on *TV*; and the significantly positive coefficients of dummy variables of district imply the *TV* of branches in east and central is higher than that of branches in west.

Table 2. Regression Estimates of Branch Equation

Variables	Variable Meaning	2008 M	2007 M	2006 M
NIU	Average of Internet Users	0.116***	0.206***	0.121***
RS	Resident Savings	0.0279	0.051**	0.093***
GGDP	Growth of GDP	0.0155**	0.013*	0.009
IC	Investment Propensity	0.200***	0.201***	0.145***
POP_CLUSTER	Urban population / city population	-0.091	-0.012	-0.101
COMPETETION	The reciprocal of Branch numbers in each city	0.391***	0.328***	0.338***
AVE_ASSET	Average of Total Assets	0.644***	0.495***	0.551***
AGE	Years Founded	0.001	0.005*	0.004
ALR	Assets Liability Ratio	1.040***	0.482***	0.733***
nb2	Dummy variable for number of branches (nb), nb2=1 if 20<nb≤45, nb3=1 if 10<nb≤20, nb4=1 if 3≤nb≤10 Else is 0.	-0.063**	-0.063**	-0.057
nb3		0.024	0.031	0.051
nb4		-0.015	-0.149**	-0.089
EAST	Dummy variable for region, they equal to 1 when the branches belong to the corresponding district, Else is 0.	0.152***	0.196***	0.272***
CENTRL		0.161***	0.232***	0.229***
EASTNORTH		-0.047	0.006	0.096
Constant		-0.651	0.300	-1.420**
R-squared		0.250	0.255	0.288
F		63.22	57.67	61.25
p		0	0	0

Note: ①*** p<0.01, ** p<0.05, * p<0.1; ②NIU, RS and AVE_ASSET are log forms.

5 Conclusion

The empirical test confirms our hypothesis that most of regional factors emerge with positive sign significantly when controlling the bank-specific characteristics such as branch network size, scale of assets, etc. Then the coming questions are why and so what, if the regional factors or spatial distribution of branches play important role to the performance of banks and their branches in such an internet era so far.

Branches location is influenced by the regional economic and social factors, since their customers are mainly locals and the characteristic of them is branded by regional factors. Then indirectly, the performance of banks is influenced by regional factors since it is the sum of their affiliations'. Yet different regional factors may work in their own way to the performance of branches. And our research put forward some explicit and interesting finding. Brokerage is the main revenue of branches and banks, which is connected closely to fortune and security investment activities. Higher *GDP* in a city may reflect that there are more rich people and firms in the developed city relatively, together with higher scale of economic activities, which may contribute to more security trading. And higher investment propensity means that the investors in the city incline to trade in higher frequency relatively and contribute more commissions, which is related to the investment culture or custom of a city. And the investment propensity of cities keeps stable in long time. Yet the role of average annual wages depends on the explained variables, which implies that wages may regarded as average income of people' in some cases, or a kind of cost in other cases.

Obviously it is easy to understand that internet shows positive role to the performance, which is consistent with previous studies. But the question might be that why regional factors play important roles in a world with high popularity of internet. The key one may be the characteristic of banks industry, coming from the consideration of safety, cost and convenience by investors. A branch nearby at sight every day or at least in the same city will be a better choice. Similar thing may happen to commercial banks.

The result of theoretical model and empirical study may mean a lot to the practice of bank industry and firms on the location strategy and bank evaluation. First of all, it implies that a better location strategy may be to choose a city with higher *GDP* per branch or higher *Investment Propensity* for a new branch, as well as to select those places with higher internet users. It also indicates a kind of benchmark for a bank to rearrange or adjust the spatial distribution of branches to gain better performance. Secondly, it puts forward some indicators such as *WPBGDP* and *WPBIC* to evaluate the competitive power of an investment bank originated by its spatial distribution of branches, which might help investors choose a better bank to invest. Those banks with higher competitive power and better situation relatively in the industry may gain money more easy. And the power is determined by market structure, regional socioeconomic factors and the combination of them, seen the formulas of W_1 and W_2. At last, it also reminds that big size of branch network may not help to improve the performance, and it is essential to make full use of each branch instead of enlarge the scale of network.

Acknowledgment. This paper is supported by National social Science Foundation of China through project 10CGL039 and Ministry of Education of China through project 09YJA790064 and 09YJC90231, and Hunan Social Science Project 08YBA165. A draft was present at a seminar of Regional Economics Applications Laboratory (REAL) of University of Illinois.

References

1. Cohen, A., Mazzeo, M.J.: Investment Strategies and Market Structure: An Empirical Analysis of Bank Branching Decisions. Journal of Financial Services Research 38(1), 1–21 (2010)
2. Athanassopoulos, A.D.: Nonparametric frontier models for assessing the market and cost efficiency of large-scale bank branch networks. Journal of Money, Credit, and Banking 30, 172–192 (1998)
3. Buch, C.M.: Distance and International Banking. Review of International Economics 13(4), 787–804 (2005)
4. Giokas, D.I.: Cost efficiency impact of bank branch characteristics and location: An illustrative application to Greek bank branches. Managerial Finance 3, 172–185 (2008)

5. Furst, K., Lang, W.W., Nolle, D.E.: Internet banking. Journal of Financial Services Research 22, 95–117 (2002)
6. Georgios, C., Claudia, G., Alexia, V.: Efficiency and Productivity of Greek Banks in the EMU Era. Applied Financial Economics 19(16), 1317–1328 (2009)
7. de Blasio, G.: Distance and Internet Banking. Part 1 of The Changing Geography of Banking and Finance, 109–130 (2009)
8. Hirtle, B.: The impact of network size on bank branch performance. Journal of Banking & Finance 31, 3782–3805 (2007)
9. Hernando, I., Nieto, M.J.: Is the Internet delivery channel changing banks' performance? The case of Spanish banks. Journal of Banking & Finance 31(4), 1083–1099 (2007)
10. Cyree, K.B., Delcoure, N., Dickens, R.: An examination of the performance and prospects for the future of internet-primary banks. Journal of Economics and Finance 33(2), 128–147 (2009)
11. Lee, Y., Fukui: Identifying the Relationship between Area Characteristics by Social Class and Bank Branches Distribution using GIS – Case Study of Tokyo 23 Wards. Map Asia, 34–45 (2003)
12. Okeahalam, C.C.: Bank Branch Location: a Count Analysis. Spatial Economic Analysis 3, 275–300 (2009)
13. Acharya, R.N., Kagan, A., Lingam, S.R.: Online banking applications and community bank performance. International Journal of Bank Marketing 6, 418–439 (2008)
14. DeYoung, R., Lang, W.W., Nolle, D.L.: How the Internet affects output and performance at community banks. Journal of Banking & Finance 4, 1033–1060 (2007)
15. Hernández-Murillo, R., Llobet, G., Fuentes, R.: Strategic online banking adoption. Journal of Banking & Finance 7, 1650–1663 (2010)
16. Richards, T.J., Acharya, R.N., Kagan, A.: Spatial competition and market power in banking. Journal of Economics and Business 60(5), 436–454 (2008)
17. Willer, J.D.: A Spatial Decision Support System for Bank Location: A Case Study, Technical Report 90-9, National Center for Geographic Information and Analysis, Santa Barbara (1990)
18. Zardhoohi, A., Kolari, J.: Branch office economies of scale and scope: Evidence from savings banks in Finland. Journal of Banking and Finance 18, 421–432 (1994)

Research on the Sports Consumption Characteristics of Non-professional Sports Women Teachers of Hengshui Universities

Ruihong Wu, Xiuling Li, and Jianli Sun

Physical Education Department of Hengshui College, 053000, Hengshui, China
`blakehorse83@163.com`

Abstract. This paper takes the non-professional sports women teachers of Hengshui universities as the participants. It makes analysis towards their sports consumption characteristics, probes into the main influences, and put forward reasonable countermeasures, which provides relevant theoretical basis for the women teachers of universities to reasonably conduct with sports consumption.

Keywords: University, woman teacher, sports consumption.

1 Introduction

The women teachers of universities are not only the mental workers engaging in education and scientific researches, but also the creators and propagators of science and technology. They play vital roles in the education system of personnel training, with great responsibility of cultivating senior talents. Whether the university teachers are healthy or not has direct relation with the implementation of the strategy of rejuvenating the country through science and education, which influences the national economic construction and technological development. As an important group among the intellectual female of new China, its current situation of sports consumption will directly reflect their physical fitness consciousness and their enthusiasm of participating in sports activities. Besides, to some extent, it affects not only the tide and tendency of sports consumption of university students, but also the sports consumption ability of that group of the region.

Although the female sports consumption develops rapidly, there are still so few relevant researches, especially, much fewer about that of the women teachers of Hengshui universities. Therefore, it is of great importance to probe into the sports consumption characteristics of Hengshui university women teachers and gain a clear idea of the relations among each factor influencing the consumption situation, which can correctly guide them to deal with sports consumption more reasonably, drive residents' whole consumption. It plays an important role in developing market economy and cultivating mature consumer markets.

M. Zhou (Ed.): ISAEBD 2011, Part IV, CCIS 211, pp. 233–238, 2011.
© Springer-Verlag Berlin Heidelberg 2011

2 Research Object and Methods

2.1 Research Object

This paper takes the Hengshui university women teachers engaging in non-sports profession (hereinafter referred to as university women teachers) as the research object.

2.2 Research Method

This paper adopts document literature method, investigation method, mathematical statistical method, logical analysis and other methods to make research and analysis towards the sports consumption of university women teachers.

3 Research Results and Analysis

3.1 Survey of Sports Activities Condition of University Women Teachers

3.1.1 Survey of Sports Population of University Women Teachers

The criterions of judging the sports population: exercise over 3 times a week and over 30 minutes every time, and take the moderate strength as the main exercise intensity. [1] The survey result shows: The sport population of the university woman teacher occupies that of 14.5% survey amount; the population that does not do exercise occupies 29%; the population that do exercise every week occupies 56.5%. It turns out that the sports population of university woman teacher is extremely small and 71% do exercise every week. It indicates that the physical exercise is not attached great importance to by the university women teachers.

3.1.2 Analysis of the Leisure Time and Dominating Ways of the University Women Teachers

The leisure time refers to the free dominating time except teaching, scientific research, work and meeting the basic physical needs. [2] Therefore, it is an important objective reason of affecting the women teachers to do sports consumption. However, the situation of the leisure time used for taking part in sports is an important factor of determining the level of sports consumption. The survey indicates: the population of the university woman teachers whose leisure time is less than 1 hour occupies the least proportion of the survey amount, while 1 to 2 hours the largest proportion, about 46%, and the proportion of the rest decreases with the extension of the time. The result shows that the university woman teacher plays a vital role in the family environment, so that their leisure time is basically about two hours.

As for the ways of dominating the leisure time, the women teachers with high titles utilizes the time to mainly watch TV programs, surf on the Internet, do housework, make scientific researches, etc. However, the sports activity ranks 7. And the top 6 of the leisure time of the teachers with low title are surfing on the Internet, doing housework, watching TV programs, participating in social activities, assisting the children, studying, etc. and the sports activities ranks 10, which shows that the former three activities are the main dominating ways of the women teachers' leisure time. In a word, whether the woman teachers' titles are high or low, the sports activities plays a relatively low part in dominating leisure time, and it does not arouse the teachers' attention. Therefore, the consciousness of sports activities needs to be strengthened.

3.1.3 Analysis of Women Teachers' Exercise Motivation
Exercise motivation is the driving force or the reason for the sports participants to do exercise. The survey result shows: the motivation of the teachers with different titles is different from person to person, while that of the teachers with high titles is: keeping healthy and preventing diseases, curing diseases, enriching the leisure life; the motivation of the teachers with low titles is social contact, joy of taking exercise, keeping healthy and preventing diseases. It indicates that the sports function is diversified and it is to the benefit of sound mind and body. From the viewpoint of side, it reflects the university women teachers' deep understanding of sports function.

3.1.4 Analysis of the Unit Leaders' Attitudes towards the Exercise
The unit leaders' attitudes towards the exercise directly influences the teachers' taking exercise, and thus it will influence the teachers' sports consumption behavior. The survey shows: Hengshui universities that organize to do exercise and input expenditure occupies 39%; ones that only organize to do exercise instead of inputting expenditure occupies 31%; and ones that advocate doing exercise instead of organizing occupies 22%. It is thus clear that the leaders of Hengshui universities have different attitudes towards the sports organization. Some leaders maintain that sports activity is just the teachers' own problems. They neglect the importance of the physical fitness.

3.2 Survey of University Women Teachers' Sports Consumption Situation

3.2.1 Analysis of University Women Teachers' Sound Sports Concepts
The survey shows that, 90% university women teachers maintain that the health state has certain relation with exercise, and 10% teachers think the opposite is right. It means that the teachers have already realized the importance of fitness and also known that exercise is an important way to keep healthy, which indicates that their teachers have positive attitudes' towards fitness concepts. The proper fitness concept must make contributions to the sound development of guiding sports consumption.

3.2.2 Analysis of University Women Teachers' Value Concept of Sports Consumption
The value concept of sports is one of the important factors influencing people to take part in sports activities and sports consumption. It is people's cognition and view towards the sports. It directly reflects not only one's attitudes towards sports activities and sports consumption behavior, but also one's interest or sports consumption behavior of participating sports activities. [2] The survey Shows that, 15% maintain the sports consumption is valuable; 63% shows affirmative attitudes; and 22% think it is ordinary. Therefore, it means that the teachers have relatively positive value concept of sports consumption and the basis of developing sports consumption is good.

3.2.3 Analysis of University Women Teachers' Income Situation and Consumption Level

The income level directly restricts sports consumption level. And the residents' income level implies their purchasing power level, which will influence the consumption structure. The survey shows that, the income of the women teachers is in the middle-high level among the town residents of Hengshui, which lays good economic foundation for sports consumption. It turns out that, the expense from RMB101 to RMB500 used for sports consumption occupies the largest proportion in the last year; that from RMB 1 to RMB100 ranks 2; above RMB500 and zero consumption also occupies certain consumption. In general, the teachers' consumption level is still relatively low and various.

3.2.4 Feature Analysis of University Women Teachers' Sports Consumption Structure

The sports consumption structure refers to the occupied proportion of the gross expenditure of sports consumption in various sports consumption and the correlations among the various sports consumption. It is generally divided into entity-oriented sports consumption and nonentity-oriented ones. The former one refers to one's consumption behavior of purchasing various sports entity consumption materials related to sports activities, such as purchasing sportswear, equipments, sports beverage, various sports journals, etc. The latter one refers to the behavior of purchasing various sports service consumption materials. The survey shows that, the proportion of university women teachers who "purchase sportswear and equipments" is large, ranking 1; and the proportion of "participating in the training of sports club" ranks 2. It is because the sportswear can be replaced by articles for daily use to a large extent.

3.2.5 Strategic Analysis of University Women Teachers' Sports Consumption

According the survey of "what will the teachers do before they deal with sports consumption", it turns out that, conducting sports consumption according to ones' own economic condition ranks 2; that according to ones' own needs ranks 2; and the proportion of other situations (consulting family members and friends, purchasing things with friends) is basically equal. It indicates that the economic situation is the most important factor influencing the teachers' sports consumption. Besides, what the teachers have done before sports consumption is relatively reasonable. They will make purchase only if there is something they really need. And they do not consume blindly.

3.3 Factor Analysis of Influencing University Women Teachers' Sports Consumption

Among the unfavorable factors influencing university women teachers' sports consumption, the most important ones are limited economic capability, low interest, bad exercise ability, little spare time, insufficient sports consumption concepts.

Economic capability is an important factor influencing the teachers' sports consumption. The salary of most women teachers of Hengshui universities is about from 1500 to 2000. As the respondents are mainly young and middle-aged teachers, they face the responsibilities of marriage, buying houses, etc. Their daily consumption is relatively high and also their actual bearing capability of sports consumption is limited. What's more, their purchasing power is insufficient. Therefore, the economic situation is an important factor restricting the university teachers' sports consumption.

Insufficient leisure time is also an important factor influencing the university women teachers' sports consumption. When people are not well-off, they will generally choose income. Choosing income means choosing labor. Obviously, the leisure time will become less. Only if the income reaches a certain level can more people choose leisure time. Under this circumstance, the sports consumption will have the guarantee of more time. On one hand, the woman teacher plays an important role in family so that the time for her is so little. On the other hand, as the universities of our country continuously expand the scale at present, the teachers are so busy. At the same time of finishing the teaching tasks, they will be busy in various scientific research and study. During the limited leisure time, the leisure time is generally replaced by the labor.

Physical capability is the precondition of accelerating the university women teachers to take part in sports activities. The capability directly affects their interest of doing exercise. However, the teachers do not form relatively strong physical capability and various ways of keeping fitness during their school life. Consequently, it is necessary to adopt corresponding measures to improve the teachers' physical capability and push them to conduct sports consumption.

Sports consumption concept is the internal mechanism of sports consumption behavior, and an important factor influencing the teachers' sports consumption. Under the influence of traditional sports consumption concept, their consumption is mainly about entity-oriented sports consumption. The proportion of participation-oriented and appreciation-oriented sports consumption is small, and the consumption structure is sole. They haven't realized the social economic results brought by the sports consumption. Their consumption consciousness is relatively weak and consumption concept lags behind. Therefore, they need to change their old consumption concept and establish the sports consumption consciousness of "spending money on health", which can help them keep healthier and improve the life quality.

4 Conclusions

4.1 The sports population of the university woman teacher of our city is relatively small. The population of the teachers who never do exercise occupies 29% and the proportion is very high, which indicates that the population has a lot to do with the sports interest and athletic capability.

4.2 From the viewpoint of sports consumption structure, the economic level of our university women teachers is not high. It is based on entity-based sports consumption and the structure is not reasonable.

4.3 From the viewpoint of sports consumption concepts, their sports consumption concepts are relatively positive. The motive is relatively clear, while it is not fully implemented in the sports consumption behavior.

4.4 The unfavorable factors influencing the university women teachers' sports consumption are: limited economic capability, low interest, bad athletic capability, little leisure time, insufficient sports consumption concepts, etc.

5 Suggestions

5.1 Strengthen the correct guidance of social athletic directors, improve their exercise interest and capability, and accelerate the increasing of sports consumption.

5.2 During the process of economic development, enhance the income level of national economy, and increase the investment dynamics of the sports.

5.3 Correctly guide the sports consumption consciousness, cultivate good sports consumption habit, and accelerate the implementation of sports consumption behavior.

References

1. Yuanzhen, L.: Sports Sociology, vol. 6(2), p. 92. Higher Education Press (2006)
2. Qiujuan, C.: Analysis of Current Situation and Influencing Factors of Our Domestic Woman Sports Consumption. Journal of Yichun University 29(2), 185–186 (2007)
3. Xiaolong, X.: Influencing Factors of Woman Sports Consumption Psychology and Marketing Strategies. Journal of Beijing Sport University 26(1) (2007)
4. Yong, Z.: The Present Sports Consumption Situation and Research of Regular University Teachers of Hebei Province. Market Modernization 136 (2008)

Collusion with Correlated Demand

Hongxin Yao, Zongling Xu, and Jiatao Xu

Business School, Shantou University, Shantou, China
{hxyao,zlxu}@stu.edu.cn, xujiatao2106@163.com

Abstract. Under the correlated demand model, we examine the effects of the correlated coefficient and the volatility of the stochastic demand on the collusion behavior in international trade. With the symmetric cost, the motivation for collusion can be strengthened under correlated demand. In terms of the cost asymmetries, it is shown that the increase of cost difference make it more difficult to sustain collusion in a cartel as the inefficient has greater incentive to defect than the efficient. However, the increase of the correlated coefficient and the risk in stochastic demand could weaken the effects of cost asymmetries on the collusion condition in the international industry.

Keywords: Collusion, Correlated Demand, Cost Asymmetries, Cournot Duopoly.

1 Introduction

Most traditional studies on the strategic behaviors of firms and governments under international oligopoly market have a same assumption which the Cournot and Bertrand competitions are set in an environment, where the market demand of one country is certain and independent with other countries'. However, with the speed up of the global economic integration, the demands of different countries become correlated with each other in reality. In most cases, the variation of demand for energy or manufacture product of one country can in fact influence the demand of other counties in the world, thus, the assumption seems not suitable for explaining some phenomena in international trade.

Consider the reasons, Anam and Shiang [1,2] extended Brander-Spencer model [5] as a new one, where they depart from the existing literature by allowing domestic and foreign demand to be correlated. At first, they demonstrate that demand correlation alone can be a basis for dumping, i.e., dumping may arise in the presence of correlated demand when it would not have occurred had the markets been stochastically independent. More interestingly, they are able to show that covariance-based pricing strategy can lead to a new possibility of dumping below costs. For another, they examine that when the firms play the Cournot-Nash game in two stochastic and positively correlated markets, it may be optimal to tax exports to the more volatile market while subsidizing it in the other. The policy combination reduces the amplitude of aggregate profit and raises the utility of the risk-averse firm in a manner similar to the theory of portfolio choice.

Another literature for the paper concerned about the collusion behaviors, Friedman [7] shown that collusion, where all firms could obtain higher profits than in the static

M. Zhou (Ed.): ISAEBD 2011, Part IV, CCIS 211, pp. 239–248, 2011.
© Springer-Verlag Berlin Heidelberg 2011

Nash equilibrium, could be sustained as a subgame-perfect equilibrium using Nash-reversion trigger strategies provided the discount factor was sufficiently large. Recently, the sustainability of collusion with asymmetries has been addressed in a number of different oligopoly markets. Bae [4], Lambson [8, 9], Rothchild [10], Collie [6] have been considered the Cournot or Bertrand duopoly model to examine the impacts of asymmetric capacity or marginal cost on the collusion condition, such as in Rothchild and Collie' studies [6, 10], they examine that the inefficient firm has greater (weaker) incentive to defect from the cartel without (with) altering the allocation of output quotas. We will extend the literature into a collusion model under correlated demand.

In our paper, we are interested in how the correlated demand impacts on the condition of sustaining collusion. In the case of symmetric cost, the relation between the critical discount factor for collusion and the correlated demand has been considered; it is shown that the motivation for the collusion can be strengthened under the correlated demands. What is more, with the cost asymmetries, we examine the increase of the correlated coefficient of the stochastic demand may weaken the effects of cost asymmetries on the collusion condition in an international industry.

The paper is organized as follows. The basic model with symmetric cost is presented in the section 2, and we extended the Anam and Shiang model to examine the collusion behavior under the correlated demand. In section 3, we consider whether the cost asymmetries effect on the collusion condition and whether the correlated demand can compensate for the effects from cost difference. Concluding remarks are contains in section 4.

2 The Model

In our model as in the Anam and Shiang model [2,3], we assume that there are two firms, one domestic and one foreign, producing a homogeneous product both for local demand and exports, and the export competition takes place in not one but two neutral markets. In contrast to their model, however, two identical firms compete as Cournot duopolists in an infinitely repeated game with a common discount factor: $\delta \in (0,1)$.

Demand for the homogeneous product is linear

$$p_i = a - x_i - y_i + e_i, i = h, f$$

Where x_i and y_i represents the domestic and the foreign firms respectively, h and f represents the domestic and the foreign market. For simplicity, the assumption for the stochastic demands of bilateral markets is similar to Anam's model [3]. We postulate that (e_h, e_f) has a multivariate distribution with $E(e_h) = E(e_f) = 0$, $E(e_h^2) = E(e_f^2) = \sigma^2$, and $E(e_h e_f) = \sigma_{hf} = \rho\sigma^2$, where ρ is the correlated coefficient . Given that $-1 \le \rho \le 1$, the value of ρ is thus bounded by σ^2 and $-\sigma^2$. Thus we can gain some insights into the impacts of the correlated coefficient and the stochastic demand on the collusion behaviors.

Under the condition of stochastic demand, the aggregate profit functions of the firms are given by

$$\pi_h\left(x_h,x_f,y_h,y_f,e_h,e_f\right)=\left(a-x_h-y_h+e_h\right)x_h+\left(a-x_f-y_f+e_f\right)x_f-c_h\left(x_h+x_f\right) \quad (1)$$

$$\pi_f(x_h,x_f,y_h,y_f,e_h,e_f)=\left(a-x_h-y_h+e_h\right)y_h+\left(a-x_f-y_f+e_f\right)y_f-c_f\left(y_h+y_f\right) \quad (2)$$

where c_i is marginal cost of the country i, the profit functions of two firms under certain demand ,the same as the Brander-Krugman model[5] , are be shown as

$$\pi_h(x_h,x_f,y_h,y_f,e_h,e_f)=(a-x_h-y_h)x_h+(a-x_f-y_f)x_f-c_h(x_h+x_f) \quad (3)$$

$$\pi_f(x_h,x_f,y_h,y_f,e_h,e_f)=(a-x_h-y_h)y_h+(a-x_f-y_f)y_f-c_f(y_h+y_f) \quad (4)$$

According to the Anam and Shiang model, the total expected profit of the two risk-averse firms can be denoted as a quadratic utility function, so we have

$$\Pi_i(x_i,x_j,y_i,y_j)=\pi_i(x_i,x_j,y_i,y_j,0,0)-R/2(\pi_i(x_i,x_j,y_i,y_j,e_i,e_j)-\pi_i(x_i,x_j,y_i,y_j,0,0))^2 \quad (5)$$

where $R>0$ is a risk-aversion index.

If the two firms collude with each other for product quantities in bilateral markets, thus they will optimize the profit of the international industry, which yields

$$\Pi = E\sum_i \Pi_i, i = h, f \quad (6)$$

In the first place, let $c_h = c_f = c$ for simplicity. Since the firms are assumed as Cournot duopolists, thus we can derive the optimal output and revenues under international collusion and Cournot-duopoly competition as follows

$$x_i^{na} = y_i^{na} = \frac{(a-c)}{3+\Delta}, \quad x_i^{co} = y_i^{co} = \frac{(a-c)}{4+\Delta}, i = h, f \quad (7)$$

where $\Delta = R(1+\rho)\sigma^2$,the notation na and co denote the Cournot-Nash and collusion condition respectively. Then, substitute equation (7) into the profit function (5), we have

$$\Pi_i^{na} = \frac{(a-c)^2(2+\Delta)}{(3+\Delta)^2}, \quad \Pi_i^{co} = \frac{(a-c)^2}{4+\Delta}, i = h, f \quad (8)$$

Now consider the defecting output and profit in the supergame using Nash-reversion trigger strategies. If the output quota gives each firm higher profit in cartel than in the Cournot equilibrium, then collusion can be sustained provided that the discount factor is sufficient larger. The equilibrium strategies involve each firm choosing its output quota in the first stage and in subsequent stages if both firms have chosen their output quota in all previous stages of the supergame. If any firm has defected from the cartel and chosen an output other than its output quota in any previous stage of the super-game, then the other will choose Cournot equilibrium output as punishment in all subsequent stages. However, the firm who deviating from the cooperative output quota in advance will get more profit in the first defecting stage, we can derive the defecting output and revenue under this condition as follows

$$x_i^{de} = y_i^{de} = \frac{(a-c)(3+\Delta)}{(2+\Delta)(4+\Delta)}, \quad \Pi_i^{de} = \frac{(a-c)^2(3+\Delta)^2}{(2+\Delta)(4+\Delta)^2}, \quad i = h, f \qquad (9)$$

From the above equations, it is obvious to show the excess profit from sustaining collusion and deviating from the cooperation path

$$R_i = E\Pi_i^{co} - E\Pi_i^{na} = \frac{(a-c)^2}{(3+\Delta)^2(4+\Delta)} \qquad (10)$$

$$R_i' = E\Pi_i^{de} - E\Pi_i^{co} = \frac{(a-c)^2}{(4+\Delta)^2(2+\Delta)} \qquad (11)$$

From equations (10) and (11), we know Δ is inversely proportion with R_i (or R_i') while Δ is in direct ration with ρ and σ^2. As for one-shot stage game, both firms choose the duopoly competition is a unique Nash equilibrium analogous with the prisoner dilemma, even if the profit from the collusion is larger than from the competition. But under the supergame framework, collusion is sustainable for both firms, the present discounted value of the profits which comes from being partner in a cartel is no less than the present discounted value of deviating from the collusion for one stage followed by the punishment in all subsequent stages. Thus, the critical dis-count factor can be given by the follow equation:

$$\delta^* = \frac{\Pi_i^{de} - \Pi_i^{co}}{\Pi_i^{de} - \Pi_i^{na}} \qquad (12)$$

After a little math transformation, we obtain

$$R \le R'\frac{\delta}{(1-\delta)} \Leftrightarrow \delta \ge \delta^* = \frac{R}{R+R'} = \frac{(3+\Delta)^2}{17+12\Delta+2\Delta^2} \qquad (13)$$

given R, δ^* will drop with the increase of R', thus, as $\partial R'/\partial\Delta < 0$ and $\partial\Delta/\partial\rho$ (or σ^2) > 0, so δ^* can be heighten by the increase of the ρ and σ^2; on the contrary, given R', δ^* will be raised by the increase of R', then, as $\partial R/\partial\Delta < 0$ and

$\partial\Delta/\partial\rho(\text{or }\sigma^2)>0$, δ^* can be lowered by the increase of the ρ and σ^2. From above, it turn out that Δ has two contradicted impacts on the δ^* through different paths, however, the second impact has larger effect than the first one, so δ^* has been lowered by the increase of ρ and σ^2.[1]

Lemma 1. *The increase of* σ^2 *or* ρ *result in the decrease of* δ^*.

From the Lemma 1, the effects of correlated factor and the risk of stochastic demand on the condition of international collusion can be shown in the following proposition:

Proposition 1. *Since correlated coefficient and risk in stochastic demand can lead to the decrease of critical discount factor, so the motivation for collusion can be streng-thened under the correlated demands.*

The Proposition 1 deliveries the idea as follows. As the market demand is certain, if any export firm deviates from the collusion quota, it will has a strategic response to the collusion quota of the competitor which sustain the cartel at this game stage, and the defecting firm can capture more larger market share and profit through the extended output. However, since the market demand is stochastic and demand be-tween the markets is correlated, it subjectively restrict the outputs of both firms, and limit the extended output for strategy response also, as a result, it certainly weaken the defective motivation of each firm. Generally, the more profit could be gained from the shortened output, the more strong incentive to sustain a cartel they have under this situation.

3 Collusion under the Asymmetric Cost

In the above section, the collusion condition has been derived under the symmetric cost, as a matter of fact, the collusion always formed by the firms with differentiated cost. As in Collie[6] and Rothschild [10] , cost asymmetries make it more difficult to sustain collusion in a cartel that allocates output quotas to maximize total-industry profit as the inefficient firm has a greater incentive to defect than the efficient. In our paper, we examine whether the correlated coefficient and risk of stochastic demand can change the impacts of cost asymmetric on the collusion condition. For the pur-pose on that, we assume $c_h = 0$ and $c_f = c$, thus c can be treated as the cost dif-ference between the domestic and foreign firms. Since the collusion pattern in terms of cost asymmetry has some specialty unlike symmetric cost above, consequently, two cases are considered: (1) a general case where $-1<\rho\le1$ and (2) a special case where $\rho=-1$.

---

[1] Form(12) ,we know $\dfrac{\partial\delta^*}{\partial\rho}=\dfrac{-2(3+\Delta)(\partial\Delta/\partial\rho)}{(17+12\Delta+2\Delta^2)^2}<0$, $\dfrac{\partial\delta^*}{\partial\sigma^2}=\dfrac{-2(3+\Delta)(\partial\Delta/\partial\sigma^2)}{(17+12\Delta+2\Delta^2)^2}<0$.

3.1 Case 1 $-1 < \rho \le 1$

In this case, we are interesting in how the correlated demand change the collusion condition of cost asymmetries. Like in the case of cost symmetries, we need to consider the revenue of each firm from Cournot competition, collusion and defection at first, thus, solving for the Cournot output and profits yields

$$x_h^{na} = x_f^{na} = \frac{a - 2c + (a - c)\Delta}{3 + \Delta(4 + \Delta)}, \, y_h^{na} = y_f^{na} = \frac{a(1 + \Delta) + c}{3 + \Delta(4 + \Delta)}$$

$$\Pi_h^{na} = \frac{(2 + \Delta)(a(1 + \Delta) - c(2 + \Delta))^2}{(3 + 4\Delta + \Delta^2)^2}, \Pi_f^{na} = \frac{(2 + \Delta)(a + c + \Delta)^2}{(3 + 4\Delta + \Delta^2)^2} \quad (14)$$

Given asymmetric cost, when the firms collude, they are assumed to behave as a cartel that maximizes total industry profits. It is straightforward to calculate the joint profit-maximizing output and profits of each firm:

$$x_h^{co} = x_f^{co} = \frac{(a - c)\Delta - 2c}{\Delta(4 + \Delta)}, \, y_h^{co} = y_f^{co} = \frac{a\Delta + 2c}{\Delta(4 + \Delta)}$$

$$\Pi_h^{co} = \frac{(a - c)(a\Delta - c(2 + \Delta))}{\Delta(4 + \Delta)}, \Pi_f^{co} = \frac{a(2c + a\Delta)}{\Delta(4 + \Delta)} \quad (15)$$

Suppose that home (foreign) firm defect from the cartel from the first stage, then it will maximize its one-period profits in the stage given the collusion output of the competitor. Solving for the output and profits of the defecting domestic (foreign) firm yields

$$\Pi_h^{de} = \frac{(a\Delta(3 + \Delta) - c(2 + 4\Delta + \Delta^2))^2}{\Delta^2(2 + \Delta)(4 + \Delta)^2}, \Pi_f^{de} = \frac{(a\Delta(3 + \Delta) + c(2 + \Delta))^2}{\Delta^2(2 + \Delta)(4 + \Delta)^2} \quad (16)$$

Consider the supergame with asymmetric cost, for avoiding prisoner dilemma and forming the cartel, the collusion profit of domestic and foreign firm should be larger than from the deviating behavior (collusion, duopoly) or (duopoly, collusion). Compared with the symmetric case, the output and profit of the domestic and foreign firms is different with each other due to the asymmetric cost, so the discount factors of the home firm is still not in accordance with the foreign one. But only as both firms have motivation to sustain the collusion, there is an actual cartel in the international industry. In order to compare different δ^* between the two firms, from the equations (14)-(16), we have

$$\left(\Pi_h^d - \Pi_h^c\right) - \left(\Pi_f^d - \Pi_f^c\right) = \frac{(a\Delta + 2c)}{\Delta^2(2 + \Delta)(4 + \Delta)^2} > 0 \quad (17)$$

$$\left(\Pi_f^d - \Pi_f^n\right) - \left(\Pi_h^d - \Pi_h^n\right) = \frac{(a-1)\Delta(\Delta+2c)(\Delta+a(2+\Delta))}{(3+4\Delta+\Delta^2)^2} > 0 \quad (18)$$

In (18), we assume the market size a is much larger than cost difference c for simplicity, so we can substitute $c=0$ into the results of the equation (18).[2]Consequently, we obtain lemma2

Lemma 2. *Since* $\pi_f^{de} - \pi_f^{na} > \pi_h^{de} - \pi_h^{na}$ *and* $\pi_f^{de} - \pi_f^{co} < \pi_h^{de} - \pi_h^{co}$, *so we have* $\delta_h > \delta_f$.

As there exists $\delta^* \in [\delta_f, \delta_h]$ [3], the inefficient firm has no incentive to sustain the collusion, the collusion could be realized as $\delta^* > \delta_h$, so we have no need to consider the δ_f. Substitute equations (13)-(15) into the (12), we have

$$\delta_h^* = \frac{(B^2-1)^2[a(B-2)+2c)]}{[A-c(B^2+2)][A(2B^2+4B+9)-c(B^2+2)(2B^2+1)]} \quad (19)$$

where $A = a\Delta(1+\Delta)$ and $B = \Delta+2$ .For simplicity and according to the assumption, we can substitute $c = 0$ into the result of $\partial \delta_h^* / \partial c$, which yields

$$\frac{\partial \delta_h^*}{\partial c} = \frac{2(2+\Delta)(4+\Delta)(3+\Delta)^2(11+10\Delta+2\Delta^2)}{a\Delta(1+\Delta)(17+2\Delta(6+\Delta))^2} > 0 \quad (20)$$

The equation above shown that as the cost difference is increasing, the inefficient firm (domestic firm) will have stronger incentive to compete as duopolists in international trade, the result is the same as the propositions in Rothschild [10]. Furthermore, consider whether the correlated demand can change the collusion behavior with cost asymmetries, the equations below can be derived

$$\frac{\partial^2 \delta_h^*}{\partial c \partial \rho} = \frac{\partial^2 \delta_h^*}{\partial c \partial \Delta} \frac{\partial \Delta}{\partial \rho} < \frac{\partial \delta_h^*}{\partial c} \frac{\partial \Delta}{\partial \rho} (-\frac{5}{17+12\Delta+2\Delta^2}) < 0 \quad (21)$$

$$\frac{\partial^2 \delta_h^*}{\partial c \partial \sigma^2} = \frac{\partial^2 \delta_h^*}{\partial c \partial \Delta} \frac{\partial \Delta}{\partial \sigma^2} < \frac{\partial \delta_h^*}{\partial c} \frac{\partial \Delta}{\partial \sigma^2} (-\frac{5}{17+12\Delta+2\Delta^2}) < 0 \quad (22)$$

---

[2] Collie [6] use the same approximation method to examine the impacts of cost parameters on the critical factor also, as the math solution is too complex.

[3] As $c \geq 0$, no matter how c varies, it can not change the fact that $\left(\pi_h^d - \pi_h^c\right) - \left(\pi_f^d - \pi_f^c\right) > 0$ and $\left(\pi_f^d - \pi_f^n\right) - \left(\pi_h^d - \pi_h^n\right) > 0$,so there always exists $\delta_h > \delta_f$ under our assumption.

Proposition 2. *Cost asymmetries make it more difficult to sustain collusion in a cartel as the inefficient has greater incentive to defect than the efficient. Moreover, the increase of the correlated coefficient and risk in stochastic demand will weaken the effects of cost asymmetries on the collusion condition in international industry.*

The Proposition 2 implies the economic intuition as follows. An inefficient firm expected to extend the profit by capturing more market share from the defecting behavior, and the profit from sustaining the collision in the future can't completely compensate for the one-period profit from deviating the cooperative path, then, as the cost difference become more larger, the inefficient firm has stronger motivation to defect from the collusive trade. However, as the risk in stochastic demand and the correlation between the two market demands has been increasing, two firms need to avoid the uncertainty in the market by limiting their output, thus the inefficient firm can't obtain more profit from the defecting behavior as under the certain condition, so the stronger motivation for deviating from cartel caused by cost asymmetries has been weaken by the correlated demand.

3.2 Case 2 $\rho = -1$ ($\Delta = 0$)

As the market correlation factor is near to -1, the meaning behind the figure is delivery the fact that the demand risk of the two countries is completely substituted, the demand of one country dropped with the same increment of demand of the other. Even if the case is very special, but we still need to consider the cooperation behavior under this condition in theoretic.

Lemma 3. *As $\rho = -1$, the inefficient firm will abstain the output on the condition of collusion, the efficient one will be an actual monopolist.*

Proof: omit

In this case, the total demand is limit but the demand risk is completely in reversion in two different markets. Consequently, the inefficient firm has no motivation to produce in terms of collusion and the efficient firm will be an actual monopolist in this industry, for compensation the efficient firm will provides the subsidy to the inefficient one from the monopoly revenue.

Proposition 3. *The revenue from the monopoly in terms of $\rho = -1$ is larger than aggregate revenue of two firms in Cournot equilibrium, so both firms could benefit firm the cooperation in this case.*

Proof. As the efficient firm is a monopolist in industry, the profit of the firm can be denoted as,

$$\Pi_f^m = E\Pi_f(0,0,y_h,x_f)$$

$$= \pi_f(0,0,y_h,y_f,0,0) - \frac{R}{2}(\pi_f(0,0,y_h,y_f,e_h,e_f) - \pi_f(0,0,y_h,y_f,0,0))^2 \quad (23)$$

$$= (a-y_h)y_h + (a-y_f)y_f - \frac{R}{2}\sigma^2(y_h^2 + 2\rho y_h y_f + y_f^2)$$

As $\rho = -1$, we have the monopoly outputs and profits as follows

$$y_h = y_f = \frac{a}{2},\ \pi_f^m = \frac{a^2}{2} \tag{24}$$

From (14), we have the Cournot outputs and profits as follows

$$x_h^{na} = x_f^{na} = \frac{a-2c}{3},\ y_h^{na} = y_f^{na} = \frac{a+c}{3}$$

$$\Pi_h^{na} = \frac{2(a-c)^2}{9},\ \Pi_f^{na} = \frac{2(a+c)^2}{9} \tag{25}$$

Thus, we have that

$$\Pi_f^m > \Pi_h^{na} + \Pi_f^{na} \qquad\qquad \text{Q.E.D}$$

Proposition 3 states that the two firms could obtain more aggregate revenue from cooperation compared with in Cournot EQ. The intuition behind this result is obvious. Since the demand risk is can not be averse through export on the condition of $\rho = -1$, so the monopoly revenue is optimal choice by the collusive firms, and they can share the revenue surplus through bargaining, but bargain arrangement is not a focus in our paper.

4 Conclusion

With the symmetric cost, since the correlated demand results in the output limit in bilateral markets, it is shown that the motivation for collusion can be strengthened from uncertainty and correlation of the demands. In the case of the cost asymmetry, it turn out that the increase of cost difference make it more difficult to sustain collusion in a cartel as the inefficient has more strong incentive to deviate than the efficient. However, as the inefficient firm can't profit from the defecting behavior as under the certain condition, the increase of the correlated coefficient and the volatility in stochastic demand will weaken the effects of cost asymmetries on the collusion in the international industry.

Even if all these conclusions in our paper are derived under the stricter assumption, the results still provide a helpful understanding for the effects of the correlated demand on the collusion behavior in international trade. Both the firms with symmetric or asymmetric cost will have a greater incentive to sustain collusion under the condition of the correlated demand, it means the volatility and the correlation of demands will be available for the collusion behaviors. However, the influence of the correlated demand and collusion behavior on the whole world economy and social welfare of countries needs to further research.

References

1. Mahmudul, A., Chiang, S.-H.: Dumping with correlated demand. Southern Economic Journal 62, 1072–1078 (1996)
2. Anam, M., Chiang, S.-H.: Export market correlation and strategic trade policy. Canadian Journal of Economics 33, 41–52 (2000)
3. Anam, M., Chiang, S.-H.: Price discrimination and social welfare with correlated demand. Journal of Economic Behavior and Organization 64, 110–122 (2004)
4. Bae, H.: A price-setting supergame between heterogeneous firms. European Economic Review 31, 1159–1171 (1987)
5. Brander, J., Krugman, P.: A 'reciprocal dumping' model of international trade. Journal of International Economics 15, 313–320 (1983)
6. Collie, D.: Sustaining collusion with asymmetric cost. Presented to the Royal Economic Society Conference at the University of Wales, Swansea (2004)
7. Friedman, J.W.: A non-cooperative equilibrium for supergames. Review of Economic Studies 38, 1–12 (1971)
8. Lambson, V.E.: Some results on optimal penal codes in asymmetric Bertrand supergames. Journal of Economic Theory 62, 444–468 (1994)
9. Lambson, V.E.: Optimal penal codes in nearly symmetric Bertrand supergames with capacity constraints. Journal of Mathematical Economics 24, 1–22 (1995)
10. Rothschild, R.: Cartel stability when costs are heterogeneous. International Journal of Industrial Organization 17, 717–734 (1999)

The Research of Measurement of Goodwill Based on Enterprise Resource Theory

Xi Wang

Center of China's Merger and Acquisition Research, Beijing Jiaotong University
wangxi198@163.com

Abstract. As a capital operation, M&A is chosen by many companies to expand the scale of enterprises. Increasing attention is paid to confirm and measure goodwill. We should find a way to confirm and measure it. In the first the paper introduce the nature of this goodwill, in the second part it make a brief review of enterprise resources theory, considering goodwill as a valuable enterprise, rarity, imperfect imitability and irreplaceable nature of the specific resources and business-specific capabilities. In the third part, it put forward the concept of the index of goodwill to measure the goodwill based on enterprise resource theory. The index of goodwill is to evaluate the corporate profitability (ROE) which exceeds the industry average ROE.

Keywords: Goodwill, enterprise resource theory, the Index of goodwill.

1 Introduction

The size of M&A on global is increasing. The goodwill takes great proportion in the purchase price. For example, Philip Mooris spent $1.29 billion to acquire Kraft Inc of which 90% is goodwill. In the Time Warner M&A case, $13 billion out of $14 billion is goodwill. Increasing attention is paid to confirm and measure goodwill. The current internationally accepted practice is to only confirm the combined goodwill, not the generated goodwill. In fact, the essence of both is the same. Because of uncertainty and immeasurability, the generated goodwill isn't confirmed which will make the financial statements contrary to the principle of comparability.

1.1 The Reviews on the Nature of Goodwill

Currently the main reviews on the nature of goodwill are: the view of intangible resources, the view of excess profit, the view of residual values, excess resources in view of profitability.

(I) The view of intangible resources
The views of intangible resources take backs to the view of favorable impression. The perspective believes that goodwill is produced in the harmonious business relationships and customer preferences. This favorable impression may come from the advantages of corporate status, good reputation, such as exclusive privileges and good management.

M. Zhou (Ed.): ISAEBD 2011, Part IV, CCIS 211, pp. 249–255, 2011.

(II) The view of excess profit
The view of excess profit thinks that goodwill is discounted value of excess earnings. U.S. accounting expert Paton (1922) thinks "goodwill "in the broad sense is the future value of the capitalization of excess earnings, or more than the "normal " level of profitability of enterprises.

(III) The view of residual values
In current accounting practice, the measurement of goodwill is mainly based on the residual values, which is equal to the overall enterprise value of goodwill, minus the fair value of identifiable net assets. This method is simple, but the views are affected by the concept of intangible resources. Generally believed that the reason why the overall value of the enterprise will be greater than the value of the identifiable net assets is due to the existence of intangible assets not recorded or synergies exist.

(IV) Excess resources in view of profitability
China's well-known scholar Yang Rumei (1936) in the "The discussion on intangibles assets "suggests the enterprise's excess earnings dates to the enterprise of some special resource rapport with the role of other intangible assets. Because not all factors which create their excess earnings can be recognized, these unrecognized intangible assets can generally be attributed to the goodwill.

2   Explanation on Goodwill Based on Enterprise Resource Theory

Enterprise resource theory mainly explores the sources of competitive advantage on the view of the internal resources in enterprise. Enterprise resources include both tangible and intangible assets and corporate capacity. Penrose (1959) in the "business growth theory " first proposed in his book "resource based theory", she believes resources and capabilities constitute the basis for sustained growth in economic efficiency of enterprises, and enterprises depends on the accumulation of knowledge to save scarce decision-making ability resources, managers can use the savings of the decision-making ability resources to solve new problems.

Currently, the academic communities generally agree that goodwill will bring excess returning for the enterprise, but few studies research on why the goodwill can generate excess returns. Enterprise resource theory can be made to explain the excess capacity. Economists mainly discuss the formation of corporate excess profits from the perspective of production and product market imperfections. Enterprise resource theory suggests that business is a resource system, because each enterprise has the resources and ability to dominate resources differently, output efficiency will be different for each company. That those who have valuable, scarce, incomplete imitable, the specific intangible resources and capabilities to take advantage of these specific intangible assets can get excess earnings than average profits the industry obtained.

Although the profits are uncertain and will change as market conditions change. This is why the financial report did not record the goodwill in the accounts. Goodwill of these companies is essentially the specific resources and business capabilities mentioning in the above. Goodwill can bring excess earnings to the enterprise. Although the unrecognition of goodwill, we can elect a representative analysis of the factors including the relationships between business ,customers, suppliers and government, the advantage human factors, corporate culture, management system and other advantages. Enterprises take the advantage which the goodwill brings forward to implement the strategy which its competitors cannot, access to markets, improve corporate profitability. Currently in the accounting report, the accounting report did not confirm the above aspects, but the goodwill has a great impact on the enterprise's profitability, the financial report should be a true reflection of financial situation of enterprises through the confirmation of the goodwill.

Most of the resources of enterprises can bring benefits to the enterprise, but not all resources can bring excess profits. The intangible resources such as human factors, management processes, and information technology systems can create value for the enterprise, but these intangible resources cannot create sustainable competitive advantage. They are an essential resource for business operations, not reflect the nature of goodwill that can provide a sustainable advantage in resources.

3   The Construction of the Index of Goodwill

In the above talking, we know goodwill is the internal value, rarity, imperfect imitability and irreplaceable nature of the specific resources and specific business capabilities. But under the existing accounting reports, any enterprise has unrecorded intangible resources and capabilities, only those with value, rarity, imperfect imitability and irreplaceable nature of the specific resources and capabilities can generate sustained excess profits. Only these part recourses of the business can be recognized as goodwill. The general poor performance in those enterprises, intangible assets and enterprises ability can create value, but cannot sustain, because other companies also have the same advantage, or can easily copy and replace these resources. Due to the difficulty of measurement of these intangible resources, the current financial reporting system has not recognized them. So when we measure goodwill, we must exclude the value that the normal intangible resources create. Here we can distinguish between "the view of intangible resources" and "the view of enterprise resource''. although both are from the internal resources of enterprise to explain the goodwill, "the view of enterprise resource'' stressed the value, rarity, imperfect imitability and irreplaceable nature of the specific business resources and capabilities, and "the view of intangible resources" does not distinguish between specific resources and general resources.

The index of goodwill is defined as excess profits which is equal to the enterprise's ROE minus the industry average ROE. The company's index of goodwill multiplied by the net assets is defined as goodwill. We choose ROE because of its ability to best reflect corporate profits. When the enterprise's ROE can sustain higher than the industry average, then the difference (between the enterprise's ROE and the industry average) can be used to calculate the company's goodwill. In the bellowing, we take China's pharmaceutical industry as an example; calculate the value of the index of goodwill in the China's pharmaceutical industry between 2007 -2010, The average return on equity rate is 19.6163%, 17.6489%, 18.7436%, 13.0974%, these data may indicate that the income of the average level of the pharmaceutical industry, including the value the normal intangible resources create. The specific intangible resource exists in the corporate which ROE can sustain beyond the industry average. The following Table I indicates the index of goodwill in China's pharmaceutical industry between 2007—2010.

Table 1. The index of goodwill of China's pharmaceutical industry between 2007-2010

Stock number	2007 the index of goodwill	2008 the index of goodwill	2009 the index of goodwill	2010 the index of goodwill
300122	0.761737333	0.808810533	0.41746419	0.14262601
002399	0.381537333	0.534110533	1.01406419	0.08972601
300039	0.618637333	0.398210533	0.29316419	-0.02667399
300026	0.771137333	0.513410533	0.14256419	-0.06287399
000650	-0.014662667	0.094010533	0.03906419	0.09692601
300086	0.335737333	0.178810533	0.30396419	-0.01037399
002412	0.370337333	0.213310533	0.13056419	-0.02657399
002317	0.091037333	0.353110533	0.30316419	-0.03237399
002424	0.296837333	0.184210533	0.16306419	-0.05237399
300119	0.287437333	0.125210533	0.08216419	0.02962601
002275	0.195737333	0.171210533	0.08046419	0.01902601
002001	-0.099962667	0.777610533	0.25626419	0.14302601
002422	0.190637333	0.139710533	0.12216419	0.01012601
002393	0.093437333	0.160510533	0.14626419	-0.02147399
300138	-0.034662667	0.179710533	0.15626419	0.06082601
000538	0.062937333	0.117510533	-0.00763581	0.09972601
600216	-0.128362667	0.553110533	0.35746419	0.14362601
002022	0.090237333	0.133810533	0.11536419	0.14352601
002118	0.090737333	-0.02408947	-0.03593581	0.20252601
300150	0.037737333	0.030510533	0.15406419	0.08452601
002433	0.154637333	0.081810533	0.08996419	-0.05597399
000623	0.403337333	0.005810533	0.05916419	0.00152601
002007	0.001337333	0.044410533	0.24546419	0.18992601
002349	0.125337333	0.072810533	0.08026419	-0.04497399
000963	0.143237333	0.076610533	0.21456419	0.06792601
002038	0.081737333	0.156810533	0.09626419	0.12322601
600276	0.086137333	0.052210533	0.09866419	0.11352601
300110	0.007537333	0.046810533	0.04676419	-0.00157399
002370	0.067337333	0.056910533	0.04376419	-0.07227399
300016	0.102937333	0.085310533	-0.00503581	-0.07997399
600829	0.042037333	0.019710533	0.00226419	0.08342601
002219	0.072437333	-0.01098947	-0.04453581	0.00212601

Table 1. (*continued*)

600781	0.048637333	0.037810533	-0.04763581	-0.02707399
300049	-0.008862667	0.022010533	0.05096419	-0.05627399
300006	0.072837333	0.092010533	-0.02143581	-0.07457399
002004	0.168537333	-0.05208947	-0.02773581	0.01512601
300009	0.001237333	0.076810533	0.00056419	-0.02757399
002099	-0.137162667	-0.12898947	-0.13233581	0.01322601
600196	-0.018562667	-0.00098947	0.29186419	-0.01597399
002332	-0.016662667	0.002110533	0.03916419	-0.01907399
000423	-0.017762667	0.039110533	0.02376419	0.03012601
600161	-0.022362667	0.028110533	0.04546419	0.06242601
002198	0.061337333	-0.11398947	-0.12293581	-0.03077399
000513	0.108837333	-0.14848947	0.06156419	0.04842601
600557	-0.007462667	0.053110533	-0.03203581	-0.00287399
600535	-0.094462667	-0.04068947	-0.02283581	0.07962601
600436	-0.042462667	0.012810533	-0.01513581	0.03532601
600195	-0.047462667	-0.03318947	-0.00023581	0.09152601
002107	-0.084862667	-0.05588947	-0.10833581	-0.28387399
600993	0.006437333	-0.06918947	0.02046419	-0.00737399
600750	-0.077562667	-0.01798947	0.01116419	0.10532601
600420	-0.004162667	-0.07538947	-0.03253581	0.03052601
600267	-0.089362667	-0.03998947	-0.02443581	0.03202601
600479	0.035767333	-0.02361547	-0.03833581	-0.04277399
002019	0.356037333	-0.10258947	-0.14203581	-0.14447399
600664	-0.071562667	-0.01538947	-0.03053581	0.00312601
002030	-0.073562667	-0.06488947	-0.05173581	0.01182601
600518	-0.097562667	-0.06568947	-0.05043581	-0.02577399
600062	0.021137333	-0.03738947	-0.04973581	0.01032601
600521	-0.052262667	-0.02968947	-0.04283581	-0.05527399
000788	-0.144962667	-0.12718947	-0.05853581	0.26962601
000566	-0.310262667	-0.02588947	-0.01373581	-0.04907399
000919	-0.011662667	-0.12918947	-0.06343581	-0.03027399
600351	-0.066362667	-0.03678947	-0.03183581	0.02472601
000522	-0.001562667	-0.07808947	-0.06193581	0.07182601
600572	-0.052362667	-0.07128947	-0.08073581	0.03332601
600085	-0.104162667	-0.08238947	-0.09003581	-0.02227399
600079	-0.119162667	-0.09588947	-0.03083581	-0.01427399
600594	0.003117333	-0.00150947	0.00280419	0.03911601

Table 1. (*continued*)

600380	0.087947333	-0.18596947	-0.02297581	0.08098601
000597	-0.144662667	0.144910533	0.07756419	-0.10447399
600607	-0.119962667	-0.07498947	0.01356419	-0.13097399
000989	-0.073762667	-0.01428947	-0.06813581	-0.04547399
600201	-0.053462667	-0.07278947	-0.09613581	-0.01617399
000952	0.139937333	-0.04168947	-0.13153581	-0.11437399
600666	-0.078162667	-0.06618947	-0.07803581	-0.03047399
000999	-0.088462667	-0.00738947	0.02556419	0.07992601
000739	-0.145862667	-0.13658947	-0.14243581	-0.10057399
600252	-0.099862667	-0.06788947	0.05996419	0.11642601
600332	-0.081562667	-0.11768947	-0.12183581	-0.05287399
000915	-0.154762667	-0.13228947	-0.08453581	0.05242601
600771	-0.196162667	-0.17648947	-0.18743581	-0.13097399
600422	-0.144262667	-0.12208947	-0.09573581	-0.00857399
000661	-0.173362667	-0.12108947	-0.00413581	0.04962601
600488	-0.175162667	-0.14178947	-0.14353581	-0.07237399
600285	-0.064262667	-0.15798947	-0.13553581	-0.09217399
000990	-0.138962667	-0.15138947	-0.15893581	-0.11797399
600129	-0.145862667	-0.15798947	-0.15673581	-0.10317399
600513	-0.157762667	-0.12848947	-0.12753581	-0.07807399
600222	-0.154862667	-0.13278947	-0.13333581	-0.09379899
600976	-0.184462667	-0.15468947	-0.12253581	-0.04127399
600329	-0.257862667	-0.01718947	-0.00203581	0.04642601
002020	-0.191062667	-0.23776947	-0.17497581	-0.08930399
000078	-0.148762667	-0.19188947	-0.16913581	-0.06047399
000705	-0.179862667	-0.15118947	-0.15123581	-0.08957399
000766	-0.161662667	-0.14498947	-0.13503581	-0.11057399
000153	-0.187262667	-0.15438947	-0.15263581	-0.07917399
000606	-0.133762667	-0.14708947	-0.21723581	-0.13007399
600867	-0.139562667	-0.14558947	-0.13593581	-0.05537399
600277	-0.162002667	-0.24288947	-0.16883581	-0.06887399
000756	-0.172162667	-0.15618947	-0.11913581	-0.07287399
000790	-0.191462667	-0.16338947	-0.16933581	-0.10187399
600812	-0.147062667	0.018310533	-0.54113581	0.10932601
600789	-0.178062667	-0.15308947	-0.16233581	-0.04937399

4 Conclusion

Enterprises which average return between 2007--2010 is negative are excluded in the above table. Those enterprises has been in the net assets below the industry average, therefore, it is removed. As can be seen from the above data, the index of goodwill can be positive or negative. Positive index of goodwill indicates that companies' return on net assets exceed the industry average, having competitive resources. The index of negative goodwill indicates that competitive advantage is yet to play out .Index of goodwill can give suggestions to the M&A party in paying a appropriate premium to the combined party. That M & A party is ready to pay a premium to the combined party which ROE is beyond the industry level, and the index of goodwill continues to remain positive in the recent years, the premium will be more apparent.

Enterprises in the merger process may pay a premium to the company which have a negative index of goodwill, which is determined by the M & A targets. That is to say the acquiring party may consider it as strategic acquisitions. In our current accounting system, measurement of combined goodwill may include the price which does not reflect the essence of goodwill. This view is different from the essence of goodwill as a valuable, scarce, incomplete replicability and irreplaceable nature of the specific resources and capabilities. The measurement of goodwill must reflect essence of goodwill which can create value for the enterprise, and keep the ability to get excess earnings. In this view, we believe that only those with positive index of goodwill have specific resources and enterprise capabilities and create value for the enterprise.

Despite the goodwill of the index will be inflected by the financial market volatility, we can choose the companies which sustain to exceed industry standards or calculate the average index of goodwill. But this method measures and confirms the goodwill from the point of view of essence of goodwill. Business managers can manage goodwill through the change of index of goodwill. At the same time the index of goodwill can give advice managers to pay an appropriate premium for the combined company.

References

1. Tang, Y., Qian, F.: Accounting Theory. Shanghai Financial Press, Shanghai (1997)
2. Miller, M., Hopkins: Goodwill-an aggregation issue. The Accounting Review (1973)
3. Paton, W.A.: Accounting Theory. John Publishing Company, New York (1922)
4. Walker, George, T.: Accountants' present concept of goodwill depends upon unusual earning power. Journal of Accountancy (1951)
5. Yan, D.: Reconstruction of Goodwill Accounting Theory - Comment on goodwill accounting Three Theories. The school journal of Zhongnan University of Economics and Law (1997)
6. Yang, R.: The discussion on Intangible assets, 3rd edn. China Financial and Economic Publishing House, Beijing (1936)
7. Ge, J.: Current Issues in financial accounting–derivative financial instruments, generated goodwill and uncertainty. Accounting research (1) (1996)
8. Dong, B.: Generated goodwill Studies - a resource based view of competitive advantage. Xiamen University (2004)
9. Li, Y.: The accounting element based resource theory. Accounting research (2006)

Research and Design of Logistics Management Information System of Chinese Small and Medium-Sized Enterprises

Zhigang Zha and Nan Li

School of Business, Jiangsu Teachers University of Technology,
213001 Changzhou, China
dxzg800@163.com, linan @jstu.edu.cn

Abstract. At present, the management of goods distribution and supply scheduling is mainly operated by workers according to their experience in most of small and medium-sized enterprises (SMEs), which is unfavorable to the improvement of working efficiency, and is more difficult to deal with the complicated situation. The logistics management information system and its operation procedure designed in this article can enable the goods distribution and supply scheduling procedure of some qualified SMEs tend to standardize and principled. It is a convenient way for SMEs to control and manage accurately.

Keywords: Logistics Management, Distribution, Supply, Scheduling.

1 Introduction

The goods distribution scheduling of most SMEs s are mainly operated by workers at present. Dispatchers mainly rely on their own experience to carry on the connection, scheduling and loading of vehicles, while rarely consider uniform scheduling of vehicles on the external supply of goods such as materials and purchased parts. This model can basically meet the needs in the low season of shipment, but will produce some outstanding issues to some aspects of the enterprise that cause the temporary confusion and disorder in the peak season of shipments.

2 Overview of Design Philosophy of Goods Distribution and Supply Scheduling Management Information System (GDSSMIS)

2.1 Positive Significance of Implementation of GDSSMIS

Specifically, operation and implementation of GDSSMIS and its procedure is expected to bring at least the following aspects of the positive effects:

Eliminate the Confused Situation that Vehicles from Outside Waiting in the Crowded Warehouse in Busy Season, While Allowing the Carrier Cooperate

M. Zhou (Ed.): ISAEBD 2011, Part IV, CCIS 211, pp. 256–261, 2011.
© Springer-Verlag Berlin Heidelberg 2011

with the Enterprise to Arranges the Vehicle in a Planned Way at the Same Time, Strengthen the Coordination Between Enterprises and the Carrier.

Reduce the Unordered and Blindness of Scheduling and Storage Department, Reduce the Duplication of Work, Reduced the Labour Intensity and Improve Work Efficiency.

It Is Easy to Track the Situation of Shipped Goods in Transit, Enhance the Security and Reliability of Transportation.

Allow Customers to Understand the Precise Time that the Goods Send and Reach and the Situation in the Course More Accurately.

The Selection of Economic Line and the Optimization of Loading Scheme Will Save the Costs for Enterprises to a Certain Extent, the Portfolio that the System Counts Accurately can Offer More Accurate Reference Basis for Settlement of the Freight Charges at the Same Time.

It Is Convenient for Administrative Department Obtains More Accurate Information in Time, and to Make Management Decisions More Scientific.

2.2   Structure and Function of GDSSMIS

GDSSMIS mainly consists of the following function modules:

The Basic Information Set and Maintenance Function Module

Set of Basic Information. Set up the product information database, including materials such as the name of product, edition, the specification, type, quota weight and the volume after packaging; The basic information database of vehicle, including materials such as the specification, type, loading capacity; The basic information database of the warehouse, including materials such as warehouse name, address, storing products classification, capacity.

Maintenance of Basic Information. Maintain and back up all business data and store information and manage data, support the information inquiry function at the same time, inquire about all information in the system according to the sales slip, by the shopping list, by the license number, by customer's name, by the destination or by time at any time.

Comparison of Inventory Check Function Module. The main function of this module will be automatically to compare the number of goods need to ship on sales notice with the number stock in the warehouse that can be transferred after certain time to see whether can satisfy the demand. If can be satisfied, the system reminds feasible; If can not satisfied, the system reminds to wait, and forecast the time of waiting according to produce progress.

Loading Function Module. According to the information such as the name, specification, type and quantity of the goods need to be shipping on the sales notice, this module channel the basic information material of the products and the vehicle into the system, calculate data such as the volume and weight of the goods need to be shipping, and then according to the loading rules such as the big do not press the small, the heavy do not press the light, avoid pollution, proposed three kinds scheme on loading and vehicle matching for choosing. The system supports the function such as one order many cars, try hard to transport rounded up, pay the utmost attention to the self-provided car, the selected scheme can carry on the artificial adjustment of a certain degree and revise, offer the knowledge database for self-study at the same time, the module has a certain extension functions service for new requirements such as increase the loading rules and increase the loading plans.

Geographical Information System (GIS) Module. This module can list two economic lines (domestic area) automatically according to the origin point and end point information obtained for selection, and indicate the line length, the average running time of vehicles (within a certain speed), the main three waypoints and other information. Program can be adjusted manually to a certain degree. System has the function of manually adjustment of the knowledge database memory or selected final scheme to offer appropriate line scheme intelligent at the similar business.

Queuing Function Module. This module calculate the number of vehicles required per hour mainly based on queuing theory of operations research , and then calculate the average time interval per vehicle enter into the warehouse , arrange vehicle timetable more scientific and accurate.

Vehicle Trips Tracking Management Function Module. The module supports the operation of vehicle trips cancelled, and record the delivery vehicles to coming, shipping, via the designated place, reaching the destination and the time information and a brief case of all other aspects.

3   Operation Procedure of GDSSMIS

3.1   The Flow Charts

The Beginning and Ending of the Business Flow Chart Indicated with Hollow Arrows;

The Transferring of the Subsystem, Insertion of the Data Also Used Hollow Arrows;

Business Processing Steps Indicated with Real Lines Add Arrows;

The Information Transferred Automatically in System Indicated with Increases with Dashed Lines Add Arrows.

3.2   The Flow Charts

Inventory Checking and Comparing Subsystem Call in Related Finished Goods Inventory Data According to the Sales Notice Information Has Been Already Input and Compare It with the Quantity of the Goods to Be Shipped Automatically to See Whether Can Satisfy the Demand. The principle of checking comparison operation is: the current inventory number minus scheduled shipment number, minus reserve inventory number, plus storage number produced in extended hours, comes to plan inventory number.

The current inventory number $-$ scheduled shipment number $-$ reserve inventory number $+$ storage number produced in extended hours $=$ plan inventory number.

Then compare the number of all types of goods to be shipped in the sales notice with the relevant plan inventory number of finished product, if $\sum$plan inventory number $\geq \sum$ the number of goods to be shipped, then system to remind feasible, On the contrary, the system remind to wait, and calculate the waiting time according to unit time average output rate to meet the demand of shipping. As expected waiting time over one day, notify the sales department to contact customers and make explanation, contact the production department to step up producing at the same time; As expected waiting time is less than one day, wait after contacting the production departments directly. Once the plan inventory number can satisfy the demand, the system reminds feasible, business treatment enters the next link.

Loading Subsystem Aimed at Providing Loading Scheme for Transportation of Truck-Load, If Less-Than-Truck-Load Transport, Just Draw the Total Weight and Volume of the Goods, Do Not Have to Select Vehicle Type, and Let the Transport Companies to Matching. If self-provided vehicle has already come into operation, the system predicts its time to return according to tracking the statistical information, and compare with the deadline of the length of extended hours, for instance: return time predicted≤deadline of the length of extended hours, use the self-provided vehicle, otherwise they will outsource transport. In this way, it can get more sufficient use to self-provided vehicle.

Geographical Information Subsystem Can List Two Economic Lines (Domestic Area) Automatically According to the Origin Point and End Point Information Obtained for Selection, and Indicate the Line Length, the Average Running Time of Vehicles (Within a Certain Speed), the Main Three Waypoints and Other Information. Program can be adjusted manually to a certain degree. System has the function of manually adjustment of the knowledge database memory or selected final scheme to offer appropriate line scheme intelligent at the similar business.

After Route Scheme Selected, We can Print Out the Result in the Form of Transport Requirements List. It includes warehouse name, address, destination, goods name, specification and type, quantity, weight, transportation route, three main passing through points, customer, contact, telephone number, invoice number, order number, sales department, vehicle type and loading scheme requirements and so on, and leave carrier's name, license number of matching vehicle, specification and type, loading capacity, driver's name, telephone number, and other blank columns.

If scheme printed out requires self-owned vehicles, enter the vehicle arrangement procedures after the relevant staff filling in the requirements list, and then, If scheme requires outsourcing the transport, can fax transport requirements list to the carrier. Carrier allocate vehicle and driver according to the transport requirements list, and fill detailed contents in the blank before re-fax the list to the scheduling department.

The Scheduling Department Input System the Contents Filled in By the Carrier and Queue Vehicles After Receive the Requirements List Returned. The principle of the queuing system is: According to queuing theory, arrival process of the vehicle that come to the warehouse to load and unload the goods seen as a Poisson flow, the subject parameters of arrival time is the negative exponential distribution of λ ; the subject parameters of each vehicle's loading and unloading time (from beginning to go through the formalities until leave the storage) is the negative exponential distribution of μ; while at the same time can serves for S vehicles' loading and unloading . So, can set up a set of M/M/S waiting queuing model:

The idle probability of loading place in the finished storehouse:

$$P_0 = \left[\sum_{n=0}^{s-1} \frac{\rho^n}{n!} + \frac{\rho^s}{S!(1-\rho_s)} \right]^{-1} \qquad \rho = \frac{\lambda}{\mu} \quad \rho_s = \frac{\lambda}{s\mu} \tag{1}$$

Average queue length

$$L_q = \frac{P_0 \, \rho^s \, \rho_s}{S!\,(1-\rho_s)^2} \tag{2}$$

$$L = L_q + \rho$$

The System Will Print Out the Details Information Table of the Vehicle Trip Scheduled. According to different purposes of coming vehicles, information table can be classified as "supply vehicle coming time notice" and "dispatch delivery vehicles task list". Among them, the "supply vehicle coming time notice" transferred to the supply department, and faxed to the supplier by the supply department in form of shopping list. And to require suppliers to notify the supply vehicles to arrive at the appointed warehouse according to the scheduled time strictly. "Dispatch delivery vehicles task list" includes the relevant information in the sales notice, vehicle information, loading programs, drivers name, telephone, transportation routes, the main three via point, line length, the time entering warehouse, estimated shipping time, estimated time of arrival and other content, which (together with the timing of delivery vehicles) will also be transmitted by the system to the gate keeper and warehouse (the gate keeper can only see time table and the corresponding coming vehicle information for reason of authority). Scheduling department re-fax the vehicle dispatch list printed out to the carrier or directly notify the driver of self-provided vehicle, and require all drivers to enter the warehouse according to the time table strictly, must not be ahead of time or delay.

Once the Special Circumstances Appear, Need to Cancel the Vehicle Trips that Have Already Scheduled, Then to Carry on the Operation of Cancelling Vehicle Trips. If vehicle trips be cancelled are delivery vehicle, Comparison of inventory check subsystem will reduce corresponding "the number of shipments been scheduled." automatically. If the time difference between the vehicle trip cancelled and the former or later vehicles is greater than or equal to the fixed time interval of vehicle queue, and: If the time difference between the vehicle trip cancelled and the former or later vehicles is greater than or equal to the fixed time interval of vehicle queue, and:

Time of vehicle trip cancelled $\geq$ formality time＋come vehicle traveling time＋current time, the time cancelled can be filled in by the new sales notice behind, but must meet another condition at the same time: time difference of the adjoining vehicle trips from the vehicle trip cancelled to newly added vehicle trip less than double the fixed time interval of vehicle queue (newly added vehicle trip time＝formality time＋formality time＋come vehicle traveling time ＋current time).

Formality time is the necessary time from input the basic information of the sales notice newly arrived to the dispatch vehicle list sent to driver, can set up into fixed value after calculating. The same methods handle with come vehicle traveling time.

4   Relevant Problems Needing to Solve

4.1 The Primary Premise of This System's Effective Operation Is that Can Grasp the Finished Goods Inventory Timely and Accurately. Therefore, the finished goods warehouse must be unified planning, and adopt scientific inventory checking means to improve the speed and accuracy of inventory, conditional enterprise can be equipped with special inventory utensils such as scanner.

4.2 The Stacking and Storage Conditions of Some Enterprises' Materials Warehouse Are Relatively Poor, The Confused Situation Often Occur that Need to Look for the Place for the Reaching Goods to Be Piled Up Temporarily, Which Led to Vehicles Stuck in The Warehouse Area for a Long Time. So, must further improve existing warehouse management rules and regulations according to the specific situation, and urge warehouse staff to comply with the rules and regulations strictly, eliminate the phenomenon of cluttered, so that make warehouse management more principled and standardized, and thus make a good use of existing warehouse resources rational and effective.

4.3 The Normal Running of This System Needs Mutual Cooperation and Coordination Between Related Departments and Relevant Work Links as the Guarantee, Especially Cooperation and Coordination Among Production and Storage, Purchase, Transportation Scheduling And So On. Therefore, it is necessary to strengthen the mutual communication and convergence between the relevant departments and work links, only really understood each other subjectively, could be getting the result of cooperating more closely and coordinated objectively.

4.4 The Set of Relevant Data of the System Should Be as Accurate as Possible. Before setting up the data, should carry on calculating carefully, and consider of the possibility and range of data change at different time and under different conditions comprehensively, make every effort to obtain the true and reliable average value of data which accords with the actual conditions.

Reference

1. Hu, Y., Guo, Y.: Operations Research Tutorial, pp. 291–305. Tsinghua University Press, Beijing (2000)

The Research on the Policy of Debt Financing for the Scientific Middle and Small Enterprises

Zheng Zhang

School of Business Administration
South China University of Technology
Guangzhou, China
sprite@scut.edu.cn

Abstract. The current situation of debt financing for the small and middle enterprises (SMEs) was analysis, and highlights current policies and measures supporting the debt financing for small and middle enterprises in some parts of China. By learning the experience and successful practices, some suggestions and recommendations on policy for supporting the scientific small and middle enterprises debt financing was proposed.

Keyword: Scientific middle and small enterprises, Debt financing, Policy.

1 Introduction

In recent years, the important status and role of small and middle enterprises (SMEs) in the economic and social development of China has been widely recognized by all society, causing all levels of government attention as well. Up to the end of October 2006, registered SMEs in China has reached more than 430 million, which created the value of all final goods and services accounting for 58.5% of GDP, accounting for taxes paid 50.2%, absorbing 75% of urban employment population and 75% of the rural migrant workers. Among them, scientific SMEs represent one of the most dynamic and potential of the backbone. The open mind, innovation and vitality of scientific SMEs influence the development and advancement of science and technology in China significantly. According to statistics, SMEs which accounts for 3.3% of the SME, has contributed more than 65% of patented inventions, more than 74% to technological innovation and 82% of the new product development. However, the SMEs' main problem are financing from the date of birth. The availability of stable sources of funds, getting the funds timely and sufficiently, are essential to all enterprises, including SMEs.

Currently, the SME financing mainly includes debt financing and equity financing. The debt financing is that the Enterprises finance through debt. The capital suppliers as a debtee entitle to recover the principal and interest due the financing. Debt financing of SMEs in China mainly include bank loans, bond financing, credit guarantee financing, private debt financing and financial leasing financing etc. At present, the equity financing system is just established. The newly established small and medium

M. Zhou (Ed.): ISAEBD 2011, Part IV, CCIS 211, pp. 262–267, 2011.
© Springer-Verlag Berlin Heidelberg 2011

enterprises board and GEM (Growth Enterprises Market) board can only help a small number of large-scale financing for SMEs in short time. Expanding and improving the financing system for SMEs have become a priority.

2   The Current Status of SME Financing

Currently, SMEs generally face the same problems: lacking the funds to support the transform for technology and rapid and healthy development for enterprises. Source of financing, including limited circumstances, bank credit remains the main channel for SME financing. But for the loan transaction and monitoring costs are high, lack of credit, lack of collateral assets, and many other reasons, the situation of unwilling to provide a loan by bank to the SME remains widespread. Corporate bond market is still very high threshold issue. The chance for the SME to public offering loans is slim. Private finance although has played a role in some economically developed areas in China, it has greater blindness and uncertainty for the lack of the necessary legal specification and management. In addition, the SME credit guarantee system for financing is still underway. As for venture capital, it bears a higher credit risk. In our country, it is basically still in the exploration and the initial stage, and the underdevelopment of capital markets makes the benign cycle of investing, training and dropping out impossible.

3   Advanced Experiences and Measures in Some Regions of China

Currently, parts of the country have taken various measures and means to broaden the channels for SME debt financing and have made some experience and achievements.

By issuing "Regulations for promoting SME development in Zhejiang Province" and "The opinions on construction of interaction and cooperation mechanisms for SMEs ", Zhejiang Province in 2006 strengthened supporting the financing and taxing for SMEs. The branch Bureau of People's Bank of China Banking in Zhejiang province tried to play a policy-oriented role in encouraging investment. It encouraged in many ways the establishment of SME credit guarantee institutions and requires the establishment of the Commonwealth of financing for SMEs to explore with the banks to establish a standard enterprise credit evaluation system; Zhejiang Provincial Government also introduced some guidance document to encourage non-public capital taking part in regional financial institutions and financial intermediation services systems.

By introducing "the guidance on speeding up the construction for province's social service system on SMEs", Jiangsu Province emphasized on supporting SME financing in 2007. The guidance claimed to provide multi-level finance, security services for venture capital for SMEs, financing guidance, loan guarantees, credit collection and evaluation. It tried to cultivate a group of large-scale, management practices, good credit guarantee agencies, and improve credit assessment and risk control system, strengthen the supervision of credit guarantee institutions. It also constructed a credit guarantee incentive and risk compensation mechanism, improved the management system of the provincial security agencies and the operation mode.

Since the beginning of 2006, Chongqing city tried to build a new "four in one" model of financing including government, bank, social intermediation and enterprises. The core is the cooperation between government and bank system. The specific operation is that the county government set up the Leading Group for SME lending, SME debt office and Credit Association firstly. To Applying for loans, the SMEs must first join the Credit Association, reporting the real state of its assets, credit record and financial data. After evaluation by the authorities from government, the lending enterprise is selected and reported to the development banks. Development banks give the loans after lending credit assessment. To reduce the risk, the security center has to pay a certain deposit, lending according to the proportion of 1:5.

Beijing proposed a "North set bonds model". The program is that 12 scientific enterprises in Beijing Zhongguancun Science Park issued 400 million Yuan bundled bonds, adopting a form of "unified distribution, unified security, unified rating, and their liabilities". The period of the bond is 2 -3 years, and the interest rate is about 5%. The Zhongguancun Science and Technology Co., Ltd. provided the security guarantees.

4   The Suggestions on the Policy for SMEs Debt Financing

Scientific SMEs in China are on the stage of vigorous development. To guide and support its development, the government should take more measures to expand the channels for SME debt financing on the nowadays conditions that the equity market is not mature yet.

4.1   To Guide and Encourage Banks and Other Financial Institutions to Strengthen the Banking Governance, Communication and Cooperation between Banks and Enterprises

The cooperation between the government and the China Banking Regulatory Commission, state-owned and commercial banks should be strengthened. The SMEs classification standard, provisioning ratio of verification measures and accountability systems should be studied and established immediately. The banks should be encouraged to change concepts in their work, improve the loan incentives and develop financial products for SMEs. At the same time, the power to approve loans to SMEs should be gradually delegated, and the lending rates for SMEs can be determined by the actual situation of the market risk pricing mechanism. Second, policy should encourage financial institutions to give key support on the transformation from technology to project, and scientific industrialization projects. By the ways of available funds, interest subsidies and guarantees, the financial institutions can guide and support the SMEs' innovation and industrialization. In addition, the Government's industry and commerce, taxation and other departments should further strengthen cooperation with the banking institutions to fully use its regulatory powers to overcome the information asymmetry of the negative factors, and monitor the financing of SMEs effectively. What's more, the establishment of the self-regulatory organization such as trade association should be encouraged. It can improve the transparency of information disclosure for SMEs.

4.2   To Reduce the Threshold for Bond Issues for SMEs to Explore the Issue of Bonds Model of Innovation

There are signs that the day of SMEs to issue bonds is not far away. It is reported that the new "Regulations for the corporate bonds," is expected in the near future. The new regulations will make a greater adjustment to reduce the threshold for the bond issue. According to the national "Eleventh Five-Year Plan" proposal, some SMEs with independent intellectual property rights and some pricing power will also be included in corporate bond market.

At this stage, the main work can be done in following aspects. The first is the bonds model innovation. First of all, under existing policies, the enterprises on the infrastructure such as irrigation, hydropower, roads, bridges and other projects are suitable for issuance of bonds. The government can approve these SMEs to issue corporate bonds. And then, SME bold bonds Innovation, such as "a collection of bonds North mode" in Beijing should be encouraged. The second work can be done is the establishment of the "SME Bond Fund". This fund is to invest on the SMEs and the concept that high-risk come with high return should be known by the investors. Nowadays, domestic private finance is prosperous. Many investors are willing to take high-risk to seek high return. In addition, high quality financial companies can be release to enter the inter-bank market. Moreover, the city commercial, rural credit cooperatives and other regional operations can lower lending conditions. If the China Banking Regulatory Commission and other regulatory authorities can issue some management approach on the bank investment on low-grade bonds, the small banks would be motivated to buy the bonds.

4.3   To Strengthen the Credit Guarantee System

At present, China's credit guarantee system framework is "One body, two Wings and three-tier". That is, the policy security policy is the main body, along with the mutual assistance and commercial security organizations for the two wings, and it is divided into national, provincial and municipal security levels, in which policy security accounts for about 95%. At present, China's security law and related management practices or policy aimed at the security agencies. The scope is narrow and also uncomplicated. The regional government should further amend the relevant policy documents, and develop more detailed rules especially for the commercial security agencies and mutual guarantee institutions' access to the industry, risk prevention, compensation mechanism, while further complete the mechanism for the corporate credit rating, registration, upgrading and releasing, and provide guide to the construction of credit guarantee system. Five models can be considered to use: Firstly, governments at all levels can establish a common fund, and consign a professional organization to manage it. The second model is to encourage the establishment of mutual funds in the SMEs' industry, commissioned by professional agencies. The third way is the establishment of provincial, city, county and other multi-level reguarantee mechanism, which can further diversify risk. Fourthly, we can expand the guarantee agency business methods, such as Shenzhen "Scientific investment", which consists of investment and guarantee operations as well. In addition to provide security for innovative SMEs effectively, it also increases the value of the guarantee fund successfully. Finally, the government could develop compensation mechanism of financial funds and tax incentives for the security agencies.

4.4 To Divert and Make Use of Private Finance Correctly

Although private financing have played a role in some of the more economically developed regions in China, it still have some blindness and uncertainties for the reason of lacking necessary legal norms and management. To use it, we should adopt a "sparse block" approach. Firstly, the monitoring system for the private finance should be established. It can collect relevant data regularly. The second way is to improve relevant laws and regulations, strengthen legal advocacy efforts, and let all people know the risk of private lending as much as possible. Thirdly, the credit intermediary management agencies can be established in the private finance prosperous regions to provide the necessary legal advice and protection. Finally, we can strengthen the guidance on private finance, improve the investment environment, open access to all areas of private capital and expand private investment channels. In addition, even though the development history is short and the scale is not large enough, the angel investment, a form of private financing, have special significance for the SMEs pre-financing. The publicity for the angel investment could be further strengthen and the laws and taxation could be improved step by step, while the communication platform between the angel investors and entrepreneurs could be built.

4.5 To Support the Development of Financial Leasing

Currently, the development of financial leasing in China is relatively slow, and it did not play its due role for the financing of SMEs. It is mainly due to several reasons such as the lack of support from government for financial leasing, the lag in legislation for finance leasing etc. we can learn something form Zhejiang Province which make some achievement in lease financing in the last 20 years. Above all, we can support the development of lease financing from the following aspects. One is to increase the policy support for financial leasing industry, by the way of develop some preferential policies for the financial leasing such as accelerated depreciation, investment tax, lease credit guarantees, rent subsidies etc. The second is to accelerate the speed of financial leasing legislation, and to improve the legal environment for financial leasing. There are still some limitations on the scope and legal effect for the document of "Regulations for the Financial Leasing Companies" and "Announcement on the issues about finance leasing business" which were introduced in China from 2000 to 2005. The local governments should establish relevant local laws and regulations as soon as possible to provide legal basis for protection and available references for the leasing business embarked on a standardized way, and laid the foundation for future development. The third way is to encourage the financial leasing business combination with the local economy to strengthen the business innovation. The development of enterprises should be fit for local conditions. The enterprises should make innovation on project selection in the leasing, leasing the subject of enterprise development etc. And at the same time, the enterprises should strengthen understanding and cooperation with bank and other financial institutions to reduce the risk of leasing business.

4.6 To Encourage the Development of Risk Investment and Expand New Channels for Debt Financing

Venture Capital is that the specialized investment company invests on the unlisted small and medium enterprises which are potential for development, expansion type and recombinant, and take part in the enterprise management as well. The characteristics of venture capital determine that the SMEs are one main objective.

In 2005, the documents of "Interim Management Regulations on Venture Capital Company" and "Announcement on the issues about SME financing promotion" were introduced. The documents declare that venture capital can apply for loans from banks to increase investment capacity. This opened a new venture capital financing channels. It is a good chance for the local government to establish corresponding regulations supporting the administration regulations for the venture capital companies, to improve the legal protection system for venture capital and to encourage social capital to enter the field of venture capital. And under the permission of laws and regulations, the government can support the insurance companies to invest in venture capital companies, allow securities companies to carry out venture capital business, permit venture capital companies to increase investment capacity by getting loans from banks and other debt financing way.

In the model of venture capital business investing on SMEs, it can be bold and innovative, such as the model of "debt-equity swap". Specifically, it is to combine the loan guarantee business and investment business. For some larger risk projects, we can give loan guarantees to support the enterprise, while subscribe the condition of "debt-equity swap" with the enterprises. This gives the venture capital business a chance to change the debt investments into equity investments at the appropriate time. This model can do a great help for the early stage of SMEs financing.

References

1. Yang, J.: The Financing structure of Middle and Small Enterprises: the Theory and Experience from China. China Economy Press, Beijing (2008)
2. Cheng, J., Sun, X.: The Financing of Middle and Small Enterprises. Tsinghua University Press, Beijing (2006)
3. Bruton, G.D.: An institutional view of China venture capital industry–Explaining the differences between China and the west. Journal of Business Venturing, 233–259 (2003)
4. Berger, A.N., Undell, G.F.: Small business credit availability and relationship leading: the importance of banking organization structure. Economic Journal, 32–54 (2002)

Forecasting of Litopenaeus Vannamei Prices with Artificial Neural Networks

Dongsheng Xu*, Xinchun Li, Chao Wang, and Danhui Zheng

School of Business, Sun Yat-sen University,
Guangzhou, 510275, China
xudsh@mail.sysu.edu.cn

Abstract. The shrimp industrial has been growing very fast in the past decade in China. L.Vannamei is the major kind of shrimp cultured in China and its production contributes over 60% of the total production volume in 2010. The price of L.Vannamei is particularly important to L.Vannamei farmers and the upstream and downstream firms. However, it is difficult to predict as it is affected by many macro and micro factors. In this paper, we introduce an approach to apply artificial neural networks (ANNs) to forecast L.Vannamei prices. Experiments shows that our approach achieves 2.64%'s error in the past months on an average. This is the very first work in applying ANNs in this area.

Keywords: Litopenaeus Vannamei Shrimp, Artificial Neural Networks, Forecasting.

1 Introduction

Litopenaeus vannamei is the major cultured shrimp in China. As one kind of Tropical prawns, it can tolerate 18^oC or even lower water temperature. More relaxed requirements on the salinity(euryhaline nature) and stronger immune system make it favored by the majority of farmers. In China,L.vannamei was firstly cultured in Guangdong and Hainan province in 1998, and then cultured in many provinces.

L.vannamei is often referred to as white-leg shrimp, it is rich in nutrition. Because of its big size and good taste, it sells well on the market. L.vannamei farmers made a good living from 1998 to 2007. However, with the increase of environmental pollution and other negative factors, many farmers experienced loss for the first time in recent years.

Shrimp culturing has been a high-risk industry. There are about 20 kind virus infecting shrimp. In 1990s, a lot of Fenneropenaeus chinensis and Penaeus monodon died because of White Spot Syndrome. Shrimp production reduces to 60,000 ton from 200,000 ton. Since 2008, Litopenaeus vannamei has been threatened by virus despite of its strong disease resistance. In addition to virus, LP (L.vannamei post larvae, LP for short) quality is also very worrying. Most farmers buy LP from commercial hatcheries.

---

* Corresponding author.

M. Zhou (Ed.): ISAEBD 2011, Part IV, CCIS 211, pp. 268–274, 2011.
© Springer-Verlag Berlin Heidelberg 2011

Heidi L.Atwood, Shawn P.Young and Joseph R.Tomasso conduct experiments to determine salts' influence on L.vannamei (see Heidi.etc[1],2003). Dissolved oxygen (DO) and PH are also critical factors affecting output. Formers have to detect water quality regularly. Once quality becomes worse, farmers should take measures timely. Shrimp culture techniques is indispensable without a doubt. Many farmers don't notice it, and their investments are blind. Price forecast can help agriculture practitioners make decisions and help the government make policies.

This paper is the very first work in applying Artificial Neural Networks (ANNs hereafter) to forecast the price of L.vannamei. The remainder of the paper is organized as follows. Section 2 introduces the history and the applications of ANNs. Our ANNs model is presented in Section 3. The numerical experiment and forecasting results are shown in Section 4 and conclusion remarks are provided in Section 5.

2   Artificial Neural Networks

Artificial neural networks mimic how the human brain works. There are roughly 10^{11} neurons in the human brain. Many researches have suggested that the networks consists of a large number of neurons can sort information and make analysis. D.M.Rodvold.etc [5] gave detailed descriptions of the theory on ANNs, they also illustrate why ANNs can perform prediction.

The pace of ANNs application has increased recently. In environment field, many model results are reflected by mass factors. Artificial neural networks are applied in forecasting for its flexibility and intelligence. Several characteristics, including built-in dynamism in forecasting, data-error tolerance, and lack of requirements of any exogenous input, render ANNs attractive for use in river stage prediction in hydrologic engineering. (K.W. Chau, 2006[2])

In economic research, ANNs are very useful when creating forecasting models because of its non-linear mapping structures. ANNs can be used without understanding of the relationship between input and output, just like a kind of "black-box" approach. HE Yan-hui.etc [7] employed the ANNs to forecast the price of Tilapia and obtained satisfactory results. B.R.Szkuta.etc [8]forecasted short-term electricity price by using ANNs, the ANNs generated forecasts appeared to fit the curves relatively closely.

ANNs can identify and learn correlated patterns between input data sets and corresponding target values, what we called supervised learning. For supervised neural networks (models with specific actual/desired outputs), one of the most effective and popular technique to minimize the error function is the back-propagation (BP) algorithm.(Yu-Ren Wang, 2010[6]). Rumelhart and Hintont firstly found back-propagating errors method in 1986. It has a more broad field of application now.

In biology, Extending from the neurons are tendril-like axons, by which neighboring neurons connect with each other. These axons are also transmission channels of electrochemical signals. The neuron generate different electrochemical

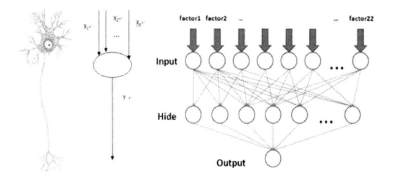

Fig. 1. Transfer functions and Artificial neural networks

signals according to signals it received. ANNs mimic this function by transfer functions.

In a network with BP algorithm, there are many neural units distributing in three layers (input/hide/output). We take our following model as an example, the number of neural units in each layers is 22,16 and 1, respectively. The input is the value of 22 factors we select, the neurons in the input layer transfer value to the neurons in the hide layer, then the value are transferred to the output layer.

The unit in the output layer output the forecasting price, and we take the real price as a desired value. We get the error through comparing the output against the expectation. We expect the error as low as possible. The method adjusts the factors affecting the output unit to induce the error: Supposing the error is positive (the forecasting price is higher than the expectation), if value transferred by one unit in the hide layers makes for increasing the output, the method reduces the influence from the unit through adjusting weight; else if value encouraged is lessening the output, the influence is increased.

The same procedure is adopted for each unit in the hide layer. A similar situation occurred when the error is negative. After all neurons accomplish these operations, one new output value generates. Then compare and adjust, time after time, until that the error can be received. Finally, we get a trained network, with which we entry the related information and get the forecasting price.

3   Model Construction

By the macro and micro economic analysis, we select 22 factors from various aspects, as follows.

The first category of the factors is from macro-economy aspect. The factors including GDP growth rate, money supply volume (M1), the per capita disposable income.

The second category is the price index set, including consumer price index growth rate (CPI), consumer price index growth rate (CPI).

International market also affects the national shrimp market. Therefore, we consider important international economy factors as well. The GDP of USA and US Dollar index are taken into account.

The fish meal is the major food of L.Vannamei, so its cost is a major component of L.Vannamei's price. As the fish meal price in China depends up the import price, we collect the data published by Huangpu Port monthly.

We can also find that the price varies with seasons, festivals and holidays. Therefore, we create season index and festival index as factors. Season index is based on the historical prices in past 5 years and festival index is given based on expert system. To be specific, we assign different values to the month containing different notional holidays, such as 1 for month Containing spring festival and 0.5 for International Labor Day. For special consumption habits of Chinese people, we also set index as 0.4 for the previous month Chinese New Year and 0.2 for the following month.

The market price of L.Vannamei varies among different markets and sizes. We take the average price of L.Vannamei traded in Humen market, one of the most important Shrimp market in China, as a benchmark. This price is published online everyday. We refer it as L.Vannamei market price in this paper. It is in unit of RMB per kilogram.

To illustrate the relations between input and output, we calculate the covariances between individual factors and L.Vannamei market price, which are illustrated in Table 1.

Table 1. Input factors and their covariances with the price

Factors	Covariance	Factors	Covariance
Price of the previous month	0.73347	Price of the 9th month before	0.22895
Price of the 2nd month before	0.41580	Price of the 12th month before	0.52000
Price of the 3rd month before	0.21445	Price of the 24th month before	0.68910
Price of the 4th month before	0.04688	GDP growth rate	-0.14961
Price of the 5th month before	-0.12988	CPI growth rate	0.26194
Price of the 6th month before	-0.17326	Money supply(M1)	0.40883
Factors	Covariance	Factors	Covariance
Disposable income per capita	0.54898	U.S. unemployment	0.38600
Shopping basket index	0.45851	Dollar index	-0.19899
Consumer price index	0.03368	Price of fish meal	0.44870
Price index of agricultural products	0.46157	Festival index	0.13803
GDP growth rate in the USA	-0.14749	Season index	0.57799

We use MATLAB to construct ANNs, train ANNs and do the forecast. The ANN toolbox in MATLAB provides many functions for training back-propagating networks, such as activation functions, learning functions and training procedures. such as that 'Newff' can be used to create a feed-forward back propagation network.

Transfer functions calculate a layer's output from its net input. We select 'tansig' and 'purelin' as transfer functions. MATLAB introduce 'tansig' as follow:

"TANSIG is named after the hyperbolic tangent which has the same shape. It differs in that it runs faster than the MATLAB implementation of TANH, but the results can have very small numerical differences."

We select 'trainbr' (Bayesian regularization) as training functions for its tolerance to data. The function characterizes the training effect by mean squared error performance function (MSE) and sum squared error performance function (SSE).As a gradient descent method, only the target achieve the required standard or the number of iterations meet the requirements, training process stops.

In order to accelerate the training speed, we need do data preprocessing at first. 'premnmx' in MATLAB can normalize data for maximum of 1 and minimum of -1, with 'postnmx' provides the reverse operation. Experience has shown that when the input and output are in the closed interval $[-1, 1]$, the training function 'trainbr' shows best performance.

4   Experiment and Forecasting Results

We conducted the numerical experiment on a computer with a Duo CPU with two 2.80GHz processors and 1.0GB RAM. MATLAB version 7.0 was employed and the training procedure was completed in 10 to 20 minutes in our computational environment.

We collect the data from January 2005 to December 2009 as training data set, the data from January 2010 to September 2010 are be used to test. The result are as follows:

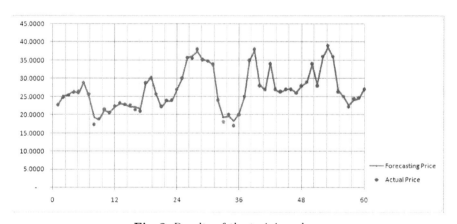

Fig. 2. Results of the training phase

The result suggests that forecasting L.vannamei price with ANNs is desirable, the figure 1 illustrates the effect of supervised learning after training. The forecasting value can be adjusted to very close to the true value.

With the trained network, we can compare the forecasting results with the real prices (see Figures 3 and 4). Test results are satisfactory.

Month	Real price	Forecasting	Error (%)
Jan 2010	41	41.8720	0.8720
Feb 2010	34.3	36.6490	2.3490
Mar 2010	33	33.9080	0.9080
Apr 2010	33.7	34.1060	0.4060
May 2010	31.3	36.0390	4.7390
Jun 2010	27	32.8610	5.8610
Jul 2010	27.5	32.1680	4.6680
Aug 2010	27.5	30.5730	3.0730
Sep 2010	41	41.8720	0.8720

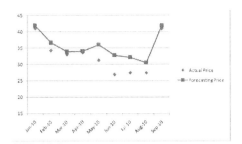

Fig. 3. Comparison between the forecasting prices and the real prices when testing

Fig. 4. Comparison between the forecasting prices and the real prices when testing

Since October in 2010, we have forecasted shrimp monthly price in the beginning of every month and announced it in public conference, and we also have compared the forecasting accuracy in the end of the month. The results are shown in Table 2.

Table 2. Comparison of the forecasting prices and the real prices (Forecasting is made at the beginning of December 2010)

December 2010 result		
Forecasting result	Real price	Percentage error (%)
27.95	28.00	0.19
January 2011 result		
Forecasting result	Real price	Percentage error (%)
31.12	31.33	-0.67
February 2011 result		
Forecasting result	Real price	Percentage error (%)
37.80	40.67	-7.06

Price forecasting in February is particulary difficult. The reason is twofold. First, from the demand prospect, Chinese new year, Spring Festival, is in February in 2011. Therefore, the demand peak makes great uncertain in this month. Second, from the supply prospect, the L.Vannamei production is very low as the temperature disallows many regions to culture. Moreover, the spread of shrimp disease made the supply decreased.

5 Conclusion

This paper represents the first step in applying ANNs to predict the price of L.Vannamei. The results suggest that this approach is possible. When the 22 factors vary with other factors remaining unchanged, the forecasting value is worthy of belief. A rolling horizon scheme can be applied to include incoming data and update the ANN model each period. A number of research directions are worthwhile. The first is to include more affecting factors which are significant to L.Vannamei prices, for example, the data of environment, shrimp disease, etc. Moreover, more parameters and algorithms in ANNs can be tested to improve the forecasting accuracy. Furthermore, we can employ econometrica models to do the forecasting. We can employ existing systematic approaches to combine the different models to make the forecast more robust and accurate.

Acknowledgement. This research was supported by the Ministry of Agriculture of China through the fund of the Industrial Economics team under China Shrimp Technology System. We would like to thank a number of Anonymous members in the system for providing data and suggestions. The second author was supported by the Fundamental Research Funds for the Central Universities.

References

1. Atwood, H.L., Young, S.P., Tomasso, J.R.: Survival and growth of pacific white shrimp litopenaeus vannamei postlarvae in low-salinity and mixed-salt environments. ournal of the world aquaculture society 34, 518–523 (2003)
2. Chau, K.W.: Particle swarm optimization training algorithm for ANNs in stage prediction of Shing Mun River. Journal of Hydrology 329(3-4), 363–367 (2006)
3. Lek, S., Guegan, J.F.: Artificial neural networks as a tool in ecological modeling, an introduction. Ecological Modelling 120(2-3), 65–73 (1999)
4. Zupan, J.: Introduction to Artificial Neural Network (ANN) Methods: What They Are and How to Use Them. Acta Chimica Slovenica 41(3), 327–352 (1994)
5. Rodvold, D.M., McLeod, D.G., Brandt, J.M., Snow, P.B., Murphy, G.P.: Introduction to Artificial Neural Networks for Physicians: Taking the Lid Of the Black Box. Journal of Management in Engineering 21(4), 164–172 (2005)
6. Wang, Y.-R., Edward Gibson Jr, G.: A study of preproject planning and project success using ANNs and regression models. Automation in Construction 19(3), 341–346 (2010)
7. He, Y.-h., Yuan, Y., Zhang, H., Gong, B., Wang, H.: Application of BP Artificial Neural Network in Tilapia Price Forecasting. Journal of Anhui Agriculture Science 38(35), 20443–20445 (2010)
8. Szkuta, B.R., Sanabria, L.A., Dillion, T.S.: Electricity Price Short-Term Forecasting Using Artificial Neural Networks. IEEE Transactions on Power Systems 14(3), 851–857 (1999)

Yunnan Informatization Level Measurement and Analysis of Its Contribution on Economic Growth

Liangtao Sun

Business College,Honghe University,Mengzi, China
liangtaosun@qq.com

Abstract. According to the experience of developed countries, promoting industrialization by informatization not only can improve products' level and
quality, but also could upgrade the production environment, reduce consumption on energy and raw material, and increase economic benefit. The government and people pay more attention on how many contributions have been
made by informatization level on economic growth in Yunnan. At the beginning, this paper estimates the informatization level in Yunnan by informatization index determination. Then, it analyzes the contribution of informatization
development level of Yunnan on economic growth through regression analysis
modeled in improved Cobb-Douglas production function. At last, it gives
some suggestions on how to improve the informatization level of Yunnan and
promote economic growth.

Keywords: Yunnan, information, measuring economic growth, contribution.

1 Introduction

17th CPC National Congress distinctively proposed the brand-new proposition of
combined development of informatization and industrialization for the first time,
endowing a new historic mission for informatization construction and providing an
unprecedented opportunity for it. The report regarded informatization, along with
industrialization, urbanization, marketization, internationalization, as the significant
situation and task. This will inevitably make all the people in China realize, ponder
and promote the informatization as an important situation and task that has universal
meaning to all works. According to the experience of developed countries, promoting
industrialization by informatization not only can improve products' level and quality,
but also upgrade the production environment, reduce consumption on energy and raw
material, and increase economic benefit. It can be said that the penetration and combination of information technology will have a core role in improving the level of
industrial technology of every departments in national economy. In 2001, a test made
by UN in the world found out that in a city with the population of 1 million, the initial
realization of informatization would boost its gross product by 2.5 to 3.1 times in the
condition of same level of investment. The combination of information technology,
network technology and traditional economy will produce multiple benefits, propelling the economic development greatly.

M. Zhou (Ed.): ISAEBD 2011, Part IV, CCIS 211, pp. 275–280, 2011.
© Springer-Verlag Berlin Heidelberg 2011

The government and people pay more attention on how many contributions have been made by informatization level on economic growth in Yunnan. At the beginning, this paper estimates the informatization level in Yunnan by informatization index determination. Then, it analyzes the contribution of informatization development level of Yunnan on economic growth through regression analysis modeled in improved Cobb-Douglas production function. At last, it gives some suggestions on how to improve the informatization level of Yunnan and promote economic growth.

2 Determination of Informatization Index of Yunnan

2.1 Choice of Indexes

The informatization index determination proposed by Japanese scholar Seisuke Komatsuzaki in the late 1970s focuses more on evaluating social information and information competence to reflect social informatization level. However, the specific informatization index is not suitable for our current informatization development. In order to describe the informatization level of Yunnan, this paper follows the representative and operative principles in choosing the indexes. It picks 5 first level indexes and 16 second level indexes. The first level indexes include: information quantity (Q), information communication level (B), information equipment rate(E), communication subjective level(P), information consumption level (U). The second level indexes in information quantity are: patent application number for ten thousand people and publishing number for ten thousand people. The second level indexes in information communication level include: internet user number, annual mail volume per capita, annual telecommunication volume per capita, annual newspaper volume per one hundred people. The second level indexes in information equipment rate are: phone number per one hundred people, television capacity per one hundred urban households, television capacity per one hundred rural households, computer capacity per one hundred urban households, and computer capacity per one hundred rural households. The second level indexes in communication subjective level are: employment rate for tertiary industry, university student number per ten thousand people, and scientific staff number per ten thousand people. The second level indexes in information consumption level include: incidental expenses (expenses except food, cloth and shelter) rate in personal consumption of urban dwellers, incidental expenses (expenses except food, cloth and shelter) rate in personal consumption of rural residents.

2.2 Calculation Method and Results

As there is no unified standard for the effects of all indexes in informatization, and this paper aims to analyze the contribution of informatization factors on Yunnan economic growth through the measurement on Yunnan informatization level, as for the convenience of data comparison, this paper will identify all indexes value of Yunnan in 2000 as 1, and the other years' value will be converted into indexes accordingly. Then, calculate the informatization level indexes of Yunnan over the years by two-step arithmetical method with the help of software Excel:

I = 1/5 [1/2 (Q1+Q2) + 1/4 (B1+...+B4) + 1/5 (E1+...+E5) +1/3 (P1+...+P3) + 1/2 (U1+U2)]

The results are shown in table 1.

Table 1. Informatization level index of Yunnan over the years

Year	2000	2001	2002	2003	2004	2005	2006	2007	2008	2009
I	1.00	1.34	1.43	1.67	1.84	2.04	2.16	2.45	3.10	3.63

Data source: calculated in line with *Yunnan statistical yearbook*.

3 Analysis of Contribution of Informatization Level of Yunnan on Economic Growth

3.1 Choice of Model

Production function refers to the relation between the number of production factors in production and the maximum amount of production under the same technological condition. Cobb—Douglas production function was proposed by mathematician Cobb and economist Douglas in 1930s. The early Cobb—Douglas production function presumed there were only two production factors in production: labor and capital. The function form was $Y = AL^{\alpha}K^{\beta}$. In it: α is yield elasticity of labor, and β is yield elasticity of capital. In the actual analysis, as technological advancement also has impact on yield, the technological impact is introduced into it—technological factor. Welfens (2002) decomposed technological advancement factor into two parts: $A = A_0 I^{\gamma}$. In it, I means informatization level, γ is yield elasticity of informatization level, A_0 represents other technological advancement factors besides information technological advancement. These technological advancement factors impacts are decomposed into information technological impact and non-information technological impact. The improved C-D function becomes $Y = A_0 L^{\alpha}K^{\beta}I^{\gamma}$. Get the logarithms on both sides, $\ln Y_t = \ln A_0 + \alpha \ln L_t + \beta \ln K_t + r \ln I_t + U_t$ can be gained. In it, α, β, γ respectively represent yield elasticity of labor, capital, and informatization level.

3.2 Results Analysis

As for the convenience for comparison analysis, on the basis of the above measurement of informatization level of Yunnan, this paper converts GDP (Y), social fixed asset investment (K), labor employment number (L) in Yunnan province over the years into indexes (regarding year 2000 as base year), and conducts logarithm processing on all indexes values. The results are shown in table 2.

Table 2. Yunnan Province GDP and all production factors data from 2000 to 2009

Year	Y	L	K	I	LnY	LnL	LnK	LnI
2000	1.00	1.00	1.00	1.00	0.00	0.00	0.00	0.00
2001	1.06	1.01	1.05	1.34	0.06	0.01	0.05	0.29
2002	1.15	1.02	1.19	1.43	0.14	0.02	0.17	0.36
2003	1.27	1.03	1.46	1.67	0.24	0.02	0.38	0.51
2004	1.53	1.05	1.91	1.84	0.43	0.05	0.65	0.61
2005	1.72	1.07	2.51	2.04	0.54	0.07	0.92	0.71
2006	1.98	1.10	3.18	2.16	0.68	0.09	1.16	0.77
2007	2.37	1.12	4.01	2.45	0.86	0.11	1.39	0.90
2008	2.83	1.15	5.05	3.10	1.04	0.14	1.62	1.13
2009	3.07	1.17	6.49	3.63	1.12	0.16	1.87	1.29

Data source: calculated in line with *Yunnan statistical yearbook*.

Taking advantage of the data in table 2 and in line with the above model, after the linear regression method, the results are as follows:

$$\ln Y_t = 0.259 \ln L_t + 0.672 \ln K_t + 0.069 \ln I_t + U_t$$

F=663.928, sig=0.000<0.05, $R^2 = 0.998$. These show that this function is significant, meaning these three variables have significant influences on equation. Elasticity of GDP index on informatization index is 0.069. This represents that maintaining the investment and labor input, the informatization index of Yunnan will increase 1%, GDP index 0.069%. It is far less than the elasticity of GDP index on capital and labor. In recent years, though Yunnan has achieved a lot in informatization development, it has late start and low starting point in informatization industry. Therefore, with less contribution on national economic growth, its industry scale is still very low compared with that in more developed regions. As a result of these, promoting informatization level in Yunnan and facilitating the combination of information technology with traditional industry will become important driving forces for propelling economic restructuring and promoting transformation of economic development patterns.

4 Suggestions on Improving Informatization Level of Yunnan and Promoting Economic Growth

4.1 Strengthening Information Network Infrastructure Construction

The information infrastructure of Yunnan is still very weak. In the aspect of information network infrastructure, some infrastructures cannot meet the development demand of new technologies. Yunnan should give full play to its advantages of newcomers, utilizing the latest fruits of high and new technologies, especially the digital technology and network technology development, as well as planning promotion of information and communication network construction as a whole. The "triple play" of internet, telephone network, broadcasting network will save trillions of cost in information infrastructure. Besides, it will improve the popularization of information greatly.

4.2 Cultivating Talents on Information Vigorously, Innovating Talents Training and Access Mechanism

Yunnan is in lack of talents who can promote the informatization construction. Yunnan should actively encourage and support universities of higher education to cultivate the versatile talents who master knowledge of information technology and industrial and economic management. It has to speed up the training of leader talents and advanced technical talents in all fields of scientific researches. Besides, Yunnan could introduce foreign intelligent resources, attracting students abroad to go back to China for work. Furthermore, it could stick to the focus on people, improving information quality of staff and retraining in information technology for engineering technical staff at their posts.

4.3 Implementing and Acting on the National Informatization Development Strategy in Real Earnest, Promoting the Combination of Informatization and Industrialization

The core of the combination of informatization and industrialization is informatization support and pursuit of sustainable development model. It is the urgent demand of transforming economic growth pattern by improving the combination of informatization and industrialization. It can not only promote the economic growth from depending on increase of material resources consumption to depending on technological advancement, workers' quality improvement and management innovation conversion. The effect of information technology in green, low-carbon, intelligent and sustainable development can be given full play Consider information network technology application as an important content in technological upgrading, upgrading traditional industry, cultivating strategic budding industry and promoting energy saving and emission reduction as well as environment protection. Meanwhile, boosting the combination of informatization and industrialization can give informatization development continuous impetus. Industrialization not only lays a solid material and technological foundation for informatization, but also proposes extensive application demand to informatization development, facilitating development of the information industry and innovation of information technology, driving the popularization application of information technology and equipments.

4.4 Promoting the Combination of Information Technology with Primary and Tertiary Industry, Developing Modern Agriculture and Modern Service Industry

The government should energetically promote agricultural informatization construction, narrowing the digital gap between urban and rural areas. Government can strengthen countryside information infrastructure construction and informatization training, establish information service system, intensify application and dissemination of information technology and advance countryside informatization, offering on-time and effective information service for farmers' living and production process. These include all aspects in market, science and technology, education, public health, health care and other social and economic life. Meanwhile, government should also consolidate the resource integration of information involving in agriculture, perfect agricultural information service platform, serving the modern agriculture. Taking e-commerce development as the entry point, develop rural modern circulation pattern and new circulation types vigorously.

In service industry, upgrade traditional service industry, promoting the development of modern service industry. Yunnan has to develop network equipment, bar code and other digital equipments and build information service platform facing the domestic and foreign markets. Promote the combination of information technology with financial insurance industry, modern logistic industry, management consultation industry, information service industry and modern tourism, boosting development of modern service industry. It should attach more attention on the support of software industry, internet industry, information service industry and other budding industries, following the trend of modern economic and scientific development.

4.5 Improving E-Government and E-Commerce

Establish and complete unified e-government platform and enhance the construction and networking of important business systems in government departments at all levels. Promote the connection of e-government network, realizing business collaboration and information sharing cross-level longitudinally and cross-department horizontally. Improve work efficiency and public service level. Meanwhile, government should lead the society to gradually establish and complete business credit, online payment, logistics and secure authentication system, encouraging e-commerce development.

Acknowledgment. Many thanks to the support of Honghe College Scientific Research Foundation for Masters and Doctors on this project titled: "A Study of the Influences of E-commerce on the Economic Development in Yunnan", Project Number: XSS08023.

References

1. Lijun, G.: Historical opportunity: Integration of Informationization and industrialization, Guangming daily (January 30, 2008)
2. Liu, H., Zhen, F., Zhou, H.: Analysis of urban economic growth of Nanjing information. Journal of Tianjin Normal University (natural science Edition) 9, 78–80 (2006)
3. Jin, X.: Analysis of the influence of Informationization on economic growth. Statistical research 5, 74–80 (2010)
4. Statistics Bureau of Yunnan province. Statistical Yearbook of Yunnan, pp. 47–436.China statistics press, Beijing (2010)
5. Statistics report on Internet development in China, http://www.cnnic.com.cn

Analysis on Land-Lost Rural Aging Labors' Integration into City in the Course of Urbanization

Min Chen

Economics and Management School
Chongqing Three Gorges University
wanzhou, chongqing, China
37223411@qq.com

Abstract. Land-lost Rural Aging labor is a vulnerable group in fringe gradually due to their own physical and skill constraints. Many obstacles this aging group have encountered in the course of their integration into city and urbanization. The existence of system isolation barrier, urban-rural cultural conflicts as well as spatial and social segregation, has exacerbated their poor living condition increasingly. In view of integrating themselves into urban life, we should stress the combination of their short-term living condition and long-standing developing potential, to adopt a package of policies to sharpen their competitiveness and survival capacity in the course of urbanization, for instance, to promote the institutional environment innovation and to create special and cultural environment for them, meanwhile, to modify their employment and living surroundings as well as reform the re-employment skills training modes.

Keywords: Land-lost Rural Aging labor Integration into City Weakness Countermeasures.

1 Necessity Analysis on the Land-Lost Aging Labors' Integration into City

Aging rural land-lost labor is a dynamic concept in comparison with the young labor force, which mainly refers to the landless urbanized rural group who are more than 40 years of age and still having the weak working ability. Owing to the special historical background and limited literal and physical fitness, this group becomes the most disadvantageous one in fringe by their own technical limitations, in urgent need of focus and attention from the society and government significantly.

1.1 The Land-Lost Aging Labor's City Inclusion Is the Inner Needs of Urbanization

The current accelerated process of urbanization is in conflict with the city inclusion of the above-mentioned group prominently, especially the social security and employment issues of this aging labor group. They have been deprived of land they living on for decades, and living under a weak and helpless circumstance; the passive

M. Zhou (Ed.): ISAEBD 2011, Part IV, CCIS 211, pp. 281–286, 2011.
© Springer-Verlag Berlin Heidelberg 2011

urbanized status drives them into an embarrassed inadaptable condition. As far as urbanization is concerned, it's not only the realization of urban residence identification, also the integration and assimilation of resource acquisition, spatial location, living style as well as value concepts.

With poor adaptability and heavy family burden, the aging labor and their Incompatibility with urban life highlights the issues of peasants' city inclusion.

To guarantee the urbanization process successfully, aiming at the improvement of their urban social ideology and survivability, it is crucial to take the city inclusion of the above-mentioned group into account, to create a good social environment to develop their living potential to adapt themselves to the city.

1.2   The Integration into City Is the Essential Need of Social Stability Objectively

The city inclusion of the rural aging land-lost labor is not only the intrinsic needs of current harmonious urban-rural development and urbanization, also is an important factor in social stability. Because the existing value of concepts and literal degree, these people are distinguished themselves from citizens with the nature of obvious weakness and pervasiveness. Their serious urbanization and assimilation problems call for highly attention and effective measure to deal with. Once they can't be accepted and assimilated by the city, they will be isolated or marginalized. The existence of behavioral and psychological or social differences, as well as the widespread rural culture in their city life, will result in the emergence of second-class citizens, which will make them neither residents of rural collective community nor traditional urban residents. Therefore, marginalization of the group will seriously affect the harmonious development of urban society, together with the sustainable urban economic development and social stability.

1.3   The Integration into City Accelerates the Urban-Rural Economic Development

The requisition of land and the urbanization of the expropriated peasants are inevitable due to the acceleration of industrialization and urbanization. As one of the most vigorous factors contributing to the economic development, the use of non-agricultural has promoted the ascending of the non-agricultural economic gains significantly, in addition, the output of production factors, for example, land and labor, will actively be promoted by optimal allocation noticeably. Simultaneously, as a special disadvantageous group with a huge population, their urbanized identity adjustment has not only improved the relative efficiency of agricultural output, also stimulated the development of the agriculture industrialization. The land-lost aging labor has been emancipated from land and then been engaged in the agricultural processing industry as well as secondary and tertiary industries, which plays a strategically important role as to harmonious urban-rural economic development and healthy optimization of industrial structure.

2   Barriers Analysis on the Aging Land-Lost Labor's Integration into City

Compared with other land-lost groups, this aging group's city inclusion is relatively reluctant and passive. Being cut off the inevitable contact with the rural, they are forced to receive new knowledge and skills to survive in the city, and to adapt themselves to the urban culture. Therefore, they have suffered much vulnerability from the existence of system isolation barrier, urban-rural cultural conflicts as well as spatial and social segregation, which has exacerbated the poor living condition of this special rural group increasingly.

2.1   The Barrier Deriving from System Isolation

The aging land-lost labors' city inclusion requires creating a good system environment, and requires the government implementing its responsibility and obligation as a major function body. At present, due to the lack of the relative institutional system and governmental function, the aging landless labor is in a rather embarrassed condition, and facing unexpected difficulties to integrate themselves into the urban life. As to the group's social security urbanization, it plays as an extremely important role as their urbanized identification. Aiming at improvement and standardization of the construction of the social security system for the urbanized land-lost peasants, the government has promulgated a set of regulations in the purpose of making up the land-lost' loss they suffered in the course of performance of early incomplete requisition compensation and security system.

  As a special group aging between the strong young labor and the aging group living on allowance without working ability, though the aging labor group has benefited the generalized improvement of the system than before, the margin of benefits they obtained is improved merely slightly compared with other groups. Since this disadvantageous group is generally facing the problems of high costs of pension payment, children's education expenses, and the family's medical care outside the medical security system and as well as increasingly soaring price on account of recent inflation, they are living in a considerable difficult situation with heavy social and family burden, and become the city's most poor group due to the age, quality limitation of the labor as well as long-term social prejudice against them.

2.2   Cultural Difference Hindrance against the Aging Labor's Integration into the City

The urbanization of the aging rural labor is a dramatic transformation regarding their lifestyle, ideology as well as occupation, requiring not only realizing their identification urbanization, also keeping pace with the establishment of corresponding public services, social security and capacity development system. Adapting to urban mainstream culture is the prerequisite for the aging rural labors' integration into urban society, therefore it will takes a rather long process to realize the identity transfer as well as assimilation of urban culture because their urban identification is an institutional one arranged by the government.

Compared with the urban peers, this aging group's urban survival skills and competitiveness are considerably poor because they are inherent in the rural empirical knowledge and social orientation. Owing to the swept effect of small-sized agricultural economy and keen dependence on the land for decades, it's difficult for this aging group integrating themselves into the city on account of cultural differences and hindrance.

2.3 The Barrier Deriving from Spatial and Social Segregation

The spatial and social segregation between the landless aging group and the original urban inhabitants is one of the most important reasons why it is extremely difficult for them to realize city inclusion and integration. As in the urbanization process, the land-lost peasants mostly will be relocated in the form of concentrated resettlement, and this single relocation form will lead to serious separation from city and wide spreading of rural or sub-urban culture in the resettled community. By this means, it's undoubted that the objective existence of separation will influence the urbanization and city inclusion of the land-lost relocated, especially this aging group due to their poor adaptability and knowledge.

2.4 The Barrier Deriving from Quality and Skill Difference

The Quality and skill difference is an important constraining factor in the course of the aging landless labor's integration into city, and the group's culture, technology, psychology limitation drop them into an worse disadvantageous condition. Without capacity of competing with the urban residents, they usually face unemployment and being laid off or undertake to the inferior occupations with lower earnings even find a position with tremendous efforts. Even some members of the group partially involve in the integration of city life, it is still a low-level and incomplete inclusion. Without stability and security in their lives as well as the high costs of urban life, the difficulties they encounter in their lives are in conflict with their expectation dramatically.

3 The Countermeasures Available

As to the countermeasures of the land-lost aging labor's integration into city, we should combine their short-term life quality and long-term viability to cultivate their sustainable development capacity on the basis of ensuring sufficient short-term compensation for them. The flexible polices should be applied to prevent the occurrence of social exclusion and separation, and to reinforce their further development potential effectively.

3.1 Promoting System Environmental Innovation by the Government

Aiming at the vulnerable characteristics of rural aging land-lost labor's social security and employment, the local government should take full advantage of the leading, directing and supporting function, to modify the established land compensation system, social security system and employment system in a sound and innovative way. The aging group mentioned bears the obligation to support the family, so the systems ought to be improved is closely related to the survival and development of the whole family. The earlier land requisition compensation system is monopolized and compulsory by the state so that the land-lost including the aging ones are excluded from the interest contribution system, which is immensely against the mechanisms and principles of market, characterized by a low purchasing price of land in contrast to a rather high selling price. Based on the rural collective ownership and respect for property rights of peasants, the government should apply to available measures in the transformation of construction land from rural usage, ensuring the land-lost group sharing the achievements of urbanization commonly. As for the Innovation of social security system, the Government should focus on promoting the legislation and effective implementation of the aging land-lost labor's unemployment insurance, pension insurance, medical insurance and industrial injury insurance system, to propel the establishment and perfection of environment innovation for the labors.

3.2 Focusing on the Construction of Assimilated Spatial and Cultural Environment for the Labor's Integration

For the relocation of the land-lost, we should adopt flexible centralized or decentralized resettlement form, sufficiently considering the full use of resources, centralized management of the labor, as well as their nature of being disadvantageous. For the centralized relocated, they may be resettled near schools or businesses in order to be engaged in service industry; or be provided with shops to operate or lease in accordance with the government programs. For the scattered resettlement of the land-lost, the government should promote the participation and enthusiasm in accepting the aging labors initiatively, strengthen the community liaison system, make full use of community resources to build community public service organizations, establish a sound information management system for the aging labor, as well as strengthen the neighborhood and interaction with urban residents.

3.3 Reducing the Labor's Employment and Living Risks by Diversified Forms of Employment

3.3.1 Strengthening the Enterprises' Employment Capacity by the Government

We should strengthen the enterprises' employment capacity by the government to explore more positions for the urbanized aging labor, especially the enterprises who expropriate the land. As the same government leading and central function in the process of urbanization, the aging labor's employment is still in badly need of the promotion and supervising form from the state. The government should adopt preferential policies to attract the whole society to hold the aging labor actively with diversified employment forms. As to the labor's non-agricultural employment, we should place emphasis both on the government's promotion function and the aging labors' ability acceleration. To develop some labor-intensive industries properly and guide them be engaged in some modern service industries, such as the food and beverage industry, modern logistics, housekeeping and other industries, and to stimulate labor exporting development, are scientific and appropriate approaches to settle the employment problem for the aging urbanized labors.

3.3.2   Encouraging Pioneering Businesses and Creative Employment

Considering the characteristics of the aging labor, the government should provide policy and operation convenience for them, encouraging pioneering businesses and creative employment, and expanding the employment channels to assist the labors' social and self actualization. Taking advantage of their own hard-working and entrepreneurial spirit, the aging labor are encouraged to establish their own businesses, for instance, some private enterprises, including construction materials, wholesale and processing of agricultural products, handmade crafts and other special industries, which will help them moving steadily into the city life without difference from the original citizens based on their economic survival potential progress.

3.3.3   Enhancing Further Exploration of Their Agricultural Potentials

Compared with other groups whose land was expropriated, the aging labors are more dependant on the land and more anxious about land losing. On the one hand, we should strengthen their market analysis and controlling ability, continue to develop their expertise in agriculture, extend the industrial chain of agriculture products, and develop agro-industries and urban agriculture as well as tourism and leisure industry in a sound way. By this means, both the aging labor and the agricultural economy will be developed beyond expectations.

3.4   Improving the Employability by the Reforms of Skills Training Models

The aging urbanized labors are characterized by being older, low literacy levels, inferior labor skills, which is obviously insufficient to adapt themselves to the fierce competition in the job market. Though the traditional generalized pre-job training system helps them with re-employment, it turns out not to be satisfactory yet. With a view to expanding their comprehensive employability, the re-training issue of the aging group should fall into the training system of urban staff, to improve the quality of the overall employability of the group. Based on combination of the training with the labors' age, cultural background and interest, the training plans should be carried out with different targets and levels, such as different levels of training regarding community security guard, housekeepers, manual processors, etc…

References

1. Gan, M.-t.: Farmer-turned Migrant Workers and Triple Social Structure In China Today. Fuzhou University Journal (Philosophy and Social Science Edition) (2001-2004)
2. Wu, S.: Research Progress of the Identity Recognition of Land-lost Farmers during the Process of Urbanization. Journal of Anhui Agricultural Sciences (2008)
3. Yi, G.: On the Land-Expropriated Farmers in the Process of Urbanization. Reformation & Strategy (July 2009)
4. Ng, Y.-K.: Welfare Economics: Introduction and Development of Basic Concepts. Macmillan, London (1983)

The Application of Principal Components Analysis on Residents' Living Level Evaluation of Our Country

Chao Sun

Department of Management Engineering, Shenyang Institute of Engineering,
Shenyang, 110136, P.R.China
sie5722@163.com

Abstract. Purpose: to evaluate and arrange the residents' living level of our country, offer reference for the decision-making of governments at all levels about the people's livelihood. Procedures: at first, established the evaluation index on residents' living level in our country, evaluated and arranged the residents' living level of our country with the method of principal components analysis. Conclusions: this ranking makes every provincial government envisage its own actuality and location, further make the structural and strategic regulation according to the actual situation.

Keywords: principal components analysis, residents' living level, evaluation.

Principal components analysis is a method which simplifies many indexes into few indexes at the same time keep the relativity of initial data in a maximal degree. Its characteristics are concentrating information, simplifying index structure, make the analysis procedure more simple, visual and effective, therefore it is applied on every field widely. This paper used the method of principal components analysis, by setting up index system to reflect relative factors of residents' living level in our country, evaluated the residents' living situation in every region of our country, and arranged them in a sequence.

1 Problem Posing

Residents' living level counts for much of the social development and stability. Because residents' living level is the most basic problem of people's livelihood, namely people's livelihood and living, also is the problem that is closely related to the people's life, including clothing, food, shelter, means of travel, learning, birth, old age, sickness, death and other aspects. Certainly, with the vicissitudes of times as well as economic and social development in the different period, the connotation of people's livelihood will change constantly.

The implementation of basic state policy of reform and opening-up made the living level of most urban and rural residents improve in a great degree. Annual analysis report(2009)(*Blue Book of China's Society*), issued by China Academy of Social Sciences in 2010 showed, our country's per capita GDP in 1978 was under the 400 US dollars, and it added to the more than 800 US dollars in 2000; in 2003, our country's per

M. Zhou (Ed.): ISAEBD 2011, Part IV, CCIS 211, pp. 287–292, 2011.

capita GDP exceeded the 1000 US dollars, while in 2006, it exceeded the 2000 US dollars and exceeded the 3000 US dollars in 2008. In 2009, Engel's Coefficient of urban and rural resident in our country reduce to the 37% and 43% respectively. According to the standard of Food and Agriculture Organization of the United States our country has entered into the well-off residents' living level and consumption phase.

It need to be paid attention, under the development background in a high speed a series of people's livelihood problems appear clearly which are prominent all along and are paid more attention by common people, involving employment, income distribution, social security, high housing price, selecting school in the compulsory education phase, enrollment difficulty of rural works' family, difficulty and high cost of getting medical service, food and drug security, unsound payment for labor, big treatment difference in endowment among different groups, constant widening of urban and rural income gap and so on. People's livelihood in some fields are brewing and inspiring social unstable factors, will result in all kinds of group matters. Both social problems reflected by "Dwelling Narrowness" and "Ant Tribe", and anxiety brought by enrollment difficulty and high housing price for salariat reveal that there is fall need to be repaired urgently between public production supply and social requirement. This advances the new requirement of people's livelihood construction in the new period for us. Therefore, our country put the social cause development which took people's livelihood as main body on the total socialistic cause arrangement with Chinese Characteristics in 2006. Report to the Seventeenth National Congress of the CPC emphasized that social development is closely related to the people's well-being. More importance must therefore be attached to social development on the basis of economic growth to ensure and improve people's livelihood, carry out social restructuring, expand public services, improve social management and promote social equity and justice. We must do our best to ensure that all our people enjoy their rights to education, employment, medical and old-age care, and housing, so as to build a harmonious society.

It is encouraging, under the push of a series of state important polices on benefiting people's livelihood and promoting development, governments at all levels promulgate the policies and measures related to people's livelihood in succession, as well as increase the funding for people's livelihood development. By improving people's livelihood promote the economic resuscitation and development, and achieve the certain effects.

Under this situation, we need to arrive at a common understanding on the issue of people's livelihood as well as create on the aspects of system and mechanism among the multi-interest pattern. It is important to place the people's livelihood improvement on the height of strategic orientation. To evaluate and arrange the residents' living level of our country, offer reference for the decision-making of governments at all levels about the people's livelihood, have the important significance for the economic and social development as well as social stability of nation and regions.

2 Establishment of Evaluation Index on Residents' Living Level of Our Country

Facts prove that many factors influence the residents' living level. According to the acquirability and integrality of data, this paper considerd some factors from the aspects of social environment, consumer's income and expenditure and so on, as following:

2.1 Social Environment

(1) GDP,(2)Employment volume (this paper applied the percentage of city's employment volume to the regional population),(3) Consumer price index.

2.2 Resident Income

(1) Total income
(2) Per capita annual disposable income of urban household
(3) Per capita net income of rural household
(4) Average wage of employee
(5) Savings deposit

2.3 Resident Consumption Expenditure

(1) Per capita annual consumption expenditure of urban household
(2) Consumer level index
(3) Number of automobile per 100 urban households

In order to analyze expediently, we give the above indexes the corresponding variables respectively, shown as table 1:

Table 1. Residents' living level index factor and its code

	Factor	Variable
1	Savings deposit	X1
2	Per capita annual disposable income of urban household	X2
3	Total income	X3
4	Number of automobile per 100 urban households	X4
5	Per capita net income of rural household	X5
6	Consumer price index	X6
7	Average wage of employee	X7
8	Per capita annual consumption expenditure of urban household	X8
9	GDP	X9
10	Consumer level index	X10
11	Employment volume	X11

3 Evaluation of Residents' Living Level of Our Country Based on the Principal Components Analysis

Principal components analysis is a statistic method of reducing dimension, it may replace numerous initial data with as few integrative index as possible, and reflect the information of initial data to the best. Except the linear correlation among data it may find out every integrative index to influence residents' living level and make integrative indexes turn into the linear combination of initial variables. Therefore, integrative indexes not only preserve the main information of initial variables, also irrelative each other, as well as have more predominant features than initial variables. It make us easy to grasp the main conflict when evaluate residents' living level.

This paper selected the data from *2010 China Statistical Yearbook* according to the indexes in table 1, and utilized method of principal components analysis and used the statistical software of SPSS(11.5), calculated the factor load matrix, eigenvalue, contribution rate, cumulative contribution rate of factors. According to the factor load matrix, selected the common factor whose contribution rate to above 11 variables was the greatest among all common factors, namely the load sums of 11 variables on this common factor was the greatest, took it as the first main factor and second as the second main factor, analogized in turn. Because the contribution rate sum of the first and the second main factors reached the 78.2%, it explained this two main factors contained the information of 11 indexes basically. Thereby, this paper analyzed the first and the second factors. Analysis results were shown as table 2 and table 3.

Extraction Method: Principal Component Analysis. A 2 components extracted.

We can see in the table 2, the contribution rate of the first main factor is 61.85%, and explains that it is dominant among all factors, the loads of X1, X2, X3, X4, X5, X7, X8 and X11 are bigger, many of these are related to the residents' income and consumption expenditure. The contribution rate of the second factor is 16.346%, the lode of X9 is bigger, it is related to the economic development level of region.

Table 2. Total Variance Explained Total Variance Explained

Component	Initial Eigenvalues			Extraction Sums of Squared Loadings		
	Total	% of Variance	Cumulative %	Total	% of Variance	Cumulativ e %
1	6.809	61.896	61.896	6.809	61.896	61.896
2	1.798	16.344	78.240	1.798	16.344	78.240
3	.920	8.365	86.605			
4	.620	5.638	92.244			
5	.396	3.597	95.841			
6	.226	2.051	97.891			
7	.121	1.098	98.990			
8	.064	.580	99.569			
9	.031	.281	99.850			
10	.016	.142	99.992			
11	.001	.008	100.000			

Extraction Method: Principal Component Analysis.

Table 3. Component Matrix (a)

	Component	
	1	2
VAR00001	.707	.577
VAR00002	.981	-.055
VAR00003	.983	-.081
VAR00004	.828	.065
VAR00005	.948	-.107
VAR00006	-.513	-.473
VAR00007	.788	-.471
VAR00008	.958	-.057
VAR00009	.579	.690
VAR00010	-.168	.570
VAR00011	.794	-.436

Constructed the integrative evaluation function:
The main components of this sample are as follows:

$Z1=0.707X1+0.981X2+0.983X3+0.828X4+0.984X5-0.513X6+0.788X7+0.958X8+0.597X9-0.168X10+0.794X11$

$Z2=0.577X1-0.055X2-0.081X3+0.0650X4-0.107X5-0.473X6$ $-0.471X7-0.057X8+0.690X9+0.570X10-0.436X11$

There fore we can calculate the important factors according to the following models. (Shown as table4)

$Z= 0.61896Z1+0.16344 Z2$

According to the above results analyzed and arranged the residents' living situation of 31 provinces and municipalities in our country, this paper selected the top 12, results were shown as table 4.

Table 4. The top 12 provinces ranking of residents' living situation in our country

Province	Ranking
Beijing	1
Guangdong	2
Shanghai	3
Zhejiang	4
Jiangsu	5
Shandong	6
Tianjin	7
Fujian	8
Liaoning	9
Hebei	10
Henan	11
Sichuan	12

4 Conclusions

Facing numerous indexes of 31 provinces and municipalities and using the method of principal components analysis may replace numerous initial indexes with few integrative indexes. By first two main components may understand clearly the residents' living level of every region, consequently further analyze the economic development and people's living situation of every region. Shown as the table 4, several provinces on the top mostly are the provinces which locates the southeast coast of China with developed economy, yet only Sichuan Province among wets provinces of China is on the list and ranks at last. In this sense, the State Strategy of Developing The Western Region should go on unswervingly. In a word, this ranking makes every provincial government envisage its own actuality and location, further make the structural and strategic regulation according to the actual situation. To develop regional economy and increase residents' income energetically are of paramount importance. Viewing on the economics, economic gross and structure are the two indispensable aspects, the increase of residents' income and consumption level also involves the absolute quantity and consumption structure difference. Therefore, the significance of sound consumption structure of residents' income still is deep and important. Sound structure concerns not only the people's immediate interests also the sustainable development of economy and society, as well as the basis of social stability. The significance to make overall arrangement of consumption level of urban and rural residents' income is very prominent.

References

1. Report on people's livelihood in Chinese city, http://www.calss.net.cn/n1196/ (August 2, 2010)
2. 2010 China Statistical Yearbook. Chinese Statistics Press, Beijing (2011)
3. Jianyin, L., Renke, Z., Xu, L.: The principal components analysis of factors to influence residents' income distribution difference. Journal of Hunan University of Arts and Science (Natural Science) (3), 18–20 (2007)
4. Wenxiu, H., Yanlin, Y., Jianlin, F.: Study summary on Chinese residents' income difference. Economy Research Reference 83(1), 13–29 (2003)
5. Jiewen, C., Yong, C., Haiming, L.: Problems should be paid attention during applyes the principal components analysis. Statistics and Decision-making (8), 140–141 (2009)

Gradient Transfer of China's Textile Industry: The Perspective from TFP Comparative Advantage

Naiquan Liu[1], Ying Li[1,2], and Jin Dai[1,3]

[1] Research Center for Regional Economy,
Shanghai University of Finance and Economics, Shanghai, China; 200433
lnq@mail.shufe.edu.cn
[2] School of Economics, Henan University, Kaifeng, China; 475004
liyingshufe@163.com
[3] Pinghu Campus of Jiaxing University, Pinghu, China; 314200
earl@hz.cn

Abstract. As viewed from the TFP comparative advantage of textile industry, this paper analyzed the multiregional transfer of textile industry in China's three regions. Based on the data of China's manufacturing firms in 2001-2007, this article measured industry TFP with a semi-parametric estimation method. Through the work for comparative analysis of TFP between textile industry and other industries in China's three regions, we find that the TFP comparative advantage in eastern region has declined obviously since 2003, whereas ascended in central and western regions; namely, the internal motivation mechanism of gradient transfer has already formed for China's textile industry. Furthermore, in order to accelerate the mass gradient transfer of textile industry smoothly, some effective policies concentrated on firms are still needed to remove obstacles in the way.

Keywords: Textile Industry TFP, Regional Disparities, Comparative Advantage, Gradient Transfer.

1 Introduction

Although China has carried out the strategy of "transferring spindles from East to West" since the mid of 1990s, the total output proportion of textile industry has still raised from 80.2% in 1995 to 81.7% in 2001, and reached as high as 93.3% in 2005 in eastern region (Qi Shi and Jiliang Zhang, 2007). With the promulgation of *the Plan of National Textile Industry Adjustment and Revitalization* in 2009, the transfer of textile-clothing industry from east to west and central region has been accelerated in recent years. However, the overall progress of transferring is still very slowly in China. In July of 2010, *the Guidance Law of Promoting Transferring of Textile Industry* by MIIT (Ministry of Industry and Information Technology) noted further that it is particularly urgent to push forward the progress of transferring in order to boost the structural adjustment of textile industry and optimize industrial distribution. Furthermore, the external policy of industrial transfer should be combined with enterprises to play an active role in market economy. Therefore, it's of great

M. Zhou (Ed.): ISAEBD 2011, Part IV, CCIS 211, pp. 293–299, 2011.
© Springer-Verlag Berlin Heidelberg 2011

significance to seek internal impetus for textile industry's gradient transfer, which makes industry transferring policy run effectively.

It is well known that transferring studies concerned have a long history. Kaname Akamatsu (1936), Vernon (1966) and Kiyoshi Kojima (1978) explained industry transfer by the theory of comparative advantage, though they studied from different angles. Since the 1990s, study upon industry transfer turned to microeconomic level. Dunning (1993) employed an O-L-I model to show the behavior and expansion of foreign investment. Recently, Chinese scholars carried out some studies concerned. Jianjun Chen (2002) and Houkai Wei (2003) interpreted transferring motivation from the angle of firms. They thought industry transfer is the result of many firms' migration. In addition, Tangjun Yuan (2009) suggested that firms should pay the most attention to TFP (Total Factor Productivity) and TFP analysis based on the data of firms is the most close to reality.

The main questions of this article devoted to as following: Is there regional differences of textile TFP? How about the changing trend of textile TFP comparative advantage? Is there a firm's intrinsic motivation for the gradient transfer of textile industry?

The rest paper is organized as below. Section 2 introduces model and data processing. Section 3 analyzes measurement results. We conclude in section 4.

2   Model and Data

2.1   Model

As for the study of firm's productivity, it is of crucial significance to resolve the simultaneity bias and selection bias emerged from the estimation of production function. In order to estimate firm-level production function more accurately, this paper adopts the method of Levinsohn and Petrin (2003, hereinafter referred to as LP method), who proposed a better semi-parametric solution to the two biases by employing intermediate goods acting as agent variable. Suppose the production function adopt Cobb-Douglas form and its logarithmic form as formula (1).

$$y_{it} = \beta_0 + \beta_l l_{it} + \beta_k k_{it} + \beta_m m_{it} + w_{it} + \eta_{it} . \tag{1}$$

Where, i, firm, t, year; y_{it}, firm gross output value deflated by PPI (Based on 2001); l_{it}, firm's employment; k_{it}, firm's capital, this paper adopted perpetual inventory method to get firm's net value of fixed assets, and investment referred to Kuan Chen's approach (1988), and we take net value of fixed assets at the beginning as firm's initial capital; m_i, intermediate inputs deflated by purchasing price index of raw materials, fuel and power (Based on 2001).

With LP method, we could get estimated coefficients of capital, labor and intermediate input, and then the logarithmic form of productivity for firm i in t year could be calculated by formula (2).

$$\hat{w}_{it} = y_{it} - \hat{\beta}_l l_{it} - \hat{\beta}_k k_{it} - \hat{\beta}_m m_{it} . \tag{2}$$

From dynamic perspective, the growth of industry productivity depends on the advance of technical level and reallocating or combining of resources among heterogeneous firms (Yuhong Li, 2008). Here we define w_{it} as the productivity of firm i in industry j at time t, and then we get total industrial productivity by formula (3).

$$w_t = \sum_{i \in N} z_{it} w_{it} \ .$$

(3)

Where, z_{it} is a weight to depict the allocation of resources among firms, here we measure it by firm's output share in its industry, and N is the set of firms in this industry at time t.

2.2 Data

The source data of this paper comes from the database of China industrial firm in 2001-2007, which rooted in annual investigations by China's national bureau of statistics, and the statistic objects including all state-owned firms and non-state-owned firms with designated scale (the income of main business more than RMB 5 million), and the industrial section of China statistical yearbook was based on this database. To make clear the comparative advantage of TFP in textile industry, we adopt the firm data of 29 manufacturing industries from this database. The sample covered all designated scaled firm's annual business data in 2001-2007. This paper divided China's 31 administrative regions into three areas, eastern, central and western, to analyze industry TFP. Eastern region includes eleven provinces: Beijing, Tianjin, Hebei, Shanghai, Jiangsu, Zhejiang, Shandong, Guangdong, Fujian, Hainan and Liaoning. Central region includes 8 provinces: Shanxi, Anhui, Jiangxi, Henan, Hubei, Jilin, Heilongjiang and Hunan. Western region includes 12 provinces: Guangxi, Inner Mongolia, Chongqing, Sichuan, Guizhou, Yunnan, Tibet, Shanxi, Gansu, Qinghai, Xinjiang and Ningxia.

In order to get the desirable sample, we deal source data with the steps below, and we finally get matched data as displayed in Table 1. Firstly, regroup industries. Based on standards of industrial classification, the paper regrouped the data in 2001 and 2002 accordingly, and deleted industry C43, "the industry of recovery processing for wasted resource and recycled materials", and then we got 29 industries with double-digit code. Secondly, eliminate abnormal values. The adopted data is up to the standards below: A. the inputs and outputs of firm are both positive. Here we exclude firms employed fewer than eight people (Qianli Xie, 2008). B. the original value of fixed assets is greater than the net value of fixed assets. C. the gross output value is greater than the value-added of industry or the intermediate inputs. D. the adopted data is only from the firms keeping on running. Thirdly, unify statistical standard. Only the firms with designated scale are adopted.

Table 1. Total firms with designated scale in 2001-2007

Year	2001	2002	2003	2004	2005	2006	2007
Total Firms	132768	142104	160947	235215	221411	246504	287071

Source of data: China industrial firm databases (2001-2007).

3   Measurement Results and Economic Analysis

3.1   Analysis of Estimation Results for Firm's Production Function

We respectively apply formula (1) to 29 manufacturing industries with double-digit code, then use LP and OLS methods to estimate firm's production function with 2001-2007 sample data. 20 of those 29 industries passed LP test, which account for 72 % of total observation. Therefore, we only choose the data of those 20 industries to facilitate comparison. The coefficients of labor and capital in 20 industries (except pharmaceutical manufacturing) match with the theoretical conclusion of LP, that is, if corrected by LP estimation method, the coefficient of capital would increase and the coefficient of labor would decrease. Undoubtedly, LP semi-parametric estimation method is effective to correct coefficient bias, which lay a solid foundation for the following accurate TFP estimation. Due to the limitation of space, Table 1 only listed the coefficient and significance of LP and OLS for textile industry.

Table 2. Estimated coefficients of production function for textile with LP and OLS

	ln$l$	ln$k$	ln$m$
LP	0.064***	0.033***	0.881***
OLS	0.076***	0.02***	0.892***
OLS coef. bias	+	−	+
N. of obs.		114983	

Note: 1. The superscript "* * *" said it's significant at 1% significance level. N. is
sample size, "+" and "-" means high and low respectively.
2. The software we used is STATA10.0.

3.2   Regional Differences Analysis of Textile Industry's TFP

Firstly, we calculated regional TFP of textile and other 19 industries in 2001-2007 according to formula (3).The annual regional TFP of textile is shown in Table 2. Obviously, the absolute advantage of textile TFP in eastern region is the highest, lower in central region, and western region is the lowest. Additionally, as viewed from dynamic changing trend of textile TFP in 2001-2007, the TFP of three regions tends to convergence numerically in 2003, which means the regional gap of absolute advantage over textile TFP tends to decrease.

Table 3. Textile TFP in three regions

year	2001	2002	2003	2004	2005	2006	2007
Eastern	0.83	0.86	0.9	0.88	0.83	0.82	0.82
Central	0.8	0.83	0.87	0.84	0.82	0.8	0.81
Western	0.77	0.8	0.84	0.82	0.8	0.78	0.8

Secondly, we analyzed respectively the regional TFP rank of textile among 20 industries in the same region. As showed in Table 3, the comparative advantage of textile TFP in eastern region had declined obviously since 2003. On the contrary, it displayed an ascendant trend in central and western regions. In order to achieve a better allocation, the capital in central and western regions would draw out from the industries with a lower TFP. Meanwhile, when the eastern capital gradually turned to other industries with higher TFP comparative advantage, the total supply of textile would decrease and its price would rise. Consequently, the capital in central and western regions would flow in the textile industry to capture this long-term profitable opportunities. Here we can safely approach the conclusion that firm's rational choice is endogenous driving power for gradient transfer of textile industry, and the shift of investment is its exterior market performance.

Table 4. Rank of textile TFP in three regions

year	2001	2002	2003	2004	2005	2006	2007
Eastern	6	7	8	9	11	11	12
Central	8	8	7	7	6	5	5
Western	10	9	8	7	7	6	6

Thirdly, we studied the difference between the textile TFP and the TFP mean of other industries with a higher rank than textile in eastern region. The difference is respectively 0.06, 0.07, 0.08, 0.1, 0.11, 0.13 and 0.17 in 2001-2007, displayed an expanding tendency, which indicated other industries with higher TFP rank attract more and more capital from textile industry, that is, the push motivation become stronger for firms to abandon textile in eastern region. On the other hand, the new capital in the central and western regions would take over the transferred textile industry from eastern region, which generated an increasing pull forces. However, if only depended on the market mechanism, textile industry would transfer slowly due to asymmetric information, market failure, etc. Therefore, as this endogenous push-pull mechanism came into being and improved gradually, the local government should seize the favorable opportunity to promote and accelerate the gradient transferring process of textile industry by the agency of offering feasible policies and eliminating resistance.

3.3 Analysis of Resource Allocation Effects upon Textile TFP

The analysis above reveals there is a significant difference between trans-regional textile TFP, and the internal impetus of transferring already formed in eastern textile firms. And then, we would put forward the questions below. Will the production factors flow to the firms with high marginal productivity spontaneously and improve the TFP level by reallocating resources? Is there an efficient resources allocation or gradient transfer of textile occurred from east to west and central region?

In order to find these answers, we refer to the method of Foster (2001) who decomposed TFP growth into five effects, effect within firm (WE),effect between firms (BE),crossover effect (CE), entry effect (ENE) and exit effect (XNE) , as the five orderly corresponding items depicted in the right side of formula (4) .

$$\Delta w_t \equiv \sum_{i \in C} z_{it-1} \Delta w_{it} + \sum_{i \in C} \Delta z_{it} (w_{it-1} - \overline{w}_{jt-1}) + \sum_{i \in C} \Delta z_{it} \Delta w_{it} + \sum_{i \in E} z_{it} (w_{it} - \overline{w}_{jt-1}) + \sum_{i \in X} z_{it-1} (\overline{w}_{jt-1} - w_{it-1}).$$ (4)

Where, i, j, t respectively represent firm, industry and time; z the output share of firm i in industry j; w_{it} TFP of firm i in industry j at time t, $\triangle w_t$ the change of productivity in year t; C, E, X refer to always existing, new entering and exiting firms in 2001-2007; and the bar symbol is the mean of the industry.

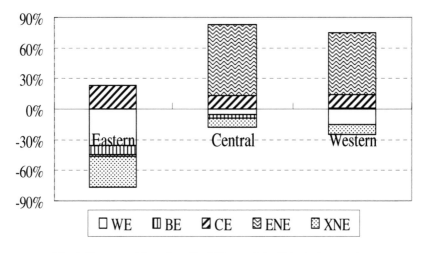

Fig. 1. Decomposition of textile TFP growth in China's three regions

Fig. 1 depicted the contribution of the abovementioned effects to the textile TFP of three regions in 2001-2007. Firstly, WE performed negatively in all three regions, which indicated firms' technical efficiency was deteriorated by itself. Secondly, negative BE indicated the market share of surviving firms decreased, which reduced sharply in eastern region, followed by the central and western regions. Meanwhile, CE performed positively in all three regions, which showed the resource allocation was optimized in regional surviving textile firms, and the resource optimization effect is better in eastern surviving textile firms than in the central and western ones. Finally, the contribution of ENE to textile industry was greater in central and western regions than in eastern region. Negative XNE is the largest in eastern region, which led the textile productivity up in central and western areas and down in eastern region. Now we can say that the textile TFP growth in three regions comes mainly from resource optimization among firms, particularly ENE and XNE indicates that central and western regions are more attractive to the textile resources to flow in, as also indirectly reflected gradient transfer of textile industry from east to west and central region in 2001-2007.

4 Conclusions

This paper uses microeconomic data, data of firms, to measure TFP of textile and other industries. The measurement results indicated there was a regional TFP difference of textile industry in China's three regions. The regional gap of TFP absolute advantage displayed a descendent trend after 2003. Meanwhile, the TFP comparative advantage has declined obviously in eastern region since 2003, whereas ascended in central and western regions. That is, the endogenous push-pull motivation of textile industry's gradient transfer came into being and increased gradually. Moreover, the textile TFP growth in three regions mainly comes from optimized resource allocation among firms, particularly the allocation effects of ENE and XNE indicate that central and western regions are more attractive to the textile resources to flow in. Consequently, we could safely draw the conclusion that the endogenous transferring motivation of textile industry already exists in China's three regions, and there is a premise for the external motivation to act smoothly. However, in order to accelerate the mass gradient transfer of textile industry, some effective policies concentrated on firms are still needed to remove obstacles in the way.

Acknowledgement. This paper is supported by the philosophy social Foundation of Shanghai (NO.2010BJL002).

References

[1] Dunning, J.H.: Multinational Enterprises and the Global Economy. Addison Wesley, Wokingham (1993)
[2] Foster, L., Haltiwanger, J., Krizan, C.J.: Aggregate Productivity Growth Lessons from Microeconomic Evidence. In: Hulten, C.R., Dean, E.R., Harper, M. (eds.) New Developments in Productivity Analysis, The University of Chicago Press, Chicago (2001)
[3] Jefferson, G.H., Rawski, T.G., Zhang, Y.: Productivity Growth and Convergence across China's Industrial Economy. China Economic Quarterly (3), 809–826 (2008)
[4] Wei, H.: The Development Trends of Industrial Shift and Its Impacts on Competitiveness. Fujian Tribune (An Economics & Sociology Monthly) 4, 11–159 (2003)
[5] Chen, J.: Industrial Regional Transferring at China Current Stage and Its Power Mechanism. China Industrial Economy 8, 37–44 (2002)
[6] Levinsohn, J., Petrin, A.: Estimating Production Functions Using Inputs to Control for Unobservable. Review of Economic Studies 70, 317–341 (2003)
[7] Kojima, K.: Direct Foreign Investment: A Japanese Model of Multinational Business Operations. Praeger, New York (1978)
[8] Chen, K., Jefferson, G., Rawski, T., Wang, H., et al.: Productivity Change in Chinese Industry: 1953—1985. Journal of Comparative Economics 12, 570–591 (1988)
[9] Shi, Q., Zhang, J.: Harmony of Regional Industry Transferring and Industrialization for Underdevelopment Area. Industrial Economics Research 1, 38–44 (2007)
[10] Yuan, T.: Total Factor Productivity Performance of Chinese Firms. Economic Research Journal 6, 53–64 (2009)
[11] Li, Y., Wang, H., Zheng, Y.: Firm Evolution: Important Path of Industrial TFP Growth in China. Economic Research Journal 6, 12–24 (2008)

The Application of Real Options Analysis in the Risk Decision of Overbooking in Airlines

Guangxi Wu

School of Management, Xiamen University, Xiamen, Fujian Province 361005
Wgx87@qq.com

Abstract. Overbooking is an important tool for revenue management. This paper, which is based on the perspective of producers of perishable goods - the airline, proposes to introduce a new tool in reducing and avoiding these two kinds of risks while making decision on the volume of overbooking. This paper also probes into the problems of overbooking and the feasibility of the introduction of options, also builds a model of real options in overbooking and utilize a simple example to analysis the feasibility of real option in aviation -- overbooking.

Keywords: management overbook real option application.

1 Introduction

In the overbooking system of Airline Revenue Management, the overbooking amounts confirm is very important, which is the key to determine overbooking sales effectiveness. There are two perspectives to confirm the optimal overbooking amount form risks of No show and DB, it is a risk decision-making problem. In enterprise risk decision-making, real options analysis is a historical mature decision-making theory which is superior and valuable in the determination of optimal schemes, risk measurement and management. In fact, revenue management problem is a branch of business risk decision-making, so it can also adopt advantages of real options analysis to optimize decision-making and handle this issue. Some scholars have introduced real option analysis into revenue management, including: (1) Anderson introduced real option analysis model into car rental industry to determine the minimum price and the corresponding booking limit level. (2) In 2004, McAfee and Te Velde established a dynamic pricing model for the aviation industry to adjust current price based on future sales option value. (3) 2006, Rolf discussed how to price stock with option contract in air cargo. But these studies are not mature enough, and it is still an issue about how to introduce real option analysis method in revenue management system. In order to determine overbooking amount in revenue management, it can also introduce the powerful real option analysis to decision-making and risk control. However, there are few studies on overbooking with real option analysis. This article will focus on the overbooking amount decision-making and risk management with real option analysis method.

M. Zhou (Ed.): ISAEBD 2011, Part IV, CCIS 211, pp. 300–307, 2011.

This paper proposes an indirect screening method for optimal overbooking amount, which can determine the optimal overbooking amount, but a little cumbersome. However, the key of this method lies in finding real options hidden in decision-making while determining the best overbooking amount, so we can directly apply financial option pricing theory and risk management methods to effectively manage and avoid risk during overbooking amount confirmation, and there are prominence and innovation of this paper.

2   The Bottleneck of Current Overbooking Risk Management

There are two risks in practical operation: one is "No show" which means virtual sales, the other is "DB" for the damage compensation of clients and business integrity loss.

Establishing a more reliable, ultra-sound system is the most direct way to reduce risk. Overbooking system prediction is complex and random, and considering the current overbooking system accuracy, it is still a bottleneck to optimize overbooking system within a short period. ZHOU Yan, ZHU Jin-fu propose recall method to reduce DB ticket losses. When the actual demand of flight space is greater than forecast, take use of recall system to meet high-end customer demands which solves partial DB problems; while in the low flight space the actual demand is greater than forecast demand, recall system can be used to promote. However, this method also has disadvantages: strictly speaking it is not revenue management method because this method is really just taking use of price differences to reduce risks between recallable ticket price and the reserve price which NO show clients would like to pay (clients who do arrive at airport and need to take a flight but there is no ticket left). This method does not show the essence of revenue management theory – in No show circumstance, simply recall tickets and inform clients that these maybe recalled and raise the price to Go show clients, so Go show clients pay much more because selling price has to be higher than recall price, let along the loss of clients whose ticket has been recalled. Gao Qiang, ZHU Jin-fu proposes to control and manage overbooking risk with indefinite ticket which need not adjust flight, just allocate tickets among different flights, thus to achieve high seat kilometer utilization. Because the selection is among multiple flights, it may effectively avoid DB. But there are also some shortcomings: the premier of this method is to deploy within flights on the same day, which means there have to be a large airline scale and enough flights for choose, or it cannot make the most advantages from indefinite tickets allocation.

Considering above issues, this article will expatiate overbooking risk management and avoidance from a different point of view. Taking use of real option model to determine best overbooking amount and find out the real option from decision-making, which provides the foundation for utilizing real option analysis to determine overbook risk management and decision making.

3 Feasibility of Applying Real Option in Overbooking

According to real options characteristics, real options analysis should be used to make investment decisions in the following conditions:

When there is or possible investment decisions, traditional investment decision-making methods can not accurately estimate the value of this investment opportunity.

When the uncertainty of investment projects is large enough that more information is needed to avoid investment mistakes.

When the value of investment projects is determined mainly by future growth value rather than current cash flow.

When uncertainty is large enough that flexibility has to be taken into consideration, the only way to evaluate investment with active options is real option method.

When in project update or when the strategic break.

Overbooking amount can be regarded as airline company investment during overbooking process. In this decision, because the number of No show is random and unknown, it is impossible to make accurate investment decisions with traditional investment decision-making program. In addition, the investment decision variables – choice of overbooking amount is an OR decision-making power, so airline company overbooking problem meets the prerequisite of real options.

The investment decision-making in airline overbooking, investment revenue is the amount of investment income received after airline tickets are overbooked, while investment cost is the possible loss caused by DB, decision-making uncertainty is the number of No show. Overbooking can be treated as the gained assets, while the other as abandonment options, if choose the first decision, then it means giving up implementing options, if select the second decision, then implement abandonment option, therefore, this issue contains an issue of giving up real options.

To make an effective analysis of real options theory, the following chart lists input parameters correspondence of real options decision-making and financial option pricing theory:

Table 1. Input parameters correspondence between financial options and real options

Financial Options	Real Options
Current stock price S	Project cash flow present value of earning P
Exercise price X	Uncertainty of project value V
Option expiration date T	Project investment opportunity duration T
Uncertainty of stock prices σ	Uncertainty of project value θ
Risk-free interest rater	Risk-free interest rater

In overbooking decision-making, the present value of project cash flow yield P is overbooking additional revenue, project investment cost V is DB damages, the project investment opportunities duration T lasts from start selling tickets to takeoff time, the project value uncertainty θ is relevant to number of No show probability distribution.

4 Real Option Model and Application in Overbooking

4.1 Real Option Model Assumptions and Model Description

The followings calculate model details and list assumptions:

One Assumption on air overbooking Model
Full sale of airline overbooking.

For No show passengers, in order to simplify the study, assuming that the number of No show passengers meet the binomial distribution, that is: each No show passenger are independent, and each one has the same No show probability q. According to aviation industry experience in sales statistics, q is usually 10% -15%.

DB loss consists of two parts: direct economic compensation for DB customers and business credit losses. In order to investigate more practically, assume that the value of economic damages are approximately equal with air fares (if compensation cost is much higher than ticket revenue, then airline overbooking is completely meaningless.) This compensation does not include returned air ticket fares. The loss of business reputation is generally not linear, and Airline Company will set a nonlinear function table of losses. In order to get model core idea and avoid complexity caused by minutiae of mathematical calculations without affecting results, it can be assumed that loss of business reputation is a multiple of DB number. Fare loss value = $\sum^i$ * fare (i is the i DB passengers).

There is only one kind of flight position in this model (in reality, the number of economy class in most cases are far more than other types, so upgrade impact can be ignored.).

After deciding overbooking amount, the opportunity cost is not considered if No show number is too many which leads to inefficient overbooking.

Assumptions of real options analysis.

Two decision-making options in the model are given in two different overbooking amounts with unknown No Show number. By pair-wise comparison of all overbooking amounts, select scheme with best optimal benefits. Now computers are widely used, Bubble sort algorithm can be used to easily select the best one. Therefore, this model only focuses on the two given overbooking decision-making problems.

In alternative scenario, regards additional income as investment revenue and DB damages as investment cost.

Since ticket sales are different from general investment, the period is very short, so we can ignore the risk-free interest rate.

Different No show circumstance, no risk probability is equal to the number of different No show number.

These are assumptions and descriptions before building and derivate model.

4.2 Real Option Model Building and Derivation

Seating capacity of an aircraft is M, two decision alternatives are known,

overbooking capacity K_1, No show number N_1, N_1 is a random variable, subject to b (q, M), the value of this program (overbooking revenue) is A.

overbooking capacity K_2, No show number N_2, N_2 is a random variable, subject to b (q, M), the value of this program is B.

Known, N_1 and N_2 are independent and identically distributed, and all loss of business reputation due to DB customer is C, ticket price is p, then: the objective is to find Max (A, B);

Order: No show number i, the probability is:

$$q_i = C_M^i * q^i * (1-q)^{M-i} \tag{1}$$

(Binomial distribution formula for the distribution of column);

At this point, the decision scheme 1, overbooking earning is

$$A_i = q_i *(K_1 *p\text{-Max} (K_1 \text{-i}, 0)*2*p\text{-} C_1) \tag{2}$$

(without considering opportunity cost loss when No show number is larger than overbooking, in fact, over booking amount is model premise, there is no visible loss of opportunity cost. 2 * p includes loss of refund to DB passengers and financial compensation.)

For decision scheme 2, overbooking earning is:

$$B_i = q_i *(K_2 *p\text{-Max} (K_2 \text{-i},0)*2*p\text{-} C_2) \tag{3}$$

$$\text{其中} : \text{Max}(K_1 \text{-i}, 0)= \begin{cases} 0, i>K1 \\ K_1-i, 0<=i<=K1 \end{cases} \tag{4}$$

$$A=\sum_{i=0}^{M} A_i = \sum_{i=0}^{M} q_i *(K_1 *p\text{-Max} (K_1 \text{-i},0)*2*p\text{-}C_1) \tag{5}$$

$$B=\sum_{i=0}^{M} B_i = \sum_{i=0}^{M} q_i *(K_2 *p\text{-Max} (K_2 \text{-i},0)*2*p\text{-}C_2) \tag{6}$$

It is assumed that when No show number is N, overbooking number is K, DB number is: K-N. Then by the arithmetic series summation formula, get the loss of business reputation at this time:

$$C= \frac{(K-N)^2 + (K-N)}{2} *p \tag{7}$$

(6) - (5) then substituted into (7), we have:

$$B\text{-}A = \sum_{i=0}^{M} q_i * (K_2\text{-}K_1) * p + \sum_{i=0}^{M} q_i * [(Max(K_1-i,0) - Max(K_2-i,0)) * 2 * p + (C_1-C_2)]$$

$$= (K_2 - K_1) * p + \sum_{i=0}^{M} q_i * 2 * (Max(K_1-i,0) - Max(K_2-i,0)) * p +$$

$$\sum_{i=0}^{M} q_i * (\frac{Max^2(K_1-i,0) + Max(K_1-i,0)}{2} - \frac{Max^2(K_2-i,0) + Max(K_2-i,0)}{2}) * p \qquad (8)$$

$$= \sum_{i=0}^{M} q_i * (\frac{Max^2(K_1-i,0) + 5Max(K_1-i,0)}{2} - \frac{Max^2(K_2-i,0) + 5Max(K_2-i,0)}{2}) * p$$

$$+ (K_2 - K_1) * p$$

The above (8) is the ultimate expression of this model. It can be used to compare two overbooking scheme values, when (8) is greater than 0, then choose the second overbooking program, and q_i represents No show risk-neutral probability. In (6) Max (K_1-I, 0) and Max (K_2-i, 0) can be seen as trading as European sales right of two conventions, so that (8) is regarded as a function of two European put options. Based on the Black-Scholes pricing formula of European put option, real option prices can be calculated, which are hidden in two different overbooking schemes.

In practical overbooking operations, its amount is an unknown number based on No show variables. From above modeling and derivation, optimal scheme actually can only be selected from the two given overbooking amounts. If you want to directly find the best unknown overbooking amount, due to the amount of overbooking is a positive integer, first list all possible acquired overbooking amount, and then compare multiple overbooking amounts cons and pros with above decision-making methods until the best overbooking amount is found. In fact, airline policy makers have a lot of experiences in deciding overbooking amount, overbooking amount is set within a small range (such as 2% -5%) excluding a large number unreasonable overbooking amounts; on the other hand, with computer applications, even a large number of screening calculations can be completed in a relatively short period of time; so in summary, this model can better carry out overbooking decision-making under above assumptions.

4.3 Numerical Example of Real Option Model

For above deducted overbooking real option decision-making model, take the following example to make a specific analysis.

Example: an aircraft seating capacity is 100 people, known two decision-making schemes:

A: overbooking amount is 3, No show number N_1, N_1 is a random variable, subject to b (0.15, 100), the value of this scheme (that income got from this scheme) is A.

B: overbooking amount is 5, No show number N_2, N_2 is a random variable, subject to b (0.15, 100), the value of this scheme is B.

Known, N_1 and N_2 are independent and identically distributed, the i-DB customers cause marginal loss of business reputation is 600 * 1 yuan, ticket price is 600 yuan.

Pilot analysis is the profit from scheme A and scheme B to make investment decision.

Objective function in this case is to get Max(A,B) ;

When No show number is i, the probability is:

$$q_i = C_{100}^i * 0.15^i * (1 - 0.15)^{100-i} \tag{9}$$

Put known data into (8) and get:

$$B\text{-}A = \sum_{i=0}^{100} q_i *(\frac{Max^2(3-i,0) + 5Max\ (3-i,0)}{2} - \frac{Max^2(5-i,0) + 5Max\ (5-i,0)}{2}) * 600 \tag{10};$$

$$+\ (5-3)*600$$

and get : B-A=1200-0.0054*600 ; =1196.78 yuan

It is seen that overbooking number should be more than 5 people, and because 1196.78 is approximately equal to 1200, which shows the two excess DB loss risk is almost negligible.

For the first calculation, take use of computer programming and recursive function to solve.

After deciding optimal overbooking amount of each time, use computer screening to select the best overbooking amount among superior items from pair-wise comparisons. Bubble sort method should be used to screen optimal overbooking amount when the number is N, follow these steps:

Comparison of two adjacent numbers, small number in the front and large number at the back; numbers on the back.

Perform the above operation, comparison from 1 to N.

Repeat operation 1 and 2; repeat N times like this, then N sort is completed.

4.4 Optimal Analysis of Real Options

In above model, the most clever part is to clearly differentiate exceeded benefits with investment costs and measure benefits apart from overbooking revenue, DB loss is investment cost of overbooking decision-making, and two overbooking amount selections are self-decided real options, by which means overbooking issues can find corresponding variables, uncertain factors and real options hidden in decision-making process within real options framework

I believe that, we can also start from options expansion, if regarding overbooking as a non-executed overbook, when profit has been made (without execute overbooking, the airline tickets have been sold), because there are investment project with good yields (spare seats) and a good market conditions (clients possibly will take the flight but have no tickets), this is the expansion of investment. We could also treat overbooking as conversion options, flexibly switch among various investments in dynamic overbooking process, thereby changes investment decisions.

In short, real option can be introduced from different perspectives of overbooking issue. Within overbooking model of real options, the more relations of real options in each step, the more clear these relations are, the more advantageous we can get from real options.

References

1. Smith, B., Leimkuhler, J., Darrow, R., et al.: Yield management at American Airlines. Interface 1(1), 8–31 (1992)
2. Fitzsimmons, J.A., Fitzsimmons, M.J., Command Cheng, F., et al.: Service management, operations, strategy, information technology, 5th edn. China Machine Press, Beijing (2007)
3. Bodie, Z., Kane, A., Marcus, A. (Annotation). Investments (English the 6th of original). Mechanical Industry Press, Beijing (2007)
4. Mun, J., Li, Q.: Real options analysis and techniques for valuing strategic investment and decisions. China Renmin University Press, Beijing (2006)
5. Hu, M., Zhu, J.-F., Wang, X.: Airline Revenue Management Pricing Based on Game Analysis [. Forecast 25(6), 45–49 (2006)
6. Anderson, C.K., Davison, M., Rasmussen, H.: Revenue management: A real options approach. Naval Re2search Logistics 51, 686–703 (2004)
7. Feldman, J.M.: To rein in those CRSs. Air Transport World 28(12), 89–92 (1991)

The Effect of Bounded Rationality Types on Project Evaluation

Haitao Li and Xiaozhi Ma

College of Management and Economics
Tianjin University,Tianjin, P.R.China, 300072
lihaitao@tju.edu.cn

Abstract. In project activities, bounded rationality has an impact on the project inevitably. But for different projects, the impacts of bounded rationality also have important differences. For some projects, there are much risks and uncertainties that people's cognitive ability can't cope with them, and the impact mainly shows as cognitive bounded rationality. While for some other projects, the problem of the project's conflicting interests is prominent that it is difficult to achieve the optimization of the overall project effectiveness, and the impact shows as interests bounded rationality. Of course, there are many projects impacted by the both. Therefore, the project evaluation under bounded rationality requires distinguishing different circumstances, and giving different evaluation packages aiming at different bounded rationality types. At the same time, it should understand the characteristics of the project deeply, classify the project in accordance with the impact of bounded rationality, and then select the appropriate evaluation packages.

Keywords: project evaluation, uncertainty, cognitive bounded rationality, interest bounded rationality.

1 Introduction

It is generally believed that the main impact of bounded rationality on project evaluation is that the consequences of decisions can not be optimal and satisfied due to the limited cognitive abilities of people or some unpredictable factors [1].But we believe that it is just the first layer meaning of impact of bounded rationality. The impact of bounded rationality on project evaluation and project decision should implies three meanings: First, rationality is bounded that some uncertainties can not be mastered in project and some dissatisfied consequences may happen; Second, people strive to be rational that decision-makers will try to investigate and interpret these dissatisfied consequences and take the bounded rational consequences in the future project activities into consideration; Third, striving to rationality doesn't mean that all these unsatisfactory consequences can be predicted and only some corresponding arrangements can be made.

2 Bounded Rationality and Bounded Predict

Only from the perspective of "correct" or "incorrect", a effective project evaluation needs two conditions: The first one is to own information about project activities and

M. Zhou (Ed.): ISAEBD 2011, Part IV, CCIS 211, pp. 308–314, 2011.

it is also the foundation of project evaluation; the other one is to own the intelligence and wisdom to form effective decisions by calculating and operating with the help of information. The meaning of rationality contains these two conditions which are needed by effective project evaluation. A rational decision-maker knows anything and can do anything. To know anything means that he has the information to make decision. To do anything means that he has the intelligence to make decision.

But the realistic decision scene can not fully meet the requirement of rationality. The information and intelligence are hard to be satisfied in practice. But the people with bounded rationality are smart enough to try to meet the requirements of decision-making through all kinds of methods. Compared with the information, the intelligence is easier to be satisfied. All kinds of technical methods, supplementary measures and decision-making models are developed to eliminate the limitation of individual intelligence hence some satisfactory results can be generally achieved. But it is not easy to achieve such effects for information because technology can not essentially play a key role for it. It surely does not deny the fact that technology can reduce the difficulties and costs of acquiring information.

In the view of the need of project decision-making, project information can be divided into two parts: One part is the information about "now". Since the information exists already, the key is how to collect it. It usually presents decentralized distribution and is respectively mastered by different people who are related to the project activities. Therefore, using dispersed information and playing total power in decision-making should be focused on. There are two models to cope with this problem: One is the centralized model that to submit the dispersed information to the decision-maker who make the decision finally; The other one is the dispersed model that decision-making power are scattered to the information owners while the information isn't needed to be transferred.

The other part refers to the information about "future". Since the state of future is not occurred yet, the information about "future" can be abstained only by forecast rather than by collect. Many theoretical models and methods are developed about forecast which could do some auxiliary help to forecast. But the main problem is not the method. It is always unclear what information could play a significant role to predict the future. Therefore, it is more important to select information, but people often encounter infinite information and get disoriented; On the other hand, some acute decision-maker often find opportunities and clues from faint information. Therefore, if bounded rationality such as intellectual and information can be made some appropriate remedies in some way, the predict of "future" information may often depend on the decision makers' sudden inspiration, although some technical assistances can be made, there are still some areas which rationality can't reach.

3   Bounded Predict and Mechanism Arrangement

The bounded rationality plays a particular prominent role in predicting. Although there are some areas that the rational can not reach, it doesn't mean people can do nothing about it. Actually, although people can not predict the future exactly, they do know their drawbacks and do not fallaciously want to eliminate bounded rationality completely. On the one hand, they try to reduce bounded rationality to some degree through mechanism arrangement; On the other hand, they appraise the impact of bounded rationality in decision-making process. Decision-makers with bounded rationality can not predict all the future project activities perfectly, what also means that the future filled with uncertainties which include not only the cognitive aspects of project activities information, but also the interactive relationship between project participators in the cooperation and conflict. Different types of uncertainties will be given different treatments in the prior evaluation.

3.1   The Treatment and Evaluation of Cognitive Bounded Rationality

Usually, people have two different attitudes toward the uncertainties caused by cognitive bounded rationality. Sometimes, people emphasize the possibilities of loss brought by uncertainties. Uncertainties may cause project activities stop if the loss is hard to bear. Therefore, the prior evaluation emphasizes the ability of risk aversion. A project is advisable if it can achieve the expected target and has a strong ability of risk aversion. Conversely, a project is abandoned possibly if it has great uncertainties and weak ability of risk aversion, although it may achieve the target and the expected revenue is high. Traditional project evaluation also emphasizes risk and uncertainty analysis [2].But sometimes, for uncertainties caused by cognitive ability, people don't just negatively avoid. Prior evaluation also emphasizes the possibility of excess returns and actively creates the conditions for generating excess returns. To those projects such as technological innovation projects, exploration and development projects, people develop them although they do known there are many uncertainties in the future. Obviously, to against downside risks is also part of the project work, but in quite a secondary position. It is another tendency to appraise uncertainty that to value the opportunities brought by the risks and uncertainties of the project.

3.2   The Treatment and Evaluation of Interest Bounded Rationality

Project activities are usually done by relevant participants together. The coordination among relevant participants is the essential condition of the project activities' success. But the communications are often not smooth enough. More important, it will make the coordination of project activity difficult because the respective interest demands conflict. Obviously, to manage the project activities through some mechanism arrangements is an important measure to eliminate interest bounded rationality. Since the interest bounded rationality will bring uncertainty, the degree of coordination harmony should be investigated and the ability to avoid this kind of uncertainty should be analyzed in the prior evaluation. The project activity will not only bring the bounded rationality created by the interest conflicts among project actors, but also effect on the people out of the project. Different from the conflict within the project, the relevant participants can produce a stable and harmonious collaboration by game, of course, it is only a possibility under certain conditions; However, the impact of projects on the outside can not automatically adjust to the state of harmony by game, but only through government and other control units, relying on rules limiting and policy to coordinate the project impact outside and eliminate the interest bounded rationality outside.

4   The Bounded Rationalities of Different Project Types

4.1   Bounded Rationality and the Dimensions of the Project

As the performances of bounded rationality of different projects are different, the emphases of evaluation are very different. Although there are common properties and management features among various projects, there are differences among different projects due to the peculiarities of project. So it is necessary to classify the projects further to grasp the specific characteristics of different types of projects, and give different evaluation packages aiming at different bounded rationality types. There are usually various ways to classify projects. The main dimensions of classification include: project risk, time span, project subject, role, scale, etc. A certain project usually has multi-dimensional feature. In project evaluation, different combination of dimensions will lead to quite different performances of bounded rationality. Correspondingly, different investigation methods will be used in decision evaluation.

4.2   Bounded Rationality of Different Types of Projects and the Key of the Decisions

There is bounded rationality in any project. Although people can eliminate it to some extent, it is impractical to eliminate it completely. The severities of bounded rationality in different project are different and the presentation ways also have great differences. Since people's attitudes toward risks and uncertainties are different, a same problem may be solved in different ways. Sometimes, people value the potential loss, and sometimes value the potential benefit; sometimes, people pay attention to the coordination within the project, and sometimes pay attention to the harmony outside the project. The type and scene of the project (not the preference) determine the focus of the decision-making.

1. Public Project

Public project is essentially provided by government which includes public welfare project and infrastructure project. Public welfare project does not target profits and has great social benefits. Infrastructure project has a natural monopoly, a big investment scale, a long construction cycle and unapparent benefits. In a word, public project essentially target at meeting the public demands which includes improving the investment environment constantly, optimizing the industrial structure, achieving the sustained macroeconomic growth, and improving various welfare such as public education, public health and public safety [3] .Obviously, this kind of projects service to the public rather than take the interest of the participants within the project. Therefore, it has serious interest bounded rationality. Besides, as the decisions are always made by government officials, the phenomenon of self-interest pursuit and short-term interests may occur, without regarding to the interests of society and the long-term interests. There will also be principal-agent problem between government and contractors [4]. The rent-seeking phenomenon is usually in the principal-agent problem. Therefore, the effective evaluation of the interest bounded rationality is essential to public project.

2. Large Project

Large projects tend to cause impacts of externalities. Many large projects have positive externalities and negative externalities. Large projects will generally have impacts of regional externalities and positive effects on driving the development of regional economy and effect on employment. In ecological aspect of environment, it may bring impacts on geology and climate; large-scale industrial projects will generate large amounts of pollutants emission. A lot of impacts are very subtle and can not be forecasted in initial stage, they may emerge after several years or even decades. For example, there are benefits and drawbacks in the large Three Gorges Project (TGP). On the one hand, it brings great comprehensive benefits. On the other hand, it does serious harms to the riverbed, the geologic structure and environment, and so on. Over all, large project should be given full consideration.

3. Cross-enterprises Project

Cross-enterprise project is carried out by several different companies for a common cooperation goal. The motivation is to fill the gaps of resources and technology, improve the competitiveness, disperse and reduce the business risks, and so on. What should be taken note is that the main purpose is to reduce the risks of individual enterprises and uncertainties, but it does not reduce the uncertainties itself. New problems will emerge among cooperation partners after the project takes the cooperation form. For cross-enterprises projects, the conflict of interest is inevitable. The benefit goals of the companies are not identical. Some enterprises are not to pure profits, but to coordinate the enterprise strategic goals. Individual rationality could eventually lead to collective irrationality on the premise when benefit goals deviate. Whereas, some enterprises transfer their costs to the investment project and damage the interests of other cooperative enterprise in order to maximize their own interests. For example, common supply chain projects formed by many enterprises often have information asymmetry. Since lack of effective oversight and control mechanisms, there will be some phenomenon of moral risk and meeting self-interest by damage the downstream interests of partners [5].The most common conflict types of cross-enterprises project include: human resource, equipment and facility, capital expenditure, cost, technical advice and trade off, priority, management procedure, schedule, responsibility, cultural diversity, personality Collision, and so on. The relative strength of every conflict will change with the cycle of project. As the relationship of the cooperative participants is one of the key factors, project decision should be made by investigating the harmony of the relationships among participants.

4. Long-period Project

As the name implies, the long-period projects have long life cycles that generally can last 10-20 years or even longer. The length of project cycle is closely linked with the uncertainty. This kind of projects inevitably has the characters of high uncertainty, which bring challenges to project management and take difficulties to prior evaluation. First, decision-maker should determine a clear objective and make a schedule in the concept stage because there are many uncertainties in the whole process and decision-makers have bounded rationality. Second, the investment estimate of project, project schedule, design plan, procurement plan, construction plan, quality plan and financial plan should be made in the development stage. It will bring great difficulties to forecast the problems which may happen in the future. Third, there may be lots of problems during the construction stage; decision-maker will obtain more information as the project ongoing and the surrounding environment changing. Surely, new uncertainties will increase, and some problems will inconsistent with the initial evaluation they considered. Due to the cognitive bounded rationality of decision-maker, there are many uncertainties, including how many quantities will be changed, how fast the construction progress, whether the amount of investment increase, and so on. At last, in the examining and the maintenance stages, the uncertainties are mainly reflected in the operation and maintenance cost. Decision-maker should evaluate the cost for the last years in the evaluation stage. The evaluation result entirely depends on the experience of decision-maker. Because of the concession period, it is more difficult to evaluate the cost of operation and maintenance for the projects such as BOT. It probably can not recover the investment if the estimation is far from the actual value. Although long-period brings many uncertainties, it brings some advantages to the decision. First, long-period projects are implemented in several stages, so the decisions can be flexible. Second, experiences can be taken because the leaning effect in the process is very significant. Therefore, cognitive bounded rationality is almost throughout the whole period which brings out both high uncertainty and potential revenue of flexible decision that should be paid significant attentions and given sufficient evaluations.

5. Strategic Project

Strategic projects support the long-term missions of organization whose goals are often to increase the revenue and expand the market share. From the view of the long-term development, it is very important to invest on strategic projects. For enterprises, the strategic projects include creative projects that control the market share and master the core resources. Some have high added value; some can be a core competitiveness that play a key role in the future development and the improve competitiveness in the industry. The strategic projects are risk-loving because they seek the future opportunities, pay more attention to the value of risk (uncertainty), and abound with uncertainties and bounded rationality. In the view of decision-making, the strategic projects do not take the revenue for a moment as the main objective consideration, but value "Today's effort is for tomorrow's harvest". Therefore, in project evaluation, not only the revenue of the project should be investigated, but the opportunity value and the associated drive value are more important.

6. Conservative Projects

Some projects do not have any "ambition" and just want to get basic profits to survive which could be called conservative projects. Conservative project usually is a strategic choice in mature period when steady development is the most important concern to a company. Those projects with good future and in conformity with the abilities are advisable to enterprises, while those too aggressive and risky are inadvisable. Some social security projects also belong to conservative projects. These risk-averse investment community investment evaluation goals are not to maximize profits, but slightly profitable on the basis of preservation. How to evaluate this kind of project effectively is the bottleneck of project development. Same projects will show different behavior orientations because the economic statuses and the investment motivation of the investors are different. For conservative project, to acquire satisfactory profits securely is an important investigation term of decision, which should be reflected in the evaluation system.

7. High-tech Project

There are too many uncertainties in high-tech projects which are mainly caused by technology, market and management, etc. The technological uncertainty comes from the exploration of unknown in technology development and innovation. The market uncertainty is of enterprise competitive advantage which is brought by the high-tech project itself or the changes of environmental factors, and comes from the variations of unpredicted or unpredictable competitive conditions. The uncertainty of management refers to the uncertainties throughout the innovation process of high-tech project. Technology innovation will inevitably change the state of organizational management, this change in turn to bring unpredictable impact to technological innovation and increase the number of uncertainties further more. Although there are too many uncertainties in high-tech projects, people are still keen to develop them because they could bring high return. If they are successful, several times or even thousands of times profits will be brought to investors. As a venture capital, high-tech project is an innovation of intensive production and management technology product based on high-tech and knowledge. Since it values the potential opportunities, the value contained in uncertainties should be emphasized in project evaluation.

Acknowledgements. This paper is supported by the MOE Youth Foundation Project of Humanities and Social Sciences at Universities in China (10YJC790128).

References

1. Edward, R.J.: Decision Behavior, pp. 66–68. Beijing Normal University Press, Beijing (1998)
2. Jiaji, F., Yunhuan, Q.: Industrial Technology Economics, pp. 88–156. Tsinghua University Press, Beijing (1996)
3. Xizhen, G., Tong, C.: Based on the sustainable development the public investment project evaluation index system. Statistics and Decision 2008(1), 67–69 (2008)
4. Haizheng, W., Yun-Hwan, Q., Yi, T.: Plural values of the Public project evaluation method. China Soft Science 2006(6), 138–149 (2006)
5. Xiangyang, Z.: Risks and countermeasures between supply chain partners. Finance and Trade Research 2006(3), 151–152 (2006)

Study on Production Logistics Based on SCM Integration Models[*]

Guojing Xiong

School of Economy and Management, Nanchang University
Nanchang, Jiangxi Province, China
xiongguojing@ncu.edu.cn

Abstract. Production logistics is the core business, only it has the rational organization of production logistics, it can make the production process always at its best. Logistics information system can improve logistics management system, achieve production logistics functions the transition from functionalization to integration and establish enterprise logistics management information system. Reasonable allocation of manpower, material resources can make allocation of resources more optimal and make the relevant parts no longer waiting for each other, so this can avoid flow stagnation. This article defines supply chain integration models to fulfill synergy in the supply chain and core competence of single enterprise within the supply chain.

Keywords: Production Logistics, Model, SCM, green logistics.

1 Introduction

Production logistics is the logistics activities in internal production process which responsible for transportation, storage, loading and unloading of materials and other tasks, it's the foundation of the continued product and constitutes the whole process of the internal logistics activities. The management of Production logistics should meet the requirements in order to ensure stable production and coordinated manner, shortening the production cycle, improves product quality and reduces product consumption.

Supply chain management (SCM) is total systematic view of management, which is defined as the design, planning, execution, control, and monitoring of supply chain activities with the objective of creating net value, building a competitive infrastructure, leveraging worldwide logistics, synchronizing supply with demand and measuring performance globally, also the systemic, strategic coordination of the traditional business functions and the tactics across these business functions within a particular company and across businesses within the supply chain, for the purposes of improving the long-term performance of the individual companies and the supply chain as a whole.

---

[*] This work is supported by the Jiangxi Province Office of Education Social Science Foundation Grant # JC0918.

M. Zhou (Ed.): ISAEBD 2011, Part IV, CCIS 211, pp. 315–321, 2011.
© Springer-Verlag Berlin Heidelberg 2011

Production logistics should meet the requirements of specialized production to face the specific logistics needs instead of facing the society and the general logistics needs. Therefore, logistics achieve higher efficiency by the means of specialization and standardization, and would adjust the scale of business to the changing clients. Thus we can implement our planning more accurate and precise and using the effective means of resource management systems to achieving lean logistics.

2 The Main Factors and Shortage of Influence the Production Logistics

2.1 Production Logistics Management Is an Important Segment of the Supply Chain Management

It's based on the optimized resources and capabilities to produce the best product in a lowest cost, fastest speed and quickly to meet user's requirements such as variety, quality, quantity and delivery in order to improve enterprise responsiveness and efficiency as well as reduce non-value-added services. It started when companies accept orders including contract processing, organize to apply raw materials, the production planning, manufacturing, formulation and issued the command, control and adjust of the production process, production and performance of collection and sorting until the process of tissue products manufactured.

2.2 The Main Factors of Production Logistics

Type of production: the product variety, structure, complexity, accuracy class, process requirements and raw materials are different from production types. These characteristics affect the composition of production logistics and the ratio between each other.

The scale of production: The scale of production is the output of products per unit time(usually expressed in annual output). While the Production scale is larger, more complete composition of the production process, the greater the amount for the logistics. On the contrary, while production scale is small, there are no very fine conditions to divide composition of the production process small as well as small of the logistics capacity.

The level of business professionalism and collaboration. as the raising level of social specialization and collaboration, the enterprise will tend to streamline the production process and shortened the logistics process. Thus some of the basic stages of the process semi-finished products such as rough, spare parts, components, etc., can be supplied by the other specialized factories.

2.3 The Main Shortage of the Production Logistics

(1) Infrastructure, technology and equipment level falls behind. (2) The sharing of information of network is in a low level, information transmission lag. (3) The market mechanism is not perfect and the order of competition is not standardized, the existing rules and regulations and management is not adapted to the modern logistics development. (4) The concept of supply chain management is weak; the degree of

logistics standardization is not high. (5) Inventory management level is low; except for a few enterprises realize zero inventory management, the production and logistics management are still not high. (6) The inventory takes up a lot of money, production and logistics cost accounting unreasonable.

3 Measures Are Suggested in Building Supply Chain Integration Models Beginning with Logistics Management

3.1 Find Out Core Competence, and Choose Proper Partners to Build Up Strategic Cooperation Relationship

Non-core business with low self-managing ability should be outsourced to partners, while the key business should be focused on. The factors considering choosing partners include business performance, business structure, production capability, quality system, and environment. Fist of all, enterprise should analyze own internal resources and abilities to define the core competence, afterwards, evaluate numerous partners and select proper ones to set up strategic cooperation relationship, outsourcing non-core business to partners make for cost reduction, capital saving, risk sharing, ability raising, quality improving, and particularly supplementary value-created business creation which is difficult or costly by self-completing.

3.2 Optimize SCM, and Prompt Informatization in Logistics

Modern information system with advanced IT is vital difference between traditional freight transportation and modern logistics. High degree on information sharing and integration leads to overall value creating through valid coordinate combination of transportation, warehousing, packaging, loading and unloading, handling, processing, distribution, etc. only if key data about orders, inventory, stock-out, production plan, transport schedule, etc. are highly shared and integrated, the valid control could be realized, such as rapid adjustment according to changeable environment, zero inventory, quick response.

3.3 Control Logistics Cost, and Integrate Resources in Whole Process

Logistics costs deduction is main objective for developing SCM, and become crucial part in boosting enterprise competence. First strategic decision on self-running or outsourcing should be judged from costs that all the expenditure and resource occupation during whole logistics process, after comparing to TPL services, the ultimate decision should balance minimizing costs and maximizing service through resources integration and process optimization. There are many methods to downsize supply chain costs, first is to decrease times of transportation by efficient distribution, increasing loading rate, making out proper transportation schedule, and choosing optimal transportation tool, second is outsourcing, third is to utilize modern logistics information system, forth is to reinforce consciousness of employee on costs reduction through whole process from product designing, manufacturing to sales, fifth is to achieve complete SCM to maximize profit.

3.4 Develop Green Logistics for Achieving Sustainable Development

Within supply chain, every node from acquirement of raw materials to transportation generates waste causing environmental pollution threat to human health and ecosystem. Green logistics pursue compatibility with the environment, which leads to sustainable development, and thus affect positively greatly to social benefits. To take environmental friendly methods to maximize use ratio of resources, such as reverse logistics, to avoid penalties because of pollution, to ameliorate working conditions helpful improving working efficiency are all starting points of green logistics. However, a great many paradoxes and inconsistencies will arise if the application goes further in details, green logistics is a significant issue facing more difficulties than might have been expected on first encounter. In addition, for customers, green logistics contributes to establish correct attitude towards consumption and proper sense of social value.

4 The System Model of Production Logistics and Optimization

4.1 Enterprise Production Logistics Based on Lean Logistics

Lean Logistics uses lean idea into the management of logistics activities. The core of lean thinking is the elimination of all waste, which is providing the right amount of product at the right time, right place. It stresses an idea which is the customer first, timely and accurate, the overall optimization, continuous improvement and innovation. Lean production Logistics is the concrete manifestation of lean production in the process of enterprise manufacture activity, is based on the theory of lean manufacturing requirements of the production logistics, production logistics, no waiting, no continuity of current flow, thereby reducing the waste of the production process and shorten the production cycle, reduce production costs and improve efficiency, it is the basis for achieving lean logistics. Lean Logistics on the establishment of the production logistics system helps to extensive changes in the management of manufacturing concepts helps to improve core competitiveness of enterprises. Information logistics system is the key to achieving lean logistics and is a prerequisite for the implementation of lean logistics.

4.2 Model Based on the Lean Logistics of Enterprise Production Logistics

Enterprise will change traditional production logistics operation model into lean production logistics operation model, from the user requirement and requirement of information flow to reverse pull production logistics flow. In the production process, the next working procedure as customers, by the next working procedure demand instructions to perform production and supply. Follow the principle, according to the needs of customers JIT the time, place, quantity, quality and price production and supply products, the realization of zero inventory, zero defect and zero fault production logistics services. (Figure 1).

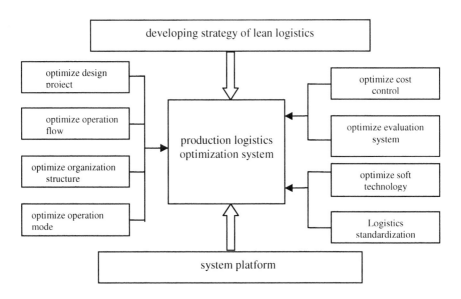

Fig. 1. Model of production logistics system based on the lean logistics

4.3   Enterprise Manufacturing Logistics System Optimization Strategy

Enterprise production logistics operation mode optimization strategy. Dynamic control and adjustment in the whole production and logistics process from raw materials to the plant products factory, ensure to finish production plan and the provisions of the contract product punctually, quality, quantity. Strengthening production and logistics process control solve the production scheduling optimization preparation, logistics tracking, production scheduling, etc.

Enterprise production logistics cost management optimization strategy. Enterprise production logistics cost management goal is minimum inventory, integrating transportation, assure product quality, etc. Implement manufacturing logistics cost accounting management; make the production logistics cost accounting specialization, the exposition.

Enterprise production logistics standardization and management technology optimization strategy. Logistics standardization is promoting lean logistics base, is China's logistics and international strong foundation. Enterprises as logistics standards implementation unit should cooperate with standards and conscientiously implement the national standards.

Enterprise production logistics performance appraisal system optimization strategy. Logistics performance evaluation for reducing logistics cost, improve the management efficiency has a pivotal role. Accordingly, we should focus on the strengthening of the enterprise culture construction and to improve the staff of logistics performance management knowledge, and logistics performance evaluation result with employee's reward hooks.

4.4 The Strategy of Enterprise Manufacturing Logistics System Optimization

To implement material handling distance shortest configuration. Reasonable decorate each workshop and within the workshop of each process position, avoid material handling in various processes between circuitous handling, round-trip handling, backflow handling. And try to improve handling the batch and reduce the number of handling, make handling distance retreat to a minimum. The use of reasonable production mode. In the early period meet production and users of prophase and tried to compress inventory, reduce the intermediate in-process inventory of storage, had better be completely just-in-time production.

Enterprise workshop reasonable decorates. First, the enterprise internal workshop, position and within the workshop working procedure, and the workshop layout of the finished product area, semi-finished area, excipient area as well as other relevant auxiliary facilities position distribution. Reasonable decorate can make the material or product handling the minimum amount. Secondly, logistics line is determined thing, big part of the problem is to choose the appropriate handling equipment.

Coordination and balance production logistics bottleneck link. Adopt optimized production logistics management method, to bottleneck resources plan is analyzed and more effective coordinated project plan, which is beneficial to the key project plans, at the same time, also can overcome pure traditional production logistics in a bottleneck resources a possible ability waste. In addition, through to the bottleneck resource capacity balance, discovered early capacity, in order to take measures, gaps assure integral production plans.

Improve production logistics control efficiency. In the integrated system, mobilize workers' enthusiasm and creativity, the production process control and harmonious by mutual is directly linked to finish production workers. The dispatcher only when necessary, such as how to change the process route, change processing equipment, that is executed control and coordination function, this helps to reduce the complexity of dispatching work, improve the scheduling the quality of work, so as to raise productivity.

5   Conclusions

The design, plan and management of good production logistics are the keys to improve labor production quota and produce quality. Only reasonable production logistics of organization can make the process of business production always in the best state. This article that analyzing the main factors and shortcoming that influence business production. Discussed the way that solve the problems and obstacles of business production logistics, constructed the model of business production logistics system based on lean logistics, put forward the tactics that optimize production logistics system, reduce the logistics cost, renew the management sense of business production logistics, improve the key advantage of business.

Production logistics management should begin from standardizing enterprise management data, it carries out real-time monitoring and precautionary during production logistics process. So the problems can be found in the shortest time to correct and remedy. Based on the basic data, establishing a reasonable production management plan, optimizing production scheduling, strengthening production logistics process control can make logistics, cash flow and information flow of the logistic activities in the best state, thus achieve significant economic benefits and social benefit.

References

1. Krikke, H.R., Le Blanc, H.M., et al.: Product Modularity and the Design of Closed-loop Supply Chains. Calif Manage Rev. 46, 23–39 (2004)
2. Li, Y.-f., Liu, W.-s.: Logistics Planning Based on Industry Supply Chain. Commercial Research (400), 207–209 (2010)
3. Li, Y.-s., Jiang, W.-s.: Logistics System and its Reconstruction Model Based on Agile SC. Logistics Technology 27, 41–43 (2008)
4. Budoff, S., Krupinski, V.: Supply Chain Alliances Offer Added Value for the Power Industry. Power Engineering 107, 110–114 (2003)
5. Shen, W., Ma, S.-h.: A Scheduling Model for Logistics Capability in A Time-based Multi-stage Supply Chain. Operations Research and Management Science 16(3), 20–25 (2007)
6. Zheng, P.-F., Tian, Q.-h.: Research on the Typical Production Logistics System and Modeling Technology 20(5), 148–152 (2006)
7. Zheng, Y.-q., Zhang, X.-y.: The Lean Improvement Method and Application Based on Production Process Analysis. Manufacture Information Engineering of China 38, 18–22 (2009)

Tianjin CO$_2$ Emissions: The Status and Empirical Analysis of Factor Decomposition[*]

Zhimei Tao[**] and Beijia Hao[***]

School of Public Management, Tianjin University of Commerce,
P.R.C., Tianjin, 300134
taotao@tjcu.edu.cn, cubei@126.com

Abstract. Under the background of the international and domestic attention focusing on the research on CO$_2$ emissions, Tianjin's theoretical literature in the study of CO$_2$ emissions measurement and mechanisms is still scarce. We analyzed Tianjin's total CO$_2$ emissions, carbon intensity, per person CO$_2$ emission and three major industries' variation in CO$_2$ emissions from 1996 to 2008, and compare the three departments' terminal energy use of total CO$_2$ emissions. Adopting LMDI decomposition method, we set up a decomposition model of Tianjin incremental factors in CO$_2$ emissions and quantitatively analyzed influences of CO$_2$ emission increment which cased by economic scale, industrial structure, technical progress and energy consumption structure during in 1996-2008. Through the research, we found that economic scale is a positive factor; technical progress is negative factor; the influence of adjustment of industrial structure and energy consumption structure is relatively weak.

Keywords: carbon emission, IMDI, Tianjin, industrial structure.

1 Introduction

Global warming has become an important factor which endangers the survival and development of human society. The international community generally agrees that reducing the emissions of greenhouse gas, especially the emissions of CO2, is the best way to solve the problem. American Lawrence Berkeley national laboratory's studies showed that in 2006 China's CO2 emissions relating to energy has more than the United States'[1]. The Chinese government has voluntarily undertaken the international commitments to reduce CO2 emissions, and on 26 November 2009 has officially declared the clear quantitative targets to control the emissions of greenhouse gas, by 2020 the emissions of CO2 produced by one unit of GDP should be dropped 40%-45% compared with it in 2005. As the economic center of Bohai rim region, Tianjin's researches of CO$_2$ emissions' situation and the development mechanism and

---

[*] Supported by Program for Tianjin Science and Technology Development Strategy Research Program "The research of low carbon economy development mode and regional industrial upgrading" (No. 10ZLZLZF04600).

[**] Associate professor, master, 86-13132535498.

[***] Postgraduate student, 86-15122287651.

M. Zhou (Ed.): ISAEBD 2011, Part IV, CCIS 211, pp. 322–327, 2011.
© Springer-Verlag Berlin Heidelberg 2011

trend have an important role in promoting and demonstrating the work of energy conservation and emission reduction in our country.

2 CO₂ Emissions LMDI Decomposition Method

2.1 Date Sources and Measurement Method of CO₂ Emissions

We selected Tianjin energy consumption of three major industries and industrial output data from various industries in 1996-2008 to analyze the three major industries' changes in the consumption of final energy. The output data in 1996-2008 come from "Statistical Yearbook of Tianjin" (to eliminate the influence of price changes, we translated the nominal value into actual value by using consumer price index and producer price index). The terminal energy consumption of three industries came from "Statistical Yearbook of Tianjin", "Tianjin Energy Balance", and "China Energy Statistical Yearbook".

2.2 The Research of Energy Burning CO₂ Emissions' Changing Mechanism

The large number of studies at home and abroad shows that no matter from the theoretical background, practical, feasible, or the results' expression LMDI (Longarithmic Mean Divisia Index) is an excellent method of researching the CO2 emissions' changing mechanism[3-5]. CO2 emissions can be expressed as:

$$C_t = \sum_i \sum_j \frac{E_{it}^j}{E_{it}} \times \frac{C_{it}^j}{E_{it}^j} \times E_{it} = \sum_{i=1}^m P_t a_{it} e_{it} \left(\sum_{j=1}^F ef^j s_{it}^j \right) \tag{1}$$

Among them, Ci says the economic system's total CO₂ emissions at stage t; E_{it} says the total energy consumption in sector i at stage t; E_{itj} says sector i's energy consumption of j at stage t; C_{itj} says the CO2 emissions caused by the energy consumption of j in sector i at stage t; S_{itj} says the structure proportion of energy consumption of j in sector i at stage t; e_{fj} says the energy CO2 emissions coefficient of j; P_t says Tianjin value of production at stage t; P_{it} says value of production in sector i at stage t; a_{it} says the sector's contribution rate of economic system in sector i, namely the ratio of output value in sector i in local output; e_{it} says the energy intensity in sector i at stage t, namely the ratio of energy consumption and output; m says the classification number of economic system; F says the number of energy.

Refer to the Ang LMDI decomposition formula without residual items and formula (1), the changes from year t to t+1 can be expressed as:

$$\triangle C = \Delta C_{scale} + \Delta C_{str} + \Delta C_{int} + \Delta C_{E,str} \tag{2}$$

Among them, ΔC_{scale} says the changes of CO2 emissions caused by the effect of economic scale; ΔC_{str} says the changes of CO2 emissions caused by the effect of industrial structure; ΔC_{int} says the changes of CO2 emissions caused by the effect of technological progress; $\Delta C_{E,str}$ says the changes of CO2 emissions caused by the

effect of energy consumption structure. The specific formula is:

Here we define $w_i(t) = \left(C_i^{t+1} - C_i^t\right)/\left(\ln C_i^{t+1} - \ln C_i^t\right)$;

$$\Delta C_{scale} = w_i(t) \cdot \ln(P^{t+1}/P^t) \tag{3}$$

$$\Delta C_{str} = w_i(t) \cdot \ln(a_i^{t+1}/a_i^t) \tag{4}$$

$$\Delta C_{int} = w_i(t) \cdot \ln\left(e^{t+1}/e^t\right) \tag{5}$$

$$\Delta C_{E,str} = w_i(t) \cdot \ln\left(\sum_{j-1}^{F} ef^j S_{i(t+1)}^j / \sum_{j-1}^{F} ef^j S_{i(t)}^j\right) \tag{6}$$

2.3 The Result and Analysis

2.3.1 Tianjin Changes in CO_2 Emissions from Energy Combustion in 1996-2008
In 1996-2008 CO2 emissions from energy combustion of Tianjin Industrial terminal increases from 7,439,000 tons to 10,264,000 tons, and its average annual growth rate is 3.16%.According to the research of Qianjie[6], in 1994-2005, CO2 emissions resulted by energy combustion in Shanghai increases from 3299.7×104t to 4493.4×104t and its average annual growth rate is 2.9%. CO2 emissions of Tianjin have grown faster than Shanghai but lower than the level of 4.0% of average annual growth rate of China CO2 emissions in 1994-2004[7].

2.3.2 Tianjin Mechanism Research of Changes in CO_2 Emissions from Energy Combustion in 1996-2008
In 1996-2008 CO2 emissions increased by 2.825 million tons in Tianjin. The factors of stimulating growth in CO2 emissions are the rapid economic growth and the change in industrial structure, and they respectively account for 19.46%, 523.87%. The inhibition

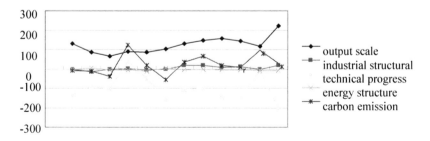

Fig. 1. Accumulated effect of carbon emission increment from 1996 to 2008 in Tianjin

factors of emissions mitigation are technological progress and the change of consumption structure, and they respectively account for 425.79%, 17.53%. So the key factor of inhibition of CO2 emissions growth is technological progress and it means the reduction of energy intensity.

2.3.3 Scale Effect of Economic Development

According to real economic value, in 1996-2008, GDP of Tianjin increases from 102.929 billion Yuan in 1996 to 602.882 billion Yuan in 2008, it increases by 486% and its average annual growth rate is 40.47%. In 1996-2008 the fast development of economy is the key factor of CO2 emissions growth. Because of amplification of economy scale, CO2 emissions increase by 2,825,600 tons and stimulating effect of amplification of economy scale to CO2 emissions growth has an increasing trend (Fig.2). The fast growth of secondary industry and tertiary industry is the key factor of CO2 emissions growth (Fig.1) and secondary industry accounts for 73.76% and tertiary industry accounts for 24.61%. So the way of slowing down CO2 emissions is slowing down the economic growth scale and speed of secondary industry.

2.3.4 Effect of Adjusting Industrial Structure

Effect of industrial structure has always little influence to CO2 emissions. It has little change in different years and its contribution rate is between - 0.55%〜 135%. It haves positive effects in most years and annual average value is 1.62%. It indicates that adjusting industrial structure has promoting effect in CO2 emissions growth. So contribution rate of slowing down CO2 emissions caused by adjusting industrial structure fluctuates a lot and it is yet not very stable. We can find that mechanism of adjusting industrial structure to the change of CO2 emissions is reflected by adjusting structure of secondary industry and there is a high degree of consistency between the two from the result of temporal decomposition which structure change of different industrial sectors affects CO2 emissions of Tianjin. (Fig.2).

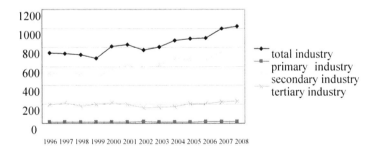

Fig. 2. Decomposition of production and total industry effect into sectors from 1996 to 2008

2.3.5 Effect of Technological Progress

Effect of technological progress is often reflected by energy consumption intensity. In 1996-2008, effect of energy intensity is -12,031,400 tons totally and effect of energy consumption intensity has the increasing tend . This indicates that reduction of energy consumption intensity is always the key factor of slowing CO2 emissions and the inhibition effect is reflected by declining of energy consumption intensity in secondary industry. In 1996-2008, energy consumption intensity of primary industry decreases form 0.2269 to 0.1389 and average change is 2.7%. Energy consumption intensity of secondary industry decreases from 4.4989 to 1.5418 and average change is 4.5%. Energy consumption intensity of tertiary industry decreases from 0.8778 to 0.3566 and average change is 4.2%. So we can find that energy consumption intensity of secondary industry and tertiary industry increase steadily and energy consumption intensity of secondary industry is the largest. It is as 16 times as primary industry and it is as 4.58 times as tertiary industry. So reduction of energy consumption intensity of secondary industry is the main way to promote energy efficiency.

2.3.6 Effect of Structure of Energy Consumption

Structure of energy consumption of CO_2 emissions by unit thermal coal is 36% and 61% higher than oil and gas[8]. In 1996-2008, the change of structure of energy consumption played a promoting role in CO_2 emissions growth and change of coal consumption has the evident inhibition effect to increasing CO_2 emissions and change of oil has the evident promoting effect to increasing CO_2 emissions, however, in general speaking, adjusting of structure of energy consumption has little effect in CO_2 emissions . According to the carbon emissions of different energy types, ratio of CO_2 emissions of coal which accounts for the total carbon emissions has decreased from 78% in 1996 to 48.75% in 2008 and ratio of CO_2 emissions of electric power which accounts for the total carbon emissions has increased from 14.7% in 1996 to 41.27% in 2008. But CO_2 emissions of coal and gas are stable relatively and CO_2 emissions of gas increased a little, which has increased from 2.13% in 1996 to 8.51% in 2008. It is to say that in recent 14 years the constitution of CO_2 emissions of energy in Tianjin has become from coal-based to the situation of electric power and coal accounting for each half.

3 Conclusion

This paper researches mechanism characteristic of the change of CO_2 emissions of Tianjin and analyzes scale effect of economic development, adjusting industrial structure, technological progress and structure of energy consumption to driver and mechanism of the change of CO_2 emissions. The research findings indicate: in 1996-2008, average annual growth rate of CO_2 emissions of terminal in Tianjin is about 3.16% and is higher than the level of Shanghai and lower than the average level of entire country. The key factor of affecting CO_2 emissions is fast economic development and the key factor of depressing CO_2 emissions is the effect of technological progress in macroscopic. In 1996-2008, in the promoting effects of CO_2 emissions growth in Tianjin, fast economic development accounts for 523.87% and the promoting effect of CO_2 emissions growth increases year by year. In the economic development to promoting effects of CO_2 emissions growth, contribution rate of the fast growth of secondary industry accounts for 73.63% and contribution rate of tertiary industry accounts for 24.61%. Effect of technological progress is the key factor of depressing fast growth of CO_2 emissions in Tianjin and its contribution rate is 425.79% and also energy consumption intensity has the gradual increasing tend and the inhibition effect of energy consumption intensity is reflected by reduction of energy consumption intensity in secondary industry mainly. The change of structure of energy consumption plays a catalytic role in slowing down growth of CO2 emissions in Tianjin, but time series analysis indicates that contribution of adjusting industrial structure has decreased gradually in reduction the growth of CO2 emissions.

In the process of our research and analysis, due to the limit of current statistical data, we only obtained credible conclusions to the four factors above. In future research we will add more detailed and richer data for the analysis of additional factors. In addition, we will complement the LMDI decomposition method with some regression based methods to improve the credibility.

References

1. Levinem, D., Adenn, T.: Global Carbon Emissions in the Coming Decades: the Case of China. Annual Review of Environment and Resources 3(11), 1239 (2008)
2. 2006 IPCC Guidelines for National Greenhouse Gas Inventories,vol.2: Energy, pp.2.11, http://www.ipcc-nggip.iges.or.jp/public/2006gl/index.html
3. Ang, B.W.: Decomposition analysis for policymaking in energy:Which is the preferred method. Energy policy 32(9), 1131–1139 (2004)
4. Ang, B.W., Zhang, F.Q.: A survey of index decomposition analysis in energy and environmental studies. Energy 25(12), 1149–1176 (2000)
5. Ang, B.W., Lee, S.Y.: Decomposition of industrial energy consumption: some methodological and application issues. Energy Economics (16), 83–92 (1994)
6. Qianjiang, Zhongjie, Y.: Research of the contribution of fossil fuel in emitting CO2 in Shanghai. Shanghai environmental science 22(11), 836–881 (2003)
7. National Development and Reform Commission, China's national plan to respond to the climate changes (2007)
8. National Coordination Committee on Climate Change, the Energy Research Institute of National Development and Reform Commission. China's research of greenhouse gas inventory. China environmental science press, Beijing (2007)

Research on Maturity Model of Enterprise NPD Project Management

Yue Ma[*], Yu Chang, Hanyu Zhu, Chunyu Xia, and Zhichao Chang

College of Management, Northwestern Polytechnical University,
710129 Xi'an, China
mayue215@nwpu.edu.cn

Abstract. Facing high risks and the high failure rate in developing new products, it seems to be necessary to assess the management of a company in its new product development projects. Combining with the PMI-OPM3 model and features of the organizational environment, this study creates a new model to manage the maturity of a product development project, aiming at providing a useful tool to enhance the success ratio of the product development projects.

Keywords: new product development projects, project management capability, maturity model.

1 Introduction

The implementation of the new product development (NPD) project is an essential way for companies to survive in the fierce competition of the world. The successful cases are numerous, for example, Glaxo became the world's second pharmaceutical manufacturers because of its new anti-ulcer drug and Microsoft, a giant in the software industry keeping its position by updating operating systems [1].

However, the NPD projects always face problems of high risks and failure rate. A research conducted by the Product Development and Management Association (PDMA) claimed that the success ratio of new products is just around 59%[2], which shows a great command for enterprises to improve their NPD management level. Combining with the complexity and ambiguity of the NPD project management maturity assessment, this article creates an advanced Project Management Maturity Model (PMMM) based on Fuzzy Comprehensive Evaluation Method, which can be used to enhance the NPD project management ability markedly.

2 Construction of Maturity Model of NPD Project Management

Enterprises always need to restart a NPD project, because the original ones can't meet customers' requirements, and because launching several NPD projects at one time could diversify the risks. We regard the maturity model of enterprise NPD project

---

[*] Corresponding author.

M. Zhou (Ed.): ISAEBD 2011, Part IV, CCIS 211, pp. 328–335, 2011.

management as a comprehensive evaluation which could reveal the enterprises' NPD projects management level based on the overall capacity of managing NPD projects on organizational level.

As NPD project could be influenced by external environment easily, enterprises should focus on multiple NPD project portfolio management ability when constructing enterprise-level maturity model of enterprise NPD project. Furthermore, the traditional maturity of project management only covers the rigid measures, but ignores the importance of "project management concept and culture" in the organization. Yet, considering the increasingly significance of projects, many enterprises gradually realize the enormous function. Thus the management concept and culture will be absorbed into the organization and play a vital role in the indexes.

Given the above analysis, this thesis will reference the three-dimensional structure of PMI–OPM3 model combined with the NPD project and its organization environment features to set a three-dimensional model: the first dimension stands for NPD project life cycle (denoted by X), the second is the knowledge system of NPD project management (denoted by Y) and the third is the maturity level of the enterprise NPD project management (denoted by Z). As has been showed in figure 1.

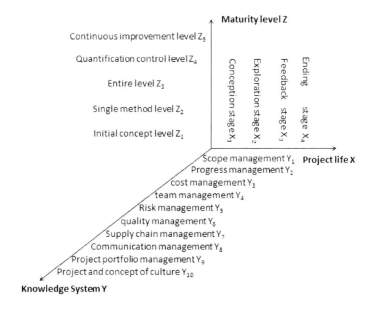

Fig. 1. Construction of the maturity model of enterprise NPD project management

2.1 The Enterprise NPD Project Life Cycle Dimension

According to the project life cycle theory, the traditional projects include five stages, namely start-up, planning and organizing, implementing, controlling and closing.

However, the NPD project needs to explore and select the best solution of new products to meet the shifting market demand concerning the feedback information, which appears to be similar to the biological evolution process [3]. Thus, based on the operation characteristics of NPD project, we may divide NPD project life cycle into four stages-conception, exploration, feedback and ending.

2.2 The Knowledge System of Enterprise NPD Project Dimension

In accordance with the PMBOK and features of NPD project, the management of NPD project management could be illustrated as 10 aspects, namely scope management (Y_1), progress management (Y_2), cost management (Y_3), team management (Y_4), risk management (Y_5), quality management (Y_6), supply chain management (Y_7), communication management (Y_8), project portfolio management (Y_9), project and the concept of culture (Y_{10}).

2.3 Levels of the Maturity of Enterprise NPD Project Management

Project management capacity, also called maturity level, can help improve project management capability during the process of maturing of project management. On one hand, it is used to describe the constantly evolving process of project management. On the other hand, it is also the periodic goal of the growth of the ability of project management [4]. In order to differentiate conveniently, this thesis will divide the maturity of NPD project management into 5 levels, taking the practice of the maturity model of CMM and the common stage type partition, among which level 1 stands for the lowest grade of the project management maturity, while level 5 stands for the highest [5]. These 5 grades are: initial concept level, single method level, entire level, quantification control level and continuous improvement level. The relationship among them has been showed in figure 2.

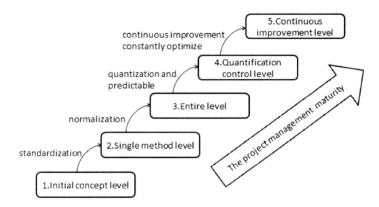

Fig. 2. The 5 levels of maturity of enterprise NPD project management

3 Evaluation of the Maturity of Enterprise NPD Project Management

3.1 Establish Evaluation Index System

Based on the characteristics of the project, this paper adopts the fuzzy comprehensive evaluation method to evaluate the NPD project management maturity. First, we could establish an index system (showed in table 1) that helps to measure the maturity of the enterprise NPD project management according to the 3d model built above. In this table, U_i (I = 2,3, … 10) stands for the score of first level of index, W_i stands for the corresponding weights, U_{ij} (I = 2,3, … 10; j≤4) stands for the score of second level of index and W_{ij} stands for the corresponding weights.

Table 1. The index system of the maturity of enterprise NPD project management

Life Cycle Dimension / Knowledge System Dimension	NPD Project Life Cycle			
	Conception Stage	Exploration Stage	Feedback Stage	End Phase
Scope Management U_1 (Weight W_1)	Analysis of Product Feasibility $U_{11}(W_{11})$			
Progress Management U_2 (Weight W_2)	Design of the R&D Overall Process $U_{21}(W_{21})$	Classification Test of Design, Production, Manufacturing Process $U_{22}(W_{22})$	Revise the Research and Development Process $U_{23}(W_{23})$	R&D Process Evaluation $U_{24}(W_{24})$
Cost Management U_3 (Weight W_3)	Cost Budget $U_{31}(W_{31})$	Cost Input Try $U_{32}(W_{32})$	Cost Control and Adjustment	Cost Accounting $U_{34}(W_{34})$
Team Management U_4 (Weight W_4)	Design organization structure, formulate human resources plan $U_{41}(W_{41})$	The Nurturing and Managing of the Project Team $U_{42}(W_{42})$	Adjustment of the Organizational Structure and Project Team Personnel	Dissolution of the Project Team $U_{44}(W_{44})$
Risk Management U_5(Weight W_5)	Risk Identification Analysis $U_{51}(W_{51})$	Risk Response $U_{52}(W_{52})$	Risk Control $U_{53}(W_{53})$	
Quality Management U_6 (Weight W_6)	Decision of the Product Quality Standard $U_{61}(W_{61})$		Quality Monitoring $U_{62}(W_{62})$	The final Inspection of Product Quality $U_{63}(W_{63})$
Supply Chain Management U_7 (Weight W_7)	Choose and Determine the Supply Partner $U_{71}(U_{71})$	R&D with Supply Chain Partners $U_{72}(W_{72})$	Adjust Supply Chain Partners $U_{73}(W_{73})$	Partnership Dissolution $U_{74}(W_{74})$

Table 1. *(continued)*

Communication Management U_8 (Weight W_8)	Design the Information Transmission Carrier and Mode $U_{81}(W_{81})$	Design Communication Network to Prompt Communication $U_{82}(W_{82})$	Information Transfer Status Feedback and Adjustment $U_{83}(W_{83})$	Summary Communication Results $U_{84}(W_{84})$
Project Portfolio Management U_9 (Weight W_9)	Multiple NPD Project Worked $U_{91}(W_{91})$	Coordination Multiple Projects $U_{92}(W_{92})$	Adjusting Individual Project $U_{93}(W_{93})$	
Project the Concept and Culture U_0 (Weight W_0)	Preliminary Form of Project Concept and Culture $U_{01}(W_{01})$	Popularization Ideas and Culture $U_{02}(W_{02})$	Perfect Philosophy and Culture $U_{03}(W_{03})$	Inheritance Ideas and Culture $U_{04}(W_{04})$

3.2 Define the Grade of Enterprises' NPD Project Management Maturity

According to defined five grades of project management maturity, we set the span of the scoring of the evaluation indexes at different levels [0, 5]. The individual span at different levels is: original concept level (0, 1], single method level (1, 2], overall standardization level (2, 3], quantization control level (3, 4], continuous improvement level (4, 5].

Meanwhile, the concept of Key Area, KA, has been introduced to embody the major aspects related to the grade of project management maturity and judge the required standard at different levels of the grade of project management maturity. KA is the key areas which must be accomplished and possessed if the project management wants to reach certain level of the grade of maturity. These key areas stand for the comprehensiveness and maturity level of the content of project management [6]. Based on the features of enterprises' NPD project management, this article treats project team, integration management, element management and the process of management as 'key areas'. So this article will judge the standard of the grade of enterprises' NPD project management maturity at different levels from these four aspects (indicated as Table 2 below).

Table 2. The different levels and features of the grade of maturity of enterprises' NPD project management.

Maturity degree	Interval	Features
Original Concept Level	(0, 1]	It is an individuation management which differs from person to person. The concept of project management is introduced at an original level and there are no identical management regulations and requirements, no clear project procedure plan, as well as organization and plans. The application of project management tools and methods relies on experiences.

Table 2. *(continued)*

Single Method Level	(1, 2]	It is a conscious management. The management procedure has clear plans and the efficient and effective project team has been established. The missions and responsibilities are clear; the measurements are guaranteed. The project organization can pursue similar and repeatable work.
Overall Standardization Level	(2, 3]	It is an overall standardization management. The project management has been into the stage of standardized procedure management. It has established standardized management procedure by elements such as range, quality, progress, cost, risk. The project team has been more effective and mature. The system has been more complete.
Quantization Control Level	(3, 4]	It is an elaboration management. The elements such as time, cost, and resource are evaluated accordingly. It has learnt and improved from success and failure. The pre-arranged plans are prepared for emergencies; the examinations are pursued based on standards; the control is implemented under measurements. And the repeatable management plans are gradually established.
Continuous Improvement Level	(4, 5]	It is a dynamic optimization management. The project management level has gradually become mature and excellent. It is under a continuous improvement condition. At this time, the principles and best practice of project management has been combined and the innovations constantly come up.

3.3 Evaluate the Grade of Enterprises' NPD Project Management Maturity

This article will evaluate the grade of enterprises' NPD project management maturity by fuzzy synthetically evaluation, while based on the features of complexity and fuzziness of the evaluation on the grade of NPD project management maturity and combining the features of NPD project itself, the application process is as below:

(1) The definition of evaluation index weight W.

Weight affects the ultimate evaluation result. Sometimes, different Weight will result in different conclusion. This article will define index Weight W by AHP (Step Analysis). The specific steps are as follows:

① Establish the panel of experts. The panel generally consists of 9 people including experts, enterprisers or scholars. They shall remain active in academic field, and possess profound scientific attainments and rich research experiences.

② Establish the Judgment Matrix for evaluation indexes at different levels. Judgment Matrix sets certain element from last level as evaluation standard. It defines the elements of matrix by comparing the indexes at this level in pairs; the following is the format of Judgment Matrix:

$$\text{Judgement Matrix } B_j = \begin{pmatrix} b_{11} & b_{12} & \cdots & b_{1n} \\ b_{21} & b_{22} & \cdots & b_{2n} \\ \cdots & \cdots & \cdots & \cdots \\ b_{n1} & b_{n2} & \cdots & b_{nn} \end{pmatrix}.$$

In the Judgment Matrix, b_{ij} indicates the importance scale of index i comparing to index j, and $b_{ij}=1/b_{ji}$. The ratio scale chart of relative importance has to be established, so that the experts can make judgment easily. This article adopts nine-level ratio scale. '1' means equally important, '3'means a little important, '5' means obviously important, '7'means very important, '9'means extremely important, and '2, 4, 6, 8'means the mid-value of adjacent judgment.

③ Compute Weight of indexes at different level of Judgment Matrix. Relative Weight of different second level indexes under first level index U_i is supposed to be $W_i=(W_{i1},W_{i2},\ldots W_{in})$, so the computational formula of W_i is:

$$B_i W_i = \lambda_{max} W_i. \tag{1}$$

And λ_{max} is the max-Eigen value of Judgment Matrix B_i.

④ Consistency examination. The computational formula of the consistency degree is:

$$CR = \left(\begin{array}{ll} 0 & \text{when } n=1.2 \\ \frac{\lambda_{max}-n}{n-1} \cdot \frac{1}{RI} & \text{when } n\geq2 \end{array} \right). \tag{2}$$

And CR is random consistency ratio; n is the dimension of matrix Bi; RI is random consistency index value and its magnitude is related to n. Please check related records for specific numerical value. When CR≤0.1, the computing result from Judgment Matrix passes consistency examination, it also means its relative Weight coefficient is acceptable. Or the Judgment Matrix needs to be modified and recomputed.

(2) Fuzzy Synthetically Evaluation

① Organize the experts to mark. A nine-people panel was formed, including domestic experts and scholars with rich experience on enterprises' NPD project management. They have marked second level indexes separately according to the level of the grade of maturity. In order to simplify it, we herein assume the values at different levels are 1, 2, 3, 4, and 5, so the markings of indexes are integers.

② Set up Membership Grade Matrix R. After doing statistics on experts' marking charts, the Membership Grade Matrix R of the grade of enterprises' NPD project management maturity is: $R=(R_1,R_2,\ldots R_i,\ldots,R_{10})^T$, $R_i =(r_{ij})_{n\times5}$, R_i is the Membership Grade Matrix of the first level index Ui. rij is the ratio of experts who think the marking of the second level index Uij shall be j (j=1,2,3,4,5).

③ Comprehensive evaluation on the grade of enterprises' NPD project management maturity. Firstly, compute the evaluation vector S1 of evaluation indexes at different levels:

$$S_i = W_i \cdot R_i = (s_i)_{1\times5}. \tag{3}$$

Then, compute the comprehensive evaluation vector of enterprises' NPD project: $P=W \cdot S=W_{1\times10} \cdot (S_1,S_2,\ldots S_i,\ldots,S_{10})^T_{10\times5}=(P_i)_{1\times5}$.

At last, compute the grade of maturity of enterprises' NPD project management C:

$$C = P \cdot E .\qquad\qquad(4)$$

And $E = (1,2,3,4,5)^T$.

4   Conclusions

The features of NPD project is of high risk and failure rate. So it is necessary to evaluate the grade of enterprises' NPD project management maturity. This article uses the structure of PMI-OPM3 model for reference, combines the features of NPD project and its organization environment, and builds a three-dimensional structure model of the grade of enterprises' NPD project management maturity. The first dimension of this model is the lifecycle of the project, the second is the knowledge system of the project management, and the third is the maturity grade of the project management. And then the application of AHP and fuzzy synthetically evaluation give some instructions on how to evaluate the maturity grade. During the research process, we can quantificational compute the maturity grade which enterprises' NPD project management ability can reach and find the weak link in project management ability. After that, we can provide methods for continuous improvement to the grade of enterprises' NPD project management maturity. Moreover, increasing enterprises' NPD project management ability can somehow lower the risks of the project.

Acknowledgments. Thanks my supervisor for his help during the research. And thanks for the sponsorship of humanities and social sciences and management sciences, Funding of Northwestern Polytechnical University (RW200807).

References

1. Fang, W.: Research on Critical Elements of New Product Research and Development Project Success. Northwestern Polytechnical University, Xi'an (2006)
2. Griffin, A.: Drivers of NPD Success: The 1997 PDMA Report. Product Development & Management Association, Chicago (1997)
3. Qu, H., Shan, M.: Discourse on the Value of CAS Theory to Research and Development Project Management. Science, Technology and Management Research 7, 478–480 (2008)
4. Yuan, J., Ou, L., Wang, W.: Research on Shenzhou Spaceships Project Management Maturity Model. China Space Science and Technology 5, 1–9 (2005)
5. Paulk, M., Curtis, C., Weber, C.: Capability maturity model for software. Carnegie Melton University 7, 320–332 (1986)
6. Fan, H., Tang, D.: Research on Scientific Research Project Management Maturity Model in Colleges and Universities. Science, Technology and Management Research 3, 141–142 (2009)
7. Liu, Y., Qin, Z.: Analysis of Project Management Maturity Model on the Basis of the Grey Theory. Value Engineering 12, 126–128 (2008)
8. Andersen, E.S., Jessen, S.A.: Project Maturity in Organizations. International Journal of Project Management 21(6), 457–461 (2003)

An Optimization Model for Client Relationship Management of Third-Party Logistics Enterprises

Dawei Sun, Sanyuan Zhou, and Yuqing Song

Beijing Wuzi University, Tongzhou District, Beijing 101149, China
sdw19870315@sina.com, zsy624206@sohu.com, songyuqing@139.com

Abstract. There has been widespread acceptance and adoption of client relationship management (CRM) since the late 1990s. Although some organizations have realized benefits from CRM, many problems persist. CRM of third-party logistics (3PL) enterprises has developed an ordinary operation and process improvement cost optimization model, and the optimum period of re-design logistics services process for minimum cost is defined. The model provides a basis for the establishment of implementation procedures for CRM systems, it is efficient in different stages of 3PL enterprise developing with different objectives.

Keywords: Client relationship management, optimization model, third-party logistics.

1 Introduction

The implementation of CRM systems is technologically and economically an elusive problem, especially for third-party logistics enterprises. Its technological problems, which depend on the methods of application, on the tools of assessing, on the features of logistics industry, on the relationship between services providers and customers and the enterprises market orientation, are never ending. Its cost of application, operation and relationship maintenance has never been assessed properly.

This paper develops a model whose optimization identifies the average relationship performance level and the period of process improvement at minimum cost for CRM system in 3PL enterprises. The objective function of cost involves both the costs of system application, operation and management, the cost to the clients and the opportunity cost of client loss. The objective evaluated parameters with objectively measured properties make the model suitable also for comparative evaluation and selection of alternatives. For a given 3PL enterprise and its clients, the relationship between any client and the enterprise can be established by the same function just with particular value of parameter. In general, the model solution provides the period of logistics service improvement or process redesign at minimum cost. Such model, especially needed for the features of 3PL industry, is quite different comparing with other industries.

In the 3PL industry, competition is extremely fierce. The logistics services provided are relatively homogenous, and the homogenization trend is gradually evidence. The

M. Zhou (Ed.): ISAEBD 2011, Part IV, CCIS 211, pp. 336–341, 2011.

main reason is that almost each 3PL enterprise or entity has already spared no efforts to explore the potential efficiency or productivity, with the limited resources and technology, only to achieve the consequence that the performance of their logistics services is within the same level. The mere difference between 3PL entities' various logistics services is the price and the core client relationship. Therefore, for avoiding involving in the fierce price war, the only way to maintain differential competitive advantages is to keep a comparative high level of client relationships. Although 3PL enterprises have ultimately recognized the significance of this problem, on the other hand, a scientific theory or procedures are lacking to guide them into the track of scientific and economic way of core client management, including the client relationship maintenance. Even in large-scale 3PL enterprises, core client management performance is practically depended on the personal ability of the service operator who is in charge of the business, not on a sound 3PL client management mechanism, neglecting the balance of efficiency and economy. That is also what this paper aims at.

2 Assessing of CRM Determinants

The relationship performance P of a CRM system in a 3PL enterprise should be evaluated most properly by the accurate operation-relative data, which is objective and collected by statistics methods. After we get the exact data, it may be easier to assess the performance. Among the multitude of attributes, the average order processing time E, defined by the response time, and its error rate R, defined by order accuracy, seem to be the most sensitive to client relationship performance and the easiest ones to measure, are selected to define the 3PL client relationship performance according to prior research. A proper function relating performance and attributes seems to be provided by:

$$P = P_0 E^\alpha R^\beta. \tag{1}$$

The evaluation of attributes E, R is obtained by objective statistic measurements from the actual enterprise operation data. Reviewing prior research of client management, especially for 3PL enterprises, the evaluation of attributes E, R is increasing from the original peak value with the increasing of time, that is to say, they are positively correlated to time.

By numerous logistics operation data regression analysis, the appropriate correlation between E and t can be expressed by:

$$E = a_1 t^2 + b_1 t + E_0 . \tag{2}$$

Where E_0 is the minimum average order processing time, when P reach its maximum value P_m just after the whole client-related logistics service procedures and operation activities are improved or redesigned. a_1, b_1 and E_0 are constants which can be identified and measured through enterprise history performance data by one variable linear regression model. The variation in order processing time corresponds to the variation in the client relationship performance. According to the performance history, for ensuring (1) to be a monotonic increasing function when $t \geq 0$. So, the constants a_1, b_1 must satisfy:

$$a_1 > 0, \; -\frac{b_1}{2a_1} \le 0. \tag{3}$$

With respect to another important client relationship performance attribute, order accuracy r, has the same correlation with time t, and may also be expressed with a similar structure, as:

$$R = a_2 t^2 + b_2 t + R_0. \tag{4}$$

Where the constants a_2, b_2 and R_0 can be identified from the actual order processing data in 3PL enterprise. Similarly, for the same reasons given above, the following constraint condition (5) must be satisfied.

$$a_2 > 0, \; -\frac{b_2}{2a_2} \le 0. \tag{5}$$

3   The Total Cost Function

The maintenance of CRM system at any relationship performance level involves a cost. It is the objective of this section to derive the cost function and identify the level of performance at which the cost is minimum. This is equivalent to identifying the time of improving or redesigning at which the cost is minimum and this will also identify the relationship performance.

The average cost of application per day, C_a, when improved or redesigned after T days, is defined as:

$$C_a = C_0/T = (C_f + C_s + C_i)/T. \tag{6}$$

Where C_0 is the initial cost of the improvement or redesign of the whole logistics service operation for a particular client, with C_f the cost of adding fundamental logistics facilities and equipments, C_s the salary cost of staff who have to invest time and mental or physical labour for improving or redesigning, and C_i the necessary cost of investigation for obtaining the actual and practical operating data, which can be depended on to conduct analysis. Although C_0 may change with time, for each improvement may varied as the quantity and quality of facilities is different and the time and labour needed is also different. However, compared with a relative long time span T, the overall difference dispersed on each single day will be same. What's more, if T is assigned with a fixed value, the difference of improving cost for a particular client can be viewed as a constant. Because the logistics service operation improvement cost mainly depends on the scale of the business and the complexity of the logistics processing procedure and the features of the service, which are all independent from the model itself and the statistics data of these features can only be obtained from the client-related logistics service. In a word, with the hypothesis above, the application cost C_0 is a fixed quantity variable if the improvement periods T is constant.

The average client cost C_c per day due to a decrease in performance and the increase of the order processing time, as it can be specified from (6), is defined by:

$$C_c = \frac{1}{T}\left[C_E \int_0^T (E - E_0)dt + C_R \int_0^T (R - R_0)dt\right]. \tag{7}$$

Where E_0 is the minimum order processing time at maximum client relationship performance P_m, and E the time corresponding to performance P at any time t. The C_E defines the average order processing time delayed cost, for any time added to the logistics operation process indicates extra cost, for instance, the cost of time, labour or opportunity. C_R defines the cost of reduction of any percent in order accuracy, which is equivalent to the increase of order error rate. Though the 3PL provider has the privilege to reduce the order accuracy to an agreed degree, any percent reduced in order accuracy needs the 3PL client side to compensate.

Inserting (5) and (7) in (10) and performing the indicated integrations one gets:

$$C_c = \frac{1}{3}(a_1 C_E + a_2 C_R)T^2 + \frac{1}{2}(b_1 C_E + b_2 C_R)T. \tag{8}$$

Another important cost is the client loss opportunity cost. 3PL industry has an extreme high level homogenization of logistics service among different 3PL enterprises. Technology advantages can't last for long because traditional logistics is a capital or labour intensive industry, not technology-intensive. There exists no absolute loyalty between clients and 3PL enterprise, the only connection is the balance of price and service performance. Maintaining a relative low client relationship can ensure a small operation cost, however, on the contrary, this will directly lead to a high opportunity of client loss. According to history statistics data about client loss probability φ and client relationship performance P, the correlation between these two variables approximately obeys negative exponential distribution. Given that P is also the function of time t, φ can be defined by monotone increasing function with t, as:

$$\varphi = a_3 t^2 + b_3 t + \varphi_0. \tag{9}$$

Where φ_0, representing the minimum probability when P is assigned the peak value or the time is initialized 0, is constant and can be identified. Also, for the reason of monotone increasing in probability function (9), a_3, b_3 must meet:

$$a_3 > 0, \ -\frac{b_3}{2a_3} \leq 0. \tag{10}$$

Losing core client means a sharp decline of 3PL enterprise profit and wasting substantial surplus productivity, including staff labour and facilities. Considering the specificities of the fierce competition, the total cost function much include client loss opportunity cost, which is expressed by:

$$C_l = \frac{1}{T} C_I \int_0^T (\varphi - \varphi_0) dt = \frac{1}{T} C_I \int_0^T (a_3 t^2 + b_3 t) dt = \frac{1}{3} a_3 C_I T^2 + \frac{1}{2} b_3 C_I T. \tag{11}$$

Where C_I indicates the average profit obtained from the certain client.

The sum of (6), (8) and (11) gives the cost per day for the maintenance of client relationship management system up to time T at which its average relationship performance level is P_T, as:

$$C = C_a + C_c + C_l = C_0/T + \frac{1}{3}(a_1 C_E + a_2 C_R + a_3 C_I)T^2$$

$$+ \frac{1}{2}(b_1 C_E + b_2 C_R + b_3 C_I)T. \tag{12}$$

The next step is the calculation of T which minimizes the total cost and determines the period of improving logistics service and the corresponding relationship level. Take the first derivative of (12) with respect to T and set it equals to zero. This gives:

$$AT^3 + BT^2 - C_0 = 0. \tag{13}$$

Where $A = \frac{2}{3}(a_1 C_E + a_2 C_R + a_3 C_I)$, $B = \frac{1}{2}(b_1 C_E + b_2 C_R + b_3 C_I).$ (14)

As (13) is a cubic equation, it can be solved by many methods such as Cardan formula method, Shengjin formula, dichotomy classification method, tangents method and so on. With the solution of Cardan formula method, (13) can be standardized by substituting $T = z - B/\varepsilon A$, as:

$$z^3 + pz + q = 0. \tag{15}$$

Where $p = -\frac{B^2}{3A^2}$, $q = \frac{2B^3}{27A^2} - \frac{C_0}{A}.$ (16)

According to the definition of Cardan formula method, 3 roots of the equation (15) can be obtained as:

$$z_1 = \sqrt[3]{y_1} + \sqrt[3]{y_2}, z_2 = \sqrt[3]{y_1}\omega + \sqrt[3]{y_2}\omega^2, z_3 = \sqrt[3]{y_1}\omega^2 + \sqrt[3]{y_2}\omega. \tag{17}$$

$$\omega = \frac{-1+\sqrt{3}i}{2}, y_{1,2} = -\frac{q}{2} \pm \left[\left(\frac{q}{2}\right)^2 + \left(\frac{p}{3}\right)^3\right]^{\frac{1}{2}}. \tag{18}$$

With (14)-(18), we can get 3 roots of (13), they are T_1, T_2 and T_3. Meeting constraint conditions, (3), (5) and (10), we come to a conclusion that the cost function C in (12) is the sum of one monotonically increasing and the other two monotonically increasing. However C_0 is comparatively a large value, the function will first monotonically decrease then increase when $t \geq 0$. So it is a convex function with a single minimum. Finally, insert T_1, T_2 and T_3 in (12), and the one which is positive and minimizes cost function C is the optimum periods T_0.

And with the optimum period of client relationship improvement, T_0, the average relationship can be obtained as:

$$\bar{P} = \frac{1}{T_0} \int_0^{T_0} P_0 E^\alpha R^\beta dt. \tag{19}$$

4   Conclusion and Discussion

The implementation of this model needs the identification of the correlation (2), (4) and (9), but the correlation provided by this paper is not the exclusive form. Other forms of correlation, such as linear correlation, exponential correlation, may better express the relationship depended on the specific problems. However, the advantages of this model is that all the parameters are obtained from actual logistics operation data, and the performance can be objectively evaluated, distinguished from prior subjectively assessing method.

The cost function (12) provided for a specific client includes the opportunity cost of client loss. All relative client loss rate φ can be estimated by analogy of the clients with similar features. This kind of cost is not contained in most total cost for optimization, but for a 3PL enterprise, the loss of a core client is significant and the opportunity cost must be considered. Because of the client loss cost, the 3PL enterprises must keep a relative high level of client management performance.

The total cost includes a large part of client cost, which is another constraint condition enforcing the 3PL enterprise keeping superior client management relationship performance. If there was no cost to the client, there would be no reason to improve or redesign the performance. Therefore, the selection and measurement of parameters which define this cost in a model is important.

C_E, C_R and C_I can be viewed as cost, however, when necessary, they function as coefficients of the 3 kinds of cost and can be artificially increased or decreased by the operator according to market orientation. Therefore, this model is efficient in different stages of 3PL enterprise developing with different objectives, it provides a basis for the establishment of implementation procedures for CRM systems.

Acknowledgements. Grateful acknowledgement is my supervisor Mr. Zhou Sanyuan who gave me valuable instructions and suggestions. Without his patient instruction, insightful criticism and expert guidance, the completion of this paper would not have been possible. In addition, I deeply appreciate the contribution to this paper supported by 2304 Deepening the Talents Education Planning—Innovation Team.

References

1. Law, M., Lau, T., Wong, Y.: Marketing Intelligence and Planning, 3rd edn. China Renmin University Press, China (2003)
2. Feinberg, R., Kadam, R., Hokama, L., Kim, I.: The state of electronic customer relationship management in retailing. International Journal of Retail & Distribution Management (2002)
3. Chich, Y.: O.E.D.D. Symposium on Road User Perception and Decision-Making. Bologna Serendipita Editrice. In: Rome 5th Session (1972)
4. Reinartz, W., Krafft, M., Hoyer, W.: The Customer Relationship management Process: Its Measurement and Impact on Performance. Journal of Marketing Research Press (2004)
5. Rheault, D., Sheridan, S.: Customer relationship management systems: Implementation risks and relationship dynamics. Qualitative Market Research: An International Journal (2002)
6. Tanoury, D., Pease, J.: Exploding some myths about customer relationship management. In: 2nd IEEE International Conference on Information and Financial Engineering. ICIFE (2010)

Research on Knowledge-Intensive Services Trade Competitiveness

Lei Chen

School of Economics
Wuhan University of Technology, Wuhan, China
chenlei19830921@126.com

Abstract. The article selects statistical data on trade in services from 2000 to 2010, measures knowledge-intensive services trade competitiveness index of TC and MI. It is concluded that the overall services trade in knowledge-intensive in China is lack of international competitiveness.

Keywords: Knowledge-intensive Services Trade, TC index, MI index.

1 Introduction

With the industry trade structure enhanced constantly in the world, knowledge-intensive services trade has been becoming the most important part in the international services trade and a competition hotspot. The gravity center of international services trade has been turning from traditional labor and resource-intensive services trade to modern knowledge-intensive services trade. For china, to speed up the development of knowledge-intensive services trade can promote service trade structure optimization and upgrading, enhance the international competitiveness of services trade, promote the continuous growth of the national economy, save resources and protect the environment sustainable development effect.

2 Literature Review

Knowledge-intensive services trade is also called knowledge service trade. There is no unified definition; it generally refers to international trade in services which provides all kinds of knowledge service for the main standard and transaction object. (QianYan, 2001). The organization for economic cooperation and development (OECD) in the report of "innovation and knowledge-intensive services" defines it as the service activities of production and integration which enterprise or public sector in manufacturing or services background is engaged in, they can be combined with manufactured products, also can be a single service. Thus, knowledge-intensive services generally refer to those services with higher density and value-added input of technology and human capital. It has a high degree of knowledge, technology, interaction and innovation. This article defines knowledge-intensive services trade as: service providers with high level of knowledge and skills through commercial

M. Zhou (Ed.): ISAEBD 2011, Part IV, CCIS 211, pp. 342–346, 2011.

presence or movement of natural persons, etc provide consumers in his country with high knowledge and technology intensive and interactive, innovative services products, and obtain the corresponding income in these business activities.

China divides services trade into 12 categories, respectively is: (1) transport; (2) tourism; (3) communications services; (4) construction services; (5) insurance services; (6) financial services; (7) computer and information services; (8) proprietary rights fees and license fees; (9) consulting; (10) advertising, publicity; (11) film, audio and video; (12) other business services. For the analysis of the competitiveness of trade in knowledge-intensive services, considering the availability of data, with reference to China's international balance of payments statistics classification and classification of academic research on knowledge-intensive service industries, according to the statistical classification of China's services trade, seven categories of communication services, insurance services, financial services, computer and information services, royalties and license fees, consulting, advertising in services trade are studied as knowledge-intensive services trade.

3   Selection and Analysis of the Competitiveness Index

Currently, there are many competitiveness indexes to evaluate trade competitiveness. Domestic and foreign scholars selected international market share, trade competitiveness index TC, revealed comparative advantage index of RCA, revealed comparative advantage index of competitive CA, net export revealed comparative advantage Index NRCA index and Michaely index, etc. China's services trade statistics caliber is similar but not exactly the same to the GATS of WTO. For example, royalties and service fees in WTO on trade in services statistics is absent, and the three kinds of comparative advantage index of RCA, CA, NRCA require the world's total export data of the project, which results that RCA, CA, NRCA can not be calculated. Thus, it does not apply to the research on knowledge-intensive services trade in this paper. For the same reason, the international market share does not apply to the competitiveness of knowledge-intensive services industries. Therefore, to study the competitiveness of knowledge-intensive services trade, TC and Michaely index are selected as trade competitiveness index.

3.1   Trade Competitiveness Index TC

Trade competitiveness index is often used to measure international competitiveness of trade in services of a country or region. It indicates that the overlap between import and export trade of a country accounts for the proportion of the total import and export trade, and it is usually used to analyze the international competitiveness of an industry in a country. Computation formula is shown below:

$$TC = (X_{ij} - M_{ij}) / (X_{ij} + M_{ij}) \tag{1}$$

X_{ij} represents that i country exports j commodity, M_{ij} represents that i country imports j commodity. The index of TC is the range of [-1, 1]. If the index is close to 0, indicating a comparative advantage such products or services close to the international average; if TC> 0, the index shows a strong comparative advantage, meanwhile, the closer to 1, the stronger the competitive industry; if TC = 1, it indicates that the country or areas have only the export of products or services; if TC <0, shows weak comparative advantage, and the closer to -1, the weaker the competitive industry; if TC =- 1, it shows that the country or region have only the import of products or services. Table 1 shows knowledge-intensive services trade sub-item TC index of China between 2000 and 2010.

Table 1. Knowledge-intensive services trade sub-item TC index of China between 2000 and 2010

Year	2000	2001	2002	2003	2004	2005	2006	2007	2008	2009	2010
knowledge-intensive services trade	-0.35	-0.51	-0.55	-0.49	-0.45	-0.39	-0.34	-0.26	-0.18	-0.15	-0.12
communications services	0.7	-0.09	0.08	0.2	-0.04	-0.11	-0.02	0.04	0.02	0	0.04
insurance services	-0.92	-0.85	-0.88	-0.87	-0.88	-0.86	-0.88	-0.84	-0.10	-0.75	-0.81
Financial services	-0.11	-0.12	-0.28	-0.21	-0.19	-0.05	-0.72	-0.42	-0.30	-0.27	-0.04
computer and information services	0.15	0.14	-0.28	0.03	0.13	0.06	0.26	0.33	0.33	0.34	0.51
proprietary rights fees and license fees	-0.88	-0.89	-0.92	-0.94	-0.90	-0.94	-0.94	-0.92	-0.90	-0.84	-0.88
consulting	-0.29	-0.26	-0.34	-0.29	-0.20	-0.07	-0.03	0.03	0.15	0.16	0.20
advertising, publicity	0.05	0.04	-0.03	0.03	0.10	0.20	0.20	0.01	0.06	0.07	0.18

Note: The data is calculated according to China's services trade guide nets.

It can be seen from Table 1, in the year 2000-2010, the overall competitiveness of knowledge-intensive services trade is not strong (average -0.38). In the view of sub-item, the TC index of communications services in 2000 reached 0.70, but TC index fluctuated around 0 after 2001, reflecting the competitiveness and comparative advantage close to the world average recently. The TC index of financial services always has been fluctuating and negative. And the TC index in the year 2006, 2007 was large, showing a greater impact by the international financial situation. The items of insurance services, royalties and license fees are at a disadvantage, especially in royalties and license fees (-0.94 in 2005, 2006, -0.88 in 2010). In the short term, there is no sign of improvement. Consulting services has been steadily increasing after 2007, in the long run, there is great potential.

3.2 Michaely Index

Michaely index is also known as "Michaely volatility index." The formula is:

$$MI = X_{ij}/\sum X_i - M_{ij}/\sum M_i \tag{2}$$

X_{ij} is the export of j product for i country, M_{ij} is the import of j product for i country. $\sum X_i$ is the total export for i country, $\sum M_i$ is the total import for i country. MI index inspect the relative value, which is the share of the trade volume of import and export of j commodity in the total trade volume, the range of [-1, 1]. A positive number indicates a comparative advantage, the greater the value, the stronger the competition, the negative number indicates a comparative disadvantage, the greater the value, the weaker the competition. Table 2 shows knowledge-intensive services trade sub-item MI index of China between 2000 and 2010.

Table 2. Knowledge-intensive services trade sub-item MI index of China between 2000 and 2010

Year	2000	2001	2002	2003	2004	2005	2006	2007	2008	2009	2010
knowledge-intensive services trade	-0.060510	-0.112431	-0.158160	-0.086180	-0.140800	-0.132640	-0.129370	-0.101550	-0.067670	-0.030599	-0.032260
communications services	0.037870	-0.000120	0.003770	0.005970	0.000500	-0.000690	0.000460	0.001290	0.001440	0.001714	0.001320
insurance services	-0.065338	-0.062560	-0.065140	-0.076460	-0.079390	-0.079140	-0.082030	-0.075072	-0.070400	-0.058760	-0.071810
Financial services	-0.000120	0.001040	-0.000660	-0.000970	-0.000410	3.81E-05	-0.007300	-0.002420	-0.001737	-0.001316	0.000351
computer and information services	0.004420	0.005170	-0.008390	0.004880	0.008880	0.005380	0.015023	0.018630	0.022690	0.030050	0.038800
proprietary rights fees and license fees	-0.033070	-0.046310	-0.064200	-0.062380	-0.059000	-0.061851	-0.063880	-0.060560	-0.060740	-0.066770	-0.062580
consulting	-0.006040	-0.011460	-0.024470	-0.022250	-0.015310	-0.002340	0.002080	0.011210	0.038086	0.059300	0.055060
advertising, publicity	0.001760	0.001810	0.000920	0.002130	0.003930	0.005960	0.006290	0.005370	-0.003000	0.005170	0.006593

Note: The data is calculated according to balance of international payments.

As is shown in table 2, in the year 2000-2010, the overall competitiveness of knowledge-intensive services trade is relatively weak (average MI -0.116645). For sub-item, The MI of Communication services, financial services, computer and information services, consulting services and advertising is floating around 0, the competitiveness of which is average in the world. And the MI of computer and information services and consulting services is on the rise in recent years, competitiveness has been enhanced accordingly. While the MI of insurance services and Royalties and license fees has been negative and still a downward trend, both of them lack international competitive advantage.

4   Concluding Remarks

(1) The overall services trade in knowledge-intensive in China is lack of international competitiveness. TC index or MI index, both reflect comparative disadvantage in the world, which is related with immaturity of knowledge-intensive services industry in

China to some degree. China is shortage of large enterprise and globalization enterprise groups, and less knowledge-intensive services enterprises participate in the competition of foreign market. Knowledge-intensive service sector in China is relatively backward, and lack capacity of independent innovation, To some extent China's economic growth mainly relies on natural resources, capital, labor and other input. The diffusion of knowledge, science and technology progress have lower contribution rate on the economic growth.

(2) From TC and MC index, we know that insurance services, royalties and license fees have obvious disadvantage. On one hand, these two services have greater demand for overseas market, on the other hand, China's manufacturing technology have a wide gap compared with international advanced level and lack industry professionals. Knowledge-intensive services industries are based on knowledge and human capital, from the personnel quality structure, we lack talents familiar with foreign laws, international conventions and the market environment related with knowledge-intensive services industries closely, such as insurance, consulting, financial and other professionals. Thus, it is difficult to adapt to the international market demand, restricting improvement of international competition of KIBS.

References

1. China Statistical Yearbook (1999-2009)
2. Yin, Chen, X.: An Empirical Study on the Influencing Factors of International Services Trade and China's Competitiveness. Journal of International Trade (2), 61–69 (2009)
3. He, W., Wu, X., Gao, C.: Positive Analysis on Factors that Have Impact on Competitiveness of China's Service Trade. International Trade Journal (2) (2005)
4. Peng, L., Wenxin, W.: Comparative Advantage and the Optimization of Chinese Service Trade Structure. Journal of Shijiazhuang University of Economics 31(1), 10–13 (2008)
5. Zili, S.: Analysis on Influencing Factors of China's Service Trade Competitiveness and Its Improving Countermeasures. Research on Economics and Management (4) (2007)
6. China's services trade guide nets,
   http://tradeinservices.mofcom.gov.cn/index.shtml
7. Lichao, W.: An analysis on the situation and promoting countermeasure of the international competitiveness of service trade in China. Journal of Capital University of Economics and 1, 96–100 (2008)

SME Reverse Logistics Outsourcing Risk Analysis and Strategies Based on Fuzzy Comprehensive Evaluation

Yang Zhou, Yi Zhang, and Ke Zong

Shandong University of Science and Technology, Taian 271019, China
tazhy@126.com

Abstract. This paper uses fuzzy comprehensive evaluation method to analysis Reasons and risk factors of SME reverse logistics outsourcing. Sorting of risk categories, it Puts forward that information risk is the most important risk. Finally, this paper propose five management strategies to prevent reverse logistics outsourcing risk。

Keywords: Reverse Logistics, Outsourcing Risk, Fuzzy Comprehensive Evaluation.

1 Introduction

Reverse logistics rapidly becoming a new growth point of modern logistics with the development of new resources and the environment concept. But SME is unable to operation reverse logistics because of high investment and high risk. Therefore reverse logistics outsourcing has become a basic mode of reverse logistics.

In recent years, many scholars began to study logistics outsourcing problem, but research focused on forward logistics, reverse logistics outsourcing is only in its infancy. [1]

The Research of reverse logistics outsourcing focused on two aspects: one focused on the Advantages and disadvantages of reverse logistics outsourcing [2]; another focused on the mode selection of reverse logistics outsourcing. However, the study of the reverse logistics outsourcing risk has not attracted enough attention, especially SME. [3]

2 SME Reverse Logistics Outsourcing Risk Analysis

2.1 Strategic Risk

Strategic risk mainly refers to uncertainty of future operating factors. First, at the strategic level, business will lost core advantages [4]. The strategic advantages of Reverse Logistics outsourcing is that businesses can outsource non-core reverse logistics, so that enterprises can pay more attention to the cultivation of core competitiveness. If SME do not understand the core elements accurately enough, although the reverse logistics outsourcing reduce logistics costs in the short term,

M. Zhou (Ed.): ISAEBD 2011, Part IV, CCIS 211, pp. 347–353, 2011.
© Springer-Verlag Berlin Heidelberg 2011

SME may lose the core competitive advantage. Companies take the strategic risk may be greater in the background of Service competition.

Second, enterprises may face risks of the different strategic objectives. Collaborators will give more consideration to their own interests and less to consider the common interests of both partners, because of differences in management, corporate culture and economic interests. That will make the enterprise can not run normally.

2.2 Decision Risk

There are three main reasons of reverse logistics outsourcing decision-making errors. First, The enterprise did not realize the real demand of outsourcing. Second, outsourcing environment is not appropriate. Third, reverse logistics is a new form of business and there is no standards for the choice of third-party logistics service providers.

2.3 Information Risk

Information risk includes two aspects. One is risk of Hidden information. Third-party logistics service providers may hide some certain information that against himself, in order to get more benefits in cooperation. Another is risk of asymmetric information. SME lack the ability to manage reverse logistics and can not control reverse logistics activities directly. That will easily make logistics service providers to reduce service quality or raise prices, so that enterprises suffer from credibility crisis.

2.4 Technical Risk

Technical risks include the loss of basic technologies and loss of core technical material risks. Outsourcing reverse logistics services for SME need to provide product design information, including raw materials, product composition, structure design and so on, in order to the third party logistics service providers disassemble and category, which could lead to patented products or high-tech products information Leak. Meanwhile, third-party logistics service providers grasp the business data, customer information and other important information, once the information was leaked to the enterprise's competitors, that will give the company serious economic losses.

2.5 Market and Financial Risk

Reverse logistics outsourcing will face the market risk and financial expenses risk. SME can not respond quickly to market, because third party logistics providers directly handle enterprise's terminal after-sales service. [5]

That will make the enterprises lose the best time of improving technologies and products. Reverse logistics cost, including recovery of goods, transport, processing, storage and other aspects of costs and expenses. Reverse logistics cost include the costs and expenses of recycling, transportation, treatment and storage. The reverse logistics costs that SME paid to the third-party logistics providers is more than the cost of reverse logistics, because it includes the logistics outsourcing management fees and cost of enterprise transpose. At the same time, there are a lot of hidden costs when SME look for a suitable third-party logistics service provider. The logistics complexity leads to financial risk.

3 Reverse Logistics Outsourcing Risk Evaluation

3.1 Fuzzy Comprehensive Evaluation Principle

We assume that $U = \{u_1, u_2, \cdots, u_m\}$ is factor set of evaluation and $V = \{v_1, v_2, \cdots, v_n\}$ is Level set of evaluation. M said that the factor number evaluation and n said that the grade number evaluation. According to different situations, Level set of evaluation have different choices.

Evaluation matrix $R = \begin{pmatrix} r_{11} & r_{12} & \cdots & r_{1n} \\ r_{21} & r_{22} & \cdots & r_{2n} \\ \vdots & \vdots & \vdots & \vdots \\ r_{m1} & r_{m2} & \cdots & r_{mn} \end{pmatrix}$, r_{ij} said that the i factor is the degree

j Level of evaluation. At the same time $0 \le r_{ij} \le 1$, $i = 1, 2, \cdots, m; j = 1, 2, \cdots n$.

We must focus on all of the factors when we evaluation of an object. So before evaluate, we should consider weight set of evaluation $A = (a_1, a_2, \cdots, a_m), 0 \le a \le 1, i = 1, 2, \cdots m$. Then, we consider $B = A \circ R = (b_1, b_2, \cdots, b_n)$ as the final evaluation.

3.2 An Empirical Study

3.2.1 Evaluation Index System of Outsourcing Risks on Reverse Logistics

The outsourcing risk of reverse logistics is complex, so it is difficult to use a single indicator to evaluate. We must evaluate it from more views, to establish a

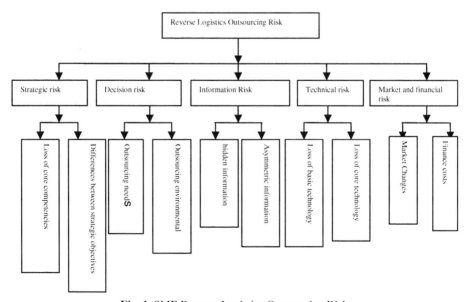

Fig. 1. SME Reverse Logistics Outsourcing Risk

comprehensive index system. The assessment analysis of reverse logistics outsourcing risk may carry out a comprehensive consideration from five factors. Evaluation index system is divided into two levels. That is, the target layer-U, indicators of a layer Ui, secondary level indicators Uij. There are 5 types of 10 indicators. The risk evaluation index of reverse logistics outsourcing shows in Fig. 1.

3.2.2 Establish Evaluation Set and Weight Set

In order to the needs of judging, the degree of risk of various evaluation will be divided into five grades of unity. V={V1,V2,V3,V4,V5}=(low risk, lower risk, general risk, higher risk, high risk). The weight of risk of various evaluation is $A = (a_1, a_2, a_3, a_4, a_5), \sum_{i=1}^{5} a_i = 1$, The weight of second risk of various evaluation

$a_{ij}(i = 1,2,3,4,5; j = 1,2)$, $\sum_{j=1}^{2} a_{ij} = 1(i = 1,2,3,4,5)$.

3.2.3 Data Collection

Based on the enterprise's point of view, we can get the data, including the weight of various risks, range of risk assessment level and various risk membership grade (table1, table2, table3).

Table 1. Risk factor weight

Risk Category	Strategic risk		Decision risk		Information Risk		Technical risk		Market and financial risk	
U	u_1		u_2		u_3		u_4		u_5	
Weight a_i	0.1		0.2		0.3		0.2		0.2	
Second Risk Weight u_{ij}	u_{11}	u_{12}	u_{21}	u_{22}	u_{31}	u_{32}	u_{41}	u_{42}	u_{51}	u_{52}
Weight a_{ij}	0.5	0.5	0.5	0.5	0.5	0.5	0.5	0.5	0.5	0.5

Table 2. Risk rank and range

Risk rank	low risk v_1	lower risk v_2	general risk v_3	higher risk v_4	high risk v_5
Range	$(0,20)$	$(20,40)$	$(40,60)$	$(60,80)$	$(80,100)$

Table 3. Various risk membership grade

r_{ij} \ u_{ij}	r_{i1}	r_{i2}	r_{i3}	r_{i4}	r_{i5}
u_{11}	0.1	0.2	0.4	0.2	0.1
u_{12}	0	0.2	0.4	0.3	0.1
u_{21}	0.3	0.3	0.2	0.1	0.1
u_{22}	0	0.2	0.2	0.3	0.3
u_{31}	0	0.1	0.2	0.4	0.3
u_{32}	0	0.2	0.4	0.2	0.2
u_{41}	0.2	0.4	0.2	0.1	0.1
u_{42}	0	0.1	0.2	0.4	0.3
u_{51}	0.1	0.2	0.4	0.2	0.1
u_{52}	0	0.2	0.3	0.3	0.2

3.2.4 Single Risk Assessment
Single risk fuzzy matrix is

$$R_1 = \begin{pmatrix} 0.1 & 0.2 & 0.4 & 0.2 & 0.1 \\ 0 & 0.2 & 0.4 & 0.3 & 0.1 \end{pmatrix} \quad R_2 = \begin{pmatrix} 0.3 & 0.3 & 0.2 & 0.1 & 0.1 \\ 0 & 0.2 & 0.2 & 0.3 & 0.3 \end{pmatrix}$$

$$R_3 = \begin{pmatrix} 0 & 0.1 & 0.2 & 0.4 & 0.3 \\ 0 & 0.2 & 0.4 & 0.2 & 0.2 \end{pmatrix} \quad R_4 = \begin{pmatrix} 0.2 & 0.4 & 0.2 & 0.1 & 0.1 \\ 0 & 0.1 & 0.2 & 0.4 & 0.3 \end{pmatrix}$$

$$R_5 = \begin{pmatrix} 0.1 & 0.2 & 0.4 & 0.2 & 0.1 \\ 0 & 0.2 & 0.3 & 0.3 & 0.2 \end{pmatrix}$$

The weight of risk factor is: $A_1 = A_2 = A_3 = A_4 = A_5 = (0.5 \quad 0.5)$, according to $M(\bullet, \oplus)$, we can calculate B

$$B_1 = A_1 \circ R_1 = \begin{pmatrix} 0.05 & 0.2 & 0.4 & 0.25 & 0.1 \end{pmatrix}$$

$$B_2 = A_2 \circ R_2 = \begin{pmatrix} 0.15 & 0.25 & 0.2 & 0.2 & 0.2 \end{pmatrix}$$

$$B_3 = A_3 \circ R_3 = \begin{pmatrix} 0 & 0.15 & 0.3 & 0.3 & 0.25 \end{pmatrix}$$

$$B_4 = A_4 \circ R_4 = \begin{pmatrix} 0.1 & 0.25 & 0.2 & 0.25 & 0.2 \end{pmatrix}$$

$$B_5 = A_5 \circ R_5 = \begin{pmatrix} 0.5 & 0.2 & 0.35 & 0.25 & 0.15 \end{pmatrix}$$

According to table 2, we can choose the high score $\{ c_{hi} = (20\ \ 40\ \ 60\ \ 80\ \ 100) \}$, low score $\{ c_{li} = (0\ \ 20\ \ 40\ \ 60\ \ 80) \}$ and the middle score $\{ c_{mi} = (10\ \ 30\ \ 50\ \ 70\ \ 90) \}$ in every range, and calculate the average score. The following is the final score.

Table 4. The single risk score

score	Strategic risk	Decision risk	Information Risk	Technical risk	Market and financial risk
S	u_1	u_2	u_3	u_4	u_5
S_h	63	61	73	64	65
S_m	53	51	63	54	55
S_l	43	41	53	44	45
$\overline{S}$	53	51	63	54	55

From the table 4, we can see that information risk is the highest risk, the following is Market and financial risk, technology risk, strategic risk, decision-making risk. Therefore, when SME choose reverse logistics outsourcing, they should pay more attention to information risk and take the necessary measures on prevention.

4   Reverse Logistics Outsourcing Risk Management Strategies

Based on the above analysis, we propose five Reverse Logistics Outsourcing Risk Management Strategies: first, strengthen the information communication between Reverse Logistics Outsourcing partners; second, strengthen the capacity to respond to market changes unexpectedly and a reasonable allocation of expenses; third, strengthen the core technical innovation capability and enhance the basic technical level; fourth, Improve core competitive capability and establish a common strategic goals; fifth, analyze needs of Outsourcing correctly and improve the ability to adapt to the environment.

References

1. Andel, T.: Reverse logistic: a second chance to profit. Transportation and Distribution 38(7), 61–63 (1997)
2. Klausner, M., Hendrickson, C.: Reverse-logistics strategy for
3. Cottrill, K.: Return to sender. TraNc World 262(7), 17–18 (2000)
4. Discount Store News. Outsourcing: reverse logistics push into high gear 38(6), 8–10 (1999)
5. Gooley, T.: Reverse logistics:0ve steps to success. Logistics Management and Distribution Report 37(6), 49–55 (1998)

Regional Policy in the Baltic States

Ilze Stokmane

Latvia University of Agriculture, 2 Liela Street, Jelgava, LV3001, Latvia
Ilze.Stokmane@llu.lv

Abstract. Regional development in nowadays have focus primary on local governments and interests and initiatives of their inhabitants. After accession to the European Union, the regional development legislation base in the Baltic States is governed by EU regional policy. Therefore countries that make up the European Union have joined their sovereignty to gain power and influence upon the world – something they could not have reached on their own. Practically, the joint sovereignty means that the member states delegate part of their decision making power to different entities set up by the member states to make sure that the decisions made on the European level ensure democracy and common interests. The main instrument that is used to implement the regional policy in the EU member states are the European Union Structural Funds.

Keywords: Regional policy, Baltic countries, Structural Funds.

1 Regional Policy Development

Along with setting up goals for economies and social cohesion during mid eighties, the European community expressed the necessity to develop a new and joined policy that would be built on solidarity between member states and regions by promoting integrated and solid development, decreasing the structural differences between the regions and the countries and setting a principle that all regions and their populations should have a security of equal rights for economical and social development [3].

Starting with the Treaty of European Union, the conception about cohesion was further defined and was understood the decrease of developmental levels between the different regions, not the general division between the regions. But not the Single European Act, nor the Treaty of European Union did not provide the definition for cohesion to establish the policies that needed to be applied to reach it. According to both of these agreements, the conception of cohesion expressed only the need to decrease both the economical and social differences between the regions within the Community.

The European Commission emphasizes that cohesion is not homogeneity; therefore the purpose of cohesion should be consummation of equal economical and social opportunities. EU has clearly identified the economical variables in practice that are being used to measure the main developmental differences between different regions and then apply the cohesion policies. The output that was produced in the EU and the workforce used are the key figures for the levels of economical welfare in the region and it is being calculated from the gross domestic product and unemployment rate.

M. Zhou (Ed.): ISAEBD 2011, Part IV, CCIS 211, pp. 354–362, 2011.
© Springer-Verlag Berlin Heidelberg 2011

It is equally important for the EU member states to maintain the social welfare, to provide conservation actions, health security, and educational system, decrease the crime rate, increase the quality of services and provide growth and development for scientific work and development in general.

So with the Treaty of Europe (1993) and later the Treaty of Amsterdam (1997), the European Commission [5] defined that the economical and social cohesion is a process and its goal is to secure the communities solidarity with the lesser privileged countries, regions and populated areas.

The new cohesion policies of 2007-2013 key goals are to further development, employment and competitive capacity. This strategy is based on three elements. First of all, the strategical guidelines made on EU level that set separate measures about priorities of cohesion policies, that are anticipated by the Lisbon's strategy for development and employment. Secondly, member states in their annual reports about the Lisbon strategy dedicate a separate chapter for information how the cohesion policy has furthered the implementations of state reform programs. Besides that, in 2009 and 2012 the member states will hand in a report dedicated entirely to the cohesion policy, where will be stated the goals reached in the developmental and employment programs. And lastly, at least 60% from the finances of the cohesion policies in the lesser developed regions (75% in other regions) must be put towards development of growth and employment strategies. Therefore the cohesion policy is the base of EU economical administration system as the main instrument of growth and employment promotion.

Based on the institutional analyses on the European Union action principle and formation of the regional policy done before, the author understands that terms for long lasting economical growth are development, competition and employment.

The life rhythm in modern day Europe is fast. To solve problems that affect us not only in Europe, but also outside it, the legislation needs to adjust to the fast growing technological development and need to further innovations that could protect the wellbeing and security of the inhabitants of Europe. The public offices and authorities need to be effective, flexible and determined. These are the standards that the European Commission [5] has set for themselves.

The public authorities adopt legislations for the society to reach numerous goals - to provide fair trade and competition, provide health security and security, further innovations and protection the environment. When developing the policies and legislations the government tries to obtain betterments – make sure that the right instruments are used for the corresponding task, the gains are maximized and the negative influence is minimized, and they make sure to listen to those who are directly influenced by these actions. Therefore the author is convinced that the legislation is a tool that makes policies become reality and realizes the needs of citizens.

The international dialog and collaboration is extremely important not just because of security of high consumer rates and social and environmental protection, but also from the perspective of business development. Just like the creation of a single market in the Europe was set by the company needs to get rid of the unreasonable differences in norms between the member states, the international collaboration motivation is to scale down or liquidate excessive formalities between the business partners.

In a century where the modern economy is developing fast, the public offices in Europe want to reduce excessive formalities and get rid of the superfluous bureaucracy. And the European Union is no an exception. The European Commission puts much of its energy towards betterment of their legislations, they want to get rid of similar rules and to make the legislation easier to understand, including making the decision making process more accessible and to involve a bigger circle of people in the policy making process.

Thanks to all fields of politics, the inhabitants of Europe are secured with different liberties, many jobs have been created and growth and development is promoted. But for this to work in reality there is a need to pass a set of rules that would be applied throughout Europe consequently.

In the last decades not only the country, using the central governing institutions and local authorities, is active in the implementation of the regional policy, but also the European Commission and other international organizations [10].

There can be observed quintessential social economical differences between the regions in the EU. The big social economical differences slow down the EU in general, as a whole, and each region of each state, even the wealthiest slow down in growth. Therefore one of the EU priorities by realizing the solidarity principle [9] is the economical and social reconciliation (cohesion).

Within the framework of the European Union (European Community before) the goal of convergence (cohesion) has existed since the Treaty of Rome in 1957 and it is measured by "the level in which the social and economical disproportion of wellbeing between the different regions of the Community are politically and socially acceptable". In the Treaty of Europe (1993) the goal of reaching cohesion was particularly stressed.

Competitive capacity and cohesion are the cornerstones of EU expenses, therefore the means spent in the time period of 2007-2013 are increased by 23% comparing to the means spent in the previous seven years. By not using the EU and state regional policy means and by not preventing negative influence of market economy, not only the difference between the economically strong and weak regions would be maintained, it would increase even more. The author agrees to the statement [2] that the economically stronger regions have better grounds for investments: growing infrastructure, qualified personnel, availability of different services, etc.

Usually the key goals and tasks of the regional policy are said to be balance of the regional economical growth, the balanced and effective use of material, natural and other resources in all regions of the state, the decrease in regional differences by, firstly, the income on one citizen and the unemployment rate as well as the stimulation of the economical growth in the poor regions.

The policy of the state can be viewed from two sides:

– first of all, the whole policy of the state that has an immediate and important territorial influence, like, in employment, housing,etc.;
– second of all, as a regional policy where the main focus is on the territory and territorial growth. The understanding with growth is that it is a positive change, but in the context of regional policy the definition is more precise – with growth is understood the change process furtherment of nature, environment, culture and social environment for the betterment of society.

The author agrees to the member's of the European Parliament, Ineses Vaideres, statement that regional policy is a complex of concrete and organised measures for the security of growth and development throughout the whole country. The regional economical policy or the regional planning includes all forms of public interference that are meant for the geographical placement of economical activities. The regional policy tries to adjust the free market economy to reach two mutually connected goals – economical growth and betterment of the social allocation.

The English economist Harvey Armstrong [1], [3]. [4] by evaluating the goals reached in the approximately 20 years in the European regional policy admits that the results are not unequivocal. The cohesion process in the European Community founding states was quite fast and it was accompanied by remarkable inner and outer trade activities. In the periphery, which was the main goal of the regional policy, the results are not that conclusive either. For example, Ireland and Spain projected good growth, but Greece, which in the 1960's in the conditions of autocracy was developing and growing quite fast, showed some relative deterioration despite of major funding – approximately 30% from all public investment. Some problems that the Greek economy was facing remind of Latvian economical policies. The European funds in Greece were mainly used to subsidize the gigantic public sector - electricity, telecommunications, aviation and railways, but they were not modernizing them. Therefore the regional policy made the structural reorganization process rather slower than faster. The other problem was the short term wage subsidation for those who went back to work. The method that was meant to get the unemployed individuals back in to the job market was used by companies to get subsidies, namely they were letting individuals go and hiring new employees. Therefore human resources and capital were lost. And the third problem was that the regional program preparation and implementation process was sketchy and it was done by unprepared and unqualified representatives of regional and local authorities. And last but not least, the regional policy funds were mainly used in the public sector - approximately only two percent of the European funds reached the profitable private sector investments. If these funds were to be put towards modernization of the infrastructure, that could be thought of as a positive thing, but, unfortunately, these funds were mainly used to create non-profitable jobs in the public sector. Therefore the unemployment rate was low, but the public sector had a huge personnel.

The problems stated are referable to the regional policy as such, but the real obstacle for the economical growth was the investor unfriendly and public sector-oriented economical policy as well as the socially unstable situation. Therefore the author thinks that the blame can not be put only on the regional policy. Referring to the example that was described, the author concludes that a successful regional policy can only be reached in a market oriented competitive environment.

There are many distinguished types of documents of regional development process: Development planning documents for policies, documents for institutions of administration and documents for territorial development plans.

The policy planning document states goals and tasks, and action for one or more political direction, sector or under sectors development furtherment. The development planning documents are developed in a national, regional or local level.

The regional and local level long term territorial development planning documents state the priorities in development of the corresponding territory and dimensional development perspectives, but in the intermediate term development planning documents – the complex of concrete measures needed for realization of the priorities.

The Baltic States construct their legislation according to the declarations of International global organizations, the legislation in force in the European Union, taking into account other joint organization policies and development documents.

The main instrument that is used to implement the regional policy in the EU member states are the European Union Structural Funds. European Fund for Regional Development (EFRD), European Social Fund (ESF) and Cohesion Fund (CF) give their contribution to consummation of three goals of the regional policy – convergence, regional competitiveness and employment, territorial cooperation in Europe.

2 Support for Regional Development in Baltic States

The EU structural fund development documents are used in Estonia for regional development, development of human resources and improvement of infrastructure.

In the time period of 2007-2013 the Estonian structural fund policy is set by these documents [6]:

–   In the Estonia National Strategic Reference Framework 2007-2013 the general strategically approach to the organization of support measures for structural funds is set. The Framework document also serves as the basis for the development of three operational programmes and determination of implementation principles.
–   Operational Programme for Human Resource Development;
–   Operational Programme for the Development of Economic Environment;
–   Operational Programme for the Development of the Living Environment;
–   Along side with the structural funds the support for rural, agricultural and branches of fishery is being secured by implementing the Estonia Rural Development Plan 2007-2013 (for implementation of European Agricultural Fund for Rural Development – EAFRD) and the Estonian Fisheries Strategy 2007-2013 (for implementation of European Fisheries Fund – EFF).

Table 1.

Beneficiaries	Cohesion Fund	EFRD	ESF	EAFRD	EFF
State institutions	xxx	xxx	xxx	xxx	xxx
Municipalities	xxx	xxx	xxx	xxx	xxx
Legal entities	xxx	xxx*	xxx	xxx**	xxx**
Private entities	-	-	x	xxx	x
Non-governmental organizations	xx	xxx	xxx	xxx	xxx

x - Participation possible directly

xx - Participation as partner

xxx - Participation possible both directly and as partner

*   except private and legal entities of agricultural and fishery branches

** available only for private and legal entities of agricultural and fishery branches.

By studying the EU Structural fund availability to the Baltic States, the author has separated the five main groups that could claim finances from structural funds by implementing projects alone or in partnership- governmental authorities, local authorities, legal entities, private entities and non-governmental organizations. Table 1 shows the EU instrument availability in Estonia.

Governmental and local authorities and legal (business) entities in Estonia can receive the support of structural funds either directly or by joining a project as a partner. The biggest difference between the accessibility of the structural funds for private entities and for non-governmental institutions are that a person can involve the ESF and EFF in their projects for raising their qualification or other developmental processes as well as implementing a project directly or within a partnership with the EAFRD. In Estonia non-governmental institutions can enter for a partnership in the Cohesion fund projects, therefore securing the publicity principle in adaption of remarkable financial funds in infrastructural and environmental object maintenance important to the state.

In Latvia, as well as in Estonia and Lithuania, the structural fund development documents that bring direct support for the state institutions, local authorities, non-governmental institutions, legal and private entities for development of competitiveness, for 2007-2013 have been developed in detail [7]:

- Latvia National Strategic Reference Framework 2007-2013 is the main structural fund and cohesion fund development document that secures the link between the cohesion policy and national priorities and substantiates the choice of these priorities as well as sets the strategy for acquisition of the funds, frame of administration and secures the coordination between the programmes of work and other financial instruments;
- Operational programme "Human Resources and Employment" (ESF);
- Operational programme "Entrepreneurship and Innovations" (ERDF);
- Operational programme "Infrastructure and Services" (CF/EFRD);
- Along side with the structural funds the support for rural, agricultural and branches of fishery is being secured by implementing the Latvia Rural Development Programme 2007-2013 and Operational Programme for the Implementation of the European Fisheries Fund Support in Latvia for 2007 – 2013.

Table 2.

Beneficiaries	Cohesion Fund	EFRD	ESF	EAFRD	EFF
State institutions	xxx	xxx	xxx	xxx	xxx
Municipalities	xxx	xxx	xxx	-	xxx
Legal entities	xxx	xxx*	xxx	xxx**	xxx**
Private entities	-	x	-	x	x
Non-governmental organizations	-	-	xxx	-	xxx

x - Participation possible directly
xx - Participation as partner
xxx - Participation possible both directly and as partner
*   except private and legal entities of agricultural and fishery branches
** available only for private and legal entities of agricultural and fishery branches.

The availability of the EU instruments in Latvia is shown in Table 2. Governmental (state) and local (municipality) authorities and legal entities (business) in Latvia can receive the support of structural funds either directly or by joining a project as a partner. For the local authorities EU, EFRD, CF and EFF funds are available.

Private entities the means of structural funds for raising their qualifications or other activities may involve EFRD, EAFRD and EFF in their projects.

The non-governmental organizations in Latvia may apply directly or as partners in the ESF and EFF projects when taking part in solving issues of social matter in the state or local offices.

In Lithuania, just like in the other Baltic States a separate programme of action and support for attracting the means of structural funds.

In the Lithuanian Republic for the local and regional authorities, state institutions, non-governmental institutions as well as legal and private entities such EU structural fund documents for 2007-2013 should be of interest [8]:

−   National general strategy: the Lithuanian Strategy for the use of European Union Structural Assistance for 2007-2013;
−   Operational Programme for the Development of Human Resources for 2007–2013;
−   Operational programme for the Economical Growth for 2007–2013;
−   Operational Programme for Promotion of Cohesion for 2007–2013;
−   Along side with the structural funds the support for rural, agricultural and branches of fishery is being secured by implementing the Lithuania Rural Development Plan 2007-2013 and Operational Programme for the Lithuanian Fisheries Sector 2007-2013.

In the Lithuanian Republic, similar to Estonia, the governing bodies, local and regional authorities and business entities can get the support of the structural funds directly or joining in on a partnership.

But private entities can hand their projects in to EAFRD and EFF. The non-governmental institutions in Lithuania can join all of the processes of the structural funds and activities that have been included in the analyses in Table 3, but the Cohesion fund and EFRD they can join in on partnership.

Table 3.

Beneficiaries	Cohesion Fund	EFRD	ESF	EAFRD	EFF
State institutions	xxx	xxx	xxx	xxx	xxx
Municipalities	xxx	xxx	xxx	xxx	xxx
Legal entities	xxx	xxx*	xxx	xxx**	xxx**
Private entities	-	-	-	xxx	x
Non-governmental organizations	xx	xx	xxx	xxx	xxx

x - Participation possible directly
xx - Participation as partner
xxx - Participation possible both directly and as partner
*   except private and legal entities of agricultural and fishery branches
**   available only for private and legal entities of agricultural and fishery branches.

In all three Baltic States the emphasis in the structural fund mean management is on the growth of infrastructure, human resources and competitive economy.

In a time of globalisation where the boarders for services, goods and travelling have been removed the citizens are expecting security and wellbeing from their governments and the businesses want equal rights in the market and furthered competitiveness. Legislation plays a big part in reaching these goals. To create a good legislation is a difficult task – all level public offices in Estonia Latvia and Lithuania have to provide such level of security that is expected from the consumers and the citizens and at the same time they have to create an environment for local companies so they could compete successfully and would become innovative in the harsh global competitiveness. Legal regulations have different alternatives nowadays that should be evaluated by governments of the Baltic States, for example, how to reach individual political goals cheaper and more effective by not using regular methods, but common conduct (the goals set by the legislation could be trusted to social partners or non-governmental institutions) or self conduct (private structures agree from their own free will to commitment for the solving of issues involved).

3 Conclusions

The regional policy often is called the structural policy because in the result of implementing the regional policy the regional and state economical and social structures change.

The Baltic States construct their legislation according to the declarations of International global organizations, the legislation in force in the European Union and taking into account other joint organization policies and development documents.

There are different types of legislations in Europe. The EU directive can be applied to the member state rights, but they have to do it themselves, therefore the legislation can be applied to the local conditions. But the regulations are directly applicable in each and every member state – the legislation is adapted to every member state. The local policy planning document states goals and tasks, and action for one or more political direction, sector or under sectors development furtherment. The development planning documents are developed in a national, regional or local level.

The regional and local level long term territorial development planning documents state the priorities in development of the corresponding territory and dimensional development perspectives, but in the intermediate term development planning documents – the complex of concrete measures needed for realization of the priorities.

For the regional development and promotion of competitive capacity in the Baltic States in 2007-2013 large means of structural funds for different programmes of business activity and research development therefore promoting the state and individual region competitiveness from the European Union are available.

References

1. Armstrong, H.W.: Convergence among Regions of the European Union, 1950-1990. Reg. Science 74(2), 143–152 (1995)
2. Armstrong, H.W., Read, R.: Microstates and Subnatural Regions: Mutual Industrial Policy Lessons. Int. Reg. Science Review 26(1), 117–141 (2003)

3. Armstrong, H.W., Taylor, J.: Regional economics and policy, 3rd edn. Blackwell, Oxford (2000)
4. Armstrong, H.W., Wells, P.: Structural funds and the evaluation of community economic development initiatives in the UK: A critical perspective. Reg. Studies 40(2), 259–272 (2006)
5. European Commision homepage. EU policy, http://ec.europa.eu/policies/index_lv.htm
6. European Union Structural Funds in Estonia, http://www.struktuurifondid.ee/
7. European Union Structural Funds in Latvia, http://www.esfondi.lv
8. European Union Structural Funds in Lithuania, http://www.esparama.lt/en/pasirengimas/
9. Summaries of EU legislation, http://europa.eu/legislation_summaries/regional_policy/index_en.htm
10. Vaidere, I., Vanags, E., Vanags, I., Vilka, I.: Reģionālā politika un pašvaldību attīstība Eiropas Savienībā un Latvijā (in Latvian) Rīga, Latvijas Universitātes Akadēmiskais apgāds, Latvijas Statistikas institūts (2006)

Reflections on Water Resource Sustainable Development in Wuhan Metropolitan Area

Xiaohua Dou, Renzhong Liu, and Xinzheng Chen

The College of Urban and Environmental Sciences, HuaZhong Normal University, CCNU
Wuhan, China
douxiaohua@yahoo.com.cn

Abstract. Water resource, as fundamental material basis for economic and social development in Wuhan metropolitan area, becomes currently a heated focus in society under the idea of "resource-saving and environment-friendly" social construction and sustainable development. Through the analysis of current situation of total water capacity, water exploration and utilization in Wuhan metropolitan area, the thesis points out existing problems of water resource utilization, such as water shortage and high pollution, lack of uniform water resource management system, disparity of water consumption between urban and rural area. Based on these problems, the thesis, therefore puts forward relevant solutions from the perspective of reinforcement of comprehensive regulation and management in water resource, industry restructure, reasoning industry arrangement, reform of water policies, innovation of water-saving technology, and optimization of irrigational infrastructure and sewerage facilities.

Keywords: Wuhan metropolitan area, water resource, sustainable utilization.

1 Current Water Resource Situation in Wuhan Metropolitan Area

Wuhan metropolitan area is located in the middle reaches of Yangtze river and east of Hubei province, is one of areas abundant in water resource area. In boasts profusions of lakes and ponds, crossing rivers and reservoirs, and is also abundant in precipitation, surfical flows and ground water. Moreover, Wuhan city, which is the key parts in the area is dubbed as "river city", and "city of hundreds of lakes". The total area in this region is 58081.9km2, and its water area covers 10%. There are about 300 rivers with the length larger than 5km, and 565 lakes with the area more than 66700m2 [1]. Since the vast majority of cities in this area is adjacent to rivers and lakes, and since economic centers within the area are evidently bordering Yangtze river, Han river or their branches, economic and social development of Wuhan metropolitan area are characterized by "both prospering via water and restraining via water".

M. Zhou (Ed.): ISAEBD 2011, Part IV, CCIS 211, pp. 363–369, 2011.

1.1 Total Water Capacity in Wuhan Metropolitan Are

Wuhan metropolitan area is in the center of sub-tropical monsoon climate, and boasts abundant annual precipitation. By the aspect of annual precipitation, the average annual precipitation for years is 1200mm; rains mainly appear from April to September, which covers 70%-90% of annual precipitation [2]. The annual precipitation in 2007 is up to 9491.5mm, 3.23% higher than the previous year, while 8.83% lower than the average annual precipitation in this area. By the aspect of total water capacity, Wuhan metropolitan area covers 25,386,000,000m3, including surficial water capacity 23,773,000,000m3, and 76,250,000,000m3 of ground water capacity. According to the latest demographic statistics, per capital water resource within the area is 808.37m3, which is just more than 1/3 below the national average (2400m3); water resource per 667m2 agricultural used area is 1284.44m2, which is 84.6% of the national average. By the aspect of water reserve, the area at present covers 11 lakes, 101 reservoirs, and the total water reserve is to 4,705,000,000m3 [3]. Moreover, annual water on average derived from other regions is 716,900,000,000m3, is 20 times of self-produced water resource, which contributes a lot to industry and agriculture development within Wuhan metropolitan area. By the aspect of spatial distribution of water resource total water resource in Wuhan, Xiaogan, Huanggang and Xianning within the area is 78.7% of the whole area. (see figure1). The general distribution of water resource within the area is in accordance with the total area of each city. According to statistics, due to discrete demographic density within the area, per capita water resource in Wuhan is merely 374m3, whereas Xianning is 1566m3, which signals a disparity of per capital water resource within the area.

Fig. 1. The spatial distribution of water resource of wuhan metropolitan area

1.2 Status of Water Resource Development and Utilization

Water resource is a strategic resource, just like energy. If water has been exhausted, production will not be normally continued, and human lives will be at risk. At present, by the aspects of water supply, the majority of supply comes from surficial water in Wuhan metropolitan area, and the total water supply is up to 14,497,000,000m3 in 2007, in which surficial water supply is 96.3% of the total water supply. By the aspect of water consumption, the total water consumption is 14,497,000,000m3 in the whole year. According to former statistics, agricultural-used water is 7,345,000,000m3, which is 51% of total water consumption; industrial-used water is 5,546,000,000m3, which is 38% of total water consumption; livelihood water is 1,607,000,000m3, which is 11% of total water consumption. In recent years, water consumption requirement in each field all exhibit an upward trend(see figure 2), and each city show different trend according to industrial and agriculture development status. According to new statistics, production water consumption is 13,337,000,000m3, which is 92% of total water consumption; living water consumption is 1,154,000,000m3, which is 8% of total water consumption; Eco-water is zero. By the aspect of water loss, Comprehensive water loss is 6,598,000,000m3, and water loss rate is 25.99%, including agriculture water loss, industrial water loss and living water loss are respectively 4,200,000,000m3, 1,546,000,000m3, 852,000,000m3. and water loss rate are respectively 57.18%,27.8%,53.2%. By the aspect of construction of water conservancy facilities, stem embankment length is 1503km, including 725.7km in Yangtze rive and 566.6km in Han river, DongJing embankment is 210.2km; the number of drainage pump station is 1200, and pump 3600. These water conservancy facilities resolve initially water shortage of "two years drought in three years".

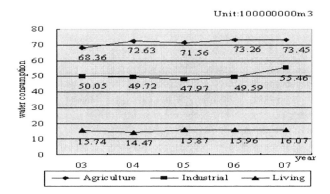

Fig. 2. Structure of water consumption of wuhan metropolitan area

2   Analysis of Sustainable Utilization of Water Resource in Wuhan Metropolitan Area

2.1 Shortage of Water Resource

In recent years, according to the consumption trend of total water capacity and water consumption capacity in Wuhan metropolitan area, total water capacity appears decreased while total water consumption capacity increased considerably. Some cities like Wuhan, E'zhou and Xiantao can not satisfy their demanding requirement for water. Especially, per capita water consumption in E'zhou is 52.8% more than that in the whole area, thus water resource shows in alarming shortage in the area. Moreover, lakes and marshes in the area decline sharply due to exponent pace of urbanization in intra-area cities and human activities of urban construction. Set Wuhan as an example, its water area declines 55% from the dubbed "hundreds of lakes" city in the

1950's to merely 27 lakes at present [4]. The decreasing water resource contributes directly to the slicing of total water resource in the area, thus the contradiction between water consumption and water supply shows exasperation. Meanwhile, the efficiency of water consumption within the area is relatively low at present, performed by industry-used water recycling ratio at 74.78%, even only about 20% in some regions, while a good many enterprise manifests no water recycling; agriculture-used water coefficient is 0.4 on average, which is less than the national level; the fact that water-leaking prevails in urban water-distributing pipes and water devices leads the waste in livelihood-used water is more than 20%. Moreover, the waste of public-used water deteriorates the strained situation of water shortage.

2.2 Pollution of Water Environment

In the process of water exploration and consumption, water quality is one crucial index for water environment. Currently, surficial water in the area is generally in low quality except some major reservoir rivers and water quality in some cities is considered as V level, which will not be suitable for drinking. Thus over-exploration of ground water in some regions like Xiaogan breeds adverse effect on future urban development. As economic development and population increase faster their pace, the discharged capacity of polluted water in urban area therefore follows suit, which results in serious pollution is gravely neglected so that ecological damage arises. By the aspect of waste-water discharge, further and widespread river-toward waste water discharge rises appreciatively as waste water discharge for livelihood, second and tertiary industry accelerates. Wuhan, Huangshi and Huanggang are among those whose waste water discharge is more than 300,000,000T. According to the statistics from "water resource communiqué in Hubei province" in 2008, the waste water discharge in Wuhan metropolitan area is up to about 3,200,000,000m2, 70% of total waste-water discharge in the province. Water environment in the area deteriorates as large amount of unprocessed waste water for livelihood and industry use are discharged into rivers and lakes, and the waste of pesticide, fertilizer after agriculture production are randomly placed, which results in pollution with various degree among 90% lakes, and 80% medium and small-sized rivers[5]. By the aspect of water quality, due to low water-flowing in lakes, slow water circulation, and indiscriminate discharge of waste water in urban residential area, the worsening of water quality is in a striking position, performed b some lakes at IV or V level in water quality. Tianmen, the principle drinking water source within the area, has only annual suitable water quality ratio at 66.7%.By the aspect of eutrophication, some representative reservoirs within the area are basically in medium- eutrophication degree concerning water quality, and the pollution elements are ammonia, nitrogen and phosphor. In addition, Hanjiang, crossing the area, has several-time algae bloom phenomenon, and the frequency, along with the resulted economic loss show no sign of slowdown, which has not only   tremendous influence on life environment in the area, but also causes huge disasters toward lower-reach urban areas.

2.3 Lack of Uniform Management System of Water Resources

With regard to water resources management of metropolitan area, on the one hand , urban districts have many phenomenon ,such as the discrepancy on levy departments of water resources and standards, the disagreement on urban water quality, water quantity, management of water supply and flood control and decontamination property, and the dispersion of administration management of water sector. Lack of unified regulations and management system of rational water value will not only affect the effective and efficient management of water resources, and become a great obstacle to optimal allocation of water resources, but also result in empty areas of water management due to the dispersion of benefits, thereby causing a serious waste of water resources, On the other hand, in aspects of water supply, water consumption and decontamination between urban and rural districts, there is a huge gap on water consumption and water supply because that a more complete urban infrastructure investment in fixed assets is higher than rural areas. At present, per capita daily water consumption of urban living in Wuhan metropolitan area is about 173L, per capita daily water consumption of rural living is about 52L, there is a big gap between the two of water consumption.There does not exist any sewage treatment sector in rural areas, emissions of waste water is a essential random state, which not only affects the water quality of groundwater resources, but also causes serious damage to the ecological environment in rural areas.

3 Countermeasure Study of Protection and Sustainable Utilization of Water Resource in Wuhan Metropolitan Area

3.1 Improvement in Comprehensive Management of Water Resources

First, build a management system of water resources for Wuhan metropolitan area and make the management of water resources in every area of the circle be a complete unit. In each area, the usage and development of water resources and sewage disposal should be arranged to Drainage Services department. Secondly, water management system of Urban-rural integration in Wuhan metropolitan area should be enhanced and the huge distance in water use between city and country should be reduced increasingly. On the one hand, the increase in investing the infrastructure of water use and sewage disposal for the inhabitant in village will improve water quality in village and the environment of sewage disposal and advance the water quality in village. On the other hand, the irrigation management of agricultural production should be reinforced and Non-point source pollution should be controlled. Improve the irrigation skill, reduce the waste of water resources, reinforce the supervision on the use of pesticides and chemical fertilizer, forbid the use of highly toxic p pesticides, carry out formulated fertilization, encourage to use fertilizer and return straw back to field, control the mount of nitrogenous fertilizer to reduce groundwater pollution caused by agriculture production. Last, the management of water resources should transfer from district to area. The middle-route project of the South-to-North water transfer project in Yangzi and Han river and the frequency and disorder in developing and stopping flow in the upper reaches of Yangzi river have influenced greatly water resources in the circle, therefore, it is necessary to make the water management in upper, middle and lower reaches into a unit. Through supporting the protection for water and ecological environment in the upper reaches, the water safety in the region will be maintained. For example, build Water ecological compensation mechanism, close the enterprises in the upper reaches that greatly pollute and destroy water environment of lower reaches, the lower region should offer the upper region reserve fund to maintain water and earth and protect water environment.

3.2   Reasonably Adjusting Industrial Structure and Planning Industrial Layout and Water Resources Allocation

At present, in Wuhan metropolitan area, water use in agriculture and industry occupies 88.92% of the total, that in agriculture occupying 56.98%, which shows obviously partial to farm. Because of lagging skills in irrigation, the water use rate in agriculture is up to 57.18%, which leads to serious water waste, in addition, the use of fertilizer and pesticide pollutes groundwater badly. Compared with GDP in other industries in metropolitan area, water use in agriculture and GDP produced by it present obvious and unmatched features, so in order to improve the continuous development of economy in the city circle, the industrial structure shall go on being adjusted. What's more, combining industry development and layout of every area in the circle, considering the comprehensive use and the development of water in taking, pollution discharge system, on the one hand, the development of industries with low consumption of water, slight pollution and highly benefit should be supported while the industries with water waste, serious pollution and low benefit should be forbidden to expand. The building of pollution discharge system in the area where heavy industry is dominant should especially be paid attention to. Bath, washing car and swimming pool should be restricted and managed to improve the development of water-based service industry. Water resources should be used reasonably and effectively to make the consumption of water and the discharge of water pollutants in the range that total amount index limits. On the other hand, adjust the industry layout of each area in the circle to build the enterprises in the circle into an order industrial chain step by step. Recycle resources to decrease output of waste to least. For example, remove the highly water waste industry in Wuhan city, such as the industry for auto parts and steal, to Huanggang and Xiaogan region. Through the transfer of some industries and population, reduce the amount of water use in city.

3.3   Strengthening Water Pollution Governance, Control Water Environment

In order to reduce water shortage of Wuhan metropolitan area caused by pollution of water resources and water environment, the related measures should be taken to reduce the coexistence of non-point source pollution and point source pollution, the multiplicity of domestic pollution and industrial pollution, the compound of various new and old pollution and secondary pollution. On the one hand, we can fasten the building of different types of sewage treatment plant in the city circle and impel the construction of wastewater interception pipeline network and concentrated sewage treatment plant in the city to improve the standard of sewage treatment. On the other hand, we should reduce water pollution in the countries caused by discharging pollutants at random through proceeding the towns and the villages with good condition with the comprehensive treatment for domestic sewage and livestock pollution. Besides, it is necessary to improve the lake ecological management around the city circle and search water eco-compensation mechanism. For instance, through implementing protection and recovery project of lakes and wetlands, the direct discharge of sewage from residential area around the lakes should be forbidden, as well as possible action causing water pollution because of cultivation in lake. Reclaiming land from lakes and cultivation leading to the reduction of lake water area should be forbidden. On the premise of not departing from ecological laws, operate connection project between huge lakes in Wuhan metropolitan area, improve self-purification ability of the lake which supply living water in the circle to realize self-recovery of lake ecological system.

References

1. Tao, T.: Do a good job of water development of Wuhan metropolitan area and provide reliable support for "resource-saving and environment-friendly" social construction. The internet of Yangtze River Water Conservancy,
   `http://www.cjw.gov.cn/news/detail/20090422/`
   `113445.asp,2009-4-22`
2. Chen, s.: Some problem of sustainable utilization of water resources in wuhan metropolitan area and countermeasures.the internet of Hubei Provincial Committee of CPPCC,
   `http://www.hbzx.gov.cn/newsdetail.jsp?id=200908271549590490,`
   `2009-8-13`
3. Hubei Water Conservancy internet. Water Resources Bulletin of Hubei province in (2007),
   `http://www.hubeiwater.gov.cn/inews/Index/Catalog88/`
   `11568.aspx,2008-9-3`
4. Huang-zhiyong.Some thought of flood resource utilization,
   `http://www.hbqx.gov.cn`
5. Mo, H.: The study of water sustainable and utilization in Shenzhen. China's rural water conservancy and hydropower 8, 81 (2004)

Research on Plyometric Training: Interpretation and Application

Zhi Xiang Li

Department of Physical Education, Shandong Institute of Business and Technology, Shandong Yantai China

Abstract. Some researches showed that plyometric training has an important role for improving the speed ability. However, in spite of the fact that this method has played a significant role, it also has not been utilized and understood. So, for understanding and using the method objectively, the study analyzes origin and definition of the concept, physiological basis, the effects, methods of the training. The results showed that the outstanding role is to improve the speed ability of human body other than maximum muscle. Finally, based upon such analysis, the author hope that this article can improve the application of plyometric training in sport.

Keywords: Plyometric Training, Interpretation, Application, speed strength.

1 Introduction

In traditional sports training, the skeletal muscle contraction can be divided into isometric, centripetal contraction and eccentric contractions, but in training practice, the three forms can not be seen alone. In human movement, especially, when the speed strength is development, the centripetal and eccentric contractions of muscles will ensue successively, the phenomenon was called plyometric. Plyometric exercises are widely used to develop muscular power, and to improve the athletic performance. There is solid research evidence that plyometric training is an effective way for enhancing ballistic and maximal strength. For example, Tomas B(2008) pointed out that plyometric training can improve the strength-speed ability for basketball players. however, several authors have show that for optimising maximal strength training, the combination of training modalities (i.e., plyometric and aerobic training) is recommended rather than only a single modality.

In short, the characteristics of plyometric training are not clear, the effect of it on training is unclear and induced some controversy in modern training (e.g., the strength speed or maximal strength), thus, all factors that need to be considered when prescribing plyometric training. Therefore, For using the modality correctly, this article analyzed the plyometric training, on the one hand, it can express the definition of plyometric training, and on the other hand, it can provide some conferences for sport training.

M. Zhou (Ed.): ISAEBD 2011, Part IV, CCIS 211, pp. 370–374, 2011.
© Springer-Verlag Berlin Heidelberg 2011

2 Comprehension to Plyometric Training

The use of plyometric training as a new training intervention in sport has been increased in the last few years, it is original from track and field, it refers to exercises that are designed to enhance neuromuscular performance, for example, in regard to the sprint training, some studies have found that plyometric training had a significant effect on running velocity when resistance training was combined with plyometric training on consecutive days. Fig.1 shows that the strength speed of lower limber can be developed by jumping which is a kind of plyometric training. Of course, the plyometric training can also develop the upper limber (see figure 2), by different resistance, the strength speed of upper limber can be improved.

However, with the development of plyometric training, some characteristics and effects are unknown, Randall L (2007) reported that the intensity and rate are important factors in plyometric training, quantifyling plyometric-training intensity requires consideration of both the mass of the mode of resistance or athlete and the acceleration of that mss. So, the plyometric intensity also has been defined as the amount of stress placed on involved muscles, connective tissue, and joints and is dictated by the type of plyometric exercise that is performed. Above of all, the plyometric training causes higher muscle tension compared to conventional resistance, the velocity of exercise is the main characteristics for plyometric training.

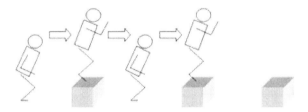

Fig. 1. The strength speed Training of lower limber

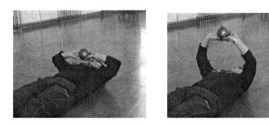

Fig. 2. The strength speed Training of upper limber

3 Effect of Plyometric Training

In order to know plyometric training, this article examined the influence of various factors on the effectiveness of PT using a meta-analysis approach (see table 1). Statistical significant was set at $P \leq 0.05$ for all analyses. The magnitudes of the ESs were considered either trivial ($<$ 0.35), small (0.35-0.80), moderate (0.80-1.50), or large ($>$ 1.5). The analysis revealed that the average ES of plyometric training on strength speed was significant, all ESs are almost above 0.80, therefore, this indicated that plyometric training is an effective way for improving the strength speed in sports training.

With regards to the study characteristics, the results indicate that there are significant effect between different study features, for example, as far as sport level is concerned, whether the national level or no athletes, the ESs is higher than 0.8. So, we can suggest that the results of analysis support numerous previous studies that PT is an effective training method for the improvement of muscle power, the present meta-analysis offers robust quantitative evidence for this conclusion and provides some value information concerning the importance of controlling some determinant variables for the improvement of performance.

Table 1. The meta-analysis of independent variable of subject characteristics

Independent variable	F	P	ES	SD	N
Previous	14.83	$<$ 0.01			
experience			0.93	0.59	9
Familiarized			1.52	0.97	17
Not familiarized					
Fitness	15.32	$<$ 0.01			
Bad			1.69	1.23	4
Normal			1.85	0.85	15
Good			1.61	0.70	12
Elite			0.80	0.62	13
Gender	8.56	$<$ 0.01			
Male			1.43	1.64	11
Female			1.36	1.87	13
Sport level	9.32	$<$ 0.01			
National			0.82	0.74	14
Regional			0.89	0.84	10
No athletes			1.92	2.03	4

4 The Physiological Mechanism of Plyometric Training

4.1 The Optimum Muscle Length of Stretch

It is well known that with the increasing of the muscle length, the effect of muscle contraction will increase gradually, when the muscle length achieve certain degree, the power of muscle will produce the maximum level. therefore, we can image that plyometric training stretch the muscle length at the first, this will improve the ability of muscle contraction by adding the number of horizontal bridge in muscles, according to this, plyometric training improve the effect of centripetal contraction. Of course, due to the difference of sport level and sport activity, when they play the plyometric training, the optimum muscle length is different, so, it is necessary to individualized training.

4.2 The Connective Tissue of Muscles

Connective tissue plays an important role in aiding the contractile actions of muscle, because that the connective tissue sheaths contribute the "elastic component" of muscle, muscle can be stretched slightly and the elastic energy is subsequently partially recovered in the stretch-shortening cycle (eccentric elongation of the muscle prior to a rapid shortening of the muscle). This elastic property increases power output by 20-30% during rapid movements, such as during jumping. Plyometric training can make the elastic component get longer, this will increase the elastic energy in human movement, therefore, by which, the muscle power is strengthen in sports training.

4.3 The Activated Ability of Stretch Reflexes on Neuromuscular

There is no doubt that stretch reflexes play an important role for muscle strength training, stretch reflexes may make a net contribution to muscle stiffness already during the period of plyometric training, this could be a logical consequence of how muscle spindles and Golgi tendon organs operate in the control of muscle length and tension, some study evidence that in plyometric training, the reflex contribution to total EMG can be substantial due to a great number of motor units. Thus, there seems to be sufficient support for the argument that the stretch reflex contributes significantly to the activation of neuromuscular which will improve the strength power. Recent growing evidence indicates that the plyometric training is an effective way for improving the activated mode of skeletal muscle and neuromuscular ability.

5 The Insufficient of Plyometric Training

5.1 The Inconformity of Training Methods and Special Technology

The plyometric training can be see as a combination exercise of centripetal contraction and eccentric contraction for most coaches in sports training, it resulted in that some athletes have fine ability of centripetal and eccentric contraction, but they have not good performance in special technology, this inconformity of strength and technology influences the performance of athletes. Therefore, plyometric training should pay attention to the integrity of centripetal and eccentric contraction, meanwhile, the training methods of plyometric should combined with sports event.

5.2 The Inconformity of Training Load and Special Events

Training load is an important issue in plyometric training, although the plyometric training significantly improves strength performance, the training load is often neglected in the past years, such as the height of training, intensity, frequency and interval time, it can say that the study of training load is very insufficient at present, because of it, whether the sprinter or long distance, the training load of plyometric is the same, then, the effect of training will be reduced. Thus, we hope that when adapting the method, the training load should pay attention to the sports event.

6 Conclusions

In conclusion, The present study demonstrates that PT significantly improves strength performance, especially, the meta-analysis indicated that PT have important role for strength speed (ESs> 0.80). Generally, the plyometric training involved primarily two-foot takeoff jumps or single foot jumps. Of course, for upper limbers, it can adapt some methods of pushing balls. In addition, the plyometric training have some insufficient, for example, the intensity of plyometric training are unclear, and it is difficult to control the training load, especially, when combining with special technology. However, it is sure that plymetric training should be strengthened in modern sports training. Meanwhile, it is necessary to say that it can more beneficial to combine plyometrics with others training method than to utilize only the plyometric training.

References

1. Tomasz, B., Jerzy, U.: The Effect of Plyometric Training on Strength-Speed Abilities of Basketball Players. Med. Sport Press 14(1), 14–20 (2008)
2. Randall, L.J., William, P.E.: Quantifying Plyometric Intensity Via Rate of Force Development, Knee Joint, and Ground Reaction Force. Journal of Strength and Conditioning Research 21(3), 763–767 (2007)
3. Eduardo, S.S., Bernodo, R., Robert, U.N.: Dose Plyometric Training Improve Strength Performance? A Meta-analysis. Journal of Science and Medicine in Sport 13, 513–522 (2010)
4. Christos, K.: Effect of Plyometric Training on Running Performance and Vertical Jumping in Performance Boys. Journal of Strength and Conditioning Research 20(2), 441–445 (2006)
5. Adam, H.P., Michael, G.M., William, R., et al.: The Effects of High Volume Aquatic Plyometric Training on Vertical Jump, Muscle Power, and Torque. International Journal of Aquatic Research and Education 4, 39–48 (2010)
6. William, J., Barry, A.: Skeletal Muscle Physiology: Plasticity and Responses to Exercise. Plenary overview 25, 1–16 (2007)
7. Markus, U., Wolfgang, T., Albert, G., et al.: Training-Specific Adaptations of H- and Stretch Reflexes in Human Soleus Muscle. Journal of Motor Behavior 39(1), 68–78 (2007)

A Research of the Feature Effectiveness of Volleyball in the Body Development of Middle School Students and Its Channel of Exertion

Zewen Xiong, Bin Ji, and Chaochao Zhao

The P.E College of the Southwest University, Chongqing, China, 400715

Abstract. Among the many sport activities, volleyball possesses its own unique effectiveness of body -building. In this article, the authors adopt some research methods, including the method of analyzing documents and materials, to conduct a research on the utilization of volleyball's feature effectiveness in the body development of middle school students and its channel of exertion. Hence hope to provide a certain option for the implementation of the new curriculum reform in P.E.

Keywords: New Curriculum Reform, Middle School Students, Volleyball, Feature Effectiveness, Development of Body, Channel.

1 Introduction

The physical education (PE) is an important component of ability-oriented education. Since our nation attaches great importance upon the ability-oriented education and the implementation of New Curriculum Reform of PE, the status of PE is becoming more and more significant. To carry out the exercise of volleyball is of importance to PE, not only because of its role of transferring the culture of specific sport, but also because of its unique value of feature effectiveness which would be unfolded in the present thesis. The implementation of new curriculum reform of PE is a brand-new design of the overall situation of PE which would involve some re-consideration to the arrangement of PE program in schools. Among the many sports items, if there are some deep investigations into those which possess unique feature effectiveness and make use of them effectively, it would operate anxo-action to the reasonable arrangement of the layout of PE within the framework of new curriculum reform. The present thesis conducts the research, based on the importance of volleyball mentioned above, on the utilization of volleyball's feature effectiveness in the body development of middle school students and its channel of exertion, hoping that the exploration of a logical conclusion would provide some useful theoretical guidance to the arrangement of PE in new curriculum reform.

2 Research Methods

2.1 The Document-Data Method

The author of the present thesis extensively refers to and collects information and sources relevant to the present thesis through the databases, like cnki, and so on.

M. Zhou (Ed.): ISAEBD 2011, Part IV, CCIS 211, pp. 375–380, 2011.
© Springer-Verlag Berlin Heidelberg 2011

2.2 The Observation Method

The author of the present thesis obtains abundant first-hand emotional material through the long-term observation on the condition of implementation of volleyball in middle-schools of the southern part of Shanxi Province, Handan city of Hebei Province, Beibei county of Chongqing city, etc.

2.3 The Logical Analysis Method

The author of the present thesis adopts the method of induction to arrange and analyze the relevant document and to card the logical order of the research data in order to find out the internal relation among the objects of study and then make a conclusion.

3 Research Result and Analysis

3.1 The Definition of the Feature Effectiveness of Volleyball

The feature effectiveness is the specific function effectiveness possessed only by the sport item and cannot be substituted by other ones. The basic skills of volleyball include passing, under-passing, smashing, blocking, serving and so on. Among these skills, the obvious feature of a smashing is to exert oneself to jump up on the basis of quick run-up, unfolding the muscle of thorax and abdomen (to appear the form of a recurved bow), and then contract thorax and abdomen and wingding-up; a blocking requires jumping up with all one's strength and contract the muscle of thorax and abdomen so as not to touch the net. The operation structures of these two actions have the function of exercise the muscle of thorax and abdomen, as well as stretching the body vertically, which can not only reduce the "carnosity" viz. fat deposits, of thorax, enhance the strength of the muscle of thorax and abdomen, but also profit the vertical development of ossature and muscle. Therefore, it is self-evident that the action of smashing and blocking in volleyball perform a role of "body heightening and shaping", viz. promoting the organism heightening and beautifying.

There exist plenty of actions which can exercise the muscle of thorax and abdomen and provoke the vertical development of ossature; however, there is no other collective sport item than volleyball which can organically connect the two exercises and reach a certain kind of intensity. For instance, among the sports with net, volleyball requires striking the ball over the net with higher jump height than tennis and badminton, which demands a fuller vertical extension of the muscle. Basketball also demands vertical extension to get the backboard recovery, but it does not need the radian of recurved bow required in the action of volleyball; hence its impact on thorax and abdomen is not as intense as volleyball's. Though the requirement of jumping height and arched body in fosubry flop are not lower than those of volleyball's, due to its high difficulty and classification of solo sport item which lacks playfulness of collective ones, the reason of implementing it is thus relatively lowered. All in all, it is not difficult to find out that among the many sport items which are with similar action structures, the action combination of volleyball's smashing are more effective in the aspect of body heightening and shaping; moreover, its extent, intensity and playfulness are all helpful for the actualization of the target of body heightening and shaping. There are some researches show that "bouncing is the first element of heightening and speed is the second" , and the action of smashing and blocking in volleyball are both on the basis of the combination of rapid movement and utmost bouncing. Therefore, it is obvious that volleyball has unique value both in body heightening and shaping.

3.2 The Fit Degree between Volleyball's Feature Effectiveness and Body Expectation of Middle-School Students

Medical statistics shows that in China, the heights of 60% of the adolescents in urban areas and 65% in rural areas are under the height standard. No matter being with tall or low height, students are all have the expectation of body heightening. If one can design the height and weight of oneself, there is a great difference between the actual body mass index (BMI) and the ideal one of college students. Among them, male students expect to be taller (88.9%) and fatter (79.8%) which is consistent with the research abroad (Ps: the "fatter" is a confusion of "robust" and "fat". If the numerous side-effect of obesity is truly understood, perhaps male students prefer "robust".); Female students hope to become taller (90.1%) and thinner (53.2%) (Ps: "thin" and "robust" are on the sense of fitness; the latter one is more natural and the former one is much more like the female's self-concept of aesthetic; however males prefer females fit with the beauty of "robust" in real life.) Researches show that compared with weight, height is a more crucial element determining the satisfactory towards body. Both male and female students commonly expect a taller height and the female students' hope of "becoming thinner" is mainly realized through the way of raising height. According to the investigation of random sampling of one thousand senior middle school students(five hundred boys and five hundred girls) and one thousand junior middle school students(five hundred boys and five hundred girls), there exist not a conspicuous or very remarkable gulf between the consciousness of height and figure in middle school students and students in universities and colleges(P⟩ 0.05 or P⟩ 0.01). Consequently, the consciousness of "raising height and fashioning figures" does not recede with the increase of their age during the period from junior middle school to universities when their outlook on life emerges. In daily life, middle school students, in order to achieve the goal of "raising height and fashioning figures", usually wear high—heeled shoes, eat raising height medicines, keeping diet to lose weight, and exercise and so on. But some methods of them may be not "green", as the side-effects of human bodies are obviously and hard to define at this time. However, volleyball, a natural kind of exercise is relatively "green", and it is not difficult to find out the similarities between middle school students' expectation on their body and volleyball feature effectiveness. No doubt it provides the theoretical support for middle school students' employment volleyball, a kind of "green" exercise according to their aims to raising height and fashioning figure.

As for the goal of raising students' height and fashioning their figures, the application of the curriculum reform of physical education, beyond doubt, serves as a great opportunity for the realization of this goal. The new curriculum reform of physical education is under the premise of the principles of "People first" and guided by the ideology of "Health comes first", being a radical reformation of physical classes of schools. Where the new curriculum reforms concerned, the Nation Ministry of Education and State Sport General Administration jointly issued several concerning circulars in 2002, such as "Students' Fitness Health Standard", "Standards of Full-time Compulsory Education in Ordinary High School Physical Education and Health Course (The Experimental Edition)" and " The Guiding Sketch of Physical Classes of National Universities and Colleges" (shorted for the Sketch), which mainly aims at solving the gulf between the physical education classes in elementary schools, junior middle schools and senior middle schools, bettering students' health as well. Amid all these documents, "Principles of Course in Physical Education and Health" came up with four fundamental concepts regarding to the reformation of classes about physical education, that is, adhering to the guiding ideology of "Health comes first"; prompting the well development of students; stimulating students' sport interest; cultivating the consciousness of life-long education; concentrating on students' development; paying much attention on fortifying students' foremost position; keeping eyes on individual differences and various needs; ensuring every student's benefits. Therefore it is not difficult to perceive by comparison that the special benefits of volleyball on raising height and fashioning figure and students' expectation on their own body also meet the support of the "Principles of Course in Physical Education and Health".

3.3   Affecting Matters of Realization of Volleyball Feature Effectiveness in Middle Schools

Compared to the development of basketball classed in middle schools, volleyball sports own the comparatively huge space to its development. Through research, disadvantages of realization of volleyball feature effectiveness are listed as follows: for example, students' enthusiasm for volleyball still needs improving; their learning motivation also needs cultivating; they do not have the good knowledge and practice on basic actions and techniques; they badly lack courts and facility, and so on. The number of students who really love volleyball in Guangzhou city only occupies 8.7% of the total number of students investigated. Only four schools have volleyball court in thirty schools inquired. And the volleyball courts have been functioned as others in seven schools of them. There also exists great insufficiency of facilities. The top four favorite sport kinds of students are respectively basketball, badminton, football and volleyball, which is in the fourth place. Students who love volleyball occupy 28.6% of all students surveyed in Changde city. There are all together forty-six courts in nine schools, so every school has five in average. However, volleyball is located still in the fourth place after basketball, badminton and table-tennis in students' after-class activities. Both the above places belong to the comparatively developed places, and so volleyball class is developed preferably well, but volleyball still locates in the fourth place, and students' likeness in it is relatively low. Peeping one spot, and one can see the complete picture. Thereby the condition in other places is no pleasant. The writer of the present paper, by enquiring the physical education classes in the southern part of Shanxi Province, Handan city of Hebei Province, Beibei county of Chongqi city, comes to a conclusion that the general provision of volleyball classes in middle schools is indeed relatively weak, which is the potent evidence and addition for the above premise. Moreover, via investigations of the random samplings of some freshmen's mastership of volleyball in Chongqi's universities and colleges, more than ninety percent of students cannot even master digging volleyball-one of the most fundamental technique of volleyball. The contemporary conditional also verifies the above premise. In a word, it is much probable that the general provision of volleyball in middle schools is weak, which on the other hand, reflects the grand space of its development.

3.4 Accesses for Promoting the Realization of Volleyball Feature Effectiveness in Middle Schools

Formulation and Unification of the Consciousness of Volleyball Feature Effectiveness. Volleyball feature effectiveness, a highlighting function of volleyball sports, relies on the support of the new curriculum reform of physical education. Leaders of the new curriculum reform of physical education play a decisive role, where the development of it is concerned. And the mastership of physical education teachers and the logistic guarantee (provision of courts and facilities included) function as a bridge in the applications of its feature effectiveness. At last, students' understanding of awareness of volleyball feature effectiveness decides the retention of its after-class effectiveness. Therefore it is easy to perceive that the formulation of volleyball feature effectiveness concerns the unification of several ideologies, including leaders of the new class reformation, physical education teachers and practitioners, providers of logistic guarantee(containing headmasters and the decision layer of schools), and beneficiaries of volleyball feature effectiveness(students). That obviously compose a resonance system of volleyball feature effectiveness, and the declination of any one layer in it will restrain other parts. And in this process, leaders of the new curriculum reform should bear the responsibility of dredging and connecting the feature effectiveness.

The effective teaching media and method of the volleyball characteristic obtained by conditions improvement
Provoking the student's interests through the material transformation of volleyball 1. The material transformation of volleyball may have effective influence on the encouraging of the student's interests. Especially the fully implement of Soft Volleyball, Gas Volleyball.etc. Since the volleyball's degree of hardness changed a lot that may increase the controllability of the ball on some degree, it also makes the entertainment of the ball stronger, at any rate, that stimulate the interests of the student to control the ball, the teacher also can request the student have more rapid reaction of the handling the volleyball's direction on the basis of the deepened interests toward the ball gradually.

 The flexibility use of the volleyball rules is conductive to promote the student's volleyball technique from easy one to difficult 2. In Middle-school's volleyball teaching goal's setting in, it is not suitable to act with undue haste. If there is the hard -like six people in the volleyball competition, the adult volleyball net is a high 2.24 meters (female) and 2.43 meters (male), then the Middle School student can use the "first rise then fall" principle when they practice smash the ball, namely, the teacher need to keep the altitude of the net in a place easy to smash the ball, then increases the net to a high altitude based on this, it can improve the student's skill gradually, then that will improve the success rates, cultivate the student's confidence and interests. Certainly, there also have other rules to make corresponding changes, such as, holding, double hit's relaxation and so on.

4 Conclusions and Suggestions

The Middle-school students attain the extremely crucial phase of the body growth. The volleyball properties benefit and the high expectation for the health condition requests the New Curriculum Reform supplied a powerful support. However, the volleyball still belonged to development "to dive the superiority" project compared to the popular item, such as, basketball, badminton of those projects are took considered. As the article shows that, if we want to transform "to dive the superiority" into "obviously the superiority" this kind of qualitative change, there need all sorts of beneficial condition to make it come true. Therefore, there have more following tips: to strengthen the enhancement of propaganda; to improve the people's cognition level toward volleyball characteristic; to enlarge the investment efforts of "Soft Volleyball" and "Gas Volleyball"; to improve the teacher's teaching skill; To develop more volleyball competitions among the schools or at the campus to activate the campus volleyball culture.

Acknowledgments. The research was funded by "2009 the project granted by special funs of the basic scientific research operation cost from Southwest University Chongqing", China (Grant No. SWU0909676).

References

1. Ruihua, H., Shanbin, L.: To Analysis the Games in Application and Utilization of the Middle School's Teaching Project. China Education Innovation Herald 471, 202–205 (2007)
2. Feng, L.: A Present Study on the Developing of Chang De Middle School's Volleyball Game. Journal of Huaihua College 28, 134 (2009)
3. Tonghui, L.: Research on the Actuality of Developing the Volleyball Games among the Middle School Students in Guangzhou Hubei Radio and Television University Journal. 7(28), 157 (2008)
4. Songping, Z., Xia, H.: The Exercise Therapy to Accelerate Growth. Chengdu Sports College Newspaper 2(19), 94 (1993)
5. Congshu, Z., Chen, L.: Investigation on Degree of Satisfaction toward the College Student's Body and Weight. China Journal of Health Psychology 8(17), 979 (2009)
6. Huncheng, Z., Ruike, L.: A Present Analysis the Teacher's Teaching Ideology Since the Implement of Sketch and New Curriculum among the Middle school and Primary School Student. Sports and Science 1(28), 85 (2007)
7. Yong, Z.: Study on the Standard of Carrying out the New Curriculum. People (middle) 10, 12 (2008)

Operation Patterns of Chinese Commercial Real Estate: Based on Value Chain Theory

QiXue Kang

School of Economics and Management, Beijing Forestry University, Beijing, China
kangqixue631@163.com

Abstract. This paper gives the model of the value chain of commercial real estate. On the background of the development of Chinese commercial real estate, we analyze the three main operation patterns: entire-sale, entire-lease and sale-leaseback. Conditioned on analysis of the importance and shortage of different patterns, the conclusions and policy applications are put forward.

Keywords: Operation pattern, commercial real estate, value chain theory.

1 Introduction

The purpose of this paper is to probe the operation models of commercial real estate and the value chain. The concept of value chain was first put forward by Michael E. Porter in his book The Competitive Advantage of Nations in 1985. Since then, the theory of value chain has been applied in different fields. The value chain of commercial real estate is composed with complex principals. In China the commercial real estate is on the stage of diversification. Niechong and Fangyaojing (2007) mention the difference between commercial and residential real estate and then the pattern of value chain. Liyangdi (2007) and Gaoguangzhi (2004) analyzed the relationship between developers and commerce tenants. Wudeyun (2004) and Liubo (2009) described typical cases about their operation patterns. Up till now, researches on the patterns of commercial real estate grounded on the theory of value chain are deficient.

The paper proceeds as follows. Second 2 is devoted to building the model of the value chain of commercial real estate. The different patterns of commercial real estate such as entire-sale, entire-lease and sale-leaseback would be analyzed in second 3. Finally, the main conclusions would be delineated.

2 Model of the Value Chain of Commercial Real Estate

2.1 Main Principals

Commercial real estate covers the features of both real estate and commerce. The different principals that consist of developer, investor, operator, commercial tenant and consumer interact and make up the value chain of commercial real estate. On the

M. Zhou (Ed.): ISAEBD 2011, Part IV, CCIS 211, pp. 381–387, 2011.

whole, all the values by different principals can be classified into two: commerce value created by consumers, operator and commercial tenant and property value created by developer, owners or investors and operator.

2.2 Model of Value Delivery

Fig.1 shows the value delivery net of commercial real estate.

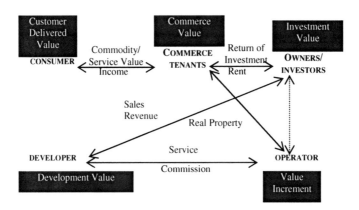

Fig. 1. Value Chain of Commercial Real Estate

As Fig.1 shows above, one commercial real estate is developed by its developer. The delivery of real right to owners or investors generates development value. Investors or owners get investment value when the value of the real property increases. Generally speaking, operator is hired to manage the real property so as to enhance the whole financial return. Commerce tenants rent the real estate from owners or the developer or the operator and achieve commerce value by merchandising. Consumers get customer-delivered-value when they buy commodity and service from commerce tenants.

Here we produce a value chain model which doesn't contain suppliers as the general value chain model often describes because we want to find out the pure interest flowing between the main principals. The process of the value delivery forms a longitudinal value chain. And there is no value leak when one value is transferred to another. Customer-delivered-value counts a lot because it is what customers gain from those such as commodity, service, convenient transportation and fine shopping environment. So, customer-delivered-value determines the other values. The value flowing procedure is customers→commerce tenants→operator→owners/investors→developer.

2.3 Relationship between the Two Main Values

Property value depends on commerce value as the following equation indicates.

$$V = \frac{A_1}{1+Y_1} + \frac{A_2}{(1+Y_2)^2} + \cdots + \frac{A_n}{(1+Y_n)^n} \tag{1}$$

Here, V is property value. A is net income which would be rental receipts or income from joint operation. Y is yield rate. It can be seen that when Y is fixed, the higher rental receipts or operation income comes with the higher property value.

3   The Operation Patterns of Commercial Real Estate

Primarily speaking, there are three patterns of commercial real estate. In order to cash out timely, developers invariably sell the commercial real estate by segments to investors. It is the pattern of entire-sale. Entire-lease pattern fits the traits of commercial real estate because the profit is caught not by sale but by long-term operation. Most of the time, the ownership and the right of operation and management which is crucial are detached. Sale-leaseback falls into between the other two patterns.

3.1   Development of Commercial Real Estate in China

With the breakthrough of real estate commercialization in 1998, the entire-sale pattern of commercial real estate massively turned up. Since 2004 when retail industry was overall open, the development of commercial real estate has been developing in swift and violent way. Meanwhile, the financing channels are narrow for developers. Additionally, professional operation and management of commercial real estate is not well. So entire-sale is still the dominating pattern. At the same time, along with experience of operation and management being richer and richer, the patterns of entire-lease and sale-leaseback grow up.

Fig.2 shows the sales and investment of Chinese commercial real estate over years. In recent years, the amount of capital investment and average price of commercial real estate have been keeping uptrend. While the trend line of saleable area of commercial real estate presents shape of parabola before 2008 and sharp rise after 2008. The

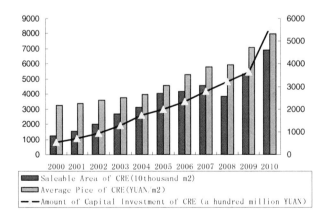

Fig. 2. Sales and Investment of Chinese Commercial Real Estate over Years
Data Sources: Statistical Bureau of China

tendency of these three indexes implies diversification of the operation patterns of commercial real estate with entire-sale still the main pattern. More and more developers such as WANDA are inclined to entire-lease. These had promoted the slow increase or even decrease of the saleable area of commercial real estate between 2005 and 2008. On the background of the financial crisis from 2008, commercial real estate which is less risky than other industries has caught more attention from developers. Some of them are involved in commercial real estate for the first time and apply entire-sale pattern due to little experience of last-stage operation. That is why the saleable area and the amount of capital investment of commercial real estate appear the sharp rise since 2008.

3.2 Pattern of Entire-Sale

Strictly speaking, different from residential real estate, before doing business, a commercial real estate which has been completely constructed is still semi-production. Entire-sale is the pattern that the commercial real estate is sold like house though it is just semi-production. Invariably, developers break down the property right into segments and sell them to different investors and get back their capital investment rapidly. The ignorance of the last-stage operation and management produces results of out-of-order development, in adaptation of produce function and service function to the needs of merchandising enterprises and then the impeded increase in value of commercial real estate.

The following figure (Fig.3) shows the mechanism of entire-sale pattern.

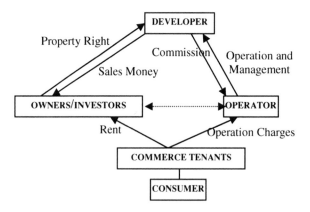

Fig. 3. The Mechanism of the Entire-Sale Pattern of Commercial Real Estate

When developers apply the pattern of entire-sale, they would sell the property to owners or investors for earning sales money and would organize operator to canvass commerce tenants in at first stage. On the stage when the real estate has been sold and the developer is off, the owners may cancel the employment relationship with the designated operator. That is why dotted line between owners or investors and operator is used in Fig.3.

Commercial risk can be reduced by recovering investment money quickly in pattern of entire-sale. But since there are too much small property owners, it is not impossible to unify their suggestions. The lack of unified management leads to lower commerce quality. Without unified plan, multiple function of the real estate can't come true. Without unified marketing spread plan, the maximum profit of tenant can't be got. Without unified operation and management, the maximum commercial value and property value can not be achieved.

3.3 The Pattern of Entire-Lease

There are small number of property owners, usually the developer and its sponsor, in the pattern of entire-lease. They get high rent or partial merchandising income from long-term operation. As customer-delivered-value attaches more importance to developers, the realization of property value is related with the beginning link of the value chain. So, the pattern of entire-lease makes the value chain an organic whole and provide persistent cash flow to the developer. Relatively speaking, because of many risks and slow yield, this operation pattern requires highly rich capital strength and highly perfect operation capacity.

There are two types in the pattern of entire-lease: self-restraint operation and committed operation. With self-restraint operation pattern, developers would transform themselves into operators. As there are no small investors or owners, a developer is both owner and operator. In committed operation pattern, a developer would entrust professional teams to canvass business orders and professional operators for well business. A developer is the property owner and gets rental income.

The pattern of entire-lease is the trend of commercial real estate because the value of different principals in the value chain is accomplished through long-term and professional operation. With long-term market plan and position, the customer-delivered-value orientation is established. With unity of management, service and marketing spread, commerce tenants can profit from the save of cost and increase of income. With long-term operation, developers can gain rather good rent return. Though there are many advantages by using this pattern, there is highly requirement for nearly perfect operation capacity and capital strength which few developers can live up to.

3.4 The Pattern of Sale-Leaseback

When developers sell commercial real estate to owners or investors, they promise them to rent their real properties by some yield rate in due time. During the period of time, the professional operator would be hired and return income to the owners or investors. In deadline of leaseback, the market would have been developed and developers retreat. In this way, both developer and property owners win the commerce market for the developer can withdraw its capital investment in short term and the owners can obtain commercial real properties with mature market.

Fig.4 shows the relationship between different pricipals in this pattern.

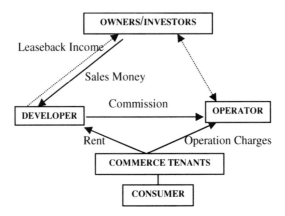

Fig. 4. The Mechanism of the Sale-LeaseBack Pattern of Commercial Real Estate

There are two pairs of relationship in the chain: seller-buyer and tenant-lessor. The buyers or the owners are lessors and the seller or the developer, the tenant. When developers finish selling the property, they lease back the real estate from owners and correspondingly pay leaseback return to them. As the same time, the developers would hire professional operators and pay commission to them. This pattern comprises two types in reality: financing sale-leaseback and operating sale-leaseback. The difference between them is that the developers would repurchase the property in the former type, but no repurchase agreement in the latter.

On the basis of income approach, the price of commercial real estate can be described as following equation.

$$V = \sum_{t=1}^{n} \frac{R_0 + R_1}{(1+r)^t} + \frac{P}{(1+r)^n} . \tag{2}$$

Here, V is property value. r is discount rate. R_0 is developer's rental return. R_1 is the leaseback return to the owners. P is residue value at the deadline of leaseback.

Leaseback agreement is always the marketing tool of developers in selling the property. As developers have gained their profit from owners, many of them don't care about the business of owners and their tenants. So, it is risky for owners or investors to buy such commercial real estate when the developer violates his promise. Further more, there are too many property owners who cannot reach consensus in operating and management. These lead to the long-term value loss of the commercial real estate.

4 Conclusions and Policy Applications

We have presented the model of value chain of commercial real estate. On the basis of the model, the three patterns of commercial real estate were analyzed. On the whole, professional and unified operation is central to commercial real estate. Undoubtedly, entire-lease pattern is the ultimate trend. As most of developers in

China can't afford the abundant funds requested for in the application of this pattern, diversified financial tools and wider channel are needed.

It has taken no more than 30 years for Chinese developers to develop commercial real estate. On the background of complex factors, the entire-sale pattern is yet the most important one for most of developers. Because of interest decentralization of numerous and small owners, agglomeration of business can't act. Therefore, both the commerce value and property value can't be accomplished. This pattern is suitable for small-scale development which has little requirement for professional operation.

For the sake of the deficiency of entire-sale pattern, the pattern of sale-leaseback turns up. As a transitory pattern, sale-leaseback pattern is applied by more and more developers. In this case, there should be complete regulations to safeguard the interest of different principals in the value chain and guarantee the realization of commerce value and property value.

References

1. Brown, R.K.: Tax Considerations in Sale-Leaseback Transactions. Appraisal Journal (10), 562–568 (1969)
2. Rutherford, R.C.: Empirical Evidence on Shareholder Value and the Sale-Leaseback of Corporate Real Estate. Journal of the American Real Estate (4), 522–528 (1990)
3. Chao, G.: Status of Business Area in Urban Development. Shanghai Business (2), 10–11 (2009)
4. Chen, J.: Analysis on the Value Chain of Commercial Real Estate. Modern Business (9), 39–40 (2009)
5. Wang, L.: the Differentiation between Commercial Real Estate and Residential Real Estate. Productivity Research (17), 120–122 (2008)
6. Weng, N., Lin, P.: Operation Pattern of Commercial Real Estate. Commercial Times (24), 27–28 (2006)

The Researches on Some Questions about the Same Structure of Industries

Fan Liu

Dept. of Economics and Management, Jiangsu Teachers University of Technology,
Changzhou, China

Abstract. The author measured the same structure degree with the structure familiar coefficient and the division degree with the structure difference index of the manufacture industry in Yangtze delta in this article. Based on my analysis I got the special data about the negative relation between structure familiar and structure difference, at the same time, I got the exact data about the relation between structure coincide degree and structure difference degree, and defined a basic numerical value to judge the same structure degree. According to my analysis, I think the same structure degree of the manufacture industry is dropping and the division degree is rising in Yangtze delta area in recent years.

Keywords: Yangtze delta; manufacture industry; same structure; division.

1 Introduction

In recent years, the question about the same structure of the manufacture industry in Yangtze delta is paid more attention by the personalities of various circles. And a lot of scholars put in time and energy to study the reasons of the same structure to compose, the methods to measure the same structure, the effect of the same structure and how to deal with it etc. and all of the positive results of the study made the people realize the question more and more science and reasonable. As a matter of fact, the division degree is the very important coefficient to indicate the close degree of economic connection and integration between the different areas but a lot of scholars ignored the question. I think, it is very necessary for us to study the division degree and its changing tendency and judge the relation between structure and division when we try to discuss the question about the same structure, especially for the Yangtze river delta area, because the members of the area are putting their best to achieve the economic integration.

2 About the Method to Measure the Same Structure

The same structure means the same or familiar degree if we compare the two different areas in the field of manufacture industry. Based on the industry structure theory, the narrow sense of the industry structure indicates the composition of the trades and their mutual relation. And in the real studying, the mutual relation indicates the proportion relation among the various trades in the manufacture industry. So, to measure the same

M. Zhou (Ed.): ISAEBD 2011, Part IV, CCIS 211, pp. 388–393, 2011.
© Springer-Verlag Berlin Heidelberg 2011

structure degree is to measure the same or familiar degree of the proportion relation among the various trades in manufacture industry. We can use the structure familiar coefficient and the structure coincide index to measure its familiar or same degree.

2.1 Structure Familiar Coefficient

The method is offered by the international industry studying center of UN, and it is used to reflect the industry same structure degree by measuring the familiar degree of the industry in different areas. The formula to count the same structure is following

$$S_{ij} = \sum_{k=1}^{n} (X_{ik} X_{jk}) \Big/ \sqrt{\sum_{k=1}^{n} X_{ik}^2 \cdot \sum_{j=1}^{n} X_{jk}^2} \tag{1}$$

About the parameters of the formula: Sij means the structure familiar coefficient; i, j means the two different areas to be compared; n means how many trades are included in the manufacture industry, and k = 1, 2, …, n; Xik means the proportion of the number k trade is in total industry in area i; Xjk Means the proportion of the number k trade is in the total manufacture industry in area j.

2.2 Structure Coincide Degree Index

The structure coincide reflects the coincide degree of the industry structure in different areas, and it is got by reforming the export structure familiar index offered by Finger and Kiernan. The formula is following

$$SSI_{ij} = \sum_{k=1}^{n} \min(X_{ik}, X_{jk}) \tag{2}$$

About the parameters of the formula, SSIij means the structure coincide degree index and the other parameters is same as formula (1). Based on the math implication, SSIij is to get the least number value that the same trade proportion in two different areas first, and it means to get the "common portion", and it reflects the coincide degree of the single trade and to get the total coincide degree of the manufacture industry in the different areas by adding the related parameters. So, the index can be used to measure the same structure degree of the different areas.

The value of Sij and SSIij is between 0 and 1, the manufacture industry structure is total different in two areas if the value is 0; it is all same in two areas if the value is 1. And the value trends more to 1 the situation is to indicate the manufacture structure in two areas trends more to same. And the above is to examine the question of the manufacture structure by static state angle. If we take the trend angle, we can check the changing situation of the manufacture industry in special period of the special time and to make the correct judgment based on the related numbers. Example, if the value of Sij and SSIij trends to rise, it indicates that the manufacture structure in these areas trends to "same", and if the value of them trends to drop, it indicates that the manufacture structure in these areas trends to "difference".

3 The Method to Measure the Division

I take the method, offered by Paul Kerugma, measuring the difference degree index in different areas to measure the different division in various areas. The formula is follow

$$SI_{ij} = \sum_{k=1}^{n} \left| X_{ik} - X_{jk} \right| \qquad (3)$$

About the parameters of the formula: SIij means the structure difference degree index and the other parameters is same as formula (1); The value of the index is between 0 and 2, if the trade structure is all same in two areas, the value is 0 and if the trade structure is all different in two areas, the value is 2 (because all of the industry portion of every area is added.), and the bigger value indicates the more difference of the trade structure in different areas.

4 The Relation between Same Structure and Division

4.1 The Measurement about the Structure Familiar Degree, Structure Coincide Degree and Structure Difference Degree of the Manufacture Industry in Yangtze Delta

According to the national trade classification standard issued by national statistical bureau, the manufacture industry is belonged to a special category and the category includes the large, medium and small scale industries. But all of the public reference

Table 1. The Measuring Result about the Same Structure and Division Degree of Manufacture Industry in Yangtze Delta

age	Structure familiar degree	Structure coincide degree	Structure difference degree
1990	0.914	0.771	0.458
1991	0.919	0.785	0.430
1992	0.915	0.780	0.440
1993	0.907	0.773	0.454
1994	0.922	0.806	0.388
1995	0.930	0.814	0.372
1996	0.894	0.804	0.392
1997	0.882	0.805	0.390
1998	0.831	0.792	0.416
1999	0.837	0.789	0.422
2000	0.875	0.816	0.368
2001	0.851	0.799	0.402
2002	0.865	0.806	0.388
2003	0.859	0.799	0.402
2004	0.861	0.795	0.410
2005	0.851	0.786	0.428
2006	0.829	0.767	0.466
2007	0.822	0.765	0.470
2008	0.805	0.748	0.504

(example, the statistic almanac issued by the different areas) only issued the data of the category and large trades and lack the information about the medium and small scale industries. Additional, the specific of the structure familiar coefficient, structure coincide index and structure difference index is that we can not count the same structure degree or division degree of the top industry unless we can master the information of the lower industry. Limited by the source of the reference and the measuring method, the main question I studied and certified in this article is about the category. Based on the methods to measure the same structure and division, I counted the same structure degree, structure coincide degree and structure difference degree of the manufacture in Yangtze delta and the time included from 1990 to 2008. The result is demonstrated in table1.

I'd like to illustrate that the data of the table is counted based on the formulas and the original data come from the different magazines like Jiangsu statistical almanac, Zhejiang statistical almanac and Shanghai statistical almanac, and the special procession is to count the structure familiar coefficients every year between Jiangsu and Zhejiang, Jiangsu and Shanghai, Zhejiang and Shanghai first, and then to get the average value of the three coefficients and the average value represent the structure familiar of all manufacture industry in Yangtze delta. And I got the other two indexes with the same way.

4.2   Relation Analysis about the Structure Familiar Degree and the Structure Difference Degree

Based on the table1, we can find that the least value structure familiar of the manufacture industry in Yangtze delta is 0.805 in the examining period, and the largest value is 0.930, extreme difference is 0.125. The absolute value is in the higher level although the change is small in over the years. So we can get the result that the same structure of the manufacture industry in Yangtze delta is in the higher level if we only check the situation with the category angle. The least value of the structure difference degree is 0.368 and the largest value is 0.568, the extreme difference is 0.2. So, we can get another result that the structure difference degree fluctuates more than the structure familiar, but its absolute value is in the lower level.

With the trend angle, the fluctuation of the structure familiar taken a procession from rising and dropping, and the change of the structure difference degree is negative, its fluctuation is from dropping to rising. According to my counting, the Pearson related coefficient is -0.372, and the Spearman related coefficient is -0.489 and the former is not very notable if its level is 5%, but the later is very notable if its level is 5%. So we can deduce that the negative relation indeed exists between the structure familiar and the structure difference of the manufacture industry in Yangtze delta. But what quantity relationship existing between the two indexes needs us to make more study and discussion. Because of this, we should take the regression analysis method to get the correct result.

$$\Delta Y_t = \alpha_0 + \alpha_1 t + \alpha_2 Y_{t-1} + \sum_{i=1}^{k} \beta_{t-i} \Delta Y_{t-i} + \mu_t \qquad (4)$$

For avoiding the falsehood regression, I checked the smooth of the two group numbers first because all of the numbers in this article is time list. To judge whether or not the time list is smooth, we can take the method of unit radical, and the popular unit radical to be used is ADF(Augmented Dickey-Fuller Test), and the basic principle of the test method is to use n times different value to make the no-smooth list change to the smooth list. The special method is estimating regression formula.

About the parameters of the formula, α_0 means constant, t means time trend, k means lag class number (the best lag unit), μ_t means deficient difference unit. The test 0 suppose is $H_0 : \alpha_0 = 0$; the reserve suppose is $H_1 : \alpha_0 \neq 0$ and if the value of the ADF of α_2 is bigger than the critical value, the former suppose H0 will be refused and H1 will be accepted, the situation indicates that Y_t dost not exist unit radical and it is the smooth list. If the situation is negative, it indicates that the unit radical exists and it is not the smooth list, and it needs to test again. The goal to add the k lag class numbers is to make the deficient difference unit be without noise.

If S_t indicates the structure familiar of the manufacture industry in Yangtze delta in t years, and SI_t indicates the structure difference of the manufacture industry in Yangtze delta in t years, we can use the above basic model test to check the unit radical of S_t and SI_t , the result is showed in table2.

Table 2. The ADF Test Result for St, and SIt

variable	ADF test value	5% level critical value	conclusion
S_t	-1.1311	-3.0114	No-smooth
SI_t	-1.5959	-3.0114	No-smooth
$D (S_t)$	-3.6031	-3.0199	smooth
$D (SI_t)$	-5.1157	-3.0199	smooth

Critical value, the result is that the two lists are no-smooth. But after adjusting, the values become -3.6031 and -5.1157, the value is smaller than 5% horizontal critical value and the situation indicates that the two lists are smooth. The two lists are one class and single total. Based on the knowledge of time list metrology economy, for the two no-smooth time lists, their linear combination may be smooth if they are same single total class number. It means that it is possible to qualify the coordinate relationship between them. And it can avoid the mistakes when we take them to the linear regression if they qualify the coordinate relationship.

5 Conclusion

Although we can get the conclusion that the same structure and the division exist the negative relationship no matter we use any indexes to count the same structure of the manufacture industry, the high-level same structure degree indicates that the division degree is lower in the area and it indicates that the economic integration degree is not very high.

References

1. Xueqing, J.: Analysis about the same structure tendency of the manufacture industry in Yangtze delta. Reform (2), 48–52 (2004)
2. Jianjun, C.: Analysis about the same structure and structure position in Yangtze delta area. Manufacture economy of China (2), 19–26 (2004)

Policy Proposals on Promoting the Development of "Guanzhong—Tianshui Economic Zone"

Yuhong Liu[1] and Xin-an Wang[2]

[1] School of Economics
[2] Business school, Xi'an University of Finance and Economics, 710061 Xi'an, China
lunwen200807@163.com

Abstract. Located in the center of Eurasia Continental Bridge, Guanzhong and Tianshui play a centrally leading role in coordinating regional development. "Guanzhong—Tianshui Economic Zone" has practical significance in strengthening self-development capacity, enhancing their own internal function, integrating innovation resources, gathering innovation elements and establishing advantage-prominent regional innovation system. While the basic role of market is given the full play in allocating resources, the policy support and reform and improvement of system play a key role in coordinating various scientific and technological resources. The macro-strategy for promoting the development of "Guanzhong—Tianshui Economic Zone" has been put forward in terms of fiscal and taxation policy, investment and financing policy, "Agriculture, Countryside and Farmer Issues" and industrial policy.

Keywords: Guanzhong—Tianshui Economic Zone, economic growth, innovation of regional system, policy proposals.

1 Fiscal and Taxation Policy

1.1 Optimize the Policy on Fiscal Spending

Strengthen fiscal support and optimize the developing environment of economic zone. Since the Guanzhong—Tianshui economic zone is weak in its infrastructure, the government should strengthen its fiscal support in hardware environment input and software environment input to key industries, key fields, eco-industrial parks, major technical fields and major projects in economic zone such as environmental infrastructure industry, major water conservancy project and rising high-tech recycling industry which are strong in externality, high in industrial correlation and occupy the exemplary and leading place, while the basic role of market is given the full play in allocating resources.

Broaden fiscal financing channels and improve the service efficiency of funds. Adhere to the principle of giving the guiding role to fiscal funds, giving the basic role to the market operation and encouraging the participation of multiple investors; change the previous direct fiscal investment; adopt finance discount, financial subsidies, investment in shares, injection of capitals and loan guarantee; vigorously

M. Zhou (Ed.): ISAEBD 2011, Part IV, CCIS 211, pp. 394–400, 2011.
© Springer-Verlag Berlin Heidelberg 2011

broaden sources and channels of capital for economic zone development; energetically channel and encourage all circles of the society to participate in investment of funds; put focus on gaining preferential loans from financial agencies such as China Development Bank, China Construction Bank and the Agricultural Bank of China; expand the scale in use of foreign funds; zealously channel the input of the non-government fund, investment from eastern region in particular; actively expand the input scale of loans of the World Bank, loans of foreign government and treasury bonds in the economic zone; work hard for gaining finance from central government to establish economic development funds and gather the finance to support major infrastructure and industrial projects which play the key role in the region.

Strengthen support for technical advance of medium-sized and small enterprises. Establish and improve the system for supporting the technical advance of medium-sized and small enterprises as well as the laws and regulations favorable to promote the development of medium-sized and small enterprises to provide the system guarantee for the technical innovation of medium-sized and small enterprises. Government can strengthen the support for technical advance of medium-sized and small enterprises by tax preference, fiscal investment and financing and government procurement. In order to promote the technical progress of medium-sized and small enterprises, functional departments of government may provide the support for these enterprises with informational service, training for technical personnel and other services.

Support development of farmer specialized cooperative and leading enterprise in agricultural industrialization. Accelerate the building-up of integrated urban and rural development network and information service system and develop the rural intermediary organization and service sector; formulate the "Green Box Policy" to support and protect the agricultural development and establish and improve the relief subsidies for natural disaster, investment subsidies for adjustment in structure of agricultural production and subsidies for regional development.

Strengthen the financial supervision. Implement interest subsidy system, subsidy system and bidding system of engineering projects as well as budget and settlement system of project capital; detail the budgeting of projects by strictly observing the available budget account, carry out annual budget and rolling budget for major projects and strictly prepare and render the final accounting reports. Carry out the treasury single account system. Use the platform of "GFMIS" to directly pay the financial funds in intensive manner and establish the fund information system and fund monitoring network. Establish examination and approval procedures of fund use strictly, strengthen the supervision and inspection over the management and use of funds, especially over the funds in great sum and seek to build up a set of scientific, reasonable and feasible performance appraisal system on construction capitals used for supporting Guanzhong—Tianshui development fiscally.

1.2 Adjust the Structure of Tax Preferential Policy

In terms of tax policy, the central government may consider to grant the following supports: increment and sharing can be carried out in duty of "Guanzhong—Tianshui Economic Zone" to support the construction of infrastructure such as border ports, harbors, airport and railway. Set up "Guanzhong—Tianshui" bonded zone, develop businesses including international transfer, international distribution, international procurement, international switch trade and export processing following operational models of free port, international hub port and free trade zone, carry out the policies such as port bonded for foreign stock keeper, tax-deductible port for domestic stock keeper and tax-free for processed products in the port. The enterprises in the economic zone can be granted with reduction of income tax of 10% within 10 years. Work hard to gain the preferential tax policy for Guanzhong—Tianshui economic zone from central government.

1.3 Adjust the Distribution Policy of Non-tax Revenue Properly

Put forward reform of tax distribution system and improve the local fiscal system; divide the fiscal power of government of different levels, explore debt financing system of local government, provide fully steady sources of fiscal revenue for local government in the economic zone and lighten the dependence of local government on non-tax revenue. Meanwhile, make a reasonable comprehensive financial budget to meet the reasonable spending needs of departments, achieve the separation of incomes and expenses in real terms and cut off the relation between non-tax revenue and interests of departments.

1.4 Improve System of Transfer Payment

Put forward legislation for transfer payment; standardize specialized transfer payment system and implement fiscal management reform such as immediate control of provincial-level departments over the county-level departments and fiscal management of county and township; make greater efforts to carry out standardized transfer payment; annul the return of tax completely when the economy develops to a certain level and system is sophisticated; continue to optimize the structure, increase general fiscal transfer payment to financially-weak rural area of Tianshui economic zone; transfer part of lending capitals of national bonds of public projects to appropriate funds and increase the medical service subsidies to low-income groups and elderly people in the economic zone; enhance the efforts in transfer payment subsidy in Guanzhong—Tianshui economic zone. The central financial department shall return the part of Four Kinds of Taxes which is allocated to central government from economic zone. The decrease in income of local government and increase in expenditure of local government resulted from the resources conservation, the issue brought along with West-East natural gas transmission Project, should be subsidized by the central and provincial-level financial departments by general transfer payment.

2 Investment and Financial Policy

2.1 Vigorously Introduce Financial Institution and Establish Guanzhong—Tianshui Development Bank

Integrate local financial resources and actively promote the merger and restructure of urban commercial banks and urban credit cooperatives; promote the development of new rural financial institution and try to establish rural banks and fund mutual cooperatives. Support the reform and restructure of urban commercial banks in economic zone, vigorously develop the local financial agencies and work hard for preferential loans from international financial organizations, Asian development banks and foreign governments by integrating property and introducing strategic cooperative agency. Try to establish Guanzhong—Tianshui industry investment funds and entrepreneurial venture investment funds and support competitive industries and prop enterprises to issue bonds and seek financing by listing on the stock market; encourage the development of private financial institutions and establish micro-credit companies, guarantors and pawn companies to increase the support in medium-sized and small enterprises financially.

2.2 Innovation of Financing Methods

Develop innovation investment and equity investment; develop loan transaction of medium-sized and small private enterprises and micro-credit operations of farmers; actively develop debt financing tools such as corporate bonds, short-term financing bills and medium-term note; encourage the investment of equity fund in enterprises and projects where the resources can be recycled, encourage the investment of social funds by means of equity participation and financial claim in industries where the resources can be recycled, channel the social fund to set up venture investment of enterprises and projects where the resources can be recycled; reform issue of new shares; improve restriction mechanism for enquiry and subscription offer to further form pricing mechanism of market, optimize issue mechanism on line, separate the participants for subscription on line and off line and cap the individual subscription account on line and strengthen the risk reminder of new share subscription.

2.3 Improve the Establishment of Financing Platform Actively

Support the establishment of demonstration base for reform in coordinating scientific and technological resources in Xian, give necessary support to bases for advanced manufacturing, high-tech industry and modern agricultural high-tech industry; gradually increase input in public or public-based project constructions in fields including rural infrastructure, ecology protection and social programs and abolish or reduce supporting funds at the county level and below; enhance the efforts in attracting investment, give priority to enterprises outside the zone, especially competitive industries and energy-saving and environmental protection programs of economic zones invested by the western enterprises in terms of project approval and authorization on the even ground; allow and encourage non-government funds to participate in restructure of the state-own assets by equity participation, share holding, merger and acquisition following national policies and regulations.

2.4 Strengthen the Prudential Oversight over Finance

Guard against potential systematic risks caused by the financial market-cross or field-cross development, pay close attention to study on establishing and improving frame of prudential oversight, develop macro-oversight tools, study on furthering provisions and fund requirements for upwind loan loss, keep the financial system steady and promote the stable and sustainable development of economy by enhancing market-cross and industry-across comprehensive oversight; establish the new mobile injection mechanism, establish national quick response mechanism to emergent financial risks; pay attention to the off-site inspection of off-site inspection, intensifying risk-based inspection, keep a watchful on the key issues and improve the regulation system.

2.5 Pilot Projects for Cross-Border Trade Settlement in RMB

In order to conform to the demands of markets and enterprises at home and abroad and keep the normal trade development between Guanzhong—Tianshui economic zone and its neighborhood and create more favorable environment for enterprises, the settlement for the cross-border trade in RMB can be started by learning the experience of South-East Asian Nations as well as borrowing ideas from the decision of the State Council made in April 8th, 2009 that the pilot projects for cross-border trade settlement in RMB were first started in Shanghai and four cities of Guangdong provinces, i.e., Guangzhou, Shenzhen, Zhuhai and Donguan and this pilot projects would be carried out in the such area outside the border as Hong Kong and Macao for the time being.

3 "Agriculture, Countryside and Farmer Issues"

3.1 Energetically Develop County Economy and Labor Economy

Integrate training resources, establish employment training base for transfer of rural labor in Xian and Tianshui with existing agencies and facilities, intensify the training for capability of rural labor in transferring employment and starting business; make even greater efforts in implementing training projects for rural labor transfer; actively exploit the labor market, support the development of labor intermediary organizations, strengthen the coordination between the labor import and export regions, vigorously build the labor brand; encourage the farmers to transfer their jobs in the neighborhood, support the improvement of farmers' pioneer parks and support the migrant workers to return their hometown to start their own business; strengthen the guarantee for the rights and interests of migrant workers, accelerate the reform of household registration system and actively research and formulate the plans for transferring the farmers with stable jobs and permanent residence to urban households.

3.2 Establish Permanent Mechanism for Sustained and Stable Development of Grains

The grain producing areas of Guanzhong—Tianshui economic zone can be divided into core area, non-core area of main grain production, non-major country of main grain production, reserve area and other areas; transfer developing manners in terms of basic conditions, level of equipment and technical progress to continuously enhance the comprehensive grain production capacity, anti-risk capability, international competitiveness and sustainability, to protect and arouse the initiative of farmers in planting grains and further to promote the steady increase in output of grains; improve the market environment for the flow of agricultural products, strengthen the green channel construction, standardize and improve the forward market of agricultural products, establish perfect immediate subsidy system of agricultural finance and use the supporting measures for protecting the price of agricultural prices reasonably.

3.3 Establish Protecting System for Rights and Interests of Migrant Workers

Eliminate and abolish all the discriminative and restricted policies to the migrant workers who will reside in the city permanently , introduce protecting policies for their rights and interests, properly resolve issues such as industrial injury, medical care, unemployment, support of the aged and household register; establish state-led mechanism for rural infrastructure construction, accelerate the development of irrigation and water conservancy facility and promote the development of rural roads, improve disaster prevention and reduction system, enhance the disaster resistant capability of grain production, strengthen the development of agricultural ecology and environment protection system, conserve water and soil resources, prevent and control widespread pollution from the overuse of fertilizers and pesticides in rural area and improve the warehouse and logistics system of grains.

4 Industrial Policies

4.1 Give Priority to Fostering and Strengthening Competitive Industries

With the advantages of Guanzhong—Tianshui economic zone, adjust industrial layout, optimize industrial structure, accelerate the promotion of major industries such as petrochemical industries, energy processing and processing of grains, oils and foodstuffs, tourism and logistics, vigorously support processing of electronic information industry, logistics base construction, convert the potential resource advantage and location advantage into external economic advantage and competitive advantage and promote the rapid rising of Guanzhong—Tianshui economic zone.

4.2 Put Focus on "Integration between Military and Civilian"

In Guanzhong—Tianshui economic zone, military technology resources play the most part in technology resources. Thus, it is imperative to integrate military and industrial science and technology resources and civil science and technology resources. As for the western region, defense security comes first and it is needed to integrate the economic development goal with defense security goal as well as the economic development strategy with defense development strategy so this base is also needed. First, strengthen and expand the equipment manufacturing industry of "integration between military and civilian" and then extend to manufacturing industry. Once the base is set up, "integration between military and civilian" will become the only advantage and feature of western region. With its feature, it will occupy an important position correspondingly in the country. With such banner set up, "integration between military and civilian" programs and enterprises all over the country or even all over the world will be attracted to invest in the zone.

4.3 Strictly Enforce Market Access Rules

Strengthen the appraisal on environmental influence of industry program of economic zone; programs failing to pass environment appraisal and approval are not allowed to be started and developed; manufacturing enterprises failing to meet the emission standard of pollution or exceed the aggregate indicators of pollutants must undertake treatment within a prescribed limit of time and those enterprises failing to meet the standard within the limit must be shut down; provide and use land strictly following laws and regulations; establish departments joint information distribution system; expand and strengthen competitive state-owned enterprises in market-based way by assets reorganization, combination and merger; by aggregating income from transferring enterprise property, land grant fee of enterprises and financial budget allocation, actively raise funds for reform to specially support reform of state-owned enterprises.

References

1. Writing Group of Development Research Center in the State Council.: Key Words of China's Economy, pp. 148–201. China Development Press, Beijing (2009, 2010)
2. Wei, H.: Influence and Corresponding Strategies of China's Regional Economy on Financial Crisis. Economy and Management Research, 30–38 (April 2009)

Fiscal and Tax Policy Research on Adjustment of Industrial Structure

Yang Hongxin

Henan Polytechnic, Zhengzhou, 450046, China
yanghxin@yeah.net

Abstract. Tax policy is mainly the after-tax price by changing the product to change the product supply and demand, thereby affecting economic activities, the relationship between benefits and costs, and ultimately affect the industrial structure. Specifically, the setting is through taxes, the choice of tariff lines, the establishment of tax basis, tax rate setting, the implementation of tax incentives and other measures to make different products, different economic behavior, different companies, different industries bear different tax burdens, leading to different economic activities of the original difference in tax revenues or costs incurred due to changes in industrial structure and ultimately affect the evolution.

Keywords: Fiscal and tax policy, industrial structure, Adjustment.

1   The Tax Policy to Influence the Industrial Structure of Demand

Tax policy can change the structure of demand, while the transmission mechanism in a relatively healthy market economy, the demand structure changes will impact on the final changes in the supply industry structure.

1.1   The Tax Policy Changes Affecting the Structure of Demand among the Industrial Structure

Tax policy can influence the progress of technology directly on the raw materials, intermediate products such as the use of energy efficiency impact of the replacement of intermediate products also have an impact, thereby changing the industry's intermediate input rate and the demand structure of the intermediate products, ultimately affect the proportion of intermediate goods-based industries and its internal structure [1-2].

1.2   The Consumption Structure of Tax Policy Changes Affecting the Industrial Structure

Regulation of income distribution tax is an important policy tool, by changing the settings related to property taxes and property stock distribution of incremental condition, private consumption demand changes in the structure, and thus the industrial structure related industries affected. In addition, comparison of tax can change the price of consumer goods or consumer goods producers compare costs and make a different

M. Zhou (Ed.): ISAEBD 2011, Part IV, CCIS 211, pp. 401–407, 2011.
© Springer-Verlag Berlin Heidelberg 2011

take on different consumer goods, tax burden, thus changing the structure of consumer demand.

Meanwhile, the proportion of GDP, tax revenue, the tax burden will cause changes in national income in the private sector and government departments, the allocation pattern changes, the Government and private sector trends and consumer preferences completely different, resulting in demand for private consumption and government consumption a corresponding change in the proportion of demand structure, which led to the different structure of supply, and ultimately affect change in industrial structure [3].

1.3 The Tax Policy Changes, Thus Affecting the Structure of Investment Demand, the Industrial Structure

Tax policy can change the ratio of consumption and savings, and different tax policy can change the comparative advantage of consumption and savings, private savings preferences and marginal propensity to consume. According to the national income identity, it will affect the ratio of consumption demand and investment demand, and ultimately change the industrial structure.

Demand for private investment, the tax can change the comparative yields of different industries, affecting the private purchase of a particular preference for investment goods, thus affecting the investors in the purchase of investment goods structure. While similar, the level of tax burden can also affect the demand for private investment and government investment demand ratio, thus affecting the industrial structure [4].

2 The Impact of Tax Policy Affecting the Supply of Industrial Structure

2.1 The Tax Policy Change in the Quantity and Quality of Labor and Thus Affect the Industrial Structure

Social Security taxes for the establishment and improvement of the quantity of labor can bring the most direct impact of the tax increase can be achieved by improving education, labor force quality. First, to provide the necessary tax revenue for education funding. Second, the optimization through the tax system to improve civic education preferences. Again, through tax expenditures-the-job training means to improve corporate preferences and encourage the development of the education industry [5-6].

2.2 The Amount of Capital Tax Policy Changes Affecting the Industrial Structure and the Orientation

Tax policy mainly through the following channels affect the amount of capital: first, the government can tax measures to attract foreign direct investment. Second, the government can tax measures to increase domestic investment. First, as mentioned above, the relevant tax policy can increase the savings rate, capital formation so as to provide adequate funding base. Second, the government can invest through tax policies to increase the conversion rate of savings.

Tax policy on the different industries and different products, the tax burden imposed by the inevitable changes in related industries and products of the original rate of return, which directly affect the capital to different industries and product preferences, change the capital to invest. Changes in the capital to invest in different industries will inevitably affect the capital stock, thereby affecting the industry value added and employment.

2.3 The Impact of Tax Policies Affecting the Industrial Structure and Technological Progress

Tax Policy on the main determinant of technological progress - R & D investment level, education level, scientific and technological achievements into industrial level could constitute a significant impact. Tax policy on education levels mentioned above, tax policy can also be a variety of tax expenditure measures, such as the expense deduction, tax credits, accelerated depreciation and other applications, to encourage increased R & D investment; transfer of income through the scientific and technological achievements tax relief to encourage the transformation of scientific and technological achievements; scientific and technical personnel through income tax incentives to encourage workers to use the technology training and workforce orientation.

3   Give Full Play to the Government in Promoting the Role of Industrial Structure Adjustment

The process of economic restructuring, the Government has a very important role. In a market economy, the market is a basic form of the allocation of resources, but the government has an irreplaceable function and role. Especially in the restructuring and transformation process, the role of the government's macro regulation and control is more important. Has certain social restructuring, market can not determine the direction of its long-term development, combined with imperfect competition markets, externalities, the existence of such factors as spillover, structural adjustment process can not fail to consider the Government's participation. According to the general need for social and economic development of the strategic objectives, a number of key industries in need of support and focus the direction of the necessary guidance and support. Including policy support and financial support to accelerate the structural transformation process. Practical experience has shown that no country's economic restructuring is carried out entirely from the government.

Developed countries in the process of economic restructuring, there are basically two types of role. Early major industrialized countries tend to play to the market mechanism itself to solve the evolution of industrial structure, the various contradictions in the form of economic structure, industrial self-adjustment mechanism. Nevertheless. But the government still attach importance to the use of industrial policy and its financial policies to promote development of relevant industries, to structural adjustment has an important role. Then send the country, for as soon as possible to shorten the gap with advanced countries, tend to strongly with government forces, the evolution of industrial structure. The Government has a clear organizational goals and objectives of the structure, the main direct intervention and indirect means of intervention combined to promote the realization of industrial restructuring.

Compared with developed countries, developing countries lagging behind the general economic development, the gap is larger, industrialization, urbanization, modernization of developmental delay, only the more developing countries with the power of government to develop a clear structure of goals, a clear industrial policy in order to to speed up economic restructuring and accelerate economic development. On the other hand, developing countries do not improve the market mechanism, market competition, efficiency and relatively poor, developing countries than in developed countries, only to play a stronger role for the government to correct market distortions, to solve market failures in order to accelerate economic development.

In accordance with the requirements of the central and unswervingly push forward reform of rural taxes, phasing out agricultural tax, the effective system should reduce the various townships unreasonable burden in order to fundamentally solve the farmers, there is hope the problem. Reduce the costs of the farmers-tax losses, to reduce the real burden of the peasants. From China in recent years to increase the tax increment transfers to rural areas, increase investment in agriculture and rural infrastructure investment, to achieve the sustainable development of rural areas, a solid foundation of primary industry. Especially developed to strengthen the support for agricultural development, and establish a more complete relief of agricultural support system, and promoting regional agricultural economic structure adjustment and optimization.

Tax to actively support the construction of agricultural industrialization, support the agricultural base, the development of competitive advantage of agricultural products, agricultural products base to play in the process of industrialization of agriculture an important role. Making full use of financial discount, tax incentives and other policies to support the development of agricultural products have an advantage, and promote value-added agricultural processing and conversion, promote agricultural industrialization. Through various tax incentives and other measures to promote agricultural science and technology community and social service system and other investments, establish a sound system of agricultural information network marketing organization to promote agricultural production, processing, marketing information services building, to improve the agricultural value-added services. To promote agricultural technology, and promote the adjustment of industrial structure in rural areas increased.

As mentioned earlier, the high level of macro tax burden will undermine the market in allocating resources to the basic role of structural distortion of consumer demand and investment demand structure and ultimately distorted industrial structure. Therefore form a reasonable level of tax burden to promote industrial upgrading is very important. Be appropriate to reduce the main tax rates. China's value-added tax and corporate income tax rate compared to most countries at a high level, the production of value-added tax, if the conversion rate for the consumer of its rise from the current 17% to 23% -24%, In addition, From the international comparison, the income tax rate is lower than many countries China, such as: Germany is 25%, 28% of Australia, Britain, Japan, India and other countries 30%, the U.S. imposed 15%, 18%, 25% , 33% of the four progressive rates, the former of lower than third gear, the top marginal tax rate was the same in China, and China is 33%, therefore, value-added tax and income tax rates should be appropriately reduced. Another tax clearance fee legislation to eliminate the phenomenon is overrun charges of large-diameter lower level of the key steps of macro tax burden. In addition to the fees in rural areas outside of clean-up, clean up all kinds of unreasonable charges in urban areas is also an important step. Qing Li after-tax charge, due to excessive management fees to eliminate the cost and lack of supervision led to the diversion of revenue to waste, and income will greatly enhance the efficiency, so will the new tax burden is lower than the original macro tax burden of large diameter.

Tax Legislation by the current unreasonable and improper fiscal management system has led to a certain extent, the proliferation of tax charges, tax efficiency can not fully reflect the role. Tax Legislation should be so divided in a "centralized-based, decentralized, supplemented by" the principle of separation of powers reasonable and appropriate delegation. Under the premise of a unified tax administration, given the right to place the appropriate Shuizhengguanli. Create the conditions for the progressive realization of a unified urban and rural tax system. Clearance fees with tax legislation, setting new taxes, the appropriate cancellation fees. The local tax base according to the local, negative tax capacity and public expenditures on the local tax system to make the necessary adjustments. But also the financial management system must be adjusted to increase the central and local transfer payments to local governments, especially at the grassroots level with more financial resources to make it commensurate with the scope of its powers necessary to regulate financial resources. To maximize the efficiency of the tax effect, to further promote the industrial structure adjustment increase. Improve other local tax system, reform, urban construction tax, expanding the scope of taxation, foreign units into the tax base will no longer be prescribed by administrative division rate tranches, the provisions could be considered the central rate of duty, according to the specific tax rate by the provincial government local economic development and urban construction developments identified. Implemented in accordance with the requirements of the central urban construction tax reform, in particular, to reform and improve the existing land use tax and property tax system, when conditions are ripe for the introduction of a standardized real property tax. Expand the scope of stamp duty tax, Jane and Tax Rates, collected by the obligor clear, change "three-self" tax for the tax declaration. Expand the scope of resource tax assessment, reflecting on the environmental engineering and ecological environment construction of tilt, the appropriate resources to enhance the rate of non-renewable resources, limit excessive exploitation of resources in the resource fees into taxes, to regulate the collection and management, reduce the cost of collection, and promote Tax Reform. Merge the foreign travel tax system.

The perfect addition to value-added tax should be appropriately reduced its tax rate, should also be changed from production-based value-added consumer to avoid the production of VAT-induced reverse transformation of industrial structure adjustment. Appropriate to relax the conditions of the general taxpayer identification, to minimize the tax on the de facto discrimination against small enterprises, encourage private investment. Upgrading of industrial structure in accordance with the objective requirements of the tax adjustment of consumption tax, the alcohol, automobile tires and other investment goods removed to the entertainment industry, luxury service industry, "Need" goods, some high-end health products, should be included. Appropriate to reduce the car's consumption tax rate to encourage car consumption, and promote the development of automobile manufacturing. Further improve the financial and insurance industry, business tax policies in order to avoid excessive tax burden and impede the development of financial and insurance industries.

Progressively to foreign enterprises income tax, in the current economic situation, domestic and foreign-funded enterprises in the general tone of the fair tax burden, the special offers to foreign investors give special provisions. Prevent foreign investment due to a major tax policy changes in the flow. Adjust the tax payroll deduction provisions. Higher average wages to reduce the tax burden on the industry can also be combined with industrial policies, the state encourages the development of high-tech industry, intelligence consulting services, finance and insurance and other industries to improve their taxable wages alone, or allow it to pay costs deducted. High-tech talent in the technical achievements and technical services revenue from royalties, mutatis mutandis, by taxable income reduced by 30%; appropriate expansion of scientific research and development personnel for technical achievement awards range of personal income tax exemption. Adjust the employee education expenses deduction requirements. For education expenses for employees should be allowed to deduct business, faster for some industries and technological progress, and even allows a certain percentage of its accordance with the additional deduction in order to enhance their preference for continuing education for employees. Promote the development of related industries. Wage should be raised from personal income tax in the cost of the standard deduction. Classification of the progressive realization of the comprehensive transformation of the income tax, and labor income due to lower marginal tax rates, so that the overall tax burden on labor income does not exceed the one hand, non-labor income, personal income tax makes the tax burden tends to be more reasonable.

Imposition of Social Security tax. This is driving consumption, promotion of labor in the smooth transfer between industries, reduce the growth rate of labor force is significant. Urban areas can now have a pension, health care, unemployment insurance premium included in the basic tax track, in order to improve collection rates, reduce management costs, improve efficiency in the use of funds. When the conditions, and then gradually extended to rural areas. Introduction of education tax. The current surcharge for education and other educational fees combined, the introduction of education tax, and according to the needs of education spending to determine the appropriate rate, to ensure education funding.

Science and technology are primary productive forces, so tax policy should actively encourage technological development. According to economic development and high-tech industries at different stages of system planning and design development of tax incentives and dynamically adjusted. In accordance with national legislation on science and technology, speed up the pace of technology tax legislation and improve the tax laws of the authority of science and technology. Tax incentives should follow the following principles: to obey the principle of national development plans; not be encouraged by the principle of dependent arising; the principle of equal encouragement; financial sustainability principles.

Tax incentives should be based on whether a company is really based on high-tech enterprises. Technology Development Fund to encourage enterprises to self. Development Fund or sales by enterprises to invest a certain percentage of the amount of provision, and allow a deduction in taxable income before, so that enterprises can reduce the risk of development of technology to enhance technological innovation initiative. Preferential tax policies have long focused on high-tech industry has focused on the production and sale of two areas, while the innovation process is not favored. Preferential tax policies for the future should focus falls on product research and development, technology transfer areas, and promote technological innovation and improve the formation mechanism. Tax incentives to achieve the "beneficiaries" to specific research projects, the development of specific aspects of change. Should be based on the characteristics of high-tech research and development, through the project benefits, research and development aspects of incentives to stimulate technological innovation with meaningful actions.

High-tech industry through tax incentives, for the second and tertiary industries to support the strategic adjustment. Should also pay attention to accelerate the development of information industry and Internet economy, handle the new economy and traditional economic relationship between the two can not be separated against each other. On the one hand to take full advantage of high-tech means to transform the traditional economy, continue to play the advantages of the traditional economy; the other hand, take advantage of the new features of the economy needs to create, expand demand and promote economic development.

References

1. Zhi, Y.: Introduction to Industrial Economics. The Chinese People's University Press (1985)
2. Zhenhua, Z.: The structure of modern economic growth effects. The Shanghai Joint Publishing Company, Shanghai People's Publishing House (1995)
3. Jun, G.Y.: Industrial Structure. Shanghai Finance University Press (2002)
4. Red, Z.: On the present stage of industrial restructuring and tax policy analysis. Earth 20 (2003)
5. Levin.: Tax policy and industrial structure. Finance at Renmin University of China Research Center, Public Economics Review
6. Zheng, Z.T.: To accelerate the development of China's preferential tax policies for high-tech industry choice. Fujian tax (7) (2002)

Research on Internal Control Optimization of Enterprises Based on Accounting Informatization

Hong Lv and Hua Feng

Shandong Women's University, Accounting School
Jinan, china
namelvhong@163.com

Abstract. Based on enterprise accounting Informatization, this paper focuses on internal control optimization. Firstly, the dialectical relationship between accounting Informatization and internal control optimization is studied dialectically. Then, the author makes further analysis on current problems about company internal control and proposes new ideas on optimizing internal control environment based on accounting Informatization.

Keywords: Accounting Informatization, Internal control, Risk, Optimizing.

1 Introduction

In recent years, with the publication of "Strategy on National Informatization Development" and "Guidance on Promoting Accounting Informatization comprehensively " issued by the Ministry of Finance, people all over the country are involved into the study of accounting Informatization. Meanwhile, the Ministry of Finance, Securities and Futures Commission, the Audit Commission, China Banking Regulatory Commission and China Insurance Regulatory Commission, jointly issued "regulations of basic norms of internal control" and "internal control support Guidelines "in May 2008 and April 2010, respectively, which highlight the great attention paid by our government to enterprise internal control. "Internal control" and "Informatization" were regarded as two of the top ten key words in accounting area during the year 2010. With these social backgrounds and the development of accounting Informatization, internal control has become a distinct sense of this era.

From the aspect of current accounting Informatization development, there are two reasons for unsuccessful businesses operating, accounting information being distorted and unlawful operations occurring after implementing accounting Informatization. One reason is that enterprises spare too much money on purchasing or developing accounting software to achieve accounting Informatization. The other reason is that the importance of internal control system construction within accounting information system is ignored which is mainly attributed to inadequate and ineffective internal controls. How to combine them together and improve internal control in accounting Informatization is major problem for enterprises vigorously conducting Informatization and internal control.

Based on enterprise accounting Informatization, this paper focuses on internal control optimization. Firstly, the dialectical relationship between accounting Informatization and internal control optimization is studied dialectically. Then, the

M. Zhou (Ed.): ISAEBD 2011, Part IV, CCIS 211, pp. 408–414, 2011.

author makes further analysis on current problems about company internal control and proposes new ideas on optimizing internal control environment based on accounting Informatization.

2   The Relationship between Accounting Informatization and Internal Controls

In April 2010, relationship between accounting Informatization and internal control was first put on the agenda at the ninth annual meeting of the national accounting Informatization. Most participants had reached a consensus that the two are mutual penetrating, influencing, complementing and collaborative developing. The relationship between them should be analyzed from two aspects: the influence of accounting information on internal control and the reaction to the former.

2.1   Accounting Informatization Influence on Internal Control

Accounting information has characteristics of openness, dynamics, integration and diversity, which brings great impact to original system. The influences include the following fields.

Increase Internal Control Content. As well as original manual accounting, accounting Informatization now also refer to purchase, sale, storage, production, human resources and other management aspects, which increases the work scope of internal control. In addition, after the implementation of accounting Informatization, companies add some vacancies as system administrators. The changes of business organizations and job division have also brought innovations to internal control content.

Chang the Form of Internal Control. After implementing accounting Informatization, the original manual processing of internal control lost its need of existence, such as reconciliation, account and voucher checking, categorized accounts summary and so on. There are some internal controls processes are completed by computers, such as voucher debit balance check, voucher type control and trial balance ledger and so on. Accounting information on has less dependence on traditional internal control functions, but more on a centralized data processing and high efficiency, which replace existing internal control measures gradually by the corresponding program functions. Original system-oriented internal control is transformed into the co-existence of both program and system control and favor the program control constantly.

Enrich Internal Control Environment. Accounting Informatization has changed traditional accounting environment, which mainly involved in computer and network accounting. Computer intelligence, high-speed computing capacity, network sharing and remote operation capability make internal control environment more complex.

Change Internal Control Object. Under the background of accounting Informatization, stuff in corporate business execution changes from traditional financial personnel to computer and systems, so the corresponding internal control objects also changes to Man-Machine System.

2.2 The Reaction of Internal Control to Accounting Informatization

Accounting informationizaiton influences the internal control in full aspects, in the mean time, enterprise internal control quality will also react to the process of accounting Informatization. This mainly reflects in the way that high quality of internal control ensures the accuracy, security and reliability of accounting information systems data. Stable accounting information system depends on continuous optimization and improvement of internal controls.

3 Enterprise Internal Control Problems under Current Accounting Informatization Environment

3.1 The Original Internal Control System Not Suitable for the Needs of Accounting Informatization

Accounting Informatization is an important part of enterprise Informatization and gives a tremendous impact on traditional internal control systems, the internal control system under original manual accounting environment cannot adapt to the needs of enterprise Informatization, which requires the integration of financial and business processes, new audit criteria and balance for identifying business goals and clear job responsibilities. Under this circumstance, the internal control is actually an intensive enterprises management tool, which put new challenges to the construction and improvement of the internal control system.

3.2 Hard to Mutual Restraint among Accounting Positions

Accounting information data processing is highly integrated and automated, and a large number of the original complicated work which was processed by multiple personnel is now unified done by computer. The role of accounting personnel is transformed from checking and calculation to management. Traditional manual processing between the various positions is completed in the form of signature, seal and accounting as the core of the control system, which is difficult to play a role in accounting Informatization environment. Therefore, if there are no effective mutual restraints, supervision and controls among positions, the risk of error and fraud will greatly increase.

3.3 Potential Safety Hazard of Magnetic (Optical) Storage Media of Accounting Files

Accounting information is stored on paper in traditional work process as voucher, account book, reports and so on, the accounting system strictly prohibits cutting and mending, scraping, smearing and bleaching with solutions, modifications like add, delete, modify on accounting documents or books have to be verified and controlled through handwriting and seal of the accounting personnel. But physical accounting form will decrease greatly in accounting Informatization than original manual accounting system, various accounting data will be stored in the magnetic (optical) media, and there is no traces of operations like add, delete, modify, and copy, so data can be easily tampered or stolen, which may result in distortion or leakage of accounting information. At the same time the hard disk, CD-ROM hardware and software may also fail due to quality problems or viral infections to make enterprise information security threatened.

3.4 Security Risk Increases in an Open Network Environment

A major feature of accounting Informatization is to bring original closure of local accounting system to an open Internet world, which brings serious challenges to the accounting system security. In the open network, various enterprise data is stored in the server which is connected to the network or client's machine, due to internet openness, it gives some malicious visitors an opportunity to exploit. Meanwhile, rampant viruses on the Internet are also huge risk to accounting information system. A large number of accounting information is transmitted through the open Internet, and it is difficult to ensure its authenticity and integrity. In the past, local-computer-oriented security method has not applicable now, which increases difficulties to control accounting information system security.

3.5 Increase Difficulty in Fraud Control

A lot of software provide functions like "Cancel Check Out", "restored account (canceled account)", "Cancel audit", "cancel cashier (or supervisor) signature " in accounting Informatization which may lead to no traces of change vouchers, books or forge accounting information after settling or keeping accounting, it would greatly increase the difficulty of controlling fraud. On the other hand, each user's authorization control relies mainly on the division of labor and password, each user's password is stored in the computer system. So once the password is compromised, it may lead to unpredictable losses.

3.6 Error Repetition and Unlimited Magnification Based on Controls of Applications

Internal control is under manual and program control together in accounting Informatization, and gradually tilted to the latter. The effect of process control depends on the accuracy and validity of application system. If an application system has errors, it may cause repeated error occurrence, while the operators have long-term trust and reliance on system operation and this circumstance will make errors difficult to spot. On the other hand, due to the enterprise information system covering multiple sectors' data, even a minor error may lead to errors in a series of relevant links, and its harm can be hugely magnified.

3.7 Enterprise Facing Huge Risk under the Dependence on Software Systems

Under the environment of accounting informationizaiton, responsibilities are highly concentrated in the information software systems, once program data is tampered with or infected with malicious viruses, it can affect system stability and safety and cause serious system crash and incalculable damage to enterprises. Accounting information system in general composed by accounting software at clients' end and back-end database, all kinds of data are stored in the database. In the mean time, there may be potential safety hazard due to insufficient protection of database. At the same time, imperfect software design may uncover some security breaches, and some kinds of software do not abide with modular design under system security requirements, so that software system inner structure is illogical. To prevent these system risks, accounting systems should seek more measures to enhance the safety and be more vigorous.

4 New Thoughts on Enterprise Internal Control Optimization in Accounting Informatization

4.1 Build Internal Control System Based on ERMF and COBIT4.1 Framework

From the perspective of globalization, in enterprise Informatization, the latest results of enterprise risk management are ERMF framework published by COSO and COBIT framework controlled by modern information technologies.

In 2004, Treadway Commission (the Commission against financial fraud) issued a new COSO report – "Enterprise Risk Management-Integrated Framework" (referred to as ERMF). ERMF summarizes a decade achievement of COSO reports, and upgrade the internal control from "process" to "risk", incorporates internal control into risk management and it becomes an important part of the business management process.

"Control Objectives for Information and related Technology"(Referred to as COBIT) issues by the Information Systems Audit and Control Association in 1996, has been updated to version 4.1. COBIT is a widely used international information technology framework. It provides a set of authoritative internationally recognized standards information for enterprise Informatization, which aims to standardize and improve the information technology governance, effectively prevent and control risk, increase the perception of management control with authoritative and internationally recognized standards.

ERMF and COBIT are all based on the theory of internal control, and a natural extension, development and improvement of the internal control framework. Both focus on monitoring and evaluation of internal control activities, highlighting the validity, reliability and compliance of relevant laws and regulations, emphasizing on the importance of risk assessment and human resource management and so on. business control framework represented by ERMF mainly assess control value from the perspective of general fiduciary responsibility, which focuses on a new internal control framework proposed for all enterprises, but it is lack of the control on elaboration of information and instructions; And COBIT4.1 control framework aims at government or enterprise application and control of technology. ERMF is strong in theoretical way and COBIT4.1 is more on practicality and feasibility. Enterprises should consider their actual situations, and effectively integrate the two to construct a suitable internal control of accounting information system.

4.2 Role-Based Personnel Permissions

The establishment of a clear job responsibilities and labor rights division structure in the internal control system can give a mutual restraint among different positions, which could prevent or reduce the incidence of fraud and error. Role-based access control solution is to empower, modify or cancel the roles of authorized users. First, system administrators define a variety of roles and set the functional rights, then empower user with roles according to rights, responsibilities and interests, one role may correspond to multiple users and one user may need to be defined with more roles. The Access control process includes two parts: functions associated with roles, roles with users, which enable a logic division between user permission and function, and it is more convenient and effective to distribute and manage permissions.

4.3 Improve Accounting Information Files Management System

Files are stored in a magnetic (optical) or paper-based media in accounting Informatization environment. First, to improve files management system, we should make clear regulations on file storage methods, storage conditions and store men, then conduct these regulations strictly to form an effective constraint mechanism. Also accounting files should be backed up regularly, two or more backups are necessary and save them in different locations, which increase file security. For example at 911 events, Morgan Stanley's financial data is transmitted as 100 km away per day to the telecom backup center, so they can resume business shortly after the accident.

4.4 Improve Software Performance, Enhance Network Security Control

Take strict inspection and test before using software on fault tolerance, database security capabilities and information system to ensure its legality, compliance, qualification and security. Regular maintenance and management are needed during using process: file integrity checking to ensure no unauthorized modification and deletion; identify and correct errors in program to improve system performance; eliminate software failures to increase system efficiency; regular backup system data and so on.

On the other hand, network security is also an important problem under the internal control of Informatization. With the rapid development of network technology, enterprises should strengthen the entire financial network security at all levels of financial system. Such as taking use of authority control, authentication control, identification, data encryption and other security technologies to formulate a well-developed network security operating system, and establish a comprehensive multi-level security network system.

5 Conclusion

The implementation of accounting Informatization is not only a revolution on technology, but also on management theories and thoughts. Enterprise internal control based on accounting information optimization is a research hotspot at home and abroad. Under the background of accounting Informatization, only enterprises in continuous optimization and improvement on internal control can enhance economic efficiency and occupy a space in the fierce market competition.

References

1. Zhounan, Y., Hailin, W., Qinhong, W.: Accounting information system- financial business-oriented integration. Electronic Industry Press, Beijing (2009)
2. Yuting, L.: Application and dissemination XBRL, Promote accounting Informatization construction. Accounting Research (11), 3–9 (2010)
3. Yuting, L.: Discuss about accounting Informatization development strategy of our country. Accounting Research (06), 3–10 (2009)
4. Liangbin, L., Bai, Z.: Internal control research during Enterprise Informatization process. Accounting Research (05), 69–75 (2008)
5. Xiongsheng, Y.: Internal control theory obstacles and outlet. Accounting Research (02), 53–59 (2006)

The Positive Analysis of the Trade in Goods of China and Japan Based on the International Trade Theory

Yuli Tian

Shandong Women's University, Jinan, Shandong, China
jadebeautiful@163.com

Abstract. In this paper, the trade current situation, trade combination degree, revealed comparative advantage, competitive advantage and the trade complementarity are analyzed between China and Japan by using the international trade theory. By using the positive ananlysis method based on the trade theory and the analysis consequence, we can conclude the trade situation between China and Japan and find the way of how to improve the trade amount and depth cooperation between China and Japan.

Keywords: Trade combination degree, revealed comparative advantage, competitive advantage, the trade complementarity.

1 Introduction

As a big trade partner country, Japan are very important for Chinese international trade. In this paper, we will give the measurement consequence and persue the further space and countermeasure cooperation between China and Japan by using the analysis of their trade combination degree, revealed comparative advantage, competitive advantage and the trade complementarity.

Considering the probability of the statistics and the representativeness of the data, I use the SITC classification standard and choose ten kinds of commodities according the UNCTAD data to measure the trade situation between them.

2 The Current Situation and the Trade Combination Degree between China and Japan

2.1 The Current Situation of Trade between China and Japan

Because of the impaction of the financial crisis, the amount of the trade between China and Japan was decreased greatly in 2009 after it is increased constantly about 10 years from 1998 to now. Along with the recovering of the global economy, the trade amount between them starts to increase, the following figure 1 gives the detail information.

M. Zhou (Ed.): ISAEBD 2011, Part IV, CCIS 211, pp. 415–422, 2011.
© Springer-Verlag Berlin Heidelberg 2011

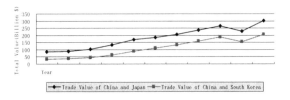

Fig. 1. China and Japan Trade Value from 2000 to 2010

2.2 The Analysis of the Trade Combination Degree between China and Japan

The Trade Combination Degree (*TCD*) is an index which can measure two countries' trade close degree and interdependent degree. The bigger the *TCD* ratio, the closer realationship between them. We can write the *TCD* calculation formula (1) as follows:

$$TCD_{ij} = \frac{X_{ij}/X_i}{M_j/M_w}.$$ (1)

In this formula, *TCDij* means the Trade Combination Degree of country *i* to country *j*, *Xij* means the export volume of country *i* to country *j*, *Xi* means the whole export volume of country *i*, *Mj* means the whole import volume of country *j*, and M_w means the import volume of the whole world. If *TCDij*<1, that means the realationship between two countries is not very close, and vice versa. We can calculate and obtain the fluctuation of the *TCD* index by using the UNCTAD data, the calculation results are as figure 2.

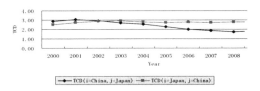

Fig. 2. The fluctuation of the TCD index

3   The Revealed Comparative Advantage and Competitive Advantage Analysis of China and Japan

3.1   The Revealed Comparative Advantage Analysis of China and Japan

Comparative advantage, an economic theory, first developed by 19th-century English economist David Ricardo, attributed the causes and benefits of international trade to the differences among countries in the relative advantage of producing the same commodities. So the comparative advantage will impact the trade flow and the change of the trade. And this theory also can be applicable to the trade between China and Japan.

The most popular measurement index is the Revealed Comparative Advantage (*RCA*), first developed by American economist Balassa in 1965, which measure one kind of commodity comparative advantage of the country by the *RCA* index. *RCA* index can be indicated as follow formulua (2):

$$RCA_{ik} = \frac{X_{ik} / X_i}{X_{wk} / X_w}$$ (2)

In this function, RCA_{ik} means the country i Revealed Comparative Advantage (*RCA*) index of commodity k, X_{ik} means the country i export volume of commodity k, X_i means the whole export volume of country i, X_{wk} means the whole world export volume of commodity k, X_w means the whole world export volume. If $RCA_{ik}>1$, that means country i has the comparative advantage of commodity k, and vice versa. The calculation results of the *RCA* index of China (RCA_C) and Japan (RCA_J) from 2001 to 2009 are as table1:

Table 1. RCA Index of China and Japan in Commoditys

Commodities Classification	Primary Commodities						Manufactured Goods			
	Food, basic	Beverages and tobacco	Agricultural raw materials	Ores and metals	Pearls, precious stones	Fuels	Chemical products	Machinery and transport equipment	Iron and steel	Textile fibres, fabrics clothing
2001 RCA_C	0.80	0.35	0.51	0.61	0.22	0.33	0.52	0.88	0.55	3.25
RCA_J	0.11	0.10	0.29	0.47	0.22	0.04	0.79	1.66	1.56	0.30
2002 RCA_C	0.73	0.32	0.46	0.59	0.19	0.28	0.46	0.97	0.45	3.09
RCA_J	0.07	0.09	0.31	0.49	0.20	0.04	0.77	1.67	1.65	0.29
2003 RCA_C	0.66	0.25	0.38	0.59	0.18	0.25	0.42	1.09	0.45	3.01
RCA_J	0.07	0.08	0.30	0.49	0.24	0.03	0.78	1.70	1.55	0.28
2004 RCA_C	0.56	0.24	0.33	0.60	0.18	0.22	0.42	1.16	0.78	2.91
RCA_J	0.07	0.08	0.29	0.49	0.22	0.04	0.80	1.69	1.38	0.28
2005 RCA_C	0.54	0.20	0.34	0.53	0.17	0.17	0.45	1.23	0.83	2.97
RCA_J	0.08	0.09	0.33	0.52	0.24	0.05	0.84	1.70	1.52	0.27
2006 RCA_C	0.51	0.16	0.32	0.51	0.16	0.13	0.45	1.26	1.08	3.09
RCA_J	0.08	0.09	0.34	0.53	0.42	0.06	0.87	1.71	1.49	0.27
2007 RCA_C	0.45	0.15	0.31	0.41	0.14	0.12	0.47	1.30	1.23	3.05
RCA_J	0.08	0.08	0.37	0.55	0.44	0.09	0.87	1.74	1.40	0.27
2008 RCA_C	0.39	0.14	0.33	0.40	0.12	0.13	0.53	1.39	1.35	3.09
RCA_J	0.07	0.09	0.41	0.58	0.52	0.14	0.85	1.82	1.54	0.28
2009 RCA_C	0.40	0.16	0.33	0.31	0.09	0.12	0.44	1.43	0.71	2.98
RCA_J	0.08	0.11	0.48	0.70	0.47	0.13	0.91	1.69	1.93	0.28

Data Resource: statistical analysis according to the UNCTAD data.

3.2 The Competitive Advantage Analysis of China and Japan

We can acknowledge whether one of country's industry is competitive by analyzing the trade competitive advantage. In this paper, I use the Trade Competitiveness Index to estimate the trade competitive advantage. It can be indicated as follow formula (3):

$$TC_{ik} = \frac{X_{ik} - M_{ik}}{X_{ik} + M_{ik}}$$ (3)

In this function, TC_{ik} means the country i Trade Competitive Advantage (TC) index of commodity k, X_{ik} means the country i export volume of commodity k, M_{ik} means the country i import volume of commodity k. If $TC_{ik} > 0$, that means country i has the trade competitive advantage of commodity k, and vice versa. The calculation results the TC index of China (TC_C) and Japan (TC_J) from 2001 to 2009 are as table 2:

Table 2. TC Index of China and Japan Trade in Commoditys

Commoditys Classification		Primary Commodities						Manufactured Goods			
		Food, basic	Beverages and tobacco	Agricultural raw materials	Ores and metals	Pearls, precious stones	Fuels	Chemical products	Machinery and transport equipment	Iron and steel	Textile fibres, fabrics clothing
2001	TC$_C$	0.20	0.36	-0.63	-0.51	-0.08	-0.35	-0.41	-0.06	-0.55	0.53
	TC$_J$	-0.88	-0.85	-0.69	-0.52	-0.30	-0.96	0.10	0.48	0.66	-0.53
2002	TC$_C$	0.23	0.43	-0.64	-0.51	-0.15	-0.39	-0.44	-0.04	-0.61	0.57
	TC$_J$	-0.91	-0.85	-0.64	-0.49	-0.37	-0.96	0.13	0.50	0.73	-0.51
2003	TC$_C$	0.11	0.35	-0.68	-0.54	-0.14	-0.45	-0.43	-0.01	-0.64	0.60
	TC$_J$	-0.91	-0.86	-0.64	-0.50	-0.17	-0.96	0.14	0.50	0.69	-0.52
2004	TC$_C$	-0.02	0.38	-0.73	-0.57	-0.13	-0.54	-0.43	0.03	-0.26	0.61
	TC$_J$	-0.91	-0.86	-0.64	-0.49	-0.28	-0.96	0.17	0.50	0.61	-0.53
2005	TC$_C$	0.06	0.20	-0.71	-0.61	-0.12	-0.57	-0.37	0.10	-0.15	0.66
	TC$_J$	-0.90	-0.86	-0.60	-0.50	-0.25	-0.94	0.16	0.48	0.58	-0.55
2006	TC$_C$	0.10	0.07	-0.72	-0.54	-0.14	-0.67	-0.32	0.12	0.20	0.69
	TC$_J$	-0.89	-0.87	-0.60	-0.51	0.15	-0.93	0.17	0.49	0.64	-0.57
2007	TC$_C$	0.01	0.00	-0.70	-0.66	-0.17	-0.67	-0.28	0.17	0.36	0.74
	TC$_J$	-0.88	-0.85	-0.55	-0.52	0.24	-0.90	0.18	0.50	0.61	-0.55
2008	TC$_C$	-0.16	-0.11	-0.71	-0.71	-0.16	-0.68	-0.20	0.21	0.45	0.76
	TC$_J$	-0.89	-0.84	-0.54	-0.52	0.37	-0.87	0.12	0.51	0.59	-0.57
2009	TC$_C$	-0.12	-0.09	-0.70	-0.80	-0.23	-0.72	-0.29	0.18	-0.06	0.77
	TC$_J$	-0.87	-0.84	-0.45	-0.39	0.43	-0.87	0.12	0.45	0.71	-0.62

Data Resource: statistical analysis according to the UNCTAD data.

4   The Trade Complementarity Analysis of China and Japan

Trade Complementarity is a impetus to enlarge the scale of international trade and develop the depth of international trade. We can obtain two countries common benefit focus by analyzing the trade complementarity. In this paper, I use the Austrilia economist Peter Drysdale's basic idea: Firstly, we should find the RCA_{ik}^x of the export country i of commodity k, that is the formula (4):

$$RCA_{ik}^x = \frac{X_{ik} / X_i}{X_{wk} / X_w}$$ (4)

Secondly, we should find the RCA_{jk}^{m} of import country j(it is the parter of the country i) of commodity k, that is the formula (5):

$$RCA_{jk}^{m} = \frac{M_{jk} / M_{j}}{M_{wk} / M_{w}}$$ (5)

In function (5), M_{jk} means the country j import volume of commodity k, M_{j} means the whole import volume of country j, M_{wk} means the whole world import volume of commodity k, M_{w} means the whole world import volume.

If one commodity has more comparative advantage in export country and less competitive disadvantage, that means there is strong complementarity between the export and import country. So we can obtain the trade complementarity index, that is the formula (6):

$$C_{ijk} = RCA_{ik}^{x} \times RCA_{jk}^{m}$$ (6)

Table 3. Trade Complementarity Index Between China and Japan

Commoditys Classification	Primary Commodities						Manufactured Goods			
	Food, basic	Beverages and tobacco	Agricultural raw materials	Ores and metals	Pearls, precious stones and non-monetary gold	Fuels	Chemical products	Machinery and transport equipment	Iron and steel	Textile fibres, yarn, fabrics and clothing
2001 C_{CJk}	1.46	0.49	0.86	1.01	0.10	0.67	0.37	0.61	0.19	3.72
C_{JCk}	0.06	0.02	0.67	0.92	0.06	0.03	1.03	1.85	3.03	0.33
2002 C_{CJk}	1.33	0.43	0.74	0.99	0.10	0.58	0.32	0.69	0.14	3.43
C_{JCk}	0.03	0.01	0.66	0.91	0.06	0.03	0.95	1.97	3.29	0.27
2003 C_{CJk}	1.11	0.33	0.61	1.00	0.08	0.53	0.30	0.78	0.16	3.39
C_{JCk}	0.04	0.01	0.60	0.96	0.06	0.02	0.85	2.05	3.33	0.23
2004 C_{CJk}	0.94	0.32	0.52	1.02	0.09	0.44	0.29	0.83	0.32	3.35
C_{JCk}	0.04	0.01	0.62	1.07	0.05	0.03	0.85	1.98	1.90	0.22
2005 C_{CJk}	0.86	0.26	0.49	0.90	0.08	0.32	0.30	0.85	0.37	3.37
C_{JCk}	0.04	0.01	0.71	1.23	0.06	0.04	0.91	2.01	1.93	0.20
2006 C_{CJk}	0.72	0.22	0.47	0.89	0.06	0.24	0.30	0.85	0.39	3.57
C_{JCk}	0.04	0.01	0.78	1.05	0.12	0.05	0.91	2.10	1.29	0.20
2007 C_{CJk}	0.61	0.18	0.43	0.76	0.05	0.24	0.32	0.87	0.47	3.45
C_{JCk}	0.04	0.02	0.81	1.28	0.12	0.07	0.90	2.08	1.01	0.17
2008 C_{CJk}	0.48	0.16	0.43	0.69	0.03	0.26	0.36	0.87	0.54	3.41
C_{JCk}	0.05	0.02	0.94	1.59	0.12	0.12	0.84	2.14	0.99	0.16
2009 C_{CJk}	0.52	0.20	0.42	0.50	0.02	0.23	0.33	0.95	0.24	4.01
C_{JCk}	0.05	0.02	1.03	2.25	0.10	0.11	0.86	1.98	1.75	0.14

Data Resource: statistical analysis according to the UNCTAD data.

At last, we can add up all of commoditys' trade complementarity by using every commodity's weight coefficient and obtain the comprehensive trade complementarity index, that is the formula (7).

$$C_{ij} = \sum_k C_{ijk} \times (W_k \div W) \tag{7}$$

In this function, W_k means the whole world trade volume of commodity k, Wmeans the whole world trade volume.

If $RCA_{jk}^m < 1$, that means country j has the comparative advantage of commodity k, and the less the value, the more comparative advantage. If $C_{ijk} < 1$, that means country i and country j's trade complementarity of commodity k is feeble, and the less the value, the less trade complementarity. If $C_{ij} < 1$, that means country i and j's comprehensive trade complementarity is feeble, and the less the value, the less comprehensive trade complementarity, and vice versa. According to above functions, we can obtain the trade complementarity index of China(C_{CJk})and Japan (C_{JCk})and the comprehensive trade complementarity index of China (C_{CJ})and Japan(C_{JC}) from 2001 to 2009, the calculation results are as table 3 and table 4:

Table 4. Comprehensive Trade Complementarity Index of China and Japan

	2001	2002	2003	2004	2005	2006	2007	2008	2009
C_{CJ}	0.89	0.87	0.87	0.85	0.80	0.78	0.77	0.72	0.79
C_{JC}	1.20	1.25	1.26	1.19	1.19	1.19	1.18	1.15	1.16

Data Resource: statistical analysis according to the UNCTAD data.

5   The Analysis and the Conclusion

5.1   According to the Situation as a Whole, the Trade Scale of China and Japan Is Changing with a Tendency to Continuously Going Up, However, the Trade Combination Degree do Not Change in the Same Direction

According to the figure 1, the trade scale of China and Japan goes up continuously from 2000 to 2010, only decreased in 2009 because of the world financial crisis. The increasing of the mutual trade scale is realated with our country's rapid trade development and the price that we used when we make the statistic. Because the trade volume is calculated by using the price multiplie the quantity, the price will be impacted by the fluctuation of the inflation and exchange rate, so the trade volume will be affected by the price.

According to the figure 2, because of all the $TCD > 1$, so we can obtain that the trade relationship between China and Japan are very close, and it is changing with a relatively smooth tendency. By obseving the chart 2, we can conclude that the trade combination degree between China and Japan showed a downtrend curve since 2002, however, the TCD between Japan and China remain stable, and we also can find that China to Japan's TCD index has been lower than the index of Japan to China, this means that the trade penetration of China to Japan is not so high. But Japan' trade penetration to China is very high. So we should strenghten our country's trade penetration.

5.2 According to the View of the Trade Commodities's Structure, We Can Conclude that Most of the Trade of China and Japan is Based on the Intra-industry Trade。The Trade Not Only Based on the Factor Endowment, But Also on the Intra-industry Trade. So the Two Countries Have Possessed the Basic Factors to Improve the Cooperation Depth and the Level of Mutural Trade

According to the table 1, we can conclude that, for the primary commodities, China and Japan's primary commodities have not any trade comparative advantage. For the manufactured goods, two countries' commodities such as the machinery and transport equipment, iron and steel are all in high comparative advantage, textile fibres, yarn, fabrics and clothing are the China comparative advantage goods, so we can conclude that only the textile fibres, yarn, fabrics and clothing trade is based on the factors endowment, however, the trade of the machinery and transport equipment, iron, and steel are all intra-industry trade.

According to the table 2, we can conclude that the commodity that china has the most competitive advantage is textile, secondly is the machinery and transport equipment, which competitive advantage is not very strong. Iron and steel have the strong competitive advantage since 2005, but it decreased severely in 2009 because of the financial crisis. Other commodities are all in the disadvantage status. However, for Japan, the order of the commoditity which has stong competitive advantage is iron and steel, the machinery and transport equipment and the chemical products, it still has no competitive advantage of the primary commodities.

According to the table 3, we can conclude that the trade complementarity of China and Japan is also most from the intra-industry trade. For the primary commodities, the food basic and the ores and mentals of China have stong trade complementarity to Japan, and Japan has not trade complementarity in primary commodities. For the manufacture commodities, the machinery equipment, transport equipment, the iron and steel have strong complementarity.

According to the table 4, we can conclude that trade complementarity index of Japan to China has exceeded to 1, but the complementarity index of China to Japan has not exceeded to 1, that means China will be the very important role for further development of the international trade between them.

5.3 From the View of China and Japan International Trade Dynamic Development, the Comparative Advantage, the Competitive Advantage and the Complementarity of Both Parties Have Changed in Various Degree in Recent Years

Firstly, the primary commodites comparative advantage of China have tended to decrease year by year in the recent development ten years. However, the manufactural commodities comparative advantage, especially the machinery and transport equipment, irons and steels have tended to increase year by year since 2000, but the *RCA* index is not very high. The textils' comparative advantage decreased in little degree, and the chemical products comparative disadvantage have changed little. For Japan, the primary commodities comparative advantage is low, and the *RCA* index of irons, steels, machinary and transport equipment which are all manufactural commodities is high, however, all of them has been stable since 2000.

Secondly, for China, the primary commodities competitive advantage also have tended to decrease a little year by year in the recent development ten years. For Chinese manufactural commodities, the textiles competitive advantage have increased by small margin, the chemicals products competitive disadvantage has increased more, the machine and transport equipment has changed from the competitive disadvantage goods to the competitive advantage goods since 2004, and the changes degree of the irons and steels are most obvious, the increasing degree is big, but its competitive advantage is decreased greatly in 2009 because of the financial crisis. For Japan, all of the primary commodities and the textile commodties are still not the competitive advantage goods, the manufactural goods except the textile are still its competitive advantage goods, and the degree of them has changed a little..

At last, though the trade complementarity indext of China and Japan all exceeded 1, but they are all relatively steady. That means the two countries possess the foundation of developing the trade of China, and there are immense space in the mutual international trade development.

By using the above analysis, we can give the follows advice:

(1) Further improve the mutual international trade development by utilizing the higer trade combination dgree, and the complementarity of China and Japan;

(2) Accelerat the pace of our country's industrial restructuring, strenghten independence research and development and encourage innovation. By the analysis of the comparative advantage, we can conclude that the bilateral trade between them based not only on the factores endowment but also on the inter-industrial trade and the competitive advantage. Two counties all concentrate in the manufactural commodities, so the key factors that we can enhance our county's trade statue will be depended on our county's technique level;

(3) Establish the Free-Trade-Area of China and Japan by stages and hierarchically based on the APEC. We can utilize the bilateral geographic advantage and improve the coopertion degree.

References

1. Xu, P.-y., Tang, J.: Study on Sino-Japanese Intra-industry Trade and its Influencing Factors. International economics and trade research (2009) (in chinese)
2. Zhao, F., Li, J.: An Empirical Analysis on Intra-industry Trade between China and Japan and Its Influence Factors. World Economy Study (2010) (in chinese)
3. Li, C.-n., Chen, M.: Analysis and Suggestions of China's Trade Dependence and Competitive Ability upon Japan. Journal of Yanbian University (2007) (in Chinese)

Energy Saving Strategy of China's Green Hotel

Rixin Li

School of Tourism and Cuisine, Harbin Commercial University, Harbin, China
liri@hrbcu.edu.cn

Abstract. In the context of sustainable development theory,the creation of green hotel has become the inevitable trend of hotel industry development.This paper takes green hotel in china as an example,studies on the measures for energy saving, such as adopting advanced technology, green procurement,green room,green food, green service, government's economic policy support, and so on.

Keywords: Green hotel, environment, sustainable development, technology, green service, economic policy.

1 Introduction

Because of the deteriorating global environment,environmental protection, protection of human health has received worldwide attention. "Comments on accelerating the development of the tourism industry by the State Council"promoted energy saving as one of the main tasks of tourism. It claimed that we should vigorously promote tourism energy saving and emission reduction. Water consumption,electricity consumption of star hotels,a-level scenic should be reduced by 20% within five years. As a pillar industry of tourism,the efforts of Hotel industry on effective protection of the environment and rational utilization of resources is directly related to the healthy development of the tourism industry and affect the sustainable development of society. Create "Green Hotel"is an important part of the hotel environmental management. Create green hotel has become the future development trend of the hotel industry.

2 The Meaning and Basic Principles of Green Hotel

2.1 The Meaning of Green Hotel

In the "Green Hotel" Standards enacted by China National Tourism Administration in 2006, green hotel is defined that a hotel with the concept of sustainable development, adhering to clean production, promoting green consumption, protecting the environment. Its core meaning is that the hotel should strengthen the sustainable protection of the environment and rational utilization of resource in the production process.

2.2 Basic Principles of Green Hotel

At first, reducing. Under the premise that without affecting the quality of products and services,the hotel should use less material and energy inputs. The hotel's product

M. Zhou (Ed.): ISAEBD 2011, Part IV, CCIS 211, pp. 423–428, 2011.

volume and product weight can be reduced, the package can be simplified in order to reduce costs, reduce waste, achieve the established objectives of economic and environmental benefits.

Secondly, reusing. Under the premise that without reducing the standard of facilities and services, items should be multiple used or transfered,not be discarded easily. Reduce the use of disposable supplies.

Thirdly, recycling. Items are recycled after they are used and become renewable resources after treatment.For example, the installation of water system is a common way to recycle water for the hotel. There are two sets of pipelines within the hotel,one is drinking water pipeline,the other is non-drinking water pipeline.Sewage generated from washing, laundry and toilet was sent to non-potable water pipes to flush toilets, clean cars, cool or heat after treatment.

At last, replacing. To conserve resources, reduce pollution,,the hotel use pollution-free goods or renewable materials to replace certain items.Such as the use of standard bath, cleaning supplies which are organic and no phosphorus.

3 The Significance of Energy Saving in Green Hotel

Creating green hotel is the best way of sustainable development for the hotel,is the way to enhance the competitiveness of the hotel, will create good social and environmental benefits.

3.1 Meet the Needs of the Customers

With the gradual enhancement of environmental awareness, green consumption has become the choice of most people in many countries. The green hotel can offer the customers a good natural space through the indoor and outdoor green environment.The indoor and outdoor environment of the green hotel comply with a safe and healthy standard.The green hotel provide consumers with healthy service and enjoyment. The construction of green hotel meet the new trends in consumption.It is conducive to attract more tourists and increase market share.

3.2 Reduce Operating Costs

Green Hotel can save energy by strengthening energy management and the use of energy-saving technology. Green Hotel can reduce daily consumption by taking a large number of measures such as recovery of waste heat,recycling of supplies for hotel guests.Then reduce the cost of hotel operations, increase economic efficiency in general. It can not only use resources rationally, but also save money and improve the competitiveness of the hotel to achieve sustainable development. For example,in April 2009, Shanghai Longbai Hotel introduced the project of ground-source heat pump, realized zero emissions of the smoke and dust pollution,saved 269.4 tons standard coal and saved 80 million cost one year.

3.3 Create a Good Corporate Image

Creating green hotel can reduce the abuse of nature and society, protect the environment.Green Hotel is an important symbol of participating in environmental protection, providing the public with safe and comfortable space, improving management level continuously. The enterprise concerns about environmental protection can win government's support and the goodwill of consumers, establish a good corporate image easily. Creating green hotel can make the hotel won the respect and trust of consumers and enhance the visibility of the hotel, improve the intangible assets and brand's effectiveness, so the hotel has a good reputation and attract more guests.

4   Measures for Energy Saving in Green Hotel

4.1 Extensive Use of Energy-Saving Technology

Energy-saving is not difficult, the key is that energy is saved under the premise that the the service's standard doesn't be reduced. Under the premise of the guests' satisfaction ,tourism hotels should adopt environmental protection measures to achieve business targets and achieve energy saving effect, so achieve hotel's sustainable development.

Ground-source heat pump technology is the leading way of energy-saving. The use of ground-source heat pump technology can provide the hotel with cooling, heating, hot water 24 hours year-round. The other technology is water storage technology. In order to reduce the cost of operation,hotel may use the electric power price policy of peak and valley,store energy to the energy storage device in low power time at winter or summer night, release the energy be stored during the peak power time in the day. Use heat recovery technology in freezing Host equipment, swimming pool air-conditioning equipment, fresh air system at the same time.

Frequency technique and intelligent control technology can be used to save electricity.Control elevators, air conditioning units, air coil, hot and cold water regulation by using frequency or variable flow.Transform the secondary chiller and the overall lighting, use electric meter classification, compensation capacitors, infrared sensors, and other energy-saving facilities.

Use solar energy.In October 2008, Power Valley Jinjiang International Hotel's Solar wall generate power officially. The first five-star hotel in China which use solar power was shown in the world. It installed more than 500 establishments such as solar street lights, landscape lights, lights, lawn light, solar logos, solar water heaters.

4.2 Green Procurement

Green procurement refers to procure products which have no negative impact on the environment or small negatively affect relatively. In product procurement,green hotel should consider the following characteristics of products fully:healthy; security; energy saving; durable, can be reused or recycled; low noise, no radiation, low pollution or pollution-free; less waste;easy to be degraded and be disposed or conducive to recycling; packaging moderate or no packaging.

Energy-saving and environmental protection products should be the procurement direction the hotel must adhere to. Hotels should adhere to the implementation of green procurement, the product should have the "environmental mark ".Try to purchase large package guest supplies. For example,the disposable supplies in the room should be discarded and be instead by continue filling soap, bath liquid container. Green procurement of raw materials, choose safe, pollution-free green food ingredients, it can indirectly reduce the impact on the environment, safeguard the customers' health and safety meanwhile. Procurement of energy-saving products, such as purchasing energy-efficient bulbs, electrical appliances, air conditioners, boilers and chillers. Procurement of recycled products, paper, glass and aluminum products.are the most common recycled products.

4.3 Provide Green Products

Green room ,green food, green service are three elements of green hotel's green products.

At first, green room.Green room refers to the non-pollution of the construction, renovation, noise of the room.The room's indoor environment meet the requirements of human health. All items, appliances, and their use in the room are in line with environmental requirements. The focal point is there are no harmful substances radiate from the furniture, appliances, decorative materials, cotton. There are moderate outdoor air to ensure clean air. Clean air conditioning ducts and fan coil regularly to ensure that the bacterial content is not excessive.At the same time, the drinking water comply with the standard.

Green room request that the environmental conduct of the whole process from design to provide products must comply with environmental requirements. The housing must be designed to use green building materials.The rooms use ecological building materials,natural paints and decorative materials such as wood, natural stone,etc. The decoration of the kitchen can be ceramic tile, stainless steel or glass and other non-polluting materials. The supplies in the room should be green products as possible. Reduce the use of the disposable supplies, use the disposable supplies repeatedly as far as possible. The bedding should be pure natural cotton fabric. Use the pure natural oil soap. Use green stationery, green refrigerators, energy-saving air-conditioning and lighting.Reduce the washing times of the room items. Use the classified trash and water-saving toilets, shower facilities. Display some lively green plants and flowers useful to human to reduce the room noise.The non-smoking floors or small non-smoking building may be available in green hotel.

Secondly, green food. Green food means that Food and Beverage department provide pollution-free, non-polluting, safe, fresh, healthy green food and organic food.To meet the requirements of green food,the vegetables are not allowed to use any chemical pesticides, fertilizers, and hormones.The operating process from the production, storage to packaging must meet the standards. Does not sell the wild animal be protected and be prohibited to sale by the country. In the food production process, comply with environmental regulations strictly, product cleanly, and deal with food and beverage containers and wastes in an environmental protection way. Non-smoking areas can be set up in A la carte restaurant and breakfast room.

At last, green service.Green service means that use environmentally friendly facilities, equipment, appliances in the service process,and advocate green consumption. Green service focuses on implying, advocating moderate consumption through the details of the service and creating an atmosphere. Hotels should propagandize and guide the guests to green consumption through a variety of ways.The implementation of green service requires the participation of hotel staff and consumers.

Employees can communicate green awareness to their customers, guide customers to green consumption, advocate thrift and environmental protection during the consumption.Give discount in the checkout price or appropriate gifts to the guests who conduct "green consumption".

In room services, recommend no-smoking room to the customer timely when the customer making a reservation under the specific circumstances of the customer. Pass the green information, propagandize hotel's environmental program through the brochure at the reception, letters sent from General Manager and Service Guide. Set card about green washing, card about advice of using disposable supplies, promotional materials,newspapers,periodicals,books on environmental protection in the room. Propose guests reduce replacement frequency of bed sheets, towels. It requires washing the sheet per 3 days in Green room's standard in china.The guests who doesn't require washing sheets everyday can enjoy laundry services or fruits free.

In the food service, promote rational consumption, recommend green food and drink for the guests appropriately.Introduce affordable, nutritionally balanced, reasonable quantity dishes. Provide good "package" services if guests have leftovers. Some hotels also keep leftover wine for the consumer to drink next time.The hotel set up specialized storage cabinet to set the wine the guests left, put up a label on the wine-bottle which labeled guest's name, address, telephone, and store date.

4.4 Economic Policies Support from the Government

The hotel industry's energy saving should take full account of borrowing and relying on relevant policies and measures. Especially for green development needs of the hotel, the government must develop appropriate economic policy measures to ensure the construction of green hotels.In order to guide the work of environmental protection and energy conservation,some policies should be issued for different levels of green business,such as tax support, electricity and water fees are charged by level, government incentives.So that each hotel has the awareness of saving resources, provide green products, create green consumption environment. The hotels reduce the operating costs and enhance competitiveness, at the same time receive economic support by the state government, it can be described as double benefit.

5   Conclusion

With the economic development, the concept of circular economy increasingly popular, people's environmental awareness and health consciousness gradually increased, and "green" will become a development direction of modern hotel industry. Environmental management is important effective ways and means for the green hotel to improve management level and enhance efficiency. Environmental management is a good opportunity to win the guests.Implementation of environmental management is necessary and feasible for all levels, all types of hotel. In this process, the hotel should improve its awareness and management. government, industry and the public should stirve together.So the hotel can achieve sustainable development and maintain its good competitiveness in the increasingly fierce internal and external competition.

References

1. Jinzhi, X.: Green Hotel Experience of energy saving. Hotel Modernization 2, 64–65 (2008)
2. Gong, Z., Haiying, L.: Hotel accelerate low-carbon process. Hotel Modernization 10, 33–34 (2010)
3. Yansong, L.: Green Hotel Development Strategy in the mode of circular economy. Economic Forum 1, 47–49 (2010)
4. Mingzi, P., Fang, X.: Key elements and the path to enhance the competitiveness of Green Hotel. Environmental Engineering 26, 51–52 (2008)

Fiscal Compensation Mechanism for the Coordinated Development of Post Three Gorges Reservoir Area under the Main Functional Division System[*]

Jilian Hu

Economics and Management
Chongqing Three Gorges University
Wanzhou, Chongqing, China
hjl212@163.com

Abstract. As an important freshwater resource base in China, post Three Gorges reservoir area's ecological and economic construction goals and the natural conditions itself determined the main orientation of limited regional development function. The implementation of preferential policy in the restricted developing area is out of the essential need of coordinated regional development imperatively. Our central government and state council have regarded the fiscal and taxation policies as an important policy tool and leverage to promote the coordinated development in China in the main functional areas. The compensatory fiscal policy is not only the main way to implementing the succession plans, but also strong support for the protection of water resources and coordinated development in the limited development zone. Aiming at the orientation of important function as well as the problems, this paper places emphasis on the significance of the preferential policies and some fiscal and taxation measures are put forward to promote the coordinated development in the post Reservoir area.

Keywords: The Main, Functional Division System, Post Three Gorges Reservoir Area, Coordinated Development, Fiscal Compensation Mechanism.

1 Introduction

With the construction and fully running of the Three Gorges reservoir, the main orientation and function of the reservoir has been accelerated. In the period of planning and construction, the Three Gorges project was mainly functioned as flood controlling, clean energy base and shipping. As to the orientation of Three Gorges Reservoir, Chongqing government proposed the function strategy of Three Gorges' water pool reserve in 2006, and set the guideline of regarding this area as the resettlement area for the millions of the relocated. After the period of eleventh five-year plan, according to the national main function zone construction system, the reservoir area is divided into ecological and economic zone, restricted and prohibited development zone respectively.

---

[*] This work is partially supported by Chunhui project of national educational Dept. # S2007-1-63002, and fianancial research project of Chongqing 2010.

M. Zhou (Ed.): ISAEBD 2011, Part IV, CCIS 211, pp. 429–432, 2011.
© Springer-Verlag Berlin Heidelberg 2011

2   Problems Regarding Coordinated Development in the Post Three Gorges Reservoir Area

2.1   The Increasingly Exacerbated Environment Caused by the Three Gorges Project

2.1.1   Increased Soil Erosion and Geological Disasters

Owing to the large-scale resettlement of a large number relocated in a rather centralized time in the Three Gorges reservoir area, as well as the poor geological conditions and surface morphology, in addition to the complex geological structure, these areas have suffered a lot of ground-breaking and soil erosion from the human's activities.

2.1.2   Ascending Sewage and Garbage Treatment Difficulties and Reduced Self-purification Capacity of the Yangtze River

The urban pollution control facilities can not keep up the increasing pace of urban population, hence the increasing sewage, garbage and other wastes emissions induced environmental pollution Intensively. With the accomplishment and application of The Three Gorges Project, the water flow rate has been slowed down, and the self-purification of water dilution and environmental capacity also reduced.

2.1.3   Extremely Difficult Management Regarding Comprehensive Treatment in Hydro-fluctuation Belt

Since the accomplishment of Three Gorges project, the reservoir water varies from 1.45 to 1.75 meters annually and periodically, therefore a hydro-fluctuation belt of 48.93 square kilometers has been formed. In this special area, it is difficult to find suitable plants capable of surviving on such infertile land and under weak biographical situation. At present, we haven't found such plants growing well both under 30 meters water and on land. Reservoir water level fluctuation have caused the frequent collapse of the mountain and possible land sliding, and the cross-contamination from the two surfaces of water and land is likely to induce outbreaks of epidemic disease occurrence.

2.2   Requirements of Industrial Optimization from the Function Orientation of Ecological Economic Zone

According to relevant research, now the population density in the reservoir area is of 302 persons per square kilometer, which is 2.1 times higher than that of the country's and 4.5 times than the similar areas, and it has far exceeded the modest capacity of the environment. The orientation of ecological function in the Three Gorges reservoir area require its industrial restructuring optimization should be led by eco-industry, specialized industry, and tourism service industry.

2.3   Heavy Task of Ecological Relocation

"The country should initiate the feasible implementation of the ecological resettlement program, and strive for to completing 500 million ecological migrants' resettlement with10 years." the deputy director of the former State Environmental Protection Administration, Jin Jianming said in the 11th annual meeting of China Association for

Science in 2009. The ecological relocation in this area confront a wide range of problems indeed, such as weak environmental capacity, a large number of the relocated, incomplete policies and systems, lower subsidies and so on.

2.4 Serious Problems Left over and Inferior Public Services

Influenced by the missed investigations and national policy adjustments, many problems have been left regarding the current relocation and resettlement, many serious problems are emerged gradually. there are schools and hospitals in heavy debts due to movement, and non-cultivated land without compensation, short funding for the bankrupted and closing state-owned enterprises, etc…

3 Policies and Countermeasures Regarding the Coordinated Development of Post Three Gorges Reservoir Area

To promote the coordinated development of the restricted development zones in the post three gorges reservoir area, the state should attach more importance to some crucial issues, such as environmental recovery and protection, ecological relocation, industrial development and optimization as well as the equalization of public services and so on.

3.1 Corresponding Countermeasures against Ecological Restoration and Protection

3.1.1 Setting Special Fund for Ecological Environment Construction and Protection in the Three Gorges Reservoir Area

The ecological environment construction and protection need large amount of fund which is beyond the local government's solvency ability.

As to the source of funding, the government should abide by the principle that who develops, who restores, and who profits, who compensates.

3.1.2 Modifying the Relevant Tax Policy to Protect the Environment

Collecting the environmental protection tax is one significant way to compensate and develop the ecological development in the three gorges reservoir area. According to the actual situation in our country, we may transform the current collection fees for excessive emission and ecological environment restoration to environmental protection tax. Simultaneously, we may expand the collection range to highlight the feature of being widely used.

3.1.3 Taking Advantage of Bonds to Promote Ecological Improvement and Accumulate Environmental Protection Fund

To make up the deficiency of the capital of three gorges ecological construction, we should accelerate issuing the bonds towards ecological construction increasingly. By the means of employing inter-external experiences, the government should speed up issuing bonds through different financing platforms and thus obtain long term ecological construction fund.

3.2 Enhancing the Establishment of Preferential Policies for the Ecological Resettlement

We should enhance the establishment of preferential policies for the ecological resettlement through different channels as follows:

To start with, setting up special fund for the ecological relocated is essential and necessary. Through the financial dial and transferred payments for the ecological emigration, the basic migration compensation and social security will be guaranteed then. In addition, we should increase financial investment in the construction of industrial park in different resettlement, and guide the relocated transfer to safe ecological regions.

3.3 Measures of Promoting Industrial Optimization and Development

Resorting to flexible and preferential tax policy is a good way to promote the development of characteristic and specialized industries and the ecological protection. The above-mentioned industries can enjoy business tax and enterprise income tax preference, deferred tax, as well as accelerated depreciation tax policies to promote the development and reduce their business risks, thus realize the accelerating growth of regional industrial optimization.

3.4 Measures to Equalize Public Services in the Reservoir Area

We should adopt some effective measures to improve the public service quality while expanding investment. In detail, In order to make up for the deficiency of local solvency ability, we should increase the local government transferred payment to ensure the smooth operation of security agencies and professional training mechanism in the reservoir area, thus the labors are capable of accepting the professional education and skill trainings constantly to meet the market demand. Next, to enhance the horizontal transfer payment system is greatly beneficial to the public service quality improvement, which means the provincial government in lower Yangtze river should increase a longer county financial compensation in reservoir area in a certain proportion of increased financial revenues.

References

1. Jia, K., Ma, Y.: Research On the Finance and Taxation Under the Main Function Area in China. Finance and Accountance Research (January 2008)
2. Zhu, J., Wan, X.: The Research on Some Issues Concerning the Optimization of the Ecological Compensation Mechanism in China. Environmental Science and Management (December 2007)
3. Wang, K.: On Establishment of Comprehensive Ecological Compensation System. Journal of Hefei University, Social Sciences (June 2007)
4. Zou, H.-m.: Research on Practical and Consideration of Mechanism for Eco-Compensation. Economy and Management (July 2007)

On Henan's Development of Special Cultural Tourism by Exerting Its Advantages of Cultural Resources

Guiying Zhou

School of Economics and Management
Zhengzhou University of Light Industry, 450002, Zhengzhou, China
zhgy95@126.com

Abstract. Henan is the main origin of Chinese nationalities and the cradle of Chinese civilization. Its cultural resources are rich and have several advantages. However, there still exist some problems in tourism development. In order to develop special cultural tourism in Henan effectively, some measures should be taken: to integrate cultural resources effectively, to strengthen the pertinence and adaptability of cultural tourism products, to attach more importance to visualization and delighting of cultural tourism, to develop exellent cultural tourism brands and to strengthen the marketing of Henan cultural tourism.

Keywords: Henan's cultural resources, advantages, special cultural tourism, countermeasures.

1 Introduction

Tourism is playing a more and more important role in national economic development. There is an inseparable relationship between tourism and culture, that is, culture is the soul of tourism while tourism is the carrier of culture. Tourism without culture will look pale and hollow while culture without tourism will lack of vigour. Henan is the main origin of Chinese nationalities and the cradle of Chinese civilization. Its brilliant culture has been formed after thousands of development, and it is the core quintessence of Chinese culture. The problem is how to develop these rich cultural resources effectively to promote the economic develoment of Henan, which is an important project which is worth studying.

2 Avantages of Henan's Cultural Resources

Henan is endowed with rich cultural resources, which grants many advantages to the development of Henan cultural tourism industry.

2.1 Profound Cultural Background

In the long history of China, more than twenty dynasties set up their capitals in Henan or moved their capitals to Henan. There are 8 ancient capitals, 4 of which are in Henan: Zhengzhou, Luoyang, Anyang and Kaifeng. Henan has 7 famous nation-levelled historical and cultural cities. It has about 30,000 historic interests, 97 of which belong to important nation-levelled protection units, and 666 of which belong to province-levelled

M. Zhou (Ed.): ISAEBD 2011, Part IV, CCIS 211, pp. 433–439, 2011.

protection units. Henan is in the leading position in the amount of the unearthed cultural relics possessed, and it has about 1,300,000 pieces of various relics and covers about one eighth of the total in China. From what is said above, we can see that Henan's cultural resources are rich with more historical relics and high time continuity, which is quite rare in China. So Henan is called "China's natural museum of history" by historians.

2.2 Longstanding and Well-Established History

Culture in Henan can be traced back to about seven or eight thousand years ago if the culture of Peiligang was regarded as the origin or it has a history of about six or seven thousand years if it is counted from the Yangshao culture. The appearance of the He tu (River Map) and Luo shu (Luo Chart) is the important symbol of the origin of Chinese culture. Meanwhile, the Yin Ruins' Oracle-Bone Inscriptions start the skriba historio, which symbolizes the new stage of the development of Chinese culture.

2.3 Rich Endowments and Great Variety of Cutural Resources

Henan is one of the main birthplaces of Chinese culture. In the long history of China, Henan used to be the central area of China's polictics, economy and culture for three thousand years, which leaves a great deal of precious historical and cultural relics such as the first flute of China, the first dragon of China and the first sword of China. Henan is endowed with rich cultural resources. They can be classified into several categories as illustrated in table 1.

Table 1. Henan Cultural Resources and Evaluation

Types of cultural resources	Content	Evaluation
Culture of ancient capitals	Kaifeng, Luoyang, Anyang and Zhengzhou	very rich
Cultures of origin	origin of Chinese civilization, origin of surnames and source of national thoughts	very rich
Culture of emperors	Taihao Mausoleum, Hometown of Huang Emperor, Royal Mausoleum of Eastern Han etc.	very rich
Culture of historical celebrities	Lao Zi, Zhuang Zi, Mo Zi, Zhang Zhongjing, Zhang Heng, Li Shangyin, Bai Juyi, etc.	very rich
Religious culture	Buddhism culture: White Horse Temple, Shaolin Temple, etc. Taoism culture: Wangwu Mountain, Song Mountain, etc.	very rich
Culture of red tourism	Xin county, the hometown of the Red Army and the cradle of generals, the Memorial Hall of the Huaihai War in Yongcheng county, the Red Flag Irrigation Ditch in Linzhou county, Erqi Striking Monument in Zhengzhou and Nanjie village-----a model of communist community, etc.	rich
Culture of martial arts	Shaolin boxing, Chen's Taiji	rich

From table 1, we can see that Henan not only has more cultural resources in amount but also their variety is greater. That is, almost all different types of cultural resources are covered. Of course, many other cultural resources are still not listed here.

2.4 High Taste of Culture

Many of Henan cultural resources have higher historic value. For instance, the first script in China—the Yin Ruins' Oracle-Bone Inscriptions in Anyang, China's first pass—Hangu Pass in Lingbao, Taihao Mausoleum, Hometown of Huang Emperor, Shaolin Temple—the first temple in China and the White Horse Temple, the temple in which the founder resided are all well-known humane landscapes. In addition, Longmen Grottoes in Luoyang and Yin Ruins in Anyang have been inscribed on the World Heritage List by UNESCO. All these indicate the high taste of culture in Henan.

2.5 Reasonable Distribution with Regional Differentiation

The cultural resources in Henan are scattered in many counties and cities, but they are relatively centered along Longhai railway line, Jingguang railway line and around major cities of Henan, which provides convenience to their development. In addition, different places have different regional culture features, such as Yin Shang culture in Anyang and Zhengzhou, Song culture in Kaifeng, Chu culture in Xinyang, Han culture in Nanyang, culture of Three Kingdoms in Xuchang, culture of several dynasties in Luoyang, etc..

3 Problems Existing in Developing Cultural Tourism Resources in Henan

Though Henan is endowed with rich cultural resources, advantages of its resources have not been fully exploited. There still exist some problems.

3.1 Lack of Deep Digging of Connotation of Cultural Resources

Henan cultural tourism products lack of competitiveness due to their low level of development without deep digging the rich and deep connotation of cultural resources. So the phenomenon is that the resources in Henan are the first class, but the products developed are the third class and the package is the fourth class, which makes the sightseeing of Henan tourist spots discounted and dull. Guangchun Xu, the former governor of Henan Province, once said that there were numerous historical celebrities, but that could not be reflected in Henan tourism because cultural spots lacked of attractive stories and legends, which led to their dullness. The key is to exploit the deep connotation and specialty of the cutural resources and provide tourists with rich cultural information and humane spirits, which can make tourists educated and inspired.

3.2 Lack of Efficient Marketing and Publicity

Henan's marketing philosophy of cultural resources is very backward. Cultural tourism should be regarded as products, which requires a series of package, publicity, scheme and communication. Henan's input in tourism marketing is relatively less and it lacks of scientific and proper marketing means. Therefore, marketing philosophy must be changed and input in marketing must be increased. Meanwhile various marketing means should be utilized such as participating various tourism exhibitions and fairs, distributing tourism materials by various means, going to other provinces to publicize Henan special cultural tourism.

3.3 Lack of Systematic Integration of Cultural Resources

As illustrated in table 1, Henan has rich cultural resources, but what it lacks is integration. The cultural resources are scattered in different places of Henan, so they are developed by various local governments, which lacks a whole planning and uniform designing. Aslo they are developed at different levels, which makes them look in disorder and lack of superior quality. The most important is that they should be planned and exploited uniformly according to different themes such as a tour to ancient capitals, a tour to the Yellow River, a tour of Martial Arts, a tour to red tourist attractions, a tour of seeking origins, a tour to religious sacred temples, etc.. Only in this way, can cultural tourism be influential.

3.4 Lack of Famous Brands

As we know, brand is invisible but quite powerful, which is beneficial to the substainable development of any industry. However, most of cultural tourism products in Henan do not have high tastes, and their content is coarse and vulgar, which makes them little known or even have a bad reputation. If some famous brands of cultural tourism products are set up, they will promote the great development of the whole tourism in Henan.

4 Countermeasures to Be Taken in Developing Special Cultural Tourism in Henan

Henan has rich cultural resources, but they are independent respectively and scattered in different places. The outstanding features of culture tourism are open, disperse, relevant and scarce. The facilities in many cultural tourism attractions are deficient or worn out or in disrepair, which makes them sound interesting but lack of good visual effect. The key point to develop cultural tourism greatly is to integrate them and allocate them efficiently, strengthen the pertinence and adaptability of cultural tourism products, attach more importance to visualization and delighting of cultural tourism, set up exellent cultural tourism brands and strengthen the marketing of the cultural tourism.

4.1 To Integrate Cultural Resources and Forge the Special Cultural Tourism Products

Cultural resources in Henan are characterized by richness and diversification, but they need to be integrated into tourism products with special themes in order to satisfy the needs of tourists. In this way, they can complement each other's advantages, which is the best way to improve the overall quality of cultural tourism products. So special cultural tourism products with different themes can be developed. For instance, there were many historical celebrities in Henan such as Da Yu, the hero of water control, Lao Zi, the originator of Taoism, Zhuang Zi, the successor of Taoism, Chen Sheng, the leader of the peasant uprising at the end of Qin Dynasty, Zhang Heng, the famous scientist, Zhang Zhongjing, the medical sage, Du Fu, the famous poet, Tang Xuanzang, and Yue Fei, the famous national hero in Southern Dynasty. Therefore, a garden for these historical people can be set up in honor of them, which can also make modern people review history and inspired. Meanwhile, their former residences can be rebuilt or renovated. All these can make up a special tourism product with the theme of historical celebrities. In addtition, four of eight ancient capitals are in Henan, so it is quite feasible to develop an exellent tourism product with the theme of ancient capitals, or set up a museum of ancient capitals in Zhengzhou or Kaifeng to exhibit the prosperity of ancient capitals. Henan is also the sacred place of Buddhism with many historical remains like the White Horse Temple, the temple in which the founder resided, the Shaolin Temple, the first famous monastery in China, the great aid-the-dynasty monastery in Kaifeng, the royal temple of Northern Song Dynasty and the Longmen Grottoes in Luoyang, all of which have great value not only in terms of architecture art but also in the development of Buddhism. The tourism product with the theme of Buddhism sacred places, accompanied by various activities of the Buddhism cultural festival, can be developed.

4.2 To Strengthen the Pertinence and Adaptability of Cultural Tourism Products

The essence of tourism is to experienc pleasant feelings brought about by tours. So tourism is different from education because the main purpose of tourism is not to acquire knowledge though tourism can broaden one's mind and increase one's knowledge. At the same time, the majority of tourists are common people and they are willing to accept those visual things and have pleasant experience. So the cultural tourism products should be adapted to the taste of customers—common people. Qingming Riverside Landscape Garden, which has brought about much social and economic benefits, is a good example. The key to its success is that its tourism service and construction projects are more tourist-oriented, which emphasizes tourists' participation and entertainment. Many marketplaces reflected in the Riverside Scene at Qingming Festival are presented in this garden such as construction of official posthouse to provide lodging, Sun Yang Zheng Dian to render catering service, which combines culture with services. In addition, there are many other interesting activities to present some scenes in classic literatures such as Yang Zhi selling knives, Bao Zheng meeting guests, spraying fire by Qigong, and the ministry councillor Wang selecting the groom for his daughter, in which people are inspired to participate. The Bianhe River Water's transport of grain to the capital is also a very good show indicating busy picture of waterage at ancient times. The practice shows a great success, so other scenic spots can learn something from that and adjust the cultural tourism products to the need of tourists. Only in this way can cultural tourism be attractive and prosperous.

4.3 To Attach More Importance to Visualization and Delighting of Cultural Tourism

Visualization means that the destroyed architectures and things should be restored or renovated authentically by following the principle of restoring the old things as old things and that ancient cultural elements should be encoded into modern language and expressions easily understood to make tourists grasp the true essence of the traditional culture. Delighting requires that in developing cultural resources and designing cultural products, not only the rich connotation and historical value of cultural resources should be presented but also they should be understood and accepted in a pleasant way. So some legends can be adopted and inserted into the tourism products as well. And the form of their embodiments should be novel and make tourists willing to take part in, which can improve the entertainment of tourism products greatly.

4.4 To Set up Exellent Cultural Tourism Brands on the Premise of Effective Protection, Reasonable Planning and Innovation

Culture protection is ahead of the development of cultural resources to guarantee their diversity, variety and ecology. Meanwhile tourism economy should be planned properly with the scientific arrangement of developing levels, developing orders, regional integration and overall image, which makes the coordination between upper levels and deep levels, parts and the whole, the short-term and the long-term and the potential and the current. Innovation in the mode of communicating deep cultures and proper publicity is also quite important in order to improve the prestige of cultural tourism products and promote the deveopment of economy. On the premise of all these, the establishment of special brands is critical to the the success of cultural tourism. Of course, the special brands should be based on careful study of special features of central plain culture.

4.5 To Strengthen Marketing of Henan Cultural Tourism

Marketing means of cultual tourism in Henan should be innovated by networking, informationization and virtualization. Tourism marketing should establish informationized flow and operational system and perfect the information flow of sound, image and color. Many marketing activities such as the organization of tourism products, pricing, management, advertisement planning, publicity and sponsoring should be made on line to make marketing convenient, swift, rich, effective and efficient. Besides, some short films can be used for publicity such as "The Soul of Shao Lin " which is a good example in publicizing the Shaolin Temple effectively. On the other hand, more attention should be paid to distribution channels in order to improve the promotional effect. The first is to attach importance to the market development of individual tourists. The second is to regulate the services of agency. The third is to establish offices of travel agencies both domestically and abroad.

Acknowledgement. This research is sponsored by Henan Provincial Government Decision-Making Bidding Projects (Project No. 2011B911).

References

1. Zhang, C.: Identification of Cultural Resources in Henan Province and Analysis of Its Competitive Advantages. Henan Social Science 11, 91–93 (2006)
2. Wang, X., Jia, B.: SWOT Analysis of Sustainable Development of Tourist Economy with Historical and Cultural Heritage in Central Plain. Journal of Jiangsu University of Science and Technology (Social Science Edition) 3, 43–48 (2008)
3. Feng, J.: The advantages of Henan's Cultural Tourism Resources and Their Developing Strategies. Henan Technology 7, 16–17 (2006)
4. Henan Statistics Bureau: Yearbook of Henan Statistics 2005, pp. 96–108. China Statistics Press, Bejing (2006)
5. Hou, Y., Sun, H.: Research on Central Plain Culture and Innovation of Henan Tourism Products. Journal of Henan Business College 1, 83–86 (2008)

The Evaluation Study on Knowledge Transfer Effect of Supply Chain Companies[*]

Ping Kang[**] and Wei Jiang

Xi'an college of finance and economy, Shanxi, Xi'an, 710100, China
`pkang_ufe@126.com`

Abstract. This paper aims to improve the level and efficiency of knowledge transfer among Supply Chain Companies, strengthen the companies' knowledge and knowledge innovation skill and enhance the advantage of supply chain competition. Using AHP and GRAP, this study analyses the influence factors of knowledge transfer among Supply Chain Companies, construct evaluation model of knowledge transfer effect. Thus, through the calculation and comparison of grey correlation among different influential factors, this study concludes the order of knowledge transfer effect among Supply Chain Companies. Therefore, based on the results of the study, this paper tends to improve the efficiency of knowledge transfer among Supply Chain Companies under effective control.

Keywords: Knowledge transfer, effect evaluation, AHP, GRAP.

1 Introduction

The effective supply chain management can make the enterprises on the chains obtain and maintain the stable and lasting competitive advantages. Nowadays, in the era of knowledge economy, the supply chain is no longer merely limited to the physical distribution., the information flow and the fund flow, The knowledge flow are also added into the supply chains, which is considered as one of the important strategic resources that affect the whole competitive advantage of supply chains. If the knowledge can effectively transfer among the enterprises in supply chains, it will help to enhance the core competitiveness of enterprises as well as improve the overall competitiveness of the supply chain. Therefore, the study on the knowledge transfer effect evaluation in the supply chain has a more important significance.

At present, the domestic and the foreign scholars have conducted a series of research on the knowledge transfer effect. Hamel has attributed the successful knowledge transfer to the following three factors: the learning intentions or motivation of partners, the ability of transferring knowledge to the partners and the ability of accepting knowledge of the partners. At the same time, he has also further elaborated the determining factors that influence the knowledge transmitting ability

---

* Supported by the Natural Science Foundation of Shanxi Province (SJ08ZP14, 2009JM9008) and the Foundation of Shanxi Educational Committee (09JK437).

** Kang Ping (1961-), professor, mainly engaged in information management, knowledge management and enterprise informatization research. Jiang Wei (1987-), master, mainly engaged in information management and knowledge management research.

M. Zhou (Ed.): ISAEBD 2011, Part IV, CCIS 211, pp. 440–447, 2011.

and the knowledge accepting ability[1]. Simonin has pointed out that the organization difference degree, the organization cultural distance, the mentality of organization members and some others will influence the knowledge transfer and the receiving [2].

Gupa A thinks that the wishes for obtaining knowledge from the knowledge resource and the learning ability of organization are the main factors to influence the knowledge transfer effect [3]. Nowadays, there are also some researches studying the knowledge transfer in supply chain at home. For example, in the papers of "Study on the knowledge transfer and diffusion" and "The formation and sustainability of knowledge capital in enterprises", Wang Kaiming et al have conducted a tentative statement about the transfer process of knowledge in enterprises and compared the knowledge transfer cost as well as proposed the incentives of enterprises [4-5]. Then we can find that they have different emphases on the knowledge transfer effect based on supply chain companies. However, as the knowledge has the explicit and implicit characteristics and the implicit knowledge is more complex than the explicit knowledge which is more difficult to express and quantify, so the researches that study the evaluation of effect are still at relatively early stage. This paper has analyzed the influence factors of knowledge transfer effect between supply chain companies and constructed the grey comprehensive evaluation model based on AHP (analytic hierarchy process) so as to make the comprehensive evaluation of enterprise's knowledge transfer effect in supply chains become a reality.

2 The Analysis of Influence Factors of Knowledge Transfer Effect between Supply Chain Companies

As the knowledge has the strong complementarity and dependence between enterprises in the supply chain nodes, so this paper has mainly analyzed the effect problems that influence the knowledge transfer from the knowledge senders, the knowledge receivers and the enterprise cooperation scene between the supply chain companies.

The knowledge sender. In the process of knowledge transfer, whether the knowledge senders are willing to share knowledge with others, in which degree they are willing to share with others as well as the investment of knowledge sharing, these three factors will directly determine the effectiveness of knowledge transfer [6]. The knowledge sender is in the driving position. If the knowledge sender is lack of effort or has reservations about the transferred knowledge, then the efficiency of knowledge transfer will be greatly reduced. The knowledge transfer ability of the knowledge senders are mainly reflected in the following two aspects: the cost of knowledge transfer and the diffusion speed of knowledge transfer. The cost of knowledge transfer is the primary factor that influences the knowledge sender to diligently transfer the knowledge. If the cost is too high, or even higher than the economic benefits brought by the knowledge transfer, then the knowledge sender will give up the knowledge transfer. The diffusion speed of knowledge transfer is another factor that influences the knowledge transfer effect. The diffusion speed of knowledge transfer refers to the time interval in which the knowledge senders transfer the knowledge to the receivers and the effective knowledge quantity is obtained by the receivers under the effective cooperation scene. The shorter the time lasts, the faster the diffusion speed of transfer is, which also shows that the knowledge transfer ability of knowledge senders is stronger and vice versa.

The knowledge receiver. The knowledge receiving ability of knowledge receivers is also the key factor that influences the knowledge transfer effect. In this paper, it is mainly reflected in two aspects: knowledge learning motivation and knowledge absorptive capacity. The knowledge learning motivation refers to the phenomenon that the knowledge receivers are willing to learn the knowledge transferred by knowledge senders. If the learning motivation is stronger, the knowledge transfer effect will be better and vice versa. The knowledge acceptance ability can be measured by the effective utilization rate of knowledge, which refers to the effective rate between the knowledge actually employed by the enterprises and the total knowledge transferred by the knowledge senders. If the ratio is bigger, and it will indicate that the knowledge acceptance ability is stronger. Then the knowledge transfer effect will be better and vice versa.

The cooperation scene. As the cognitive structure and the enterprise culture of each company in supply chains are different, so this difference will always lead to the communication barrier, which also influences the transfer, the receiving and the absorption of knowledge. The greater the difference is, the more difficult the communication will be. Then the efficiency of knowledge transfer will be lower. If the communication is smooth, it will also improve the efficiency of knowledge transfer.

3 The Evaluation Methods of Knowledge Transfer Effect in Supply Chains

When the enterprises in supply chain perform the knowledge transfer activities, they will be affected by many factors. However, these factors are usually difficult to quantify and they have greatly influenced the knowledge transfer effect. The knowledge transfer system in supply chain is actually a grey system. From another point of view, this paper has introduced AHP and grey relational analysis methods (GRAP) according to the influence factors of knowledge transfer in supply chains without excessively pursuing the accurate data results. Then discuss the evaluation ways of knowledge transfer effect in supply chain, which can not only compare the order of knowledge transfer effect of each enterprise in supply chains, but also provide some mathematical language that can be judged for the analysis of influence factors. So it can be obtained which factors affect in a big way, which factors affect in a small way, which factors need to be improved and which factors need to be suppressed, etc. Then it will be helpful to improve the efficiency of knowledge transfer in supply chain companies.

4 The Establishment of Grey Synthetic Evaluation Model Based on AHP

The analytic hierarchy process is a multi-objective decision making method that systematically and hierarchically analyze the problems. However, GRAP method is usually used for analyzing and processing the vertical sequence (such as the time series) [7]. This paper has combined the AHP method and the GRAP method to establish the evaluation model of knowledge transfer effect in supply chains, and the basic idea is: the hierarchy structure relational diagram is constructed through AHP method. The relative weight of each influence factor in the criteria layer and the program layer is quantitatively calculated according to the judgment matrix. Then through the GRAP method, the non-inspected pattern vector formed by the importance degree of each influence factor in criteria layer and the characteristic matrix of knowledge transfer effect composed by the relative weight of each influence factor in program layer have been got. According to the interrelatedness computation, the order of knowledge transfer effect of each enterprise in the supply chain will be also obtained.

(1) The establishment of hierarchical structure model.

Based on the analysis of influence factors of knowledge transfer effect of supply chain companies, we will regard the influence factors as the criteria layer so as to construct the hierarchical structure graph about the evaluation system of knowledge transfer effect between supply chain companies, which can be shown in Figure 1.

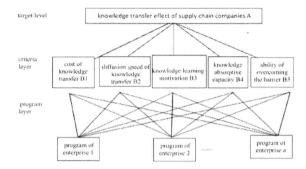

Fig. 1. The hierarchical structure graph of knowledge transfer effect of supply

Note: The n program of enterprise represents the knowledge transfer model of the five evaluation indexes contained by some enterprise. The future research can implement the empirical study through collecting the specific data and discussing the specific programs.

(2) Determining the weight ratio of influence factors in criteria layer on the target layer.

According to the five influence factors in criteria layer, the experts have been invited to compare the influence degree of knowledge transfer effect of supply chain companies in target layer through the 1~9 scale method. Then they will determine the scale value and construct the judgment matrix which can be shown in Table 1.

Table 1. The judgment matrix of each influence factor in criteria layer and the weight ratio on target layer

A	B1	B2	B3	B4	B5	sorting value
B1	1	3	5	1	5	0.351
B2	1/3	1	3	1/5	3	0.133
B3	1/5	1/3	1	1/5	3	0.078
B4	1	5	5	1	5	0.388
B5	1/5	1/3	1/3	1/5	1	0.050

Using the AHP software we can get

λ max =5.287, CI=0.072, RI=1.120, CR=0.064 <0.10.

CR <0.10, therefore, the judgment matrix can be passed consistently after checks and have the satisfactory consistency. Otherwise, the judgment matrix also needs to be adjusted.

The above results have shown that the importance values of each influence factor of knowledge transfer effect in supply chains are: the knowledge absorptive capacity (0.388), the cost of knowledge transfer (0.351), the diffusion speed of knowledge transfer (0.133), the knowledge learning motivation (0.078) and the ability of overcoming the communication barrier (0.050).

(3) Determining the weight ratio of program layer in the five influence factors

The calculation principle is the same as above. This paper has selected three enterprises as the examples and determined the influence degree of the three enterprises under five factors. And the specific judgment matrix and the weight ratio value of each enterprise can be shown from Figure 2 to Figure 6. Meanwhile, C is on behalf of enterprise's programs and α is regarded as the sorting.

$$\begin{bmatrix} B1 & C1 & C2 & C3 & \alpha \\ C1 & 1 & 5 & 3 & 0.637 \\ C2 & 1/5 & 1 & 1/3 & 0.105 \\ C3 & 1/3 & 3 & 1 & 0.258 \end{bmatrix}$$
λ max = 3.039, CI = 0.019
RI = 0.580, CR = 0.033 < 0.10

Fig. 2. The weight ratio of program layer in cost index of knowledge transfer

$$\begin{bmatrix} B2 & C1 & C2 & C3 & \alpha \\ C1 & 1 & 1/5 & 1/3 & 0.101 \\ C2 & 5 & 1 & 4 & 0.674 \\ C3 & 3 & 1/4 & 1 & 0.226 \end{bmatrix}$$
λ max = 3.086, CI = 0.043
RI = 0.580, CR = 0.074 < 0.10

Fig. 3. The weight ratio of program layer in diffusion speed index of knowledge transfer

$$\begin{bmatrix} B3 & C1 & C2 & C3 & \alpha \\ C1 & 1 & 5 & 6 & 0.717 \\ C2 & 1/5 & 1 & 3 & 0.195 \\ C3 & 1/6 & 1/3 & 1 & 0.088 \end{bmatrix}$$
λ max = 3.094, CI = 0.047
RI = 0.580, CR = 0.081 < 0.10

Fig. 4. The weight ratio of program layer in the index of knowledge learning motivation

$$\begin{bmatrix} B4 & C1 & C2 & C3 & \alpha \\ C1 & 1 & 7 & 5 & 0.731 \\ C2 & 1/7 & 1 & 1/3 & 0.081 \\ C3 & 1/5 & 3 & 1 & 0.188 \end{bmatrix}$$
λ max = 3.065, CI = 0.032
RI = 0.580, CR = 0.055 < 0.10

Fig. 5. The weight ratio of program layer in the index of knowledge absorptive ability

$$\begin{bmatrix} B5 & C1 & C2 & C3 & \alpha \\ C1 & 1 & 4 & 1/3 & 0.280 \\ C2 & 1/4 & 1 & 1/5 & 0.094 \\ C3 & 3 & 5 & 1 & 0.627 \end{bmatrix}$$
λ max = 3.086, CI = 0.043
RI = 0.580, CR = 0.074 < 0.10

Fig. 6. The weight ratio of program layer in the index of the ability of overcoming the communication barrier

(4) Giving the typical characteristic matrix of knowledge transfer effect and the non-inspected pattern vector

There are five factors that influence the knowledge transfer effect in supply chain, namely n=5. There are three enterprises waiting for assessment, namely m=3. And then we will find the typical characteristic matrix of knowledge transfer effect.

$$T_K = \begin{bmatrix} T_{K1} \\ T_{K2} \\ T_{K3} \end{bmatrix} = \begin{bmatrix} 0.637 & 0.101 & 0.717 & 0.731 & 0.280 \\ 0.105 & 0.674 & 0.195 & 0.081 & 0.094 \\ 0.258 & 0.226 & 0.088 & 0.188 & 0.627 \end{bmatrix}$$

Similarly, we can also get the non-inspected pattern vector composed by the importance degree of each influence factor.

$$X_\Pi = \{e_1, e_2, e_3, e_4, e_5\} = \{0.351, 0.133, 0.078, 0.388, 0.050\}$$

(5) Calculating the correlation degree

$$X_\Pi = \{e_1, e_2, e_3, e_4, e_5\} = \{0.351, 0.133, 0.078, 0.388, 0.050\}$$

is regarded as the main factor and T_{ki} $(i = 1, 2, 3)$ is considered as the sub-factor. $\{x_\Pi\}$ should be carried out the initial processing.

$$X_\Pi = \left(\frac{0.351}{0.351} \quad \frac{0.133}{0.351} \quad \frac{0.078}{0.351} \quad \frac{0.388}{0.351} \quad \frac{0.050}{0.351} \right) = (1, \ 0.379, \ ,0.222, 1.105, 0.142)$$

$T_{K1} = (0.637, 0.101, 0.717, 0.731, 0.280)$ $T_{K2} = (0.105, 0.674, 0.195, 0.081, 0.094)$

$T_{K3} = (0.258, 0.226, 0.088, 0.188, 0.627)$

Calculating the sequence difference:

$\Delta_{\Pi Ki}(K) = |X_\Pi(K) - T_{Ki}(K)| \quad i = 1,2,3 \quad K = 1,2,3,4,5$

$\Delta_{\Pi K1} = (0.363, 0.278, 0.495, 0.374, 0.138)$ $\Delta_{\Pi K2} = (0.895, 0.295, 0.027, 1.024, 0.048)$

$\Delta_{\Pi K3} = (0.742, 0.153, 0.134, 0.917, 0.485)$

Calculating the maximum value and the minimum value of the two levels:

$\max \ |K_\Pi(k) - T_{k1}(k)| = 0.495$

$\max \ |K_\Pi(k) - T_{k2}(k)| = 1.024$ $\max \ |K_\Pi(k) - T_{k3}(k)| = 0.917$

Therefore $\Delta_{\max} = \max \ \max \ |K_\Pi(k) - T_{ki}(k)| = 1.024$ $\Delta\min = 0$

Calculating the correlation ratio. According to the formula $\varepsilon_{ij}(k) = \dfrac{\Delta\min + \rho\Delta\max}{\Delta ij(k) + \rho\Delta\max}$, taking $\rho = 0.5$ and then we can get the correlation ratio, which can be shown in Table 2.

Table 2. The correlation ratio

$\varepsilon_{ni}(k)$ I	k=1	k=2	k=3	k=4	k=5
i=1	0. 585	0. 648	0. 508	0. 578	0. 788
i=2	0. 364	0. 634	0. 950	0. 333	0. 914
i=3	0. 408	0. 770	0. 793	0. 358	0. 514

Calculating the correlation degree

Form the formula $\gamma_{ni} = \dfrac{1}{n}\sum\limits_{k=1}^{n} \varepsilon_{ni}(k)$, we can get

$\gamma_{\Pi k1} = 0.621$, $\gamma_{\Pi k2} = 0.639$, $\gamma_{\Pi k3} = 0.569$

Namely the correlation degree is $\gamma_{\Pi k2} > \gamma_{\Pi k1} > \gamma_{\Pi k3}$. Then we can conclude that among the three enterprises in supply chain, the effect of knowledge transfer program of enterprise 2 is the best when the knowledge transfer is conducted. From the correlation ratio value of enterprise 2, we can also find that the diffusion speed of knowledge transfer of enterprise 2 is slowly and the knowledge absorptive ability is relatively weak comparing with the other two enterprises, but the knowledge transfer cost is relatively low comparing with them as well as the strong knowledge learning motivation and the strong ability of overcoming the communication barrier. These obvious advantages can compensate the disadvantages of the other two indexes, namely the enterprise 2 has the best knowledge transfer effect in supply chains.

5 Conclusion

At present, the competition of enterprises is not just the competition between the individual companies, but also extending to the competition between supply chains. Improving the transfer effect of knowledge in supply chains can not only promote the knowledge innovation of enterprises, but also increase the competitive advantage of the overall supply chains [8]. Then the effective evaluation of knowledge transfer effect is particularly important. As the evaluation system of knowledge transfer effect of supply chain companies is a grey system. Based on this, this paper has combined the AHP method and the GRAP method to construct the evaluation model of knowledge transfer effect in supply chains. Meanwhile, through calculating the weight ratio of each layer relative to the previous layer, the correlation degree will be obtained. From this we can find the order of knowledge transfer effect of each enterprise in supply chains. According to the correlation ratio value, we can also judge in which factors the enterprises should be improved so as to effectively control them and improve the efficiency of knowledge transfer, which has a certain practical significance for the enterprises.

References

1. Hamel, G.: Competition for competence and inter-partner learning within international strategic alliances. Strategic Management Journal 12, 83–103 (1991)
2. Simonin, B.L.: Ambiguity and the Process of Knowledge Transfer in Strategic Alliances. Strategic Management Journal (9), 595–623 (1999)
3. Gupa, A., Govindarajan, V.: Knowledge management's socialdi-mension: lessons from nucor steel. Sloan Management Review 42(1), 71–80 (2000)
4. Kaiming, W., Junkang, W.: Study on the knowledge transfer and diffusion. Foreign Economies and Management 25(10), 2–7 (2000)
5. Kaiming, W., Junkang, W.: The formation and sustainability of knowledge capital in enterprises. Foreign Economies and Management 23(5), 43–48 (2001)
6. Nan, L., Yumin, L.: Study on the knowledge transfer and the diffusion mechanism in supply chains. Technology and Management Research (6) (2003)
7. Dong, D., Qinghua, P., Yan, W.: Modern Comprehensive evaluation methods and Case Selection. Tsinghua University Press, Beijing (2008)
8. Bai, Y.: Study on the supply chain performance evaluation of the dynamic alliance of auto enterprises based on balanced scorecard. Management World (8), 161–162 (2007)

An Empirical Study on the Covergence of Expenditure per Student of High School between Provinces in China

Lei Nie and Chuanyi Wang

Wuhan University, School of economics and management, Wuhan University,
School of education science, Hubei Wuhan, 430072, China
wangchuanyi1128@163.com

Abstract. This article suggest that the equity contain absolute β covergence and club covergence. It could be detect by using panel data regression to analysis. This article find that: In China, there is absolute β covergence between provinces and club covergence in most distinct except for Huanghe River area and southwest area.

Keywords: High school,expenditure per student, absolute β convergence, club convergence.

1   Definition and Review of Relevant Researches

With the increasing demands of a balanced development on basic education and reducing the high school differences among regions, Average educational expenditures is an important indicator of the differences between regional education development, therefore inter-provincial high school students average educational expenditures fund is good for analyzing inter-provincial differences in the high school education development.

Current scholars views on intro-provincial high school students Average educational expenditures fund are mainly the following: differences between developed areas and less developed areas is more and more large; compared with 2003, 2007 Average educational expenditures difference of inter-regional increased;[1]east high school average educational expenditures was significantly higher than the average national investment funds or the western and central regions, the growth rate is higher than the national and other areas, student average budget gap is widening. Growth trends of western and central regions are similar with the national rate, but much lower than the east region. Central region has the lowest average educational expenditures budget, and with the slowest growth. [2] Most of these indicators are the standard deviation, standard difference coefficient, the Gini coefficient, Sale coefficient and so on. Although these statistics may reflect the overall inter-provincial funding for high school students, and analyze intro-provincial balance features through above statistics, but it is not sufficient to grasp balance process characteristics and the control of independent variables.

There are two stages to achieve a balanced process: In the first phase, provinces with average educational expenditures fund began to increase, but it did not exceed the rate of the development of advanced provinces, provincial differences does not reduce actually, but still further expand; In the second stage, less developed provinces

M. Zhou (Ed.): ISAEBD 2011, Part IV, CCIS 211, pp. 448–454, 2011.

further enhance the pace of development, and exceed advanced provinces to narrowing the intro-provincial gap. There are some studies on only the second stage, and no fully excavation for the first phase features. This study takes use of economic convergence, proposed by Cai Fang and fellow scholars, to give a more accurate grasp on average educational expenditures balance features of the first stage[1].

Studies have divided economic convergence into the absolute β convergence, conditional βconvergence, club convergence and σ convergence, which shows the economic gap narrowing(widening) level of a country or region. [3] This study investigated the absolute β convergence and club convergence of high school average educational expenditures.(1) Absolute β convergence: the initial high school with different average educational expenditures fund levels among provinces, the low level of provinces have rapid growth, provinces with high investment growth rate slows down, the fund of these two kinds become close to the same level; (2) club convergence: provinces with similar economic conditions, policy environment and geographical location, but the initial high school average educational expenditures fund levels are different, the low level provinces have fast growth, provinces with high growth slows down, at last these two kinds tend to reach a close level. The difference between the two convergences are: comparison subject of absolute βconvergence targets at national wide, while club convergence object focuses on provinces with the same economic conditions, policy context and location, that is to control the three irrelevant variable of economy, policy and location. This paper will use the Panel data regression method to analyze intro-provincial high school average educational expenditures fund from 1999 to 2009 in order to examine these two types of convergence.

2   Research Ideas and Model Building

Absolute β convergence characteristics of high school average educational expenditures need to explore the relationship between provinces high school average educational expenditures fund and its growth rate, utilizing practices of other scholars, [4] I build the model as the following form:

$$(1/T)Ln(y_{i,t-1+T} / y_{i,t-1}) = a - \frac{1-e^{-\beta T}}{T}Ln(y_{i,t-1}) + u_{i,t} \tag{1}$$

$$y_{i,t-1+T}$$

$y_{i,t-1+T}$ And $y_{i,t-1}$ corresponds to high school average educational expenditures level at a certain time, T for the time interval between base time and report time. This paper examines the sequential growth rate, so T = 1, the original equation is

$$Ln(y_{i,t-1+T} / y_{i,t-1}) = a - (1-e^{-\beta})*Ln(y_{i,t-1}) + u_{i,t} \tag{2}$$

---

[1] Refer to Cai Fang, Duyang, China regional economic growth convergence and differnce[J]·Economic Studies, 2000, (10).

If $\beta = e^{-\beta} - 1$, then $Ln(y_{i,t-1+T} / y_{i,t-1}) = a + \beta * Ln(y_{i,t-1}) + u_{i,t}$ (3)

β is called the Growth elasticity of high school average educational expenditures level to its growth rate., investment in high school average educational expenditures level changes 1% units, then high school average educational expenditures funds growth changes β% unit.

Club convergence of high school average educational expenditures funds not only need to observe the relation between province educational development and its growth rate, but also to control three irrelevant variables as regional economic development state, policy environment and location. Therefore, improve the model (1) and get:

$$(1/T)Ln(y_{i,t-1+T} / y_{i,t-1}) = a - \frac{1-e^{-\beta T}}{T} Ln(y_{i,t-1}) + \sum a_i * X_i + D_i + u_{i,t} \quad (4)$$

X_i Represents economic development and marketing degree, D_i refers to target provinces location. Similarly, we make T=1, $\beta = e^{-\beta} - 1$; ; The original equation changes to:

$$Ln(y_{i,t-1+T} / y_{i,t-1}) = a + \beta * Ln(y_{i,t-1}) + \sum a_i * X_i + D_i + u_{i,t} \quad (5)$$

β is the growth elasticity of high school average educational expenditures funds and its growth rate, that is in provinces with similar economic development, policy environment and geographical location, every 1% units change of high school average educational expenditures funds, its growth changes β% units.

To explore the convergence features of intro-province high school average educational expenditures funds, we propose the following two assumptions:

Assumption a: there are absolute β convergence characteristics of intro-provincial Education Funds;

Assumption a proof is equivalent to the negative relationship between high school average educational expenditures funds and its growth rate, which proved the model (3) $\beta < 0$;

Assumption b: there are club convergence characteristics in intro-provincial high school average educational expenditures funds;

The proof of assumption b is equivalent to prove Negative relationship between intro-provincial high school average educational expenditures funds and its growth rate after controlling three irrelevant variables of economic development, policy environment and location, which proves model (4) $\beta < 0$;

3 Variable Selection and Descriptive Statistics

Induced variable in this study is educational development rate, independent variable is educational development level, and control variables are the level of economic development, policy environment and geographic location. The measurement indicators of all variables and data sources as follows:

Table 3.1. Variable measure and data sources

	variables	Measure	Data sources
induced variable	Growth rate of average educational expenditures funds	sequential growth rate of average educational expenditures funds	China Education Finance Statistics Yearbook(1999-2008)
independent variable	average educational expenditures funds level	lagged one period average educational expenditures funds	China Education Finance Statistics Yearbook(1999-2008)
control variables	economic development level	Gross domestic product	China Statistical Yearbook(1999-2008)
	Police environment	Market Indices	China's market index(2009)— Regional marketing process report
	location	Eight regional division[2]	

The selection of measurable indicators is based on educational development level with average educational expenditures funds as core, GDP to measure economic development level, and marketing indicators[3] proposed by Fan Gang as index of regional policy environment. Eight economic regions: south coast (Guangdong, Fujian, Hainan);Eastern coastal areas (Shanghai, Jiangsu, Zhejiang); northern coastal areas (Shandong, Hebei, Beijing, Tianjin); Northeast area (Liaoning, Jilin, Heilongjiang); Middle reach of Yangtze River region (Hunan, Hubei, Jiangxi, Anhui); Middle reach of Yellow River region (Shaanxi, Henan, Shanxi, Inner Mongolia); Southwest area (Guangxi, Yunnan, Guizhou, Sichuan, Chongqing); Northwest area(Gansu, Qinghai, Ningxia, Tibet, Xinjiang) their indicator data are Panel Data, the descriptive statistics as follows:

---

[2] Refer to "China plan to establish eight economic regions to replace previous western-eastern division [DB/OL]· http://news· sohu· com/2004/06/05/85/news220398505·shtml·

[3] Market indices include five parts: relation between government and market, non-state economy development, production element market development, market agencies development and legislation improvement, now many scholars use market indices to measure system environment.

Table 3.2. Descriptive statistics of each index

index	observed value	mean value	Standard deviation	Max	Min
sequential growth rate of average educational expenditures funds	310	0.0991	.1268	1.2448	-1.1053
Logarithm of average educational expenditures funds	310	8.2166	0.511	9.9725	7.1196
GDP	310	5702	5751	36796	91.5
Market Indices	279	5.6781	2.1308	11.71	0

4 Model Result

To explore if there is absolute convergence characteristics in high school average educational expenditures funds, we put provincial educational fund, I have funding for education in the provinces high school students and sequential growth rate of average educational expenditures funds into model (3), index data span from 1999 to 2008. Taking use of statistical software STATA 11.0 and fixed effects model[4] to estimate and the results show in Table 4.1.1.

Table 4.1.1. Absolute convergence characteristics of high school average educational expenditures funds

Independent variable	coefficient	Standard deviation	T value	P value
Constant	0.5401	0.2177	2.48	0.014
high school average educational expenditures funds	-0.0536	0.0264	-2.03	0.044

From the result we can get β=-0.0536 , that is from 1999 to 2008, each 1% increase of high school average educational expenditures funds, its growth rate decreases 0.0536%, the two has a negative relationship, which indicates that there is absolute βconvergence characteristics at intro-provincial high school average educational expenditures funds. Assumption one is confirmed.

(B) Research on club convergence characteristics of intro-provincial high school average educational expenditures funds

To explore if there is club convergence characteristics of intro-provincial high school average educational expenditures funds, we input provincial high school average educational expenditures funds, its sequential growth rate, provinces GDP and Market Indices into model(4), indexes span from 1999 to 2008, take use of STATA11.0 and block estimation method in fixed effect model, result shown in 4.1.2:

---

[4] The selection of random effect model or fixed effect model depends on the results of Hausman test.

Table 4.1.2. Relative convergence characteristics of high school average educational expenditures funds

region independent variable	Southern coastal areas	Eastern coastal areas	Northern coastal areas	Northeast area	Middle reach of Yangtze River region	Middle reach of Yellow river region	Southwest area	Northwest area
Constant	6.5957(4.11)	3.9477 (0.40)	4.1236 (3.82)	4.8243 (4.4)	-2.5335 (-4.52)	-0.8678 (1.69)	0.919 (1.51)	-1.7467 (-2.77)
high school average educational expenditures funds	-0.9544 (-4.24)	-0.5047 (-3.83)	-0.5351 (-3.65)	-0.6216 (-4.27)	-0.3289 (-4.26)	-0.1503 (-1.37)	-0.1181 (-0.136)	-0.2346 (-2.75)
controlled variable：								
GDP	-12.4 (-0.63)	-2.66 (-0.56)	4.17 (0.95)	29.7 (1.28)	42.4 (3.31)	20.1 (1.74)	13.9 (0.89)	1.61(0.03)
Market Indices	-0.2021 (-2.47)	0.0797 (4.19)	0.0754 (2.71)	-0.0357 (-0.88)	-0.0091 (-0.46)	-0.007 (-0.22)	0.0119 (0.45)	0.0696 (3.12)
Model F value	2.1	5.38	5.73	2.43	4.38	5.59	1.53	1.99

Note: Figures in brackets are T values examined by parameters.

From above table we can see that the Growth elasticity of high school average educational expenditures funds and its grow rate have passed T examination in southern coastal area, eastern coastal area, northern coastal area, northeast China, Middle reach of Yangtze River and Northwest regions, that is after controlling the gross domestic product and the market index, high school average educational expenditures funds significantly influence its growth rate , and the two have a negative relationship. This shows that there are club convergence characteristics in above areas, that provinces with similar geographical location, economic development and policy environment have similar high school average educational expenditures funds. Middle reach of Yellow River region and the Southwest area do not show convergence characteristics but their high school average educational expenditures funds difference have not further expanded.

5 Conclusions and Discussions

This paper studies if there is absolute convergence and club convergence characteristics in intro-provincial high school average educational expenditures funds, taking use of Panel Data recession method to analyses high school average educational expenditures funds from 1999-2008 Year and find out there does exist absoluteβconvergence characteristics that intro-provincial investment differences narrows. This expresses a negative relationship between high school average educational expenditures funds and its previous investment; provinces with more high school average educational expenditures funds have a lower growth rate than those with less investment.

Meanwhile, club convergence characteristics exist in most intro-provincial high school average educational expenditures funds, that is provinces with similar geographical location, institutional environment and economic development have narrows investment gap difference, which is very obvious in the southern coastal area, eastern coastal area, northern coastal area, northeast China, middle reach of the Yangtze River region and the Northwest area, among which the middle reach of Yellow River region and the southwestern region have less clear club convergence, but there is no trend of expending their investment funds.

References

1. Youlu, S., Hao, C.: Difference analysis on national wide average fund of ordinary high school students. Education and Science 12(11) (2009)
2. Sun, Y.: Research of average fund of national ordinary high school student status Our. Master's thesis, Fudan University (2010)
3. Tang, X., Chen, X.: Economic convergence and its influencing factors analysis of eight regions. Journal of the Renmin University of China 106(1), 106 (2007)
4. Wang, C.: Balance analysis of primary school development among provinces- empirical research on 1999-2008 average fund of primary school students. Journal of Tianzhong 6(1) (2010)

Factor Analysis of College Students' Travel Motivations in the Tourist City: A Case Study for College Students in Taian City[*]

Shuzhen Peng, Leiting Wang, Feifei Qu, and Wei Zhang[**]

College of Tourism, Resources and Environment, Taishan University,
271021 Taian, China
shuzhepeng@sohu.com, zhrenwei@163.com

Abstract. The travel motivations studies are necessary for the tourist behavior studies; both tourist market performance measurement and tourism marketing plan depend on travel motivations studies. In this article, the travel motivations of the college students from four universities in Taian city were investigated. The college students' travel motivations were divided into six types by using factor analysis and ANOM (Analysis of Means). The results showed that decompression type, learning type, amusement type were the primary tourism motivations of the college students, the decompression type became the all-important motivations gradually. Maybe the causation was the increasing pressure from the family, school and social environment. The Taian city is famous for the Mount Taishan, mountain traveling can offer the decompression tourism environment. It indicated that the local tourism environment could impact the college students' travel motivation directly.

Keywords: Travel motivations, Factor analysis, College students, Taian city.

1 Introduction

Tourism consumptions become more and more popular with the rising of the people's living standard. College student is an important and unattached part in the tourism group. They have certainly economic independent; enough time, more venturesome spirits and dreams, and can stand on their feet. These are the reasons for the college students' tourist boom. The number of college students in China has been increasing year by year; Chinese college students' tourism has been a large market. So tourism managers and researchers have given more attention to the college students' tourism behavior. Study of travel motivations as a part of study of tourism behavior can offer direct guidance to the plan of tourism picture, and is the direct power to the tourism behavior.

Although the study of travel motivations began early, there were fewer results. The college students' travel motivations were various; Culture or spirit, communication were the main motivation [1]. The main college students' travel motivations concentrated in sound body and mind, seeking beauty and culture; there was no

---

[*] Shandong Soft Science Fund (No. 2009RKB440).
[**] Corresponding author.

obvious differences between boys' travel motivations and girls'[2]. Travel motivations, education levels, leisure and consumption structure were the advantages in college students' tourism behaviors, the restrictive factors mainly concentrated in government and related departments, tourism enterprises, social environment and so on [3]. According to Yang et al., knowledge, slow pressure with owner ship, entertainment and emotion, practice and visiting friends were the main college students' travel motivations [4]. Xue et al. considered that leisure and entertainment, knowledge, new life experience, seeing the places of interest, seeing history relics, seeing the local conditions and customs were the main travel motivations of college students [5]. Zheng et al. identified that there were five push factors, which were "learning", "culture", "health", "communication" and "reputation"; and five pull factors, which were "abundant resource", "good image", "facilities of convenience", "distinctive characteristics" and "diversity of entertainment". The push factors were not significantly affected by the personal characteristics of temperament, but the push factor of "learning" was affected by the majors; gender and personal consumption levels could impact on the pull factors significantly [6].

In short, the college students' travel motivations change according to the times and tourism environment. The changes and developments of college students' travel motivations should be studied in the detailed tour activities and environment. In this article, the college students in Taian city were taken as the objects of study, the travel motivation scale was set up; the college students' travel motivations were compartmentalized by using the reliability analysis, factor analysis and ANOM based on the questionnaires in order to guide the exploitation of the college students' tourism market.

2   Methods

2.1   Variables Selection of Travel Motivations

In this article, many travel motivations variables in the literatures were taken as references to reflect back the college students' travel motivations. At last, nineteen indicators were chosen in the scale by combining the investigation and in-depth interview, and part of indicators were modified to make the indicators more clear. The detailed realizations were as below. First, twenty indicators about the college students' travel motivations in the literatures were chosen; Second, twenty college students taken at random were investigated experimentally; Third, according to the results of investigations, the last indicators were defined by combining the results of ten interviewees who were interviewed again in depth.

2.2   Design of the Questionnaire

There were two parts in the questionnaire. The first part was about the individual and demography characteristics of the interviewees; it was used to analyze the differences caused by the differently individual characteristics and search the root of the individual travel motivation. The second part was about the measurements of the motivations; the interviewees used Richter scale to evaluate the nineteen subliminal reasons about tourism.

2.3 Datum Collection

Method of random sampling was used in the survey. 200 questionnaires were sent out randomly to the college students in the Taishan University, Taishan Medical University, Shandong agricultural University, Shandong University of Science and Technology. 194 questionnaires responded, and the numbers of valid questionnaires were 184. The response rates (97.5%) and effective rates (92%) could meet the study requirements. The sex and grade information was shown in the Table 1. The sex distributions: male 45.1%, female 54.9%. The interviewees were from all grades, but most from junior (51.6%).

Table 1. Survey of the samples that were investigated

Categories	Sex		Grade			
	male	female	Freshman	Sophomore	Junior	Senior
Numbers	83	101	17	37	95	35
Percentage	45.1%	54.9%	9.2%	20.1%	51.6%	19.0%

2.4 Analysis Methods

The factor analysis in SPSS 16.0 was used to analyze the datum of the questionnaires. Principle components and variance-max were chosen in the factor extraction and rotation respectively. The ANOM was used to get the main travel motivations of college students after the factor analysis.

3 Results Analysis

3.1 Factor Analysis of the College Students' Motivations

The variances of common factor of the 5th (Taking part in group activities conducted by the school societies and classes, deepening the understanding and friendship between classmates) and 7th (deepening the emotion between the lovers) item were less than 0.4, so these confidence estimations were lower. These two items were removed. 17 items were analyzed by the factor analysis at last. The results of factor analysis showed that the KMO was 0.7; it indicated that there were common factors in the correlation matrix of the 17 items; the samples were suitable for the factor analysis.

The factors loading, eigenvalues and accumulative total of variance contribution were shown in the Table 2. According the results of factor analysis, the college students' travel motivations were classified, called and explained. The names and explanations of six types of travel motivations were as below.

1st factor was called "common type", including four items as below, "expedition/hunting for novelty", "prevent disease/Keeping in good health", "visiting the places where the idols or celebrities lived", and "meeting new friends". The variance contributions were 12.1%, and the factors loading were 0.82, 0.62, 0.62 and 0.41 respectively. These four items were the benefits of travel considered by most of tourists, e.g. newness, health, and friends. So it was called "common type".

2nd factor was called "prestige type", including two items as below, "trying new food and local snacks", and "gaining the envy and respect from schoolmates or peers". The variance contributions were 11.1%, and the factors loading were 0.82 and 0.74 respectively. These college students tried new food and local snacks in the traveling, and flaunted these traveling to the classmates and friends. They thought that oneself could be envied or respected. So it was called "prestige type".

3rd factor was called "relaxation type", including two items as below, "adjusting frame of mind", and "getting a change from busy study and life". The variance contributions were 10.6%, and the factors loading were 0.85 and 0.83 respectively. These college students made a trip for getting a change from busy study or life and adjusting frame of mind, so it was called "relaxation type".

4th factor was called "learning type", including four items as below, "understanding the local conditions and customs/culture and art", "travel when accomplishing professional activities (e.g. practice, scientific research, social practice, commercial activity)", "visiting scenic spots when looking for a job", and "traveling natural scenery because of the description in film or TV". The variance contributions were 10.3%, and the factors loading were between 0.4 and 0.75. The values of "understanding the local conditions and customs/culture and art" and "accomplishing professional activities" were higher, reached 0.75 and 0.73 respectively. According to these items, this factor was called "learning type".

5th factor was called "economic type", including three items as below, "choosing favorite commodities", "visiting friends and relatives", and "momentary impulse because of no own visits". The variance contributions were 9.3%, and the factors loading were 0.74, 0.66 and 0.44 respectively. These college students were short in tourism funds. Travel was not ther true purpose, but the accessory of something. They always went to the free or lower price scenic spots, and the tourist expenditure was mainly used in the trip. So this factor was called "economic type".

6th factor was called "pleasure type", including two items as below, "enjoying the sights of mountains and rivers", and "travel because of religious cult". The variance contributions were 9.3%, and the factors loading were 0.74 and 0.68 respectively.

There was hardly a religious belief in Chinese college students, their travels to temples were just for entertainment too. So this factor was called "pleasure type".

The results of factor analysis indicated that there were six types of travel motivations in the college students. All types were as below, "common type", "prestige type", "relaxation type", "learning type", "economic type", and "pleasure type".

Table 2. Factor analysis results of the college students' travel motivations

Factors	Items	Factor loading	Rotated eigenvalues	% of variance contribution
1st factor	Expedition/Hunting for novelty	0.82		
	Prevent disease/Keeping in good health	0.62		
	Visiting the places where the idols or celebrities lived	0.62	2.06	12.1
	Meeting new friends	0.41		
2nd factor	Trying new food and local snacks	0.82		
	Gaining the envy and respect from schoolmates or peers	0.74	1.89	11.1
3rd factor	Adjusting frame of mind	0.85		
	Getting a change from busy study and life	0.83	1.81	10.6
	Understanding the local conditions and customs/culture and art	0.75		
4th factor	Travel when accomplishing professional activities (e.g. practice, scientific research, social practice, commercial activity)	0.73	1.74	10.3
	Visiting scenic spots when looking for a job	0.44		
	Traveling natural scenery because of the description in film or TV	0.40		
5th factor	Choosing favorite commodities	0.74		
	Visiting friends and relatives	0.66	1.58	9.3
	Momentary impulse because of no own visits	0.44		
6th factor	Enjoying the sights of mountains and rivers	0.74	1.52	8.9
	Travel because of religious cult	0.68		
KMO=0.7；accumulative total of variance contribution=62.3				

3.2 Main Travel Motivations in College Students

These six travel motivations were analyzed by ANOM to understand the main motivations more clearly. The Richter values of the seventeen items were ranked, and then we got the average of rank. The results were shown in Table 3. The average of rank in "common type" were 9.8, the average of rank in "prestige type" were 10.0, the average of rank in "relaxation type" were 2.0, the average of rank in "learning type" were 6.0, the average of rank in "economic type" were 13.7, and the average of rank in "pleasure type" were 9.5. Comparing the averages, it was found that there were three main travel motivations in college students as below, "relaxation type", "learning type", and "pleasure type".

Table 3. Frequency analysis and rank of the college students' travel motivations

Type of motivations	Items	Averages	Rank	Average of rank
common type	Expedition/Hunting for novelty	2.78	9	
	Prevent disease/Keeping in good health	2.53	11	9.8
	Visiting the places where the idols or celebrities lived	2.42	13	
prestige type	Meeting new friends	3.30	6	
	Trying new food and local snacks	3.16	8	10.0
	Gaining the envy and respect from schoolmates or peers	2.46	12	
relaxation type	Adjusting frame of mind	4.25	3	2.0
	Getting a change from busy study and life	4.37	1	
learning type	Understanding the local conditions and customs/culture and art	4.26	2	
	Travel when accomplishing professional activities (e.g. practice, scientific research, social practice, commercial activity)	3.59	4	6.0
	Visiting scenic spots when looking for a job	2.53	11	
	Traveling natural scenery because of the description in film or TV	3.20	7	
economic type	Choosing favorite commodities	2.30	15	
	Visiting friends and relatives	2.60	10	13.7
	Momentary impulse because of no own visits	2.05	16	
pleasure type	Enjoying the sights of mountains and rivers	3.49	5	9.5
	Travel because of religious cult	2.42	14	

4 Conclusions and Discussions

In the article, a scale of travel motivations composed of 17 items was created. The travel motivations of college students in Taian city were analyzed by factor analysis and ANOM. The results showed that the travel motivations could be divided into six types; they were "common type", "prestige type", "relaxation type", "learning type", "economic type", and "pleasure type". According to ANOM, "relaxation type", "learning type", and "pleasure type" were the main travel motivations in the college students in Taian city .

Comparing the conclusions in the article with the literatures', we found that: First, "learning type" is one of the main travel motivations in college students in 21st century; it was in the top three from 2000 to 2007. Second, the status of "relaxation type" was rising after 2007, which was the primary motivation in the article; perhaps, contemporary college students needed to relax to respond to the increasing pressures from family, schools and society environment. Third, the properties of tourism resources in Xi'an city are mainly on the historical humanity landscapes; however, it is mountain scenic in Taian city, the difference cause the primary travel motivation of college students in Xian was "learning type" and in Taian was "relaxation type"; the college students' travel motivations were impacted directly by the tourism environment where the college sited in. According to the discovery, the researches of development and change of college students' travel motivations should be associated with the tourism environment.

The development of tourism market should associate the resource characteristics. The peculiar tourisms should be the major, and other tourism items should be given consideration too. The purpose is to meet the needs of the diversification of the college students' travel motivations and attract more and more college students to travel during holidays, which can not only expand the development of tourism, promote the national economic development, but also let college students get relaxation under the study pressures, promote development of the students' body and mind.

References

1. Li, L.M., Bao, J.G.: A Study on Tourism Behavior of College Students—the Case of Zhongshan University. Journal of Guilin institute of tourism 11(4), 45–54 (2000)
2. Jin, P.B., Lang, F.P.: Analyses on Tourism Behavior of University Students—Illustration of Hangzhou City. Tourism Tribune 4, 19–22 (2004)
3. Meng, R., Zhao, W.L., Liu, J.W.: A Study of Undergraduates' Touristic Behaviors. Tourism Science 18(2), 15–19 (2004)
4. Yang, R., Bai, K., Cai, P.: Factor Analysis of University Student's Tourist Motives—Take Universities Students Of Xi'an As An Example. Journal of Baoji University of Arts and Sciences (Natural Science) 27(1), 81–85 (2007)
5. Xu, P., Xu, C.W.: Diagnose of Tourist Motivations of College Students. Modern Enterprise Education, 113–114 (2008)
6. Zheng, Z.Q., Lai, Z.J.: An Empirical Study of College Students' Tourism Motivation Based On the Push And Pull Factor Theory: A Case Study For Students In South China Normal University. Journal of south China normal University (Natural Science Edition) (2), 121–128 (2008)

The Design of "1+N" Curriculum under Flexible Education Perspective

Li Zheng

Wuhan Textile University, School of Management, Wuhan, 430073,China
franck_1010@yahoo.com.cn

Abstract. Starting from the existing personnel training model of higher education, the paper has put forward flexible curriculum based on the concept of flexibility in higher education; and then elaborated basic ideas and frame structures of flexible curriculum plus assurance measures of building a new curriculum. People-orientation is emphasized to combine scientific personnel training with respect for individual students. Elastic and flexible way of education will be adopted to cultivate flexible talents adapting to modern social needs.

Keywords: Higher education, flexible education, curriculum systems.

1 Introductions

Under the conditions of mass education, the need for high-quality talents shows more and more obvious characteristics of the times. It determines that "the mass production" type of homogenization training cannot satisfy the needs of the society. Rigid curriculum with same courses cannot respond to market changes timely. Forceful division of professional courses and training model for vocational talents are much more detrimental to cultivate inter-disciplinary talents, and not conductive to the long-term career development of students as well. "Application-orientation, capacity-building" is considered as basic orientation for the higher education adapting to social needs. In order to do this, personnel cultivation model should be reformed systematically, and the original and traditional training model should be broken through.

Based on the merits learned and absorbed in a variety of curriculum, the paper tries to propose "1+N" flexible curriculum which not only adapts to the needs of economic and social, but also fits for internal principles of higher education and development of students' personality under the guidance of the concept of flexible education. It is hoped that will be a significant exploration for the curriculum reform of higher education.

2 Overview of Flexible Education

As a value orientation of higher education reform, the philosophy of flexible education firstly proposed and implemented by universities from U.S. in 1990s has set

M. Zhou (Ed.): ISAEBD 2011, Part IV, CCIS 211, pp. 462–468, 2011.

off a global wave of educational reform. Such innovative measure was adopted in the environment of global informatization when U.S. had flexible needs for talents. The so-called flexible education refers to a kind of education, which is based on the tenet of satisfying the objective requirements of evolving social technology and economy, and cultivating students for the purpose of the future adaptation. Meanwhile, in curriculum system, teaching plans, contents of courses, teaching management, teaching methods and other aspects, flexible education has greater composability, alternative and sustainable develop ability [1]. In fact, flexible education requires to get rid of the rigid personnel training mode under traditional educational system, emphasizing the essence of education lies in people-orientation and promoting the comprehensive development of human beings. To cultivate flexible talents adapting to modern social needs is to making use of elastic and flexible teaching methods, and paying attention to students' ability cultivation, potential exploration and the overall quality enhancement.

As for educational objectives, higher education is required to produce "skills and knowledge adapting to national productivity and prosperity. Young people should be fully developed. They can acquire a range of skills from higher education, dare to take responsibilities to himself and his actions, and then take positive measures under all the situations and pressures" [1]. As for educational practices, higher education is required to take "student orientation" and "concerning about students' employment" as strategies. "Capacity cultivation" should be implemented. Students can be trained and developed their agility and flexibility of their responsiveness to educational activities, especially imparting "skills of transferability" to students in classes design, teaching activities and practical teachings.

The philosophy of flexible education guides the reform of personnel training mode, which firstly manifests itself in reforming universities' curriculum, strengthening flexibility of higher education, changing the rigidity of the structure and operation mechanism, and providing flexible services and brilliant teaching security for personnel training system. Under guidance of the philosophy of flexible education, many countries such as U.S., Britain, France, Germany and Japan have implemented a full range of reformations in curriculum, courses, teaching methods and educational evaluation of higher education in order to responding towards challenge brought by social economic development. Although different countries took various measures, they all followed some common beliefs such as emphasis on professional orientation, promotion of integrative curriculum, focus on cross-training, respect for students' diversity, encouragement of individual development and attention to cultivate creative and open mind etc.

3   The Design of "1+N" Curriculum under Flexible Education Perspective

3.1   Description of "1+N" Flexible Curriculum

In modern society, the characteristics of diversity, dynamics, complexity and independence are demonstrated between social needs and personnel training, which imposes new challenges for higher education. Diversified combination of modular curriculum is required to satisfy the diversity of students' development. Scientific personnel cultivation should be combined with respect for the individuality of students to cultivate flexible talents meeting needs from modern society. Therefore, flexibility should be strengthened in universities firstly to response to the challenges towards professional setting and teaching contents by social development, career changes and undated knowledge. Students should be taught some necessary flexible skills and provided with corresponding educational conditions and services. Secondly, students should be allowed to choose professions and learning contents according to their interests, strengths and practical situations, making maximum use of independence of students to look for their own career paths.

Based on the above acknowledges, the basic fixed position of "1+N" flexible curriculum is characterized by the curriculum structure of "one platform plus N modules" under the premise of "big profession+ small orientation". In the system, basic abilities and professional capacities need to be cultivated simultaneously. One platform refers to a cultivation platform for basic abilities consisting of public courses and professional courses from bottom to up layer by layer. N modules indicate that modules of professional orientation for professional capacity composed of N relatively independent modules with complete knowledge. Figure 1 shows it as follows:

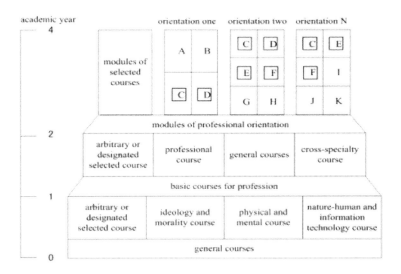

Fig. 1. Platform of "1+N" curriculum

(1) Implementation of personnel training mode ladder characterized by "1+1+2". Based on the reality of many universities in China carrying out teaching management system with combination of the "academic year" and "credit", the mode is a kind of innovation. That's to say, students will be cultivated by professional categories in the first two years regardless of professional orientation. After entering schools, students receive platform curriculum. General education will make them have necessary capabilities to be modern talents laying foundation for their future development. Students will finish general courses in the first year, and in the second year study

basic courses for profession. After that, in the following two years, students can select their professional orientation according to their personality, interests, strengths and needs with the principle of "voluntariness and assessment". Competition and incentive mechanisms will be introduced to achieve secondary divided-flow into the stage of professional education. Students will be cultivated to develop their professional capacity in the career, placing emphasis on direction, application and reality.

(2) "1 — platform curriculum" is set on basis of common development and professional characteristics of different students. It is constituted of general courses and basic courses for profession, highlighting "solid foundation" as the characteristics, occupying about 60% of total curriculum hours. The emphasis on the foundation, comprehensiveness, compatibility, and intercrossing reflects the basic specification of personnel training and the common requirements of integrated development with the purpose of enhancing the overall quality and developing potential of university students to cultivate talents strongly adaptive to the society with deep foundation and wide caliber.

(3) "N — modular curriculum" is required to set a number of modules of professional orientation selectively according to social needs, professional characteristics and career development in the last two years, constituting "menu" module library for students to choose under the guidance of the instructors with 40% of total curriculum hours. It emphasizes the combination of professional characteristics and individual requests of personnel training and market demand in order to achieve diversion of personnel cultivation. Actually, it has resolved the docking problem between the wide aperture of higher education and the refinement of social diversion of labor.

3.2   The Structure of "1+N" Flexible Curriculum

Based on the environment of credit system management, "1+N" flexible curriculum is divided into "1-platform curriculum" and "N-modular curriculum" two parts.

(1) General courses of higher education are open to all the students including ideology and morality course, physical and mental course, nature-human and information technology course and arbitrary designated selective course etc. Such courses aim to realize quality-training requirements of university students; establish a correct outlook on life and values; and then improve comprehensive quality and master basic knowledge and abilities. The main courses touch upon college English, college Mathematics, college Chinese language and literature, computer, "two courses", music, art appreciation, mental health, legal basis and college sports etc.

(2) Basic courses for profession require the students with the same major to learn for professional training objective. That's to say, students in a major must learn the basic theory and techniques of that profession, which play an important role for students to acquire specialized knowledge, learn science and technology lay a solid foundation to develop relative capacity, improve professional quality and optimize the knowledge structure. It is conductive to academic exchanges, professional exchanges and art and science pervasion. Basic courses for profession mainly include professional course, cross-specialty course, partial general courses (English, Mathematics, "two courses" etc), arbitrary selective course and designated selective course etc.

(3) Modules of professional orientation refer to a variety of professional orientation according to different orientations of same profession. Each profession is required to set more than three modules of professional orientation (shown as the figure 1 the orientation one, orientation two, orientation N...). Each module of professional orientation is composed of several "curriculum units" (shown as the figure A, B, C, D...) which is in connection with a specific theory of professional courses, skills or practices with clear learning objectives, training standards and relatively independent contents. "Curriculum units" are selected from required professional courses, restricted selective course, arbitrary selective course, laboratory course, all sorts of practices, curriculum design, diploma project (paper), scientific research project, social survey and practices and extracurricular scientific and technological activities. Each module consists of different "curriculum units" in flexible combination, which can not only timely adjust the teaching contents with the objective needs of social and economic development, but also achieve educational resource training among different modules. For example, the curriculum module of professional orientation one is constituted of curriculum units A, B, C, D, etc. The curriculum two is divided into curriculum units C, D, E, F, G, H etc. And the curriculum module of professional N consists of curriculum units of theories and practices C, E, F, I, J, K and so on.

3.3 Features of "1+N" Flexible Curriculum

Compared with traditional curriculum based on linear type of "general courses---basic disciplinary courses---professional courses", "1+N" flexible curriculum possesses the following characteristics:

(1) "1+N" flexible curriculum refers to a flexible and hierarchical curriculum system consisting of "knowledge point---units---modules---platform" with compact internal logic links in accordance with learning rules. The system will break down into knowledge points from systematical knowledge. The knowledge points are combined to relatively independent units according to the internal logic. Then in the direction of training orientation of students, the units will be combined into a module. And different combinations of modules form the platform organically.

(2) With comparison of currently advocated personnel training mode "achieving professional shunt after large-scale training of disciplines", "1+N"flexible curriculum characterized by "large-scale training of disciplines at first, then considering orientation shunt" is much more closer to current situation of higher education. It becomes much more realistically maneuverable and directive, which is conducive to reduce resistance of reforming traditional educational mode and lower the cost of reformation. Meanwhile, it is in line with current tendency of much more refined socio-professional division to improve the quality of personnel training.

(3) Learning incentive effects can be generated through medium term segregations. During the process of professional orientation shunt, competition and incentive mechanism will be introduced according to the principle of "voluntariness and assessment". Based on academic performances and individual performances, the diversion project will be carried out according to fairness, justice and merit, which is conducive to motivate students to study hard, make proactive progresses and strive for good overall scores in order to acquire the priority of the choice of profession orientation.

4 Assurance Measures of Taking "1+N" Flexible Curriculum into Practice

4.1 Improving Class Teaching Style

The basic principles of improving the teaching methods in class lie in cultivating and strengthening the critical thinking and learning ability of students, paying attention to the communication between professors and students, and enhancing the teaching effects. During the classroom teaching, student-centered teaching ideas should be implemented to actively guide students, activate classroom atmosphere, increase communication in class, realize the interaction between professors and students and continuously improve the independence of students' learning. Gradually, the acquirement of knowledge mainly depends on students self-learning out of class. The classroom is transformed into a place for discussion, communication and self-assessment, and a place for capacity cultivation instead of a place for imparting knowledge in unidirectional way.

4.2 Paying Attention to Career Planning

Universities should fully exploit advantageous resources and guide students to think about and plan their careers from three layers---profession, career, endeavors with combination of the characteristics of students and schools. Vocational planning education needs to be developed to alert students' career awareness, cultivate career planning capabilities of students and excavate the potential of students, enabling students to combine their individual strengths, interests, and social development and determine the career paths.

4.3 Reforming the Examination forms and Advocating New Evaluation Methods

Evaluation towards students should fully reflect comprehensive contents, flexible approaches, multiple measures and diversified forms. The examination tendency of paying less attention to the practice and capacity with too much importance attached to the theory and knowledge should be corrected in order to break traditional pattern of test domination. The implementation of flexible and diversified evaluation methods, focusing on the actual abilities of students, characters and morals, mental outlook with organic combination of self-assessment by students, and evaluation by parents, schools and society makes students reveal true faces in the society.

References

[1] Wu, X.-Y.: Gentleness Education: The New Tendency of American Higher Education. Studies In Foreign Education 4, 56–61 (2001) (in Chinese)
[2] Liang, W.-M., Yin, J.-T.: On the enlightenments of American university's flexible education to the implementation of Chinese university' quality education. Journal of Yunnan Normal University 3, 16–20 (2002) (in Chinese)

[3] Jiang, R.-C.: The validity of the personnel training pattern based on curriculum structure systems of "platform + module. Higher Education of Science 2, 103–106 (2006) (in Chinese)

[4] Li, Y.-H.: Surveying the course structure of "platforms+ modules. Journal of Fujian University of Technology 2, 243–246 (2006) (in Chinese)

[5] Xu, Z.-Y., Zhenl, L.: The Design for "1+N" curriculum systems under on the flexible education concept. Liaoning Education Research 1, 69–72 (2008) (in Chinese)

[6] Jiang, L.-P.: The research of curriculum structure with wide base and flexible module. Chinese Vocational and Technical Education 3, 50–53 (2002) (in Chinese)

[7] Dewit, H.: Internationalization of Higher Education in the United States of America and Europe: A Historical, Comparative, and Conceptual Analysis. Greenwood, Westport (2002)

[8] Trow, M.: From mass higher education to universal access: the American advantage. Minerva (37), 1–26 (2000)

[9] Jeroen, H.: Accountability in higher education: bridge over troubled water? Higher Education 48, 529–551 (2004)

[10] Kogan, M., Hanney, S.: Reforming Higher Education, vol. 32. Jessica Kingsley publishers (2000)

[11] Scott, P.: The Meanings of Mass Higher Education, pp. 1–158. SRHE and Open University Press, London (1995)

[12] Peter, T.M.: Globalization and Higher Education. University of Hawaii Press, Honolulu (2004)

Discussion and Research about the Permanent Mechanism of Professional Career and Growth of Clinical Nursing Staff

Xiumei Ma[1], Xiuwen Gao[1], Qinggang Xu[2], and Haijun Wang[3]

[1] The second affiliated hospital of Qiqihar Medical University, 161006
[2] The second affiliated hospital of Qiqihar Medical University, 161000
[3] Adult Education College of Qiqihar Medical University, 161006

Abstract. With the continuous advancement of personnel system reform of China's medical understaking, the proportion of contract nurses increases year by year. However, the high loss rate of contract nurses has always been an important issue faced by nurse managers. Our hospital, with the starting point of improving occupational qualities and abilities of clinical nursing staff and stabilizing nursing team, makes in-depth discussion and research about such aspects as concept, personnel, continuing education, professional ability assessment, service, etc, and also enacts a series of systems and measures in terms of personnel and nursing management [1]. For example, increase the basic salary of contract nurse with rights of having prize money, participating assessment and having paid leave of cadre. This acquires significant effect.

Keywords: Clinical nursing staff, professional career and growth, permanent mechanism, discussion and research.

1 Introduction

At present, problems of nursing staff in our country are becoming increasingly apparent, such as obviously insufficient manning quotas, heavy workload, huge psychological pressure, high-level demand and longing for continuing education. Therefore, it is imperative to establish a permanent mechanism of professional career and growth of nursing, in order to ensure the sound development and great progress of our nursing undertaking.

2 Purpose and Significance of Research

2.1 Purpose of Research

① Investigate reasons for the loss of nursing staff; ② Be affirmative about the professional status of nursing; ③ Improve comprehensive quality and social practice

M. Zhou (Ed.): ISAEBD 2011, Part IV, CCIS 211, pp. 469–474, 2011.
© Springer-Verlag Berlin Heidelberg 2011

ability of nursing staff; ④ Establish a scientific and effective permanent mechanism enhancing professional career and growth of nursing staff.

2.2 Significant of Research

Starting from the source of practice, establish an effective permanent mechanism that enhancs professional career and growth of clinical nursing staff, so as to avoid and reduce the loss of nursing professionals, increase the number of nursing staff and the quality of their professional career and growth, and meet the requirements of social development.

3 Research Methods and Object

3.1 Research Methods

Investigate the effect on professional career and growth of clinical nursing staff of the new mechanism by methods of experimental research, questionnaire survey and statistical analysis.

3.2 Research Object

Select 109 nursing staff with one to four years' experience from the second affiliated hospital of Qiqihar Medical University as the research object. 59 nurses with one to two years' work experience constitutes the experimental group and 50 nurses with three to four years' work experience constitutes the control group.

4 Research Contents

Investigate the effect of the new personnel and nursing management system on professional career and growth of clinical nursing staff in our hospital.

5 Implementation Process

5.1 Investigate Current Working Situations of Nursing Staff with 3 to 4 years' Work Experience in Our Hospital

There are now 38 nursing staff with 3 to 4 years' work experience in our hospital, of which 20 are contract nurses, accounting for 52.7%. Conduct anonymous questionnaire surveys on these 20 contract nurses from March to May of 2009 and reclaim 20 questionnaires with a reclaim rate of 100%. Refer to table 1 for results.

Table 1. Factors in nursing work enthusiasm of contract nurses

Factors	Number	Percentage(%)
Poor welfare and remuneration	17	85
Low wages	18	90
Huge working pressure	16	80
Weak awareness of active service	10	50
No opportunity of further education abroad	12	60
Weak awareness of continuing medical education	8	40
Weak awareness of nursing career planning	7	35

Conduct anonymous questionnaire surveys on 18 registered nurses from March to May of 2009 and reclaim 18 questionnaires with a reclaim rate of 100%. Refer to table 2 for results.

Table 2. Factors in nursing work enthusiasm of registered nurses

Factors	Number	Percentage(%)
Tired or not tired for being a nurse	18	100
Injury from pinprick, drug, radiation, mentality or even violence	13	72.2
Inequality between giving and receiving	7	38.8
Still choose to be a nurse or not if given a new chance, or no idea	4	22.2

5.2 Construct and Implement the New Personnel and Nursing Management System to Establish a Permanent Mechanism that Improves Professional Career and Growth of Nursing Staff

① Improve and make clear treatment of contract nurses; ② Establish practical and feasible incentive mechanism; ③ Implement a scientific and reasonable promotion system; ④ Formulate career planning for nurses[2]; ⑤ Define nursing concept and update nursing management mode[3]; ⑥ Introduce continuing education administration and carry out multi-level training: the content of assessment for training of less than 2 years includes core competences of three basics and three stricts, all-subjects base /professional basis; the content of assessment for training of two to four years includes core competences and professional enhancement[4][5]; ⑦ Stabilize nurses' emotions and improve the ability of coping with stress, fully mobilizing their work potential; ⑧ Change the concept and enhance the awareness of active service[7][8]; ⑨Strengthen labour protection against occupational hazards.

6 Results Analysis and Discussion

6.1 Research Results

Statistical results of new nurses loss of the experimental group and the control group are illustrated in table 3.

Table 3. Statistical table of comparative analysis on loss rates of the two groups

Group	Category of new nurse	Total number	Loss number	Loss rat (%)
Experimental group	Contract nurse	45	6	13.3
	Registered nurse	14	0	0
Control group	Contract nurse	32	12	37.5
	Registered nurse	18	0	0

Results: it can be found that the new nurse loss rate of the experimental group declines significantly compared to the control group through comparative analysis.

Statistical results of professional ability examination pass rate of the experimental group and the control group are showed in table 4.

Table 4. Statistical table of comparative analysis on professional exam performance of the two groups

Group	Number	Professional exam performance analysis of clinical nursing							
		excellent		good		pass		fail	
		number	rate	number	rate	number	rate	number	Rate
Experimental group	53	31	58.5%	20	37.7%	2	3.8%	0	0%
Control group	38	15	39.5%	9	23.7%	11	28.9%	3	7.8%

Results analysis: according to chi-square test ($x2$ test), $P < 0.005$. It has statistical significance. It can be found that performance of the experimental group is significantly improved compared to the control group.

Statistical results of all-subjects ability examination pass rate of the experimental group and the control group are showed in table 5.

Table 5. Statistical table of comparative analysis on all-subjects exam performance of the two groups

Group	Number	All-subjects exam performance analysis of clinical nursing							
		excellent		good		pass		fail	
		number	rate	number	rate	number	rate	number	Rate
Experimental group	53	18	33.9%	30	56.6%	4	7.5%	0	0%
Control group	38	3	7.9%	21	55.3%	10	26.3%	4	10.5%

Results analysis: according to chi-square test (x2 test) , $P < 0.005$. It has statistical significance. It can be concluded that performance of the experimental group is significantly improved compared to the control group.

Conduct questionnaire surveys about patient satisfaction rate in departments of nurses of the control group and the experimental group relatively in May 30th of 2009 and May 30th of 2010. Refer to results in table 6.

Table 6. Statistical table of comparative analysis on patient satisfaction rate of two groups of nurses

Group	Number	Patient satisfaction rate					
		Satisfied		ordinary		unsatisfactory	
		(number)	rate	(number)	rate	(number)	rate
Experimental group	200	192	96%	6	3%	2	1%
Control group	200	162	81%	30	15%	8	4%

Results analysis: according to chi-square test (x2 test), $P < 0.005$. It has statistical significance. It can be concluded that patient satisfaction rate of the experimental group is significantly increased compared to the control group.

7 Discussion

According to statistical analysis, poor welfare and treatment, low wages and huge working pressure are important factors in affecting work initiative of contract nurses. Factors like low social status, imbalance between giving and receiving, few opportunity of further education abroad and others also dampen enthusiasm and initiative of nurses to a large extent.

For a long time, nurses have formed a mindset of making disease the center and making rigid operational task the key point of work. They ignore other needs of patients and fail to take the initiative to find problems of patients, causing a low patient satisfaction rate.

Through constructing and implementing the new permanent mechanism that enhancs professional career and growth of clinical nursing staff, sense of responsibility of nursing professionals as a master and the spirit of unity and cooperation have been formed preferably, fully mobilizing the subjective initiative. Thus, the loss rate of contract nurses in our hospital is less than or equal to 20%; the pass rate of professional ability examination is equal to or more than 95%; the pass rate of all-subjects of nursing examination is equal to or more than 95%; the patient satisfaction rate reaches more than 95%. It largely solves the problem of contract nurses loss, effectively improves the overall quality and level of nurse team, and preferably promotes professional career and growth of nursing staff.

References

1. Xin, L., Wenfang, W., Dessler, G., et al.: Human Resource Management, 6th edn., pp. 239–239. China Renmin University Press, Beijing (2002)
2. Lei, Y., Xiaoping, L.: Professional Career Planning and Growth. Chinese Journal of Nursing 39(10), 777–779 (2004)
3. Guirong, C.: Nursing Management Fascicule, vol. 88. People's Medical Publishing House, Beijing (2003)
4. Zhenbo, Q.: Human Resource Management, pp. 166–167. Tsinghua University Press, Beijing (2006)
5. Xian, L., Hongyu, C., Hong, W.: Standardized Training and Assessment of Contract Nurses. Chinese Nursing Research 18(1), 162–163 (2004)
6. Shi, C.: Problems and Thinking of Human Resource Management of Nursing. Chinese Nursing Management 6(1), 39 (2006)
7. Shi, J., Wu, L., Wei, Y., et al.: Enlightenment of Nursing Satisfation Investigation on Improving Nursing Service. Chinese Rural Health Service Administration 25(4) (2005)
8. Xi, Y., Yijia, S., Yu, S.: Improve Inpatient Satisfaction Degree by Active Service. Family Nurse 5(10), 67–68 (2007)

Research of Behavioral Structure in Sports Lifestyle of Elder People

Zhong Zhang

Physical Research Department, Qiqihar Medical University, Qiqihar, Heilongjiang 161006

Abstract. This article uses document-data method, questionnaire survey and mathematical statistics to make a study on behavior constitution, physical characteristics and other aspects in sports lifestyle of elder people, proposes a construction model of sports participation behavior for the elderly, analyzes their purposes of training, programs and places, and suggests that they should take exercise in the moderate intensity, which provides a theoretical basis for scientific guidance and intervention of sports lifestyle of the elderly.

Keywords: Elder people, sports lifestyle, behavioral structure.

1 Introduction

Sports lifestyle refers to the stable forms and behavioral characteristics of all physical activities of individuals, groups and all the members in the society which are guided by a certain values to meet the multi-level needs under the constraint of a certain social objective conditions. The three provinces in the northeast of China are located in the high latitudes which belong to the severe cold district. Exploring the status of sports lifestyle of the elderly there has far-reaching significance to develop senior sports and improve their life happiness and quality of life.

2 Research Objects and Methods

2.1 Research Objects

Randomly select 300 respondents in Qiqihar City. These subjects actively and voluntarily participate in fitness activities.

2.2 Research Methods

Document-data Method. In the process of studying this topic, through looking up relevant information at home and abroad, this method can ensure the effectiveness of the article.

Questionnaire. Survey. Recovery and effective rate of questionnaire survey.This study issues 300 questionnaires. The survey situation can be seen in Table 1. The questionnaire recovery is 100.0%, and the effective rate is 93.0%.

M. Zhou (Ed.): ISAEBD 2011, Part IV, CCIS 211, pp. 475–479, 2011.
© Springer-Verlag Berlin Heidelberg 2011

Table 1. Questionnaire issuance and recovery

category	Issue questions	recover questions	recovery (%)	effective questions	effective rate (%)
respondent	300	300	100.0	280	93.3

Mathematical statistics. Use Spss10.0 and Excel to analyze the data obtained.

3 Behavior Constitution in Sports Lifestyle

Sports lifestyle is a lifestyle to maintain exercise habits, which needs to meet the basic conditions for sports population. Sports participation behavior is an expression of sports lifestyle. Combined with the characteristics of physical activities, according to the physical and mental health of elder people, a construction model of sports participation behavior can be proposed.

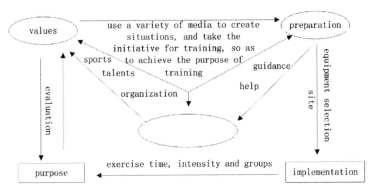

Fig. 1. The behavioral model of sports participation of elder people

As shown in the above figure, in order to achieve physical well being, people first enter the preparatory stage, which includes the selection of activities and the corresponding training sites. In the implementation phase, participants need to decide the participating groups, time, intensity and so on. The purpose they want to achieve after exercise is directly determined by their values. Meanwhile, the two stages are influenced by natural environment, social environment and other factors. At last, through the evaluation on whether the intended purpose has been achieved, modify the forms and contents of activities, so as to decide whether to participate it again or still to participate other physical activities. People's values have a decisive role in the purpose and evaluation of sports behavior. Also, as the environment changes, people's values also have subtle changes, so as to affect the purpose of people's participation in physical activities.

4 Analysis of the Situation in Elder People's Physical Activities

It can be seen from Table 2 that, elder people have a definite purpose for their sports lifestyle, which is mainly to achieve a healthy body and mind, and the number of people account for 55.36% of the total. From the point of view of the exercise program, elder people mainly choose those of smaller intensity without a specific equipment place and consumption. People in walking and jogging account for 46.07%, and it can be seen that physical exercise for the elderly is a phenomenon of "zero" sports consumption. The new concept of "spending money on health" is only applicable to a very few elder people. Some do not or do not fully understand the true value and effects of sports. From the point of view of exercise places, they are mainly grouped in the park plaza and open space in the community, and this part of people account for 46.79% and 34.64% respectively. The figures reflect that most elder people like to choose free sites for exercise, which are very limited and also cater to their sports consumer psychology and their habit of relatively fixed fitness sites. Thus, we should help elder people form a good sports lifestyle, and suggest relevant departments strengthening the construction of public sports facilities and opening public sports revenues, so as to avoid the embarrassment that there is no place for the elderly to take exercise. From the point of view of forms of physical activity, elder people usually exercise alone, followed by exercising with family and friends, with a ratio of 35.36%. There are a smallest number of elder people to participate in club activities, with a ratio of 5.71%. It can be seen that sports associations and clubs for the elderly need to be further improved. The establishment of the mass sports fitness club is a tendency for mass sports development, and is also the best way for the elderly to form a good sports lifestyle.

Table 2. The survey of the participation of elder people in physical exercise （n=280)

item	content	Number of people	percentage
purpose	physical and mental health	155	55.36%
	recreation	81	28.92%
	cultivate the temperament	27	9.64%
	communication	19	6.78%
exercise programs	walking, jogging	129	46.07%
	chesses & cards	82	29.29%
	body-building exercise and fitness dance	58	20.71%
	body-building apparatus	11	3.93%
site selection	park plaza	131	46.79%
	open space in the community	97	34.64%
	fitness centers	10	3.57%
	street side	42	15%
sports forms	individuals	114	40.71%
	associations and clubs	16	5.71%
	with family and friends	99	35.36%
	exercise organizations	51	18.21%

5   Physical Characteristics in Sports Lifestyle of Elder People

The static way of life is a serious threat to physical and mental health of elder people, so we must increase our efforts to guide its transformation to a dynamic sports lifestyle, rationally design exercise time, frequency and intensity, and guarantee adequate relaxation exercise after the load. To evaluate the sports lifestyle of the elderly in a well-off society from the social, physical and psychological systems, a good sports lifestyle should reach the basic standard of our sports population. Namely, exercise time should be more than 30 minutes each time, over 3 times per week, and the exercise intensity should reach moderate, of which exercise intensity is a factor that is the most difficult for elder people to determine in physical training.

5.1 Intensity Scale of Physical Activities for Elder People

Exercise intensity refers to the degree of physiological stimuli by physical exercise, which is one of the factors that constitute the amount of exercise. The heart rate is used to measure its size. Generally, less than 120 times/min represents a small amount of exercise; 120～150 times/min represents a moderate amount of exercise; 150～180 times/min or more than 180 times/min represents a great amount of exercise. Different exercise intensities may produce different effects on one's body and mind. According to elder people's physical conditions and physiological and psychological characteristics, this study divides intensity into three groups of large intensity, medium intensity and small intensity. In small intensity, the range of the heart rate is 90－100 times/min; in medium intensity, the range of the heart rate is 100－120 times/min; in large intensity, the range of the heart rate is 120－130 times/min.

5.2 Intensities of Physical Activities Participated by Elder People

When people walk into the old-age group, their physical health is significantly lowered, and their physiological and psychological functions also have a series of age-related changes. But scientific research shows that reasonable physical exercise makes the body able to withstand a certain exercise stress which can promote blood circulation and slow down the degenerative changes in elder people's organs, so as to improve their health. Elder people take physical exercise mainly of moderate intensity, accounting for 53.95%. From the point of view of sports sociology, one of the conditions sports population must have is that exercise intensity should achieve the medium intensity, and elder people need to reach over half of the standard intensity for sports population. More than half of the elderly feel good for exercise results. After two months of exercise, among the impacts of the three different intensities on body weight of elder people, exercise of the medium intensity leads to the largest reduction in weight and significant improvement of physical conditions, which indicates that scientific body-building methods have an obvious effect on the improvement of physical fitness for elder people.

Table 3. Intensities of physical activities for elder people

	small intensity	medium intensity	large intensity
number of people	88	151	41
percentage	31.43%	53.93%	14.64%

6 Conclusion

Elderly population is made up of people of different ages of 60–90 or more, who have different physiological and psychological characteristics at different ages. Therefore, we need to organize some sports activities which comply with the physiological and psychological characteristics of elder people of different age groups. We also need to concern about the social needs of elder persons of different ages, establish perfect sports facilities, and effectively play the role of sports talents and fitness instructors. The elderly should also strengthen their means to obtain sports knowledge, choose their appropriate sports activities and exercise intensity, and enhance their awareness to protect their own health.

Acknowledgment. This article is one of the research results of "Research of sports attitudes of elder people in Qiqihar City" (Project No.: 11552342) which is the project of Humanities and Social Science of Education Department of Heilongjiang Province.

References

1. Dapei, M.: On sports lifestyle. Beijing Sport University Press, Beijing (2004)
2. Xin, W.: The trend for sports life in the new century. Sports Culture Guide 5, 36 (2002)
3. Zhou, X., et al.: A study and survey on the present situation of ault people's physical exercises in Fujian Province. Sports Science (5), 43–45 (2002)
4. Zhang, X.: Study of prescription on the life style and sport exercises of the old people in Hebei Province. Journal of Hebei Institute of Physical Education 18(4), 11–12 (2004)
5. Li, M.: On the sports and healthy lifestyles. Journal of South China Normal University (3), 114–116 (2002)

Study on the Restriction Factors of Rural Sports Development in Qiqihar City and the Related Countermeasures

Zhong Zhang

Physical Education Department, Qiqihar Medical University, Qiqihar, China
chinard@126.com

Abstract. This study has analyzed the restriction factors of the new rural sports development in Qiqihar city by employing the data statistics and summary methods. It is concluded that the factors restricting the development of new rural sports mainly include the following aspects: the sports awareness of famers is insufficient, the sports population are few, the sports facilities are short and the sports management is blind, etc. For its causes, this paper has proposed that the development of new rural sports requires to strengthen the rural economic development, rely on the scientific management and enhance the construction and the maintenance of sports facilities as well as some other strategies.

Keywords: Qiqihar city, new countryside, sports development, restriction factors, countermeasures.

1 Introduction

The issues of agriculture, rural areas and farmers have always attached great attention from the party and the government, which are also the key aspects to build the moderately prosperous society and the socialist modernization. The development of rural sports is the important part of building the new socialist countryside and the construction of new socialist countryside has provided a strong platform for the development of rural sports [1]. The development of new rural sports has become the urgent need for the sports course and the new rural construction. Heilongjiang is a big province with large population and strong economy, which is also a major agricultural province. The development of rural sports will directly influence the popularity of body-building activities in the whole province. The total area of Qiqihar city is 43,000 square kilometers and the total population is 561 million. It has governed seven districts, one city and eight counties, which is the important economic center and transportation center in the western region of Heilongjiang. In order to comprehensively and accurately understand the current status of rural sports in Qiqihar city, this study has analyzed the previous survey data and analysis so as to objectively understand the current status of rural sports in Qiqihar city. At the same time, it has also found the strategies and measures for developing the rural sports, which has provided reference for implementing and exploring the healthy and sustainable development of rural sports in north of Henan and Heilongjiang Province.

M. Zhou (Ed.): ISAEBD 2011, Part IV, CCIS 211, pp. 480–486, 2011.
© Springer-Verlag Berlin Heidelberg 2011

2 The Current Status of the Development of Rural Sports in Qiqihar City and the Restriction Factors

2.1 The Awareness of Physical Exercise of Farmers Is Insufficient

With the rapid development of rural economy and the continuous changes of farmers' lifestyle and concept, the demand for physical exercise of some farmers in China has become stronger and the awareness of actively participating in sports activities has been also enhanced. However, for some farmers, the understanding of sports has the characteristics of simplicity and one-sidedness. They haven't formed the proper understanding for the sports functions. From the survey we can find that some grass-roots leaders of rural villages always believe that "the sports activity is just a joke. It wastes money and can't get any benefits. The loss outweighs the gain." However, the farmers who work all day long think that "it is not necessary to exercise" and "the productive labor can substitute for the sports exercise". Some people even believe that "the sports exercise will influence the productive labor". A survey on the rural sports in Qiqihar city has shown that [2]: there are mainly four factors that influence the farmers in Heilongjiang Province not to participate in the physical exercise: they don't have the time, they are not interested in sports, the family income is low and there are no relevant facilities. And the people in these four aspects are respectively 24.0%, 22.1%, 29.4% and 31.9% of the total surveyed people. Therefore, the factors that the family income is low and there are no relevant facilities are the main reasons to influence them not to participate in the physical exercise. Meanwhile, in the vast rural areas in Qiqihar city, as the information and the transport are not convenient as well as the economic income of famers is single, so the people can't devote additional effort to the physical exercise. And the factors that they don't have the time and they are not interested in the physical exercise are also the important restriction factors for the rural sports development in Qiqihar city.

2.2 The Sports Population Is Few and the Structure Is Irrational

The criteria for sports people in our country are: the frequency of physical activity is more than three times per week, the intensity of each physical activity is higher than the medium degree and the time for each physical exercise is more than half an hour. The sports population is an important indicator for social sports, which reflects the participation level of people in sports. In the total 561 million population in Qiqihar city, the urban population accounts for 39.92% and the rural population accounts for 60.08%. At the same time, the sports people account for 32.56% in urban populations and the sports people account for 10.43% in rural populations. In rural areas, the people who participate in the exercise mainly refer to the old or some patients who are compelled to exercise. In addition, there are also some pupils in school. As for the middle-aged people or the young people, they hardly participate in the sports. Thus, not only are the sports people in rural areas too few but also the age structure is irrational.

2.3 The Severe Shortage of Sports Facilities

In rural areas, the sports facilities are always short. The per capita stadium area and the per capita investment for sports facilities in Qiqihar city are both lower than the national average level. In addition to the primary and secondary school in rural areas, there are no sports facilities in the majority of rural areas. At the same time, there are also some existing problems in the rural sports fields, such as the few facilities and the poor quality, which are difficult to meet the needs of sports activities. In 2006, the fifth survey statistics of sports fields in Qiqihar city has shown that there are more than 900 sports fields in this city in which the ones located in towns only account for 8.12% and the ratio is less than 10%. As for the sports venues, there are more than 297 venues with different types in this city in which the towns that occupy 18.7% of the total city areas and 40% of the total populations have accounted for 79.8% of the whole sports venues. However, the vast rural areas which occupy 81.3% of the total land areas and 60% of the total populations only account for 20.1% of the sports venues resources. In order to achieve the goal of constructing the new rural sports, the weak rural sports hardware resource is always the primary concern.

2.4 The Sports Activities Are Few and the Sports Items Are Simple

According to the survey, most towns in the sixteen counties (cities, districts) of Qiqihar city have organized no more than two times influential sports activities every year in average. And the number of people who participate in activities is fewer than 5% of the total town populations. Even some towns don't carry out a large scale sports activity over the years, which has a certain gap with the requirements of "Selection Conditions of National Sports Advanced County" for the towns, that is "it is necessary to organize more than four times sports activities every year and the number of people who participate in activities should reach 5% of the total populations". Apart from the students in primary and secondary schools, the number of adults who usually participate in the exercises is less than 10%. And the items are still confined to the traditional "three balls and one pull", namely the basketball, the table tennis, the badminton and the tug of war.

2.5 There Are Dead Zones in Sports Management

In China, the sports management system has covered the county-level units and the towns as well as villages haven't been touched by the tentacles of this system, which are regarded as the dead zones of sports management. The nation has established the General Administration of Sport. The province and the county have established the Sports Committee. However, there is no professional department that charges the sports activities in towns, even if someone is responsible in some towns, they are mostly doing the part-time job. As for the natural villages and the administrative villages, there is also no department and personnel in charge of sports. No one is interested in the sports management. In this sports management model, Qiqihar city is no exception. The data has shown that the most popular leisure skills mastered by farmers include playing chess, playing cards and playing mahjong, etc. The number of people accounts for 57.5% of the total populations. And the number of people who choose to play balls just accounts for 20.4%. The number of people who practice the martial arts, practice the swordsmanship and dance is even fewer, which is less than 5%. The rural sports instructors are of great shortage and the farmers can't get the specific fitness guidance.

3   The Reasons That Influence the Development of Rural Sports Activities in Qiqihar City

3.1   There Are Erroneous Zones Existing in the Understanding of Rural Sports Fitness for Town Leaders and the Sports Is Not Taken into Consideration

In some towns of Qiqihar city, the leaders always think that the sports activities are just face-saving projects, which will waste a lot of money and have no income. And the fitness awareness of the farmers who work all day long is weak. They usually believe that the farm work equals the physical exercise and it is not necessary to participate in the sports activities. What's more, the improvement of life quality produced by physical exercises is a long gradual process, which will not bring some direct and immediate benefits to the farmers and that will also influence the enthusiasm of farmers to participate in the physical activities. The current top-down administrative system requires that the various tasks of higher authorities should be implemented at the grass roots which makes the town leaders become the duty officers and the performers of the target responsibility system ordered by the higher authorities. In the current performance evaluation system, some social development projects including the rural sports haven't been contained [3].

3.2   The Economic Base and the Management Guidance of Towns Are Weak

As the restriction of transport, history, ideas, information and others, the economic development of the western part of Heilongjiang which is located in central inland has lagged far behind the eastern coastal developed regions since the reform and opening up policy was implemented. The towns and the villages have higher debt ratio and the financial condition can't make ends meet. Let alone the input for public welfare and the public administration, sometimes it is difficult for the township units to pay the normal salary. Thus the construction of sports fields and the development of physical exercises have become the river without water. As for the public sports which concern the entire national health quality and especially the rural sports, the sports department has paid less attention, which has caused the serious imbalance between the competition and groups, the urban and the rural areas in the sports development[4]. And most of town cadres come from the rural areas. Even if the college students or the junior college students graduating in recent years, in the current educational system, they haven't been nurtured by the systematic sports knowledge and they generally lack the sports quality.

4   The Strategies of the Rural Sports Development in Qiqihar City

4.1   Developing the Rural Economy and Increasing the Incomes of Farmers

The farmers may have the demands for the higher level sports cultural entertainment under the condition that the living security is solved and the basic level of material life is improved. Then they will devote more energy to the specialized training and various sports activities [5]. Therefore, increasing the incomes of famers and improving the living standards of farmers should be firstly solved in the process of promoting the rural sports development.

4.2 Increasing the Propaganda of Rural Sports and Training the Farmers to Have the Proper Sports Values

At present, the understanding of sports fitness for the farmers in Qiqihar city is still in the relatively low level. It is necessary to increase the propaganda and use the sports media and other channels to publicize the exercise methods and sports culture. We should pay more attention to the competition and the people simultaneously and increase the support. It is required to propose that the financial departments at all levels should incline to the mountainous rural areas on funds and materials as well as put the support of Sports Lottery Fund in the construction of sports facilities in rural towns. The three activities to the countryside, which contains the delivery of the physical fitness knowledge, the sports performances and the sports health tests, has transmitted the sports culture information and created the sports fitness atmosphere. The government departments at all levels in Heilongjiang Province as well as the principal leaders in Qiqihar city should pay more attention to the construction of new socialist countryside which is a project that will benefit the people. Taking Beijing Olympic Games in 2008 and Guangzhou Asian Games in 2010 as the opportunities, it is required to carry out various forms of sports activities and spark the enthusiasm of farmers. At the same time, it is also necessary to publicize and promote the characteristic folk sports items by using the popular television and radios in rural areas as well as communicate and promote the experience of rural sports model villages. What's more, we can also improve the interest of farmers in sports by focusing on the propaganda of "health promotion" function of sports.

4.3 Increasing the Fund Investment for Rural Sports Development and Achieving the Diversification of Financing Channels

As there are some characteristics in the rural areas of Heilongjiang Province, for example, the residents are much more, the personnel are disperse and the demands are various, so the shortage of funds is always the primary problem for the rural sports work. According to the local economic and social development status, the construction status of sports fields and the development goals of sports cause, the governments and the sports departments at all levels should make the overall planning for the construction of sports fields and rationally allocate the urban and rural sports funds and resources so as to ensure the investment for rural sports. In addition, it is necessary to enhance the development capacity of rural areas and make up for the shortage of rural sports funds. We should attract more organizations and individuals to invest. And we can also broaden the sources of funds through a series of ways so as to ensure the orderly and healthy development of rural sports.

4.4 The Diversification of Rural Sports Forms

Because of the complexity of rural areas' characteristics, the socialization process of rural sports will be difficult and endless in the next long period of time. Therefore, it is required to analyze diversely and explore a sports healthy development path that is suitable to the characteristics of rural areas in order to promote the sports development of new socialist countrysides [6]. The sports development of new socialist countryside should take the road that uses the features to promote the popularization and the development. It should be also rooted in nostalgia and foster the new features of rural sports. In the future, we should further establish the characteristic concept, continuously study the nostalgia and create the new rural sports features. It is necessary to promote some new characteristic fitness events which are rich in local cultures, integrating the locality and the tradition, rooted in the people and easy to be promoted.

4.5 Strengthening the Construction and the Maintenance of Sports Fields

The development of new rural sports must have the sports fields. With the accelerated construction of new countryside, the fitness concept of farmers has been changed and the demands for fitness are also increased. The fitness needs the appropriate venues and facilities. With the sports fields and facilities, the leisure life of people will be interesting. And with the rich sports activities, the neighborhood will be harmonious. The government and the related sports departments at all levels in Qiqihar city should increase the support for rural sports facilities, uniformly put the construction of sports facilities into the urban construction planning and do a good job in the construction of rural fitness path as well as arrange the full-time staff to regularly maintain the sports facilities.

4.6 Sticking to the Concept of People-Oriented and Creating the Fitness Environment

The rural sports fitness activities should focus on strengthening the ones that are close to people, convenient for people and beneficial to people. Taking the scientific fitness as the main line, we should carry out various sports fitness activities, not only introducing some modern fitness items, but also fully digging up and promoting the rural traditional fitness events. The rural sports are the most local and distinctive items in folk sports, such as dancing yangko, walking on stilts and playing drums. We should seek the best combination between "tradition" and "modern". In addition, it is necessary to rely on the social forces, the rural sports meeting and some large-scale activities.

In short, the development of new rural sports is a long-term and systematic project, which requires the government and the leaders at all levels to make great efforts to integrate the wide range of resources. Expected that the above analytical study will have a certain reference value for the related departments to formulate and implement the new rural sports policy.

Acknowledgment. This paper is one of the research results of "the application of northeast minority traditional sports on physical teaching in universities" (item number: 6295) which belongs to the humanities and social science project of Heilongjiang Educational Department.

References

1. Zhao, C., Ma, Z.: Study on the rural sports and the development strategy in Yimeng Mountain. Journal of Jilin Institute of Physical Education 23(16), 189–190 (2007)
2. Jun, C., Jun, Y., Hui, C.: Consideration on Developing Rural Areas Sports Activity under the Construction Objective of Socialistic New Rural Areas. China Sport Science and Technology 6, 8–12 (2006)
3. Yong, W.: On the influence of urbanization on the rural sports—Revelation of the rural sports development in Zhangjiang Town in Shanghai. Sport Science and Technology 26(1), 31–36 (2006)
4. Ning, L., Zeng, Q.: Current Situation of Rural Fitness in Jiangxi Province and the Conception of its Development. Journal of Chengdu Sport University 1(31), 35–39 (2005)
5. Wang, J., Hu, Q.: Human Beings Oriented-New Ideal of Scientific Development of Rural Sports. Journal of Beijing Sport University 12, 1602–1609 (2005)

Quantum Chemical Studies on All-Inorganic Catalyst for the Oxidation of Water to Dioxygen ([{Ru$_4$O$_4$(OH)$_2$(H$_2$O)$_4$}(γ-SiW$_{10}$O$_{36}$)$_2$]$^{10-}$): Electronic Property and Redox Tunability

Mo-Jie Sun[1,*], Yong-Hua Lin[2], Peng Wang[1], Quan Hu[1], and Yong-Quan Wang[1]

[1] College of Chemical Engineering
Northeast Dianli University
Jilin City 132012, P.R. China
smoj@sohu.com
[2] Harbin Power Vocation Technology College
Harbin 150030, P.R. China

Abstract. The development of catalyst for the oxidation of water that operates at PH 7, 1 atm, and room temperature is a fundamental chemical challenge. As a all-inorganic catalyst for the rapid oxidation of water to dioxygen working in aqueous solution at PH 7, ruthenium-containing polyoxometalate (POM), [{Ru$_4$O$_4$(OH)$_2$(H$_2$O)$_4$}(γ-SiW$_{10}$O$_{36}$)$_2$]$^{10-}$, have been reported by two research groups, respectively. But the details of this mechanism are still lacking. A description of the electronic structure and demonstration of redox tenability of this catalyst are herein provided by means of density functional theory (DFT) calculations. The results show that [Ru$_4$O$_4$(OH)$_2$(H$_2$O)$_4$] core in this POM is the withdrawing electron group, the FMO of this POM delocalizes over the [Ru$_4$(μ-O)$_4$(μ-OH)$_2$] core, which indicate that ruthenium and oxygen atoms are the redox centers. The role of POM ligand in this catalyst has been evaluated according to our DFT calculations; the results show that it is the key structural factor in determination of stability for this catalyst. The POM ligand's effect significantly changes the redox properties of these clusters. A linear dependence between the one-electron-oxidized energy and the anion charge is found, with a slope of average 0.21 V per two unit charges for tungstates, and 0.13 V per two unit charges for molybdates. The first oxidization step becomes more difficult as substitution of POM ligands (X=Al, Si, P, S). For the same total charge of clusters in tungstates and molybdates, the first oxidization step of tungstates becomes more favorable compared with molybdates.

Keywords: Aartificial photosynthesis, solar energy, density functional theory.

1 Introduction

Artificial photosynthesis is a promising strategy for accomplishing collection and store of solar energy based on splitting water into oxygen and hydrogen [1-2]. The splitting

---

* Corresponding author.

M. Zhou (Ed.): ISAEBD 2011, Part IV, CCIS 211, pp. 487–494, 2011.
© Springer-Verlag Berlin Heidelberg 2011

of water into its elements is a high energy process and can be divided into two steps [3]: the oxidation of water to give dioxygen and the reduction of water to give dihydrogen. The oxidation of water is very complexity because two molecules of water need releasing four electrons and four protons to generate dioxygen [2]. This process takes place in green plants and certain bacteria. Structural information about photosystem II has been probed by biochemical, spectroscopic, and kinetic studies, which provided considerable insight into the catalytic center and its mechanism [4]. The reaction center containing manganese, calcium, and (probably) chloride in these life-forms has been known as the oxygen-evolving complex (OEC), a proposal is that the OEC acts as an electrical accumulator [1]; it is repeatedly oxidized (successive one-electron), when the OEC has been oxidized four times, it converts water to dioxygen; the necessary energy for this process comes from sunlight.

The chemical approach synthesizes nonprotein catalysts for oxidation of water, which was pioneered by Meyer and co-worker in the early 1980s [5-7]. The ruthenium 'blue dimer' $cis, cis\text{-}[\{Ru(bpy)_2(H_2O)\}_2O](ClO_4)_4$ (bpy=2,2'-bipydine), a metal complex efficiently catalyzes the oxidation of water with a strong oxidizing agent such as cerium (IV), the two ruthenium fragments are linked by a μ-oxo bridge, which are prone to cleavage, and thus it rapidly loses its catalytic efficiency after just a few cycles [8]. The subsequent reports about ruthenium-based metal complex catalysts are focus on the introduction of new ligands (such as polypyridyl ligands) for increasing the stability and turning catalytic activity [9-11]. However, the instability of organic ligands as a main disadvantage for these metal complex catalysts always leads to deactivation of catalysts because the intermediates in the oxidation of water likely degrade organic ligands [1]. Thus, the all-inorganic catalysts for the oxidation of water with high stability are highly desirable [12].

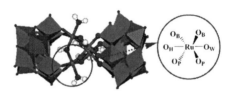

Fig. 1. Structure and atom-labeling scheme for cluster 1 (P: polyoxometalate, B: oxo bridge, H: hydroxo bridge, W: water)

A promotion in searching for catalysts that are all-inorganic compounds has now come in, when a ruthenium-containing polyoxometalate (POM) $[\{Ru_4O_4(OH)_2(H_2O)_4\}(\gamma\text{-}SiW_{10}O_{36})_2]^{10-}$ has bee synthesized and characterized by two research groups respectively [13,14]. Which are said that it catalyzes the rapid oxidation of water to dioxygen working in aqueous solution at PH 7, and it is quite stable under turnover conditions. Up to now, the details of this mechanism are still lacking. In the present paper, we report a detailed density functional theory (DFT) study on the ruthenium-containing POM, $[\{Ru_4O_4(OH)_2(H_2O)_4\}(\gamma\text{-}SiW_{10}O_{36})_2]^{10-}$ (**1**), with the aim of describing the electronic structure of this cluster, demonstrating the redox tunability of these catalysts for oxidation of water by insertion of the Ru_4O_6 fragment within other POM ligands.

2 Computational Methods

The starting geometry was the crystallographic data of $\mathbf{Cs_{10}1}$ [14]. Geometry optimizations were carried out in water using the BP86 functional [15], combined with the triple-ζ basis set of Slater orbitals (STO), which a set of polarization functions (TZP) were used to describe the valence electrons of main group atoms and the metal atoms. The 1s shell of N, O, 1s to 2p shells for Al, Si, P, 1s to 3d shells for As and Ru, and 1s to 4d shells for W, Os and Re have been treated by the frozen core approximation, and described by means of single Slater functional. The relativistic effects were taken into account by using the zero-order regular approximation (ZORA) [16]. All of the geometries were optimized with ADF 2006 [17] with symmetrical constraint D_{2d}, The integration parameter in the molecular calculations, which determines the precision of the numerical integral, was set to 6.0. The default optimization convergence criteria in the ADF were used. The continuum solvation model COSMO and a dielectric constant of water has been performed for solvent effects in this work [18]. The van der Waals radii for the POM atoms, which actually define the cavity in the COSMO, are 1.08, 1.40, 2.11, 2.07, 1.92, 1.82, 2.10, 2.09, and 2.07 Å for H, O, Al, Si, P, S, W, Mo and Ru, respectively [19].

3 Results and Discussion

A. The electronic structures of cluster 1

The four ruthenium centers in cluster **1** are in the oxidation state +4 according to elemental analysis, bond valence sum considerations, and magnetic properties (d^4-Ru^{IV} center are diamagnetic) and electrochemical measurements [13,14]. X-ray studies showed that cluster **1** had a nearly D_{2d} symmetry [14]. In this work, the structure of cluster **1** was optimized under the restrictions of D_{2d} symmetry group. The Ru-O bonds in this cluster can be divided into four sets according to whether their oxygen atoms are of water molecule (W), oxo bridge (B) of $[Ru_4O_4(OH)_2(H_2O)_4]$ core, POM ligand (P), and hydroxo bridge (H) (Figure 1). The optimized geometries of $[Ru_4O_4(OH)_2(H_2O)_4]$ core agree very well with the experimental values, and the major discrepancies appear in the Ru-O_W bonds, which are overestimated by an average of ~0.03 Å.

For the Ru core in cluster **1** possesses a formal oxidation state of +4, however, Mulliken charges are substantially low (+2.06 e), suggesting donation of ~2 e from the oxygen ligands to the Ru center. We have optimized the geometrical structure of $[\gamma\text{-}SiW_{10}O_{36}]^{8-}$ in water, compared with the POM ligands in cluster 1, it can be found that $[Ru_4O_4(OH)_2(H_2O)_4]$ is the withdrawing group, the donation electrons of POM ligands are mainly from the $W_{10}O_{32}$ cage. Comparison of the free neutral water molecule and the DFT describing water ligand in cluster **1** shows the Mulliken atomic charges for it of +0.105 e, which demonstrate that the water ligand is the electron donor. The DFT derived O-H bond length of water ligand in cluster **1** is 0.98 Å. Although X-ray studies did not provide the O-H bond length of water ligand in cluster **1**, this value is consistent with the bond length when the water ligand binds the ruthenium center in ruthenium 'blue dimer' [5].

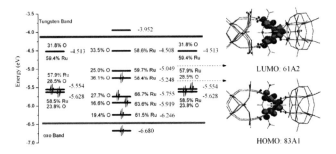

Fig. 2. The frontier orbital diagram for $[\{Ru_4O_4(OH)_2(H_2O)_4\}(\gamma\text{-}SiW_{10}O_{36})_2]^{10-}$ in water

It is well known that the redox properties of POM anions are closely related to energy and composition of frontier molecular orbital (FMO) [20], Figure 2 shows the FMO distribution of cluster **1** for the ground state. A series of occupied and unoccupied orbitals of cluster **1** are formally symmetry adapted d-ruthenium orbitals with some antibonding participation of the p-oxygen orbitals of $[Ru_4O_4(OH)_2]$ core, which are inserted between the oxo band and tungsten band of POM ligands (see Figure 2). The contributions of ruthenium core to these FMOs are rough equal, the marginal differences arise from that the participation of ruthenium orbital decreases when the energy of the FMO increases (from 66.7% to 57.9%). We did not find the large contribution from water ligands to these FMOs. The present DFT calculations give that HOMO of cluster **1** contains 58.4% Ru and 36.1% O_B characters, LUMO contains 59.7% Ru and 25% O_B characters (see Figure 2), which indicate that the one-electron-oxidized and reduced centers should be Ru and O_B atoms of $[Ru_4O_4(OH)_2]$ core. Unrestricted calculations of one-electron-oxidized and reduced species in water were performed to check predictions made by molecular orbital analysis. The spin polarizations show that the additional electron in the one-electron-reduced species is delocalized among the four ruthenium (0.19 spin alpha electrons per Ru) and four O_B atoms (0.05 spin alpha electrons per O_B) of $[Ru_4O_4(OH)_2]$ core, which is well in agreement of molecular orbital analysis. For one-electron-oxidizing species, the unpaired electron is also delocalized over the ruthenium and oxygen centers (total 0.94 spin alpha electrons) of $[Ru_4O_4(OH)_2]$ core. The geometrical structure of this POM cluster (especially the water ligands) isn't change largely in these oxidized and reduced processes.

B. Redox intermediates

For cluster **1**, the four water ligands need releasing eight electrons and eight protons to generate two dioxygens, these processes are complex acid-base equilibria and redox processes. Since these calculations would take large numbers of CPU time, we restricted the rest of study to the final structure to predict the redox and deprotonated effects on the electronic structure for cluster **1**. When cluster **1** releases eight electrons and eight protons, we obtained the deprotonated intermediate (DM). The key structural parameters of DM show that there is a significant distortion of the Ru-O_W bond. The optimized Ru-O_W bond distance is 1.744 Å, clearly shorter than the Ru-O_W bond distance of 2.149 Å in cluster **1**. This short distance reflects ruthenium-oxygen double bond character. On the other hand, the deprotonation triggers a significant increase of

Ru-O_H bond length, Δr(Ru-O_H) = 0.2 Å. This feature is very similar to that of the ruthenium 'blue dimer', μ-oxo bridge linked to the two ruthenium fragments is prone to cleavage [8], but Ru-O_P and Ru-O_B distances in cluster **1** are almost constant in this process. The geometrical distortions of cluster **1** in these processes are summarized in following expression.

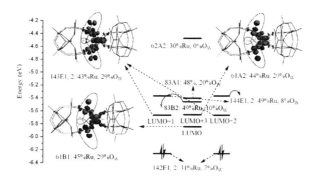

   Obviously, the result suggests that the stability of this catalyst is closely associated with the POM ligands and oxo bridges of [$Ru_4O_4(OH)_2$].

Fig. 3. The frontier orbital diagram, 3D representations of the key antibonding orbitals of deprotonated intermediate in water

   DM presents the analogous MO arrangement of cluster **1** (see Figure 3), where the FMOs localize on the [$Ru_4O_4(OH)_2O_4$] core, which are inserted between the oxo and tungsten bands of POM ligands. These processes stabilize the energy of the HOMO, which is 1.1 eV more stable than that of cluster **1**, and thus gives the larger HOMO-LUMO gap relative to cluster **1**, a sign of stability of the intermediate. It should be stressed that the shape of unoccupied orbitals, LUMO, LUMO+1, LUMO+2, and LUMO+3 in Figure 3, which provides a clue to its electrophilic reactivity. These orbital characters are best described as the Ru-O_W antibonding orbitals. Each orbital of the four antibonding orbitals contains ~29% O_W and ~44% Ru characters. According to the FMO theory [21], a good electrophile requires low-lying unoccupied orbitals with high molecular orbital compositions on the reacting atom to achieve good overlap with the FMOs on the nucleophilic reagent, in our studied system, the strong Ru-O_W antibonding orbitals are the important FMOs, the O_W atoms are the reacting atoms, which interact with the electron density of the nucleophilic reagent (such as the oxygen atom of water). These order and composition of FMOs strongly suggest that attacked mechanism of water on the O_W group proposed by Meyer [6].

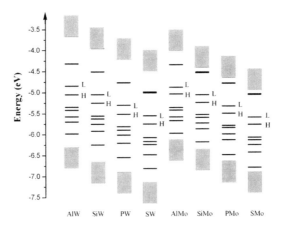

C. Redox tunability

For the α-Keggin anions [22,23], DFT calculations showed that HOMO-LUMO gap and composition of FMOs were almost independent of the nature of X, but the metal substitution can significantly affect the HOMO-LUMO gap, such as, for tungstates, HOMO-LUMO gap was computed to be ~2.8 eV, this value decreased by up to 2 eV for molybdates, and thus siliconmolybdates are more powerful oxidizing agents than the corresponding tungstates by 0.5 V. Hill and co-worker studied the di-Ru-substituted γ-Keggin POMs [24], and showed that the nature of X is crucial in determining the electronic structures of these POMs. The redox tunability of catalyst for oxidation of water is a major advantage for its practical incorporation into photosynthetic schemes [25]. Thus, we optimized a series of clusters $[\{Ru_4O_4(OH)_2(H_2O)_4\}(\gamma\text{-}XM_{10}O_{36})_2]^{n-}$ (X=Al, Si, P, S; M=W, Mo; n=12, 10, 8, 6) in water to analysis the electronic structures and redox properties. The optimized calculations show that the geometries of $[Ru_4O_4(OH)_2]$ core occur to distortion as the change of X and metal atoms, but these changes occur without significantly changing its structures, the ligand effects of X and metal atoms on $[Ru_4O_4(OH)_2(H_2O)_4]$ core are weak. The Mulliken population shows that the total charge on the XO_4 unit and $M_{10}O_{32}$ cage increase as the anion charge of the cluster goes from 6 to 12, the increase of the two parts approximately parallels the formal increment, where according to Mulliken analysis ~1 electron is added to two $M_{10}O_{32}$ cages, and the remaining 1 electron largely delocalized over the two XO_4 units as the change of the total charge of cluster. As expect, the charge of $[Ru_4O_4(OH)_2(H_2O)_4]$ core is almost constant as change of total charge of cluster.

Fig. 4. Molecular orbital diagram for $[\{Ru_4O_4(OH)_2(H_2O)_4\}(\gamma\text{-}XM_{10}O_{36})_2]^{n-}$ anions in water, HOMO and LUMO are denoted as H and L, respectively. Oxo band (bottom) and tungsten (molybdenum) band (top) of POM ligands are represented by gray rectangles (the shorthand notation without oxygen atom, charge, and $[Ru_4O_4(OH)_2(H_2O)_4]$ have been used).

The order and composition of FMOs of these clusters are almost equivalent for any X and metal atoms, which localize on the ruthenium and oxygen centers of $[Ru_4O_4(OH)_2]$ core. Analogously to other POMs, the FMO energies in Figure 4 show that smaller anion charge in tungstates and molybdates makes FMOs more stable, and the HOMO-LUMO gap is almost independent of the anion change As a simple and efficient prediction of oxidation potentials, HOMO energies of these clusters optimization in water have been compared. The results in Figure 4 show that HOMO energies decreases in the order Al>Si>P>S in tugstates and molybdates, respectively, which demonstrates oxidized energies are more positive (more difficult) for smaller anion charges. Obviously, electrostatic effects could account for this stabilization. For the same total charge of cluster in tungstates and molybdates, the HOMO energies of tungstates are lower than that of molybdates, the lower HOMO energies in tungstates means that the first oxidized step of tungstates becomes more favorable according to our DFT calculations.

References

[1] Ruttinger, W., Dismukes, C.: Synthetic water-oxidation catalysts for artificial photosynthetic water oxidation. Chem. Rev. 97, 1–24 (1997), doi:10.1021/cr950201z

[2] Kanan, M.W., Nocera, D.G.: In situ formation of an oxygen-evolving catalyst in neutral water containing phosphate and Co^{2+}. Science 321, 1072–1075 (2008), doi:10.1126/science.1162018

[3] Meyer, T.J.: Chemical approaches to artificial photosynthesis. Acc. Chem. Res. 22, 163–170 (1989), doi:10.1021/ar00161a001

[4] Hoganson, C.W., Babcock, G.T.: A metalloradical mechanism for the generation of oxygen from water in photosynthesis. Science 277, 1953–1956 (1997), doi:10.1126/science.277.5334.1953

[5] Gersten, S.W., Samuels, G.J., Meyer, T.J.: Catalytic oxidation of water by an oxo-bridged ruthenium dimer. Am. Chem. Soc. 104, 4029–4030 (1982), doi:10.1021/ja00378a053

[6] Gilbert, J.A., Eggleston, D.S., Murphy, W.R., Geselowitz, D.A., Gersten, S.W., Meyer, T.J.: Structure and redox properties of the water-oxidation catalyst $[(bpy)_2(OH_2)RuORu(OH_2)(bpy)_2]^{4+}$. J. Am. Chem. Soc. 107, 3855–3864 (1985), doi:10.1021/ja00299a017

[7] Gilbert, J.A., Geselowitz, D.A., Meyer, T.J.: Redox properties of the oxo-bridged osmium dimer $[(bpy)_2(OH_2)Os^{III}OOs^{IV}(OH)(bpy)_2]^{4+}$. Implications for the oxidation of water to oxygen. J. Am. Chem. Soc. 108, 1493–1501 (1986), doi:10.1021/ja00267a019

[8] Meyer, T.J.: Catalysis: The art of splitting water. Nature 451, 778–779 (2008), doi:10.1038/451778a

[9] Zong, R., Thummel, R.P.: A new family of Ru complexes for water oxidation. J. Am. Chem. Soc. 127, 12802–12803 (2005), doi:10.1021/ja054791m

[10] Ledney, M., Dutta, P.K.: Oxidation of water to dioxygen by intrazeolitic $Ru(bpy)_3^{3+}$. J. Am. Chem. Soc. 117, 7687–7695 (1995), doi:10.1021/ja00134a013

[11] Sens, C., Romero, I., Llobet, A., Parella, T., Benet-Buchholz, J.: A new Ru complex capable of catalytically oxidizing water to molecular dioxygen. J. Am. Chem. Soc. 126, 7798–7799 (2004), doi:10.1021/ja0486824

[12] Suss-Fink, G.: Water oxidation: A robust all-inorganic catalyst. Angew. Chem. Int. Ed. 47, 5888–5890 (2008), doi:10.1002/anie.200801121

[13] Geletii, Y.V., Botar, B., Gerler, P.K., Hillesheim, D.A., Musaev, D.G., Hill, C.L.: An all-inorganic, stable, and highly active tetraruthenium homogeneous catalyst for water oxidation. Angew. Chem. Int. Ed. 47, 3896–3899 (2008), doi:10.1002/anie.200705652

[14] Sartorel, A., Carraro, M., Socrrano, G., Zorzi, R.D., Geremia, S., McKaniel, N.D., Bernhard, S., Bonchio, M.: Polyoxometalate embedding of a tetraruthenium(IV)-oxo-core by template-directed metalation of $[\gamma\text{-SiW}_{10}\text{O}_{36}]^{8-}$: A totally inorganic oxygen-evolving catalyst. J. Am. Chem. Soc. 130, 5006–5007 (2008), doi:10.1021/ja077837f

[15] Becke, A.D.: Density-functional exchange-energy approximation with correct asymptotic behavior. Phys. Rev. A 38, 3098–3100 (1988), doi:10.1103/PhysRevA.38.3098

[16] van Lenthe, E., Baerends, E.J., Snijders, J.G.: Relativistic regular 2-component hamiltonians. J. Chem. Phys. 99, 4597–4610 (1993), doi:10.1063/1.466059

[17] ADF 2006.01. SCM, Theoretical Chemistry. Vrije Universiteit, Amsterdam, http://www.scm.com

[18] Pye, C.C., Ziegler, T.: An implementation of the conductor-like screening model of solvation within the Amsterdam density functional package. Theor. Chem. Acc. 101, 396–408 (1999), doi:10.1007/s002140050457

[19] Hu, S.Z., Zhou, Z.H., Tsai, K.R.: Average van der Waals radii of atoms in crystals. Acta Phys. Chim. Sin. 19, 1073–1077 (2003)

[20] Poblet, J.M., Lopez, X., Bo, C.: Ab initio and DFT modelling of complex materials: towards the understanding of electronic and magnetic properties of polyoxometalates. Chem. Soc. Rev. 32, 297–308 (2003), doi:10.1039/b109928k

[21] Decker, A., Rohde, J.U., Klinker, E.J., Wong, S.D., Que Jr., l., Solomon, E.I.: Spectroscopic and quantum chemical studies on low-spin Fe^{IV}=O complexes:Fe–O bonding and its contributions to reactivity. J. Am. Chem. Soc. 129, 15983–15996 (2007), doi:10.1021/ja074900s

[22] Maestre, J.M., Lopez, X., Bo, C., Poblet, J.M., Casah-Pastor, N.: Electronic and magnetic properties of α-Keggin anions:A DFT study of $[XM_{12}O_{40}]^{n-}$ (M = W, Mo; X = Al^{III}, Si^{IV}, P^{V}, Fe^{III}, Co^{II}, Co^{III}) and $[SiM_{11}VO_{40}]^{m-}$ (M = Mo and W). J. Am. Chem. Soc. 123, 3749–3758 (2001), doi:10.1021/ja003563j

[23] Lopez, X., Maestre, J.M., Bo, C., Poblet, J.M.: Electronic properties of polyoxometalates: A DFT study of α/β-$[XM_{12}O_{40}]^{n-}$ relative stability (M = W, Mo and X a main group element. J. Am. Chem. Soc. 123, 9571–9576 (2001), doi:10.1021/ja010768z

[24] Wang, Y., Zheng, G., Morokuma, K., Geletii, Y.V., Hill, C.L., Musaev, D.G.: Density functional study of the roles of chemical composition of di-transition-metal-substituted γ-Keggin polyoxometalate anions. J. Phys. Chem. B 110, 5230–5237 (2006), doi:10.1021/jp0571978

[25] McDaniel, N.D., Coughlin, F.J., Tinker, L.L., Bernhard, S.: Cyclometalated iridium(III) aquo complexes:Efficient and tunable catalysts for the homogeneous oxidation of water. J. Am. Chem. Soc. 130, 210–217 (2008), doi:10.1021/ja074478f

Forecasting the RMB Exchange Regime Using Genetic Programming Approach

Xiaobing Feng

Shanghai JianQiao College, Financial Management College
Shanghai Institute of Foreign Trade
Shanghai, China
fxb@sjtu.edu.cn

Abstract. To resolve the slow convergence and local minimum problem of BP network, an exchange rate forecast method based on Radial Basis Function Neural Network (RBFNN) is proposed.Data on economic variables is normalized, and then is put into the RBFNN in training. Corresponding parameters are got and then the exchange rate is predicted. Detailed simulation results and comparisons with Back-Propagation (BP) network show that, the operation speed of the method is faster and the forecast accuracy is higher than the traditional BP neural network can be achieved obviously. We then use genetic programming approach to achieve a better outcome compared with ANN.

Keywords: Radial Basis Function, neural network, exchange rate, forecast, Basket Regime, genetic programming.

1 Introduction

An essential problem of exchange rate forecasting is the identification of the underlying exchange rate regime, which can be problematic because it has become an undisputed fact of life that, with respect to exchange rate, countries do not practice as they declare.

There is ambivalent research that has examined whether the Chinese authority has behaved as it has claimed to be more market orientated. [1,2,3,4] all found that predominant weight was placed on the US Dollar and no evidence of a downward trend on the weight of the Dollar. They concluded that China is still in a dollar-pegged, fixed-rate regime regardless of its announcement. On the contrary, [5,6,7,8,9] discovered that the weights had slightly shifted from the US Dollar to the Euro, Yen and other currencies. There however seems no consensus on the issue. To examine the RMB exchange rate complex behavior, no-linear ANN and GP are attempted in this paper.

There are three models in ANN: BP, RBFNN and GNN. To resolve the well recognized slow convergence and local minimum problem of BP network, first, an exchange rate forecast method based on Radial Basis Function Neural Network

M. Zhou (Ed.): ISAEBD 2011, Part IV, CCIS 211, pp. 495–501, 2011.
© Springer-Verlag Berlin Heidelberg 2011

(RBFNN) is proposed. Data on economic variables is normalized, and then is put into the RBFNN in training. Corresponding parameters are got and then the exchange rate is predicted. Detailed simulation results and comparisons with Back-Propagation (BP) network show that, the operation speed of the method is faster and the forecast accuracy is higher than the traditional BP neural network can be achieved obviously.

Second, we then use genetic programming approach to achieve a better outcome compared with ANN. The GP method approaches a solution using evolutionary processes including crossover, mutation, reproduction and deletion. It involves regression models over a series of generation based on the Darwinian principle of nature selection. It starts with solving a problem by creating massive amount of basic parent random functions in a population pool. The white box characteristics is the significant advantage of the GP over black box approach of ANN. The GP model can be the best solver for searching highly non-linear space for global optima via adaptive strategies.

2 Model Specification

2.1 Formulation of Market Forces

Following research by [10,11], market forces will be determined by transactions of fundamentalists and chartists.

Fundamentalists base their decisions on the difference between the equilibrium exchange rate $\bar{S}_{t-1}$ and the actual exchange rate S_{t-1}. α is a positive parameter that reflects the speed of adjustment to the equilibrium rate: $(\Delta S_t)^f = \alpha(\bar{S}_{t-1} - S_{t-1})$. Chartists base their expectations of future rates by observing asset price movements. The following equation specifies a moving average model with declining coefficients. $0 < \beta^p < 1$, where p is lag length:

$$(\Delta S_t)^c = \sum_{i=1}^{\infty} \beta^p \Delta S_{t-1}$$

2.2 Formulation of Exchange Arrangements

In a basket regime, the central banker will arrange the exchange rate according to predetermined objectives.

$S_t^{rmb\lambda}$ is the exchange-rate arrangement against the US Dollar, s^i is the exchange rate of currency i against the Dollar. All the exchange rates in the following equation are measured in indirect quotations from the US perspective: γ_i is the weight of the US Dollar.

$$\Delta S_t^{rmb} = \sum_{i=1}^{\infty} \gamma_i \Delta S_t^i + \Delta \gamma_0$$

2.3 Non-linear Estimation

We chose three types of multivariate ANN models for this study: BP, RBF and GRNN. A single hidden-layer ANN model can be taken as an extension to non-linear from a linear regression model as follows:

$$RMB_t = \partial_0 + \sum_{j=1}^{n} \partial_j \log sig(\sum_{i=1}^{k} \beta_{ij} Var_i + \beta_{oj})] + \varepsilon_t() \tag{1}$$

Where, n is the number of the unit in the hidden layer, K is the number of independent variables, logsig is a logistic transfer function, β denotes a matrix of parameters from the input to the hidden layer units, and ε_t denotes the error term.

We consider three factors as explanatory variables: chartist, fundamentalist and exchange-rate arrangements:

$$RMB = \partial_0 + \sum_{j=1}^{n} \partial_j \log sig(\beta_1 F + \beta_2 C + \beta_3 B + \beta_o)] + \varepsilon_t \tag{2}$$

2.4 Linear Modeling

Equation (3) is a simple linear combination of market forces and exchange-rate arrangements to estimate the rate:

$$\Delta S_t^{rmb} = \delta_1 (\Delta S_t)^f + \delta_2 (\Delta S_t)^c + \delta_3 \Delta S_t^{rmbA_i} \tag{3}$$

3 Data and Estimation Results

The daily exchange rates from July 2005 to July 2009 were culled from the Federal Reserve database and from the Central Bank of Russia. The trade data used for weights in the basket rate are from the Ministry of Commerce.

3.1 Non-linear Modeling

ANN creates non-linear forms-for-regression models that automatically handle non-linearities, explanatory variables' interactions, model switching and other complex phenomena. Three non-linear optimization algorithms are applied to implement the models.

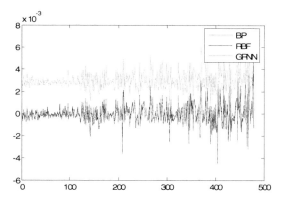

Fig. 1. Comparison of Estimation Errors among BP, RBFand GRNN

Fig 1 and 2 show estimation and forecasting errors. It is evident that errors from BP are larger than those from RBF and GRNN networks. It is, however, difficult to distinguish between RBF and GRNN as the lines are linked to each other. We therefore rely on the performance evaluation to separate them.

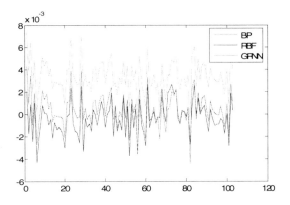

Fig. 2. Comparison of Forecasting Errors among BP, RBF and GRNN

3.2 Performance Evaluation and Economic Implication

Three indicators, MAPE, MAE and RMSE, are applied to evaluate the forecasting performance of the non-linear ANN models:

$$MAPE = \frac{1}{n} \sum_{t \in P} \left| \frac{(x_t - \hat{x}_t)}{x_t} \right| \tag{4}$$

$$MAE = \frac{1}{n} \sum_{t \in p} (\hat{x}_t - x_t) \tag{5}$$

$$RMSE = \sqrt{\frac{\sum_{t \in P} (\hat{x}_t - x_t)^2}{n}} \tag{6}$$

Where P is sample size, $\hat{x}_t$ erates, and x_t is the real rates. Results are presented in Table 1, which show that the RBF model has the lowest MAPE, MAE and RMSE. It is conclude that RBF performs the best among them.

The economic implication of the estimation is that the explanatory variables including: fundamentalist, chartist and basket arrangements contain significant power in interpreting the behavior of the basket rate.

Table 1. Comparison of Performance across Models

	Non-Linear ANN		
	BP	RBF	GRNN
MAPE	1.6887	0.6274	0.9431
MAE	0.3581	-0.0355	0.0423
RMSE	0.0034	0.0016	0.0016

3.3 Genetic Programming

The weakness of an ANN algorithm is that it may converge to local minima instead of global minima. ANN is also considered something of a black box, one which provides no specific functional form for the system. Genetic programming 2 is therefore attempted to overcome these problems.

Genetic programming model is selected as a means to compare against ANN model to meet the various demands in this study. Strengths of the GP includes the evolutionary approach, the nature selection process and the white box characteristic. The evolutionary process and natural selection techniques embedded in the GP model would allow the screening of the multiple input variables to be executed inherently for achieving the best result. The white box character of GP model can reveal internal structures with specific functional forms of the examined system, which one cannot find in ANN modeling. GP also provides a functional form which best fits the data while ANN cannot produce any specific function.

Four input variables including the market force variables are used in this model. We decide on this by trying all the possible combination of one, two, three and four variables. The software by Sara Silva [20] is used to perform all the GP runs.

Table 2 presents the final results after various experiments. It shows that all the factors—Chartist, Fundamentalist and currency arrangements—have the power to determine the rate because they all appear in the end nodes.

Based on the function specified by GP, we calculated the forecasting errors using Sum Square Error. We then compared the results with that from ANN in Fig. 3. Two lines are again mingled with each other, therefore, we calculated the SSE and arrived at 0.001557, 0.001555 for ANN and GP respectively. Thus, GP outperforms ANN.

Table 2. The Configuration of GP

Generation	100
Population	200
Algorithm	+,-,*,sin, cos, ln, /
End nodes	{X1 X2 X3 X4}
Fitness Criteria (RSS)	0.205609
Depth of the Tree	10
Mutation Rate	0.01
Stop Criteria	GP runs for 100 generations

Note: X1, X2, X3, and X4 are four input variables including fundamentalist, chartist and B4, B11 exchange arrangements.

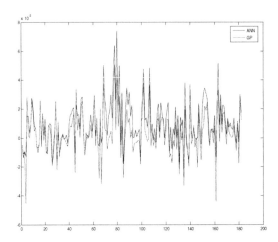

Fig. 3. Estimation Performance Evaluation of ANN and GP

4   Conclusions

Two models: ANN and GP are specified, estimated and used to generate the out of sample forecast over the period since China has announced a shift from a single dollar peg to a more market orientated basket peg.

The long-term aim of China's exchange reform has been to develop a much more flexible exchange-rate system with market forces to play a critical role. Both the Non-linear artificial neural network model and non-linear genetic programming estimations show that the market force has contributed to the formulation of the current basket regime.

Acknowledgment. This project is financed by the Innovation Project of Education Committee (2009AASH0904) and Shanghai Natural Science Foundation (09ZR142 0000). Financial support from Shanghai Education Commission for Major Subject Construction project (J51201) is also appreciated.

References

1. Jen, S.: Chinese RMB basket still a mystery, Global Economics Forum. Morgan Stanley, San Francisco (2005)
2. Shah, A., Zeileis, A., Patnaik, I.: What is the new Chinese currency regime? Unpublished memo the Department of Economics. Monash University (November 2005)
3. Frankel, J.: On the yuan: The choice between adjustment under a fixed exchange rate and adjustment under a flexible rate. In: Illing, G. (ed.) Understanding the Chinese Economy, CESifo Economictudies, Munich (2006) Also in NBER WP No. 11274
4. Eichengreen, B.: China's exchange rate regime: The long and short of it, revision of paper for Columbia University's conference on Chinese money and finance held in New York (February 2-3, 2006)

5. Yamazaki, K.: Inside the currency basket. Columbia University and Mitsubishi UFJ Trust and Banking Corporation (December 2006)
6. Xu, J., Shao, H., Tang, G.: Empirical study on China basket currency system. Journal of Shanghai University of Economics and Finance 66, 72–76 (2007)
7. Xu, S., Tang, Q.: An empirical research on China's exchange intervention byreferring to currency basket. Studies of International Finance 9, 68–72 (2008)
8. Frankel, J., Wei, S.J.: Assessing China's exchange rate regime. NBER WP13100 (2007)
9. Zhou, J.: The Reference Basket for RMB: Composition, Stability and Commitment. World Economy 3, 16–22 (2009)
10. Frankel, J., Froot, K.A.: Short-term and long-term expectations of the yen-dollar expectation: Evidence from survey data. Federal Reserve Board, International Financial Discussion Paper no. 292 (1986)
11. Frankel, J.: Using survey data to test standard proposition regarding exchange rate expectations. American Economic Review 77, 33–53 (1987)
12. Frankel, J.: New Estimation of China's Exchange Rate Regime. NBER 14700 (2009)
13. Bénassy-Quéré, A.: Opimal pegs for Asian currencies. In: CEPII 1997, October 14 (1997)
14. Bhandari, J.: Experiments with the optimal currency composite. Southern Economic Journal 51(3), 711–730 (1985)
15. Camerer, C., Loewenstein, G., Prelec, D.: Neuroeconomics: How neuroscience can inform economics. Journal of Economic Literature XLIII, 9–64 (March 2005)
16. Levy Yeyati, E., Sturzenegger, F.: Classifying exchange rate regimes: Deeds vs. words. Universidad Torcuato Di Tella (2000), http://www.utdt.edu/~ely
17. Marquez, J., Schindler, J.: Exchange rate effects on China's trade: An interim report. International Finance Discussion Paper, No. 861, Federal Reserve Board, Washington, DC (2006)
18. Sun, F.C.: Advances in neural networks-ISNN 2008: Proceedings 5th International Conference of Symposium on Neural Networks (2008)
19. Thorbecke, W.: How would an appreciation of the RMB & other East Asian currencies affect China's exports?, RIETI working paper (2008)
20. Silva, S.: GPProgramming,
http://sourceforge.net/mailarchive/forum.php?
forum_name=gplab-users

The Establishment and Application of Labour Market Monitoring and Evaluation Model

Jing Wang

School of Labor Economics, Capital University of Economics and Business,
P.R. China.100026
wangjingdxc@126.com

Abstract. This paper establishes a labour market indicators system by reference to the labour market indicators system of International Labour Office and according to the actual situation of Chinese labour market. It puts forward labour market monitoring and evaluation methods and applies the methods to analyzing the present situation of Chinese labour market. Moreover, it points out that the research on labour market monitoring and elevation model should be established on the basis of detailed and reliable data, so that it's necessary to complete labour survey system and reform existing indicators and survey methods to meet the needs of information, consultation and monitoring.

Keywords: Labour Market, Monitoring Model, Evaluation Methods.

1 Introduction

Reliable, complete and timely labour market information is an important condition to ensure the normal and efficient operation of labour market. Therefore, International Labour Office establishes a labour market indicators system consisting of 20 major indicators. The system is an international comparison and analysis standard recognized and adopted by countries around the world and also an effective guidance for a country to establish a labour market indicators system. In recent years, with the development of Chinese market economy, Chinese labour market has gradually been established and improved, but there is no complete labour market indicators system or labour monitoring and evaluation method. Under the severe employment situation of the world, many countries intensify the management of labour market and take various measures to boost economic development and employment. However, China's employment promotion task is more onerous, so that it is urgent to establish and improve a labour market indicators system and labour market monitoring and evaluation methods to provide employment guidance.

2 Construction of Labour Market Monitoring and Evaluation Model

According to the labour market indicators system of International Labour Office and the specific circumstances of China, I think that Chinese labour market monitoring

M. Zhou (Ed.): ISAEBD 2011, Part IV, CCIS 211, pp. 502–509, 2011.

indicators system should consist of labour resource supply indicator, employment indicator, unemployment indicator, labour flux indicator, labour quality indicator, wage and labour cost indicator, labour productivity and unit labour cost indicator, and poverty indicator. The eight indicators are selected for the eight aspects center on labourer and can evaluate the basic condition of labour market in a more comprehensive way. The specific monitoring model is as below:

2.1 Composite Index Linear Synthetics Evaluation Method

Composite index linear synthetics evaluation method is to get all levels of composite indexes and general indexes by weighted analysis of standard values of all evaluation indicators. The formula is $Y = \sum_{i=1}^{n} W_i X_i^*$, of which Y refers to composite index, W_i refers to weight coefficient, and X_i^* refers to standard values of indicators. In order to select the weights (W_i) of all indicators in a scientific way, it's acceptable to adopt Analytical Hierarchy Process. Analytical Hierarchy Process is a systematic analysis method which is applicable to decision problems with very complicated structures and many decision criteria that are not easily quantifiable. Essentially, analytical hierarchy process is a decision-making and thinking mode and it divides a complicated problem into groups by primary and secondary or dominance relations to shape an orderly hierarchy structure, determines the relative importance of the factor of each hierarchy by comparison and judgment, synthesizes the importance in hierarchy structure to get the total arrangement of decision factors relative to the importance of general objective, and finally analyzes the arrangement result to solve considered problems. We adopt this method for the purpose of arranging many original indicators in a scientific way and endowing all indicators with reasonable weights. Moreover, the method can be used to make preparations for the fuzzy comprehensive evaluation below. Labour market monitoring and evaluation indicator system includes three hierarchies. The first hierarchy has eight indicators, the second hierarchy has twenty-eight indicators, and the third hierarchy has thirty-five indicators. The system utilizes Analytical Hierarchy Process to arrange general objectives to get single arrangement and total arrangement. The calculation results are as shown in Table 1 below.

Table 1. Single Hierarchical Arrangement of Indicators at All Levels and Total Arrangement of Last-Level Indicators

First-Level Indicator		Second-Level Indicator	Third-Level Indicator	Total Arrangement
A1	Labour Supply 0.1410	B1	Labour Resources(0.5421)	0.0772
		B2	Labour Force Participation Rate (0.4579)	0.0637
A2	Employment Status 0.1410	B3	Total Employment (0.1684)	0.0238
		B4	Employment Rate (0.1596)	0.0225
		B5	Elasticity of Employment (0.1171)	0.0165
		B6	Flexible Employment Rate (0.1266)	0.0179
		B7	Weekly Working Hours (0.1340) — C1 Employment Ratio during Weekly working Hours0.4579	0.0084

Table 1. *(continued)*

			C2	Weekly Working Hours Per Capita (0.5421)	0.0104
			C3	Employment Proportions of Identities(0.1510)	0.0036
			C4	Employment Proportions of Occupations (0.1510)	0.0036
			C5	Employment Proportions of Industrial Sectors (0.1426)	0.0034
		B8	Employment Structure (0.1684)	C6	Employment Proportion Urban vs. Rural 0.1346	0.0032
			C7	Employment Proportions of Industries0.1507	0.0036
			C8	Employment Proportions of Enterprise Scales (0.1431)	0.0034
			C9	Employment Proportions of Registration Statuses0.1270	0.0030
		B9	Underemployment Related to Working Hours 0.1259		0.0177
		B10	Unemployment(0.2151)		0.0303
		B11	Unemployment Rate (0.2151)		0.0303
		B12	Unemployment Duration (0.2044)	C10	Average Unemployment Duration (0.4405)	0.0127
				C11	Long-term Unemployment Rate (0.3772)	0.0108
				C12	Long-term Unemployment Incidence 0.1823	0.0053
A3	Unemployment Status 0.1410			C13	Pre-Unemployment Occupation Proportion0.1798	0.0046
				C14	Pre-Unemployment Employment Proportions of Industrial 0.1912	0.0049
		B13	Unemployment Structure (0.1827)	C15	Pre-Unemployment Industry Proportions0.2247	0.0058
				C16	Pre-Unemployment Employment Proportions of Registration Statuses (0.1795)	0.0047
				C17	Proportions of Unemployment Causes (0.2247)	0.0058
		B14	Cultural Qualities of Unemployed Population (0.1827)		0.0258
		B15	LabourFlux Summary (0.2489)	C18	Employment Inflow Rate 0.2605	0.0069
				C19	EmploymentOutflow Rate 0.2784	0.0073
				C20	Reintegration Rate (0.4611)	0.0137
		B16	LabourFlux Structure (0.1566)	C21	Inter-Industry Flow (0.2639)	0.0047
A4	Labour Force Flux 0.1120			C22	City andCountryside Flow 0.2361	0.0041
				C23	Industry Flow (0.2639)	0.0047
				C24	Regional Flow (0.2361)	0.0041
		B17	Occupation Introduction Assessment (0.5942)	C25	Number of Employment Agencies (0.1702)	0.0110
				C26	Job Opening-to-Application Ratio (0.2128)	0.0142

Table 1. *(continued)*

			C27	Occupational Max. Match Ratio (0.2128)	0.0142
			C28	Job Seek Success Rate 0.2021	0.0136
			C29	Max. Job Seek Success Rate 0.2021	0.0136
A5	Labour Quality 0.1128	B18	Annual Average Training Hours (0.3704)		0.0423
		B19	Educational Level (0.3541)		0.0399
		B20	Technique Grade &Professional Qualification (0.2755)		0.0306
A6	Wage and Cost 0.1341	B21	Wages (0.7509)	C30 Average Wage (0.2831)	0.0292
				C31 Actual Wage Index (0.3221)	0.0325
				C32 Inter-IndustryWage Difference (0.3948)	0.0390
		B22	Labour Cost Per Hour (0.2491)		0.0334
A7	Labour Productivity 0.1055	B23	Labour Productivity (0.4023)	C33 Value Added Per Capita 0.2065	0.0097
				C34 Value Added Per Hour 0.2736	0.0114
				C35 Industry Structure of Labour Productivity 0.520	0.0220
		B24	Unit Labour Cost (0.5977)		0.0624
A8	Poverty Status 0.1128	B25	Poverty Incidence (0.2216)		0.0251
		B26	Total Working Poor (0.2502)		0.0282
		B27	Registered Unemployed Persons in Urban Areas 0.2637		0.0298
		B28	Gini Coefficient (0.2645)		0.0298

2.2   Fuzzy Comprehensive Evaluation Method

Fuzzy comprehensive evaluation method is to apply Analytic Hierarchy Process to analyzing the indicators system in a systematic way and establish the weighting arrangement of indicators; then utilize the thought of fuzzy comprehensive evaluation to give early warning signals on the present situation of the indicators system by a group of traffic control signs, including red, yellow, green, and blue lights, and judge the trend of Chinese labour market in future according to the signals to achieve the purpose of early warning. Considering the knowledge of the present situation of Chinese labour market, we choose several experts from Ministry of Human Resources and Social Security of the People's Republic of China, National Bureau of Statistics of China, Beijing Human Resources and Social Security Bureau, and many universities and apply Experts Grading Method to the fuzzy comprehensive evaluation of Chinese labour market.

2.2.1   Determine Factor Set, Evaluation Set and Weight Set in Fuzzy Comprehensive Evaluation

Factor Set—A classical set consisting of all factors affecting the object of evaluation, represented by U: $U = \{U_1, U_2, \cdots, U_m\}$, U_i $(i = 1, 2, \cdots, m)$ represents the indicators of all factors affecting labour market.

Evaluation Set—A set consisting of various total evaluation results that may be given by experts on the object of evaluation, represented by V: $V = \{V_1, V_2, \cdots, V_n\}$, V_i $(i = 1, 2, \cdots, n)$ represents various total evaluation results. In the early warning system, we'll divide indicators into four regions respectively represented by red, yellow, green and blue lights. Blue light V_1 = safe, green light V_2 = problematic, need attention, yellow light V_3 = problematic, need special attention, and red light V_4 = dangerous.

Weight Set—Utilize the weights of indicators of total arrangement obtained by adopting Analytic Hierarchy Process as the weights of fuzzy comprehensive evaluation. Endowing each indicator U_i with a corresponding weight a_i $(i = 1,2,\cdots,m)$, the set consisting of the weights is so-called weight set: $\underset{\sim}{A} = \{a_1,a_2,\cdots,a_m\}$.

2.2.2 Fuzzy Evaluation on the Single Factors of All Indicators in Chinese Labour Market Monitoring and Evaluation Indicators System

Get the fuzzy evaluation matrix of single indicator factor through Experts Grading Evaluation Method. See Table 2.

Table 2. Last-Level Indicator Weights and Their Present Situations

First-Level Indicator	Last-Lever Indicator		Weight	Blue Light	Green Light	Yellow Light	Red Light
A Labour Supply Status	B1	Total Labour Resources	0.0772	0.78	0.22	0.00	0.00
	B2	Labour Force Participation Rate	0.0637	0.33	0.67	0.00	0.00
	B3	Total Employment	0.0238	0.56	0.44	0.00	0.00
	B4	Employment Rate	0.0225	0.22	0.78	0.00	0.00
	B5	Elasticity of Employment	0.0165	0.11	0.78	0.11	0.00
	B6	Flexible Employment Rate	0.0179	0.11	0.78	0.00	0.11
A Employment Status	C1	Employment Ratio during Weekly Working Hours	0.0084	0.11	0.78	0.11	0.00
	C2	Weekly Working Hours Per Capita	0.0104	0.22	0.78	0.00	0.00
	C3	Employment Proportions of Identities	0.0036	0.00	0.89	0.11	0.00
	C4	Employment Proportions of Occupations	0.0036	0.11	0.78	0.11	0.00
	C5	Employment Proportions of Industrial Sectors	0.0034	0.11	0.78	0.11	0.00
	C6	Employment Proportion Urban vs. Rural	0.0032	0.11	0.67	0.22	0.00
	C7	Employment Proportions of Industries	0.0036	0.11	0.78	0.11	0.00
	C8	Employment Proportions of Enterprise Scales	0.0034	0.00	1.00	0.00	0.00
	C9	Employment Proportions of Registration Statuses	0.0030	0.00	0.67	0.33	0.00
	B9	Underemployment Related to Working Hour	0.0177	0.11	0.78	0.11	0.00
A Unemployment Status	B10	Total Unemployment	0.0303	0.11	0.67	0.11	0.11
	B11	Unemployment Rate	0.0303	0.11	0.56	0.33	0.00
	C10	Average Unemployment Duration	0.0127	0.22	0.44	0.33	0.00
	C11	Long-term Unemployment Rate	0.0108	0.11	0.44	0.44	0.00
	C12	Long-term Unemployment Incidence	0.0053	0.11	0.56	0.33	0.00
	C13	Pre-Unemployment Occupation Proportion	0.0046	0.00	0.78	0.22	0.00
	C14	Pre-Unemployment Employment Proportions of Industrial Sectors	0.0049	0.00	1.00	0.00	0.00

Table 2. *(continued)*

A							
	C15	Pre-Unemployment Employment Proportions of Industries	0.0058	0.11	0.89	0.00	0.00
	C16	Pre-Unemployment Employment Proportions of Registration Statuses	0.0047	0.11	0.67	0.22	0.00
	C17	Proportions of Unemployment Causes	0.0058	0.00	0.89	0.11	0.00
	B14	Cultural Qualities of Unemployed Population	0.0258	0.11	0.56	0.22	0.11
	C18	Employment Inflow Rate	0.0069	0.11	0.67	0.22	0.00
	C19	Employment Outflow Rate	0.0073	0.11	0.56	0.33	0.00
	C20	Reintegration Rate	0.0137	0.11	0.67	0.22	0.00
	C21	Inter-Industry Flow	0.0047	0.22	0.67	0.11	0.00
	C22	City and Countryside Flow	0.0041	0.11	0.56	0.33	0.00
A. Labour Flux Status	C23	Industry Flow	0.0047	0.11	0.78	0.11	0.00
	C24	Regional Flow	0.0041	0.00	0.78	0.22	0.00
	C25	Number of Employment Agencies	0.0110	0.11	0.78	0.11	0.00
	C26	Job Opening-to-Application Ratio	0.0142	0.11	0.44	0.44	0.00
	C27	Occupational Max. Match Ratio	0.0142	0.11	0.56	0.33	0.00
	C28	Job Seek Success Rate	0.0136	0.11	0.67	0.11	0.11
	C29	Max. Job Seek Success Rate	0.0136	0.11	0.67	0.11	0.11
A. Labour Quality Status	B18	Annual Average Training Hours	0.0423	0.11	0.22	0.67	0.00
	B19	Educational Level	0.0399	0.11	0.44	0.44	0.00
	B20	Technique Grade &ProfessionalQualification	0.0306	0.11	0.33	0.44	0.11
A. Wage and Cost	C30	Average Wage	0.0292	0.00	0.56	0.44	0.00
	C31	Actual Wage Index	0.0325	0.00	0.67	0.22	0.11
	C32	Inter-Industry Wage Difference	0.0390	0.00	0.22	0.44	0.33
	B22	Labour Cost Per Hour	0.0334	0.00	0.56	0.44	0.00
A. Labour Productivity Status	C33	Value Added Per Capita	0.0097	0.11	0.78	0.11	0.00
	C34	Value Added Per Hour	0.0114	0.11	0.78	0.11	0.00
	C35	Industry Structure of Labour Productivity	0.0220	0.11	0.44	0.44	0.00
	B24	Unit Labour Cost	0.0624	0.22	0.67	0.11	0.00
A Poverty Status	B25	Poverty Incidence	0.0251	0.11	0.67	0.22	0.00
	B26	Total Working Poor	0.0282	0.00	0.78	0.22	0.00
	B27	Registered Unemployed Persons in Urban Areas	0.0298	0.22	0.44	0.33	0.00
	B28	Gini Coefficient	0.0298	0.11	0.11	0.67	0.11

2.2.3 Multi-factor Fuzzy Comprehensive Evaluation on Labour Market Monitoring and Evaluation System

When carrying out multi-factor fuzzy comprehensive evaluation, we should fully consider the importance of various factors. According to the results of hierarchy analysis, different factors are endowed with different weights a_i $(i = 1, 2, \cdots, m)$, and only in this way, the combined influence of all factors can be reflected in a reasonable way. Therefore, the result of fuzzy comprehensive evaluation on the object of evaluation is as below: $B = A \cdot R$, namely,

$$B = (a_1, a_2, \cdots, a_m) \cdot \begin{bmatrix} r_{11} & r_{12} & \cdots & r_{1n} \\ r_{21} & r_{22} & \cdots & r_{2n} \\ \cdots & \cdots & \cdots & \cdots \\ r_{m1} & r_{m2} & \cdots & r_{mn} \end{bmatrix}$$

$$= (b_1, b_2, \cdots, b_n)$$

Now, we monitor and evaluate the present situation of Chinese labour market. Considering that different indicators have different importance, we conduct multi-factor fuzzy comprehensive evaluation. The result is as below: $B = A \cdot R = (0.1819, 0.5447, 0.2388, 0.0346)$.

The result shows that 72.66% of experts consider that the operation of Chinese labour market is in good condition at present, but there are many problems existing in the operation that need attention (54.47%); 23.88% of experts consider that there are many problems existing in the operation of Chinese labour market that need special attention; 3.46% of experts consider that there are dangerous factors existing in the operation of Chinese labour market. Therefore, the early warning indicator light is "green light", i.e. from the present situation of Chinese labour market, there are problems that need attention and we should pay more attention to the change of early warning indicator in future in order to take measures in a timely manner.

3 The Application of Labour Market Monitoring and Evaluation Model

Analyze first-level indicators, second-level indicators and third-level indicators in proper order and make judgments according to their weights and the satisfaction of fuzzy comprehensive evaluation. The mean value of weights of last-level indicators is 0.0174. It can be seen from Table 2 that the weights of 22 indicators such as total labour resource and labour force participation rate are more than the mean value. From grouping situation, Labour Resource Supply is in good condition, there is a sufficient labour supply, and Total Labour Resource and Total Employment are mainly in blue light area, but there are problems existing in the operation of Labour Force Participation Rate that need attention. Employment status and Unemployment status are in green light area, i.e. there are problems existing in the operation of the two indicators that need attention, but 11% of experts consider that Flexible Employment Rate, Total Unemployment and Cultural Qualities of Unemployed Population are in red light area, i.e. the three indicators are dangerous and the weights of the indicators are more than the mean value, so that it's recommended to take measures to control the risks. In Unemployment Status indicator, 33% of Unemployment Rate, Average Unemployment Duration and Long-term Unemployment Incidence are in yellow light area and 44% of Long-term Unemployment Rate is in yellow light area, which indicates that there are serious problems existing in the operation of the indicator that need special attention. Although Overall Labour Flux Situation is in green light area, it has more indicators with larger proportions in yellow light area, e.g. Occupational Maximum Match Tate, especially Job Opening-to-Application Ratio that is up to 44% and needs special attention; besides, 11% of Job Seek Success Rate and Maximum Job Seek Success Rate are in red light area, so that the joint efforts of government departments, intermediary agents and job seekers, especially the effective inputs of government departments. Overall Situation of Labour Quality is basically in yellow light area, which indicates that there are many problems existing in the operation of the indicator that need special attention. 11% of experts consider that Technique Grade &Professional Qualification is in red light area and such indicators as Cultural Qualities of Unemployed Population, Job Seek Success Rate and Maximum Job Seek Success Rate are in red light area, which further indicates the sizes of the problems. For labour quality determines the sustainable development of China, it's recommended to strengthen technical training and make efforts to improve labour quality. Wage and Cost is not promising. Although the indicator is completely in green light area, certain proportions of such four indicators as Average Wage, Actual Wage Index, Wage Differences among Industries, and Labour Cost per Hour are in yellow light area, especially Wage Differences among Industries. 44% of Wage Differences among Industries is in yellow light area and 33% of experts consider that the indicator has reached red light area. Labour Productivity Status is in good condition and lies in green light area, but the proportions of Industry Structure of Labour Productivity in yellow light area and green light area are 44%, which indicates that the indicator needs special attention. Poverty Status is basically working in green light area, but Gini Coefficient is in yellow light area, which indicates there are problems existing in the operation of the indicator, and 11% of experts consider that the indicator has been on the verge of danger.

4   Conclusions and Suggestions

This paper establishes a labour market monitoring and evaluation model by completing labour market indicators system and utilizes the model to analyze the present situation of Chinese labour market in order to strengthen the macro control on labour market and promote the sound and sustainable development of labour market. However, the monitoring and evaluation of labour market should be established on the basis of detailed and reliable data. In order to grasp the status of labour market in a timely manner, it's necessary to complete labour survey system and add some indicators needed for reflecting the status of labour market; besides, it's necessary to integrate various statistical survey rules. When updating the contents of existing statistical statements, it's recommended to reform existing indicators and survey methods and mainly adopt recurrent sample survey. Only in this way, the model can meet the needs of information, consultation and monitoring.

References

1. Key Indicators of the Labour Market, Electronic Version in (May 2007)
2. Huang, R., Wang, J.: Improving and Perfecting Labor Market Statistics. Research on Economics and Management (January 2003)
3. Jing, W., Lihong, D.: Research on the Construction of Labour Market Indicators System in China, Chinese Human Resource and Social Security Development Research Report. China Labour and Social Security Publishing House, Beijing((2008)

Comparison of Predictive Models for the Mortgage Behaviours Assessment System of Default and Prepayment

Cheng-Chung Wu[1] and Po-Sheng Ko[2]

[1] Ph.D, Graduate School of Management
National Kaohsiung First University of Science and Technology
wu_0110@yahoo.com.tw
[2] Associate Professor, Department of Public Finance and Taxation
National Kaohsiung University of Applied Sciences
psko@cc.kuas.edu.tw

Abstract. This paper has debated between fractional and two part models in the context of default and prepayment behaviour, applications where a large proportion of zero observations are typically found. The predictive capacity in this paper is to provider the direction of consideration and very good fit result to the behaviours of default and prepayment for bank. From the perspective of practitioners, it could point of view the characteristics of borrowers of each variable would seem to be choosing in this paper. This paper also provides the simply looking at the extent to which policy decision of bank conclusions would differ depending upon the characteristics of customers' behaviour consideration.

1   Introduction

Due to the possessed of real estate, it seems having an apartment is a lifelong goal for everybody. Although, households would use the largest possible mortgage and the circumstances under which savings are invested in the property (Leece, 2006). By the positive causal relationship with the behaviours of mortgage, one area of the most importance to the mortgage of bank where discussion of the relative merits of these is sparser is in the combinations behaviours analysis of default and prepayment. These are all the issues that financial institutions take into careful consideration in risk management of mortgage businesses (Menkhoff and Suwanaporn, 2007). The important of the issue for these behaviours arises from the fact that in an unbearable stress at any given the recent recessions and high unemployment rates among the time a substantial proportion of people behaviours will be observed with the risk occurred probability of default and prepayment. As we will discuss in more detail about these behaviours with below this may arise for a number of reasons and hence great care must be taken in model selection.

This paper presents evidence on the issue in the behaviour of default and prepayment using data from the 7 banks in Taiwan. Our focus in this paper is on the issue of model selection and the criteria which should be used and hence the discussion of the values of

M. Zhou (Ed.): ISAEBD 2011, Part IV, CCIS 211, pp. 510–522, 2011.
© Springer-Verlag Berlin Heidelberg 2011

the estimated coefficients, per se, is somewhat brief. Meanwhile, in order to establish an understanding of the characteristics of prepayments and overdue repayments across borrowers, the analysis of the historical data of mortgages offered by the banking industry in Taiwan is the first priority and essential. To reach the objectives of this paper remainder of the paper is structured as follows: in section 2 we discuss the modelling issue involved, including the crucial matter of what criteria should be considered in terms of choosing between the different approaches. In section 3 we discuss our data and methodology, in section 4 we present our analysis results of default and prepayment behaviour and section 5 presents concluding comments.

2 Literature Review

2.1 Literature Regarding Defaults and Prepayments

The two risks that financial institutions are faced with in real estate mortgage loans are defaults and prepayments. The decision of borrowers is an option. The mortgages offered by financial institutions are equivalent to the sale of a call for prepayments and a put on defaults to borrowers (Figure 1).

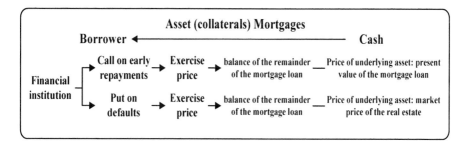

Fig. 1. Concept of Option in Real Estate Mortgages

When the market rates fall below the coupon rates, borrowers will refinance to repayment old loans because the balance of the remainder of the mortgage loan is smaller than the present value of the mortgage loan. This will allow borrowers to enjoy a lower cost of interest rates. If the market price of the real estate falls below the remainder of the mortgage loan, borrower will opt for defaults to increase their own wealth value because of the generation of negative equity. That is Hillebrand and Koray (2008) point out, there is a positive increase in interest rate volatility increases home mortgage loans. The asset of mortgages is the existence of prepayment risk while regarding as a borrower's call option with the uncertain marketing rate of interest based on the variable-rate or floating-rate.

Koutsomanoli-Filippaki and Mamatzakis (2009) argued that interest rate movements remain a key factor that affects prepayment decisions, the effect on prepayment of expected upward movement in interest rates to be stronger than that of expected downward movements. The basic model of options originates from Black and Scholes (1972) and Contingent Claim Model by Cox et al. (1985). Most of the follow-up studies apply this model on the research of real estate mortgage market. For example, Dunn and McConnell (1981a, 1981b) assumes Optimal Prepayment Policy by combining the prepayment model and interest-rate models of Poisson and apply Implicit Finite Difference Method to derive the price of the transferred securities for Government National Mortgage Association (GNMA) of the U.S. Kau et al. (1992, 1995) also use the same assumptions and consider the options for defaults and prepayments. Under this strategy, whether the borrower decides to make prepayments or not depends completely on whether the balance of the remainder of the mortgage is lower than the present value of the mortgage. Whether the borrower defaults or not depends entirely on whether the market price of the real estate is lower than the balance of the remainder of the mortgage. The finding of both approaches is that the exercise of each option hinges on housing prices and interest rates.

2.2 Application of Research Models

The frequently used empirical methods to examine the defaults and prepayments of mortgage loans include Ordinary Least Squares (OLS), Two-State Option-Pricing Model), Proportional Hazard Model (PHM) and logistic models. Most of the studies over the recent years use PHM proposed by Cox (1984) to evaluate the risks associated with defaults and prepayments of housing mortgages. Alternate or Contingency Model are proposed by Green and Shoven (1986), Schwartz and Torous (1989), Quigley and Van Order (1990).

The PHM is a survival analysis. It assumes that under the survival conditions, there is a specific default or prepayment probability at each point in time through the term of the contract. This resolves the issue of contingent claim models in association with single values. Also, PHM is able to process the problems that are difficult to address with traditional statistical techniques. The problems include Time-Dependent Covariates (Time-Varying Explanatory Variables) and censoring.

The majority of the studies that utilizing PHM examines defaults or prepayments only consider defaults or prepayments, as if the two actions are mutually independent. In other words, the estimation of defaults or prepayments is on the separate basis. For example, Schwartz and Torous (1989) assume that without default risks and combine PHM and Fixed Covariates in the empirical analysis of prepayments of mortgages offered by Government National Mortgage Association (GNMA). Green and Shoven (1986), Quigley and Van Order (1990) use PHM and time-dependent covariates and assume an absence of default risks in their empirical analysis of prepayments of mortgages.

3 Methodology

To examine that relationship we assume a two part of model for the risk rates of prepayment and default behaviours as suggested by Ramalho and da Silva (2009) they can be represented as follows.

Observed default risk: $y = DRB \overset{**}{y}$

Observed prepayment risk: $y = PRP \overset{**}{y}$

Participation equation: $ND = \alpha Z + v$, $DRB = 1$ if $ND > 0$, $= 0$ otherwise, Z are integrated variables including TL, TLR, AV, LO, LAVR, TERM, OB, GP, INC, TM, AB, SEX, (Note: there is not including the variables of OB and GP with the behaviour of prepayment) α is the coefficient value of each variable.

Default risk equation: $\overset{**}{y} = \max\left[0, \overset{*}{y}\right]$, $\overset{*}{y} = \beta DR + u$

Prepayment risk equation: $\overset{**}{y} = \max\left[0, \overset{*}{y}\right]$, $\overset{*}{y} = \beta PR + u$

Here Z and DR or PR is the regressors influencing participation and default risk, u and v are additive disturbance terms that are the random distribution with a bivariate normal distribution.

If we allow for the possibility of dependence between the disturbance terms, then if the sample is divided into those with zero default risk (denoted 0) and those with positive default risk (denoted +) the likelihood for the full default risk of mortgage model could be written as following:

$$L_0 = \prod_0 \left[1 - p(DRB=1)\, p(\overset{*}{y}>0|DRB=1)\right] \prod_+ p(DRB=1) p\left(\overset{*}{y}>0|DRB=1\right) f\left(\overset{*}{y}\middle|\overset{*}{y}>0, DRB=1\right)$$

$$= \prod_0 \left[1 - p(v>-\alpha Z)\, p(u>-\beta DR|v>-\alpha Z)\right]$$

$$\prod_+ p(v>-\alpha Z)\, p(u>-\beta DR|v>-\alpha Z)\, f(y|u>-\beta DR, v>-\alpha Z)$$

As the same results the prepayment risk could be written we presented follows:

$$L_0 = \prod_0 \left[1 - p(PRP=1)\, p(\overset{*}{y}>0|PRP=1)\right] \prod_+ p(PRP=1) p\left(\overset{*}{y}>0|PRP=1\right) f\left(\overset{*}{y}\middle|\overset{*}{y}>0, PRP=1\right)$$

$$= \prod_0 \left[1 - p(v>-\alpha Z)\, p(u>-\beta PR|v>-\alpha Z)\right]$$

$$\prod_+ p(v>-\alpha Z)\, p(u>-\beta PR|v>-\alpha Z)\, f(y|u>-\beta PR, v>-\alpha Z)$$

If we assume that the disturbance terms u and v are independent then the reduces model of default and prepayment risk of behaviour assessment to the Cragg model with likelihood could be written as:

$$L_1 = \prod_0 \left[1 - p(v>-\alpha Z)\, p(u>-\beta DR|v>-\alpha Z)\right] \prod_+ p(v>-\alpha Z)\, p(u>-\beta DR|v>-\alpha Z)\, f(y|u>-\beta DR)$$

$$L_1 = \prod_0 \left[1 - p(v>-\alpha Z)\, p(u>-\beta PR|v>-\alpha Z)\right] \prod_+ p(v>-\alpha Z)\, p(u>-\beta PR|v>-\alpha Z)\, f(y|u>-\beta PR)$$

If we allow for the possibility of dependence between the disturbance terms of default and prepayment risk assessment in this study the likelihood is:

$$L_2 = \prod_0 \left[1 - p\left(v > -\alpha Z\right)\right]\prod_+ p\left(v > -\alpha Z\right) f\left(y\middle|v > -\alpha Z\right)$$

If independence is also assumed the two part of model for the risk rates of prepayment and default behaviours reduces to a probit for participation and ordinary least squares for the default risk equation estimated over those for whom positive default and prepayment risk is observed with likelihood function as follow:

$$L_3 = \prod_0 \left[1 - p\left(v > -\alpha Z\right)\right]\prod_+ p\left(v > -\alpha Z\right) f\left(y\right)$$

Thus the two behavoirs of crucial factors in terms of modelling strategy are 1) independence of the error terms and 2) the interpretation placed upon the observed zeros which determine whether or not dominance is assumed. That is why we believe that dominance applies to our data and so the crucial choice we face is between a selection L2 of likelihood model and a two part regression model, likelihood L3.

4   Results

4.1   The Analytic Behaviour of Default

Table 1 provides the estimation of both selection and two part models for default and prepayment behaviours. Dealing with the selection equation for default behaviour first, the estimated coefficients for the two models are quite different the sign of the coefficients.

Considering first the empirical adequacy of both models, it seems that they fit the data relatively less well in all case. Indeed, the R square provides not enough explanation of functional form misspecification of all variables, although low, even some of them have quite significant of p-value results with t-test in fractional model; for the binary model, and the F-statistics is to reveal the significant of p-value results of all variables. That is, it would to say some variables in significant have enough explanation in all case.

Relative to the decision of issuing default or not of the behaviour, the estimates obtained for the binary choice model indicate that have eight variables which significantly influence that decision for all the customers who would default or not, are TLR, LO, OB, BP, INC, TM, AB and SEX. In all case, the higher positive effect of behaviour the INC variable in binary model is to reveal very significantly which has extreme trend in behaviour of default. That is, in mortgage default INC plays into the core role of defaulting whilst high INC of customer has not to default of mortgage in a tendency. Otherwise, low INC would be the most influential factor to default in mortgage behaviour. As the same results, SEX is to reveal the trend that female has the trend of default. It would be exhibited the real status of eastern society that female who's INC is more lower than male and brought out the default. AB has revealed the same situation who is elder would be to default, but has the unapparent with this default.

Table 1. Regression Results with Default Behaviour

Variables	Fractional Model	Binary Model	Influence of Default in Past Research
Intercept	9.6940447	-0.567984	Negative
TL	-0.008415	0.0025743	Positive
TLR	-0.012365	0.0076898***	Positive
AV	-0.0000001166	0.000000026685	Positive
LO	-0.00000006197	0.000000087205***	Positive
LAVR	-0.000145	-0.0000004005	Negative
TERM	-0.005693**	0.0006091	Positive
OB	0.00000033729 ***	-0.0000001012***	Negative
GP	0.0304963**	-0.032698***	Negative
INC	-3.305718***	1.3289714***	Positive
TM	-0.231119*	0.1514888***	Positive
AB	-0.010088	0.0029228*	Positive
SEX	-0.216401	0.1843804***	uncertain
Number of Observations	2717	15987	
R square	0.027462	NA	
Adj. R square	0.023146	NA	
Chi Square	NA	17429.35	
p-value<#%	0.0001	0.0001	

Note: Below the coefficients we report t-statistics and χ^2-statistics in parentheses; for the test statistics we report p-value; ***, ** and * denote coefficients or test statistics which are significant at 1%, 5% and 10%, respectively; for the binary model, we use the χ^2-statistics to test the p-value; for the fractional model, the pseudo R2 was calculated as the correlation among the predicted and actual values of ND.

For the financial status of default behaviour, the key factor of default is TM that also to show whilst lower interest or longer term of loan would not be default e.g. shorter term maybe leaded to the default, the TLR is similar. That is, the recessionary in recent years, default of customers' behaviour would be improved whilst bank could provide the more generous term to their customers who perhaps being in the edge of default. By other hand, the TL also shows the interesting result, when loan style is not the demand of living such as home, is default e.g. business. Comparison of AV, it only has a little effect in default behaviour that could be said that appraisal amount is not the major factor of default with the positive coefficient or could be said has the unapparent trend of gray area in binary model, it would be seen in the relative status clearly.

In the negative coefficients, this study has found that the real loan amount would be the major factor of default whilst the loan has small amount customer maybe not default. Otherwise, how large of the loan amount is to influence whether customers would be default or not. From the analysis of LAVR, that would be seen the trend of default but is still not very apparent. However, with the variables of OB and GP, we could see the same results whilst bank provide the strict term to their customers such as less amount of OB or shorter term of GP that causing the default, especially, GP.

Finally, we found a statistically significant positive effect of ND on our study of binary model that the external self-behaviour of customers is the major default of mortgage such as INC. That would be seen whilst too less income of customers to be paid the loan. This study not only found the external behaviour to affect the default behaviour but still providing the financial perspective to be considering for bank.

Also in contrast to the results obtained for the fractional model in this paper, we find that the different results with two part model except LAVR. That is, if response variable of data has too many zero to practice the traditional regression. But if we only consider the data of non-zero to analysis the affect of each variable with regression that would be appeared fancy of results such likes fractional model in our study.

However, the results reported in table 3 also suggest that, as discussed in this paper before, the main determinants of the probability of the default behaviour whether occurrence must based on yes or no of the real case with the two part model. That is, if the real world occurs something what the probability is that it would be occurred again next time, the two part model could provided the better solution for us. For the probability of default and prepayment would be discussed after the analysis of prepayment behaviour.

4.2   The Analytic Behaviour of Prepayment

As the same analysis of default behaviour in table 1, table 2 could be also provides the estimation of prepayment behaviours. After anglicizing of default behaviour, the estimated coefficients for the prepayment behaviour present the different results with default.

Considering first the empirical adequacy of both models, it seems that they fit the data relatively less well in all case. Indeed, the R square provides not enough explanation of functional form misspecification of all variables (adj. R square only equal 0.001881), although low, even some of them have quite significant of p-value results with t-test in fractional model, but the overall explanation is still very weakness; for the binary model, and the F-statistics is to reveal the significant of p-value results of all variables (p-value<0.0001). That is, it would to say some variables in significant have enough explanation in all case by the analysis of binary model.

Relative to the decision of issuing prepayment or not of the behaviour, the estimates obtained for the binary choice model indicate that have three variables which significantly influence that decision for all the customers who would prepayment or not, are TERM, AB and SEX. In all case, the higher positive effect of behaviour the INC variable (even only 0.0997127) in binary model is to reveal very significantly which has the tendency of behaviour in prepayment. That is, in mortgage prepayment INC plays into the more importance of prepaying whilst high INC of customer would be to prepayment of mortgage in a trend. Otherwise, low INC has not to be practiced prepayment in mortgage behaviour. As the same results, SEX is to reveal the trend that female has the trend of prepayment if she has the position of higher income. Also It would be exhibited the different with real status of eastern society that female who's INC is more less than male, but it also reveal the trend that female who has the higher income leaded to the prepayment. It is the relative with the conservatism of female. AG has the same result of SEX, who is elder would be conservatism to prepayment, but has the unapparent with this prepayment.

Table 2. Regression Results with Prepayment Behaviour

Variables	Fractional Model	Binary Model	Influence of Default in Past Research
Intercept	1.2453285***	-0.539443***	Positive
TL	0.001487	0.0012323	Positive
TLR	-0.001901	0.0008506	Negative
AV	-0.00000002609	0.00000001919	Positive
LO	0.000000039821	-0.000000000882	Negative
LAVR	-0.00001346	0.000057712	Positive
TERM	0.0007808	-0.002674***	Positive
INC	-0.175499*	0.0997127	Positive
TM	-0.00205*	0.0036221	Positive
AB	-0.001326	0.0084162***	Positive
SEX	0.1395255***	0.0747593**	Uncertain
Number of Observations	7706	12724	
R square	0.003177	NA	
Adj. R square	0.001881	NA	
Chi Square	NA	16946.14	
p-value<#%	0.0064	0.0001	

For the financial status of prepayment behaviour, the key factor of prepayment is TM that also to show whilst higher interest than investing return in mortgage or shorter term of loan would be prepayment e.g. higher term and higher rate of mortgage maybe leaded to the prepayment of customer. The TLR is similar status whilst appraisal mortgage rate is too high to endure by customer who would be prepayment. That is, the recessionary in recent years, prepayment of customers' behaviour would be improved whilst bank could provide the more generous term to their customers who perhaps being in the edge of prepayment. By other hand, the TL also shows the interesting results, when loan style attribute to the demand of business would be prepayment, contrast to the demand of living, the mortgage demand of business maybe to satisfy shortage of capital that would be more frequent to prepayment. Comparison of AV, it only has a little effect in prepayment behaviour that could be said that appraisal amount is not the major factor of prepayment with the positive coefficient or could be said has the unapparent trend of gray area in binary model. Also that, if AV is high with the higher rate and focus on the shortage demand of capital, it would be prepayment.

In the negative coefficients, this study has found that the real loan amount would be the major factor of prepayment whilst the loan has small amount customer maybe prepayment. If customer is conservatism who has the higher income or real mortgage amount could not satisfy the lack of capital needs that forms the condition of prepayment. Otherwise, how large of the loan amount is to influence whether customers would be prepayment or not. From the analysis of LAVR, that would be seen the trend of prepayment but is still not very apparent. However, with the variables of LAVR, we could see it would be prepayment in different condition whilst considering in different perspective and demand.

Finally, we found a statistically significant positive effect of NP in our study of binary model that the external self-behaviour of customers is not the major prepayment of mortgage; it must consider the internal condition with bank providing. That would be seen whilst too less income of customers to be paid the loan, they would not be prepayment or too less amount of mortgage they have the tendency to prepayment in torrent capacity. Sometimes, amount of mortgage in higher rate or shortage term would be also prepayment. It is occurring in different condition. This study not only found the external behaviour to affect the prepayment behaviour but still providing the internal financial perspective to be considering for bank.

Also in contrast to the results obtained for the fractional model in this paper, we find that the different results with two part model except TL. That is, with the same results of default analysis outlook. Sometimes, traditional regression would not be satisfied the better solution of real world. That is, we only consider the data of non-zero to analysis the affect of each variable with regression would be appeared fancy of results such likes fractional model in this study.

However, the results reported in table 4 also suggest that, the main determinants of the probability of the default and prepayment behaviour whether occurrence must based on yes or no of the real case with the two part model. The real world occurs with default and prepayment something based on the probability to decide whether it would be occurred again next time. For the probability of default and prepayment would be discussed as following section.

4.3 Probability of Default and Prepayment Occurrence

As we see in table 3, there is the predictive probability of occurrence with the default and prepayment behaviour of each variable. As the same results of our analysis of behaviour is to show the better predictive capacity to possible situation of occurrence. With the predictive default or occurring probability we would be seen that seven of twelve variables reveal the best predictive capacity to default behaviour. That is including TLR, LO, OB, GP, INC, TM and SEX, which could be said the default analysis with two part model has the exactly assessment. By other hand, in our model to predict the default trend of customers' behaviour in bank mortgage would be obtained the best solution. With the characteristics of each internal and external variable that customer and bank possessed the default could be predicted fast. That is, who would default or nor, the most important finding in our paper is to exhibit the better predictive capacity for the mortgage behaviour of borrowers.

But not everything could be one hundred percent perfect, some variables is to be shown the worse result such as LAVR, as we discussed before, LAVR is the gray edge, but however, sometimes LAVR would be leaded to default whilst some term is to be came up. That is most difficulty solution, the appraisal and available value of decision for loan amount with banker in uncertainly event, also our find in other variables could be provided the useful message to bankers whilst their customer who would borrow from them. Moreover, our predictive capacity is with 0.8 above, that is, the very good fit result to default prediction.

Table 3. Predictive Probability of Occurrence with Default and Prepayment Behaviour

Variable	Prepayment		Default	
	Threshold of χ^2	Probability	Threshold of χ^2	Probability
TL	0.7378734	0.61	1.9099166	0.83
TLR	0.6310169	0.57	28.390214	1.00
AV	1.915993	0.83	2.3757259	0.88
LO	0.0023895	0.04	13.618222	1.00
LAVR	1.4918913	0.78	5.63E-05	0.01
TERM	51.504464	1.00	1.7065672	0.81
OB	NA	NA	56.46221	1.00
GP	NA	NA	87.210538	1.00
INC	1.3491277	0.75	112.3698	1.00
TM	0.3443397	0.44	81.677164	1.00
AB	37.361801	1.00	3.1837191	0.93
SEX	4.185062	0.96	18.275638	1.00

Comparison of default, there is not best predictive capacity to prepayment behaviour except TERM and AB. Above 0.5, That is including TL, TLR, AV, LAVR, INC and SEX, which could be said the prepayment analysis with two part model has the better assessment, but not perfect. By other hand, in our model to predict the prepayment trend of customers' behaviour in bank mortgage would be observed in the analysis of ours before. With the characteristics of each internal and external variable that customer and bank possessed the prepayment could be predicted fast.

That is this study to display, prepayment occurring in different condition sometimes, to predict the exactly prepayment behaviour not only to consider the external behaviour but also to think over the internal financial perspective to the borrowers and bankers. That is, who would prepayment or nor, the most important finding in our paper is to exhibit the better outlook of prediction for the mortgage behaviour of borrowers.

But not everything could be fine, some variables is to be shown the worse result such as LO and TM, as we discussed before, LO and TM play the key factor of prepayment whilst higher interest than investing return in mortgage or shorter term of loan would be prepayment leaded to the prepayment of customer, or the difference between the loan type of business and home. However, sometimes LO and TM would be leaded to prepayment whilst some term is to be come up, contrary is not. Furthermore, for the probability of prepayment in our predictive capacity is to provider the direction of consideration for banker. In summary, that is, the very good fit result to default and prepayment prediction in two part model could be satisfied the needs of bank.

5 Conclusions

By the positive causal relationship with the behaviours of mortgage, one area of the most importance to the mortgage of bank where discussion of the relative merits of these is sparser is in the combinating behaviours analysis of default and prepayment. This paper presents evidence on the issue in the behaviour of default and prepayment using data from the 7 banks in Taiwan. Our focus in order to establish an understanding of the characteristics of prepayments and overdue repayments across borrowers, the analysis of the historical data of mortgages offered by the banking industry in Taiwan is the first priority and essential.

Thus, the nature of the questions of this study regarding default and prepayment behaviours in our data leads us to believe that dominance applies and that there is unlikely to be a latent positive expected representation which would be exactly to predict with our analysis applying the different models. Consequently, this study was carried out on three grounds of concepts with default and prepayment behaviours: theoretical, practical and the different between models and perspective. Our conclusion is that on the three grounds the two part model is to be preferred to the selection model and this preference is stronger in the case of default rather than prepayment. The predictive capacity in this paper is to provider the direction of consideration and very good fit result to the behaviours of default and prepayment for bank. From the perspective of practitioners, it could point of view the characteristics of borrowers of each variable would seem to be choosing in this paper. This paper also provides the simply looking at the extent to which policy decision of bank conclusions would differ depending upon the characteristics of customers' behaviour consideration.

References

1. Ambrose, B.W., Capone, C.A.: Modeling the conditional probability of foreclosure in the context of single-family mortgage default resolutions. Real Estate Economics 26, 391–429 (1998)
2. Black, F.M.C., Jensen, M.C., Scholes, M.: The capital asset pricing model : some empirical tests, Stuided in the Theory of Capital Market. Praeger Publishers, New York (1972)
3. Chiang, H.C.: Commercial loan borrower's optimal borrowing and prepayment decisions under uncertainty. Applied Economics 39, 1013–1020 (2007)
4. Clarke, J.A., Roy, N., Courchane, M.J.: On the robustness of racial discrimination findings in mortgage lending studies. Applied Economics, 1–19 (2008) iFirst
5. Cox, J.C., Ingersoll, J.E., Ross, S.A.: A theory of the term structure of interest rates. Econometrica 53, 385–407 (1985)
6. Deng, Y.H., Quigley, J.M., Van Order, R.: Mortgage default and low downpayment loans: the costs of public subsidy. Regional Science and Urban Economics 26, 263–285 (1996)

7. Deng, Y.H.: Mortgage termination: an empirical hazard model with stochastic term structure. Journal of Real Estate Finance and Economics 14, 309–331 (1997)
8. Dow, W., Norton, E.: Choosing between and interpreting the Heckit and two part models for corner solution. Health Services and Outcomes Research Methodology 4, 5–18 (2003)
9. Dunn, K.B., McConnell, J.J.: A compare of alternative models for pricing GNMA mortgage-back securities. Journal of Finance 36, 471–484 (1981a)
10. Dunn, K.B., McConnell, J.J.: Valuation of GNMA mortgage-backed securities. Journal of Finance 36, 599–616 (1981b)
11. Foster, C., Van Order, R.: An opiton-based model of mortgage default. Housing Finance Review 3, 351–372 (1984)
12. Gardner, M.J., Mills, D.L.: Evaluating the likelihood of default on delinquent loans. Financial Management 18, 55–63 (1989)
13. Green, J., Shoven, J.: The effects of interest rates on mortgage prepayments. Journal of Money, Credit, and Banking 18, 41–59 (1986)
14. Hillebrand, E., Koray, F.: Interest rate volatility and home mortgage loans. Applied Economics 40, 2381–2385 (2008)
15. Koutsomanoli-Filippaki, A., Mamatzakis, E.: Performance and Merton-type default risk of listed banks in the EU: A panel VAR approach. Journal of Banking & Finance (2009) (in Press, Corrected Proof(Available online 19 May 2009)
16. Kau, J.B., Keenan, D.C., Muller, W.J., Epperson, J.F.: A generalized valuation model for fixed-rate residential mortgage, Journal of Money. Credit, and Banking 24, 279–298 (1992)
17. Kau, J.B., Keenan, D.C., Muller III, W.J., Epperson, J.F.: Option theory and floating-rate securities with a comparison of adjustable and fixed-rate mortgages. Journal of Business 66, 595–618 (1993)
18. Kau, J.B., Keenan, D.C., Muller III, W.J., Epperson, J.F.: The valuation at origination of fixed-rate mortgages with default and prepayment. Journal of Real Estate Finance and Economics 11, 5–36 (1995)
19. Kau, J.B., Hilliard, J.E., Slawson, V.C.: Valuing prepayment and default in a fixed-rate mortgage: a Binomial options pricing technology. Real Estate Economics 26, 431–468 (1998)
20. Kutty, G.: Logistic regression and probability of default of developing countries debt. Applied Economics 22, 1649–1660 (1990)
21. Lawrence, E.C., Smith, L.D., Rhoades, M.: An analysis of default risk in mobile home credit. Journal of Banking and Finance 16, 299–312 (1992)
22. Leece, D.: Testing a theoretical model of mortgage demand on UK data. Applied Economics 38, 2037–2051 (2006)
23. Leung, S.F., Yu, S.: On the choice between sample selection and two part models. Journal of Econometrics 72, 197–229 (1996)
24. Menkhoff, L., Suwanaporn, C.: On the rationale of bank lending in pre-crisis Thailand. Applied Economics 39, 1077–1089 (2007)
25. Quigley, J.M., Van Order, R.: Efficiency in the mortgage market: the borrower's prespective. AREUEA Journal 18 (1990)
26. Schwartz, E.S., Torous, W.N.: Prepayment and the valuation of mortgage-backed securities. Journal of Finance 44, 375–392 (1989)
27. Smith, L.D., Lawrence, E.C., Sanchez, S.M.: A comprehensive model for managing credit risk on home mortgage portfolios. Decision Sciences 27, 291–317 (1996)
28. Schwartz, E.S., Torous, W.N.: Prepayment, default, and the valuation of mortgage pass-through securities. Journal of Business 65, 221–239 (1992)

29. Vander Hoff, J.: Adjustable and fixed rate mortgage termination, option values and local market conditions: an empirical analysis. Real Estate Economics 24, 379–406 (1996)
30. Vendell, K.D., Thibodeau, T.: Estimation of mortgage default using disaggregate loan history data. AREUEA Journal 15, 292–317 (1985)
31. Waller, N.G.: Residential mortgage default: a clarifying analysis. Housing Financial Review 7, 315–333 (1988)
32. Yezer, A.M.J., Robert, F.P., Robert, P.T.: Bias in estimates of discrimination and default in mortgage lending: the effects of simultaneity and self-selection. Journal of Real Estate Finance and Economics 9, 197–216 (1994)
33. Zorn, P.M., Lea, M.J.: Mortgage borrower repayment behavior: a microeconomic analysis with Canadian adjustable rate mortgage data. Real Estate Economics 17, 118–136 (1989)

DAIM: A Distributed Algorithm for Isolating Malfunctioning Nodes in Wireless Sensor Networks

Mohamed K. Watfa[1] and Rawad Abu Assi[2]

[1] University of Wollongong in Dubai, Computer Science Department, Dubai, UAE
[2] American University of Beirut, Computer Science Department, Beirut, Lebanon

Abstract. It has been identified that as complexity of computing and communication devices increases, fault-tolerance will gain more and more importance. Wireless sensor networks (WSNs) are exceptionally complex distributed systems where a variety of components interact in a complex way and should therefore help narrow down failures and diagnose their causes, as much as possible, with minimal physical access and interactivity. In this paper, we present an algorithm for isolating malfunctioning nodes in WSNs and provide two parallel variants of it: Naïve and Greedy. The algorithm is based on the idea that a covered node can be turned off and that turning off a malfunctioning node causes the WSN to function properly. The experiments we conducted show that the Naïve Approach is very precise in locating malfunctioning nodes whereas the Greedy Approach is very fast in finding a cover free of such nodes.

Keywords: Sensor Networks, Coverage, Malfunctioning nodes, Debugging, Sensor Networks, Greedy.

1 Introduction

Sensor networks introduce new challenges for fault-tolerance. Sensor networks are inherently fault-prone due to the shared wireless communication medium: message losses and corruptions (due to fading, collision, and hidden-node effect) are the norm rather than the exception. Moreover, node failures due to crash and energy exhaustion are commonplace. Thus, sensor nodes can lose synchrony and their programs can reach arbitrary states. Applications that impose an excessive communication burden on nodes are not acceptable since they drain the battery power quickly. Failures that often occur in wireless sensor networks can be attributed to many causes such as node failures, link failures, errors in the design, implementation errors, etc. Locating the causes of such failures is crucial to insure the reliability of the network but it is usually a challenging task due to several reasons such as the distributed nature of most protocols and applications, the energy constraints imposed on any technique, and the wide variety of faults in such networks that range from node crashes to bugs in the code running on the nodes. Since the complexity of software grows drastically with respect to its size, large scale software systems are extremely error-prone and fail frequently especially for sensor network applications, that are inherently distributed, reasoning about the system and verification of correctness are more difficult due to the lack of a centralized controller and the lack of a globally shared memory. For

M. Zhou (Ed.): ISAEBD 2011, Part IV, CCIS 211, pp. 523–530, 2011.
© Springer-Verlag Berlin Heidelberg 2011

example, Whitebox approaches for designing fault-tolerance, such as exception handling, forward recovery, recovery blocks, and application specific fault-tolerance methods assume that the implementation is fully available, and study the source code for designing fault-tolerance which are not applicable for large scale software systems because the task of studying the implementation and designing a fault-tolerant version becomes unbearable as the size of the implementation grows.

In this paper, we target failures that are caused by malfunctioning nodes that we define as the nodes suffering from a local defect i.e. the defect is not characterized as a general defect found in all nodes such as a software bug in the application code. Our approach is based on the idea that a node can be turned off if it is covered and consequently turning off a malfunctioning node will cause the network to behave properly. We propose DAIM, an algorithm which attempts to turn off such nodes and then tries to locate them. We provide two different versions of DAIM and analyse their performance and capabilities on a Java-based simulator we developed especially for this research. The rest of the paper is organized as follows: Section 2 elaborates on DAIM and its two versions, Section 3 presents the performance analysis we conducted, Section 4 discusses some related work, and Section 5 concludes the paper with some future work and in-sight.

2   Related Work

The full coverage problem, which verifies if every point in the region of interest is covered by at least one active sensor, has been studied in a variety of contexts. Our previous work [1-3] focused on the full coverage problem in 2D and 3D regions and provided algorithms to locate redundant sensor nodes in the region and deactivate them using simple geometric techniques. In [8], Gupta and Das design and analyze algorithms for self organization of a sensor network to reduce energy consumption. The work in [4] considers a large population of sensor nodes, deployed randomly for area monitoring to achieve an energy-efficient design that maintains area coverage. S. Meguerdichian, et al. in [5] consider an unreliable sensor grid-network and derive necessary and sufficient conditions for the coverage of the region and connectivity of the network in terms of the transmission radius, sensing radius, and failure rate of the sensor nodes. In [6], Lieska et al. formulate coverage problems to address the quality of service (surveillance) provided by a sensor network. The coverage concept with regard to the robot systems was introduced by Gage [7].

Concerning fault localization in WSNs, several approaches were proposed but as far as we know none of them followed our approach in searching for malfunctioning nodes. One of the proposed paradigms is to fix the faults before deployment by debugging a simulated version of the application. This approach doesn't take into consideration the physical effects of the environment on the behavior of the network and thus might overlook a wide range of faults. Another family of approaches is based on the idea of providing the developer with efficient tools to debug the network after being deployed [9-12]. Clairvoyant [10] was proposed as a source-level debugger for wireless sensor networks. It enables the developer to execute debugging commands on each node as well as on the network as a whole. Commands such as inserting breakpoints and inspecting data values help the developer monitor the execution and infer the cause of the fault. Clairvoyant doesn't require any additional hardware and no modifications need to be made to the application's source code. On the other hand, some techniques try to target specific kinds of faults based on some heuristically algorithm such as Sympathy [9] that was proposed as a tool for detecting failures that are revealed by shortage in data flows, i.e. those that result in missing data. The intuition is based on the observation that there is a direct relationship between the amount of data collected at a sink and the existence of failures in the system. The main shortcoming of Sympathy is that it is limited to specific types of faults: those that are revealed by gaps in the data flow.

3   DAIM: A Distributed Algorithm for Isolating Malfunctioning Nodes

3.1   The Definitions and Assumptions

Definition 1: We refer by Cover to any subset of the nodes that can sense the monitored phenomenon at every point in the region.

Definition 2: A passing cover is a cover with no mal-functioning nodes. In contrast, a failing cover is a cover with at least one malfunctioning node.

Assumption 1: The basic assumption we make is that all malfunctioning nodes are covered i.e. which implied that the network is dense enough. In addition, we assume that each node knows the distances separating it from each of its 1-hop neighbours and thus can know if it is covered or not using pre-existing coverage algorithms in our previous work [1-3].

Assumption 2: Another basic assumption we adopt in our experiments is that the WSN is 2-Dimensional and that all nodes have the same sensing radius. In this case, and in a similar approach to that adopted in [1], we consider that a node is covered if the intersections of all neighbouring open disks that lie inside the node's open disk are covered.

3.2   Algorithm Description

Initially, we assume that all nodes are active. The state transition diagram of the algorithm is depicted in Figure 1. At the beginning of each iteration of the algorithm, each node checks if it is covered; if so, it waits for a random time (to avoid contention between neighbouring nodes) and then decides to sleep with a sleeping probability P which will be a subject of experimental evaluation in section 3. If it decides to sleep, then it selects a set of neighbours that cover it and sends to them an invitation message (a message asking these neighbours to be active in the next iteration so that the node will be covered). We propose two ways for selecting this set in the next section which will lead to two versions of the algorithm. Then the node waits for a certain period (we call it the negotiation period). When this period expires, if it received an advertisement message from all of its invited neighbours it enters the sleeping mode. Nodes use advertisement messages to tell their 1-hop neighbours that they will be active in the next iteration. When a node enters the sleeping mode, it remains in that mode for a period of time we call application period which is the same period nodes remain in for the active mode. The idea behind this period is to allow the base station to get a feedback from the network (as part of the usual functioning of the application) so that it would be able to decide whether the current cover is passing or not. When the application period expires, a sleeping node enters the negation phase and waits for invitations from its neighbours. It is important to note that such nodes do not attempt to get active. They get active only if some neighbour invites them. In such case, they advertise that they will be active and enter the active mode.

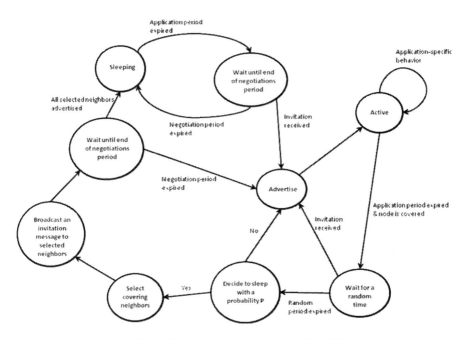

Fig. 1. The state transition diagram of DAIM

- After the application period expires, if an already active node received an invitation from one of its neighbours, then it will not attempt to sleep but rather it will advertise its presence and enter the active mode again.
- If the sleeping decision yielded a negative result, a node will advertise its presence and stay active in the next iteration.
- If a node that already broadcasted an invitation message didn't receive an advertisement message from all of the neighbours it invited, then it will advertise its presence and stay active in the next iteration. The algorithm terminates at the iteration in which the set of active nodes form a passing cover.

We present two different variations of the proposed technique. The two versions only differ in the way the covering nodes are selected. The naïve version (we will refer to it by Naïve) simply chooses the set of all neighbours whereas the greedy version (we will refer to it by Greedy) attempts to select a subset of the neighbours that didn't participate much in previous iterations. It begins by selecting one neighbour at a time in a greedy fashion (selects the one with minimum participation times) and checks if the updated selected neighbours cover it. The pseudo code of Greedy is presented in Figure 2. Isolating the malfunctioning nodes can be implemented easily at the base station by maintaining a list of the covers that were selected through the algorithm (one cover for each iteration). The algorithm terminates when a passing cover Pass is found. Then, this cover can be compared with the failing covers of the previous iterations to find the one that resembles it the most (call it similarFail). Then the malfunctioning nodes will be isolated in the set Pass - similarFail. We will refer to such set by SUSPICIOUS.

```
-------------------------------------------------------------------------
1. TEMP ← NEIGHBORS(i)
2. SELECTED ← ∅
3. while TEMP != ∅
4.      j ← NeighborWithMinParticipation(TEMP)
5.      SELECTED ← SELECTED ∪ {j}
6.      TEMP ← TEMP - {j}
7.      if isCovered(i,SELECTED)
8.              return SELECTED
9. return SELECTED
--------------------------------------------------------
```

Fig. 2. The Greedy Version Pseudo code

4 Performance Analysis

To evaluate the effectiveness of DAIM in isolating malfunctioning nodes, we define two metrics: convergence delay and isolation precision. The first is the average number of iterations taken to find a passing cover and the second is simply the size of the SUSPICIOUS set (the smaller the SUSPICIOUS the higher the precision). The first metric would be a beneficial indicator if the priority is to ensure reliability of the network (i.e. we need to make sure that the network is always supported by a passing cover) whereas the second relates to the situations in which locating the malfunctioning nodes is the top priority. We conducted several experiments to analyse the performance of the two versions of DAIM (Naïve and Greedy) under different settings and the results are presented accordingly.

We developed our own simulator in Java to analyse the performance of DAIM. Each node is associated with a thread and all communication is held through a synchronizer process. Our simulator assumes that no collisions occur by making sure that no two messages from two different nodes are sent at the same time. Invitation messages are handled using a FIFO protocol. That is, nodes that initiate an invitation message first are served first. Besides, an invitation message is cancelled if the inviter was a target of an earlier invitation. Before simulation begins, the simulator randomly generates the locations of the nodes and randomly selects the malfunctioning ones. At each iteration, the synchronizer checks the attempts of all nodes and decides the action to be taken by each of them (i.e. sleep or be active). We define three types of attempts:

- Type 0: The node might be already sleeping or active but is ready to do what the synchronizer decides.
- Type 1: The node decided to sleep. That is, it at-tempted to send an invitation message to a set of neighbors (targets).
- Type 2: The node can't be sleep-ing because it is not covered.

The synchronizer maintains two lists: Active and Sleeping which represent the nodes that will be active (resp. sleeping in the next iteration). It first handles nodes of type 2 and adds them to the Active nodes list. Then it handles nodes of type 1 based on FIFO as follows: if the node to be handled has one of its invited neighbours in the Sleeping list then it has to be active and thus added to the Active list. Otherwise, it is added to the Sleeping list. Finally, if a node of type 0 is a target of another node in the Sleeping list then it is added to the Active list, otherwise it is added to the Sleeping list. In the next iteration, nodes that are in the Active list will be active and those that are in the Sleeping list will be sleeping. The simulation variables are: nbNodes, areaWidth, Rc/ Rs, sleepingProbability, maxIterations, nbMal, selectionAlgorithm.

The first set of experiments was conducted to com-pare the performance of the two versions with respect to each other. After setting nbNodes to 20, sleepingProbability to 0.8, and nbMal to 1, we performed 16 experiments for each version and determined at the end of each experiment the values of the two metrics. The results showed that Greedy is much faster in finding a passing cover whereas Naïve is much more precise in locating the malfunctioning node. Figure 3(a) shows the performance of both algorithms in terms of convergence delay. The chart can be read in the following way: a point (x,y) on the Greedy (resp. Naïve) curve means that in (y*100)% of the experiments Greedy (resp. Naïve) finds a passing cover in no more than x iterations. For example, in 100% of the experiments Greedy didn't need more than 5 iterations to find a passing cover.

The result that Greedy is much faster than Naïve in finding passing covers can be attributed to the fact that the former tends to find new covers which consist of nodes that didn't participate much in previous iterations. On the other hand, we found out that Naïve is much more precise in locating the malfunctioning node. We can see that in 100% of the experiments Naïve isolated the malfunctioning node in a set of at most 4 nodes. The result that Naïve is much more precise than Greedy in locating the malfunctioning nodes is reasonable since the former results in covers that have large overlaps with previous ones and thus the difference between the passing cover and the previous failing covers will be small.

We also used Greedy to study the impact of node density as well as sleeping probability on the convergence delay. For each value of density (40 till 65 with step 5) we conducted 5 experiments, determined the convergence delay for each and computed the average. A similar approach was done to study the impact of sleeping probability (the values ranged from 0.2 till 0.8 with step 0.2). Concerning node density, experiments show that low densities as well as high densities degrade the performance of Greedy. In terms of sleeping probability, we found out that it performs better at lower probabilities. (Fig4(a) and Fig(4(b)).

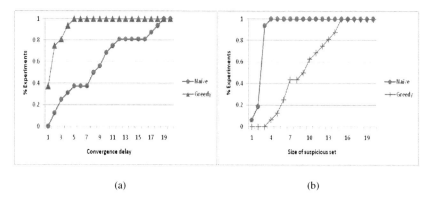

(a)   (b)

Fig. 3. (a) The convergence Delay of Naïve vs. Greedy. **(b)**The size of suspicious set of Naïve vs. Greedy

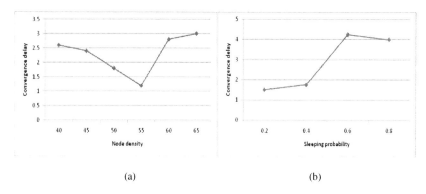

(a)   (b)

Fig. 4. (a) Convergence delay of Greedy as a function of density. (b) Delay of Greedy as a function of probability

5   Conclusions and Future Work

In this paper, we presented an algorithm to isolate malfunctioning nodes in WSNs and provided two variants of this algorithm: Naïve and Greedy. The two variants differ in the way covering nodes are selected. We found out that Naïve is more precise in locating the malfunctioning nodes whereas Greedy is much faster in finding a passing cover. On the other hand, we noticed that its precision is slightly affected by the sleeping probability. Another important observation is that when the number of malfunctioning nodes is greater than one, both Naïve and Greedy fail to isolate them.

This is left for future investigation and might be solved by forcing nodes that participate in a large number of covers to sleep. In this way, we tend to create new covers that have minimum overlap with previous covers and thus we would increase the chances of isolating the nodes simultaneously (i.e. finding a cover that doesn't contain any of the malfunctioning nodes). Another future work would be analysing the energy cost of DAIM especially that we weren't able to do it in this work because of the current limitations of our simulator.

References

1. Watfa, M., Commuri, S.: Coverage strategies in 3D wireless sensor networks. Int. J. Distributed Sensor Netw. 2(4), 333–353 (2006)
2. Watfa, M., Commuri, S.: An energy efficient and self-healing 3- dimensional sensor cover. Int. J. Ad Hoc and Ubiq. Computing 2, 121–138 (2007)
3. Watfa, M., Commuri, S.: The three dimensional coverage problem. J. Netw. 1(4), 10–20 (2006)
4. Slijepcevic, S., Potkonjak, M.: Power efficient organization of wireless sensor networks. In: Proc. IEEE ICC, pp. 472–476 (June 2001)
5. Meguerdichian, S., Koushanfar, F., Potkonjak, M., Srivastava, M.B.: Coverage problems in wireless ad-hoc sensor networks. In: INFOCOM, pp. 1380–1387 (April 2001)
6. Lieska, K., Laitinen, E., Lahteenmaki, J.: Radio coverage optimization with genetic algorithms. In: Proc. IEEE PIMRC, pp. 318–322 (September 1998)
7. Gage: Command control for many-robot systems. In: Proc. the 19th Annual AUVS Technical Symp., pp. 22–24 (June 2002)
8. Gupta, H., Das, S., Gu, Q.: Connected sensor cover: Self-organization of sensor networks for efficient query execution. In: Proc. MobiHoc, pp. 189–200 (June 2003)
9. Ramanathan, N., Chang, K., Kapur, R., Girod, L., Kohler, E., Estrin, D.: Sympathy for the Sensor Network Debugger. In: 3rd International Conference on Embedded Networked Sensor Systems (Sensys 2005), pp. 255–267 (November 2005)
10. Yang, J., Soffa, M.L., Selavo, L., Whitehouse, K.: Clair-voyant: A Comprehensive Source-Level Debugger for Wireless Sensor Networks. In: 5th International Conference on Embedded Networked Sensor Systems, pp. 189–203 (November 2007)
11. Girod, L., Ramanathan, N., Elson, J., Stathopoulos, T., Lukac, M., Estrin, D.: Emstar: A software environment for developing and deploying heterogeneous sensor-actuator networks. ACM TOSN 3(3) (August 2007)
12. Whitehouse, K., Tolle, G., Taneja, J., Sharp, C., Kim, S., Jeong, J., Hui, J., Dutta, P., Culler, D.: Marionette: Using RPC for Interactive Development and Debugging of Wireless Embedded Networks. In: 5th International Conference on Information Processing in Sensor Networks (- 2006), pp. 416–423 (April 2006)

IPurse: An Innovative RFID Application

Mohamed K. Watfa, Manprabhjot Kaur, and Rashida Firoz Daruwala

University of Wollongong in Dubai, Computer Science Department, Dubai, UAE

Abstract. RFID tags are miniscule microchips, which continue to get smaller and cheaper every day. This paper introduces IPURSE, an intelligent system built on a mobile platform which keeps track of items a user carries in their purse/handbag and also alerts the user when any item is missing from the purse/handbag. IPURSE is a unique project that brings the RFID and NFC technologies together into a single system by 'cleverly' monitoring, reminding and alerting users about their missing items based on the current weather, reminder messages and daily items usually carried by the user. We discuss the methods, equipments and technologies used to successfully implement such an application. It includes the design evolution and technical design of the system, followed by a working prototype and experimentation. The pros and cons of the application are also discussed towards the end of this paper.

Keywords: Intelligent system, Near Field Communication, NFC, RFID, Purse.

1 Introduction

This research project is committed to the forgotten items and to an apparatus and method for reminding forgotten items. This project is a computerized system that will assist in monitoring all the items carried in a purse/handbag. Humans cannot multitask – the human brain can focus only on one thing at a time; even if the focus is for a very short period (like a nanosecond). It is virtually impossible for the human brain to pay quality attention to all tasks – it eventually forgets everything that is not committed to long term memory. As a result of which, people often tend to forget and loose things. A purse/handbag is used to contain all the personal items that one needs to carry while travelling. By keeping all items in a single container, the chances of loosing things are lessened. However, it is equally difficult to monitor all the items in the carrier at all times, especially when people are engaged in other activities. At present, people set reminders to remember to carry items and repeatedly check the items they are carrying (especially in case of important documents like passports or expensive objects) at regular intervals to ensure they are not missing or stolen.

To resolve this issue, a software application was implemented which would automate the monitoring process and also incorporate additional 'intelligent' features like the alert system, real-time weather check and reminders, which would help enhance the functionalities of the overall system. The system utilizes Radio Frequency Identification (RFID) and Near Field Communication (NFC) technologies. RFID technology comprises two components: tag and reader. The RFID tag is an IC chip that

M. Zhou (Ed.): ISAEBD 2011, Part IV, CCIS 211, pp. 531–538, 2011.

can store and send information over radio frequency signals and can be applied onto different items. The RFID reader acts as an antenna for receiving and transmitting signals. NFC technology is a short range wireless connectivity technology that enables simple and safe two way interaction among electronic devices. NFC establishes faster connections compared to Bluetooth and it also provides a degree of security due to its short range communication. An NFC reader is also capable of reading RFID tags. The RFID and NFC technologies are incorporated in this software application to make it act as an intelligent system which will help in monitoring all items in the purse/handbag and also in alerting users when any item is forgotten or misplaced.

2 Method and Apparatus

For the successful working of this software application, it was important to jot down the specific requirements that the application would need to meet. The main functional requirements included providing a monitoring system, providing a web interface, providing an intelligent weather check system and an intelligent reminder system, sending alert/reminder messages at the right time to the mobile phone. Whereas, the non-functional requirements from the project included user friendliness, reliability in terms of retrieving information and sending alert messages, fast response time, error free application to offer best results and accessibility with regard to be able to create/view/modify the item list(s) at any point of time and from anywhere.

(a)   (b)   (c)
purse handbag designed   RFID tags used for   NFC enabled mobile phone
for the application   the application   used for the application

Fig. 1. Apparatus used for the IPURSE research project

IPURSE makes use of the RFID and NFC technologies as mentioned earlier in this paper. A special purse/handbag (refer Fig. 1(a)) was made that would help the users in carrying their item(s) and mobile phone and at the same time enable easy interaction between the tags and NFC mobile phone. The entry/exit point of the purse has been made in such a way that it is half-closed and half-open so as to restrict the reading space and ensure communication between the tagged item and mobile phone. The purse also has a pocket to hold the mobile phone at the front of the purse/handbag which allows the users to have fast access to the mobile phone and also easy communication with the tags. Mirfare 1K (S50 type) RFID tags (refer Fig. 1(b)) were purchased and also the Nokia 6131 NFC enabled mobile phone (refer Fig. 1(c)) which was the only available phone in the developing market for the application. Apart from the hardware, software and support was also looked at – Nokia 6131 SDK Kit and Nokia 6131 emulator were available for download at the Nokia site. JRE 1.6 and

J2ME Wireless Toolkit 2.1 were downloaded as well along with Eclipse 3.1.1 and MySQL. A few compatibility issues were faced in the beginning few weeks as the NFC based mobile phones and support for them was discontinued in the Middle East and many other countries since 2004.

When designing the system, all the requirements and functionalities of the system were taken into consideration. Different classes were defined to handle the different functionalities of the system. However, a few difficulties were faced while designing the system: One of the difficulties was to decide how frequent should the automatic scan be. The user generally would need to be reminded about the missing items before they left their home. Hence, it was decided that the user's entry and exit points of the house would be monitored. Another difficulty faced was how often the anti-losing alerts be sent. Questions like: would the users be alerted as soon as an item was taken out of the purse; what if the users remove an item from the bag, use it for some time and then forget to keep it back in purse/handbag, then after how long would an alert be sent; how often would the alerts be sent if the item was outside the purse/handbag – once or more than once; would the alerts annoy the users, etc. were considered. Finally, after enough research, a design was sought wherein every item in the carrier would be associated with a priority and the priority would define a timer for each time, so when the time went off, the users would be alerted. Three types of priority – high, medium and low were discussed, each type associated to a timer of 15, 30 and 60 minutes respectively. The design of the system is modular and function-based. It is designed in such a way that the system can easily be extended to include new functionalities. As mentioned earlier, different classes were constructed to handle different functionalities of the system. Fig. 2 shows how the classes are linked with one another. Class Asset keeps a check at the items required according to the item list set by the user.

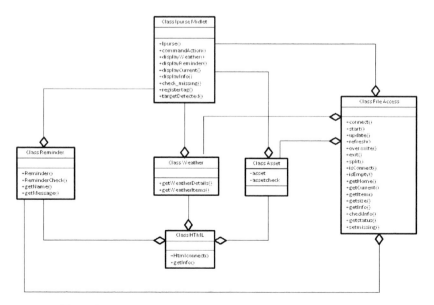

Fig. 2. Class diagram representing relationship between the classes

Class Reminder keeps in store the reminder message, the name of the person who wrote the message and also for whom it is written. Class Weather gets updated weather information for the city name specified by the user. Each of the above mentioned classes are linked to class HTML from which all the details and constraints regarding items specified by the user are received and then manipulated by the Asset, Weather and Reminder classes. Class IPURSE Midlet handles all operations made by the user via the mobile phone. All the classes, except class HTML, are linked to the class FileAccess to receive information about the items that are ether present/absent from the user's purse/handbag.

3 Working of Research Project

This project needs the user, tags and mobile phone to interact together for its smooth working. At the onset, the users need to write the item's identification data, that is, name of the item onto the RFID tags and then apply these RFID tags onto the respective item(s). Once the users have tagged the item(s), they need to specify to the system which item(s) they would want to be reminded about to carry and also on which date(s) and/or day(s) of the week. The users would need to visit the website of the application in order to make use of the application. Then, the users need to create an asset list – specify item names along with their priority level and the date(s) and/or day(s) for which they want to carry them. The system has two different scenarios that it needs to deal with – one is when the users just leave home and the other is when they are away from home. The user needs to place every item that should be carried into their carrier before leaving house. When an item is placed inside the purse/handbag, the status of the item changes from 'out purse' to 'in purse' and vice versa when taken out. An RFID tag named 'home' must also be applied to the user's main door at home so that the system can know when the user leaves or comes home. When the user passes through the door, the NFC mobile phone will interact with the 'home' tag, and the status of the user will change from 'in home' to 'out home', thereby notifying the system that the user has left home. If the status of the user is set to 'out home', then the application performs different checks – asset check, weather check and reminder check one at a time. In the asset check module, the application checks the list of the items for that specific date or day as set by the user and cross checks the item(s) with the item(s) that are present in the carrier at that time. If any item is absent from the purse/handbag and needs to be carried according to the user's asset list for that date or day; then an alert message is immediately sent to the user on their mobile phone. The user can either ignore the message or collect the item from their home and place it in the purse/handbag. In the other scenario, when the user is away from home, all the items that the user placed into their carrier are monitored at all times. Since all the item(s) are inside the purse/handbag, their status is set to 'in' and when an item is taken out of the purse/handbag, the status is changed to 'out'. The application then instantly checks the priority time that the user had set for the item, for instance, the user took out their wallet for which they had set high priority (15 minutes). The application keeps track of the time and waits for the user to place the item (wallet in this case) inside the purse/handbag before the priority time that is

15 minutes runs out. But if the user has not placed back the item in the carrier within that time, then the system sends an alert message to the user on their mobile phone informing them about the missing item. However, if the user places the item back into the purse/handbag in time, then no alert message is sent to the user at all.

4 Results

Testing was carried out for the application in two different scenarios – one when the user is at home and the other when the user is away from home. 5 participants were selected of different age groups, two being males and three females. For each scenario, same participants were called in and were briefed about the project and how it worked, after which there were given tasks to perform for application testing. At the end of the session, the participants were asked also to comment on the innovation of the application. They were asked to fill in a questionnaire based on the tasks they performed in their scenario. The answers from all the participants were collected and analyzed to get the following results:

a) When user leaves home

The participants were asked to write identification data to the tags provided to them and apply them to the respective items. Then they needed to create an asset list and specify the requirements as mentioned on the website. Later, they were asked to place their tagged items into their carrier and leave home, once by forgetting an item at home and the other time taking all items along with them. At the end of the session, the participants were asked to fill in a questionnaire which included rating (on a scale from 1-10) questions (refer Fig. 4 – x-axis for questions asked in questionnaire). The results showed that on an average all participants found the application to be easy to use including the writing data to tags. The receiving time of alert messages scored the highest on the questionnaire, while the web interface scored the least. When asked as to what they found missing in the web interface, the participants simply said that they were not accustomed to using a website as a reminder source for their required items. While the experiment was in progress, the time each participant took to put the items in to their carrier was noted, to give an average time of 20 seconds for placing 5 items in their first attempt.

b) When user is away from home

The same participants were told to purchase something at any shop/restaurant and leave the place, once by forgetting behind an item (each person left behind an item of different priority type) at the cashier's and the last time not forgetting anything. At the end of the session, the participants were asked to fill in the same questionnaire as in the scenario A with a few added questions like use of priority for items, and on the default priority time. The results for the questions repeated in this scenario were almost in sync with those in scenario A. For the additional questions, it was found from the scores that participants were pleased to have a priority timer that would allow them to assign importance levels for their items. However, the default time set for the each priority type was not liked by almost all participants. When asked for their reasons of low scoring the last priority type questions, the participants said that the time set was too long a wait and should be narrowed down for faster alerts.

c)   User leaves home VS. User away from home

For this experiment, the results received from both the scenarios were compared to find which participants were more comfortable at using the application and also where. From Fig. 3, it can be seen that the scores plotted in scenario a. and scenario b. are similar for most of the questions. The major difference in the scores among the two scenarios can be seen for questions related to web interface and response time. This variance in response time could be due to the difference in the network speed as the venues were different for both the scenarios. Also, it was found that as the participants used the apparatus more, they felt more comfortable while using the application every next time, as a result of which, the average time of putting items in carrier improved over time. Additionally, the participants seemed to be pleased with the results of scenario b. than of scenario a. as shown in Fig.3. The reason deduced for this could be that people felt vulnerable of loosing items when away from home than when they are at home.

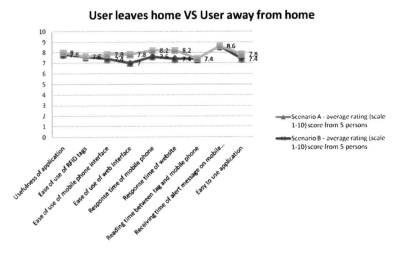

Fig. 3. Line graph showing the comparison between the two scenarios used for the evaluation of the IPURSE application

Overall, from the results it was known that the participants found this project to be very useful and user-friendly in terms of daily use and people got more comfortable with using the application every next time. The participants were also asked to suggest functionalities that they would like the application to have. All the participants who took part in the evaluation of the application, found it to be a very innovative idea. Most participants felt that the application was very useful, but said that it failed to find a solution to tackle a situation in which the user has misplaced or lost the item. In such a situation, the application cannot tell the user where the item is or at least where it was last placed.

5   Related Work and Future Directions

Some existing work with similar concept and functionalities that were found during the research phase of this project are as follows:

- Lost Item Locator [1]: this system helps in locating lost items by using a passive RFID tag and a portable reader transceiver.
- Method and System for tracking objects using GPS receiver built in active RFID [2]: this system tracks object using Global Positioning system receiver that is built in the RFID receiver.
- Electronic tether for portable objects [3]: this system issues an alarm when the distance between the module and the alert module increases by a certain value.
- LadyBag [4]: this system uses RFID technology to detect items in the bag and sends out alert with the help of LED lights if an item goes missing.

From the above stated works, it is clear that many applications have been developed but all revolving around a similar idea. Although most projects list the use of RFID technology, IPURSE is a unique project that brings the RFID and NFC technologies together into a single system. The most important advantage of this application is the intelligence part of it which 'cleverly' monitors, reminds and alerts users about their missing items on the basis of the weather, reminder messages received by the user and daily items carried by the user. Moreover, this application is cost-effective and users will definitely feel a sense of security while carrying their items away from home. Along with advantages, IPURSE also has a few shortcomings – most people feel that the web interface of the application is not needed. The participants at the application testing felt it was 'too much of work and roundabout'. The participants argued that they would not want to switch between mobile phone and computers and would prefer everything to be centralized onto a single platform. Additionally, the participants were also concerned that the reading distance between the tag and mobile phone was very small. Although, this is a valid point, it is not of much importance as the reason for using NFC in this application is to provide a cheap, handy and secure communication between the RFID tag and the NFC mobile phone. At present, there are a limited number of mobile phones which comprise NFC technology. However, in the near future, most mobile phone companies are releasing handsets that will support NFC technology. Mobile manufactures namely Nokia and Apple informed in the year 2010 that they would integrate the technology into their future handsets, with NFC-enabled smart phones expected to be available by 2011 [5]. The co-CEO of RIM, had said in the Web 2.0 conference held in November 2010, that all Blackberry phones will soon be getting NFC chips in the future [6]. Alternatively, if users do not want to purchase an NFC enabled mobile phone separately, then they can purchase NFC stickers for the same. The leading suppliers of NFC mobile phone chips – Inside Contactless and

NXP, Android NFC mobile phones will arrive in the first half of the year 2011 as well [7]. MyMax, the mobile NFC sticker created by TWINLINX says that any Bluetooth phone can be turned into an NFC terminal by simply placing the thin NFC sticker on its back [8].

Along with all the reviews obtained from the participants during the evaluation about the procedure and usability of the application, the participants were also asked to suggest their opinions and additional features they would want to be a part of the application. Participants wanted the application to include a tracking feature that would enable the users to track their missing or lost items. Other features that could also be added into this application would be – linking the users' social networking sites with the application's system so that reminder messages posted by the user's friends and family and birthday dates (of course with their permission) could be retrieved and intelligent reminder messages could be sent to the user in case they have missed to see the posts. As a final idea, the user's emails can be linked to the application so that the application can retrieve reminder messages or meeting details from the users' mailbox and intelligently remind the users to carry the required item(s) for the day. With the promising advent of the RFID and NFC technologies around the world and also the extensive use of mobile phones and smart phones, IPURSE will have a great impact on the community.

References

1. Stump, L.E., Ferri, L.: Lost Item Locator (2006),
   http://www.freshpatents.com/Lost-item-locater-
   dt20060622ptan20060132308.php
2. Chan, K.W.: Method and system for tracking objects using global positioning system (GPS) receiver built in the active radio frequency id (rfid) receiver (2009),
   http://www.freshpatents.com/-dt20091217ptan20090309731.php
3. Light, E.D., Boesch, B., Roberts, J.L.: Electronic tether for portable objects (2006),
   http://www.freshpatents.com/Electronic-tether-for-portable-
   objects-dt20060907ptan20060197658.php
4. LadyBag, http://www.talk2myshirt.com/blog/archives/447
5. Ghee, R.: NFC-enabled mobile phone – the future of the check-in process? (2010),
   http://www.futuretravelexperience.com/2010/08/nfc-enabled-
   mobile-phones-the-future-of-the-check-in-process/#
6. Rosoff, M., Yarrow, J.: RIM CEO Touts the Blackberry Playbook NFC for phones (2010),
   http://www.businessinsider.com/live-rim-ceo-jim-balsillie-
   at-web (November 20, 2010)
7. Clark, S.: Multiple NFC-enabld Android handsets to arrive from late 2010. Near Field Communications World (2010),
   http://www.nearfieldcommunicationsworld.com/2010/04/23/33506/
   multiple-nfc-enabled-android-handsets-to-arrive-from-late-
   2010/
8. An NFC terminal in every pocket. Now (2010), http://www.twinlinx.com/

Empirical Research on Impact of the Home Advantage of Referees upon Chinese Basketball Professional League

Chen Guoqian

College of Physical Education, LuoYang Normal University, LuoYang,
HeNan, China 471023
Ch_g_qi@126.com

Abstract. The referee is considered to be one of influencing factors of existing home advantage. GLM—univariate and multiple-factor variance analysis, whether the referee affects directly the home advantage or not in Chinese basketball professional leagues. The result shows that: Chinese basketball professional league exists the home advantage; The judgement of the referee is influenced by the noise. The referee is one of the most direct influencing factors of existing of home advantage in Chinese basketball professional league. Finally, some feasible suggestions are put forward for reducing the influence of the home advantage in Chinese basketball professional league.

Keywords: Referee, basketball, Professional League, GLM—univariate and multiple-factor variance analysis.

1   Introduction

It is proved that home advantage (HA for shorter) exist in various sports.Generally speaking,the home advantage came from the rules of the game ,the travelling factors,the factors of familiar with the environment and noisy factors(the support of fans) etc [1]. The rule factor and the factor of familiarity with the environment have proved to be no significant influence in Chinese basketball professional league.With the improvement of transport ,the travelling time of atheletes has been shortened ,so the travelling factor can be neglected.On the contrary, due to the noisy factor ,the influence exists very significant difference among the atheletes of two sides ,even the referee. At abroad, many researchers from different angles have proven the effects of noisy factors on atheletes. From the angle of behavioral science, resoundingcheers can spur the atheletes of the home team to achieve greater results. To explain in psychological terms,Jurkovac has found that basketball players of the home team at the university had higher contest motivation during competition period. From the Physiology, the researchers have found that players of hockey,rugby football and soccer of the home team can secrete more testicular hormone than the players of the visiting team [2]. Above results show that the players of the home team hold a "territorial stress reaction",which can strengthen their aggressive style and promote to achieve much better performance.However, these researches can't completely make sure the influence on the noisy factors to the atheletes [3]. Some other research also has

M. Zhou (Ed.): ISAEBD 2011, Part IV, CCIS 211, pp. 539–547, 2011.
© Springer-Verlag Berlin Heidelberg 2011

shown that the psychological influences do not exist between the players of the home team and those of the visiting team.At the same time,the researchers find that the judge of referees is influenced by the noisy factors.There is a significant difference from the judge to the visiting team between watching the video of match and on-the-spot [2].

To verify the influence of referees on home advantage of basketball league, we make the following proposals:firstly,if the behavior of the referees is inflenced by the noisy factors,the referees would make more or less response.Secondly,when the referees watch a lot of games,they should show individual difference. i.e.,different referees have different "territorial stress reaction" to the stress of the noise. In view of the overall situation, the judge of the referees should show individual difference. If it is neither significant nor important of the referees to dependent variables ,the behavior of the referees to this dependent variable is unanimous and impartial.On the contrary, the behavior of the referees to this dependent variable should be systematic uniform.According to the above hypothesis,and combining with the various statistical index (Fouls, Free Throws for shorter FTs , Points for shorter PTs among the home team and the visiting team) on the 2007-2008 basketball season and the 2008-2009 basketball season and the first referee of every game in Chinese Basketball Professional League. GLM—univariate and multiple-factor variance analysis, whether there is a significant influence on the dependent variable and whether the referee is influenced by the noisy factor and whether there is a significant influence on home advantage in Chinese basketball professional leagues.

2 Summary of Research Subjects and Methods

2.1 Research Subjects

Research subjects of this study is : 690 games on regular seasons of the 2007-2008 basketball season and the 2008-2009 basketball season. Among all the games, the first referees can't be ascertained in the 23th round gmae and the 30th round game in the 2007-2008 basketball season ,and two games in the 2008-2009 basketball season, so the data is unavailable and the data on the first referees of officiating not more than 10 games is invalid.i.e. ,the data on 646 games is available.

2.2 Summary of Methods

To the study of reaction of more variables on one dependent variable, many scholars, at home or abroad, generally analyze it by the stepwise regression method. However they deal with the categorical variable, especially different levels of the categorical variable, by the "dummy variable".When we deal with the statistics of more categorical varialbes,firstly ,there are more than one dummy variables;secondly ,the results of stepwise regression depend on assignment method of the dummy variable;thirdly,through this method,we can't analyze systematically to the categorical variable as a whole(levels of categorical variable more than 2). To make up for above these defects,the scholars ,at abroad, analyze the data by the Proc—Genmod of

SAS,but the scholars, at home,deal with these data by GLM—univariate and multiple-factor variance analysis of SPSS.This study involves not only in the continuously variables such as points won and points lost per game, Free Throw s , Fouls of the home team and the visiting team, but also in the categorical variables such as the referee and the season.Therefore this study adopts GLM—univariate and multiple-factor variance analysis method,which can analyse simultaneously the continuously variables and the categorical variable.

General Linear Model can fulfil the analysis of more independent variables, multiple levels,more factors,and variance-covariance of design of experiments.Among the GLM—univariate and multiple-factor variance analysis, univariate means defining only one continuously dependent variable in statistical data,multiple levels means there being more than one ,at least two levels , categorical factors in the statistical data,and covariate means the data holding continuous variables [5][6]. Comparing GLM—univariate and multiple-factor variance analysis and the stepwise regression method,dealing with the data of univariate multiple factors,the former obtains superiority [4]:

a. To categorical factors,not doing extra work of "resolution " on the dummy variable, assigning the first level of the last level of factors as "the reference level".

b. Dealing with conveniently interaction among the factors, interaction between the factor and the covariate.

c. Establishing regression equation same like stepwize regression analysis,and conducting residual analysis.

d. Filtering corresponding factors and covariates of having statistics meaning.

3   Results and Analysis

3.1   Analysis of the Current Situation on the Home Advantage of Chinese Basketball Professional League

Coumeya and Carron, US psychologists ,clearly put forward the operation definition of the home advantage,under the same times of the home and away games , the home team winning percentage is over 50%,(the home winning percentage, shorter form HWP),HWP more than 50% has been a clear criteria, a judgement whether home advantage exists or not.This standard of value is used extensively the match of having the same times of the home and away games.At the same time we can refer to other index's comparison of the home team and the visiting team.

It can be seen from Table 1 the mean of statistic index of all matches,which include 2007-2008 and 2008-2009 two basketball seasons and 2008-2009 basketball season of points difference not more than 10 in Chinese Basketball Professional League.Intwo seasons, the statistic index,which include HWP, 3-Points, Free Throws , Rebounds Rebs , Assists , Steals , Turn Overs , Block Shots and Points, of the home team all go beyond thoes of the visiting team. ,HWP are all over 60%,and HWP reaches 55.8% in the gmae of points difference not more than 10.At the same time, the two index of

Assists and Points of the home team are far above thoes of the visiting team. Fast Assists in the 2007-2008 season and Fouls in the 2008-2009 season are all inferior to the visiting team.But Fast Assists in the 2008-2009 season and Fouls in the 2007-20098 season are superior to the visiting team.From the data on points difference not more than 10 in the 2008-2009 season,all index of the home team are all superior to thoes of the visiting team. Accoring to the operation definition of the home advantage,we find out that home advantage of Chinese Basketball Professional League exists.

Table 1. Statistics of all index in 2007-2009 two seasons [7] [8]

index season		HWP	3-Points	Free Throws	Offense Rebounds	Defense Rebounds	Assists	Foul: s	Steals	Fast Assists	Turn Overs	Block Shots	Points
2007-2008	Home team	0.639	0.36	23.7	13.8	28.5	15.8	22.2	10.5	4.4	15.2	3.3	104.1
	Visiting team	0.371	0.34	22.9	12.7	27.6	12.7	22.7	9.5	6.2	16.2	2.8	100.2
2008-2009	Home team	0.622	0.356	24.0	13.4	28.2	16.8	22.2	10.9	5.5	15.9	3.8	104.0
	Visiting team	0.378	0.336	23.6	12.7	26.9	13.7	22.1	9.8	4.6	16.8	3.14	99.5
2008-2009 score≤10	Home team	0.558	0.346	24.7	40.8		15.7	22.1	10.3	5.2	15.7	3.8	101.5
	Visiting team	0.442	0.345	23.5	40.4		14.1	22.9	9.9	4.9	16.2	3.3	100.9

Note: The amount of rebounds of the home team and the visiting is total rebounds of points difference not more than 10 of 2008-2009 season。

3.2 Test on GLM—Univariate and Multiple-Factor Variance Analysis of the Referees and the Home Advantage of Basketball Professional League

In the 2007-2008 season and the 2008-2009 season,the average point of the home team was respectively higher 3.9 and 4.5 points than those of the visiting team(see Table 1). GLM—univariate and multiple-factor variance analysis of taking Points as a dependent variable, the referee factor has no significant influence on the home side point,the visiting side point,the difference of the home side points and visiting side points,the total of the home side points and the visiting side points.And the season factor has also no significant influence in above four aspects. The factors of affecting the home team points are average won of the home team（df=1,p=0.000, efficiency value=0.241） and the average loss (df=1,p=0.000, efficiency value=0.278)of the visiting team. The factors of affecting the visiting team won are the average loss of the home team （df=1,p=0.000, efficiency value=0.235） and the average won (df=1,p=0.000, efficiency value=0.126)of the visiting team.From the analysis of the efficiency value, firstly,the average loss of the opponents is the primarily factor of affecting won(namely: defensive capacity),secondly,the average won of own team. (namely:offensive capacity).lastly, the factors of affecting difference of the home side points and the visiting side points and the total of the home side points and the visiting side points are the average won of the home team and the average loss of the visiting team.(see Table 2). It can be concluded from the analysis of the above data that the won scores of the home team and the visiting team are affected by the capabilities of attack and defence of both teams,not the referee factor. There was no significant difference on points between the 2007-2008 season and the 2008-2009 season.

Table 2. GLM—univariate and multiple-factor variance analysis of taking points as the dependent variable [9]

	df	points of the home team		Points of the visiting team		the difference of the home side points and the visiting side points		he total of the home de points and visiting side points	
		P	efficiency value	P	efficiency value	P	efficiency value	P	efficiency value
referee	14	.682	.017	.188	.029	.904	.012	.217	.028
season	1	.998	.000	.260	.002	.312	.002	.500	.001
average point(home)	1	.000	.241	.019	.009	.000	.154	.000	.136
average loss (home)	1	.201	.003	.000	.235	.000	.170	.000	.116
average point(visiting)	1	.714	.000	.000	.126	.000	.112	.000	.045
average loss (visiting)	1	.000	.278	.548	.001	.000	.227	.000	.131

Note:1、 Adjusted R^2 named sequently: 0.428 ,0.332 ,0.443 ,0.353; 2、 Corrected Model named sequently: F=26.326 P=0.000, F=17.840 P=0.000, F=28.004 P=0.000, F=19.527 P=0.000。

In the 2007-2008 season , Fouls of the home team are less 0.5 than thoes of the visiting team.,but in the 2008-2009 season, Fouls of the home team are more 0.1 than thoes of the visiting team(see Table 1). GLM—univariate and multiple-factor variance analysis of taking Fouls as a dependent variable,Fouls of the home team are affected by the referees(df=1,p=0.001, efficiency value=0.057),the average loss of the home team (df=1,p=0.031, efficiency value=0.007) and the average loss of the visiting team (df=1,p=0.00, efficiency value=0.053).But Fouls of the visiting team are only affected by the average loss of the home team (df=1,p=0.00, efficiency value=0.040). The difference of Fouls of the home team and the visiting team is affected by the seasons, the average loss of the home team and the average loss of the visiting team. The total of Fouls of the home team and the visiting team is affected by the referees, the average loss of the home team and the visiting team.(see table 3).From the above analysis,there is a significant influence on the referees to Fouls of the home team ,the total of Fouls of the home team and the visiting team.But there is no significant influence on Fouls of the visiting team ,the difference of Fouls of the home team and the visiting team; there is a significant difference on the difference of Fouls of the home team and the visiting team between the two seasons.

There is no significant difference on the total of the fouls of the home team and the visiting team between the two seasons.Fouls of both teams are obviously affected by the average loss of the home team (defensive capacity),Fouls of the visiting team are only affected by the average loss of the home team(defensive capacity).

Table 3. GLM—univariate and multiple-factor variance analysis of taking Fouls results as a dependent variable [9]

	df	Fouls (home)		Fouls (visiting)		difference of the Fouls of the home side and the visiting side		the total of the Fouls of the home side and the visiting side	
		P	efficien cy value	P	efficie ncy value	P	efficienc y value	P	efficiency value
referee	14	.001	.057	.194	.029	.207	.028	.002	.052
season	1	.429	.001	.551	.001	.029	.008	.892	.000
average won of home team	1	.902	.000	.126	.004	.118	.004	.387	.001
average loss of home team	1	.031	.007	.000	.040	.003	.014	.000	.032
average won of visiting team	1	.088	.005	.735	.000	.191	.003	.197	.003
average loss of visiting team	1	.000	.053	.861	.000	.001	.018	.000	.023

Note:1、 Adjusted R^2 named sequently : 0.087 0.044 0.041 0.078 ; 2、 Corrected Model named sequently : F=4.212 P=0.000, F=2.574 P=0.000, F=2.453 P=0.01, F=3.878 P=0.000。

In the 2007-2008 season and the 2008-2009 season,the Free Throws of the home team are more than thoes of the visiting team.But in the 2008-2009 season,(see Table 1). GLM—univariate and multiple-factor variance analysis of taking Free Throws results as a dependent variable, the Free Throws of the home team and the visiting team , the difference of Free Throws of the home team and the visiting team , the total of Free Throws of the home team and the visiting team are all affected by refeferees,the average loss of the home team and the average loss of the visiting team.(see table 4), in the meantime, Free Throws of the visiting team and the total of Free Throws of the home team and the visiting team are affected by the season factors.From the angle of efficiency value ,the referee factors are respectively holding the second place,the first place,the first place and the first place. It can be known from the above analysis that there are significant influences on referees to the Free Throws of games.i.e. , The referee's decision is different and inconsistent on the Free Throws between the home team and the visiting team. there is no significant difference on the Free Throws of the home team ,the difference of the Free Throws of the home team and the visiting team between the two seasons. the difference of the Free Throws of the home team and the visiting team, the total of the Free Throws of the home team and the visiting team,are affected by the defensive capacity of the home team and the visiting team.i.e., the average loss of the home team and the visiting team.

Table 4. GLM—univariate and multiple-factor variance analysis of taking penalty shot results as dependent variable [9]

	df	penalty shot of home team		penalty shot of visiting team		difference of the penalty shot of home side and visiting side		total of the penalty shot of home side and visiting side	
		P	efficiency value	P	efficiency value	P	efficiency value	P	efficiency value
referee	14	.020	.042	.000	.075	.048	.036	.000	.075
season	1	.094	.004	.021	.008	.587	.000	.009	.011
average won of home team	1	.947	.000	.899	.000	.960	.000	.899	.000
average loss of home team	1	.000	.043	.020	.009	.028	.008	.000	.037
average won of visiting team	1	.853	.000	.999	.000	.888	.000	.905	.000
average loss of visiting team	1	.015	.010	.000	.040	.031	.007	.000	.038

Note:1、Adjusted R^2 named sequently〔0.067 0.094 0.020 0.119 ; 2、Corrected Model named sequently : F=3.427 P=0.000, F=4.517 P=0.000, F=1.694 P=0.03, F=5.596 P=0.000。

3.3   Argument and Analysis on Impact of the Home-Field Advantage of Referee upon Basketball Professional League

During the basketball competition, the statistic index ,which is most immediately affected by referees,is Fouls of the home team and the visiting team.On the other hand, the statistic index ,which is most indrectly affected by referees,is Free Throws of the home side and the visiting side and the point of the home team and the visiting team, Free Throws,which the player can earn the right for a Foul on an opponent,has an important influence on the score of the home team and the visiting team. It follows that the statistic index, the home advantage due to the referee,should be Fouls of the home team and the visiting team ,the Free Throws of the home team and the visiting team and the point of the home team and the visiting team,especially the Free Throws of the home team and the visiting team.

GLM—univariate and multiple-factor variance analysis:the point is due to the real ability(average won and lost) on each side rather than the referee factor. It is also certified the referee can not directly control the point of a contest. Fouls of the home team and the total of Fouls of the home team and the visiting side team are influenced by referees,the average loss of the home team and the average loss of the visiting team.This shows that there is a closer relation between Fouls of the home side and the judge of referees,the real ablity of the defense on each side. The data also indicates that there is a significant difference on the judge among Fouls of the home teams,i.e. the behavior of the referees to Fouls of the home team is systematic different, biased and inconsistent; Fouls of the visiting team are only affected by the average loss of the home team. the number of Fouls of the visiting team is only affected by the average loss of the home team. The difference of the Fouls on each side is influenced by the average loss of the home team and the visiting team. Combining the above analysis of the number of Fouls of the home team and the total of the Fouls of the home team and the visiting team,and the average number of Fouls on each side in two seasons(including the difference of the score not more than 10 in the 2008-2009 season),we can conclude that ,even though the judge of referees is consistent and unbiased to the visiting team,it may be an intentional control of the referee to the number of the fouls of the visiting team. There exist a significant influence of the referees and the average loss of the home team and the visiting to the Free Throws of the home team,the Free Throws of the visiting team,the difference of the home team and the visiting team and the total of the home team and the visiting team,it shows the influence of the referees and the real ability of the defense on each side to the Free Throws of the home team and the visiting team.it also indicates that there is different and inconsistent on the Free Throws of the home team and the visiting team.

According to the above allegation of the hypothesis, the behavior of the referee is influenced by the noisy factor.it lies in the actions of the referee on the number of the Fouls of the home team and the number of the Free Throws of the home team and the visiting team.On the other hand,Fouls of the visiting team ,which is influenced by the noisy factor, is a unified judgement.Combining the statistic data on the 2007-2008 season and the 2008-2009 season,we can conclude that the referee is one of the most direct influent factors of existing home advantage in Chinese Basketball Professional League.

4 Conclusion and Suggestion

There exists the home-field advangage in Chinese Basketball Professional League; the behavior of the referee is influenced by the noisy factor. the referee is one of the most direct influent factor of existing home-field advantage in Chinese Basketball Professional League.

The referees have significant influence on the home-field advantage of the basketball professional league,the first reason may be the support of the fans of the home side,the second reason is psychological mechanism of the referees. Through further detecting the level of hormone and stress,we can learn that what noise (the support of fans of the home team)and process influence the physiological mechamism of the referees and whether the behavior of the referees exist the general commonness or not. Supervisors of the league should take postive method to reduce the home-field advantage caused by the referees.one the one hand, supervisors reinforce vocational training among the referees, which improve the skill levels of referees and the impartiality of the judge under the stress.on the other hand, through the application of high-tech management(e.g. "Hawkeye" system of tennis tournament and instant replaying system in NBA games),it can decrease the subjective controversy of the referees.

References

1. Courneya, K.S., Carron, A.V.: Effects of travel andlength of home stand road trip on the home advantage. Journal of Sport and Exercise Psychology 13, 42–49 (1991)
2. Kerr, J.H., Vanschaik, P.: Effects of game venue and outcome on sychological mood states in rugby. Personality and Individual Differences 19, 407–410 (1995)
3. Carron, A.V., Loughhead, T.M., Bray, S.R.: The home advantage in sport competitions: Courneya and Carron's(1992) conceptual framework a decade later. Journal of Sports Sciences 23, 395–407 (2005)
4. Bao, H.: Gradually screening of Observational data of univariate, multiple-factor variance analysis and main influencing factors. Chinese Journal of Health Statistics 24(1), 33–42 (2007)
5. Hong, n., Wu, w.: SPSS for windows.statistical analysis tutorial, 2nd edn., pp. 156–171. Beijing Publishing house of electronics industry (2007)
6. Zhang, w.: SPSS 11,Statistical analysis tutorial(senior), pp. 1–15. Beijing hopes to electronic publishing house (2002)
7. data sources, http://cba.sports.sina.com.cn/match_result
8. data sources, http://www.cba.gov.cn/
9. data sources Chinese website of basketball referee

Research on Leg-Applied Technology in Man's Sanda Competition in the 11th National Games of PRC

Su Jianjiao

College of Physical Education, Shanxi Normal University, Linfen, Shanxi, 041000, China
Su_Jianjiao@126.com

Abstract. Using methods of literature material, video observation and mathematical statistics, this paper analyzed sanda players' leg-applied technology. The results showed that in all leg-applied technology, roundhouse leg-applied technique was used most and gained greatest success; head, body and thigh all achieved some scores, of shish body scored most while thigh struck most. The leg-applied technology of players of medium and low levels appeared relatively perfect while high level relatively monotonous.

Keywords: Games, sanda competition, leg-applied technology, research.

1 Introduction

Wushu sanda, also called sanshou, is a modern competitive game; in which two players perform dual meet unarmed the offense-defense techniques of "kick strike and wrestle" in martial arts according to certain play rules. It began in 1979. And with the constantly perfected technology and improved competitive rules, adopting and making use of excellent techniques form traditional Chinese martial arts and the overseas elite combat art, it's integrated into a new modern competitive game. Continual communication and practice make sanda internationalize quickly and to a very high extent. Especially after becoming an ad hoc game in the 2008 Beijing Olympic Games, it developed more and more quickly. How to make wushu sanda become an internationalized game is extremely imminent. Because of its vigorous development in the world and increasingly technological improvement, sanda competition becomes more stirring and heated. On the other hand, without a relatively complete sanda technical system and style in china, its rising development in Russia, Iran and Turkey changes the sanda pattern in the world and Chinese players also meet the unprecedented problems. This paper analyzed the sanda players' leg-applied technology, found out their technological characteristics and difference among different players in the sanda competition of the 11th National Games of PRC. Meanwhile, the paper provides the theory in the future leg-applied technological training for Chinese players so that they can perform more excellently in the world's sanda competition.

M. Zhou (Ed.): ISAEBD 2011, Part IV, CCIS 211, pp. 548–555, 2011.

2 Object of the Study and Research Methods

2.1 Object of This Study

The leg-applied technology of the first 16players, total 96 players in six sanda levels in the man s sanda competition of the 11th National Games of PRC.

2.2 Research Methods

2.2.1 The Literature Material
Based on lots of technical books on sanda, papers on technological application and statistics in professional journals, and the latest sanda competitive rules.

2.2.2 Video Observation
The video of man's sanda competition in the 11th National Games of PRC is turned into DVD disc, which goes on TVwith normal play, slow play and positioning observation. At the same time, the players leg-applied technology is observed and noted down.

2.2.3 Mathematical Statistics
The data associated with the players leg-applied technology is processed with Microsoft Excel software.

2.2.4 Logical Analysis
The data associated with the players technology is analyzed logically and correlatively.

3 Research Results and Related Analysis

3.1 Analysis on the Players' Leg-Applied Technology

In sanda competition, it is believed that "Fists technology provides strategy, leg-applied technology guarantees scoring and wrestling technology defeat opponent." It indicates that scoring is closely related to leg-applied technology. Table 3-1 shows that roundhouse leg s using frequency, 1907 times, accounting for 90%of leg-applied

Table 3.1. Players leg-applied Technology List

leg-applied Technology	Side kick	Roundhouse leg	Driving leg	Others	Total
Using frequency	76	1907	43	86	2112
Successful frequency	20	366	6	7	399
Success rate(%)	26	19	14	8	19

Note: others in the table refer to chopping, turning leg, etc.

frequency while its successful frequency, 366times, accounting for 92% of all leg-applied successful frequency, are far higher than those of other leg-applied technology. It is also thought that "Hands provide safety and winning depends on foot" in martial arts. In the success rate of leg-applied technology, the success rate of side kick reaches 26%, roundhouse leg 19%, driving leg 14% and others 8%. Although its success rate only reaches 19%, the using frequency and successful frequency of roundhouse leg prove that in sanda competition it is applied most frequently, scores most and has a relatively higher success rate. It indicates that roundhouse leg can react quickly, conceal easily and smite more parts of body. As for side kick, it needs higher technology. Without flexible gaits and rather a high performing speed, it's difficult to hit the opponent but easy to give the opponent counterattack opportunity, which makes side kick rarely applied in sanda competition. Driving leg and others perform slowly, smite less parts of body and need more exact attacking opportunity; On the other hand, they are easy to be perceived and observed by opponent, which give the opponent more counterattack opportunity. So they are also rarely applied in sanda competition. Other leg-applied technology such as chopping, turning leg and so on, though seldom applied, can play a surprising role so that opponent can not stand up to them. Sanda competition shows that players can score more if they own more leg-applied techniques, more flexible performing ability and better reaction. With higher development of players' various technology and their increasingly mature defensive technology, monotonous leg-applied attack is easy to be defensed and counterattacked by opponent. Only comprehensive development and improvement of various leg-applied technology, and improving leg-performing skills which are associated reasonably with the flexible fist and wrestle technology can players perform and score more in sanda competition.

3.1.1 Analysis on the Players' Leg-Applied Technology of Three Levels

In the players' leg-applied technology of three levels, roundhouse leg technology is one of the main scoring means, among which the players' using frequency of medium level reaches 661 times, high level 647 times and low level 584. Nowadays it has been the important attacking and main scoring techniques, which indicates roundhouse leg can react quickly, conceal easily and smite more parts of body. Players of low and medium levels use most side-kick technology, reaching 40 and 36 times separately. As for driving leg and others, players of three levels use them relatively less, which has certain association with player's physical conditions. Players of high level rarely use higher leg-applied technology in sanda competition, nor do players of medium and low levels. On the other hand, players of low and medium

Table 3.2. Using Frequency List of Players' Leg-applied Technology

Levels	Side kick	Roundhouse leg	Driving leg	Others	Total
Low Level	40	584	11	32	667
Medium Level	36	661	31	54	782
High Level	0	647	16	0	663
Total	76	1892	58	86	2112

levels can perform four kinds of leg-applied techniques while players of high level only score by roundhouse leg and driving leg, of which roundhouse leg becomes their main scoring technique. The above used techniques show that technology of high level is monotonous and less changeable while that of players of medium and low levels comprehensive and stable. Because of players increasingly mature various defensive technology, monotonous leg-applied attack is easy to be defensed and counterattacked by opponent. It indicates that only comprehensive development and improvement of various leg-applied technology and their free application associated reasonably with fist and wrestle technology can Chinese players of high level get better results in international sanda competition.

3.1.2 Analysis on the Players' Effective Leg-Applied Technology of Three Levels

In sanda competition players score mainly through hitting, which is a kind of corresponding effective symbol after players hit opponents using available techniques. As long as hitting opponents, players shoukd be judged by relevant scoring ofr punishing standard. Hitting standard must be in an optimal state, which depends on attacking, defensive, displacing and performing sound techniques. Scoring of leg-applied technology mainly relys on hitting the opponents' scoring parts, including head, body and shank. Therefore, players attacking and scoring also mainly depend on leg-applied technology, of which roundhouse leg scores most and becomes one of players common scoring techniques because of its small radian, high speed and effective coherence. Table 3-3 shows that the payers leg-applied and successful frequency of medium level reach 782 times and 152 times respectively, which are obviously higher than those of other levels players. Furthermore, they use four kinds of leg-applied technology and score through them, whose success rate 19.44% is also significantly higher than high level's players 18.85%and low level's players 18.25%. And equal scores and success rate show that players of medium level have higher speed, more strength, higher agility, more superb leg-applied attacking techniques and timing than those of players of low and high levels. It indicates that players of medium level have the most comprehensive leg-applied technology and achieve the best results in China's current sanda competition. However, players of high level only depend on roundhouse leg and driving leg that require relatively lower technology and score through them, which indicates they have no enough agility, harmonization, and precise timing, and coaches and players should adopt corresponding measures in the future training.

Table 3.3. Successful Frequency List of Players Leg-applied Technology

Levels	Side kick	Roundhou se leg	Driving leg	Others	Using Frequency	Successful Frequency	Successful Rate%
Low Level	8	112	0	2	667	122	18.29
Medium Level	12	120	8	12	782	152	19.44
High Level	0	121	4	0	663	125	18.85
Total	20	353	12	14	2112	399	18.89

3.2 Analysis on the Results of Players' Leg-Applied Technology

According to sanda competitive rules, there are two kinds of scoring leg-applied technology can achieve: one point and two points. If the opponent's thigh is hit, one point can be achieved. Two points is the highest scoring when players perform only one kind of technique and hit the opponent's head and body. Table 3-4 shows that players' scoring of two points is higher than that of one point while players' scoring of one point is higher than that of two points in inning score. The opponent's thigh is hit by technological performance of achieving one point, successful frequency reaching 249 times while his/her head and body are hit be technological performance of two points, successful frequency only reaching 151 times, far less than that of thigh being hit. When rivals confront each other, their legs follow closest. Therefore, the opponent's thigh is attacked first and most easily smitten, which has become players' main technological performance and leg-applied technology players adopt and score most in inning score. The rivals' heads and bodies, relatively farther from each other's, are easily defended and counterattacked by opponents. Though total scoring of two points is higher than that of one point, its successful frequency and inning score indicates hitting the opponent's head or body require higher technology and their utilization rate.

Table 3.4. Scoring List of Players' Leg-applied Technology

Score	Streak	Innings	Scoring	Inning score
One point	108	233	249	1.29
Two point	108	233	302	1.07
Total	108	233	551	2.36

3.2.1 Analysis on Scoring of Players' Leg-Applied Technology of Three Levels

Sanda competition is a process of control and anticontrol, play and counterplay. Lacking of counterattack awareness shows that when facing strong attacks, players cannot organize quick effective counterattack, control opponent's attack, make use of their own advantages and regain the initiative. Table 3-5 indicates that players' total score 208 points and inning score 2.48 of medium level is higher than players' 168 points and 2.29 of low level, and players' 178 points and 2.31 points of high level. As to one point, players of high level score most, reaching 110 points; players of low level score least, only 59 points. As to two points, players of medium level score

Table 3.5. Scoring List on Players' Leg-applied Technology of three levels

Levels	Strak	Innings	One point	Two point	Scoring	Inning score
Low Level	36	72	59	106	165	2.29
Medium Level	36	84	80	128	208	2.48
High Level	36	77	110	68	178	2.31
Total	108	233	249	302	551	2.36

most, reaching 128 points, indicating players of high level have relatively stronger advantage in the technology of one point, score through low roundhouse leg attacking the opponent's thigh, smite the opponent's head and body less and attack relatively less parts of opponent. All this makes players of high level rarely appear in sanda competition, which shows that the players' leg-applied technology of high level is not mature enough and their three-dimensional attack technology should be improved. As for players of low and medium levels, they achieve a balanced development of various leg-applied technology, score through similar hit opponent's parts, and perform three-dimensional attack and relatively mature techniques. In recent years, with the increasing hold of various sanda competition, its rapid development and improved competitive skills, in sanda competition, especially high level of competition, it is difficult to win through monotonous technique. So, combination of different offensive and defensive technology will become the inevitable tendency.

3.2.2 Analysis on the Scoring Parts of Players' Leg-Applied Technology of Three Levels

Scoring parts of sanda competition include head, body and thigh. According to the latest sanda competitive rules made be Mratial Arts Association of China and the total score of sanda players in the competition of 11th National Games of China, Table 3-6 shows that head, body and thigh are smitten in the leg-applied technology, all of which can achieve score. Monotonous leg-applied technology has turned into three-dimensional attack technology, attacking opponent's head, body and thigh. Their total score is 551 points, of which body scores most, 278 points, thigh 249 points, head 24 points. Scoring indicates that thigh is smitten most and its successful frequency 249 times; head is smitten least and it successful frequency 12 times. Furthermore, successful rate indicates that the success rate of players of high level to smite the opponent's thigh reaches 27.57% and the using frequency also reaches 399 times while they hit the opponent's head least and the success rate is lowest. It indicates that the scoring difference of players of low and medium to smite the opponent's head, body and thigh diminish gradually and their attack techniques change a lot. Based on this, sanda's appreciation enhances greatly. Rapid continuous three-dimensional attack can divert the opponent's defensive attention to the most extent, break through his/her defensive line, achieve better attacking results. And monotonous technique cannot take effect like this.

Table 3.6. Scoring parts List of Players' Leg-applied Technology of three levels

Level	Head			Body			Thigh		
	Application	Cuccess	Successful Rate%	Application	Cuccess	Successful Rate%	Application	Cuccess	Successful Rate%
Low Level	25	6	24.00	278	47	16.91	364	59	16.21
Medium Level	34	5	14.71	326	59	18.10	422	80	18.96
High Level	9	1	11.11	255	33	12.94	399	110	27.57
Total	68	12	17.65	859	139	16.18	1185	249	21.01

4 Conclusions

In all leg-applied technology, roundhouse leg-applied technique was used most and gained greatest success. Head, body and thigh are hit scoring parts, of which body scored most while thigh struck most. The scoring of two points is higher than that of one point. The using frequency of performing of one point appeared most, scoring mainly through low roundhouse leg attacking the opponent's thigh. The scoring of two points was achieved mainly through hitting the opponent's head and body.

The leg-applied technology of players of medium and low levels appeared relative balance. The scoring difference of scoring parts increased greatly and their hitting performance also appeared relatively monotonous. They used four kinds of leg-applied technology and scored through them, which had turned into three-dimensional attack technology. The leg-applied technology of players of high level also appeared monotonous and low roundhouse leg became their main attacking technique. Players of all levels rarely sued heavy hitting leg-applied technology and lacked certain balance of attack and defence.

5 Suggestions

In spite of its higher suing frequency and successful rate, roundhouse leg is easy to be defensed and counterattacked by opponents. The balance of players various leg-applied technology should be strengthened. The using frequency and effectiveness of technical leg application should be increased. The attacking effectiveness of various leg-applied technology should be enhanced. The scoring of empty shakes, feint and second attacking should be strengthened.

The attacking performance of players of medium and low levels should be varied. The scoring difference of scoring parts should be diminished. The training of striking performance and its successful rate of various leg-applied technology should be strengthened.The scoring ability of players different scoring parts should be improved. The striking successful rate and the heavy striking of single technological performance should be improved. And the training of players attacking-defensive balance should also be increased.

References

1. Su, j.-j., Zhang, y.-h.: Analysis of sanda piayers' technological application in shanxi. Journal of coiiege of physical education,Shanxi normal normal university 25(1) (2010)
2. Sanda, W.: (shanshou)competitive referee(trial) martial arts association of china, 3-5 (March 2004)
3. Sanda, W.: (shanshou)competitive rules(trial) martial arts association of china, 3-5 (March 2004)
4. Liang, Y.-d., et al.: The Comparative Study on the Offensive and Defensive Technology of Elite Male Sanda Players at home and abroad. Journal of Wuhan Institute of Physical Education 42(11) (2008)

5. Mao, A.-H., Liang, Y.-d.: The Genreal Characteristics and comparative Study on the Technology Applied by Chinese and Foreign Male Sanda Players of High Level. China Sports Science and Technology 43(4) (2007)
6. Sun, Z.-f., Li, Y.-s., Zhang, W.-l.: Analysis on the Common Combined Performance in Competitive Sanda. Journal of Beijing Sport University 29(8) (August 2008)
7. Cui, j.-g.: Research on the combined technology of male sanda players of high level. Journal of capital 19(3) (May 2007)

The Protection and Development Research of Shaolin Martial Art' Cultural Space

Tian Wenlin [*]

Physical Education College, Zhengzhou University, Henan Zhengzhou, China
TianW_lin@126.com
tianwenlin1972@126.com

Shaolin Martial Art is a representative item of martial arts, which core content is a distinctive cultural space including more than a thousand years of history, buddhism cultural environment, monks' practicing-wushu behavior and hundreds of boxing routines and martial art methods. The protection of this cultural space is more comprehensive than the protection of Shaolin Martial Arts' technique, and is more according with the appearance and essence of intangible cultural heritage. The protection and development of Shaolin Martial Art' cultural space is discussed from the cultural space protection of the intangible cultural heritage in this paper.

Keywords: Shaolin Martial Art, Cultural space, Protection, Development.

1 Introduction

In modernization storms, it is recognized by many countries to pay attention to rescue and protect native cultural, advocate cultural diversity, enhance social identity and sense of belonging of national cultural, promote the protection of cultural resource and ecological environment, prevent blind, urgent and destructive exploitation. When globalization is strengthened, international standardization is implemented, tourism develops rapidly, and modernization is accelerated, Chinese cultural ecological environment has great changes: intangible cultural heritage suffers from more stress that some cultural heritage passed on through oral instruction and behavior is disappearing, a lot of traditional artistry is endangered, and many rare objects and data with historical and cultural value are destroyed and encounters loss of overseas. Especially, when tourism industry develops rapidly in recent years, the optional abusing and excessive development of intangible cultural heritage often happens. This destructive exploitation will damage seriously the cultural space of intangible cultural heritage and threaten its survival. Shaolin Martial Art is a representative item of martial arts, which core content is a distinctive cultural space including more than a thousand years of history, buddhism cultural environment, monk' practicing-wushu behavior and hundreds of boxing routines and martial art methods. The protection of this cultural space is more comprehensive than the protection of Shaolin Martial Art'

[*] Henan Shangqiu, Master degree of traditional sports, field:theory and practice of national and traditional sports; Phone: 13103830288.

M. Zhou (Ed.): ISAEBD 2011, Part IV, CCIS 211, pp. 556–563, 2011.

technique, and is more according with the appearance and essence of intangible cultural heritage. The protection and development of Shaolin Martial Art' cultural space is discussed from the cultural space protection of intangible cultural heritage in this paper.

2 Cultural Space and the Cultural Space Shaolin Martial Art

2.1 Explanation of Cultural Space

"Cultural Space" is one of the important key words used frequently in the current academic research. It is from the French urban theory research which Henri Lefebvre and other scholars put forward. Henri Lefebvre thought space is produced by human subject's conscious activity. Cultural space in this paper is the term of the intangible cultural heritage. So, explanation of Cultural Space must is based on the intangible cultural heritage. In the UNESCO the 155th assembly in October 1998, 'Cultural Space' is defined 'strong concentration of the intangible cultural heritage with special value. ' A place in which popular and traditional cultural activities are concentrated, or a period of time in which specific activities are regularly held. This time and space exists because of traditional cultural expression form.[2] In 2003, The protection of intangible cultural heritage convention is passed in the 32nd session of the UNESCO conference, in which the research result on the traditional folk creation and the intangible cultural heritage, and human intangible cultural heritage is reclassified. This method of classification is widely used by every country. The first is the oral and expression, include the language of the intangible cultural heritage medium. The second is performing arts. The third is Social practice, ritual, festival activities. The forth is the knowledge and practice about nature and the universe. The fifth is traditional handicraft. The define about intangible cultural heritage in this convention includes the above-mentioned five kinds:' intangible cultural heritage is identified by the communities , groups, and individuals sometimes as a part of cultural heritage, including social practice, conception expression, manifestation, the knowledge, skills and related tools, material objects, handicraft and cultural sites.

It is special to point out that 'cultural sites' is different translation from 'cultural space'. In some international document translation later, 'cultural space' is determined gradually. It is worth to be noted that 'cultural space' is a specific intangible cultural heritage phenomenon, not but is noted in the above-mentioned five kinds. But in 2001, there are five cultural space phenomenon in 19 species list of the first masterpieces of the human oral and intangible heritage is published by the UNESCO. They are the Cultural Space of the Brotherhood of the Holy Spirit of the Congos of Villa Mella, the Cultural Space of Sosso—Bala in Nyagassola, the Cultural Space of Jemaa el-Fna Square in Morocco, the Cultural Space and Oral Culture of the Semeiskie in Russia, the Cultural Space of the Boysun District in Uzbekistan. The second and third list announced in 2003 and 2005 include such cultural space projects as the Kihnu Cultural Space in Estonia, the Cultural Space of Palenque de San Basilio in Columbia, the Cultural Space of the Bedu in Petra and Wadi Rum in Jordan. 'Cultural space' is the sixth kind proposed explicitly in 'interim evaluation measures of state-level intangible cultural heritage masterpiece' promulgate by the general office of the state council of China ,except of the five above-mentioned kinds proposed by the UNESCO , is defined as a space with timeliness and spatial in which traditional culture activity is held regularly or traditional culture manifestation is showed [4]. Mr. Edmond Moukala, a official of the Culture UNESCO office Beijing, gave a more specific explanation on 'cultural space:' cultural space is concentration areas of traditional folk culture activity ,or the selected time for specific cultural events.

It is aware that cultural space is not a certain space. From cultural heritage, space is the reserved material created by human wisdom, for example mementos or relics. Cultural space is a concept of anthropology, is a space or a series of spaces in which the traditional or folk culture expression has held regularly [5].

From the define of cultural space , cultural space is the worthy cultural site and time, is the space and time in which the valuable and conventional traditional culture activities and folk cultural activities is held regularity. Because culture space is new concept and knowledge, it is not paid attention in Chinese cultural protection, and many valuable cultural space projects could be lost. Martial Art is a characteristic representative item of Chinese traditional culture, and there are much cultural space needs to be protected.

Shaolin Martial Arts is one main representative of Chinese Martial Arts, and is a huge martial art system, and is one largest school with a long history and many category [6]. There are 552 kinds of boxing and device routines, and 156 martial art methods of seventy-two unique skill, david, combat, unloading bone, point, qigong. According to the statistics on Shaolin Martial Art routines passed down and collected in Shaolin temple, there are 178 boxing routines, 139 instruments methods, 59 sparring methods, other 115 methods, adding up to 545 methods. Shaolin Temple is the biggest gathering area of Chinese martial arts sanctuary, and is Buddhism holy space. Shaolin Martial Art has formed a complete and systematic buddhist martial system though more than a thousand years' hardening, inheritance and development, which has surpassed sport, formed a unique cultural phenomenon, and is a irreplaceable part of the Chinese nation culture. Shaolin Martial Art, a important part of Chinese Martial Art Culture, is selected as the first national intangible cultural heritage in June 2006. Because Shaolin Martial Art is related closely to Shaolin Temple's special buddhist culture environment and fifteen hundred years of history and has unique social functions and cultural value, Shaolin Martial Art' core content is a distinctive cultural space including more than a thousand years of history, buddhism cultural environment, monks' practicing-wushu behavior and hundreds of boxing routines and martial art methods. The protection for this cultural space is more comprehensive than the protection of Shaolin Martial Arts' technique, and is more according with the appearance and essence of intangible cultural heritage.

3 The Protection of Shaolin Martial Art Cultural Space

3.1 Protecting Descendant

Legacy without soul is merely history's body, so we should pay attention to Shaolin Martial Art ecological environment and the descendant with Shaolin Martial Art 'culture soul' . Passing on and learning Shaolin Martial Arts should combine the Shaolin Temple traditional patriarchal system and use the oral and granted methods with skill performance. Its skill and culture is Intangible and dynamic, and any material (such as museum), static (such as books) protection could not prevent martial art to disappear, and only interpersonal dynamic inheritance could ensure the existence and development of the martial art culture. So, descendant is the most direct protection level of Shaolin Martial Art Culture heritage protection engineering. Descendant protection is the key of martial art culture space protection. In fact, descendant is the core content of martial art culture space.

3.2 Protecting the eEcological Environment of Shaolin Martial Art—Shaolin Temple

Shaolin Temple is the primary cultural site of Shaolin Martial Art's origin, development and transmission. In order that Shaolin Martial Art cultural heritage can live healthy, we should pay attention and protect cultural ecological environment which it depend on closely. So Shaolin Temple is the solid state heritage protection level in Shaolin Martial Art culture heritage protection project. Descendant inherited the deep level essence of Shaolin Martial Art, and Shaolin Temple is solid performance, and both complement each other and are the important parts of Shaolin Martial Art culture heritage conservation project

3.3 Spreading in Schools

If we want to protect traditional culture and Shaolin Martial Art, we should give full play to the role of education. Education is the main mean to inherit culture. 'School is the medium to develop the national traditional sports.' [7] It will have strategic significance to develop Shaolin Martial Art in many schools. Though progressive society and advanced education, everyone can receive school education before going into society. School education can affect the social future development. So, school with concentrated and numerous students is a good place to develop Shaolin Martial Art. 'A lot of national sports can play the important role finally in the sporting world and be to the sports and cultural wealth of all mankind though introduced ,popularized, trained, improved and perfected in all kinds of schools. Because schools are the main places to spread Japanese judo and Korean karate to teenagers, they can go to society little by little, and go to the world, and become Olympic sports. Shaolin Martial Art should be according to students' characteristic, and change content to spread in schools, and play an important role to martial art education, and make a contribution to carry forward the national spirit, and enhance national cohesion, develop itself . So Shaolin Martial Art's spreading in the school is the main method and is to promote Shaolin Martial Art culture's spreading in society.

3.4 Country and Local Government's Support

In recent years, a few national policy are promulgated successively, and laying down laws for protection becomes faster and faster, and Shaolin Martial Art is listed in 'The first recommended project list of national intangible cultural heritage'. When Shaolin Martial Art heritage protection was paid attention to by the relevant national authorities, Shaolin Temple cleared thoroughly its surrounding environment at the support of Henan local government, and planned and restored the original human and natural ecological environment according to description in historical document . This is a good example that local government give support .So Shaolin Martial Art's sustainable development should depend on national, local government's attention and related policy assistance, and the laws are laid down to make Shaolin Martial Art to be one of Chinese traditional culture protection planning projects.

3.5 Laying Down the Planning and Regulations to Protect the Cultural Space of Shaolin Martial Art

It is the most basic protection mean to lay down the regulations. Only the sound laws can ensure to receive administrative protection, financial support, the intellectual property rights protection. The protection regulations for the Cultural Space Of Shaolin Martial Art could be laid down by the cultural departments of the world human intangible heritage management department and the cultural department of Henan province. Based on the Shaolin Temple scenic region, the Cultural Space Of Shaolin Martial Art should be a original culture space with self-scrolling development and management ability in which Shaolin Martial Art is experienced, human spirit would be enhanced, creativity would be inspired, Shaolin Martial Art culture would be integrated into Xiongshan culture, and recuperation and health concept would be bought into.

3.6 Protecting the Property and Brand of Shaolin Martial Art

Now, 'Shaolin' trademark is abused by the food and pharmaceutical industries. The trademark with 'Shaolin Kungfu' content is registered in America, Europe and Japan, such as 'Shaolin Kungfu', 'Shaolin Wushu', 'Shaolin Boxing', 'All Kungfu of Shaolin'. For example, Japanese Shaolin Boxing Federation registered 272 kinds of text and graphics trademarks in Japan, such as 'Shaolin', 'Shaolin Temple', 'International Shaolin Temple'. Soon afterwards, it registered 'Shaolin' trademark in the world, and run large-scale expansion, developed 28 member countries including all the developed countries. This affected largely the true Shaolin culture' s spreading and development. Because of abusing largely and registering optionally trademark, the international community distorts Shaolin culture and Shaolin kungfu. These persons far from the real Shaolin culture space, who practice kungfu, only take care of superficies of Shaolin kungfu which is far from the true essence of Shaolin Martial Art ,and neglect spirit content. Shaolin Martial Art was came from Specific buddhist culture space of Shaolin Temple, and its core is the religious culture. Far from specific Buddhism culture space of Shaolin Temple, and far from Shaolin monks who major in Buddhism, Shaolin Martial Art will disappear.

4 Thinking about Spatial Development of Shaolin Wushu Culture

4.1 Strengthening Theory Research

Currently, Wushu researchers contact less to Shaolin Wushu spreading, meanwhile, various limitations like proffesion those limits cause less thorough research," lack of Shaolin Wushu basic theory largely restricted the Shaolin Wushu development. With a scientific insight scientific epistemology and methodology to study the Shaolin Wushu, to a certain degree ,the experts and scholars may succeed their scientific research through unremitting efforts. Thus raising the Shaolin Wushu proffessinals' level of knowledge, mastering the scientific methodology and the epistemology, is an urgent problem to be solved. Only by the experience and simple shallow oral transferring and copying with pen, will not promote mutual development of Shaolin Wushu. It is good to advise in-depth to promote Shaolin Wushu research with a scientific rational ideas of developing ,strategic measures.

4.2   Enhance Shaolin Wushu Intercultural Communication

Mr. Ji Xianlin once said: "communication is a historical development power, only through the exchange to recruit new cultural factors, generating new cultural achievements after fusion,which will continuously strengthen cultural vitality, then enhance cultural taste and style [10]. We need to use Shaolin Wushu this Chinese excellent traditional culture to embrace the world all good culture. Therefore, the past general opening up and importing Wushu field culture is not enough.It is important to face the future, exchange actively, build cross-cultural awareness , can get new idea resources through various cultural exchange and dialogue, study hard and accept the western culture, so that to prompt a big blend of Chinese and the world culture.

4.3   Strengthen and Innovate the Existing Spreading Means, Strengthen Brand Shaping and Managemen

Strengthen brand shaping and management is to make shaolin traditional culture known by the world comprehensively and accurately , and make it better inherited and developed. So taking series of means of dissemination actively is necessary.

Presently, besides the daily traditional preaching to introduce Shaolin culture , Shaolin temple successively established shaolin wushu books audio-visual library, shaolin culture institute, systematically carry out shaolin meditation, Buddist, medicine, and art shaolin culture research. In addition, the temple holds international academic seminar, compiles and plays stage opera, network communication means, to promote Shaolin culture domestically and overseas. Including application of world heritage, hold shaolin monks tour performances, shaolin monks demonstrated Shaolin treasure Yijinjing and medical and health preservation secret recipe to the world openly, authorized network game and cartoon" shaolin legend ". These series of activities are incomparable such as simple business advertising communication. With the progress of modern society, the rapid development of science and technology, make the Shaolin Wushu culture in constant socialization process of getting spread to development.The TV, Internet and media system become the important medium for Wushu culture spreading. Shaolin Wushu still need government and the shaolin temple's cooperation to further strengthen the intellectual property protection and brand maintenance management. Meanwhile shaolin wushu should continue world cultural heritage bidding and protecting work. In the mining of shaolin kung fu, sorting, improve and protect, not just focus on a detailed understanding of the firstfruits of Shaolin Kung Fu, We should focus on the not realized profound shaolin wushu culture essence, thus expanding and ascension Shaolin Wushu culture brand connotation.With the government and the shaolin temple's cooperation, further strengthen the intellectual property protection and brand maintenance management.

To shape international appealing cultural tourism brand with massive history and culture as the foundation, Songshan Shaolin temple as the main body, and promote Wushu culture and buddist culture advantages to the world. Promoting cultural and tourism resources integration through the high grade planning. To develop cultural tourism products and cultural tourism scenic spots with domestic and international oriented characteristics, and try to form industrial advantage. To speed up the development of "Shaolin buddist" imaging show projects to strengthen scenic attraction and shock ability, make Dengfeng one of the world famous cultural tourist sanctuary and first selected place for coming foreigners. At the same time,to balance the relationship between Shaolin culture protection and tourism development. Rationally developing, inheriting Shaolin culture with Shaolin Wushu culture as the foundation., Protect the Shaolin culture first when temporary contradiction between them occured , this is the inevitable request for Shaolin Wushu culture tourism continuous development.

4.4 Government Support, Create Momentum with Festival Culture

Henan provincial government and Dengfeng municipal government Pay very serious attention to Shaolin Wushu culture resources development, and list Shaolin Wushu culture one of the key projects of government cultural industry. At the same time , Dengfeng specially prepared "the martial arts industry development plan in 2006, and actively bid for "the town of Chinese martial arts culture " to China Culture Federation and Chinese Nationality Association . Provide taxation, finance preferential policies and relaxed environment for for Wushu industry development such as local Wushu Schools. In recent years, Henan province and Zhengzhou city government successively planned and organized 7 international Shaolin Wushu festivals, and began to host the world traditional Wushu festivals in 2004, furtherly promoted and enhanced the brand of Shaolin Wushu culture.

5 Conclusion

Here, borrowed the saying of Mr. Sun Jiazheng minister of culture in general preface of the series books of the human oral and immaterial cultural heritage : "In the long history of human, different state and nation created colorful, distinctive culture and form their traditional culture and cultural traditions, make the world we live in various extraordinary splendor. Accelerating modernization will benefit the development of contemporary culture, also make the survival and development of traditional culture appeared predicated. The protection and development of traditional culture has become important aspect in maintaining world cultural diversity and the human society sustainable development during the economic globalization process." As martial arts people, facing the new era-- global economic integration, the world culture dissemination, culture identification, cultural choice diversification, it is our ambitious peoples' unshirkable historyical responsibility to keep the Shaolin Wushu culture long time prosperous, cope with the already come challenge of the era, pay attention to the Shaolin Wushu, focus on destiny of Chinese Wushu culture.

References

1. Zhouxian.: Research on Modern Aesthetic Culture, p. 120. Shandong Publishing House of Literature and Art, Shandong (1997)
2. Wenli.: Martial and Martial Culture, p. 119. Renmin Sport Press, Beijing (2009)
3. Zheng, X.: Analyses of the Winning Factors of Dificult and Beautiful Events from the Development of Rules of Women's Gymnastics. China Sport Science and Technology (12), 25–30 (2001)

Research about Golf in China's Future Development

Wang Lingjuan

Institute of Physical Education, Henan Agriculture University,
Zhengzhou, Henan 450002, China
Wang_l_j@yeah.net

Abstract. This paper utilizes the literature material law, logic analysis to analyze golf history , golf's charm and limitations, the golf impact to China after Entering the Olympic Games, puts forward the need for continuing to maintain and appropriately increase different places have all kinds of golf competition, the state developing mainly, social and family developing complementary, establishing civilians golf course, make golf become common public consumption, with "people's livelihood" as the starting point adjust measures to local conditions to develop the golf with Chinese characteristics , media should carry out of golf chafing, adopt "go out and meet in" method for China to enhance the golf development level.

Keywords: Golf, China, develop.

Golf is an ancient sport; it originated in the 15th century Scotland, 17th century golf was brought to America by Europeans, 19th century into Asia. By the shepherds of killing time at game development in the world today the most popular sports, golf have its original glamour place: in the lane grass from the 1st to the 18th hole, breathing freely the nature of fresh air, bathing in the warm sunshine, elegant handsomely swung, calm ease edify sentiment. Golf 1984 was introduced into China, with the development of society and the improvement of people's living standard, the golf ball movement gradually was accepted in China. In 2009 Copenhagen 121 meeting golf entered 2016 London's Olympic success, and will stir up golf boom.

1 The History of Golf

1.1 Golf World History

Golf is English transliteration and is originated from England the ,Its meaning is struck, coincidentally it is by the green (green) and oxygen (oxygen), the sun (surface), friendship (friendship) four words to the beginning of the letters, about its origin, relatively recognized one is that originated in Scotland, the world's first golf club establishment of Edinburgh in Scotland, the most famous club is located in Scotland, namely. Andrew's royal classical golf clubs, today's golf 18 holes system is formulated by Scotland. Golf in 1457 has so far from experience for more than 500 years changsheng and its development course, in 1900 and 1904 has been listed as an Olympic sport, but not officially Olympic project, at present the world golf

M. Zhou (Ed.): ISAEBD 2011, Part IV, CCIS 211, pp. 564–569, 2011.

competition have many species, such as man professional golf tournament (PGA), lady's professional golf tournament (LPGA) and regional tournament. In all professional game, highest rank, most influential, the most popular game that the USA MingRenSai, the USA open, British open and American PGA championships, this four events known as four grand slam. Today golf in developed countries has been a very popular mass movement.

1.2 The Development History of Golf in China

In 1916,Golf was first introduced to China. In1917,Hongqiao Golf Association of Shanghai, Chinese first organization for golf, with a nine-hole golf course started to run. In 1931, Britain, the United States and China operated a golf club, with a neighborhood of Central Stadium of Nanjing cemetery 。 But later it seemed to have been disappearing for a long time in mainland。 Golf did not to re-enter China until 1984.Furthermore, Chinese Golf Association was established formally in Beijing On May 24, 1985.It was 1986 that Chinese athletes freshly took their first part in Seoul Asian Games. From 1994 to now, Chinese Golf has boosted. For one thing, both of golf courses and people joining the game increased dramatically; for another, the Chinese Golf was beginning on the way of its own Professional Development. Volvo open competition debuted in 1995, China, While October 9, 2009in Copenhagen ,when the International Olympic Committee voted that golf be an official event of the London Olympics, which means that t the game shall be popularized and upgraded highly in future all over China. Golf merely has a short history of 20 decades. But nowadays there are over 500 courses, no less than 300 million participants. However, Chinese Golf is still in its infancy, still does the first generation of players lead a vital role.

2 The Charm and Limitations of Golf

2.1 The Features of Golf Attracts Lots of People

Golf's unique movement pattern is popular. Firstly, it is rooted in nature.We can carry out exercising activity in the lovely atmosphere of the sun, air and green land. Secondly, it is suitable both for man and woman, without considering of age, posture, physical condition, on account of those practitioners can control exercise intensity as well as rate and frequency of walking according to their own characteristics during exercise. Finally, golf is characterized of competing participant himself as the most prominent characteristics of all sport. As opposed to basketball, football and other sport items, there is no direct physical collision with the opponents, nor strong antagonism, just a single people compete himself, and one can control flexibly regarding of his own conditions. It comes to a conclusion that many people will like golf.

2.2 Many People are Limited by the Conditions of Golf

Golf in China, known as the "noble sport" and "rich entertainment ", the reason is that golf requires good economic foundation to carry out. While from the current situation of golf in China, most people especially young who would like to play is confronted great difficulty affording so high cost. A result of high consumption is brought out as grand payment for the huge Construction cost. To build a standard golf course, generally ranging from 60 hectares to 100 hectares, the developers are required to invest thousands of millions. Followed by costly payment of services for the enjoyment of golf , many of the golf courses are far from the urban areas, to which needing a long drive . Therefore many people are deprived of enjoying the charm of golf.

3 The Golf 's Impact to China after Entering the Olympic Games

3.1 Chinese Golf Figures Will Appear in London Olympics Held in 2016

State Sport General Administration director of the Center of ball sports management, the CGA Vice-Chairman Xiao-ning Zhang said, it is of great significance as golf enters the Olympics for China, that is to say, both an opportunity and a challenge. If we are eager to operate handsomely in the 2016 Olympics, golf in China faces two major problems, spread and up gradation, because golf is still an emerging sport. And he believes that Chinese golf develops rather slowly comparing that of the Europe and the U.S. We are only in a second-class level, as the new China's golf are gradually developing just from the mid-80s of last century, as a result, we can not compare with the world most powerful ones, even can not with South Korea or Japan in Asia. For most part, under the general policy direction of the Olympics, golf development is relatively limited. And entering the Olympics will play a significant role in promoting the development of golf in China [1]. He presented that it is of certain to increase the investment in golf, and what we must do first is that with the approval of all respects , we must accelerate the pace of golf ' s popularity in China, earning for the right to stand on the platform of the 2016 Olympics. In order to improve sports standards, China has set up a golf team, established a system of competition and training involved of market developing, and has begun to train young people, coaches, referees, etc. Because of the weak foundation of golf in China, so it is not easy to achieve good results on the Olympic Games in a short term. We do not dare to conclude that China can achieve brilliant results during the2016 London Olympic Games, but can say that golf in China will open a new chapter on the ground of this precious opportunity.

3.2 The Number of Chinese Golf Participants Is Growing

There is not much impact of golf entering Olympics for top professional players, but much for golf itself. Some a people in this career demonstrated that, at least the so-called ' noble sport ' shall removed, which is extremely beneficial for the popularization and development of golf. In China, large population, huge potential consumers, a good economic foundation and the 2008 Olympic Games etc. are creating proper conditions for golf to develop. Golf belongs to small ball, as you know ,which have a good mass base, such as table tennis and badminton making us proud of over the world. It shows that since many small balls are on a high level of development and research, if time guaranteed, China's golf will not lag behind the others.as Golf has became an official Olympic event, for Chinese part, there shall be a golf boom whether it is " from the top to down" or "from the bottom to top".

3.3 Golf Entering the Olympic Games Will Create Numerous Developing Chances for Joint Industrial

When golf began to enter China, it is purely a leisure entertainment, without any relationship with real estate . With the arrival of the peak development of golf, property investment, tourism etc. will encounter the golden period of golf. Chinese golf course design "the Ranking-First Person " , Yu Gang said, China Golf market is facing a huge historical opportunity, relying on the huge population base and huge potential consumers. The golden ten years of golf industry will drive the term of developmental peak of real estate investment upon golf to remain one decade. A few of golf open competition has been held in Beijing or Shanghai, and once in Shenzhen only a single time since golf came to China which delicates that the world-class level professional golf tournament has not been deeply rooted in China. In 2010, the China golf open competition made a breakthrough, that leaving the golf-developed cities, "Volvo China Open Competition "was carried out in not so famous Jinji Lake International Golf Club, Suzhou. More than one hundred operators, over one hundred players and their caddies as well as their families from Europe, Australia, South Korea etc., together with one hundred Chinese and foreign journalists, over ten thousand visitors from the globe, were flocking to Suzhou ,which stimulated the local tourism industry. In addition cultural industries, accommodation services, catering and other industries will also met developing opportunities.

4 Some Suggestions for Golf in China to Carry Out Better

4.1 Continue to Maintain and Increase Various Appropriate Types of Golf Competition

In 1995, the 41st Golf World Cup was held in Guanlan Lake, Shenzhen. Since 2005 ,the HSBC Champions in Shanghai once a year and Volvo China Open Competition, make more foreigners understand more Chinese places, in turn ,more peoplet in China know golf. The 41st Golf World Cup in Guanlan Lake, Shenzhen, was the first alive golf tournament, when merely a population of 10 million people fancied golf. The thing that HSBC Champions cooperates with Tiger Woods with huge payments, the planning and operation of which turns out successfully, in the light of the fact that it attracts not only professional golf stars around the world, the eyes of the world locked in China, locked in Shanghai, but the effects that golf population are growing in a form of geometric growth. Volvo China Open Competition held in Suzhou has multiple meanings, the most important of which is that the seeds of golf widely spread in not so developed cities. The significance of a world-class golf competition can be seen from a set of data: during 1995, golf population was only 10 million people in China. By 2009, China's golf population soared to 300 million. While some experts have predicted that China's golf population will increase to 500 million up to the 2012 London Olympic Games. Early March, 2009 as a positive response to the International Olympic Committee listing golf as Olympic programs in the Summer Olympic Games of 2016 and 2020,State Sport General Administration listed Golf to be an official event of The 12th National Games in 2013. It is far-reaching for the promotion of golf in China with regard to these golf competitions in different levels and of types.

4.2 Country Mainly, Supplemented by Social and Family

China's "National System" to do sports makes China a great power stand in the world sports arena. In recent years , China's sports achievements, the sustainable steady economy, the improvement of overall national strength, quantities of success of the market operation for sports clubs , in addition snooker star Ding Junhui' s Success etc., seems to challenge the "System" continually and the continuation to implement. But for such a new project, few love it, worse still, the training cost is very high, in which conditions, obvious effect can not be achieved in a short time by the operation of the market, and more difficult based on the cultivation of a single family, so the training of golf athletes depends most crucially on government . If conditions permit, we can reconsider both the social culture and the family culture , adhere to walking on two legs.

4.3 Developing Golf with Chinese Characteristics, in the Conditions of "Livelihood" as a Starting Point

A positive atmosphere of golf in China's development will be created if Golf is listed into the Olympics. But there is resistance in the developing process of golf: First, legalization issues about golf covering land, including land acquisition, license applications and construction applications. Currently there being not any relevant regulations and laws upon the construction of golf courses, a fact that without any laws to follow exists, Investors have to rely on good relations with the local governments, secretly building golf courses, but at the risk of being ordered to shut down. In March 2010 ,during the two sessions of the NPC ,the Vice Chairman of country Law Committee Sun Anmin made recommendations that the golf course permission should be given. Our country should consider Golf as an industry to guide its development. The Second is the golf business tax issue. Our government does not approve of the golf to cover land, and golf is included in the ranks of luxury heavily taxed. If golf is taxed lower, the cost of playing will come down naturally, and there will be more people playing golf, furthermore it is not far away for common Civilians to play golf [3].the last problem is environmental pollution. Along with the growing number of domestic courts, the environment issue will not be avoided. Simple Vegetation, excessive pesticide spraying, vast water using for lawn care, destruction of arable land and occupying farmland etc., so it is called "environmental killer. "the above problems are the biggest obstacles in developing golf. Golf takes a lot of land. To ensure that people eat and to feed the additional population is a critical event on the livelihood, so the bottom line must be guarded. When considering the issue in a different way, we hold that the development of golf in China, if we want, it is the matter of transforming golf to adapt to circumstances, not us adapt to the development of golf, therefore we should focus on "people ", according to local conditions, develop golf with Chinese characteristics. Such as the establishment of civilians golf course, so that the general public are able to make a consumption of golf. When golf just entered China, many people dubbed it as "the high and rich ", implying that only high-ranking officials and wealthy businessmen play golf. Although the situation has now improved, it is still the "noble sports" in our mind. Many insiders believe that, in order to make civilians can play, the establishment of civilian golf course is a necessary .at present, and the park along the river in Hubei had this golf course. People spending 50 dollars can play a round of golf there. If the country can make it in most cities, golf will become a very common exercise, and to which degree, golf will be successful in its popularization, and it is not impossible to appear more than one people like Woods in China. Shenzhen, golf courses are across the city, low to such a degree that even the ordinary working-class can also be chic. Savvy developers seize the opportunity to introduce several of "golf conception "to residents, as a result, small golf practicing area, and the ball tells a noble residential area or star hotels [4].

4.4 The Media Should Carry Fuel to the Flames for the Game of Golf

Media plays an important role in popularizing golf. Investment Guide, Shenzhen TV, Shenzhen cable TV station, Guangzhou TV and so opened up a golf column. And the media should take its responsibility and mission that, from positive perspective report golf, which not only to attract our attention, arouse public attention, but to decline some negative news reports endangering to the development of golf.

4.5 To Improve the Developing Level of Golf with the Go-Out and Meet the Coming Approach

As exotic, Golf develops well in the United Kingdom, the United States and other countries, and has coaches, athletes, golf course managers, team sports officials of high levels; however, in our country, the situation of scarcity of talents does exist, such as lacking golf courses designing talent critically. To solve it, we can hire foreign experts to train our people, and send our staff abroad to study the relevant knowledge, to master the advanced experience of foreign countries ,then come home , through which the cost of the development of golf will be greatly reduced.

References

1. Golf into the Olympic success is of far-reaching significance: remove "noble movement" hat [EB]. Modern bulletin (October 10, 2009),
   http://www.chinanews.com/ty/news/2009/10-10/1902041.shtml
2. The arrival of the era of Luo, J.: Golf. Journal of forest and human 4, 8–17 (2010)
3. J.: Golf return Mr The anniversary of thinking. World golf 38(10) (2010)
4. JingWu, Z.: Golf: remove mysterious coat. Journal of managers 66(12), 90–91 (1999)

The Future Development and Prospect Prediction of National Fitness Campaign in Hubei Province

Chuancheng Feng and Huanan Zhai

Wuhan Institute of Physical Education, Wuhan Hubei, 430079
Ch_ch_Feng@126.com

Abstract. In this essay Delphi method, logical analysis method and social survey method are mainly deployed. It analyses the social demand of national fitness sports of the people in Hubei province from the macro, meso and micro levels. It shows the broad masses of the people have a great desire for national fitness sports and enthusiasm for sports activities and pay great attention to personal health. A prediction is made about the prospect of national fitness campaign which shows the next decade will be a good period for developing national fitness sports in Hubei province or even the whole country and the development condition of national fitness sports in Hubei is well.

1 Problem Introduction

It has been fifteen years since the State Council promulgated and implemented the "National Fitness Outline"[1] in June 1995 in order to have a fundamental change of the situation that the Chinese people are not in a good health and to promote healthy sustainable development of the mass sports enterprise under the new situation. Fifteen years is a short moment in human history, but our national fitness campaign appeared earth-shaking changes. The masses respond to the Party and country's great call of "National Fitness" and carry out profound lasting mass sports activities which have made great achievements. There are people doing sports everywhere in the vast land of China, inside and outside the Great Wall. "National Fitness" which is full of the spirit of the times has become synonymous with the people's life of sports culture. It can be said that the fitness sports campaign has become an important livelihood project of the government at all levels being in power for the people and a new rising undertaking which concerns the physical and mental health of the whole nation.

Hubei province, located in the middle reaches of the Yangtze river in mid-China, lies west to Anhui, north to Jiangxi and Hunan, east to Chongqing, eastsouth to Shanxi and south to Henan. It has a total area of 185.900 square kilometres which accounts for 1.94% of the nation's land mass[2]. Under the concern of the provincial government and the whole society, the national fitness campaign in Hubei as the same with the whole country have achieved remarkable results. Today, the heavy task of building a comprehensive well-off society and constructing the harmonious socialist

---

[1] The State Council: 《National Fitness Outline》 , 1995.6.
[2] Overview of Hubei. Hubei Provincial People's Government
.http://www.hubei.gov.cn/hbgk/index.shtml

M. Zhou (Ed.): ISAEBD 2011, Part IV, CCIS 211M, pp. 570–578, 2011.

society is set before us. Meanwhile, the anticipated target by 2010 proposed by "National Fitness Outline" has been reached, and the new target is being built, the "National Fitness Regulations" has been implemented nationwide, so our national fitness campaign is now in the new situation, the reform and innovation is still very tough. In this important moment of social transition and sports transition, on the basis of the investigation of the national fitness demands in Hubei, its future development strategies are scientifically planned which will have the extremely profound theoretical meaning and great practical significance. It helps scientifically position the Chinese characteristic national fitness system, plan in advance its future development and promote the healthy sustainable development of China's national fitness campaign under the new situation.

2   Research Method

Literature method, Delphi method, logical analysis method, mathematical statistics method, comparison method and social investigation method are mainly deployed. The idea is as follows: first, determine the preliminary scheme of social sports investigation on the basis of the expert investigation, submit to experts to examine, determine the specific investigation contents and outline; second, according to the research purpose and content need, deliver questionnaires after identify investigation subjects, and have actual survey interviews; third, statistically analyse the outcome data and various indexes, obtain the corresponding research materials as the basic of analysis and research.

The social survey contains two aspects:

2.1   General Questionnaire

Choose the investigation subjects from the general public to make social investigation, so we can know individual demand of national fitness campaign, etc. The questionnaires have two categories including 31 indexes. Before the general questionnaire experts examine first and then we take a small area investigation to test the reliability and validity of the questionnaire in order to proof it's reasonable and effective. The practical survey is organized and implemented by Hubei Sports Bureau Group which assigns the questionnaire by area and considers the balance and representative of the respondents' social stratification. 1,500 copies were delivered to the general, 1450 copies returned, and the response rate is 96.7%, including valid questionnaires 1390 copies, validity rate 95.9%. The respondents' social stratification information are shown below(table 1).

2.2   Expert Questionnaire

The experts in this study have over ten years of working experience in actual mass sports organization and management or someone who do the relevant research. The

Table 1. The respondents' social stratification   N=1390

Age		
below30	287	20.6%
31-50	786	56.6%
above50	317	22.8%
Gender		
male	724	52.1%
female	666	47.9%
Educational level		
Junior school and below	61	4.4%
Senior school︐ technical secondary school	386	27.8%
Junior college and above	943	67.8%

investigation content mainly involves the prospect of developing national fitness career in Hubei. The survey method is basically the same with the former one, that is, the Group delivers and a few chosen experts fill out. 116 copies were delivered to the relevant experts, 114 copies returned and the response rate is 98.3%, which meets the basic requirements of sociological study. The investigated experts most have department-level administrative duties or above, or intermediate specialized technical titles or above. So the investigation basically reflects the general opinion of these experts.

3   The Result and Analysis

3.1   The Analysis of the Social Demand of National Fitness Sports in Hubei

The social demand of national fitness sports must be paid attention to in order to analyse its future development. Because the starting point and the foothold of all our policy should be to satisfy the various beneficial needs of the masses to the maximum. So, what's the need of the masses for fitness sports activities? A survey is carried out. The survey results are shown in the table below(table 2).

Table 2. The investigation results of the social demand of national fitness sports in the next decade N=1390

Serial number	Investigation item	pro	%	con	%	order
1	pay great attention to national fitness sports and citizen's health	1141	82.1	249	17.9	1
2	respect and guarantee the rights of taking part in fitness sports activitie	907	65.3	483	34.7	10
3	Hope to be healthy and have the normal ability to work	975	70.1	415	29.9	3

Table 2. *(continued)*

4	The family is healthy, the personal and social sustainable development is well	941	67.7	449	32.3	9
5	The government and society organize more fitness sports activities to arouse people's sports fervour	946	68.1	444	31.9	7
6	The basic public sports service is satisfied	802	57.7	588	42.3	17
7	Pay special attention to the sports facilities, improve the basic condition of national fitness	970	69.8	420	30.2	5
8	Consider to take part in fitness sports activities if the financial condition is improved	664	47.8	726	52.2	19
9	Consume in the fitness sports activities if the financial condition is improved	707	50.9	683	49.1	18
10	Have no effort to take part in fitness sports activities with the burden of work and life	435	31.3	955	68.7	20
11	introduce more knowledge about fitness sports to exercise scientifically	942	67.8	448	32.2	8
12	Strengthen the scientific guiding on fitness sports, improve the actual effect of national fitness sports	975	70.1	415	29.9	4
13	organize more monitoring of health condition, grasp the condition of body as precaution	907	65.3	483	34.7	11
14	supply more aspects about physical and mental exercise	854	61.4	536	38.6	16
15	pay more attention to home sports and supply more home sports conditon	903	65.0	487	35.0	12
16	pay more attention to school sports and care more about the next generation's healthy growing	1052	75.7	338	24.3	2
17	pay more attention to community sports and create a good sports atmosphere	952	68.5	438	31.5	6
18	pay more attention to the rural sports and care more about the peasants'physical and mental health	879	63.2	511	36.8	13

Table 2. *(continued)*

19	establish more laws and regulations about fitness sports to guarantee citizen's rights	858	61.7	532	38.3	15
20	Fitness sports is personal matter and has nothing to do with government or policy	319	22.9	1071	77.1	21
21	Pay attention to fitness sports of the weak people	865	62.2	525	37.8	14

The masses' demand of national fitness sports can be analyzed from the macro, meso and micro levels.

On the macro level, the demand of national fitness sports shows: "hope the government pay great attention to national fitness sports and citizen's health"(pro 1141, 82.1%), "respect and guarantee the rights of taking part in fitness sports activities"(pro 907, 65.3%), "establish more laws and regulations about fitness sports"(pro 858 61.7%), and "the family is healthy, the personal and social sustainable development is well"(pro 941, 67.7%). The investigation shows the most people's good wishes for national fitness sports. Nowadays, the society is people oriented, so a responsible government is a government that cares about people's livelihood. The physical and mental health of the masses is what the government at all levels should care about. Therefore, the "National Fitness Regulations" stress: "The government at or above the county level should bring national fitness career into line with national economy and social development plan." "The state council sports department shall be responsible for the nationwide fitness work, the other relevant departments shall be responsible for the relevant national fitness work within the scope of their respective duties and responsibilities." The issue concerning guarantee people's rights about fitness sports also first appears in the "National Fitness Regulations." The "Regulations" first clearly stipulate: "Citizens have rights to attend fitness activities lawfully. The local government at all levels shall guarantee citizens' rights to take part in the fitness sports activities." Anyhow, our government is adopting all effective policy system and measures to promote family happiness of the masses and the personal and social healthy sustainable development.

On the meso level, the demand of national fitness sports shows: "The government and society organize more fitness activities to arouse people's sports fervour"(pro 946, 68.1%), "The basic public sports service is satisfied"(pro 802, 57.7%), "Pay special attention to the sports facilities, improve the basic condition of national fitness"(pro 970, 69.8%), "Strengthen the scientific guiding on fitness sports, improve the actual effect of national fitness sports"(pro 975, 70.1%), "Hope to organize more monitoring of health condition, grasp the condition of body as precaution"(pro 907, 65.3%), "Hope the government and society pay more attention to school sports and care more about the next generation's healthy growing"(pro 1052, 75.7%), and hope government and society pay more attention to home sports, community sports, rural sports and the weak people' sports, etc. While being asked if fitness sports is a personal matter and has nothing to do with the government or policy, most people hold negative opinion(con 1071, 77.1%). It can be seen that the masses have great enthusiasm for sports activities and hold good social wishes and positive attitude toward our government and society to promote national fitness sports. It can be predicted, if China's public sports service career obtains the further development and the material conditions of national fitness sports are further satisfied, people's good wishes will become a reality.

On the micro level, the demand of national fitness sports shows like that "hope to be healthy and have the normal ability to work"(pro 975, 70.1%). On the whole, people concern much about personal health. Through interview survey, it shows that due to various internal and external effect, the general public have never paid more attention to health. "Consume to buy health", "Money is not important as health" such opinions are gradually becoming the leading opinions of the society. Love for sports activities has become the new fashion of society, and the lifestyle of ignoring health and sports is excluded and abandoned by society. While being asked "Consider to take part in fitness sports activities if the financial condition is improved"(pro 664, 47.8%), "Consume in the fitness sports activities if the financial condition is improved"(pro 707, 50.9%), the respondents do not show common agreement and obvious tendency. Another investigation data also shows, while health and wealth are being compared, most people choose the former without hesitation and place the latter in the secondary place. This shows from a side that people transfer their worship of materials to the concentration about themselves, the people-oriented thoughts are quite fully applied in the field of national fitness. Promoting personal healthy sustainable development is the concrete manifestation of scientific outlook on development in personal life field.

3.2   The Development Prospect Prediction of National Fitness Sports in Hubei in the Next Decade

Expert investigation is conducted about the observation of the development prospect prediction of national fitness sports in Hubei in the next decade. The results are shown in the table below(table 3).

Table 3. The experts investigation results of the development prospect prediction of nation fitness sports in Hubei in the next decade N=114

Serial number	Investigation item	pro	%	neutral	%	con	%	order
1	Next decade will be a good period for developing national fitness sports in our province	105	92.1	6	5.3	3	2.6	1
2	The national fitness career in our province will be in the forefront of the national mass sports development	52	45.6	37	32.5	25	21.9	7
3	The number of the citizens who take part in fitness sports will be significantly increased	102	89.5	12	10.5			2
4	Restricted by the whole economic and social development level in our province, the national fitness maintains at current level	20	17.5	49	43.0	45	39.5	6
5	The citizen's sports consumption demand will have a more sharply rising	86	75.4	26	22.8	2	1.8	4
6	The sports population will grow larger	91	79.8	22	19.3	1	0.9	3
7	The people's attitude toward life is renewed, their fitness awareness is strengthened	102	89.5	12	10.5			2
8	People's condition of taking part in fitness sports is greatly improved	85	74.6	23	20.2	6	5.2	5

The results show the experts totally agree that: "Next decade will be a good period for developing national fitness sports in our province"(pro 105, 92.1%, neutral 6, 5.3%, con 3, 2.6%, its pro rate is number one). As is acknowledged by the experts, the next decade is a good period for developing national fitness sports in Hubei or even the whole country. It shows as follows: First, China is in the construction of a higher leveled well-off society in an all-round way, it's a requirement "The ideological and ethical standards, the scientific and cultural qualities and health quality of the whole nation are improved obviously, forming a rather complete modern national education system, cultural and technical innovation system, nationwide fitness and medical and health system" [3]. China's socialist economic construction, political construction, cultural construction, social construction and the construction of ecological civilization put more request for people's health and all-round development. Thus it can be seen, national fitness sports will definitely cause more attention of the whole society; Second, as our administrative regulations to develop national fitness sports the "National Fitness Regulations" draw a blue print for the development of our national fitness sports and also put forward many practical measures and methods. The promulgation and implementation of the "Regulations" can surely promote great changes in system and mechanism of our national fitness career and drive the national fitness career uprise; Third, with the accomplishment of China's first basic "National Fitness Outline", the state sums up the past experience and works out the new "National Fitness Program" in accordance with the characteristics of our time, and also will issue a series of new measures and methods about national fitness sports, which will bring a new situation of its work; Fourth, with people's awareness of sports rights, the action of defending their rights will last extensively and persistently. Taking part in the sports activities becomes an embodiment of people's sports rights and also a necessity of daily life. Therefore, the national fitnesss sports in Hubei will surely step into a new period and enter the highway of development in the next decade.

The experts agree that in the next decade "The people's attitude toward life is renewed, their fitness awareness is strengthened"(pro 102, 89.5%, neutral 12, 10.5%, con 0, the pro rate is number two), "The number of the citizens who take part in fitness sports will be significantly increased"(pro 102, 89.5%, neutral 12, 10.5%, con 0, the pro rate is number two), "The sports population will grow larger"(pro 91, 79.8%, neutral 22, 19.3%, con 1, 0.9%, the pro rate is number three), and "The citizen's sports consumption demand will have a more sharply rising"(pro 86, 75.4%, neutral 26, 22.8%, con 2, 1.8%, the pro rate is number four). The sports consciousness, sports activities, sports population and sports consumption demand constitute main elements in our national fitness sports and are complete necessities to form national fitness activities flourished. The above data show that the experts are positive about the developing trend of national fitness sports in our province and confident about its future development.

About the developing level of national fitness sports in Hubei, the experts' answers are not so optimistic. Except for 46% of the experts agree that "The national fitness

---

[3] Report from Zemin Jiang in the 16th Chinese National Congress of the Communist Party: build a well-off society in an all-round way, create a new situation in building socialism with chinese characteristics, China Daily, 2002.11.8.

career in our province will be in the forefront of the national mass sports development", 32.5 % of the experts are neutral, still 21.9% of the experts disagree. This group of data show that it's difficult for national fitness sports in Hubei to be in the forefront of the whole nation. Although the government at all levels in Hubei and the society have given full attention to national fitness sports, the situation of national fitness sports in the whole province is not so optimistic owing to our economic and social development position in the whole country. Therefore, it's necessary to take effective measures about national fitness sports in Hubei under the new situation and increase investment to promote its supernormal rapid development.

4 Conclusion

4.1 About the future development of national fitness sports in Hubei, the masses' demand of national fitness sports is analyzed from the macro, meso and micro levels. The macro level shows most people's good wishes for national fitness sports; The meso level shows the masses have great enthusiasm for sports activities and hold good social wishes and positive attitude toward our government and society to promote national fitness sports; The micro level shows people concern much about personal health. Due to various internal and external effect, the general public have never paid more attention to health. "Consume to buy health", "Money is not important as health" such opinions are gradually becoming the leading opinions of the society. Love for sports activities has become the new fashion of society, and the lifestyle of ignoring health and sports is excluded and abandoned by society.

4.2 The investigation about the prospect of the future development of national fitness sports in Hubei shows the next decade is a good period for developing national fitness sports in Hubei or even the whole country. The development trend of national fitness sports in Hubei is well, but it's difficult to be in the forefront of the whole nation. Although the government at all levels in Hubei and the society have given full attention to national fitness sports, the situation of national fitness sports in the whole province is not so optimistic owing to our economic and social development position in the whole country. Therefore, it's necessary to take effective measures about national fitness sports in Hubei under the new situation and increase investment to promote its supernormal rapid development.

References

1. The State Council of the People's Republic of China. National Fitness Outline. People's Sports Publishing House, Beijing (1995)
2. The State Council of the People's Republic of China. National Fitness Regulations. China Legal Publishing House, Beijing (2009)
3. China's Mass Sports Status Quo Investigation Group. China's Mass Sports Status Quo Survey and Research. Beijing Sport University Press, Beijing (1998)
4. Tang, H.: National Fitness Sports. Hubei People's Publishing House, Wuhan (2010)

5. China's Mass Sports Status Quo Investigation Group. China's Mass Sports Status Quo Survey and Research. Beijing Sport University Press, Beijing (2005)
6. Guo, H., Tang, H., Li, X.: Socialization Reform of Public Sports Service in China. Journal of Wuhan Institute of Physical Education (11), 1–6 (2007)
7. National Bureau of Statistics of China. China Statistical Yearbook. China Statistical Publishing House, Beijing (2007)
8. Bureau of Statistics of Hubei. Hubei Statistical Yearbook, vol. 14. China Statistical Publishing House, Beijing (2003)

Research on Status Quo and Countermeasures of Development of Core Competitive Basketball Human Resources in China

Lei Xian-liang[1,*] and Zhang Xin[2]

[1] School of Sports Exercises, Wuhan Sports University, Wuhan, Hubei, 430079, China
Tel.: +86-13871292992; Fax.: +86-027-87190268
lixianliang822@163.com
[2] School of Sports Economics and Management,
Wuhan Sports University, Wuhan, Hubei, 430079, China
Zhang__xy@126.com

Abstract. The thesis makes an analysis about the status quo of the core human resources of competitive basketball in China ----the athletes and trainers, and proposes that China should strengthen the cultivation of competitive basketball players and the construction of trainer group featuring high competence, high qualification and high teacher's ethics so that competitive basketball games can realize its sustainable development. Several suggestions on core human resources' development of competitive basketball are put forward on the basis of present situation, which are expected to promote the thriving development of competitive basketball games in the future.

Keywords: competitive basketball, core human resources, status quo.

1 Introduction

Human resources of competitive basketball are an important component of competitive sports in China. They include all the staff and personnel in competitive basketball games such as athletes, trainers, referees, administrative personnel, and researchers. However, the athletes and trainers are the core parts of human resources of competitive basketball. Our country should strengthen the cultivation of competitive basketball players and the construction of trainer group featuring high competence, high qualification and high teacher's ethics in order that competitive basketball games can realize its sustainable development.

2 Current Situation of the Development of Athletes of Competitive Basketball in China

2.1 A General Tendency of Lacking in Athletes

The vigorous development of athletics basketball games rely on the basketball athletes who stand for the main body of competitive sports. Disposing reasonable

---

* Corresponding author.

M. Zhou (Ed.): ISAEBD 2011, Part IV, CCIS 211, pp. 579–584, 2011.
© Springer-Verlag Berlin Heidelberg 2011

athletics team of basketball games can promote athletics sports enterprise to obtain unceasingly the new breakthrough. But at present there is still a problem that the number of the core talents and reserved talents is not enough and the location is not proper in our country. According to the team and the athlete registration statistics from Chinese Basketball Association, the quantity of national specialized basketball team and athletes reduced sharply. In the 1980s, our country has 75 professional men and women basketball teams and 1320 athletes in all[1].But to the end of 2010, the registration in Chinese Basket Association just had 29 teams, including 17 men teams and 12 women teams, and 387 athletes, among whom there were 234 male athletes and 153 female athletes. By contrast, the number of sports team was reduced by 46 and the number of athletes was reduced by 933. In aspect of reserved talents of basketball athletes training, the incoherence of   phenomenon is prominent. In 1980s, basketball athletes of amateur training school in china (the third line team) were counted 50529.But by the end of 2010; it doesn't reach 30000 in training. The athletes in training reduced too. Because of the athletes in training and the amateur reduced, it caused that some national youth teams in China (the second line team) were dismissed for insufficient resource. At present, national youth team (male, female in the second line team) only have 47 (31 men team, 16 women team), and less 560 in training (360 male athlete, near 200 female athlete)[2].

2.2   Unbalanced Development of Athletes among Regions

For athlete resources of athletics basketball in our country, the team of high level athletes and the reserved talents present the imbalanced development characteristic between regions in two levels. In the aspect of high level athletes, take the region distribution of 17 club teams at CBA 2010-2011 season in China for an example, they mainly concentrates in eastern area in our country. In aspect of the reserved talents, echelon of youth basketball team is integrity in five provinces that is Shandong, Hebei, Liaoning, Jilin, Heilongjiang. They are not only the best area for training work of youth basketball but also the base of athletics basketball reserve in our country; Beijing, Shanghai, Guangdong, Fujian, Hubei, Jiangsu, Henan and so on are in the second level; Near 20 provinces in mid-west section are weaker area for the training work of youth basketball in our country[3].The economic situation in imbalanced is the primary cause as the economy is the sports foundation, which rises training development of athletics basketball in imbalanced. But the level of economy development is not the dominant factor. The non-balanced has many reasons. It touches on the natural condition, the subjective cognition of people and the traditional factors of athletics sports and so on. All of factors decided that athletics basketball reserve in different provinces is imbalanced in China.

2.3   Diversified Development of Athlete Resources

"The composition of the athlete resources" means the different training methods, the quantity and proportion of main athletes in each unit .From the beginning of 1960's, the resources of athletics basketball athletes mainly depend on three levels of personnel training network and system, the amateur training school in county, the amateur training school in city and outstanding Sports Team in province in our country. After the third meeting of 11 sessions, China had gradually carried on the evolution of organizational reform. With organizational reform gradually developed, especially when our country established the socialist market economy, the planned economy is not conducive to social participation, athletics floating and professional thought stabilized and so on. The phenomenon reflected that management system malpractice was already prominent day by day in China. Therefore sports management system was reformed in the course of reconsidering and criticizing old system. To the end of 70's, sports system started comprehensive reform from socialization in order to attract the social strength to manage sports and cause sorts of different body to become principal management part of basketball athlete [4]. Simultaneously, it also makes the composition of the athlete resources multivariate in our country.

2.3.1 The Traditional Basketball Athletes

The traditional basketball athletes have near 50 year's development history in our country. Up until now, the selecting, training and transmitting of athletes mainly rely on traditional procedure and methods. They transport outstanding potential athletes of each age stage to the higher level's team for training in order to raise high level athletes. With unceasingly organizational reform of sports, it has obvious change in selection and education pattern of the basketball athletes and the direction of development is building three levels of primary training networks and varied kinds of selection and education patterns.

2.3.2 Basketball Athletes in Colleges and Universities

The athletes in colleges and universities appear in 1980's. The ordinary university attempts to sets up the high level sports team, and they raise own high level athletes basically depended on colleting the retired basketball athletes, but it does not have their own organization for raising and selecting athletes. After development in 20 years, various universities had a deeper understanding to sports function and the influence of the high level athletics. Large-scale sports events start to rise and develop in China, for example, the league tournament of CUBA, the Super Basketball League Tournament of university student and so on. Now some universities are gradually forming diverse system including own athletes' collecting system and training system.

2.3.3 The Occupational Basketball Athletes

The occupational basketball athletes take the movement training and the movement competition reward as a goal, and take sports as the occupation. Professional basketball athletes in our country occur very late. until Chinese man professional basketball league tournament firing in 1995, it occurred the first group of professional basketball athletes. At that time they were collected under the traditional policy. but in the eyes of their system, they are not professional athletes in a real sense. But through 16 years' development, this type's raising and selecting system move towards the standardization gradually, and the basketball club has formed in the own mechanism and formed the positive cycle.

3   Current Situation of the Development of Trainer Resources of Competitive Basketball in China

3.1 Smaller Quantity and Brain Drain

For 1980s, our country all levels of each kind of basketball trainer approximately 15000 people, but the data material which obtains according to the National Sports Bureau basketball movement administrative center demonstrated, at present our country basketball trainer in high, the third day level trainer's population respectively is 152 human, 357 human and 1471 people, the total number of people is 1980 people, between three level of trainer's proportions are 1/2.35/9.68.The trainer lacks the corresponding quantity, could lack the corresponding project scale and the training quality inevitably, basketball trainer quantity are few already becomes the serious athletics basketball movement ecology question. At the same time, the trainer will drain affects the basketball school or the basketball club teaching training normal development inevitably, raised quantity and the quality enhancement to the basketball athlete has also created adverse effect [5].Trainer's outflow to has had the profound influence in the hillock trainer as well as the future trainer, causes the existing trainer troop not to be unstable, and will cause the future the trainer troop to construct faced with the difficulty. Creates the reason which the trainer drains to be very many, its one, in athletics basketball funds intense situation, trainer's treatment universal somewhat low; Second, in the basketball school or the basketball club, lacks the essential equal competition mechanism, the observance of seniority still is suppressed young outstanding trainer's blooming chronic disease, third, in aspect and so on title, wages, bonus, housing difficulties and question, then becomes affects the immediate cause which the trainer drains.

3.2 Knowledge and Composition Structure Are Unreasonable in High Level Trainer to Basketball

Our country high level basketball trainer majority comes from the retirement basketball athlete, generally has the high basketball technique and tactics level and the rich experience, also has the corresponding school record and certain movement training study basic theory knowledge, but still lacked to the basketball law of motion is deeper a step understanding, lacked own to the basketball movement unique opinion, to the basketball training theory exploration insufficiency, lacked the innovation, also lacked the correlation sports discipline and other foundation discipline basic unit knowledge, has created trainer knowledge structure sole [6], was unable to utilize very well the theory knowledge in the training practice, the training still paused Trains at the experience in the low level, the scientific training level is not high. The trainer system internal structure has the decisive function to its overall performance, when composition training organized group if can carry on the reasonable arrangement according to trainer's knowledge unique feature, can display the more major training benefit. However, our country various row basketball trainer troop composes the structure to be simple at present, has the perfect training set's team to be very few. The overwhelming majority team merely provides or two coaches, between the trainer divides the work insufficiently is clear about, the responsibility insufficiently is single-minded, often forms head coach to do the work comprehensively the aspect, is unable integrity which satisfies the team to construct, many teams even lack the specialized physical ability training, the nutritionist as well as other each kind of type trainer.

3.3 The Trainers' System of Post Training Is Imperfect and Insufficient

Basketball trainer's on-the-job training not only is improves the trainer quality an essential measure, also is Our country Basketball Movement Project management Functional departments trains the trainer a basic system. According to the basketball movement rapid need to develop, the basketball trainer must stand in the career development most front, the time understood the most recent information tendency, renews own knowledge structure and the training idea unceasingly. At present our country basketball trainer participates in training the form mainly to have high, the third day level post training class carries on the trainer to train, various ranks have respective training plan, the program and the teaching material, the data material demonstrated high, the third day level post training class cannot link up, the training curriculum and the training content cannot keep pace with the times, the training form, the teaching way, the method have not had the innovation, on-the-job training teaching material construct and train the lecturer ability also to wait for enhance, is affecting one of our country basketball trainer on-the-job training situation not ideal reasons. The athlete premature retirement and the trainer on-the-job training system is imperfect, various local agency to at the beginning of intermediate trainer on-the-job training execution strength, does not lack the essential surveillance mechanism, causes the athlete who a part just retired without training to step onto the training operating post, caused the young trainer to emerge massively, creates our country high level basketball trainer whole to tend to the youth oriented. The trainer on-the-job training system is imperfect, exposes the training system and the system existence insufficiency, and similarly creates our country basketball trainer on-the-job training situation to pay no attention.

4   Feasible Countermeasures of Core Human Resources' Development of Competent Basketball in China

(1) Display government administration leading role, the break tradition education system and the sports system barrier, the display sports system and the education system combined effect, the basketball reserve talented person's raise gives the support for our country in the policy and the economy, improves and enhances athlete's training living conditions, transfers the player and trainer's enthusiasm, gradually consummates, reforms our country original training competition system, lays the foundation found for our country basketball outstanding human resources storehouse.

(2) In under the diversified market guidance, with the enterprise, the institution unites positively trains the basketball reserve talented person, forms the capital source channel to be broad, the collection fund are many, practically solves the realistic

problem which the raise unit fund is insufficient, for trains our country basketball high level reserve talented person to open the new way and the channel.

(3) Must break the region limit, establishes the basketball high level reserve human resource flow system. The sports control section should formulate the related policy and the system integrates the basketball high level reserve talented person's flowing the personnel market management the standardization and the legalization track, breaks the region limit fairly, building, the fair competition environment, consummates national and the place graduation regulation system unceasingly, for realizes our country basketball high level reserve talented person's resources sharing and the exchange lays the foundation.

(4) Formulation "the basketball young people reserve personnel training plan", the be established basketball young people working committee, establishes the reasonable national young people basketball training, the competition system, the tenable basketball young people train the research centre, strengthens the young people basketball fundamental training fundamental research, the establishment "the young people basketball training teaches the law instruction collection", instruction basic unit basketball trainer's training work.

(5) Comprehensively raises the trainer level diligently. Formulates in the trainer, the long-term raise plan, persisted walks, please come in, long-term training and short-term training, the graduation and classified training, the home and overseas training unify the principle, wears raises the basketball trainer's level.

References

1. Jia, Z.-q.: A Study on Characteristic of Competitive Basketball Development Environment in China during Society Transformation Period. Journal of Beijing Sport University 31(4), 547–549 (2008)
2. Chinese Basketball Association.The public Name List of Chinese Athlete (December 1, 2010), http://www.cba.gov.cn
3. Li, T.-y., Zhao, Y.-h.: A Research of Chinese Basketball Researved Talents. Journal of Chengdu Sport University 33(3), 68 (2007)
4. Wang, B.: Research on form and development characteristics of players in high-level basketball teams in China. Journal of Wuhan Institute of Physical Education 40(7), 69–71 (2006)
5. Zhang, X., Zhu, Y.-l.: Research on ecological Environment of human Resources of Sports Basketball in Chinese. The Journal of Sport History and Culture 4, 15 (2005)
6. Du, J., Xu, B., Gao, M.: Consideration on the Construction of Coach Team of Basketball in China in the New Period. Journal of Beijing Sport University 29(6), 852 (2006)

Analysis of Scientific Papers about Taekwondo in Core Chinese Journals during 2000-2010

Pang Junpeng

Wuhan Institute of Physical Education, Department of Heavy Athletics,
Wuhan, Hubei, 430079
PangJunpeng@yeah.net

Abstract. By using method of mathematical static and literature, we carry out stratified statistic, generalization and analysis of the scientific papers about Taekwondo in Core Chinese Journals (CCJ) during 2000-2010 according to five dimensions, including published time, the application of research methods, research fields, professional title and organization of authors, and language of citation. The result shows that not many scientific papers about Taekwondo have published in CCJ of these 11 years; research methods have been used widely, but the specific research method is rather single; contents of research are very wide; the authors are mainly lecturers and the organizations are mainly based on independent sports colleges; the major language of citation is Chinese and foreign languages are very few, especially Korean – there is no citation in Korean.

Keywords: Taekwondo, scientific papers, Core Chinese Journals.

1 Research Subjects and Methods

1.1 Research Subjects

The subjects are 126 papers published in Core Chinese Journals during 2000-2010.

1.2 Methods of Research

1.2.2 Method of Literature
By logging CNKI, we downloaded the papers about Taekwondo in the core journals during these 11 years, including Sports Science, Sports and Science, Journal of Beijing Sport University, Journal of Shanghai Institute of Physical Education, Journal of Wuhan Institute of Physical Education, Journal of Xi'an Institute of Physical Education, Journal of Chengdu Sport University, and etc.

1.2.2 Method of Mathematical Static
Make the papers quantitative through encoding the different dimensions of them. And then process and analyze the data after encoding by Table Analysis Method, Chi-square Testing Method, and Frequency Statistics Method of SPSS software to provide strong support for the studies of papers.

M. Zhou (Ed.): ISAEBD 2011, Part IV, CCIS 211, pp. 585–591, 2011.
© Springer-Verlag Berlin Heidelberg 2011

2 Result and Analysis

2.1 Distribution of Published Date

The total amount of the papers about Taekwondo published in Core Chinese Journals during 2000-2010 is 126. The amount during 2001-2002 is 11; the number during 2007-2008 is 13; and in 2009, the amount of papers published is 16, which is six more than that in 2000. From the overall situation, we can find out that it published papers every year, the number is relatively small, and the speed of rise is very slow, which shows that the level of scientific research about Taekwondo is relatively low. The major reasons maybe the following: 1. The initiative for reporting issues is not high. While the author looked up the scientific papers, he found out that the issues about Taekwondo are very few. Less than 10% of the scientific papers are the issues of Sports Administration and Provincial Sports Bureau. 2. The restriction of research facilities. Taekwondo in our country is still not mature, which restricts the development of research level. Take the establishment of research institutes for example, there is no other place yet having set up independent research institute, except Beijing, which has its own sports organization. 3. High-level Scholars in our Taekwondo academia are not many. Only Beijing Sport University, Wuhan Institute of Physical Education, Shanghai Institute of Physical Education and Hebei Institute of Physical Education have scholars with vice-senior title, while the other institutes almost have none.

2.2 The Application of Research Methods

The methods used by the researchers are mainly literature, mathematical static (including factor analysis, frequency statistics, AHP, T testing), logical analysis, expert interviews, questionnaire, experiment, video analysis, observation, which demonstrates that the research methods have been used widely. Because the development of Taekwondo is influenced by many factors, including the restriction of history, politics, economy, culture, and education, the researchers must refer to the subject knowledge of these influential factors and use different methods to study in different ways in order to study the phenomenon of Taekwondo comprehensively, correctly and profoundly. Only do like that can they reveal the nature and law of Taekwondo comprehensively and objectively. Therefore, comprehensive research methods have been used widely. Additionally, the research methods for studying Taekwondo are relatively simple, which affects the significance of their researches. "In fact, mono-method always increase the possibility of errors of results and reduce the validity of the research because of its own shortcomings, limitation or being influenced by other factors. In many cases, using mono-method can only obtain small part of information, while most information is ignored or missed. So it is difficult to draw objective conclusion, and even lose the significance of research." [1] The proportion of using mono-method of the papers about Taekwondo published in Core Chinese Journals during 2000-1010 is highest, and its up to 42% of the total papers; the proportion of using two methods is relatively low, which is up to 31% of the total papers; and the proportion of using three methods or more is lowest, which is up to 27 % of the total numbers of the papers.

2.3 Research Fields

2.3.1 Physiological and Psychological Researches

The physiological research on Taekwondo is the science that mainly studies the sports capacity and the process of response and adoption to exercises of the athletes of Taekwondo. It provides favorable reference for revealing the influence laws and mechanism of Taekwondo upon human body and for the training laws. The psychological research on Taekwondo mainly refers to provide guidance for practical work of Taekwondo through analyzing cognition, emotion and behavior in exercise context. The major representative of physiological research is Professor Lin Wenjin[2], who studies the characteristics of energy supply in Taekwondo competition by determining the biochemical indexes of five excellent Taekwondo athletes of Taiwan during the process of training and competing. The main representatives of psychological research are Professor Wang Changsheng[3] and Vice-professor Wang Junfa[4]. The former studies the impact of different logical background on effect of intuitive thinking of Taekwondo athletes, and the later analyzes the phenomenon of Taekwondo elite's instantaneous loss of attention and common college students. We can find out from the statistics (see Figure 1) (the following is same) that there are 28 theses about physiological and psychological researches on Taekwondo in the scientific papers of these 11 years, which is up to 22.2% of the total amount. It has the largest proportion of the whole research filed, which shows that the scholars in China attach great importance to physiological and psychological researches on Taekwondo.

2.3.2 Analysis of Competition

Competitive Taekwondo is the leader of the whole Taekwondo industry. The success of competitive Taekwondo is bound to have a great role in promoting college Taekwondo and public Taekwondo. If we want to have great achievements in competitive Taekwondo, it must show strength by the results of the competition of competitive Taekwondo. The statistics show that there are 18 papers analyzing the Taekwondo competition in the scientific papers about Taekwondo of these 11 years, which is up to 14 % of the total amount. In term of the research contents of competition types, it includes the studies of National Taekwondo Championships, the application situation of tactics in Asian Championships, World Taekwondo, and the development trend of Olympics techniques. In term of gender, the studies of female are more than that of male, which has a certain relation with the number of gold medal that the female won at the Olympic Games. At the same time, it shows that the scholars should carry out more researches on the male's tactics.

2.3.3 Training

Training is a process to continuously create, improve or maintain the excellent athletic scores of athletes, and it is also a process to constantly explore the athletes' potential. There are 12 papers about training of Taekwondo in the scientific papers about Taekwondo of these 11 years, which is up to 10% of the total amount. The research contents mainly consist of the following aspects: firstly, it elaborates the training methods and training characteristics: Professor Zeng Yujiu makes a relatively detailed study of skills and training methods of Taekwondo; Professor Yuan Zhenlan presents the main characteristics of training of Taekwondo; and there are also other experts and scholars explain physical training methods, control of training process, and the impact of HiHiLo and LoHiLo on improving oxidative metabolism capacity of the female Taekwondo athletes in detail to provide guidance and direction for practical training. However, it is lack of the studies of certain special training of Taekwondo, especially the exploration of laws of some tactics training.

2.3.4 Researches on Rules

Through studying the rules carefully, it can adjust training techniques and methods in time, and show strong points and hide weaknesses to make full use of own advantages and lay a solid foundation for getting good achievements. The statistics show that there are 10 theses about the rules of Taekwondo in the scientific papers of Taekwondo of these 11 years, which accounts for 8% of the total amount. The researches on rules mainly analyze and explore the penalty for rules scales, the impact brought by the revision of competition rules on competition, the effect of rules on referees, the influence of revision of rules on our preparation for Taekwondo of Olympic Games. Since Taekwondo entered into the Olympic Games, there are 10 times of large or small revision of rules. It safely says that the continuous revision of the rules is the major reason for the scholars of Taekwondo increasing studies of the rules of Taekwondo. In term of the development of its regulations, it will continue increasing the efforts to study its rules.

2.3.5 Researches on Indices

The studies of indices of body diathesis can provide powerful basis and reference for the coaches to select materials and monitor the training quality. Human resources of the youth in our country is very rich, but how to select the best athlete most quickly and in the shortest time is very important. The statistics show that there are 9 theses for analyzing Taekwondo competitions in the scientific papers of Taekwondo of these 11 years, which accounts for 7% of the total amount. The researches contents mainly include index of Taekwondo athletes' body patterning and function, measurement index of physical fitness of the excellent male Taekwondo athletes, the construction of index of exercise quality of excellent female Taekwondo athletes during their training of body diathesis, and the selection of index of body shape of our excellent Taekwondo athletes. The research contents are relatively comprehensive, which has certain function for building the specific indices of different competitive abilities needed by competitive athletes.

2.3.6 Researches on Culture

The statistics show that there are 6 theses about the culture of Taekwondo in the scientific papers of Taekwondo of these 11 years, which accounts for 5% of the total amount. The researches mainly are on the relationship between traditional Chinese culture and Taekwondo, the value of Taekwondo competition, and the origin of Taekwondo. Taekwondo is a kind of sports originated from North Korean. Many original research literatures must be obtained by Korean. However, the Research Centers of Taekwondo in Korean do not open their research achievements, which can only be referred by their inner staff. Therefore, it further increases the difficulties for the foreigners to study the culture of Taekwondo. So the researchers should provide powerful theoretical support for the studies of culture of Taekwondo by relying on other disciplines, and in different ways to reveal its core knowledge when they study.

2.3.7 Other Researches

The statistics show that there are 11 theses analyzing Taekwondo competition in the scientific papers of Taekwondo of these 11 years, which accounts for 9⫾ of the total amount. The contents conclude comparison among programs, the current situation of management, and the studies of countermeasures. The comparison of programs is mainly about the analysis of strength characteristics of athletes' body muscle of Free Fighting, Boxing and Taekwondo, comparison of competitive characteristics between Free Fighting and Taekwondo, and the comparison of political environment of development between Wushu and Taekwondo. Additionally, some scholars put forward different views and opinions on the means of communication, similarities and differences between the rules, etiquette way, and differences of Dan grading among Wushu, Boxing and Judo.

2.4 Professional Titles and Distribution of Organizations of Researchers

The professional title of the researchers is mainly lecturer, who have published 60 papers, which accounts for 48% of the total amount; and then is Vice-professor, who have published 40 thesis, which is up to 30% of the total amount; the next place is teaching assistant (TA), who have published 16 papers, which accounts 13% of the total amount; and the number of professor is lowest. From the analysis of regions, we can find out that independent sports colleges have published 62 papers, which is up to 49% of the total amount; 211 universities have published 29 papers, which accounts for 23% of the total amount; general undergraduate colleges and other schools have published 24 papers, which accounts for 19% of the total amount. Our country is increasing the discipline building of Taekwondo, and the young teachers is the backbone engaging in Taekwondo, which is a major reason for why they have published the most papers. The reason why the professors have published fewer papers is: it is short of senior scholars of Taekwondo in our country, and most of them have transferred from other programs, especially from Free Fighting and Wushu to Taekwondo, and these scholars may still focus in their origin research direction. Of course, the development of Taekwondo itself is not perfect, which increases efforts of researches. Our sports institutions have opened Taekwondo for a long time, and have an advantage of invested funds, facilities and personnel training over other types of schools, which makes certain groundwork and help for their teachers to do researches and publish papers.

2.5 Language of Citation

The information provided by literature references is very important for the readers and play a significant role in researching, especially the hot spots and key spots of the researches both at home and abroad. Therefore, the types and languages of reference literatures are rather important. From the references of citation (seeing in Figure 6), there are 104 papers published in Core Chinese Journals whose references are all in Chinese during 2000-2010, which is up to 83% of the total amount; the papers whose reference literatures with the combination of English and Chinese are 21, which accounts for 16.5% of the total amount; and the papers whose reference literatures are all in English are only one, which accounts for less 1% of the total amount. There is no paper whose reference literatures are in Korean. It shows that there is still a big gap and deficiency of English and Korean level of our scientific researchers; or it maybe because of the imperfect development of research content itself and the scarcity of research materials.

3 Conclusions

Not so many scientific papers about Taekwondo have published in CCJ of these 11 years; research methods have been used widely, but the specific research method is rather single; contents of research are very wide; the authors are mainly lecturers and the organizations are mainly based on independent sports colleges; the major language of citation is Chinese and foreign languages are very few, especially Korean – there is no citation in Korean.

4 Suggestions

During the research process on Taekwondo, the nation should establish scientific and research institutes to encourage the researchers to apply for research projects, and provide certain research funds and financial aid for the Taekwondo researchers; for the research methods, it is especially important to improve innovation, accuracy and reasonableness of methods; it should increase the researches on its teaching, management, humanities, philosophy and aesthetics; comprehensive universities should increase researches on Taekwondo; and it also need to enrich the languages of citation and use the literatures with high-quality for reference.

References

1. Huang, H.: Sport Science Research: A Methodological Exploration——Survey and Analysis Based on 300 Doctoral Dissertations of Sport Science in China. China Sport Science 29(9), 7 (2009)
2. Lin, W., Huang, L.: Researches on some sports Biochemical Characteristics of Elite Taiwan Taekwondo Athletes in Training and Competition. Journal of Guangzhou Physical Education Institute 20(2), 51–53 (2000)
3. Wang, C.: Impact of Different Logical Background on Effect of Intuitive Thinking of Taekwondo Athletes. Beijing Sport University 32(1), 67–68 (2009)
4. Wang, J., Liu, J.: Research on Phenomenon of Taekwondo Elite's Instantaneous Loss of Attention. Journal of Shanghai University of Sport 30(1), 70–73 (2006)

5. Xue, X.: Analysis on Taekwondo Athletes' "Perception", "Reaction and Reaction Time" and the Psychological Characteristics. Journal of Wuhan Institute of Physical Education 38(1), 146–148 (2004)
6. Chen, Z., Huang, H.: Characteristics of Application of Chinese Sports Social Science Research Methods. Journal of Wuhan Institute of Physical Education 42(2), 11–15 (2008)
7. Bobby, A.: Methods of Social Research. Huaxia Press, Beijing (2009)
8. Newman, L.: Methods of Social Research: Qualitative and Quantitative Approach. Press of People's University of China, Beijing (2007)
9. Xu, L.: Four Characteristics of Sports Power. Sports Culture Guide (8), 4 (2009)

Study on the Market Order of Chinese Professional Football

Weng Jian-feng[1] and Gao li-hua[2]

[1] P.E. Sect. of Panzhihua University, Sichuan Panzhihua, 617000, China
[2] Panzhihua University Libraries, Sichuan Panzhihua, 617000, China
WENGJ_f@126.com

Abstract. Through using the methods of literature, logic analysis and control variables, the concept, connotation and extension, causes and existing problems of Chinese professional football market were studied. The results show that every subjective behavior and consequence of Chinese professional football market is a problem of Chinese football market order. Analysis of the formation cause of Chinese professional football market order was conducted at the macro-, middle-, and micro-scale levels resulting in the following suggested reforms of the current system: to reform the current system to make the CFA a separate entity; to improve the legal system, developing "Football Law", and establishing sports court and sports arbitration facilities; to enhance the education of individual professional ethics and legal; to strengthen the coordination of the CFA and the justice system.

Keywords: China, professional football, market order.

Compared to the passion seen in the 2010 World Cup, Chinese professional football market is in an unprecedented predicament. Many football fans feel that there are many problems with the transactions and operation of Chinese football market. They witness various confusing phenomena and anomalies in Chinese Football League and the whole nation is disappointed in Chinese football. This gives us cause to carry out reflection. The basic premise for Chinese football getting out of this difficult position is to establish a healthy, stable and developmental order of the professional football market; it is our responsibility.

1 The Order of Chinese Professional Football Market Defined

1.1 The Concept of Order

At any given time, there are various definitions and explanations of order all over the world, but there is not a uniform definition. *Poetry Xiaoya* says, "Guests began to the feast, and to have an order". Here the meaning of "order" is "routine" and "sequence". In *CiHai* the notation of "order" is the position of people or things, abiding by rules with orderliness. John Rogers Commons considered "order" to be the operating rules of collective behavior [1]. Wang Zhiyong said, "Every idea we hold actually constitutes a

M. Zhou (Ed.): ISAEBD 2011, Part IV, CCIS 211, pp. 592–600, 2011.
© Springer-Verlag Berlin Heidelberg 2011

kind of order. We even think that the order of the rules' format is a result or performance of the order that the concept formats."[2]

According to the above literature; the authors tried to define "order" as operating rules, structure and legal systems of collective behavior of mutual constraints which is influenced by ideas. By "order" of the concept of operations, it found that the variable of "order" contains the laws, rules, systems, concepts, ethics, customs, practices, and culture.

1.2 The Connotation and Extension of Chinese Professional Football Market Order

Order is in nature, it has also long existed in human society. Therefore, order also exists in the market which is closely related to modern society. Economists think the market order is the management behaviors of the market management subject, the transactions of the market operators, the buying behavior of the market consumer, and the effect of the quantity and quality of market exchange objects on the market and the sum of its objective consequences. [3]

Review the above and combine with the "order" concept. The order of Chinese professional football market is defined as the total consequences of each corresponding objective behavior which is affected by its concepts. Therefore, the market order connotations of Chinese professional football include: behaviors of management and conduct of the CFA, business acts of professional football clubs, consumer behavior of the fans, competitive performance of athletes and referee behaviors. Because Chinese football market is different from other economic markets, the product quality is related to competitive ability of players, referees and the management of the Football Association. Production of goods is a multi-stakeholder, involving the Football Association, clubs, players, referees and so on. Therefore, the extension of the market order of Chinese professional football means the management system of the football, the legal system and the cultural and moral aspects of the subject.

2 The Problems of the Market Order of Chinese Professional Football

2.1 The Consequences and the Management and Business Behavior of the CFA

1) Behavior: One of the CFA purposes is to abide by the Constitution of the People's Republic of China, laws, regulations and national policy, and abide by social morality. The realistic situation is that a considerable part of the core management leadership in our football association management structure does not strictly enforce the laws and regulations, and "knowingly violate the law", manipulate or participate in criminal activity of "false, bets black" using their management authority. This considerable part of the core management leadership even includes the former Football Association chairman, the former director of referees, the former chairman of Super league of the AG (Football Association officials), etc. They are the direct managers or operators in the football market. When they form a common benefit chain, all dominant order is just

the fig leaf which covers their ears and eyes and the real recessive order forms spontaneously.

2) The consequences: The whole football market is in the "the vacuum" condition of false supervision when "misconduct" and "management" combine under the guise of legitimacy. The chief leaders of Chinese professional football market manipulate or participate in the market. The direct and indirect negative impact of these practices is difficult to estimate. It far exceeds the ordinary criminal activities like referees, the athletes and the club participation in "match fixing" and so on. The superficial consequences of the direct and indirect negative impact of chief leaders of Chinese professional football market manipulating or participating in the market are not only that the football association authorities are questioned and a drop in football competition market quality, but also affecting the entire football competition market brand. These serious consequences cause the whole society to question the credibility of the government in the exercise of legitimate authority.

2.2 Behaviors and Consequence of Chinese Professional Football Club Management

1) Behavior: the club's income and expenditures are unbalanced, and the club's losses are generally huge. The investigation showed that, at present, the investments of the club are maintained at more than 30 million Yuan, and the total income of the club is less than 25 million Yuan. [4] Since the regulation of the Super Committee Charter, if membership does not match the "Super Football Club standard" or the requirements of the financial system exactly, or experiences three years of continuous loss, the membership of the club with cumulative losses for three years will be cancelled after being passed by a the super-committee meeting of all members and then being approved by the CFA President. In order to keep the "shell" resources of football club, earnings must be reflected in the book; almost all clubs have to engage in false accounting.

2) Consequences: It is understandable for enterprises to withdraw after losing year after year. Six of the sixteen clubs have changed names anywhere from 1 to 6 times during the 2008 season. [5] Some consequences of frequently renaming are easily losing the assets of the club brand, credit, efficiency and faith of professional football clubs, which is suspected to lead to decrease brand loyalty and affect the brand image of the Professional Football League. [6]The short-term investments of the clubs affect the development of football talents; the enhancement of utilitarianism is not beneficial to the sustainable development of Chinese football.

2.3 Behaviors and Consequence of Fans

Development of football in each country needs the support of the fans. However, in recent years, "match fixing" has deteriorated the developing environment of football. Fans have left the football stadium, which caused the rapid decline of the football market, putting most football clubs in the red. At the same time, we also note that our fans are not very mature or rational, frequently having conflict with the other fans or players. Some fans disrupt the stadium following a few pseudo-fans with ulterior motives. Some fans disclosed that these false fans are employed by somebody, and their primary mission is to incite the audience to belittle the coach. Even some of the players disparage the coach during the game and all the actions have had remarkable results: the club considers its own benefit and the fans' call, and then some well-known coach is dismissed.

2.4 Behaviors and Consequences of Athlete and Referee Production

Because Chinese football competition's production is complex, "force" is used to describe the numerous complex behaviors and consequences of individual production. It is assumed that groups "1" and "2" of the home football team are represented by the normal forces F_{a1} and F_{a2} (the normal force shows that players play the normal exercise capacity for their team). Groups "1" and "2" of the visiting football team are represented by the normal forces F_{b1} and F_{b2}. The force of the referees is represented by F_r (force of referees is zero under normal circumstances). The force of the home team and visiting team's club are represented by "Fa" and "Fb" and the force of the home and visiting team's coaches are represented by "Fac" and "Fbc". Indirect intervention force from the illegal leadership of football is represented by Fg. All force is shown on the Schematic diagram of force (Figure1). It can be seen from Figure 1 that the real decision process and the result are comprised of the direct force of both players and the referees. The other forces belong to the indirect forces, which can occur only through direct interaction effect. Behaviors and consequences of football production will be discussed in many cases using control variables.

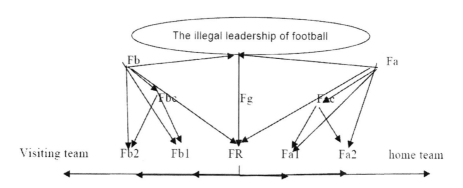

Fig. 1. The Schematic diagram of force in Chinese professional football market (the arrow indicates the direction of force)

1) When clubs, players, coaches, referees and football officials all comply with the Football Association charter.

The results: $\Sigma F= (Fa1+Fa2) - (Fb1+Fb2)$. When $\Sigma F>0$, the home team won; When $\Sigma F=0$, the result was a draw;

When $\Sigma F<0$, the visiting team won. Competition is the true reflection of the strength of both sides, as well as the rights and interests which all consumers should enjoy.

2) When the performance of a small team of players is not normal, the others are normal. "Fb1" of the visiting team intentionally lose the game for gambling interests.

The results: $\Sigma F= (Fa1+Fa2) - (-Fb1+Fb2)$, $\Sigma F= (Fa1+Fa2+Fb1) -Fb2$. It is no doubt that the result of the "competition" is the home team wining. If "Fb1" contains the main goalkeeper and defender, then the score will differ in a big way.

3) When the indirect force is zero, in the actual football game both players have bought their own failure, such as "Fa1" pay the visiting team to win, and the "Fb1" pay the home team to win.

The results: $\Sigma F= (-Fa1+Fa2) - (-Fb1+Fb2)$, $\Sigma F= (Fb1+Fa2) -(Fa1+Fb2)$. This kind of situation will cause the game to be complicated and confusing; the victory and defeat difficult to decide. Some of the players involved in gambling will lose everything. The competition scene is bewildering. For example, in the case when there is no defense formation (defender deliberately mistake), the other striker (not shot) cannot shoot at the goal frequently.

4) When players play normally and a club bribes the referees, or illegally bribes the Football Association Leadership to get the support of the referees.

The results: $\Sigma F=FR+ (Fa1+Fa2) - (Fb1+Fb2)$. If the strength is similar, it is likely that referees decide the result of the game.

The "complex" process and results have many consequences: consumers leave the football market, the national competitive level drops day by day and the brand value of Football League declines sharply.

3   The Reasons for the Formation of the Market Order of Chinese Professional Football

Order is affected by personal ideas, ideas which are restricted by an objective environment and a subjective consciousness. The market order of Chinese professional football is also affected by the subjective consciousness of microscopic individuals and the macro-objective environment. Athletes, referees, club owners and the Football Association officials are micro individual level. The club and the Football Association are middle level and the extension of the market order of Chinese professional football is macro-level. The following will analyze the reasons for the formation of the market order of Chinese professional football from three aspects.

3.1   The Social Structure of Macro-level

3.1.1   The Management System of "Deformity"
Whether the so-called "experts" or "laymen" manage Chinese Football, the results of the CFA's management show that the order of Chinese football market is very confusing. We cannot simply think that the officials of the CFA are incompetent; the deeper reason could be the combined management systems of the "football management center" and "Football Association". The CFA deals with the relationships among the international organizations, individual countries and regional associations by "association". It also undertakes the national football management and operational guidance which is accountable to the government department in the form of a "Football management center". The CFA selects the system by special privilege and adjusts the

pattern of vested interests to achieve their maximum effectiveness by using coercive means. [7] The CFA is the organizer; it is also both athletes and referees, which certainly cannot form a fair competitive environment. The management system is the source of the order of the current turmoil.

3.1.2 Legally "Unsound"

After the Wuhan Football Club withdrawal from the Super League in 2008, it gave up the lawsuit because it could not find the legal basis for prosecution of the CFA. The constitution of the CFA provides that the member associations, registered clubs and their members should ensure that they will not submit the disputes among them to the court, but only appeal to the arbitral institutions of the CFA. The FIFA recognizes the independent Court of Arbitration for Sport (CAS) with headquarters in Lausanne (Switzerland) to resolve disputes between FIFA, Members, Confederations, Leagues, clubs, Players, Officials and licensed match agents and players' agents. The meaning of the FIFA statute is that disputes are usually not submitted to the ordinary courts, but can be submitted to the independent Court of Arbitration for Sport (CAS). Since China has yet to set up the independent Court of Arbitration for Sport, the China Football Super League is independent of the law. It is in a self-contained "extra *Taoyuan*", which forms the embarrassing situation where a football club cannot sue the CFA.

3.1.3 Lack of Culture and Ethics

Some athletes and officials, who are direct participants in the football market, lack professional ethics. The material of the CFA shows that, at present, the reserve players of most Super League clubs are learning cultural lessons in the training base of the club and only a few reserve players are learning in ordinary schools. Some clubs even let their reserve players register in a school, but the players never have one day of study. Yet they can get a diploma without any guarantee of the study quality. This fully shows that our football players do not have enough culture. [8]They are involved with football skills and money all day long and lack social morality and professional ethics education. Regardless of ethics, some judges and officials succumb to the temptation of interests and step onto the criminal path.

3.2 Organization and Group (Middle-Level)

3.2.1 The CFA Power "Lacking Restraint"

The current system gives CFA supreme executive power in the field of the football market and CFA is in a dominant position in the operation and control of the franchise league by means of administrative power.

When the executive power and the right of management are highly concentrated in the hands of a small number of core leadership, to some extent the system increases the convenience for the core leadership to commit a crime. The findings of the CFA about the Qingdao Hailifeng "hanging shot" event were that it was a technical "back pass", not "match fixing". However the Ministry of Public Security's response was that Nan Yong and Yang Yimin were both involved in "false ball". How can they investigate fairly?"[9] Regulatory bodies exist in name only when "top leaders" are involved in criminal cases in the football industry.

3.2.2 Club of "Unfair Competition"

Clubs belong to the group; their essence is to seek to maximum interests of the group. Advertising effects of the club's title is the group's primary interest. Therefore, it has the important task, which was given by the super group, to keep super membership and achieve good competition results. At the expense of the interests of the market and other clubs, part of the club gains victory through improper means, such as bribing referees. CFA officials, which gradually set a standard that clubs must bribe referees for a fair game, making bribing the referee an essential expenses of the club. Bribery has become a fixed income of referees. The club is concerned that if one day the referee does not receive the "normal income", normal judgment will be carried out. Bribery not only disrupted the order of the football competition market but also potentially increased the burden on the club itself, which forced the entire football market into a vicious circle competition.

3.3 Micro Individual Criminal Psychologies

Objective environment and subjective psychology are the main causes of individual criminal activity. In the objective environment, the reform and opening up significantly improved our living environment, but also brought the West's decadent ideas of "materialism" and "carpe diem". Sharp differences between rich and poor, skyrocketing house prices and inadequate supervision causes some individuals to take the risk of crime. In subjective psychology, athletes, referees, club owners and the CFA officials involved in gambling have one kind of "luck psychology": that they obtain benefits by using their own special functions in the face of tremendous benefit returns; some football players' psychology is not balanced because the star players' salaries are several times higher than regular players. Some of the leadership of the CFA are also much more psychologically imbalanced while the leadership of other industries get more income; some people think that they worked hard all their life, it is natural for them to gain illegal wealth for their future life and for their children; some people discovered that their department or industry is betting on football, which produced the psychology of following the trend. All factors causing crime are psychological.

4 Suggestions for Establishing the Market Order of Chinese Professional Football

4.1 Reforming the Current System to make the CFA a Separate Entity

The CFA should return to the folk sports organization's nature and should become a self-sufficient and self-developing subject in the market. General Administration of Sports should no longer exercise the right of appointment and exemption and interfere with the routine business of CFA, we should put into practice that all clubs elect the leadership of the CFA independently; club and the CFA are in equal partnership. The market behavior of the subjects should be regulated mainly through legal means and economic means. The CFA should no longer expand administrative power except to fulfill some need which must be fulfilled according to legal authorization.

4.2 Improving the Legal System, Developing "Football Law", and Establishing Sports Court and Sports Arbitration Facilities

The football market is limited to the mechanism of exhausting internal remedies. The drawback is very clear: the FAC resolves its own disputes within the industry. The mechanism of exhausting internal remedies is normal sports industry rules. However, there are many illegal cases beyond the scope of sports regulation, and the mechanism cannot become an excuse to avoid legal sanctions. Instead, the judiciary should intervene in sports cases. Because sports cases require much specialty knowledge, we can establish sports court and sports arbitration facilities referring to other specialized courts, such as intellectual property courts and maritime courts. In order to improve the level of football, it is necessary to develop and promulgate "Football Law", which promotes the healthy and stable development of our Football.

4.3 To Enhance the Education of Individual Professional Ethics and Legal

We should make players engage in positive competition, referees provide impartial enforcement and officials to seriously organize games through professional ethics education, which would prevent crime from subjective thinking. We should also strengthen legal education so that they understand which behaviors are criminal, and the serious consequences of criminal activity. This would deter their behavior and achieve the purpose of reducing criminal activity. Each club cannot be "the only results first", for the education of athletes the primary goal should be educating people, talent is the second issue.

4.4 The Coordination of the CFA and the Justice System

We should request the CFA keep all competition videos, immediately investigate any anomalies in the competition, and implement "zero" tolerance of "match fixing" activities. We should also establish the judicial reporting mechanism, which intervenes in the football market quickly based on reported evidence. What's more, we should attack the network platform of gambling companies—domestic and foreign—and closely monitor the funds between gambling, for which electronic evidence can be obtained for prosecuting criminal offender.

References

1. Rogers, J.: Institutional economics. Translated by YU Shusheng. Commercial Press, Beijing (2009)
2. Wang, Z.: The definition of the order. [EB/OL],
   http://www.chinavalue.net/Article/Archive/2010/6/7/
   191652.html (June 7,2010)
3. MBA Think tank Wikipedia. Market order. [EB/OL],
   http://wiki.mbalib.com/wiki/%E5%B8%82%E5%9C%BA%E7%A7%
   A9%E5%BA%8F
4. Zhang, X.-p., Xin, L., Zhou, Y.: Research on Current Situation of Professional Football Clubs in China. Journal of Beijing Sport University 29(4), 457–459 (2006)

5. Wu, E.: Analysis on the Evolution of the "Crust" Resources for Chinese Professional Football Clubs. Journal of Chengdu Sport Universi (10), 23–28 (2009)
6. Wang, Y., Liang, X.: Discussion on Brand Establishment of Professional Football Clubs in China. Sports Culture Guide 10, 92–95 (2009)
7. Xu, X., Shan, Y., Cong, H.: Institutional environment and related problems of Chinese professional football clubs. Journal of Physical Education (5), 138–140 (2004)
8. Yan, Z., Ma, C., Jiao, H.: Comparison of training for talent-in-support of professional football clubs in China and abroad. Journal of Wuhan Institute of Physical Education (8), 76–81 (2009)
9. Wang M. Cui, D.: Talk about football gambling hanging shot" involved Nan Yong Yang and Yimin. Strait Metropolis Daily (March 24, 2010)

Research of Competitive Basketball Development in China

Zhou Xianjiang[1], Zhang Qiaoling[2], and Wang Xiangfei[3]

[1] Wuhan Institute of Physical Education, Wuhan, Hubei, 430079, China
[2] P.E.College, Huazhong Normal University, Wuhan 430079, China
[3] Wuhan Institute of Physical Education, Periodical Press, Wuhan, Hubei, China
Zhou_X_j@yeah.net

Abstract. At present, there are lots of research related to Chinese competitive basketball development, the major relevant research include Retrospection and conclusion of 50 years of development of Chinese basketball competitive sport, Current situation of professionalism of Chinese basketball competitive sport at the present stage, Constraints of sustainable development, and Strategic measures for Chinese competitive basketball development. However, current relevant research always break away from our particular historical period of society transition, thus causing the existing research to have certain dispersive ness and limitation of applicable scope. Theory of Chinese competitive basketball still requires further expanding and improving.

Keywords: Basketball Competitive Sport, Current Situation of Professionalism, Sustainable Development, Features of Basketball Sport.

At present, the research content related to Chinese competitive basketball development is quite abundant, involving sociology, economics, communication, management, sports psychology, sports medicine, exercise training, exercise physiology, etc., which are both macroscopic and microscopic. These theory relate to all aspects with respect to basketball development. The theme of this research only involves macroscopic layer, conducting summary for representative works of competitive basketball research from the angle of strategy. Major relevant research include retrospection and conclusion of 50 years of development of Chinese basketball competitive sport, current situation of professionalism of Chinese basketball competitive sport at the present stage, constraint of sustainable development, and strategic measures for Chinese competitive basketball development.

1 Retrospection and Conclusion of Development of Chinese Basketball Competitive Sport

It mainly consists of Research of features and current situation of 50 years of development of Chinese basketball competitive sport, Liu Haiying (Research of features and current situation of 50 years of development of Chinese basketball competitive sport, Journal of Beijing Sport University, 2002, 25 (3):), this research

M. Zhou (Ed.): ISAEBD 2011, Part IV, CCIS 211, pp. 601–607, 2011.
© Springer-Verlag Berlin Heidelberg 2011

performs research of features and current situation of 50 years of development of Chinese basketball competitive sport at longitudinal direction, takes historical fact of sport evolution as evidence and summaries its evolution and development. Until now, the competitive basketball development can be roughly divided into 7 periods: that is, popularity, promotion and development periods (initial stage of country establishment 1949-1957), rapid growth period (1958-1959), transitional period (1960- 1965), lag period (1966-1970), revival, recovery and adjustment periods (1971-1974), growth development period (1976-1994) as well as reform and innovation climbing period (after 1995). This research demonstrates the major problems exist in Chinese competitive basketball sport development: (1) Under planned economy system, impacted by "Olympic strategy ", the National Games strategy, the sport committees of provinces and cities eliminated basketball teams, resulting that the original three-level training network greatly shrank, reserved talents of basketball occurred discontinuity, echelon construction and layout are unreasonable, number of youth teams is lower than adult teams. Echelon construction formed unreasonable "inverted pyramid" shape. (2) Selection and cultivation of the coach has not formed scientific system, due to the negative market impact, the professional dedication and sense of responsibility of part of coaches is not strong, causing the training work short of scientific and reasonable plan and arrangement; the lacking of culture, science and technology and theoretical knowledge make the ability of scientific management, the commanding ability of training and actual match weak, basically belonging to work to meet an emergency. (3) Scientific research has not emphasized integration with practice, the basketball scientific research team is loose with popular spontaneous and individual research behaviour. Application rate of scientific research achievements is not high, forming the phenomenon of "trainer without research and researcher without training", leading that the means and methods with theory directing practice do not form own features compared with international ones. (4) Training and match system transform and advocate club professionalism measures, mostly on the situation and surface to a great extent. The thought touching essence and making deep reform should be defined, laws and regulations should be perfected, the measures should even be proper and practical. (5) Excellent sport teams and players are mostly in temporary shortage, a majority of teams have neither features in skill nor innovation in tactics. The playing methods are dull, traditional styles disappeared, new styles have not be formed yet, lacking world star. Measures related to development of competitive basketball sport: (1) Unify cognition, update concept, comprehensively boost the integrated reform, establish new order and reveal new look. (2) Starting from Chinese actual situation, make goals clear, determine proper work policy and guiding ideology for basketball training. (3) Establish new mode of basketball sport management that meets Chinese characteristics; energetically support professional basketball clubs, straighten out functions of administrative levels, clarify property rights, support self blood making function of clubs, expand autonomous power of management, gradually establish professional club mode with Chinese characteristics, promote development and industrialization process of basketball market. (4) Comprehensively plan, vigorously strengthen construction of coach team, improve comprehensive quality of players and judges, which is the hope of promoting Chinese basketball cause. (5) Master cultivation law of excellent basketball sport talents, cultivate and reserve spare talents in many ways. Establish some training and cultivation types meeting market demand, try to adopt paid training and output method, encourage society to establish basketball schools, clubs and training classes, expand cultivating layer of basketball talents. Utilize various channels to send the young players with cultivation prospect abroad to learn, send the key talents to international high-level league matches to exercise. (6) Establish Chinese novel basketball theoretical system and training practice scientific program, promote scientific training, match, management and education level.

2 Current Situation of Professionalism Research of Chinese Basketball Competitive Sport at the Present Stage

It mainly consists Basic theory of professional basketball market and research of current situation and measures for Chinese professional basketball market, Yang Tieli (Basic theory of professional basketball market and research of current situation and measures for Chinese professional basketball market, Beijing: Beijing Sport University, 2001), which analyzes the current situation of Chinese professional basketball market and indicates (1) The existing "double-track system" management system of Chinese professional basketball has not been able to adapt to the development of professional basketball under the condition of market economy system, which is the main hindrance that impacts the smooth operation of Chinese professional basketball market. There are discrepancies between State Administration Center for Basketball and professional basketball clubs in the operating purpose and cognition of professional basketball, resulting in the contradiction between two parties in profit distribution, such contradiction restricts the reform of professional basketball management system, influencing the further development of Chinese professional basketball market to a certain extent. (2) Current operating means of Chinese professional basketball are original with sole channel, a majority of clubs are not satisfied with the operating benefits. (3) The present CBA professional basketball league match is in good market market match environment. (4) Chinese cities and towns have good basketball audience foundation, this is the advantaged condition for further developing Chinese professional basketball market. (5) According to the professional distribution of scene basketball audience, staff, public servants and workers are main audience groups; based on income, those with annual income of 10,000-30,000 yuan dominate; based on age group, mainly concentrate within 20-50 years old. (6) Motives of audience to watch the game appear tendency of diversification. Motive types mainly include interest-oriented, support-oriented and feeling-oriented. According to watching form, those watch with friends, classmates and family members are most. (7) Considering the current situation of Chinese professional basketball market and specific Chinese situation, the main measures for developing Chinese professional basketball market proposed by me are: ① Further deepen reform of professional basketball system to establish one professional basketball management system that suits for the national situation of China step by step as planned. According to the successful experience of Chinese political and economic system reform, Chinese current professional basketball system should refer to "incremental" reform pattern, proceed from the operating mechanism of professional basketball market, depend on expansion of market mechanism increment to gradually intensify the marketization level of Chinese professional basketball, reduce the composition of planned economy system stock. That is, establish scientific and democratic decision-making mechanism, impetus mechanism, innovation mechanism and constraint mechanism; then perform game system reform: define the property rights of CBA professional basketball league match, establish reasonable distribution system: gradually transmit to professional basketball league. ② Take the demand of audience as starting point, improve the quality of basketball match products by increasing the level of player training and match, revising match rules, establishing cultivation system of reserved talents, creating field atmosphere, providing diversified comprehensive services and other measures. ③ Establish the strategy of comprehensive development of Chinese professional basketball market, further open up tickets, develop TV broadcasting rights, logo products, sponsoring, advertisement and other marketing channel. ④ Create the brand of CBA professional league match.

3   Research of Sustainable Development of Chinese Competitive Basketball

It mainly consists of Research of sustainable development strategy of Chinese competitive basketball, Chen Jun (Research of sustainable development strategy of Chinese competitive basketball, Beijing: Beijing Sport University, 2003), this research analyzes current situation of Chinese basketball professionalism on the basis of analysis of basketball professionalism characteristics and other theoretical issues and with reference to theoretical thought of sustainable development, and refers to the successful experience of NBA, integrates national situation of China to formulate a set of basketball professionalism development strategy system with Chinese characteristics. The research clearly points out that the basic connotation of sustainable development of Chinese basketball professionalism is: a people-oriented pattern, people actively regulate land control the composite system of professional basketball consists of economic benefits, social benefits, human resources and other key factors, enabling it to develop to be coordinated, stable and sustainable. It is basically systematic, overall, sustainable, coordinated and fair. It determines five theoretical bases and six basic principles for formulating sustainable development strategy of Chinese basketball professionalism, proposes the general objective of sustainable development strategy of 2010 Chinese basketball professionalism, that is: basically establish the operating pattern of basketball professionalism that suits for socialism market economy, meets modern basketball development law and demand of socialization and industrialization, under the macroscopic regulation and control of basketball sport management center, self-control of professional clubs and social public participation, and with Chinese characteristics; achieve social benefits (development of basketball sport), economic benefits and coordination of human resources, constantly develop, and specially emphasize that if Chinese basketball professionalism wants to realize the goal of sustainable development, "incremental" reform road should be adopted. Adopt "take match system reform as 'entry point' to establish and improve league match system" and totalling seven strategies and measures, gradually establish one professional basketball management organization adapts to socialism market economy, professional basketball league.

In Analysis of constraints of Chinese basketball sport sustainable development (Analysis of constraints of Chinese basketball sport sustainable development, Journal of Guangzhou Physical Education Institute 2007, 27 (4)), Wen Jihuai (2007) thinks that Chinese basketball sport development faces some problems and challenges: (1) Under the impact of "strategy of the National Games" and "strategy of the Provincial Games", the original network for cultivating reserved basketball teams are impacted. (2) Selection and cultivation of the coach have not formed complete scientific system. (3) Sport performance of the national team fluctuates. (4) Reform of basketball management system requires to be deepened. (5) Scientific research of basketball field should pay attention to combine theory with practice. (6) The professional basketball clubs and their management system in their true sense have not been completely established. (7) Mass-based basketball match sport in most of regions around China is still to be improved. Constraints of sustainable development of Chinese basketball sport are divided into 3 aspects: training, personnel and society. The key constraints in training consist of training system factor, scientific and technological level factor, match system factor, etc.; personnel constraints mainly consists of reserved force factor, coach quality factor, etc.; social constraints mainly consists of management system factor, economic investment factor, market development factor, etc.

In Analysis of restraining Chinese competitive basketball sport development factors (Analysis of restraining Chinese competitive basketball sport development factor, Journal of Capital Institute of Physical Education2005, 2, 11), Liu Gang (2005) thinks that the factors restraining Chinese competitive basketball sport development include: economy factor, management factor, training factor, coach factor, player factor, referee factor, laws and regulations factor, scientific research factor, reserved talents cultivation factor, environment factor, etc.

4 Strategic Measures for Chinese Competitive Basketball Development

It mainly consists of Strategic research of Chinese competitive basketball development (Strategic research of Chinese competitive basketball development, Beijing: Beijing Sport University, 2003), Bai Xilin. This research utilizes document literature method, social investigation method, expert investigation method, modern system method, logic analysis method and other comprehensive research methods, on the basis of practice, performs deep and systematic research for Chinese competitive basketball development from the layer of theory, perspectively proposes strategic measures for Chinese competitive basketball development: (1) Competitive basketball development strategy means that the national basketball authority departments propose action direction and formulate definite goals for the development of competitive basketball in certain period, then makes overall and long-term planning and management during the realization of this goal. (2) Guiding ideology of Chinese competitive basketball development strategy: under the spiritual guidance of the Sixteenth National Congress of CPC, take talent cultivation as basis, implementation of "Olympic Glory Winning Plan" as center, training and match system reform as key point, scientific research and system construction as guarantee, to accomplish the new breakthrough of Chinese basketball competition level. (3) Strategic objective of Chinese competitive basketball development: increase competition level of Chinese basketball sport, continue keeping the leading position in Asia, cultivate one high quality talent team for training and match organization management, cultivate a batch of excellent coaches proficient in scientific talent selection, training and other aspects as well s a batch of high-level players able to struggle for world basketball peak; form complete training system, match system and reserved force cultivation system: accomplish systematization and standardization of management, scientific and systematic training, socialization and marketization of match, diversification and intensification of talent selection and cultivation, rationalization of talent structure and application, strive for obtaining new breakthrough in the basketball match in the Olympic Games. (4) Key points of Chinese competitive basketball development strategy: system construction and talent cultivation. (5) Chinese competitive basketball development strategy stages are divided into short-term strategy (lay foundation and do preparation stage), middle-term strategy (comprehensive and rapid development stage), long-term strategy (stage of keeping comprehensive and rapid development) (6) Strategic measures for Chinese competitive basketball development are: ① Human resources development measures should vigorously enhance the construction of management personnel, coaches, reserved force and referee team. ② In training system, stick to the scientific training principle of "deepen implementation of 'Based on strictness, difficulty and actual competition, expanding amount of exercise', lay a solid foundation, intensify physical force, comprehensive and innovative, proficient in all aspects"; insist on rapid, accurate, flexible, defensive and cruel technical and tactics styles; implement the tactics guiding ideology of "self-centered, inside and outside integration, give priority to fastness, master rhythm, based on defence, flexible and changeable"; establish training monitoring system, comprehensively increase training quality: recover winter and summer training of teams at all levels around China, strengthen macroscopic training management, ensure the periodicity and systematicness of training. ③ In match system, accelerate match system reform, mainly establish and improve match system serves for the national team training, enhance match management and supervision. ④ In guarantee system, reform management system and operating mechanism: develop basketball market, develop basketball industry; consolidate scientific and technological service and scientific research and tacking the key research project for the national team; consolidate ideological and political work for the national team and professional moral education for players; properly control doping control work; consolidate cultural education for players; establish and improve objective responsibility system and various rewards and punishment systems; establish scientific and reasonable supervision mechanism, consolidate the all process management for strategy implementation: emphasize media publicity work.

According to the above relevant statement, there are plenty of research related to Chinese competitive basketball development. Characteristics of basketball sport often integrates the nature, law, sport practice and development trend of basketball sport, mainly expounding from sport training and sociology, it can be considered very comprehensive and systematic. The research content concerning Chinese competitive basketball development is the most abundant, comprehensive and profound, it involves multiple disciplines. In addition, may people's doctoral dissertations use the development of Chinese competitive basketball as proposition, performing deep research in strategic angle and more macroscopic layer. However, in fact, Chinese basketball is developing continuously, it will encounter various problems during its development, especially in this particular social transition period, its internal and external environment has occurred enormous changes, thus bringing about more opportunities and challenges for the development of Chinese competitive basketball. But the current relevant research is always difficult to start from this particular social transition period of China, relevant research can not realize that the development of Chinese competitive basketball must be limited at a special time and in a special space, Chinese competitive basketball will be interacted and effected each other with the big system of its social environment. The dispersiveness and limitation of application scope of the past relevant theory objectively proved Chinese competitive basketball theory should be further enhanced and improved.

References

1. Liu, H.: Research of features and current situation of 50 years of development of Chinese basketball competitive sport. Journal of Beijing Sport University 25(3) (2002)
2. Yang, T.: Research of current situation and measures for basic theory of professional basketball market and Chinese professional basketball market. Beijing Sport University, Beijing (2001)
3. Jun, C.: Strategic research of Chinese basketball professionalism sustainable development. Beijing Sport University, Beijing (2003)
4. Wen, J.: Analysis of sustainable development of Chinese basketball sport constraints. Journal of Guangzhou Physical Education Institute 27(4) (2007)
5. Gang, L.: Analysis of restraining Chinese competitive basketball sport development factors. Journal of Capital Institute of Physical Education (2) (2005)
6. Bai, X.: Strategic research of Chinese competitive basketball development. Beijing Sport University, Beijing (2003)

Application of XML Technology in Distance Education Resources Standardization

Xianmin Wei

Computer and Communication Engineering School, Weifang University, Weifang, China
wfxyweixm@126.com

Abstract. This paper discusses a XML-based courseware management tools achievement in the XML technology field of distance education applications, using the tool to generate the Web courseware to meet IMS specifications, and can achieve the standardization of distance education resources and open technology.

Keywords: XML, IMS specifications, DOM, courseware.

1 Introduction

Distance education is a teaching methods with different places same time or different places and time, the different places and time are usually Web-based approach. Web-based approach, the teaching content in the form of courseware on the Web server, learners can be anywhere at any time to learn independently. In this way the hardware configuration requirements are low, it is currently the main form of distance education.

Courseware is aid-teaching software with one point or a few of the implementation relatively complete knowledge for teaching, under the platform division, it can be divided into stand-alone version courseware and the network version courseware, the network version courseware need to be able to run in standard browsers, standalone courseware can be run via Web download or CD-ROM access, and then run in the machine. These are generally referred to courseware.

1.1 The Current Problems Facing the Development of Courseware

Web-based teaching methods, electronic courseware development is a fundamental task, at present a number of computer workers and educators are committed to the development of courseware. In order to improve efficiency and quality of courseware development, many research institutes are also working on research of courseware production management tool, but because of lack of unified standards and techniques, resulting in different systems using document formats, They independently develop courseware management systems, systems can not communicate, even within the system, content and courseware updates is not an easy thing.

In order to facilitate the integration of courseware and teaching management systems, we believe that a standard courseware production management tool to develope courseware, communication information must be able to provide the following:

M. Zhou (Ed.): ISAEBD 2011, Part IV, CCIS 211, pp. 608–614, 2011.
© Springer-Verlag Berlin Heidelberg 2011

1) describes the courseware content and structure mechanisms to ensure the same courseware for distance learning in different management systems in operation, the courseware for distance learning management system is independent.

2) describe the courseware assessment data mechanism, courseware include proxy information, so that the Web server can record the learning courseware for each course, ensure that different tools can analyze these data.

3) courseware can provide retrieval mechanisms to ensure the sharing of education resources on the Internet, courseware developers can quickly find their materials, learners can quickly find the content they are interested in learning.

1.2 Comparison of HTML and XML

The traditional courseware is based on the structure of HTML documents, HTML provides a good the data format how to display a Web page, instead of those data represents. HTML structure can not achieve in a different interaction in learning management systems courseware, it is not guarantee that students can rapidly find what they are interested in learning contents. The semantics of XML with its good and clear structure respected by the people, is the exchange data ideal format between networks, so the development standard XML education-related task is the same.

2 XML Standards and Distance Education

2.1 What Is XML

XML is eXtensible Markup Language (extensible markup language) acronym, W3C organization in February 1998 published standards. W3C XML standards organizations develop the original intention is to define a standard to exchange data on the Internet. W3C adopted a simplified SGML of strategy, based on SGML, remove the syntax part by simplifying the DTD part, and added some special elements of the Internet. Therefore, XML is also a markup language, is essentially a subset of SGML. Because XML is also DTD, so XML can also be derived from other markup languages as a meta-language. Therefore, the use of XML in the Internet world, there are two main applications, one as a meta markup language, define a variety of examples of the standard; Second, as a standard exchange language, take on the role of describing the exchange of data.

2.2 The Advantages of XML

Search in XML data can be simple and efficient. Search engine is no need to go visiting with the XML file, it needs to go look them up under the contents of the relevant tag is enough. It is no exaggeration to say, XML markup for search engines to give the wisdom!

Today's computer world, different companies in different sectors, there are many different systems. Operating system with NT, UNIX, database systems are SQL Server, Oracle ,...., succeed in these different platforms, different transmit information between the database software, had to use some special software, is very inconvenient. The different display interface, from workstations, personal computers, to mobile phones so that personalized information display has become very difficult.

Now, with XML, a variety of different systems can use XML as the communication media. XML is not only easy to read, and can mark a variety of text, image or binary file, as long as XML processing tools, you can easily read and use these data to make XML as a very good Internet language.

2.3 Education-Related Standards and Organizations

Currently, there are many standard (academic) organizations are working to standardize Web-based educational resources research, and developed a number of the corresponding norms.

1) IEEE Learning Technology Standards Committee (LTSC) P1484

IEEE LTSC P1484 is a benchmark educational standard as a basis for a number of other organizations to develop a covered learning object metadata, student profiles, course sequencing, computer managed instruction, competency definitions, localization, content packaging and so on various criteria. IEEE LTSC has also established a subcommittee ISO Joint Technical Committee 1 (JTC1) with the International Standards Organization (ISO) standards related to educational dovetail.

2) Advanced Distributed Learning (ADL) Initiative.

ADL is a U.S. federal government organization, it developed a Shareable Courseware Object Reference Model (SCORM). SCORM provides a set of educational standards based on existing guidelines and examples of implementation, provides distance education for the Department of Defense Implementation and Application Guide, in the United States armed forces can be shared among the various branches, reuse. In addition the federal government can select more than one standard IEEE LTSC and the SCORM compliance with the system provider, in other areas of distance education.

3) IMS (Instructional Management System)

Global Learning Consortium IMS Global Learning Consortium to develop educational content of the major online publishing some of the standards, including storage and use of teaching content, progress tracking, student level reports, exchange student records. IMS has the following two main objectives: the definition of technical standard for distance education applications and services; support for standards-based IMS services and products of globalization.

4) The Aviation Industry CBT Committee (AICC)

AICC was a professional and technical training international organizations, development of computer-based training in CBT (Computer-Based Training) and related training technologies, although the AICC focused primarily on the aviation industry, but some of it for many years to develop standards and experience in education Other areas are available for reference.

5) The Dublin Core

Dublin Core is one of the original data (metadata) collection of elements, used to find electronic resources, is widely used in museums, libraries, government and commercial organizations, the media, to describe their resources, to facilitate the search.

3 XML-Based Web Courseware Production Management Tools

As the network educational resources standards and specification are in the development and no criteria was release, so totally specifying a standard courseware tools also exist many difficulties. We can choose the relatively complete as a reference from current standards, after the introduction of a formal standard, can be slightly modified to run. In the current standards, IMS is relatively perfect, it provides a teaching resource metadata standard (IMS Learning Resourse Meta_Data Specifications), the content package specifications (IMS Content Packaging Specifications), the problem with the test specification (IMS Question & Test Specification), teaching management system standard (Enterprise Specification).

IMS Content Packaging Specifications describe the distance education management system data structures, the purpose is to achieve the content data exchange. It does not limit the specific content of the document and file formats, but will focus on document management structure and proposed structure of the systems approach to achieve. Microsoft LRN is the first commercial realization of IMS content package specification. Each IMS provides a tutorial should be named "imsmanifest.xml" XML documents, defining content arrangement, the content source in this document tutorial, imsmanifest.xml file structure is as following Fig 1.

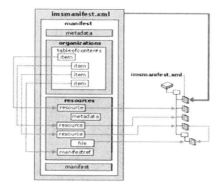

Fig. 1. Imsmanifest.xml file structure

a) metadata: the original data description of manifest, including the tutorial name, description, keywords, references Schema, shema version and other information.

b) Organizations: organizational structure of guide, description of the contents level and priority of each item on behalf of a part of the tutorial.

c) Resouces: tutorial content that are involved in resource description document, is the Organizations resources of the item by pointing to a specific document.

IMS Content Packaging Specifications is simple and clear, on the surface there is nothing very deep things, but it is obvious that the benefits of it, all to comply with this standard tutorial can communicate in different systems, easily data exchange, and because its packaging is strong, it can be directly packaged sales.

We used three levels of XML technology, one courseware database layer, including courseware code, courseware name and other information, which we call courseware tree. Second, courseware layer, including the section code, chapter names, etc., we call the tree, at this level, we used the standard IMS content packages, save the file by generating imsmanifest.xml courseware content. Third, courseware material layers, according to IMS metadata standard for tagging courseware material.

3.1   Imsmanifest.Xml File Production

In the courseware tools, in order to save the tree as a XML file, can use DOM technology. DOM stands for Document Object Model, DOM is composed of a document object model, it not only for XML, was first played in the HTML. People made development of the Web, especially those who wrote the dynamic DHTML, HTML in the document should have some concept of the object, DOM is an object model such standards. Another is a DOM interface, a language-independent interface, application through this interface and XML or HTML data within the deal. DOM-specific programming is not difficult to use and now the realization of DOM mainly provided in the form of components such as MSXML, and JAVA to achieve such as XML4J. We have adopted is MSXML3.0, using VC's COM interface. Save the XML document tree courseware is generated by this method.

3.2   XML-based Courseware Management System Model

System Model of courseware management tools is as following Fig 2.

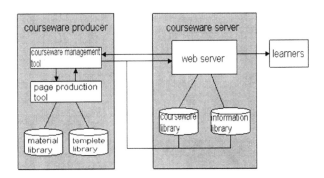

Fig. 2. System Model of Courseware management tools

1) Material Library
Material database includes text, graphics, images, animation and other common materials, including media files, audio, video and other multimedia material, these materials are provided according to IMS metadata standard notes, the material level, sharing of resources.

2) Metadata
Metadata, data about data. Such as library cards, describing a book on the theme, the location in the library. Metadata to find, easier to use a resource.

3) Template Library
Divided by the contents of electronic courseware, it can be divided into various forms of traditional audio and video courseware, teaching type and presentation type courseware, video streaming of video-based courseware, produced HTML page textbook, Java-based demonstration courseware and so on. Save the template library of these different types of courseware templates, these templates are saved with the xml file, in the production of courseware, the producers can choose template for rapid production.

4) Information Library

Learners in the process of online learning courses, the server can automatically record the learner information, such as learning time, number of visits, etc., and these data in the repository can be fed back to the courseware, that may provide other statistical analysis tools.

5) Courseware Library

Courseware can put related to data from the imsmanifest.xml file into courseware library, also available from the courseware database to generate the corresponding courseware imsmanifest.xml file.

3.3 System Functional Description

XML-based courseware management tool interface consists of three parts, toolbar, directory tree, visit the area, you can call the page production tools to create and edit pages.

1) New Courseware

A courseware production wizard, enter the courseware to the properties of information, such as course name, course code, suitable objects, introduction, key words, programs editor, then as a child node of the data into a known CourseDB. xml file and automatically generates the path information courseware. Courseware is courseware which code the only identifier used to determine whether there courseware.

2) Open Courseware

Each course has a known imsmanifest.xml courseware courseware structure file, this file uses standard IMS content packages. Open Courseware is to read imsmanifest.xml the corresponding courseware file, the directory tree structure for courseware.

3) Save Courseware

Save courseware is divided into two components, one single page of preservation, is in the courseware authoring tool to save the page, the second is to preserve the directory structure courseware and related attribute information, which is the courseware management tool by generating imsmanifest.xml file to save the.

4) Tree operation

Producers can increase node, save the node, delete node, dynamic drag nodes

5) Course upload

After courseware compiled, it should be uploaded to the server for students. Course upload content includes courseware HTML, ASP files; images, video, audio, documents and other resources; course content and structure description file imsmanifest.xml. With imsmanifest.xml file, we can achieve different database servers courseware library. In the database server, create two tables, one to record courseware directory structure, a courseware used to record access information.

6) Course Download

Courseware can download the courseware on the server for the local editing, the various source documents and courseware imsmanifest.xml content and structure description file downloaded by imsmanifest.xml documents, courseware management tools of the course open edited, you can upload to the server can also be saved locally.

7) Observation data

Courseware users access information are very important to course producers, in the user learning process, the server will automatically record each student's study time for each page and clicks, stored in the database. When the courseware producers choose observation data, the tool automatically and the database server connection, through the form, histograms, graphs and other forms of display such information. Through analysis of these data to produce students who can understand the situation, which can be adjusted accordingly courseware.

8) Preview Course

The design of courseware, if the want to know about this courseware actual effect, you can select the preview program, which is to launch the local browser is well courseware. This courseware and student access to the real effect is the same, if the author are not satisfied, can be modified in time.

3.4 XML-Based Courseware Management System Implementation

Programming tools using VC6.0, imsmanifest.xml file generation using DOM technology, XML document parsing using Microsoft MSXML3.0 parser. Server can use a variety of solutions can be WINDOWS NT + IIS platform, it can be LINUX+APACH platform, imsmanifest.xml files and database interaction, you can use multiple databases, such as: SQL SERVER, ORACLE, etc. We use is NT Server4.0+IIS4.0+ SQL Server7.0.

4 Conclusion

This paper's research was the distance education research laboratory project – "Web courseware management tool" during the development process, this project is part of the Province Natural Science Foundation in "intelligent, standardized, open and distance learning model" research. Courseware management tools in the adoption of XML-based technology, and meet IMS specifications, can achieve the standardization of teaching resources and the opening, the next step is to study how the courseware in the smart agent information, so that distance education system according to learners of different abilities and interest in providing the teaching content and teaching strategies, meet that learners on-demand learning, teachers cater for individual needs.

References

1. Holzner, S.: XMLuses. Machinery Industry Press, Beijing (2005)
2. Quin, L.: Open Sourse XML Database Toolkit: Resourse and Techniques for Improved Development. Whiley Computer Publishing (2004)
3. Geng, X.: XML Tutorial. Tsinghua University Press, Beijing (2006)
4. Dan, Z., Li, S.: XML advanced network applications. Tsinghua University Press, Beijing (2006)
5. Zheng, R., Yin, R., Tao, Y.: Practical Software Engineering. Tsinghua University Press, Beijing (2004)

Research of College Information Integration and Sharing System

Xianmin Wei

Computer and Communication Engineering School,
Weifang University, Weifang, China
wfxyweixm@126.com

Abstract. With the digital campus in recent years, the universities have developed a large number of Web-based applications and management systems, but these systems are isolated with each other, sharing data is more difficult. An important task in digital campus construction currently is to integrate various application systems to improve information sharing. This paper analyzed information system integration key technologies in the construction of digital Campus, and studied the promotion and protection mechanism.

Keywords: Information construction, integration, share.

1 Introduction

With the rapid development of information technology, all colleges and universities were in the large-scale information technology on campus, but only by adding high-strength hardware and software investment, can not achieve the required education information on the reform and traditional teaching model of the whole new education model. In the past, information technology, the application of a system just to solve a local problem, creating "islands of information." In the above context, in recent years the concept of digital campus came into being. Digital Campus is the use of computer technology, network communication technology on the teaching, research, management and life services, all information resources to conduct comprehensive digital realize the campus information resources, digital and sharing, and scientific and standardized way of information resources integration and integration. However, in the process of building digital campus, the prevailing management system is not perfect, the old system is difficult to fully integrate the new system implementation is too rushed and so many problems, leading to information sharing an "important but not effective," the embarrassment, greatly reduced the digital campus of their potential. So to solve the process of building digital campus sharing information integration, is currently an important issue be solved. Based on the current status of the development of digital campus analysis, this paper put forwards the concrete implementation plan in construction of integration and sharing of information systems.

M. Zhou (Ed.): ISAEBD 2011, Part IV, CCIS 211, pp. 615–619, 2011.
© Springer-Verlag Berlin Heidelberg 2011

2 Status

After years of development, the university has been gradually building services in teaching, research and management of a range of information management applications, such as administrative office automation system, educational management system, scientific management system, recruitment management systems. However, with the application of cumulative, gradual exposure to the new problems are the following: First, the lack of effective integration of information sharing. If dispersed in various management information system management of resources, teaching resources, and applications to the entire campus network efficiency and certainty have had a significant impact; the second is the lack of a unified system user interface. Lack of unity between the various application systems interface, access to resources and lack of a unified application interface, or even incompatible with each other; third is the application of system integration difficulties. Modules each based on different platforms is difficult to integration, system expansion and scalability is rather poor, so that the resources on campus web applications lack of effective organization and management of these problems to our users great inconvenience. In this context, the pre-construction of campus information systems one after another and digital integration of the underlying platform integration, building information-sharing systems have become integrated digital campus particularly important process of building a project.

3 Study of Information Integration Sharing Platform

3.1 Construction of the Base Support Platform

The base supporting platform, including information portal platform, and common data platforms, unified authentication platform based on digital campus.

1) Construction of Information Standards
Information standard building is one of the key management platform of digital campus, is an important component of supporting management platform. Information standards must be fully applied to teaching, research, management and service activities of the flow of information, data platforms and applications play a guiding and regulating the construction; must be a timely update and enrich the dynamic system. Therefore, the information standard system construction must have a strong compatibility, openness and manageability.

2) Information Portal Platform
Information portal platform is digital campus of the application system and user interaction service process platforms, is the digital campus internal service window, all the information resources of the organic integration into a simple, unified, personalized WEB interface and to ensure safe and consistent with the information.

3) Public Data Platform
Common data platform centralized storage and management by the data center database and data sharing, management, data integration platform, composed of two parts. Through the central database, the data of various types of data integration in schools, centralized storage, through a unified reliability, security and other design, to

provide users with stable, reliable data services. Through data integration platform for each of the business system database automatically upload the data to be integrated into the data center database, according to the subscription of the business system needs to share data distributed to business systems, unified data integration and standardization, as provide comprehensive data query and statistical analysis data base established.

4) Unified Authentication Platform

Digital campus with the gradual deepening of the campus will be built more applications. Concentrate on building a unified authentication platform for the application system provides centralized authentication service, digital campus to improve the security of application system, so users do not remember a different password and identity, through the information portal platform click Login.

3.2   Integration of Application System and Base Platform

In the building of basic supporting platform, various existing application systems must be integrated with the supporting platform, to achieve within the schools, between schools of business integration, process integration and data integration, information integration and sharing of building a real system. Integration mainly from the following three aspects:

1) Data Integration

Data integration refers to the use of public database platform, from the applications need to share the database to extract the data, so that public school within the database platform to become the only comprehensive data source, complete the data integration layer, as well as related application systems to share data access to services for the school within the comprehensive data analysis services to provide comprehensive, effective and reliable data base, integration shown in Figure 1.

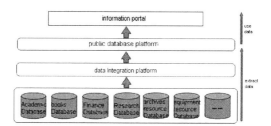

Fig. 1. Schematic diagram of data integration

2) Certification Integration

Certification integration is according to the status of integration to determine a set of user identity information, as a unified platform for identity authentication and digital identity information the authority of campus users, and establish a unified authentication platform, complete integration of the current certification system for integration, while leaving the interface for subsequent construction of the system seamless and unified authentication platform integration. User management in a unified platform for centralized authentication, application subsystems are not alone maintain user information, all user information is derived from a unified identity authentication service, in principle, requires a unified user authentication user database is relatively complete data base of information , the basic information of users of each subsystem of the system data is a subset of the user database; for some applications have been built, unified authentication platform to support the application systems to establish their own separate database, custom development background data replication services, so application system can maintain and unified authentication platform data consistency; for a Web application system, so that single sign-on.

3) Application Integration Released

Application publishing refers to the integration of the data in the public database platform based information portal platform by the teachers and students to provide personalized information services; expanding departmental information services management information system capabilities. Complete the application's main application system integration services focused on information query, enables the user to a single entrance, the use of all business applications information service provided by the system.

In information portal platform, information dissemination methods used are: a simple URL link integration; need certified systems integration (such systems need to enter a user name and password, such as the mail system, information portal to provide login credentials service, reservation system, the user name / password so that users only need to enter in the first, after clicking on the link to go directly to these systems); embedded in the pages of other systems, the use of a section of the plug-in configuration, the configuration interface in the section Enter the URL of the page embedded systems and display long high; develop specific Portlet, to achieve an integrated function of the system was released. Information portal will have carried out various application systems application integration, and through RSS, Iframe, application integration and other methods to crawl the page, the application will be part of the data generated in the information displayed in the portal page.

4   Study of the Promotion and Protection Mechanism

After completing each of these construction aspects, to build the technical aspects of information sharing system has been basically solved the problem, but the construction is completed there will still be lagging behind other issues of information, the main reason is lack of resources to share all types of information the main responsibility. Before integration in the information, university information resources development and utilization of compartmentalization is generally carried out by sector business in the development of planning, organizing, financing and institutional tranches are the roads, their own way. Information integration, the responsibilities of various departments is not clear, there is no corresponding duty of the main organization and coordination of information sharing and operational responsible for the work. There are many inter-departmental business systems, office coordination between various departments, information exchange; resource sharing is not a strong awareness and demand, buck-passing common occurrences. To enhance the development and utilization of information resources and improve utilization of information resources for teachers and students to provide timely and effective information, information resources into full play the role of development in the school, built in the system at the same time, the corresponding security mechanism to promote the building is not ignored. Safeguard mechanism to promote the construction includes the following aspects: the establishment of a sound organizational structure to strengthen the leadership of digital campus; strengthen the building, the construction of the digital campus at different stages of growth with timely technical management personnel; ensure that the funds input, so integrated planning, phased investment; the development of relevant information resources management practices, the level of information work will be incorporated into the school system of internal evaluation, public information resources, collection, storage, release, exchange, supervision, and law-based information sharing.

5   Conclusion

Digital campus has gone through several years of construction, access into information integration and sharing construction phase. The current challenge is how the university to integrate existing information systems to be able to query the user through a portal to provide all the necessary information. This feature is dependent on the integration of existing application systems. This article analyzes the Digital Campus the process of building applications on the construction status, and based this on the Digital Campus construction applications in data integration, authentication integration, application integration, three aspects of research, so as to Digital Campus Information Integration sharing provides a reference implementation of specific recommendations.

References

1. Jing, Y.: University shared database design and implementation. Shanxi Datong University (Natural Science) 5, 82–84 (2008)
2. Xu, X., Su, X., Wu, N.: University shared data center platform of the design and implementation. Modern Library and Information Technology 6, 48–53 (2005)
3. Fan, B.: Higher functions of information resource sharing implementation strategies. China Education Information 12, 51–53 (2007)
4. Liu, W., You, C.: Knowledge sharing information systems integration process on schedule impact analysis. Management Engineering 3, 141–441 (2005)

Author Index